*Church and State
in
Latin America*

Church and State
in
Latin America

A History of Politico-Ecclesiastical Relations

REVISED EDITION

by

J. Lloyd Mecham

The University of North Carolina Press · Chapel Hill

To my Mother
Lucía Preciado Mecham
in grateful memory

"Render to Caesar the things that are Caesar's, and to God the things that are God's."—JESUS.

"Our era recognizes that religion is the work of the conscience and past eras believed that religion is the work of the state."—EMILIO CASTELAR.

Preface

The Latin-American nations, preponderatingly Roman Catholic in population, and, prior to the winning of independence, having lived for centuries under a common politico-religious régime, have espoused strikingly dissimilar ecclesiastical policies. In those republics one encounters the independent Church, the established Church, and the Church burdened under oppressive State control. The present study is an inquiry into the historical evolution of the political position of the Roman Catholic Church in Latin America. This analysis of the origins and development of the somewhat anomalous present-day legal status of the predominant faith in those countries is designed to give the answer to the question so often heard in the United States when the religious conflict in Mexico was raging: What about the Catholic Church in the other Latin-American countries?

The religious disorders in Mexico were not exceptional, for the Catholic Church suffered vicissitudes in many other countries of Central and South America. Anticlericalism is a widespread movement, and in analyzing its causes and manifestations one can arrive at a clearer conception of the Mexican situation. Because of its greater importance and interest to the American public, the religious question in Mexico has been given a more lengthy and detailed treatment.

This is not a Church history. It is rather a discussion of politico-ecclesiastical relationships. Facts and events illustrative of this are mentioned; all others are intentionally omitted. Failure to include important incidents in the ecclesiastical histories of the various countries can probably be justified, therefore, as not being pertinent to the subject under discussion. Nor was this book written to prove a thesis. It seeks only to shed a little additional light on the meaning of Latin-American anticlericalism. The subject is of the author's own choosing; and in the preparation and publication of this book he received no support from any individual, institution, or organization. He has endeavored to present this subject objectively; yet when occasion demanded he has not avoided voicing personal judgment. The conclusions and opinions, which are intended to be impartial, are based upon careful study and evaluation of the facts. It is hoped that a critical examination of the work will not reveal bias.

The author acknowledges with gratitude valuable aid and suggestions which he received from Dr. Carlos E. Castañeda, Librarian of the Latin-American Collection in the University of Texas Library, and Dr. J. Fred Rippy of Duke University. He appreciates also, the courtesy of the editors of *The Catholic Historical Review* and *The Hispanic American Historical Review* in allowing him to make use of his own articles published in these periodicals. Finally, the author wishes to express the greatest indebtedness to his wife, Mabel Olive Mecham, for her invaluable aid in composition, typing, and proofreading.

J. LLOYD MECHAM
Austin, Texas, 1934

Preface to Revised Edition

Since this book first appeared in 1934, the changes in the Latin-American political scene have been frequent and often violent. These events, plus ideological changes, have affected both the legal and active status of the Roman Catholic Church. Much of the discussion, therefore, descriptive of the religious settlement of 1934, is no longer applicable to a changed situation. For this reason the author acquiesced in the urging of fellow-workers in the vineyard to bring the volume up-to-date, being fully aware of the problems involved in preparing a revision covering a period of thirty years.

The primary purpose of this revision has been to account, not only for chronological, but also for scholarly developments. In pursuance of the first objective, the discussions of post-1934 events have been added to each of the chapters devoted to the individual countries. The concluding chapter has been completely rewritten and enlarged to take account of changes in Church-State relations and the status of religious practice in Latin America. With respect to the second objective, due attention has been given to scholarly contributions published since the book was first written. When scholarship invalidated statements, they have been changed; when it added supplementary information of interest, there have been additions. Also changes have been made in the Bibliography.

In order to accommodate the addition of considerable new material, it was necessary to make many deletions throughout the volume. An effort was made to confine these deletions to the more dispensable matters in order not to impair the integrity of the volume. One of the three chapters on the Church conflict in Mexico has been deleted, without injury it is hoped, for the Church question in that country does not warrant the detailed discussion which seemed necessary thirty years ago.

Acknowledgment should be made for research aid received from the University of Texas and the Rockefeller Foundation.

J. Lloyd Mecham
Austin, Texas, 1966

Contents

Church and State
in
Latin America

———

Chapter I

Church and State During the Spanish Régime in America

Even as the antecedents of many of the political institutions of the Latin-American nations extend far back into the colonial period, so also distinctive features of the civil status of the Roman Catholic Church in those countries following independence originated under the colonial régime. During the Spanish domination the ecclesiastical power was coetaneous with the colonial system and was deeply rooted. This affiliation of the civil and religious authorities was known as the royal patronage of the Indies, or *real patronato de las Indias*. No adequate comprehension of the difficult Church problem which confronted the nascent republics when embarking upon their independent careers, and which disturbed them for many years thereafter, is possible without an understanding of the nature of the relationship which existed between the Spanish crown and the Catholic Church in America.

From an early period there existed two schools of thought on the subject of the *real patronato de las Indias*: the "regalists" and the "canonists," or "ultramontanists." Briefly, the regalists believed that royal patronage was laical in origin and therefore inherent in temporal sovereignty. The canonists contended that patronage was originally not laical but spiritual and was founded solely on pontifical concessions which were rescindable but nontransferable. According to an eminent proponent of this latter theory: "The pontifical concession of the *patronato de Indias* to the kings of Spain was a simple, juridic, unilateral act produced *motu proprio*. There were no concordats, contracts, or decrees, but only direct concession from the Holy See."[1] This conflict of interpretations became a subject of far more than mere academic interest when the Spanish colonies in America put off the control of the mother country. Then the paramount question became: Do the republics inherit the patronal rights previously exercised by the Spanish crown?

1. Faustino J. Legón, *Doctrina y Ejercicio del Patronato Nacional* (Buenos Aires, 1920), p. 186.

The regalists said Yes! The canonists said No! Innumerable treatises have been written to support the two divergent viewpoints, yet no generally accepted conclusion has been reached, and it is highly improbable that any is possible. It is not without significance that the papacy has never deviated from its position that *patronato de Indias* was not inherent in sovereignty and consequently could not be inherited by the infant republics. Furthermore, several of the new states at different periods in their histories tacitly, through the negotiation of concordats, recognized the papal claim. Keeping in mind, therefore, this very complex problem, certain features of which will be discussed in the next chapter, we shall now address ourselves to the task of explaining the nature of ecclesiastical patronage in Spain and the Indies.

Patronage is commonly regarded as the power to nominate or present a cleric for installation in a vacant benefice. The right of canonical institution to major benefices belongs to the pope; in the case of minor benefices it belongs to a bishop or to other prelates. Presentation, in reality, is only a part of ecclesiastical patronage, for the latter includes the following: (1) the right of presentation; (2) honorary rights; (3) utilitarian rights; and (4) obligations. The most important of these is the first, i.e., presentation or nomination to an ecclesiastical dignity. When a vacancy occurs in a benefice the patron proposes the name of a suitable candidate to the ecclesiastical authority empowered with the right of collation. The right of nomination is the very essence of patronage. The honorary rights include such distinctions as the granting of precedence to the patron and his family in various religious ceremonies, the according of seats of honor to them, special prayers said in their behalf, and the distinction of being buried beneath the high altar. Utilitarian privileges are found in the moral obligation of the favored religious establishment of coming to the financial aid of the patron should he ever be in straits. Moreover, utilitarian rights often included the concession to the patron of first fruits, tithes, and other incomes from the benefice. Certain obligations devolve upon the patron. He must watch over his benefice and be ever ready to defend it against attack. Patronal obligations of this character were a matter of serious moment in the days of the feudal régime. The patron's interest in caring for the welfare of his benefice gave him no authority to interfere in the administration of its property or the discharge of its spiritual duties.

According to Ribadeneyra,[2] who was an outstanding exponent of

2. Antonio Joaquín de Ribadeneyra, *Manual Compendio de el Regio Patronato Indiano* (Madrid, 1755), pp. 70-72. In addition to Ribadeneyra, Pedro Frasso (*De Regio Patronato*, Madrid, 1677) and Juan de Solórzano y Pereyra (*Política Indiana*, Madrid, 1776) were the foremost lay defenders of *regalismo*.

regalism during the colonial period, royal patronage was laical. He contended that it need not necessarily be an apostolic concession, for from the earliest days of Christianity the founders enjoyed the natural right of patronage over churches established by them. The first pontifical document in which this right of nomination or presentation was called the "right of patronage" was a decree of Pope Nicholas II in the sixth century.[3] The mere fact that there is no record of the papacy ever declaring the founder of a benefice incapable of enjoying the rights of patronage seems to indicate that this right was acquired by the mere act of founding or endowing. The popes, said Ribadeneyra, by their concessions added nothing to a natural right; indeed, the title bestowed by the pope was in fact superfluous for there was no necessity of confirming, as a reward, the temporal founders in a privilege which they were entitled to in simple justice. When Pedro of Aragon renounced the royal patronage and placed it in the hands of Innocent III, the Aragonese resisted, claiming that this right did not belong to the royal person but to the nation. This incident illustrates that the people in the medieval period believed that patronage was inherent in sovereignty.[4]

The above views are vigorously denied by the canonists—particularly the claim that the mere act of founding a church brings to the founder willy-nilly the right of patronage. The fount and source of the duties and privileges known as patronage, they contend, is the Holy See, which, having supreme jurisdiction over the Church, can do anything it desires for the advancement of its vital interests. In consequence the Apostolic Father has been accustomed to reward, *motu proprio* (of his own free will), the performance of a certain class of good works, like the founding of temples and the establishment of pious works, by bestowing the patronal concessions. The common designation of patronage in papal decretals as *ius spirituali annexum* indicates that the rights of the patron pertain to the spiritual order. Although patronage is generally called a right, says Zamora, it is more exactly a *concession*. The efficient cause of this concession is the ecclesiastical authority; the final cause, the gratitude of the Church and the desire to encourage religion and the cult. In sum, the canonists contend that patronage is a purely spiritual matter, a simple apostolic tolerance revocable at the will of the grantor, notwithstanding the fact that sovereigns exercised it like an inherent part of their secular sovereignty.[5]

3. Matías Gómez Zamora, *Regio Patronato Español é Indiano* (Madrid, 1897), p. 10.

4. Lucas Ayarragaray, *La Iglesia en América y la Dominación Española* (Buenos Aires, 1920), p. 171.

5. Zamora, *op. cit.*, p. 143; Joaquín Rodríguez Bravo, *Estudios Constitucionales* (Santiago de Chile, 1888), p. 21; Juan Manuel Estrada, *La Iglesia y el Estado* (Buenos Aires, 1929), pp. 68-74.

Thus, with respect to the essential nature of patronage in general, there are two divergent views. It has been suggested that a compromise might be effected by acknowledging that patronage derives its validity from both spiritual and temporal sources. It is civil, says an authority, because it exists before the ecclesiastical power recognizes it or gives its free consent, but it is likewise canonical because it is dependent on explicit sanction by the supreme authority of the Church.[6] No attempt will be made now to settle the issue. This must wait upon a description of the nature of the *real patronato Español* and the *real patronato de Indias*.

In Spain during the first six centuries following the immediate successors of the Apostles, it was the customary practice for the bishops to be designated by both the clergy and the people.[7] Until the time of Constantine the Great, this practice was necessary because of the obvious circumstances which did not allow to the greater number of Christian groups frank communion with the successors of St. Peter, in whom was vested theoretically the exclusive right of naming and confirming bishops. With the assurance of imperial protection and the establishment of a hierarchy of bishops and ecclesiastical provinces, the pope, who enjoyed the plenitude of power over all benefices which only he could create, in order to stimulate interest in the new religion and filial attachment to its functionaries, encouraged the practice of entrusting the elections of prelates to the clergy and the people of the city where the vacant see was located. Pope Leo I declared that "a bishop should not be given to a people who did not want him." During the first six centuries in Spain there were numerous instances of elections by clergy and the people, but none of royal nomination. There were also numerous cases of direct action of the pontiff in the creation of dioceses and in the institution of bishops. Prior to the invasion of the Arian Goths, therefore, the bishops of Spain were elected by the clergy in the presence of the people, and later under the aegis of the princes. The direct intervention of the populace in the designation of bishops frequently degenerated into strife. These riots gave the temporal lords pretext to intervene in protecting the canonical elections. At first their intervention was limited

6. Cesáreo Chacaltana, *Patronato Nacional Argentino* (Buenos Aires, 1885), p. 62. For general discussion, see Manuel Gutiérrez de Arce, "Regio patronato indiano," *Anuario de Estudios Americanos*, Sevilla, España, XI (1954), 107-68.

7. Regarding the intervention of the people in the elections some canonists claim that the suffrage of the people, presided over by the clergy, is required by divine right. They cite as evidence the election of the seven deacons (Acts 6:3). Others answer that this doctrine does not agree with historical facts, for in most cases the Apostles acted directly and by themselves. (Legón, *op. cit.*, p. 68.) For an account of the early episcopal elections see Ernest Renan, *Histoire des Origens du Christianisme* (Paris, n.d.), VI, 93 ff., and Joaquín Aguirre, *Curso de Disciplina Eclesiástica General* (Madrid, 1871), III, *passim*.

and legitimate; later the lords began to exercise greater influence in the elections, especially after the ruin of the Western Empire, and eventually they arrogated to themselves a dominant influence in the naming of prelates.[8]

In the Arian Church the influence of the crown was most pronounced. Consequently, when the Arian heresy came to an end under Reccard, the old practices of the Arian Gothic kings in ecclesiastical matters were continued. They exercised the prerogative of both universal patronage and a quasi-absolute government over the churches of the kingdom. Not only did they intervene in all the elections to ecclesiastical benefices, but they convoked national and provincial councils, established new episcopacies, and outlined the limits of the same. As can be readily imagined, the relations between Spain and Rome during this period were not intimate, although the Spanish Church, after the abolition of the Arian heresy, always recognized the pope as head.[9] Indeed, the intimacies of the first period before the Gothic invasion were not restored until the time of Hildebrand the Great.

With the invasion of the Moors the exercise of the patronage was suspended until the reconquest began to gain headway. Then, when the ancient sees were liberated, the princes appointed bishops. In general the Castilian kings followed the Visigothic tradition in their ecclesiastical relations. They founded and restored episcopal sees, elected and deposed bishops, convened councils, and judged ecclesiastical *pleitos* or causes. The right of the king to elect bishops was exercised sometimes directly, sometimes indirectly by permitting the cathedral chapter to elect, but in the event of the latter procedure the king had to confirm the election, otherwise it was considered invalid.[10]

Thanks to the efforts of Gregory VII and the other Cluniac reformers, steps were taken in the twelfth century to make the authority of the pope felt in Spain in the election of bishops and in matters of discipline. Owing to the fact that the Spanish monarchies were weak and decentralized, and that the ecclesiastical holdings had not been feudalized to the extent that they were in northern Europe, Spain was spared the disorders of the German investiture conflict.[11] Remarkably

8. Rafael Altamira y Crevea, *Historia de España y de la Civilización Española* (Barcelona, 1913-14), I, 123; Legón, *op. cit.*, p. 69; Zamora, *op. cit.*, p. 166; T. Ayuso, "El privilegio de los reyes de España en la presentación de obispos," in *Razón y Fé* (Madrid, 1904), II, 469.

9. Zamora, *op. cit.*, pp. 179-80; Ribadeneyra, *op. cit.*, pp. 43-44. For a description of the royal control over the Arian Church, see Legón, *op. cit.*, pp. 121-22, and Aloysius K. Ziegler, *Church and State in Visigothic Spain* (Washington, D.C., 1930).

10. Ribadeneyra, *op. cit.*, pp. 44-45; Altamira, *op. cit.*, I, 438-39.

11. The great controversy between Gregory VII and the German emperors Henry IV

enough, the kings of Castile coöperated with the papacy in abolishing their old privileges over the Church. They did not capitulate absolutely, however, for they insisted that the acts of the pope, to have effect in Spain, must receive the royal assent. Thus, as a result of Cluniac influence and the policy of Gregory VII, the Spanish Church became dependent on the papacy and it was freed from the interference of the civil power in ecclesiastical business. Thereafter the pope maintained in Spain legates and representatives who presided at general councils and intervened in Church questions. Gregory IX decreed that bishops in Castile were to be elected by majority vote of the cathedral chapter, and the right of confirmation was to be vested in the metropolitan. The disorders at the elections finally made it necessary for the pope, in the fourteenth century, to rule that confirmation of bishops belonged to the Roman pontiff. The question of episcopal nomination was settled sooner and more radically in Aragon than in Castile. Jaime II agreed, over the protests of the cathedral chapters, to entrust the elections to the pope himself.[12] Thus in Spain by the fourteenth century, the right of universal patronage was lodged in the Holy See where according to canonists it originally resided, after having been exercised respectively by the people, the clergy, and the temporal rulers.

Particular patronage continued to flourish in Spain after universal patronage came to an end. Its essential nature needs to be described to obviate confusion. From an early date in the history of the Christian Church it became the custom to make concessions to the founders of religious establishments. At first these privileges were conceded only to ecclesiastics. The first recorded instance was a conciliar decree of 441 which provided that bishops who founded churches in foreign dioceses with their own property or that of their diocese should enjoy the right of electing the ecclesiastics of the new churches. When patronage was conceded to laymen it was only honorary at first. For example, the

---

and Henry V centered about the imperial practice of granting to bishops and abbots, besides their titles, the possessions which constituted their benefices and the political rights which they were to exercise. Investiture meant that on the death of a bishop or abbot, the king was accustomed to select a successor and bestow on him the ring and staff, symbolic of his office, with these words: "Accept this church." Gregory VII determined to destroy all lay pretentions to the administration of the Church, and so, in 1075, withdrew from the king the right of disposing of bishoprics in future and relieved all lay persons of the investiture of churches. The resultant conflict was finally settled by the Concordat of Worms, 1122. The decision at Worms was a compromise, for a distinction was made between the ecclesiastical and secular elements in the appointment of bishops and abbots. The emperor renounced investiture with ring and staff and allowed all churches liberty of election and free consecration. The pope conceded to the lay authority the right of investing with the sceptre, signifying the granting of the temporalities.

12. Altamira, *op. cit.*, I, 124, 439; Zamora, *op. cit.*, p. 245.

patron's name or coat of arms was displayed on the church in a prominent place. Later the founder acquired the right of presentation. Originally the words "patron" and "rights of patronage" were not used, but "founders" or "builders." In the time of Justinian the rights of patronage were purely personal, that is, nontransmittable. The transmission to heirs was a later step, but when it occurred cannot be determined exactly.[13]

Some writers place the date of the Spanish origins of the practice at 655 when the Synod of Toledo granted to laymen the right of presentation to each church erected by them. The reconquest of ancient sees from the Moors and the establishment of new ecclesiastical districts in the conquered territory gave impetus to the development of particular patronage. Gregory VII in 1073 recognized conquest as the title to patronage, following the example of his predecessor, Alexander II, who had conceded to the kings of Aragon and their successors the right of presentation to the churches retaken from the Moors or those newly erected in the reconquered territory. These concessions of the Holy See were regarded as recompense for the incessant zeal which the kings of Spain displayed in the wars of the Moorish Crusade. Instead of working against this type of lay privilege, Gregory VII condemned the opposition and resistance of the ecclesiastics of Aragon to the grants made by Alexander II. Since the resistance continued, Pope Urban II in 1095 confirmed the grant of patronage over all places conquered from the Moors and over newly founded churches excepting episcopal churches. The king was also conceded first fruits and tithes of these foundations. The Fourth Lateran Council declared, "It is not just to destroy the legitimate rights of patrons."[14] From the time of Alfonso I of Castile to the conquest of Granada the Spanish monarchs exercised the privilege of particular patronage.

Some authors attempt to find in the reconquest the real origin of royal patronage. Canon law does not recognize the reconquest as sufficient title for acquiring the patronage. If it was exercised in Spain it had to be based in some special concession or some pontifical privilege. When France reacquired Roussillon in the seventeenth century the Holy See refused to recognize the right of patronage in the form enjoyed while the province was in the possession of Spain. The same principle applied when the Catholic people conquered regions inhabited by the infidel, save that they converted the mosques into churches, endowed them, and in that case acquired the patronage by foundation.

13. Legón, *op. cit.*, pp. 77-79.
14. Ayarragaray, *op. cit.*, pp. 152, 159-60; Zamora, *op. cit.*, pp. 17-18, 194, 220.

During the last two centuries of the reconquest the question of the election of bishops continued to be an element of dispute between pope and king. The general practice of the thirteenth century was that the cathedral chapters nominated the bishops, the king approved, and the metropolitan confirmed. But by virtue of papal action in the next century, the right of confirmation was taken from the metropolitan by the pope. The kings, however, did not cease to intervene in elections. Alfonso X of Castile asserted in royal decrees of 1328 and 1348 that it was an ancient custom in Spain for the Castilian kings to give consent to capitular elections of bishops and prelates. He based his claim on three factors: (1) the kings reconquered the territory from the Moors, extended Christianity, and converted mosques into churches; (2) they founded new churches; and (3) they endowed other churches. Successors of Alfonso made like declarations, always being very careful to assure to the Church new facilities for carrying on its august mission. Thus, while they prescribed ways of filling offices, the kings of Castile ordered that all pontifical dispositions should be faithfully complied with in the kingdom, and ecclesiastical lands and persons were accorded special *fueros* or privileges.

Several notable papal documents of the middle fifteenth century considerably extended the royal control over the Church in Spain. Pope Eugene IV by a concordat, in 1444, conferred upon the king of Aragon the privilege of appointing to lesser benefices. In 1448 Pope Nicholas V conceded to the king of Castile the right of nomination to the greater dignities in fifty-one ecclesiastical benefices in Castile and León. In the same year the Grand Master of the Order of Santiago was given the right of nominating to thirty ecclesiastical benefices. In 1455 Pope Calixtus III confirmed the royal right of presentation in Guipúzcoa and Vizcaya. Furthermore the pope agreed that in electing archbishops, bishops, and abbots for benefices in Castile and Aragon he would elect only persons suitable and acceptable to the king. The kings interpreted this privilege broadly, implying that it was necessary to present candidates to them in order that they might pass upon their suitability.[15]

By the time of Ferdinand and Isabella the Spanish sovereigns possessed in the traditions of the Gothic Church, in the religious character of the Moorish wars, and in numerous pontifical concessions, a juridic base upon which to establish their patronage over many churches. But it was particular and not universal patronage, and it was not easy to extend the royal authority over all the sees and prebends of the kingdom. The Catholic Kings in their efforts to consolidate the monarchy

15. Ayarragaray, *op. cit.*, pp. 151-52, 160; Altamira, *óp. cit.*, II, 90.

resolved to prevent at all cost the election of bishops in Rome. They insisted, at least, on their right of being informed and of approving the elections. When Pope Sixtus IV in 1482, without reference to the Spanish crown, appointed a foreigner to the bishopric of Cuenca, Ferdinand and Isabella protested that this was contrary to an earlier law (1476), which prohibited such a practice. When they threatened to convoke a general council to reform the Church and make it more harmonious with the interests of the state, the pope yielded and conceded to the Catholic Kings the right to supplicate in favor of candidates whom they considered qualified. Notwithstanding the pope's promise the case of Cuenca was repeated in Seville in 1485. As a consequence of this difficulty, the Conde de Tendilla, the Spanish envoy at Rome, secured from Pope Innocent VIII a notable concession to the Spanish demands. In a bull published in 1486 the pope granted to the Catholic Kings the right of universal patronage over all the benefices whether conquered or founded later within the Kingdom of Granada. Furthermore the crown was conceded the perpetual *diezmos*, or tithes, which the converted Moors had to pay to the Church. In 1494 Alexander VI confirmed the above bull and granted the crown one-third of all the tithes collected not only in Granada but throughout the monarchy.[16] The pope declared that he was motivated in making these grants because of the religious zeal of the Catholic Kings and their conquest of Granada from the Crescent. According to Zamora the bull of Innocent VIII in 1486 was the first pontifical grant of universal patronage in Spain.[17]

The famous bulls of Alexander VI and Julius II which granted patronal rights in the Indies did not affect the Spanish kingdom proper. The next step to be noted in the development of the *real patronato Español* was the grant by Adrian VI in 1523. At that time the pope conceded to the Spanish king the right of patronage over all the consistoral benefices in Spain. It was specifically declared that the patronage thus conceded was "of the same nature, vigor, force, and privilege as that which appertained to the kings by virtue of foundation or endowment." Clement VII, in 1530, extended the patronage to all the cathedral churches. In 1536 these grants were confirmed by Paul III in consideration of the services of Charles V in the siege of Tunis and the saving of Christians at that place. When Portugal was under the crown of Spain (1580-1640), Pope Urban VIII extended the *real patronato Español* to Portugal and the Algarves.[18]

16. P. Leturia, "El Origen Histórico del Patronato de Indias," in *Razón y Fé*, Vol. 78, pp. 25-26.

17. Zamora, *op. cit.*, p. 285.

18. *Ibid.*, p. 249; Ayarragaray, *op. cit.*, p. 165.

The nature and scope of the *real patronato Español* was extremely complicated. Since it was based on traditional practices and numerous grants, its complex character is understandable. Furthermore, the effectiveness of its enforcement varied in accordance with the strength or weakness of the Spanish sovereigns. The situation became acute when the first of the Bourbon kings, Philip V, brought to Spain new ideas regarding the prerogatives of the crown and the centralization of power within it. In the Concordat of 1737 a weak attempt was made to define the legal relationships of Church and State. It remained for Pope Benedict XIV and Ferdinand VI to agree, in the Concordat of 1753, on the exact nature of the Spanish patronage. The concordat was the means of reëstablishing the traditional friendly relations between Rome and Madrid, and it continued to regulate the relations of Church and State in Spain until 1851.[19]

The pope, in the concordat, recognized the right of patronage in the Spanish crown. There was put into writing what was meant by *real patronato Español* concerning which there had been much doubt and controversy. But since there was no question about the *real patronato de Indias*, because of the specific pontifical concessions, the concordat expressly excluded the Church in America from the scope of its terms.[20]

The union of altar and throne was much more intimate in America than in Spain. Indeed, it is difficult to conceive of a more absolute jurisdiction than that which the kings of Spain exercised over all the ecclesiastical affairs of the Indies. The control of the Church by the crown and its representatives in America was regarded as the most valuable of the regal attributes. Ribadeneyra describes the *real patronato de Indias* as "la piedra más rica, la más preciosa Margarita de su real diadema."[21] The patronage of the Indies existed both independent of and supplementary to that of Spain. It was based largely (in the estimation of the canonists, *absolutely*) on the following pontifical documents: (1) the bull of Alexander VI, May 4, 1493, which conceded to the Catholic Kings the dominion of the Indies and the exclusive

19. Zamora, *op. cit.*, p. 285; R. Sánchez de Lamadrid, *El concordato español de 1753 según los documentos originales de su negociación* (Jérez de la Frontera, 1937).

20. Dalmacio Vélez Sarsfield, *Relaciones del Estado con la Iglesia en la Antigua América Española* (Buenos Aires, 1889), p. 42. For the text of the Concordat of 1753, see *Nueva Recopilación* (Madrid, 1775), I, 45-65.

21. Ribadeneyra, *op. cit.*, pp. 3-4. For additional studies on the *patronato de Indias*, see Jesús García Gutiérrez, *Apuntes para la historia del origen y desenvolvimiento del Regio Patronato Indiano hasta 1857* (Mexico, 1941); Rafael Gómez Hoyos, *La Iglesia de América en las Leyes de Indias* (Madrid, 1961); Pedro Leturia, *Relaciones entre la Santa Sede é Hispanoamérica* (Caracas, 1959); W. E. Shiels, *King and Church: The Rise and Fall of the Patronato Real* (Chicago, 1961).

privilege of Christianizing the natives; (2) the bull of Alexander VI, November 16, 1501, which granted to the Spanish crown the tithes and first fruits of the churches of the Indies; and (3) the bull of Julius II, July 28, 1508, which gave to the kings of Spain the right of universal patronage over the Catholic Church in the Indies. The circumstances under which these bulls were granted and the general nature of their content will be examined.

When Columbus reported the discovery of the Indies to Ferdinand and Isabella, the Catholic Kings appealed to the pope to grant them title to the newly discovered lands. In presenting their petition they insisted that their most ardent aim was to extend the dominion of the Roman Catholic faith. With respect to Queen Isabella this may be accepted as the truth, for in her letter of instructions to Columbus (Barcelona, May 29, 1493), she declared as her first care the conversion of the natives of the new lands. Since the papacy enjoyed such great moral and political authority, the temporal rulers sought its aid to prevent other Christian princes from wresting their conquests from them. Portugal at that time was actively engaged in exploration, and it would have been easy for serious conflict to arise between the two Iberian crowns. Thus Ferdinand and Isabella sought the papal confirmation, not so much to legitimize their possession of the new lands as to avoid differences with Portugal. They felt that this could be best accomplished by papal intervention. Moreover, since the task of Christianization, which the Spanish rulers were anxious to assume, constituted a real "apostleship," it was natural and necessary that it should be done under the authority of the successor to the Prince of the Apostles.[22]

The pope, because of the great distance which separated Rome from America, as well as the lack of means to equip expeditions, was, obviously, unable to Christianize the Indies and establish there an ecclesiastical régime independent of the temporal power. The sovereigns of Spain, on the other hand, were the only ones capable of undertaking the establishment of the transatlantic Church. Thus, in proof of his impotence, and to give stimulus to the proselyting zeal of the Spanish kings, Pope Alexander VI acquiesced in their requests. By the bull *Inter Caetera*, May 4, 1493, there was conceded to the Catholic Kings title to the lands discovered or to be discovered to the west of a line drawn from pole to pole and distant one hundred leagues west of the Azores and Cape Verde Islands. A condition attached to the papal grant was the assumption by the Catholic Kings of the obligation to prosecute missionary work in the new lands.[23]

Some writers detect in the exclusive privilege granted to the kings of Spain to select and control the sending of missionaries to America, a grant of the right of ecclesiastical patronage. This interpretation sounds logical, for indeed, the exclusive right of evangelization was as absolute a delegation of authority as it was in the power of the pope to bestow. According to Ribadeneyra this bull granted the Spanish kings authority to exercise jurisdiction in all matters relating to ecclesiastical government in the Indies, "with full and complete power to act of their own free wills in all that seems to them to be most convenient for the spiritual government."[24] By the bull *Inter Caetera* the Spanish sovereigns were created a species of apostolic vicars with authority over spiritual matters in America.

On May 4, 1493, Alexander VI published another bull known as *Eximae Devotionis*. To the Catholic Kings he granted "all of the concessions, privileges, exemptions, rights, liberties, immunities, and indults" that had been granted by other pontiffs to the kings of Portugal in their overseas possessions. The most notable of these bulls was that of Pope Calixtus in 1456, which conceded the right of presentation. In addition, the same bull granted to the Order of Christ complete spiritual jurisdiction from Cape Bojador "over all Guinea unto the East Indies."[25] Pope Alexander declared that his purpose in bestowing the great privilege upon the Spanish sovereigns was to recognize and reward their Christian zeal in liberating Granada from the Moors, and in sending Columbus to distant lands to discover more people who might be won to the Catholic fold. It is possible that Alexander's nationality, he being an Aragonese of illustrious family, may have influenced him to favor the Spanish monarchs.

On November 16, 1501, Pope Alexander VI published another bull, also called *Eximae Devotionis* but to be distinguished from that of 1493. This bull most canonists regard as the third great pontifical concession of the *patronato de Indias*.[26] It increased the patronal privileges of the Spanish monarchs by granting them the use of the tithes in America. In return for the grant the crown assumed the obligation of defraying from the royal treasury all the expenses incidental to the maintenance

23. Francisco Javier Hernáez, *Colección de Bulas, Breves, y otros Documentos relativos á la Iglesia de América y Filipinas* (Brussels, 1879), I, 12-14.

24. Ribadeneyra, *op. cit.*, pp. 58-60.

25. Hernáez, *op. cit.*, I, 15-16. The validity of this bull has been contested because of its use, in 1456, of the name "East Indies." (Leturia, *op. cit.*, pp. 28-29.)

26. See N. A. N. Cleven, *Readings in Hispanic American History* (New York, 1927), pp. 248-49. For text in Spanish, see Zamora, *op. cit.*, pp. 299-301.

and propagation of the faith. In this concession can be detected another phase of the patronage, the utilitarian right, to be specific. The pope declared that the occasion of this great concession was to compensate the crown for the heavy expenses incurred by the temporal and spiritual conquest. This pontifical disposition bestowed a special character on the patronage of the Spanish kings over the Church in America which was even more comprehensive than that of Granada. In Spain the Church was supported by tithes and special rents; in America these revenues went to the crown and the Church was, in theory at least, supported by royal appropriations and regular endowments.

Although the royal authority over the Church in America was extensive, because of the bulls of 1493 and 1501, nevertheless Julius II was reluctant to recognize the patronal rights contained in the bulls of his predecessor, Alexander VI. King Ferdinand, on the other hand, entertained little doubt that the rights of patronage had been conferred, although not explicitly expressed. The question came to an issue in 1504 following Queen Isabella's request that an archbishopric and two bishoprics be created in the island of Española. Julius II on November 15, 1504, acquiesced in sanctioning the foundation of the sees, but he did not mention the rights of presentation and the royal claim to the tithes. This meant that the ecclesiastical rents belonged to the future prelates of the sees to administer just the same as they did in the dioceses of Spain. The bull was a patent violation of established policy, and can be explained only as an attempted stroke at independence by Julius II.

Ferdinand, who firmly believed in the patronal concessions of the earlier bulls, was not the type of king to acquiesce in such a policy. When the bull was received it was withheld and the sees in Española were not allowed to be founded. Ferdinand, who was a regent of Castile, now that Isabella was dead, wrote to Francisco de Rojas, the Spanish ambassador in Rome, the following instructions: "I order you to look into the bulls that were issued for the creation and provision of an archbishop and bishop in Española; in them there is not conceded to us the patronage of the said archbishop and bishop, nor of the *dignidades* and canons, prebends, and benefices with curate and without curate, which ought to be erected in the said isle of Española. It is necessary that His Holiness concede the said patronage perpetually to me and the kings who succeed to the kingdoms of Castile and Aragon, since no mention was made of it in the aforesaid bulls, as was the case of these (bulls) of the kingdom of Granada."[27]

The demands of Ferdinand were later incorporated in three petitions

27. Leturia, *op. cit.*, pp. 31-32.

to the pope. He asked that, (1) there be express grant of the right of patronage for the erection and provision of all ecclesiastical benefices; (2) those appointed to benefices should not receive more than that part of the tithes which was apportioned to them by the king; and (3) the king should have the power to determine the territorial limits of the dioceses. Ferdinand demanded that these rights be made to apply to all the Indies and that the pope act immediately. The pontiff, however, would not be hastened, and nothing was done until 1508, when Ferdinand returned to the regency of Castile after the death of Philip I. He then declared with his customary vigor that he would not permit the erection of new sees in America until the right of royal patronage was recognized; that is, until the concessions of Alexander VI were confirmed.[28]

Eventually Julius II capitulated, and by the bull *Universalis Ecclesiae*, July 28, 1508, he conceded universal patronage in the Indies to the Spanish crown. Whether it be true that this bull granted for the first time the *real patronato de Indias*, or whether it merely recognized and reconfirmed rights bestowed in earlier bulls, it is nevertheless generally regarded as the principal documentary evidence of the legal right of the Spanish sovereigns to exercise jurisdiction over the Catholic Church in America.[29] Because of its prime importance, therefore, it is presented here *in extenso*:

> Julius, bishop, servant of the servants of God. We, presiding by divine choice, although unworthily, over the government of the Universal Church, do concede voluntarily to the Catholic kings principally those things that augment their honor and glory, and contribute effectively to the benefit and security of their dominions. Since our beloved son in Christ, Ferdinand, illustrious king of Aragon, and also of Sicily, and Isabella, of cherished memory, Queen of Castile and León, after having expelled the Moors from Spain, crossed the ocean and planted the Cross in unknown lands, and subjugated many islands and places, and among these being one very rich and extremely populous named New Spain, thereby fulfilling to the extent of their ability the saying *in omnem terram exivit sonus eorum*—Therefore, we, in order that it (New Spain) might be purged of false and pernicious rites, and the true religion be planted there, have acceded to the most urgent requests of the king and queen, and do hereby erect for the greater glory of the name of Christ, a metropolitan church in Ayguacen, and two cathe-

28. *Ibid.*, p. 32.
29. Ayarragaray (*op. cit.*, p. 162), in commenting on the importance of this bull, writes eloquently of "the magnitude of its conception and the loftiness of its language."

drals in Maguen and Bayunen, and if the converts imbued by the new faith should attempt to found any church or pious place, they should do so in such a way as not to injure the new religion or the temporal dominions of the king.

In view of the fact that the said Ferdinand, who is also at present governor-general of the kingdoms of Castile and León, and our most cherished daughter in Christ, Juana, queen of the same kingdoms and daughter of the aforementioned Ferdinand, wish that no church, monastery, or pious place be erected or founded either in the islands and lands already possessed, or in those subsequently acquired, without their express consent and that of their successors; and considering that since it is convenient to those kings that the persons who preside over churches and monasteries be faithful and acceptable to them, they desire that they be conceded the right of patronage and of the presentation of qualified persons for both the metropolitan and cathedral churches already erected, or to be erected in the future, and for all the other ecclesiastical benefices inside of a year of their vacancy, and also for inferior benefices; and in case the *ordinario* should refuse without legitimate cause to grant the one presented with canonical institution inside of ten days, any other bishop, at the request of the king should grant it. We, appreciating that these privileges increase the honor, beauty and security of those islands, and also of the said kingdoms, whose kings are always devout and faithful to the Apostolic See, and heeding the reiterated demands made on us by King Ferdinand and Queen Juana, after mature deliberation with our brothers the cardinals of the Holy Roman Church, and with their advice, by these presents we concede with apostolic authority, other constitutions, ordinances, and laws to the contrary notwithstanding, to the said Ferdinand and Juana, and to the future kings of Castile and León, that nobody without their consent can construct or build in the above mentioned islands, now possessed or to be possessed, large churches; and we concede the right of patronage and of presenting qualified persons to cathedral churches, monasteries, *dignidades,* collegiates, and other ecclesiastical benefices and pious places in this manner: respecting benefices that are instituted in the consistory, the presentation is to be made to us, or our successors, within one year after the vacancy occurs; and respecting the other benefices, presentation will be made to the respective *ordinarios,* and if these refuse without cause to give institution inside of ten days, any bishop in those lands, on the petition of King Ferdinand or of Queen Juana, or the king ruling at that time, can bestow, under those conditions, free and legal canonical institution on the person presented. Nobody should deign to infringe on or act contrary to this concession, and if any one attempts to do so, let him know that he will incur the indignation of God

Almighty and of the blessed apostles Peter and Paul. Given in
Rome, etc., July 28, 1508.[30]

Since the concession of patronage was linked, in the bull of 1508,
with the creation of the ecclesiastical province of Española, fear was
felt in Spain that Ferdinand's demands for universal patronage had been
ignored. In 1510 the Council of Castile seriously considered demanding
an amendment to the bull. But it was decided to be unnecessary when
it was pointed out that the identical purpose of extending the territorial
scope of the grant could be accomplished, if, in establishing new sees,
there was an express papal recognition of patronage and presentation for
each one. Due to the rapid decline of population in Española, the
bishops for the three sees were never appointed. The king, on the
contrary, asked the pope to suppress the dioceses and create only
one bishopric in Española and another in Porto Rico, both to be dependent on the Archbishop of Seville. This was done by the bull *Romanus
Pontifex* in August, 1511. An examination of this bull, or any one of
the subsequent bulls of erection, will show that all were drawn up according to standard form and modeled after that of 1508.[31]

The most extreme canonists contend that the sole title of *real
patronato de Indias* was the pontifical concession contained in the bull
Universalis Ecclesiae. They regard it as the organic charter of the royal
right of patronage in America. Less ardent protagonists of the idea that
patronage is purely spiritual in origin, without relinquishing the contention that the privilege is based on pontifical grant, feel that these
concessions were conveyed in three papal bulls rather than in one. By
virtue of the bulls of 1493 and 1501 the Spanish sovereigns would have
exercised the absolute canonical patronage even though the bull of 1508
had never been issued. As has already been noted, Pope Alexander VI
forged three strong links in the chain of the *patronato de Indias*; they
were: (1) the concession of the evangelical mission to the crown with
the obligation in conscience of responding to it; (2) the granting of
the exclusive right to found churches and benefices as a consequence
and reward of that mission; and (3) the concession of the tithes as a
reward for those foundations.

Ferdinand believed that the crown enjoyed the right of patronage
over the churches which it founded in America even before the privilege
was formally conceded by the pope in 1508. However, it is to be noted
that Ferdinand based his claims on positive historical sources, i.e., earlier
pontifical concessions, and not on customary practices. In support of

30. Hernáez, *op. cit.*, I, 24-26; Shiels, *op. cit.*, pp. 110-12.
31. Solórzano, *op. cit.*, Lib. IV, Cap. IV, No. 11.

this assertion it is noteworthy that the Spanish sovereigns had been accustomed to petition the pope for certain "concessions." Answering their supplications the pope "conceded" with apostolic authority what had been requested of him. The bull of 1508, for example, did not "recognize" patronage as already existing by virtue of its inherency in sovereignty, but it explicitly "conceded" it. A clause in the original Latin reads: "Ad magnam instantiam quam super hoc fecerunt ac faciunt... auctoritate apostolica tenore praesentium *concedimus.*" Thus, in the natal period of the *real patronato de Indias,* the crown consistently declined to base its rights upon anything other than the papal bulls. It remained for regalism of a later period to claim patronage to be a legal right which originated simultaneously with the establishment of Spanish dominion over the Indies. Philip II was of this opinion as evidenced by his instructions concerning ecclesiastical patronage, addressed to the viceroy of New Spain on June 1, 1574: "As you know, the right of ecclesiastical patronage belongs to us throughout the realm of the Indies —both because of having discovered and acquired that new world, and erected there and endowed the churches and monasteries at our cost, or at the cost of our ancestors, the Catholic Kings; and because it was conceded to us by bulls of the most holy pontiffs, conceded of their own accord."[32] Thus, according to Philip, there was a three-fold basis of the *real patronato de Indias:* (1) the establishment of dominion through discovery and conquest; (2) the founding and endowing of churches; and (3) the papal grants. It is to be presumed that, in Philip's opinion, any one of these sufficed as legal justification for the exercise of the royal patronage.

In spite of the extensiveness of the papal grant of 1508, it will be observed that that bull contained nothing about the royal claims to the tithes and the demarcation of the dioceses—two of the three points contained in the petitions of Ferdinand. Regarding the privilege of outlining dioceses it does not appear that Ferdinand renewed his demands. This right was later conferred on the Spanish crown by pontifical concession in 1543. With respect to the tithes, however, he registered a vigorous protest, as can well be imagined, considering the practical-mindedness of this king. As a result, two bulls were issued, one on April 8, 1510, and the other on August 13, 1511, reconfirming the royal rights to the tithes.[33] The *real patronato de Indias* was won and preserved by the tenacious and absorbing policy of King Ferdinand. Had a weaker king occupied the Spanish throne in 1508 it is entirely con-

32. Cleven, *op. cit.,* p. 250.
33. Leturia, *op. cit.,* pp. 33-34.

ceivable that he would have been content to enjoy no greater privileges over the Church in America than he enjoyed in Spain. Therefore, it can be said that, to a large extent, the *real patronato de Indias* was the work of Ferdinand the Catholic.[34]

The rapidity with which the Spanish crown developed a policy of administration of the patronage was remarkable. By the end of the reign of Philip II[35] the civil control of the Church was thoroughly consolidated. Subsequent history added nothing to its essential nature, except perhaps to strengthen and expand even more the royal control. For that reason it is not necessary to enumerate the many papal bulls of erection which were issued throughout the colonial period. They extended the scope but not the nature of the royal control. Of some importance, however, in the history of the patronage in the Indies were the bulls of Benedict XIV, issued in 1753. The first (January 11) confirmed the rights of the Spanish kings as then exercised in the Indies, and the second (June 9) declared that the royal patronage was acquired "by foundation and endowment, by privilege and apostolic concession, and by other legitimate title." This bull has been frequently cited by regalists as confirmation of their claims.[36]

The ecclesiastical patronage of all Spanish America belonged exclusively to the royal crown, which was always most zealous of the conservation and inviolability of such an ample right. The zeal of the crown in protecting its rights is admirably set forth in a *cédula* of Philip II to the viceroy of New Spain:

> The King. To our viceroy of Nueva España, or the person or persons who shall, for the time being, be exercising the government of that country: As you know, the right of the ecclesiastical patronage belongs to us throughout the realm of the Indias—both because of having discovered and acquired that new world, and erected there and endowed the churches and monasteries at our own cost, or at the cost of our ancestors, the Catholic Sovereigns; and because it was conceded to us by bulls of the most holy pontiffs, conceded of their own accord. For its conservation, and that of the right which we have to it, we order and command that the said right of patronage be always preserved for us and our royal crown, singly and *in*

34. Father Mariano Cuevas, S.J., *Historia de la Iglesia en México* (Mexico, 1928), II, 47-48, doubts the authenticity of the bull because of the appearance of the name "Novam Hispaniam" (i.e., New Spain) in the papal document which was dated eleven years before New Spain, or Mexico, was discovered. Father Pedro Leturia, in a study published in 1946, *Studi e testi*, 125 (1946), 402-26, laid the whole question to rest.

35. Philip II—"a man under the illusion that he was a papal vicar." Shiels, *op. cit.*, p. 207.

36. *Dictamen sobre Provisión de Benefices Eclesiásticos* (Mexico, 1824), p. 8.

solidum, throughout all the realm of the Indias, without any derogation therefrom, either in whole or in part; and that we shall not
concede the right of patronage by any favor or reward that we or
the kings our successors may confer.

Further, no person or persons, or ecclesiastical or secular communities, or church or monastery, shall be able to exercise the right
of patronage by custom, privilege, or any other title, unless it be the
person who shall exercise it in our name, and with our authority
and power; and no person, whether secular or ecclesiastical, and no
order, convent, or religious community, of whatever state, condition,
rank and preëminence he or they may be, shall for any occasion and
cause whatever, judicially or extra-judicially, dare to meddle in any
matter touching my royal patronage, to injure us in it—to appoint
to any church, benefice, or ecclesiastical office, or to be accepted if
he shall have been appointed—in all the realm of the Indias, without
our presentation, or that of the person to whom we commit it by
law or by letters-patent. He who shall do the contrary, if he be a
secular person, shall incur the loss of the concessions that shall have
been made to him by us in all the realm of the Indias, shall be unable to hold and obtain others, and shall be exiled perpetually from
all our kingdoms and seigniories, and if he shall be an ecclesiastical
person, he shall be considered as a foreigner, and exiled from all our
kingdoms, and shall not be able to hold or obtain any benefice or
ecclesiastical office, and shall incur the other penalties established
against such by laws of these my kingdoms. And our viceroys,
audiencias, and royal justices shall proceed with all severity against
those who thus shall infringe or violate our right of patronage; and
they shall proceed officially, either at the petition of our fiscals, or at
that of any party who demands it; and in the execution of it great
diligence shall be exercised.[37]

In the above and numerous other decrees the right of royal patronage
was held to be indivisible and imprescriptible. The sovereign did not
lose it through lack of exercise and no one could acquire it through use
or custom. No person or persons, ecclesiastical or secular, were to use
the patronage except under the crown's authority and severe penalties
were provided for infringements of the royal privilege. Royal officials,
particularly viceroys, *oidores*, and governors, were cautioned to watch
over the rights and preëminences of the patronage and to issue the
necessary orders. The prelates also were ordered to preserve the patronage, and, in doubtful matters, they were to advise the Council of the
Indies. The archbishops and bishops had to vow, before entering their

37. Cleven, *op. cit.*, pp. 250-51.

offices, fealty and obedience to the crown and observance of the royal patronage.[38]

So jealously did the king guard his patronal rights that the bull of Clement VII in 1532, which granted the right of patronage to Hernando Cortés in the marquisate of Oaxaca, was retained by Charles V. A royal *cédula*, December 19, 1593, addressed to the archbishop of Mexico, reprimanded him for difficulties placed in the way of the viceroy in the exercise of the patronage. In Peru at an early period the archbishop and other prelates had usurped the patronage. In consequence Viceroy Francisco de Toledo restored the royal prerogative in spite of the strenuous opposition of the clergy. The ecclesiastical invasion was only temporarily stopped, for in 1604 Viceroy Velasco advised his successor that he would have a perpetual warfare in Peru concerning the royal patronage.[39] In Charcas in the middle of the seventeenth century occurred a case which illustrates how jealously the Spanish crown was attached to its ecclesiastical rights. A lawyer argued before the audiencia of Charcas that the royal patronage only gave extra judicial protection to the churches of the Indies and that the crown did not acquire thereby the right to hear ecclesiastical cases. The royal fiscal claimed that this argument was false, scandalous, contrary to the royal rights and to the nature, prerogatives, and dignity of the patronage. The lawyer was fined one hundred ducats and was forbidden to practice for four years. The king, when notified of this decision, approved it. The royal attitude toward the patronage might be summed up as in a *cédula* to the bishop of Cuba (July 23, 1639), "As you know, or ought to know, the said patronage is a thing which I cherish greatly, and which I cannot and ought not [to] permit to be injured."[40]

Although the patronage was held to be imprescriptible, nevertheless it could be delegated by the Spanish kings. Due to the distance between Spain and America, it was impossible for the king to exercise the patronal rights personally. Therefore he entrusted this power to his viceroys, audiencias, and governors. This delegation of powers was approved by the papacy, for Boniface VIII said that one could not expect the impossible. The laws of the Indies bestowed complete power on the viceroys, presidents, *oidores*, and governors in America to discharge the rights and preëminences of the royal patronage and to oblige

38. *Recopilación de Leyes de los Reynos de las Indias* (2nd ed.; Madrid, 1756), Lib. 1, Tit. 6, Leyes, 1, 35, 45, 47. (Hereafter referred to as *Recop. de Leyes.*)

39. Lillian Estelle Fisher, *Viceregal Administration in the Spanish-American Colonies* (Berkeley, 1926), p. 207; Angel Gabriel Pérez, *El Patronato Español en el Virreyno del Perú durante el Siglo XVI* (Tournai, Belgium, 1937).

40. Sarsfield, *op. cit.*, p. 46.

all ecclesiastical authorities to conform to their orders with respect to it. By virtue of his position as vice-patron, the viceroy had manifold duties arising from his relations with the ecclesiastical organizations. It was generally through his intermediation, or independent action, that the right of presentation was exercised, that the clergy, secular and regular, were controlled, churches established, councils held, and education, hospitals and institutions of charity were administered. "Marquina [viceroy of New Spain] declared that the authority of the viceroy was made evident by his functions as vice-patron, which caused him to be distinguished even by the ecclesiastics, who were always objects of veneration among the populace. The ceremonies whereby he was honored gave him a certain dignity of his own which surpassed that of the highest functionary." When the presidents of the audiencias exercised the privileges of the royal patronage it was always understood that they were subordinate to the viceroy. Governors in turn were generally considered as subordinate to the audiencias and viceroy. After the intendancies were established, the intendants were given a few of the patronal rights to relieve the viceroy of these duties in the provinces. By Article 6 of the *Ordenanza de Intendentes* the right of patronage in the viceroyalty of La Plata resided in the viceroy and the governors-intendants of the provinces. By the *cédula* of May 9, 1795, which modified the intendancy system, the intendants were allowed to retain the vice-patronage in their capacity as sub-delegates of the viceroys and presidents.[41]

Dating from the bull *Inter Caetera* of 1493 the Spanish crown exercised the exclusive right of licensing ecclesiastics to come to the Indies. Coincident with this power was that of controlling their movements once they were in America. Licenses were issued by the Council of the Indies and complete data relating to the age, birthplace, and the like, of the applicants were recorded. These licenses had to be scrutinized by the officials of the *Casa de Contratación* before they would allow embarkation. Expenses of transportation were paid from the royal treasury. When ecclesiastics came to America they did not go where they pleased, but where the viceroy and governor directed them. Religious who came to America without license were sent back to Spain. Whenever settlements lacked a sufficient number of ecclesiastics, the civil authorities did not hesitate to call on the regular orders for friars. If a religious wished to leave the Indies, the permission of the pope himself did not suffice; the cleric had to get the consent of the king. Even the viceroys were not allowed to grant licenses for parish priests to return to Spain. After

41. Fisher, *op. cit.*, pp. 182-84; *Recop. de Leyes*, 1-6-26, 47.

1589 an exception was made in favor of those friars who had been in America for at least ten years.[42]

In the same manner as the Supreme Pontiff was impotent in controlling the movements of ecclesiastics to and from America, so also was he legally restrained from founding churches or other pious establishments without royal permission. For the erection of cathedrals it was necessary that the pope issue an express bull, but these bulls of erection were, without exception, solicited by the crown and made to conform to royal desires and the laws of the Indies. The usual procedure in securing permission to erect a church, convent, or pious work was somewhat as follows: An *información*, or petition, accompanied by supporting documents, was drawn up setting forth the object and necessity of the desired church. This, accompanied by the opinion of the diocesan prelate, was sent to the viceroy or president of the audiencia. Then, with that officer's opinion attached, the documents were sent to the Council of the Indies, which, if it decided favorably, issued the license for the erection of the church. Due to the fact that the vice-patrons gave permission too readily for the building of convents, a *cédula* was issued on March 19, 1593, which ordered them not to grant licenses for such buildings without first securing the king's permission. This law was reaffirmed on June 14, 1616, and the viceroys were severely reprimanded for disregarding it. So insistent was the king that no ecclesiastical establishment be erected without proper license that he empowered the viceroys to demolish all religious structures which had been erected without proper authorization. This order was put into effect, too, as evidenced by numerous examples. For instance, in 1608 the viceroy Montesclaros of Peru was ordered to destroy the convent of the Mercedarians, which the Count of Monterey had illegally permitted to be established. License was even necessary for the organization of *cofradías*, or religious brotherhoods, although the object might only be spiritual and pious. If any person should build or endow a church, the king, according to the laws of the Indies, would be the patron of it. However, the crown only exercised the patronage over the cathedral churches and parishes and did not extend it to the lesser churches. A law of the Indies permitted private persons to found with their own money monasteries, hospitals, hermitages, churches, and other pious works, and to exercise the patronage over them.[43]

When the Spanish king acquired the use of the tithes in 1501, he at the same time assumed the obligation of assisting in all the expenses

---

42. Diego de Encinas, *Provisiones, Cédulas, Capítulos de Ordenanzas*, etc. (Madrid, 1596), I, 107, 122; *Recop. de Leyes*, 1-13-2, 1-14-19.

43. Fisher, *op. cit.*, pp. 186-87; Encinas, *op. cit.*, I, 145-47.

connected with the building of churches. The ordinary practice was that one-third of the cost was paid from the royal treasury, and two-thirds were paid by the encomenderos and the Indians. "In fact the Indians really bore the entire burden for the construction of churches, since they provided the manual labor, and, by working on the encomiendas, enabled the encomenderos to pay their share. They paid tribute to the king from which the portion donated by the royal treasury was taken." When a church needed repairs a petition was sent to the viceroy who submitted it to his council, which decided the amount of money that ought to be contributed from the royal treasury.[44]

Although the crown enjoyed the use of the tithes by virtue of the bull of 1501, it rarely availed itself of the grant, but donated to bishops, clergy, hospitals, etc., the greater part of what was due to it from this source. The tithes of each diocese were ordinarily divided into four parts; one part went to the bishop, and one part to the chapter. The remaining half was divided into nine parts called *novenos*. One and one-half went to the corporate body of the church which administered the temporalities; four were given to the lower clergy; one and one-half *noveno* went to the hospitals; and the remaining two-ninths to the king. All but the two royal *novenos* were variable. Generally these two were spent on churches, although the king had the right to use them for temporal matters. Whenever the tithes were not sufficient to pay the clerics the established amount due them, the balance was always forthcoming from the royal treasury. Numerous *cédulas* were directed to royal officials ordering this to be done. The royal treasury officials had charge of collecting the tithes, and it was the duty of the viceroy to see that no person escaped who was required to pay. The military orders tried to claim exemption but the king refused it. The Jesuits offered the greatest opposition. They alleged that their order enjoyed pontifical privileges which exempted the members from payment. The question was still in controversy at the time of the expulsion. It should be noted, however, that the expulsion of the Jesuits was in no way connected with *real patronato*. Other revenues to the State from ecclesiastical sources were: the income from the sale of bulls of the Holy Crusade, subsidies donated by the papacy, and the *mesadas* and ecclesiastical half-annates, or salary taxes.[45]

If there was one point in public ecclesiastical law on which the crown would not give way to Rome, it was the determining of the territorial limits of dioceses and parishes. Since the boundaries of bishop-

44. Fisher, *op. cit.*, p. 187, n. 17.
45. Cleven, *op. cit.*, p. 247, n. 1; Encinas, *op. cit.*, I, 108-11, 179-201; Solórzano, *op. cit.*, Lib. IV, Cap. IV, Nos. 26-29.

rics coincided with the political territorial divisions, the power of determining the former had to be subordinated to the temporal authority. Furthermore, the pope, being far away and not cognizant of local conditions, could not weigh all the considerations necessary for the creation of bishoprics. Only the political government of the territory was in position to know its population and resources. Sarsfield mentions that in the bull of erection for the cathedral of Tucumán, the pope believed Tucumán to be an island.[46]

The royal right of controlling the territorial extent of dioceses was based on the bull of 1508 and subsequent bulls of erection. For example: Clement VII in the bull *Sacri Apostolatus Ministerio,* which provided for the erection of a cathedral church in Mexico, and conceded the royal patronage over it, left to the decision, disposition, and order of Charles V everything relating to the erection of the said church, *even to the establishment of the limits of the diocese.* There are four laws covering this matter in the *Recopilación de Indias.* The first declared that only the king had the power to outline and divide bishoprics. The second reaffirmed that it was the king who had the power to divide bishoprics, even by acts posterior to the erection of cathedrals. The third laid down a rule for the Council of the Indies to the effect that ecclesiastical districts should be made to conform as far as possible to the political divisions; for example, archbishoprics and provinces of the regulars to conform to the district of the audiencia; bishoprics to the *gobernaciones* or *alcaldías mayores*; parishes and curacies to *corregimientos* and *alcaldías ordinarias.* The fourth law concerned the curacies: "We grant license and permission to the diocesan prelates of our Indies to, when there is necessity, divide, unite, or suppress curate benefices, provided that they have previously informed our vice-patrons in order that they may jointly issue the orders they regard as necessary." With respect to the outlining of the greater and more important districts like the bishoprics and provinces, the king acted alone in his royal council.[47]

The essence of the *real patronato de Indias* was of course the right of presentation. The origins of the privilege have already been discussed. The manner of its operation in America will now be described. Whenever a higher ecclesiastical office like an archbishopric, bishopric, or canonicate was to be filled, the candidate had to be presented by the king. The king's nominations for archbishops and bishops were presented to the Holy Father for canonical installation; the candidates for the lesser benefices were presented to the archbishop or bishop of the particular diocese.

46. Sarsfield, *op. cit.,* p. 115.
47. *Recop. de Leyes,* 1-2-8, 1-7-3, 1-6-40, 2-2-7.

Presentation to the lesser ecclesiastical positions in the Indies was entrusted to the vice-patrons. A law of April 4, 1609, gave the power of appointment to parishes and *doctrinas* entirely to the viceroys. With respect to these latter benefices, it was ordered that they should be filled in the following manner:

> When a benefice (whether a sinecure or a curacy), or the administration of any hospital or a sacristy or church wardenship, or the stewardship of a hospital, or any other benefice or ecclesiastical office, shall become vacant, or when it has to be filled for the first time: the prelate shall order a written proclamation to be posted in the cathedral church, or in the church, hospital, or monastery where such benefice or office is to be filled, with the suitable limit, so that those who desire to compete for it may enter the lists. From all those who thus compete, and from all the others whom the prelate shall believe to be suitable persons for such office or benefice, after having examined them and after having informed himself concerning their morals and ability, he shall choose two persons from them —those whom, in the sight of God and his conscience, he shall judge most suitable for such office or benefice. The nomination of the two thus named shall be presented to our viceroy or to the president of our royal Audiencia; or to the person who, in our name, shall exercise the superior government of the province where such benefice or office shall become vacant and must be filled, so that he may select one from the two appointees. He shall send that selection to the prelate, so that the latter in accordance with it, and by virtue of the presentation, may grant the appointment, collation, and canonical installation—by way of commission and not by perpetual title, but removable at will by the person who shall have presented them in our name, together with the prelate. And should there be no more than one person who desires to compete for such benefice or office, or the prelate shall not find more than one person whom he desires to receive the nomination to it, he shall send the name to our viceroy, president, or governor, as above stated, so that the latter may present him. Then by virtue of such presentation, the prelate shall make the appointment in the form above directed. But it is our desire and will that when the presentation shall be made by us, and we shall expressly state in our presentation that the collation and canonical installation shall be by title and not by commission, those presented by us be always preferred to those presented by our viceroy, presidents, or governors, in the form above mentioned.[48]

The crown was insistent that there should be no delay in filling vacancies. In the greater consistoral benefices one · year was allowed,

48. Cleven, *op. cit.*, pp. 253-55; *Recop. de Leyes*, 1-6-3, 4, 7, 15.

due to the fact that confirmation had to be bestowed by the papacy. The prelates and viceroy were ordered to notify the king of prebendaries and vacant benefices, of worthy candidates and what considerations ought to be observed in the matter of presentation. Parochial benefices and *doctrinas* could not be vacant longer than four months. In 1540 the viceroy was ordered to make new appointments when ecclesiastics were absent from their positions for more than a year. In 1574 only eight months were permitted in case of legitimate cause.[49]

The discretion of the vice-patron in the exercise of his rights of presentation was greatly circumscribed by measures designed to maintain purity of appointments. The laws commanded the viceroys always to favor the most learned and worthy candidates. Those who set the best examples by their lives were to be given preference. No cleric could hold more than one benefice. Foreigners were not to be considered for appointments unless they bore letters of naturalization. No one should be admitted to a *doctrina* who did not understand the Indian language. Furthermore, a *doctrina* was not to be presented to any relative of an encomendero. In case the governors did not present worthy religious, they were to be presented by the viceroy.[50]

The presentation having been made in due form, the canonical institution followed. As has been noted, the pope installed archbishops and bishops, and the prelate of the particular diocese conferred the other ecclesiastical benefices. It was often the practice that the prelate presented by the king would assume his office before receiving papal confirmation. Without waiting upon papal action, due to the ordinary delay because of the great distance from Rome, the king would order the ecclesiastical chapter of the vacant see to turn over the office to the bishop-elect. Although the chapters complied without opposing the least objection, nevertheless Rome never acquiesced in the practice. Before the prelates could assume their dioceses they had to exhibit to the viceroy their credentials of election and evidence of having taken the regular oath of fealty to the crown. The act of conferring the office was regulated in the following manner: "After the original warrant of our presentation has been presented, appointment and canonical installation shall be made without any delay; and order will be given to assign to him the emoluments, unless there is some legitimate objection against the person presented, and one which can be proved. If there is no legitimate objection, or if any such be alleged that shall not be proved, and the prelate should delay the appointment, installation, and posses-

49. *Recop. de Leyes*, 1-6-19, 55, 48.
50. *Recop. de Leyes*, 1-6-20, 27, 29, 30, 31, 33; Encinas, *op. cit.*, I, 97-99.

sion, he shall be obliged to pay to such person the emoluments and income, costs, and interests, that shall have been incurred by him." The prelate was supposed to institute within ten days. If he failed to act by that time, the act of institution could be performed by another prelate. If the candidate did not present himself to exercise his office within the fixed period, he forfeited the position. Those provided with benefices by the king could only be removed by royal order. The holders of lesser benefices could be removed by the prelates or superiors with the permission of the vice-patron. The royal audiencias were not to hear causes of priests removed from office in conformity with the laws of the patronage.[51]

The privileged position of the clergy in the enjoyment of its own courts was known as the *fuero eclesiástico*. This exemption from the control of the ordinary tribunals was no distinctive feature of the *real patronato de Indias*, but rather was borrowed from customary Spanish practice dating back to the fourth or fifth century. These courts, organized by dioceses, were ordinarily of three kinds: *provisorato* for Spaniards, *provisorato* for Indians, and *juzgado de testamentos, capellanías, y obras pías* (court for wills, chapels, and pious works). The powers of the last court were later curtailed by the civil probate of wills of clergymen. In 1789 the cases of *capellanías* and *obras pías* were also made cognizable in secular courts.[52]

The ecclesiastical courts had no jurisdiction over cases either civil or criminal concerning persons not Catholics. They could not inflict corporal punishment, or sentence Indians to hard labor or impose fines on them. In later times the jurisdiction of the ecclesiastical courts was reduced. By royal decree of October 25, 1795, the common courts were allowed to take cognizance of grave offenses committed by ecclesiastics. Questions of jurisdiction between the ecclesiastical and civil courts were decided by the viceroy. In Europe the papal court in Rome was accustomed to hear appeals from the decisions of the ecclesiastical courts. Such a practice was not thought to be desirable in America, for it was feared that the inevitable delay would breed scandal. Therefore, by a bull of Gregory XIII (February 28, 1578) it was provided that all ecclesiastical cases should be definitely decided in America. After obtaining the brief, Philip II did not publish it, and it remained inoperative during his lifetime because he had scruples regarding the termination of pontifical jurisdiction in such matters. Consequently appeals continued to be carried to the pope until 1606. In that year and in 1722 and

51. *Recop. de Leyes,* 1-6-23, 24, 36, 38, 39; Solórzano, *op. cit.,* Lib. IV, Cap. VII; Cleven, *op. cit.,* pp. 252-53.

52. H. H. Bancroft, *History of Mexico* (San Francisco, 1883), III, 188.

1731, royal orders provided for the enforcement of the provisions of the bull of 1578.[53]

Litigation arising out of the royal patronage, or *causas de patronato*, was not cognizable in the ecclesiastical courts. A *cédula* of 1540, directed to the president and *oidores* of the Audiencia of Mexico, fixed the jurisdiction of patronal causes in the said audiencia and expressly prohibited the ecclesiastical courts from hearing such cases. The ordinary procedure was first to have recourse to the vice-patron. If the cause originated in the territory of an intendancy, the governor-intendant was first appealed to as delegate of the vice-patron. From the decision of the vice-patron appeal could then be taken to the audiencia. Disputes between bishops, curates, canons, and dignitaries concerning benefices and canonical capacity to fill them were regarded as patronal causes or *pleitos de patronato*, and not matters for the ecclesiastical courts. In conclusion, all cases concerning the limits of bishoprics, canonical impediments to the filling of benefices, conflicts between the beneficiaries themselves over their rights and prerogatives, *pleitos* between ecclesiastical chapters and the bishops or archbishops concerning the administration of the Church, as well as all causes between curates over their respective offices, and, in general, all cases which in any way touched the *real patronato*, were attended by civil authorities and heard in civil tribunals, even though it often appeared that the subjects involved were purely spiritual in nature.[54]

In the control of church councils and synods convened in the Indies, the Spanish crown also intervened to an exceptional degree. Although the matters considered in the councils more often referred to dogma, cult, and discipline, nevertheless the laws of the Indies required royal permission for the holding of councils. Provincial church councils, as provided by the papal brief of December 6, 1610, were to be held in the Indies every twelve years, but only thirteen were actually held during the colonial period. An early law provided that the king should be consulted and his consent secured before a council could be convened. Later the archbishops of America were allowed to summon provincial councils merely with the approval of the viceroy or captain-general, without having to appeal to the king. The vice-patron attended these meetings in person and saw that the rights of patronage were not violated. In the provincial councils only the bishops could vote. The canons, su-

53. *Recop. de Leyes*, 1-9-10; Solórzano, *op. cit.*, Lib. IV, Cap. 9, Nos. 1-6.
54. *Ibid.*, III, 687-88; Lucas Alamán, *Historia de México* (Mexico, 1849), I, 68; *Recop. de Leyes*, 1-9-10, 2-15-34, 35; Solórzano, *op. cit.*, Lib. IX, Cap. 9, Nos. 1-6; Sarsfield, *op. cit.*, pp. 51, 54; Bernard Moses, *The Spanish Dependencies in South America* (New York, 1914), II, 221-22.

periors of religious orders, and the presbyters could attend but not vote. The matters discussed in the provincial councils related to morality and good conduct of the clergy, the enforcement of the decrees of the Council of Trent, and the good treatment and instruction of the Indians. The decisions of the councils were sent to the king for his approval. After the royal assent had been secured, the findings were sent to the pope who ordered them published in the provinces where the councils had been held. Thus, no measure enacted by a council could be executed without the royal approval.[55]

The Spanish sovereigns also ordered observance of a law of the Council of Trent which provided that the bishops should each year summon a synod of the prelates and clerics of their dioceses. The measures passed by the synods had to be submitted to the vice-patron, so that he could determine whether the royal rights of patronage had been observed. If he felt that the royal sovereignty had been invaded he sent the synodal constitution to the Council of the Indies. Upon receiving temporal approval the bishops published the measures that had been passed by the synod.[56]

The same motive which impelled the Spanish kings to control the councils and synods, actuated them in asserting control over the admission into America of papal bulls, briefs, rescripts, and other pontifical documents. The reason for this was the fear that the pope would trespass the limits of his divine office and legislate in purely temporal matters with a consequent invasion of the royal prerogative. This right, like that of controlling the councils, was based on ancient Spanish custom and later-day legal sanction. In following these precedents the laws of the Indies ordered the civil and ecclesiastical authorities in America not to obey briefs and pontifical bulls which did not have the approval of the Council of the Indies. A *cédula* of Philip IV in 1643 repeated the commands of his predecessors that papal bulls should be examined first in the Council of the Indies. As an additional precaution, it was ordered in 1777 that bulls, briefs, and rescripts, even though provided with the Council's exequatur, were not to be circulated without the permission of the vice-patron. Viceroys, audiencias, and governors in America were ordered to send back to the Council of the Indies all papal documents that had not been approved by it. Either the pope was very careful not to invade the royal prerogative, or the crown was liberal in its examination of papal bulls, for, according to Ribadeneyra, only six bulls were retained by the Council of the Indies. There were

---

55. Moses, *Spanish Dependencies*, II, 222-23; Fisher, *op. cit.*, pp. 218-19; Encinas, *op. cit.*, I, 137-38; *Recop. de Leyes*, 1-8-6; Gómez Hoyos, *op. cit.*, 198.

56. *Recop. de Leyes*, 1-8-6; 2-15-147; Encinas, I, 136-37.

numerous cases, however, of the viceroys stopping circulation of bulls or briefs which did not have the permission of the Council.[57]

So opposed was the crown to direct correspondence between the Church in Europe and in America, that when the papal nuncio at Madrid, without permission, published in 1642 the proclamation of a jubilee by Clement X, the act was condemned by the king. The papal legates and nuncios resided near the Spanish court, but they were not allowed to go to America. As far as America was concerned these papal representatives did not exist except in negative laws which refused them the power and jurisdiction exercised in Spain. In America all of the apostolic jurisdiction was regarded as being delegated to the metropolitans.[58]

The royal patronage embraced the regular orders quite as comprehensively as it did the secular clergy. The law of 1574 specified that the religious orders should observe and maintain the right of patronage in the following manner:

> We also will and order that the religious orders observe and maintain the right of patronage in the following form:
>
> First: No general, commissary-general, visitor, provincial, or any other superior of the religious orders, shall go to the realm of the Indias, without first showing in our royal Council of the Indias the powers that he bears and giving us relation of them; and without the Council giving him our decree and permission so that he may go, and a warrant so that our viceroys, audiencias, justices, and our other vassals may admit and receive him to the exercise of his office, and give him all protection and aid in it.
>
> Any provincial, visitor, prior, guardian, or other high official, who may be elected and nominated in the realm of the Indias, shall, before being admitted to exercise his office, inform our viceroy, president, audiencia, or governor who shall have in charge the supreme government of such province, and shall show him his patent of nomination and election, so that the latter may give him the protection and aid necessary for the exercise and use of his office.
>
> The provincials of all the orders who are established in the Indias, each one of them, shall always keep a list ready of all the monasteries and chief residences (maintained there by his orders) and of the members (resident in each) that fall in his province, and of all the religious in the province—noting each one of them by name, with a report of his age and qualifications, and the office or ministry in which each one is occupied. He shall give that an-

57. Bancroft, *Mexico*, III, 685-86; Ribadeneyra, *op. cit.*, pp. 226-29; *Recop. de Leyes*, 1-7-55, 1-9-2, 5; Shiels, *op. cit.*, pp. 169-94.

58. Alamán, *op. cit.*, I, 36-37; Sarsfield, *op. cit.*, p. 94.

nually to our viceroy, audiencia, or governor, or the person who shall have charge of the supreme government in the province, adding to or removing from the list the religious who shall be superfluous and those who shall be needed. Our viceroy, audiencia, or governor, shall keep those general lists which shall thus be given, for himself, and in order that he may inform us by report of the religious that there are, and those of whom there is need of provision, by each fleet sent out.

The provincials of the orders, each one of them, shall make a list of all the religious who are occupied in teaching the Christian doctrine to the Indians, and the administration of sacraments, and the offices of curas in the villages of the chief monasteries. They shall give such list once a year to our viceroy, audiencia, or governor, who shall give it to the diocesan prelate, so that he may know and understand what persons are occupied in the administration of sacraments and the office of curas and the ecclesiastical jurisdiction, and who are in charge of the souls for whom he is responsible; and in order that what is or must be provided may be apparent to him, and from whom he has to acquire account of the said souls, and to whom he must commit what is to be done for the welfare of those souls.

Whenever the provincials have to provide any religious for instruction or for the administration of the sacraments, or remove any who shall have been appointed, they shall give notice thereof to our viceroy, president, audiencia, or governor, who shall exercise the supreme government of the province, and to the prelate; and they shall not remove any one who shall have been appointed, until another shall have been appointed in his place, observing the above order.[59]

The houses of religious orders were under the supervision of the Council of the Indies, which was assisted in these matters by a commissioner-general. The provincial or custodian of the regulars was named by their particular general, but the latter had to notify the commissioner-general in Spain who communicated with the Council of the Indies. Without the permission of the Council the nomination was void. The creation or suppression of provinces, the founding of new convents, the sending of visitors-general to America, and like matters were all controlled by the Council of the Indies. The ordinary procedure necessary for the founding of a new mission or seminary was somewhat as follows: The province seeking permission appointed a commissioner, who personally or through his superiors, presented the request to the

59. Cleven, *op. cit.*, pp. 255-56; *Recop. de Leyes*, 1-6-49; Gómez Hoyos, *op. cit.*, 192; Shiels, *op. cit.*, 195-228.

bishop, the audiencia, and the viceroy. All of these were required to prepare exhaustive reports. The commissioner, armed with the necessary permits of the viceroy and his superior, then went to Spain and laid the matter before the commissioner-general of the Indies. The latter presented it with all the necessary documents to the Council of the Indies.

In promoting the greater spiritual and material prosperity of the Church in the Indies, the Spanish kings were even more zealous than in safeguarding their patronage. Every effort was exerted to insure morality and purity of faith and dogma. In presenting to benefices the viceroys were always charged to favor those prelates distinguished for virtue and learning. The punishment of irregularities and the settlement of religious differences was a frequent and ofttimes annoying task of the vice-patron. Whenever bishops or superiors became negligent in their manner of living it was the duty of the viceroy to adopt effective measures to compel them to obey. Also the vice-patron was ordered to help the prelates reform subordinates and oblige them to live according to their rules. Archbishops and bishops were often reminded to conform to the decree of the Council of Trent, which required frequent visitations of their respective archdioceses and dioceses. The viceroys were given absolute power to expel rebellious ecclesiastics from their viceroyalties. There are numerous examples of actual cases of expulsion of friars by viceroys. Whenever it was necessary to reprimand an ecclesiastic, the law suggested that it be done secretly, for fear that publicity might have a bad influence upon the Indians.[60]

The dreaded institution of the Inquisition, which was extended to the New World to promote the extension of the Catholic faith and to eradicate heresy, was undoubtedly the most powerful means at the disposal of the crown to maintain purity of faith and dogma. Basing his action upon the bull of Pope Sixtus IV in 1478, which authorized the Catholic Kings to appoint inquisitors who were to have jurisdiction over heretics, Philip II in 1569 announced his decision to establish inquisitorial tribunals in Spanish America. The first tribunal was erected in Peru. Two inquisitors named by the crown were installed in Lima in 1570. In 1571 two inquisitors were installed in Mexico. Prior to this time temporary representatives of the Holy Office had been sent to America.

The jurisdiction of the Holy Office extended over Catholics accused of heresy and schism. Foreigners and Protestants who were unfortunate enough to be shipwrecked in America and fall into the hands of the Spaniards were also subjected to it. The Inquisition was specifically

60. Encinas, *op. cit.*, I, 117-18; Fisher, *op. cit.*, pp. 197, 206-7, 211.

charged with vigilance against heretical intrusions of Moors, Jews, and "New Christians," or converts. The Indians were humanely excused out of tender consideration for their immaturity. In the later days of the colonial period the Inquisition came to be used more and more for political ends. In particular it was used to keep liberal ideas out of America by placing a strict surveillance over the importation of books. Not only were books of an heretical nature prohibited, but the works of the eighteenth century political philosophers were proscribed.

The Inquisition was entirely under the control of the king in the *Consejo de la Suprema y General Inquisición*; it had long before established its independence of the papacy. The inquisitors were appointed by the king and were responsible to him alone. The viceroy took an oath to aid the Holy Office and to guard its privileges and immunities. Likewise he was charged with reporting any invasion of the patronage by the judges of the Inquisition. In minor cases of conflict between the tribunal and the secular courts, an adjustment was generally worked out in a conference of the senior *oidor* and the ranking inquisitor. In the event of no compromise, the viceroy made the decision. In serious differences between the viceroys and inquisitors the matters were referred to a committee of two members of the Council of the Indies and two members of the General Council of the Inquisition in Spain. Charles III, however, gave the viceroy the final word in all questions relating to disputed jurisdiction of the Inquisition. Also, the inquisitors had to secure the consent of the viceroy before any of its edicts could be published. The alliance between the Inquisition and the civil government was evidenced by the fact that it was the latter power which executed the decisions of the tribunal. Not only did the civil authorities inflict corporal punishment when the inquisitors decreed it, but it collected and administered the fines that were imposed by the tribunal. This same close relationship of the political and inquisitorial can be illustrated by citing the kinds of offices held simultaneously by two famous Mexican viceroys. Moya y Contreras, the first inquisitor-general of New Spain, was also archbishop and viceroy. Palafox was inquisitor-general, visitor-general, bishop of Puebla, and viceroy.[61]

Since education, hospitals, and charitable institutions were largely under the control of the Church, these subjects became important divisions of the *real patronato de Indias*. Although these are important matters, and worthy of extended discussion, it will serve the present purpose to mention merely the all-pervading supervision and control of

61. The above summary description of the Inquisition is based on H. C. Lea, *The Inquisition in the Spanish Dependencies* (New York, 1908). Also see Boleslao Lewin, *La Inquisición en Hispano-américa* (Buenos Aires, 1962).

the king over these institutions. The intervention of the crown and its agents in the fostering of educational and charitable works was second only to its zeal in propagating the faith. In fact one often was inseparable from the other. The relation of the viceroy as vice-patron over the above mentioned matters has been adequately summarized in the following words: "The viceroy was likewise vice-patron over institutions of learning. He conferred fellowships and professorships in the colleges under the royal patronage, but left their administration entirely to the prelates. Some of the viceroys were enthusiastic patrons of education, culture, and science long before their English and French neighbors made any attempts to found schools. The rules of the patronage applied to hospitals and institutions of charity, as well as to schools; therefore the viceroy acted as superintendent over them."[62]

The *real patronato de Indias*, when compared with the *patronato de España*, was certainly an extraordinary patronage. Never before or since did a sovereign with the consent of the pope so completely control the Catholic Church within his dominions. This jurisdiction, as has been noted, was not confined to ecclesiastical persons and temporalities, but even encroached upon the sphere of purely spiritual matters. For this reason it can be contended with considerable truth that the king was more than a patron in America; he exercised quasi-pontifical authority. However exceptional were the powers of the crown in ecclesiastical matters, there is little doubt that the royal aid and supervision was of inestimable advantage to the Church in America. If the patronage implied the planting, protection, and promotion of the Catholic faith and the conversion of the Indians in the newly-discovered lands by endowing churches and missions, certainly the crown discharged its trust with success. The great number of churches, monasteries, convents, and missions, as well as the hospitals and charitable institutions that were established in the New World, were all tangible evidences of the faithful discharge by the Spanish sovereigns of their holy trust as patrons.

The king was amply compensated for the obligations and responsibilities he assumed with reference to the Church. Since Catholicism was indissolubly linked with royal authority, the Church was quite as effective an instrument in the conquest and domination of the Indies as was the army. It was one of the principal agents of the civil power in America for over three centuries. The clerics, being beholden to the king for great and numerous favors, served him without the slightest inclination to rebel. They felt more closely attached to him than to the pope; they were more regalist than papalist. Given the almost absolute

62. Fisher, *op. cit.*, pp. 249-50.

domination exercised by them over the minds of their ignorant flocks, the inestimable value to the crown of its control over the clergy can be appreciated.[63]

Undoubtedly the blind obedience and almost fanatical reverence of the colonials for their "most Catholic Sovereigns" were largely the result of clerical promptings. This was most ample compensation for the cares and expenses of propagating the faith.[64]

63. "The strain of religious enthusiasm could be evoked when necessary by almost any skillful ecclesiastic. Also the fact that every good Catholic attended the confessional once a year, and frequently oftener, gave to the priest the whip hand in many a difficult situation." Wilfred Hardy Callcott, *Church and State in Mexico, 1822-1857* (Durham, 1926), p. 11.

64. "Both in Spain and in Latin America the anticlerical and antireligious character of the Enlightenment, prevalent elsewhere, was muted, and political agitation for constitutional government, insignificant until the 1790's." Karl Schmitt, "The Clergy and the Enlightenment in Latin America: An Analysis," *The Americas*, XV, No. 4 (April, 1959), 381.

Chapter II

The Catholic Church and the Spanish-American Revolution

The achievement of independence by Spain's colonies in America disturbed the centuries-old politico-ecclesiastical status. The attitude assumed by the pope, the prelates, and the clergy towards the independence movement and the religious policies adopted by the revolutionaries were subjects of vital importance in this transitional period since they exercised far-reaching influences on the determination of later Church and State relationships.

Conditions within the Church of colonial Spanish-America on the eve of the outbreak of the revolt might have constituted justifiable reasons for added dissatisfaction with Spanish rule.[1] But it is an undeniable fact that religious discontent was not one of the major causes of the wars for independence. This chapter, devoted to the Catholic Church in the Revolution, is prefaced with a description of certain unsatisfactory conditions within the colonial Church, not because of their immediate bearing on the Revolution itself, but because the outcome of the revolt emphasized the necessity of finding a solution for these problems.

The most serious matter was the supremacy of the Church in the economic sphere. The vast wealth of the colonial clergy was notorious, and was represented not only in ecclesiastical buildings and their ornate furnishings, but also in revenue-producing lands and capital loaned at interest on property of individuals. In Peru on the eve of independence there was scarcely an estate of any size which did not belong in whole or in part to the clerics. In Lima, out of 2,806 houses, 1,135 belonged to religious communities, secular ecclesiastics, or pious endowments.[2] Juan and Ulloa in their famous *Noticias Secretas* also remark on the wealth

---

1. The abuses of the ecclesiastical government of the colonies as contributing cause of the wars for independence are discussed by Miguel Luis Amunátegui, *Los Precursores de la Independencia de Chile* (Santiago, 1870), I, 147-202.

2. Sebastián Lorente, *Historia del Perú bajo los Bourbones* (Lima, 1871), pp. 270-71.

of the clergy in Quito and Peru.[3] A traveler describing Lima in the middle of the eighteenth century wrote, "There are but few who do not pay rent to the Church, either for their houses or their farms."[4]

In New Spain the Church was even more strongly entrenched economically, if such a thing were possible. On the authority of Lucas Alamán, a staunch defender of the Catholic Church, the property of the Mexican Church in the last days of the colonial period consisted of one-half of the total value of all productive real estate in New Spain.[5] In 1790, out of 3,387 houses in Mexico City, 1,935 belonged to the Church. Of course, the right of mortmain possessed by it facilitated the gradual but never ending increase in the size of its properties, for land acquired could never be alienated. "The greater became the Church holdings, and they were usually of the best land in a given community, the less land was left for the laity to own, and the fewer were the chances that the very small incipient middle class would get a foothold."[6]

A writer on Mexico comments on the wealth of the colonial Church as follows: "The clergy was an economically privileged class from the beginning. The members of it received large grants of land from the crown. Many monasteries, cathedrals and individual prelates were given *encomiendas*—which had more or less the same history as those conferred upon laymen. For the erection of churches, monasteries and residences the royal treasury furnished half the money, the *encomenderos* or the Spanish population in general furnished the other half, and the Indians did the work without remuneration. Ecclesiastical capital was free from taxation—legally in the early days, virtually always. The clergy were entitled to collect tithes and first fruits of all agricultural products, to receive fees, dowries, gifts, bequests, alms, and perpetual trust funds. From the outset they had an economic advantage over even the richest *encomenderos*, who had to build their own houses and provide their own working capital, and had not the sources of income that the clergy had. So, with the immense prestige of the Church behind them, it is not surprising that the clergy dominated the colonial era economically and politically."[7]

3. Don Jorge Juan y Don Antonio de Ulloa, *Noticias Secretas de América* (London, 1826), pp. 523-25.
4. *A True and Particular Relation of the Dreadful Earthquake* (London, 1748), pp. 279-80, quoted in Bernard Moses, *Spain's Declining Power in South America* (Berkeley, 1919), p. 301.
5. Alamán, *Historia de Méjico*, I, 67.
6. Callcott, *Church and State in Mexico*, p. 14.
7. Helen Phipps, *Some Aspects of the Agrarian Question in Mexico* (University of Texas Bulletin, No. 2515), p. 45.

The considerable sums derived from various sources, like tithes, fees, proceeds from the sales of bulls, gifts, and bequests were generally invested in real estate and real estate mortgages. "As money came easily to the ecclesiastics and as the Church fulminated against usury, they were indulgent creditors. They lent at six, five, and even four per cent, and allowed the debt to run on from generation to generation, provided interest payments were prompt. Real estate mortgages, as a rule, were nominally for a period of ten years, yet the mortgagor felt perfectly sure that he would not be called upon for the principal at the end of the period, if he kept up the interest, but usually he was at liberty to pay the whole debt when he pleased. Some mortgages, however, were 'irredeemable' by agreement. The clergy preferred this form, naturally, as it gave them a perpetual investment without further effort on their part. Mortgaged property was bought and sold freely without consulting the creditor, but could not be divided. Since borrowing was so easy, it is no wonder that landowners continued to invest all capital that came into their possession in this substantial and tax-free form of wealth and to depend upon the never-failing source for their working capital."[8]

Early in the colonial period the crown became convinced of the advisability of restricting the ownership of land by the Church. Viceroy Mendoza was directed to dispose of public land but prevent its falling into mortmain. In 1576 a decree forbade religious orders from acquiring any more property. A decree of 1796 imposed a tax of 15 per cent on all property sold to the Church. The expulsion of the Jesuits in 1767 afforded the crown an excellent opportunity to recover vast estates held in mortmain. In 1804, by a royal decree, all real estate belonging to benevolent institutions, most of which was controlled by the clergy, was taken over by the State. This confiscation included sums invested as loans on properties. Abad y Queipo, bishop-elect of Michoacán, who drew up a memorial in opposition to the decree, pointed out that the withdrawal of the vast loans of the Church would paralyze agriculture and business. The united opposition of the clergy and the great landowners finally accomplished the defeat of the measure.[9]

Within the ranks of the clergy there was an amazing disparity in economic condition. Whereas many prelates enjoyed incomes of from 200,000 to 650,000 pesos, nine-tenths of the clergy did not receive more than 150 to 300 pesos annually. Alexander von Humboldt commented with surprise on this "inequality of income of the clergy, a part of which

8. *Ibid.*, pp. 56-57.
9. Alamán, *op. cit.*, I, 137.

lives in utmost misery, a step from some individuals, who enjoy incomes superior to that of many sovereigns of Germany."[10]

There was also great disparity among the clergy as to morality. Unfriendly critics of the Catholic Church seem to delight in relating in detail the worldliness, acquisitiveness, love of ease and luxuries, and loose morals of the clerics. It is true that there was grave immorality among the clergy, especially the regulars, and it was on a sufficiently large scale to warrant remark.[11] Even Alamán admits this. But to stress this side of ecclesiastical life and activity in the Spanish colonies to the exclusion of any mention of the real constructive and lasting achievements of the Church in the transplanting of European civilization to America is to distort history. Pages are devoted to particular and isolated instances of the violation of the vow of celibacy by prelates and monks, but nothing is said of the devotion and self-abnegation of the vast majority of friars and priests who labored for the faith among the Spaniards in the cities, the castes in the rural districts, and the neophytes along the far-flung frontiers. It is charged that the clergy were heartless exploiters of the Indians, but there is no mention of the fact that the Church was the Indians' staunchest defender from first to last. There are lengthy descriptions of the great wealth of the Church, but no admission that all educational and charitable facilities, insofar as they existed (and they were not inconsiderable), were supported by that institution. All this is represented as history.[12] So conspicuous was the work of the Catholic Church in the missionary field, in education, the charities, and the arts, that failure to recognize its constructive achievements would be most unjust.

That the Spanish colonials, high and low, were superficially instructed in the mysteries of religion is another story, and, unfortunately, true. To what extent the clergy were responsible for this situation it is difficult to say. In regard to the Indians, who can claim that they were promising material for conversion? Given their undeveloped, primitive minds, and their bewilderment on being thrust suddenly into a social state to which they could not adapt themselves for hundreds of

10. Alexander von Humboldt, *Ensayo Político sobre la Nueva-España* (Paris, 1821), I, 247; José María Mora, *Obras Sueltas* (Paris, 1837), I, 112.

11. Juan and Ulloa devoted a chapter in their famous secret report of investigations in Peru to the subject of clerical immorality. Their evidence has been accepted as incontrovertible. It is interesting to note that they gave the Jesuits a clean bill of health. (*Noticias Secretas*, Chap. VIII.)

12. Mr. Ernest Gruening, for example, in his book on Mexico (*Mexico and Its Heritage*, New York, 1928, pp. 171-83), in his chapter on the colonial Church has much to say about the wealth of the Church, but absolutely nothing about its work in education and the charities.

years, what could be expected of the missionaries? The Catholic Church with its imagery and ceremonials was best adapted to appeal to the savages, and realizing this, the friars quite naturally made good use of pomp and display. If the result was a thin veneer of Christianity, that at least was an achievement. The missionaries were deserving of more credit for what they accomplished than condemnation for what they failed to do. And, as for the whites, those of European origin, and the castes, their religious shallowness must have been the result of the failure of the clergy to distinguish between their mentality and that of the Indians. The priests carefully avoided making any appeal to mature and self-reliant intellects. All were treated like children; their emotions were aroused by the use of lavish ceremonials, display, and imagery. What wonder, then, that the colonials, white and colored, came to believe that the essence of the faith was its trappings? There was much profane pomp with little piety.[13] Theirs was superficial faith, blind belief with little understanding. And there was no disposition on the part of the clergy to make them understand so long as they believed. Unreasoning obedience to Church and king was inculcated by the clergy, who studiously avoided analysis of the foundations of this dual obedience.

Although the Church was drawn into the vortex of the Revolution, religion itself, superficial as it was, did not constitute a cause of the revolt from Spanish authority. Substantiation of the truth of this assertion is not difficult to find. The fact that the lower clergy generally supported the Revolution, whereas the higher ecclesiastics remained loyal to the Spanish cause is significant. It meant that the clericals participated in the movement for social, political, and economic, but not for religious, reasons. A dominant cause of dissatisfaction with Spanish rule was the monopolizing of the highest positions, political, military, and ecclesiastical, by the Spanish-born, or *Gachupines*. The American-born whites, or creoles, resented Spanish favoritism and this resentment was as bitterly harbored by the parish priest as by the sergeant in the army or the *regidor* in the municipality. Among the clergy there existed the rivalry of birth. There were actually entire religious communities made up of *Gachupines* or of creoles. The great economic inequality existent in the colonial clergy has already been alluded to. The cry of Father Miguel Hidalgo typified the spirit of creole revolt: "Down with bad government! Death to the *Gachupines!* Long live religion! Long live our most holy Virgin of Guadalupe!" In this cry was proclaimed the revolt against political, social, and economic abuses. No opposition to the Church

13. Alamán, *op. cit.*, I, 65.

was expressed; rather, adherence was proclaimed; although the invocation of the Indians' Virgin did portend a nationalization of the faith.

Not only was religion not a cause of the Revolution, but rebellion against the Church at that time was unthinkable. The colonials, for the greater part, professed a very different attitude towards religion from that felt for the State. The Church had impressed itself upon the minds of the people and had convinced them that only by its ministrations was it possible to secure the blessings of eternal salvation. So great was the power of the clergy and its influence over the ignorant inhabitants of the colonies, that the French minister Vergennes believed this alone would make secession of the Spanish colonies impossible.[14] And well it might had the whole weight of the clergy, high and low, been thrown into the balance on the side of the Spanish king. But, strangely enough, leadership was assumed by the clergy on both sides in the struggle, and at times the war was carried on almost wholly by them.

If religion was not a contributing factor to the outbreak of the Revolution, it nevertheless was dragged into the fray and made to serve personal interests. "Who would believe," asked Father Hidalgo, "that the shamelessness of the Spaniards would go so far as to profane the most sacred things in order to perpetuate their intolerable domination ...to make use of excommunications against the very spirit of the Church, to launch them when there is no religious issue whatever involved?"[15] "Religion," wrote Lucas Alamán, "served as the instrument of one and the other party, and the people did not know whom to believe, hearing its respectable name invoked in favor of the two causes."[16] For example, when Hidalgo, as a political move to secure the support of the Indians, proclaimed the Virgin of Guadalupe as the patroness of the revolt, Viceroy Venegas, to excite the religious fanaticism of the other social classes, proclaimed the *Virgen de los Remedios* "generala" of the royalist troops. Thus we have a war of the Virgins. This instance was neither the first nor the last in Mexican history in which religious prejudices were excited to serve political ends.

Perhaps nothing could evidence more emphatically the virtual non-existence of the religious issue in the Spanish-American Revolution than declarations by revolutionary leaders of loyalty to Catholicism and the inclusion in the first organic laws of clauses providing for the continuance of that religion as a privileged faith. Francisco de Miranda,

14. Bernard Moses, *The Intellectual Background of the Revolution in South America, 1810-1824* (New York, 1926), p. 69.
15. Genaro García, ed., *El Clero de México y la Guerra de Independencia* (Mexico, 1906), pp. 45-47.
16. Alamán, *op. cit.*, II, 31.

"the precursor of the Revolution," in submitting a plan of government to the *cabildo* of Caracas in 1808, advocated Roman Catholicism as the national religion. The status of the Church, including its tithes, he advised, should be preserved. But since he was saturated with the liberal doctrines of the French Revolution, it was natural that he should have advocated religious toleration "as a principle of natural right."[17]

Father Hidalgo, in the *Grito de Dolores*, as has been shown, declared adherence to the faith. Notwithstanding his denunciation by the Church as an "heretic, apostate, and follower of Martin Luther," he was always a fervent Catholic. In his manifesto of December 15, 1810, he declared that it was his intention to establish a representative congress of the Mexican people, and the principal object of that congress was to maintain the Catholic religion. Ignacio Rayón declared on October 23, 1810, in the name of the *generalísimo* (Hidalgo) : "the object of the plan of independence is nothing other than the maintenance of the Holy Religion and its dogma, the conservation of liberty, and the alleviation of the people."[18]

José María Morelos, a curate like Hidalgo, was a Roman Catholic from first to last. To the Congress of Chilpanzingo he declared himself to be in favor of the Roman Catholic religion without the toleration of any other faith. His advice was accepted and incorporated into both the declaration of independence (November 6, 1813) and the Constitution of Apatzingán (October 22, 1814).

Mariano Moreno, secretary of the Buenos Aires *junta*, and so-called "soul of the Revolution of 1810," although steeped in the philosophy of Rousseau (he translated the *Social Contract*), was nevertheless fanatical in his religious opinions. His reverence for the doctrines of the Church and appreciation of her divine mission constrained him to oppose any alteration in the position of Catholicism as the national faith.

José de San Martín, "the Protector," and Manuel Belgrano, the Argentinian military hero, advocated Roman Catholicism as the state religion. General Belgrano was a Catholic who imposed rigid religious practices on his army. He understood the value of the influence of the clergy and sought their aid. Although he was accused of being a hypocrite and of making an ostentatious display of religious practices to deceive the people, he may nevertheless have been a sincere Christian. On April 6, 1814, Belgrano wrote a remarkable letter to San Martín advising him to keep alive in his army a religious sentiment. He said that it was a war not only of arms but of opinions. "Do not cease to

17. William Spence Robertson, *History of the Latin-American Nations* (New York, 1925), pp. 35-55.
18. Vicente Riva Palacio, ed., *México á Través de Los Siglos* (Barcelona, 1889), III, 95.

implore Nuestra Señora de los Mercedes," he wrote, "and name her *generala* of the rebel armies. Give scapularies to the troops. Act like a Christian general [i.e., a Roman Catholic]. Watch your language. Say nothing disrespectful about religion." San Martín followed the advice of Belgrano. In the center of the camp a portable altar was erected on which the chaplains attached to the army celebrated mass on Sundays and feast days. San Martín's ideas on the subject of the Church are best expressed in his *Estatuto Provisorio* of 1821, proclaimed for the temporary governance of Peru. The Roman Catholic faith was declared to be the religion of the State and the government recognized as one of its prime duties the maintenance and protection of that Church, by all possible means. Whoever attacked its dogmas or principles, in public or private, was to be severely punished.[19]

Simón Bolívar was an exception among the great leaders of Latin-American independence, for he advocated separation of Church and State. Nominally a Catholic himself, the "Liberator," like Miranda, had drunk deeply of the teachings of the French philosophers and religion at best rested but lightly upon him, until the last few years of his life. Notwithstanding his liberal religious views and his unflagging efforts to have them incorporated into the organic laws of Venezuela and New Granada, Bolívar recognized the political importance of clerical support of the Revolution. No one realized better than he the strength of the hold exercised by the Church over the masses of both high and low degree. He therefore was careful not to antagonize the clergy and put aside personal opinion for the sake of the general good.[20] For example, seeing that separation of Church and State was unacceptable, he hastened to propose that a diplomatic mission be sent to Rome to conclude a concordat with the papacy. His relations with Bishops Lasso and Jiménez reveal Bolívar as a man who would not allow his personal opinions to override practical considerations in formulating a religious policy for Colombia. The Liberator's handling of the religious problem mark him as a great statesman. Thus, as indicated by the above survey, no prominent leader of the Revolution, "good" Catholic or not, was an enemy of the Church.

In the early days of the revolt the political practice in Latin America was to offer to Catholicism respect for its old privileges and exclusions.

19. Agustín Piaggio, *Influencia del Clero en Independencia Argentina, 1810-1820* (Madrid, 1912), pp. 67-69, 101; L. F. Villarán, *La Constitución Peruana* (Lima, 1899), p. 78; G. H. Stuart, *The Governmental System of Peru* (Washington, 1925), p. 4.

20. José Gil Fortoul, *Historia Constitucional de Venezuela* (Berlin, 1907), I, 160, n. 2; Carlos A. Villanueva, *La Santa Alianza* (Paris, n.d.), p. 202; Mary Watters, "Bolívar and the Church," *Catholic Historical Review*, XXI (1935), 299-313.

In the opinion of the great Argentinian constitutionalist Alberdi, this was a tactical concession upon which the success of the Revolution depended, and was comparable to the same discretion of the revolutionaries in protesting that they were fighting for the rights of Ferdinand VII.[21] It seems, however, that the analogy was poor, for the religious course adopted was a matter of both conscience and policy, whereas the political course was one of policy alone. In the writing of the religious clause of our own constitution, for example, the framers made no bid for originality; they merely guaranteed the *continuance* of religious liberty and freedom of conscience. The Latin Americans, also, chose to perpetuate what they were accustomed to, i.e., the official cult which they had inherited from Spain.

An examination of the first organic laws adopted by the nascent republics of Latin America shows that they maintained the Roman Catholic religion as the privileged faith. The first Argentinian constitutions contained this significant religious seal. The *Estatuto Provisional* of 1815 declared Roman Catholicism to be the religion of the State. A notable feature of this instrument of government was that it sanctioned religious toleration. The *Reglamento* of 1817 reproduced the religious declarations of the *Estatuto Provisional*. The Constitution of 1819 declared, "The government owes to religion the most efficacious and powerful protection, and all the inhabitants are bound to respect it, whatever might be their private opinions." Ecclesiastical dignitaries were placed in the category of State officials.[22]

The different constitutions of Chile from 1811 to 1818 contained provisions proclaiming the Roman Catholic religion to be that of the State, and excluded all others. The Constitution of 1818 declared that the protection, conservation, purity, and inviolability of the Catholic religion ought to be one of the chief duties of the State, "which will never permit any other public religion or doctrine contrary to that of Jesus Christ." The organic law of 1823 prohibited even the private exercise of the other religions.[23] As for Peru the features of San Martín's *Estatuto Provisorio* have already been mentioned. Only by a narrow margin was religious toleration excluded from Peru's next constitution, that of 1822.

In Mexico, the Congress of Chilpanzingo, when proclaiming Mexican

---

21. J. B. Alberdi, *Bases y Puntos de Partida para la Organización Política de la República Argentina* (Buenos Aires, 1914), p. 111.

22. Agustín de Vedia, *Constitución Argentina* (Buenos Aires, 1907), pp. 41, 49; Legón, *Patronato Nacional*, p. 249.

23. Alcibiades Roldán, *Elementos de Derecho Constitucional de Chile* (Santiago, 1917), p. 221; Justo Arosemena, *Estudios Constitucionales sobre los Gobiernos de la América Latina* (Paris, 1888), I, 105.

independence on November 6, 1813, declared that, in casting off the Spanish control, the Mexican people would be free "to celebrate concordats with the Holy Pontiff for the governance of the Catholic Church, in order that no other religion shall be recognized." In the Constitution of Apatzingán a great deal of space was devoted to the subject of Catholicism as the sole tolerated religion of the nation. Heresy and apostasy constituted offenses for which naturalized citizens could lose their citizenship. In the electoral system, the parish was the primary voting unit; the electors there chosen by the voters were obliged to pass into the principal church "where a solemn mass to the Holy Ghost will be [was] celebrated and an address appropriate to the circumstances delivered by the priest or some other ecclesiastic." When the electors had named a representative for Congress, they were again to attend church for a solemn *Te Deum*. The *Plan de Iguala*, announced February 24, 1821, provided as one of its three guarantees the security of the Church. Only the Roman Catholic religion was to be tolerated in Mexico, and the members of the regular and secular clergy throughout the country were to be protected in all their rights and properties. In other words, the ecclesiastical *fueros* were guaranteed.[24]

The Venezuelan declaration of independence of July 5, 1811, contained the following confession of faith: "Taking the Supreme Being as witness to the justice of our actions and the rectitude of our intentions, imploring this Divine and Heavenly aid, and protesting before Him, in the moment of our birth to that dignity which His Providence restores to us, our desire to live and die free, and maintaining the Holy Catholic and Apostolic Religion of Jesus Christ as the first of our duties." In the Constitution of 1811, the Roman faith was declared to be the religion of the State. Although the majority of the delegates were members of the school of Rousseauan philosophy, they consented to the religious article so as not to alienate the good will of the national clergy. The oath of allegiance to the Republic was as follows: "I swear to defend with my body and all my strength the States of the Venezuelan Confederation, and to conserve and maintain pure and sound the Roman Catholic Apostolic faith, one and exclusive, and to defend the mystery of the Immaculate Conception of the Virgin our Mother." Without exception the numerous revolutionary charters of government in Venezuela and New Granada were featured by clauses declaring Roman Catholicism to be the religion of the State.[25]

24. José M. Gamboa, *Leyes Constitucionales de México Durante el Siglo XIX* (Mexico, 1901), pp. 235-73, 282-83.

25. Gil Fortoul, *op. cit.*, I, 160, 175, 177; P. Pedro Leturia, *La Acción Diplomática de Bolívar ante Pío VII, 1820-1823* (Madrid, 1925), p. 74.

Not only did the revolutionary governments swear continued allegiance to the Roman faith, but, with equal unanimity, they proposed to exercise the patronage that once belonged to the kings of Spain. The problem of *patronato nacional* occupied a more important position in the revolutionary history of Argentina than elsewhere because the patronal authority of the Spanish king was never restored after the original outbreak in 1810. Mariano Moreno, secretary of the *junta,* in a set of rules drawn up for the guidance of that body declared, "The objects of the *patronato* are cared for by the *junta* in the same way as by the viceroys." The *junta* in substituting itself for the viceroy presumed to assume the jurisdiction that belonged to that official as vice-patron.[26] The colonial laws on patronage were recognized just as were Spanish laws in other matters. The *junta* not only exercised the old patronage, but with wise foresight, it proposed to extend these rights if noncommunication between the ecclesiastical authorities in the colonies and the home country made it necessary.

The deposition of the bishop of Córdova created a problem touching on the right of the *junta* to exercise the patronage and appoint to benefices. The question was submitted by Corneilo de Saavedra and Mariano Moreno, president and secretary respectively of the *junta,* to two Córdovan ecclesiastics: Dean Gregorio Funes, and Dr. Juan Luis de Aquirre y Texada. The reports of both clerics were impregnated with vigorous regalism; in brief, they were strongly of the opinion that royal patronage inhered in sovereignty, and consequently the *junta,* as the legitimate sovereign, could exercise the one-time regal patronal rights. The opinion of Funes is worth quoting: "The Spanish kings acquired their notable prerogative by their liberalities toward the Church, but these liberalities were not made with their own patrimonial goods, but with the public funds of the State, whose faithful administration prohibited them from any other use than the common good; thus they owed the right of patronage to the expenditures from the public treasury; it came to be an extension of the rights of sovereignty, which were consolidated in the crown but not in the persons who possessed or administered the regal authority."[27]

Until June 4, 1813, the revolutionary government of La Plata posed as the vice-patron upon the legal fiction that it was ruling in the name of Ferdinand VII. On that date, however, the *patronato de Indias* was formally terminated by the constituent assembly, which body proceeded to make rules for the filling of ecclesiastical vacancies. By the *Estatuto*

26. Chacaltana, *Patronato Nacional Argentino*, p. 64; Legón, *op. cit.*, p. 229.
27. Piaggio, *op. cit.*, p. 330; Legón, *op. cit.*, pp. 234-40.

of 1815 the Supreme Director was delegated authority to make appointments to vacant benefices. Finally, the inherence of the patronage in the State was specifically stated in a resolution of the Congress of Tucumán (1817), in the *Reglamento Provisorio* of 1817, and in the Constitution of 1819. Needless to say, none of the radical pretentions of the rebel government to exercise the patronage were recognized in Madrid or Rome.[28]

In Venezuela, Archbishop Coll y Prat, on July 6, 1811, proclaimed the end of the Spanish patronage. The constitution which was framed soon after vested in the government rights over the Church which had previously belonged to the Spanish crown. However, to conciliate the Archbishop and recalcitrant clergy, the government entered into negotiations with the former concerning appointments "until contact could be established with Rome." But the Republic was overthrown before an agreement could be reached. In New Granada, the Constitution of Cundinamarca, March 30, 1811, while providing for the establishment of *patronato nacional*, declared that for the secure continuance of the patronage it would be necessary to appeal to the Holy See. After the Congress of Angostura had provided for the assumption of the right of patronage by Colombia, a provisional law was passed, which declared that until a concordat could be arranged with the Vatican to settle the matter of the patronage, the vice-presidents of Venezuela and New Granada should pass upon those nominated for ecclesiastical offices below that of bishop.[29] This inclination to seek pontifical confirmation of the patronage has been interpreted by Father Leturia as meaning recognition on the part of the republics that the patronage was not inherent in their newly-won sovereignty. This is not necessarily true, for one can firmly believe in the legitimacy of his rights, and at the same time seek to have others recognize them.

It was inevitable, since the Spanish monarchs had emphasized for three centuries *real patronato* "as a traditional symbol, a ritualistic principle of power, incarnate in monarchy and in the historical entity of Spain," that the revolting colonials should regard it as an inherent, secular right, inseparable from sovereignty. What was more natural than that they, as the heirs to the prerogatives of the Spanish monarchy in America, should exercise national patronage over the Church? It has been suggested, and the explanation is plausible, that the new republics assumed control over the Church to curb its power and prevent as far as possible the interference of the ecclesiastics in the political affairs of

28. *Ibid.*, pp. 247-50, 492.
29. P. Leturia, "Alusiones en la Cámara Argentina al Origen Histórico del Patronato de Indias," in *Razón y Fé*, V, 78, p. 332; Leturia, *Acción Diplomática*, pp. 143-44.

the states. This policy was rendered doubly necessary since the higher Church dignitaries were Spanish sympathizers who frowned on the Revolution.

The support given the revolutionary cause by clericals was no inconsiderable factor in the eventual winning of independence. The nature and extent of their assistance, rendered under radically different conditions, is adequately exemplified in the revolutionary histories of Argentina and Mexico.

In Argentina, as in other parts of America, a considerable portion of the creole clergy, both regular and secular, not only favored independence but worked for it. One of the leaders of the "Revolt of May 25th" was a Dominican friar, Ignacio Grela. It is said that he did more then anyone else to maintain order. In a petition presented to the *cabildo* on the above date appeared the names of seventeen religious of different orders. An observer spoke of seeing, in the interior, more than three thousand Indians in arms under the direction of curates. Perhaps the most famous of all the clerical supporters of independence was Dean Gregorio Funes of Córdova. It was largely due to his efforts that the counterrevolutionary activities centering in Córdova were defeated.[30] Says Levene, "To its honor the Hispanic-American clergy were enrolled in the revolutionary ranks embracing the cause of emancipation. In the province of La Plata not only could numerous priests be mentioned who figured in the Revolution, but a legion of them did quiet work in favor of the revolutionary cause. These were the parish priests who after mass read to the people articles declaring principles and ideals of the Revolution."[31]

Not only did the clergy preach support of the Revolution in La Plata, but they aided it with money. "The War of Independence," says Piaggio, "was waged in large part with the money which the clergy gave personally." The influence of clerics in popular assemblies was equal to that of any other class. In the *Junta de Gobierno*, named on May 21, 1810, by the *Cabildo Abierto*, the presbyter Dr. Sola occupied a seat. A *vocal*, or member of the *Junta* of May 25 was the curate Manuel Alberti. In the Assembly of 1813 were twelve ecclesiastics. The "reporter" of this assembly was Father Cayetano Rodríguez. This same religious, as secretary of the Congress of Tucumán, was the principal author of the famous declaration of independence promulgated by that congress. Of the twenty-nine signers of the declaration, sixteen were curates. In the same congress, it was a curate, Justo de Oro, who was

30. Piaggio, *op. cit.*, pp. 21, 48-54.
31. Ricardo Levene, *Lecciones de Historia Argentina* (Buenos Aires, 1919), II, 273.

most responsible for the defeat of the monarchial project presented by Belgrano.[32]

In Mexico, in addition to Hidalgo and Morelos, "more than one hundred parish priests, including the leaders, Matamoros and Mercado, and some fifty members of the religious brotherhoods, took the field.[33] Their presence in the revolutionary ranks testified to the social ingredients of the movement, and refuted the allegations of its 'heretical' character. More in contact with the masses than the higher clergy, many of them risen from the ranks of the dispossessed, they knew and felt keenly the oppressions and discriminations of the colonial system. Like their leaders many of them died on the battle-fields or before the firing squad."[34] So active were the Mexican clergy in the Revolution that Lucas Alamán credits them with sustaining it almost alone. He says, "The clergy and disorder were precisely what sustained the Revolution; without the first there would have been a lack of chiefs; without the second there would have been no followers."[35]

Opposed to the disorganized minority of the lower clergy which supported the Revolution was the great Catholic hierarchy of Spanish America which exerted its might against the disavowal of the legitimate authority of the Spanish king. That the Church should combat rebellion was obvious, for in America it was closely identified with the monarchy. If the crown was beholden to the Church for the implanting of Spanish civilization in the New World and the inculcation in the colonials of a spirit of obedience to the king, the Church on the other hand was obligated to the crown for protection and for the innumerable privileges, exemptions, and grants which had enabled it to become great and wealthy. The American Church, therefore, would have been

32. Piaggio, *op. cit.*, pp. 19, 24, 108, 213, 233. For additional information on the contribution of the clergy of Argentina to the winning of independence, see Adolfo P. Carranza (ed.), *El Clero Argentino de 1810 á 1830* (Buenos Aires, 1907, 2 v.), and J. Francisco V. Silva, *El Libertador Bolívar y el Deán Funes* (Madrid, n.d.), pp. 106-14.

33. A list of the members of the secular and regular clergy who fought for independence in Mexico is given in Riva Palacio (*op. cit.*, III, Doc. 11, in the Appendix).

34. Gruening, *op. cit.*, pp. 187-88.

35. Alamán, *op. cit.*, III, 213. Because Genaro García disagreed with the popular opinion as expressed by Alamán that the lower clergy were very partisan toward the War for Independence, he published a set of documents (*El Clero de México y la Guerra de Independencia*, Mexico, 1906) to demonstrate that the lower clergy, except on rare occasions were unconditionally allied with the Spanish monarchy, and that the insurgents, far from giving evidence of religious fanaticism, were distinguished by lack of religious scruples. This publication does not disprove, however, that not a few curates although a small minority, were sympathetic toward the insurgent cause. For the attitude of the bishops and clerics in the various countries, see Leandro Tormo y Pilar Gonzalbo Aizpuru, *La Iglesia en la crisis de la independencia* (Madrid, 1961).

not only ingrate but short-sighted to abandon its ancient champion and benefactor and tempt fate by making a change.

In Mexico the revolutionary outbreak initiated by Father Hidalgo and continued by Morelos, another curate, and by other patriots, was "received by the higher clergy with a bolt of lightning in their hands, and maledictions on their lips."[36] This, notwithstanding the fact that Hidalgo declared that one of the principal objects of the congress he intended to summon was to maintain the Catholic religion. There is no doubt that the Church was more aroused against the *rebellion*, than against the supposed heresy of those rebelling. This is evidenced by statements and actions of ecclesiastical dignitaries and of institutions like the Inquisition.

Bishop-elect Manuel Abad y Queipo of Michoacán issued a proclamation which declared that the curate Hidalgo "a pastor of souls, a priest of Jesus Christ, a minister of the God of Peace, had raised a standard of rebellion and seduced a number of innocent people." It is to be noted that he was accused of rebellion, not against the Church, but against political authority; and because he had disturbed the peace and broken faith with Ferdinand VII he was excommunicated. Since Hidalgo was not under the jurisdiction of the Bishop of Michoacán, he denied the validity of the edict of excommunication. Furthermore, he contended that, since Abad y Queipo had been nominated by the Spanish Regency, which had no authority over the patronage in America, and since the nomination had not been confirmed by the pope, he therefore was holding his office illegally and could not exercise its powers.[37] Archbishop Lizana, however, published an edict in which he declared that the ban published by Abad y Quiepo was valid and emanated from competent authority, and the faithful were obliged under penalties to observe it. A few days later the Archbishop issued a pastoral in which he condemned the principles of the Revolution. The curate Hidalgo was branded as an heretic and the faithful were commanded to "flee from him who teaches doctrines contrary to the Holy Faith."[38]

The death of Archbishop Lizana early in 1811 made way for the nomination by the Regency of Antonio Bergosa y Jordán, Bishop of Oaxaca, as successor to the archiepiscopal see. Of all the Mexican ecclesiastics, Bergosa was perhaps the most outspoken in his condemna-

---

36. Riva Palacio, *op. cit.*, III, 127.

37. A few years later, Abad y Queipo wrote an exposition (*Breve Exposición sobre el Real Patronato*, Madrid, 1820), to prove that his nomination by the Spanish Regency was definitive. The lack of pontifical confirmation possessed no value, he said. His argument contains a strange mixture of regalistic and ultramontane doctrine.

38. Alamán, *op. cit.*, I, 390; Riva Palacio, *op. cit.*, III, 130-31.

tion of the Revolution. He celebrated with a great and solemn festival the restoration of Ferdinand VII. "It would be impossible," said Alamán, "to repeat it with equal grandeur." Notwithstanding the belligerent *Españolismo* of Bergosa and Abad y Queipo, both prelates were rewarded by Ferdinand for their untiring support of his cause by being removed from their respective sees. Since the king did not wish to confirm acts of the provisional government during his absence and since he regarded the naming of prelates as a royal prerogative which could not be exercised by the Regency, the appointees of that government were removed. Abad y Queipo returned to Spain, and Bergosa to his see at Oaxaca. Canon Pedro Font was appointed by Ferdinand archbishop of Mexico. Although not as vitriolic as Abad y Queipo and Bergosa, the other bishops of Mexico joined the chorus of denunciation. On March 28, 1811, the metropolitan chapter of Mexico issued the following: "When the future generations read with horror about the enormous crimes, the abominable projects, the incalculable evils of which on New Spain a single perfidious priest, ignorant and belonging to Satan, has been the author, they will see with the greatest pleasure the clergy of Mexico, especially all the parish priests, reproving such an iniquitous revolution, abominating the detestable means that were adopted for it, cursing the authors of so many and such horrible crimes, deploring the sins committed, preaching peace and subordination, and restraining in a thousand ways the torrent of misfortune that was about to submerge the most happy people in the world."[39]

In the following year the same archiepiscopal chapter exhorted the curates who were partisans of the Revolution to comply with the duties of their ministry and "abstain from mixing in questions foreign to their profession." Thereby exhibiting a refreshing disregard for their own extra-ecclesiastical interference. In remarking about the censures and excommunications issued by the higher clergy upon the rebels, Lucas Alamán says, "The arms of religion began at that moment to be weakened, and it cannot be doubted that employing them on this occasion as auxiliaries in political matters was one of the principal causes which contributed to lessen their effectiveness."[40]

In this ardent crusade the Inquisition took an active part. This was not to be wondered at, for the Holy Office had been used for political purposes since its establishment in America. During the revolt at Valladolid in 1808 it issued an edict to the following effect: "The sovereign pontiffs, among them Clement XI, having entrusted to the Holy

39. García, *op. cit.*, p. 112.
40. Alamán, *op. cit.*, I, 392.

Office of the Inquisition of Spain, the duty of watching over the fidelity which all their vassals owe to their Catholic Majesties, and at the same time regarding it as their duty to strengthen the throne of our august monarch Ferdinand VII, establish it as a rule ... that the king received his power and authority from God, and that you ought to believe it as divine faith."[41] Thus the Inquisition, to aid the Spanish cause in America, did not hesitate to brand as heresy the very principle of popular sovereignty which was being invoked by the Spaniards in the struggle against the French.

The weight of the Holy Office was brought to bear upon the rebellious curates Hidalgo and Morelos. On October 10, 1810, a report was published concerning the former in which violent accusations were made against his Catholicism. It was charged "that Hidalgo was a partisan of French liberty, a libertine, a formal heretic, a Judaiser, a Lutheran, a Calvinist, a rebel, a schismatic, and a suspected atheist. Three days later the Inquisition issued an edict concerning Hidalgo. In that proclamation certain denunciations which had been quietly reposing in the inquisitorial archives were published as damning evidence. Hidalgo was accused of denying that God chastised with temporal punishments. He was accused of speaking disdainfully of the popes and of intimating that a certain pope who had been canonized ought to be in hell. He was accused of accepting the doctrines of Luther in regard to the eucharist and auricular confession. With apparent inconsistency, he was accused of denying the authenticity of certain portions of the Bible. Further, it was alleged that Hidalgo had described fornication as a natural and innocent act, and that he had made a compact with a woman to foster that crime. It was stated that Hidalgo had declared war on God, his holy religion, and the fatherland. Upon pain of excommunication, the accused priest was summoned to appear before the inquisitorial tribunal in Mexico City within thirty days. It was proclaimed that, if he failed to appear, his trial would proceed *in absentia*. The edict concluded by announcing that all persons who supported the revolution, who received revolutionary proclamations, who maintained relations with Hidalgo, who failed to denounce him, or who promulgated revolutionary ideas would be punished by a heavy fine, by excommunication, and by the other punishments provided by canon law and papal bulls."[42] Because of his political activities and alleged heresies Father Hidalgo was unfrocked and turned over to the civil authorities for execution.

41. J. Pérez Lugo, *La Cuestión Religiosa en México* (Mexico, 1927), p. 15.
42. William Spence Robertson, *Rise of the Spanish-American Republics* (New York, 1918), pp. 90-91.

No sooner was the Constitution of Apatzingán adopted than the Inquisition rushed to the aid of the civil authorities in attacking it. Although that instrument of government declared Roman Catholicism to be the State religion to the exclusion of all others, it was condemned because it sought to legalize the rebellion. In this instance the Holy Office resorted to no subterfuge—it was acting openly in a political capacity.

When Morelos was captured toward the end of 1815, he was thrown into a cell of the Inquisition in Mexico City. The Holy Office declared him to be "heretic, propagator of heresy, pursuer and disturber of the ecclesiastical hierarchy, profaner of the holy sacraments, schismatic, lascivious, hypocrite, irreconcilable enemy of Christianity, and traitor to God, king, and pope." After a two days' trial, "the most expeditious in the annals of the Holy Office," according to H. C. Lea, the tribunal condemned Morelos to degradation and execution. Morelos was the last heretic sentenced to death by the Inquisition in Mexico.[43]

Not with bans and fulminations alone were the high clergy content to fight the Revolution. The most considerable material contribution of the Church to the royalist cause was its financial assistance. Church bells were gladly donated to the civil authorities to be melted into cannon. Whereas the Spaniards themselves showed little will to make contributions, the clergy dug deep into their treasures. Finally, some of the most belligerent curates actually bore arms in the royalist armies. Bishop Cabañas of Guadalajara organized a regiment of friars, clerics, and sacristans called "Los Cruzados." It drilled daily in the streets of Guadalajara to the sound of the great cathedral bell. Such was the character of ecclesiastical opposition to the Revolution in Mexico.[44] It is doubtful if, in any other part of Spanish America, the clergy were more strongly entrenched and were able to afford the Spanish authorities more valuable assistance.

After fulminating with the bitterest venom for ten years against the "heresy of rebellion," the higher clergy, and therefore the Mexican Church itself, suddenly threw its support in favor of independence. The reason for the *volte-face* was fear for the clerical interests in Mexico because of the startling anticlerical reforms adopted by the Spanish Cortes of 1820. The detested Constitution of Cádiz with its democratic features and curtailment of clerical immunities had been reëstablished; the Inquisition was abolished; liberty of the press was guaranteed; the *fuero eclesiástico* was abolished; religious orders were suppressed; and church

---

43. For the Holy Office and the Revolution, see José Toribio Medina, *Historia del Tribunal del Santo Oficio de la Inquisición en México* (Santiago, 1905), pp. 471-99.
44. García, *op. cit.*, pp. 242, 256; Pérez Lugo, *op. cit.*, p. 14.

tithes were seized. The ecclesiastical reforms of the Cortes produced a greater discontent in Mexico than in Spain because, according to Alamán, those offended by the measures were the most influential and most elevated. Consequently, "religion no longer 'condemned rebellion' when it was in the clerical interest. Forgotten were the solemn oaths of loyalty to king and constitution, and the ever-pledged support of constituted authority. Bishop Pérez of Puebla, who shortly before had held that the people's love for their king should become a 'rational delirium,' and their fidelity 'a dominant passion,' was the ecclesiastic leader of the new movement. The clergy conceived the plan, selected its military leader, supplied funds, furnished the printing press to disseminate the new idea, and worked actively in persuading the royalist soldiers to desert their banners. *Te Deums* in every temple celebrated the new order which seated an emperor on the Mexican throne with unusual pomp and glitter, established 'exclusion and intolerance of any religion but the Catholic, Apostolic, and Roman,' and ranked blasphemy with 'atrocious murder' as the only unpardonable crimes."[45] The part played by the higher clergy of Mexico in the achievement of independence deserves for them not the title of "patriot," such as belongs to Hidalgo and Morelos, but that of "traitor." There is no blacker page than this in the history of the Catholic Church in America.[46]

In the La Plata country clerical opposition to independence was in evidence during only the first stage of the Revolution. Bishops Lué of Buenos Aires, Orellana of Córdova, and Videla del Pino of Salta, being strongly royalist, although the last-named was a creole, were opposed to the establishment of the *Junta Gubernativa* in May, 1810. The general clergy, on the other hand, supported the *junta*. In the *Cabildo Abierto* of May 22, 1810, the prelate of Buenos Aires questioned the legality of both the autonomous and provisional governments. He however submitted to the *junta* which was set up to govern in the name of Ferdinand VII. Until the time of his death in 1812 all the acts of Bishop Lué fell under the suspicious vigilance of the patriot government. For example, when he asked permission to make a pastoral visit of his diocese, the *junta* refused to grant him a passport. He was told that it was best that he should not leave his see, for his presence would be beneficial in calming agitation. In reality it was feared that he would provoke trouble in the Banda Oriental. After the death of Bishop Lué the cathedral chapter elected Diego Zavaleta as ecclesiastical governor.

45. Gruening, *op. cit.*, pp. 188-89.
46. For clerical support of the Revolution in New Granada, see José Manuel Groot, *Historia Eclesiástica y Civil de Nueva Granada* (Bogotá, 1889), III, 244-45, 269, IV, 35.

The election was approved by the government which had assumed patronal rights over the Church.[47]

Bishop Orellana of Córdova was more tenacious and stubborn than Lué and consequently his fate was more tragic. He joined the counter-revolution headed by ex-viceroy Liniers, and following the victory of the Porteño forces, he was captured and narrowly escaped being executed with Liniers. On August 7, 1810, the *junta* declared the see of Córdova vacant, and Orellana was exiled. The cathedral chapter was ordered to turn over the episcopal authority to Rafael Ardreú, bishop *in partibus*. This action precipitated a veritable schism in Córdova, for the chapter was evenly divided between regalists and ultramontanists. Some considered the diocese to be headless, and others held that the lawful bishop, Orellana, was merely absent.[48]

The diocesan of Salta, Nicolás Videla del Pino, was able to maintain control of his see until 1812. In that year, during the campaign of the royalist Goyeneche against Belgrano, the Bishop was discovered to be in communication with the royalists. As a result, he was exiled to Buenos Aires by Belgrano. He was ordered first to turn over his authority to the ecclesiastical governor, the canon Zabala. Videla del Pino presented his case to the Assembly of 1813, and to the Congress of Tucumán, but without avail, and although he officiated on the anniversary of independence, he was not allowed to return to his bishopric. With his demise in 1819, there expired the last of the legal bishops of La Plata. The patronal authority of the Spanish king was definitely terminated in 1810, yet Ferdinand steadfastly refused to recognize the independence of La Plata. Consequently he declined to nominate bishops for the Republic, and after 1819, all of the sees were vacant.[49]

The Revolution in Chile afforded the same opportunity to royalist and Spanish clergy to combat independence. There is no doubt that many of the clergy, particularly the Spanish, were not sympathetic. Just as the supporters of the revolt used the pulpit to advance their cause, so the royalists used the pulpit to combat it. For example, when General Pareja occupied Concepción, Bishop Villodres preached in the name of God against the patriots, while Bishop Andre y Guerrero, in the name of God, preached to the army of General Carrera in support of the war and against the soldiers of the king. During the royalist reaction (1814-16) José Santiago Rodríguez was consecrated bishop of Santiago. He, a member of the aristocracy and unable to conceive of another order of things, was an ardent partisan of the king and called

47. Legón, *op. cit.*, pp. 463-70; Leturia, *Acción Diplomática*, p. 43.
48. Leturia, *op. cit.*, pp. 43-44.
49. Piaggio, *op. cit.*, p. 129; Legón, *op. cit.*, p. 466.

the patriots "perfidious insurgents and infamous traitors." He celebrated the triumph of the royalists at Rancagua and helped to establish
the hated tyranny. He also aided in the organization of the clergy into
a fanatically reactionary faction violently opposed to the Revolution.
As late as 1817 the clergy of Chile were hostile to the cause of independence, "with the exception of a few who wished to imitate Judas in
his treason." In the conservative society of Chile the influence of the
clergy was considerable. Joel Poinsett reported that after the overthrow
of Spanish rule the rural priests were the real rulers in the country
districts. After the patriot triumph at Chacabuco, the Chilean government ordered the expulsion of Bishop Rodríguez. He retired to
Mendoza and remained there until O'Higgins allowed him to return
to Chile.[50]

Clerical opponents of the Venezuelan Republic of 1811 were given
their big opportunity when the great earthquake of 1812 occurred.
Until that time Archbishop Coll y Prat of Caracas and his clergy viewed
the republican maneuvers of Miranda, Bolívar, and their companions
with ill-concealed distrust. The earthquake of March 26, 1812, which
destroyed the rebel centers but spared the royalist cities, was interpreted
by the Archbishop as providential punishment. The clergy attributed
the earthquake to the ire of Heaven, and friars preached to the terrified
multitudes that "the earthquake was the punishment of God irritated
against the upstarts who had refused to recognize the most virtuous of
monarchs, Ferdinand VII, the annointed of the Lord." The republican
government attempted to combat the clerical propaganda by issuing a
proclamation to the Venezuelan people declaring that the earthquake
was to be regarded either as a common manifestation of nature, or else
it might be regarded as a divine act to punish vicious morals, and was
not to be connected with political reforms.

Throughout the early period of the revolution in Venezuela, Archbishop Coll y Prat acted with the most astute opportunism. After
counselling the obedience of his clergy to the Republic, and thereby es-
caping the ban of expulsion which was being contemplated against him,
he welcomed the royalist troops of Monteverde into Caracas on October
15, 1812, with open arms. When in the following year Bolívar triumphed temporarily, the prelate feigned to be a patriot once more and
issued an edict in which he ordered the clergy to recognize independence and obey the laws of the Republic.[51]

50. Francisco V. Vergara, *Historia de Chile* (Valparaiso, 1898), pp. 252-53; Luis
Galdames, *Historia de Chile: La Evolución Constitucional, 1810-1925* (Santiago, 1926),
I, 13-26.
51. Gil Fortoul, *op. cit.*, I, 182-84.

When the course of the Revolution appeared to lead directly to independence, a reasonable regard for their temporalities induced many high ecclesiastics to manifest sympathy for the party which was destined to exercise power in the new State. These clerics, fearing the vengeance of the patriots when independence should be established, decided wisely to ward off this danger by joining the independentists. This explains why, in certain colonies and contrary to the general rule, prelates espoused the revolutionary cause.

The Catholic Church had its critics among the revolutionaries, it is true, but it is incorrect to regard their motives as entirely irreligious. Their adverse criticism was directed almost exclusively at the Inquisition and the wealth of the Church: that is, nonreligious adjuncts of the Church which seriously menaced the freedom of the State and the liberty of the individual. The most severely criticized ecclesiastical institution was the Inquisition. The *Junta* of Caracas suppressed the Holy Office in 1810. An Argentinian patriot, Monteagudo, in attacking the tribunal, charged the Church with "raising the standard of the Cross in order to assassinate men with impunity; to introduce discord among them; to deprive them of their rights; and to snatch from them the wealth which they possess in the soil of the country." On March 24, 1813, the General Constituent Assembly of Buenos Aires abolished the Inquisition and ordered it to turn over to the ordinary ecclesiastics its old function of watching over the purity of the faith.[52] There was no defending the degenerate Holy Office of the early nineteenth century, and when the Cortes of Cádiz declared the abolition of the tribunal in 1813, its decision was received with acclaim by all Catholics who had not abandoned themselves to morbid fanaticism. Following the restoration of Ferdinand VII, however, the Inquisition was reëstablished throughout the Spanish dominions with the exception of La Plata, where the revolutionaries retained control. The new lease on life accorded the Inquisition in America proved to be of short duration, for when Spanish authority was discarded definitely in the various colonies, its most detestable politico-ecclesiastical ally was abolished for all time. The abolition of the tribunal was a positive good, for: "It had spread a blight over the intellectual life of the colonists; it had smothered the spirit of inquiry; it had silenced the voice of reason; and under its malign influence Christian charity disappeared.... It is to the credit of the political reformers that they saw in the complete destruction of the Inquisition the first essential step towards individual liberty and social

52. Chacaltana, *op. cit.*, p. 66.

progress."[53] It would be preposterous to characterize the patriotic reform which accomplished the dissolution of the Inquisition in America as an irreligious action. It would be ridiculous, also, to agree with certain narrow-minded clericals that the acts of the Assembly of 1813 in Buenos Aires were irreligious. Some of these clerical reforms were: prohibition of the use of cold water in baptisms; prohibition of burials within churches; free baptisms of the children of castes; abolition of the Inquisition; and denial to Spanish ecclesiastics, not citizens, of the right to occupy benefices. Nor is it proper to attribute anti-religious motives to the attack upon the wealth of the Church. The conviction that the dominant economic position of the ecclesiastical organization curbed individual opportunity and jeopardized political freedom was well-founded. These reforms were not based on irreligion. It is impossible to ascertain to what extent Freemasonry, which was introduced into Latin America in the early years of the nineteenth century, was an antagonist of the Catholic organization. Yet there is little doubt that the Church, because of the inculcation of liberal ideas by the Masons, attributed to them a radical anti-religious program which was in the main fictitious.[54]

The foregoing survey of the Church in the wars for Spanish American independence leads one to the conclusion that throughout the struggle there was manifested undiminished allegiance to the Catholic Church. Religion did not play a positive part in causing the revolt. Yet the Church was destined to undergo, as a result of the Revolution, profound changes in its political and legal status.

53. Moses, *op. cit.*, pp. 71-72. For the decadence of the Holy Office and its extinction, see Medina, *op. cit.*, pp. 445-70.

54. Representative of the fanatical opposition of the Church to Masonry was a little pamphlet entitled *Intento de la Masonría*, which summarized the alleged purposes of the order: "We are agreed that when the sectarians [Masons in this case] preach the secularization of the source of sovereignty, that of the family, through civil marriage, when they deny the necessity of Christian baptism, when they attempt to secure possession of education, when they separate Christians from the sacraments and religious practices, when they change the appearance of towns by destroying temples and monasteries, excloistering religious communities, silencing the bells, prohibiting religious and priestly garb, secularizing charity, profaning Christian festivals, introducing death without sacraments, civil burial and [control of] cemeteries, when they despoil the Church, weave restrictions against the Holy See, elaborate constitutions and laws, open lay schools, organize masonic associations, etc., etc., in regard to all this we say: they do nothing less than fight without quarter against the reign of Christianity on earth." (Quoted in Callcott, *op. cit.*, p. 38, n. 26.)

Chapter III

Papal Relations During the Struggle for Independence

The revolt and emancipation of Spanish America created problems both perplexing and embarrassing to the papacy in its relations with Spain and that country's seceding colonies. These problems were political and religious in nature, arising from both the temporal and the spiritual character of the papal office. The principal political question which confronted the Vatican was: should the Holy See recognize the independence of the Spanish-American republics? Because of his attachment to the Metternichean system the pope was not inclined to listen to American pleas for recognition, and consequently it was not difficult for him, as a temporal prince, to find an answer to this political question. A more serious question belonging to the ecclesiastical category, which was forced upon Rome by the Spanish-American Revolution, was: how long should the patronage of the Spanish king over the American Church be observed, and, after its termination, what was to be the nature of the control to be substituted in America for it? It was mainly because of his position as visible head of the Catholic Church that the Spanish-American wars for independence created problems of extreme delicacy for the Holy Father.

The noncommunication of the Church in America with Rome, due to the breakdown of Spanish authority, and the consequent alarming decline of the Catholic hierarchy in America caused the American rebels to appeal to Rome, if not for political, at least for religious recognition. What constituted "religious recognition" was a troublesome question. The Spanish king contended that any official contact between the papacy and the colonies would be interpreted as political recognition, in fact if not in theory, and therefore injurious to Spanish interests. Furthermore, His Catholic Majesty contended that any direct intercourse between the pope and American prelates would constitute an invasion of the ancient right of *real patronato de Indias*. The pope, however, when finally constrained because of the deplorable ecclesiastical state in America to reëstablish the hierarchy, defined his action to the king of Spain as being purely ecclesiastical and having no political significance. As for his violation of the *real patronato*, he promised that if Spain's political authority were ever reëstablished in America, her old patronal rights would be restored. To the Spanish Americans, on the other hand, the pope announced that the patronage had reverted to the papacy, its original source. The American governments, however, took sharp issue with the Holy Father, for they were advancing claims as heirs of the king of Spain in America. Thus, essentially religious, in addition to political, considerations controlled papal policy towards Spain and her erstwhile overseas possessions.

In the controversy with the republics of Spanish America, the papacy, anxious to reassert its legitimate authority over the Church, consistently espoused the ultramontane theory, that is, that the *patronato de Indias* was originally a concession, therefore not inherent in sovereignty and consequently not inheritable by the republics. The latter quite as logically championed the regalistic theory, for they sincerely believed that their independence could not be guaranteed if they were not in control of the Church; and Spain, because of the forlorn hope that it would be the means of eventually restoring Spanish political authority in America, tenaciously clung to the royal patronage, threatening dire consequences if the pope dared to disregard it.

At an early date in the Revolution, the rebel governments recognized the importance of approaching Rome to secure papal confirmation of national patronage, or *patronato nacional*. Legislation which established the Catholic Church as the State-Church was generally accompanied or followed by provisions for the assumption of the old royal patronage by the new governments. For example, although the first constitution of Venezuela (1811) did not mention patronage, the Congress exercised it.[1] In New Granada authority was granted by the federal act of 1811 to negotiate with the pope for the continuation of the patronage. In 1813 the federal Congress of Tunja in New Granada again sanctioned by law the opening of diplomatic relations with the pope to settle the matter of the patronage. In La Plata provision for the establishment of State control of the patronage was contained in the *Estatuto* of 1813, in a resolution of the Congress of Tucumán in 1817, in the *Reglamento Provisorio* of 1817, and in the Constitution of 1819.[2]

The real reason for the desire of the rebel leaders to enter into an agreement with Rome was their fear that the discontent of the Catholic

1. Gil Fortoul, *Historia Constitucional de Venezuela*, I, 258.
2. Ayarragaray, *La Iglesia en América*, p. 234; Legón, *Patronato Nacional Argentino*, p. 492.

people with the isolation of the Church would endanger independence. Yet, notwithstanding their anxiety to enter into diplomatic relations with the Holy See, many years passed before their hopes were realized. From 1810 to 1814, even if the American governments had been more stable, they would still have found it well nigh impossible to treat with the pope, for Pius VII was held a virtual prisoner by Napoleon at Fontainebleau. It is thought that a meeting occurred between Pope Pius VII and Manuel Palacio Fajardo, agent of New Granada, in April, 1813. Fajardo had been sent to France to solicit Napoleon's aid. The Emperor, then preparing for the Leipzig campaign, was in no position to aid the rebels, but he suggested that Fajardo attempt to interest Pius VII in the cause of creole autonomy. Napoleon could see no objection to papal confirmation of prelates nominated by the republican governments. Whether Fajardo actually had an audience with the pope is not certain, but it is clear that he made an appeal for papal recognition. Nothing was accomplished, for Pius VII was unwilling to act, believing that any action on his part before the unquestioned establishment of Spanish-American independence would be premature.[3]

After 1814 and until 1818 the royalist reaction in America destroyed all rebel organizations capable of diplomatic action save in autonomous La Plata. It was in that region then that the only attempt, and this a feeble one, was made during these years to negotiate with Rome. Although several of the Spanish-American episcopal sees had become vacant during the first phase of the Revolution (1810-14), they were all, with the exception of La Plata, refilled by Ferdinand VII, whose nominations were confirmed by the pope. The provision of the vacant sees in La Plata constituted a serious problem which increased in intensity with the continued noncommunication with Rome. The problem was considered by the Congress of Tucumán in 1816, and 30,000 *escudos* were appropriated to defray the expenses of an envoy who was to proceed first to France to implore the support of Louis XVIII in securing a Bourbon prince for a throne in the Argentine. Then, with the aid of France, the agent was to go to Rome to urge papal provision for the vacant sees. Dr. Valentín Gómez, chosen for the mission, arrived in France in November, 1818. Failing to interest the French king in the monarchical scheme and realizing that without French support he could accomplish nothing in Rome, he did not attempt to present his petition to the pope.

Prior to 1820 the pope would not listen benevolently to the overseas

3. Leturia, *La Acción Diplomatica*, pp. 76-79. For a summary of Leturia's studies, see Guillermo Furlong, *La Santa Sede y la Emancipación Hispanoamericana* (Buenos Aires, 1957).

separatists, for it was natural and necessary that he respect Spanish rights in America. Spanish authority was rather generally reëstablished by 1820 and preparations were made to send an army against the one remaining rebellious province, La Plata. Considering the fact that all the powers, not even excepting the United States, had refrained from recognition, it would have been imprudent for the pope to violate legitimacy by ignoring the royal rights of patronage. He therefore was quite willing to listen to Ferdinand's request that he publish a brief exhorting the obedience of American subjects through the intercession of the colonial prelates. On January 30, 1816, Pius VII issued an encyclical to the archbishops and bishops of America, urging them to win over their flocks to obedience to the Spanish king. It read: "You can easily accomplish the suppression of disorders and sedition if each one of you is willing to expose zealously the dangers and grave evils of defections, and expound the noble and exceptional qualities and virtues of our dear son, and your king, Ferdinand, Catholic king of Spain, to whom nothing is more important than religion and the happiness of his subjects; and finally, if you cite the illustrious example, which should never perish, of the Spanish people who did not hesitate to sacrifice goods and life in showing their adherence to religion and fidelity to king."[4]

In 1817 the Cardinal-Secretary of State announced that he would receive no communication from the rebel governments in America. The occasion for this statement was the filing of a protest by the Spanish ambassador in Rome urging the Holy Father not to confirm the action of the Congress of Tucumán which had proclaimed Santa Rosa of Lima as patroness of their independence.[5] Finally, the most conclusive evidence of papal support of Spanish rights was the willingness of the pope during the years 1814-20 to confirm the persons presented to him by the king of Spain for the vacant sees of Santiago de Chile, Charcas, Arequipa, Mérida, Popayán, Bogotá, México, and Puebla.

After 1820, however, the papacy was not deaf to American entreaties, and papal support of Spanish policy was no longer unqualified. Between 1820 and 1822 Pope Pius VII recognized that the spiritual interests of America could not be hidden in the legitimist formula and that the ecclesiastical problems required tactful and benevolent treatment. This change of attitude was due to two causes: the achievement, or practical achievement, of Hispanic-American independence and the liberal Spanish revolt of 1820.

4. "La Encíclica 'Etsi Longissimo' de 30 de Enero de 1816," in Leturia, *op. cit.*, pp. 281-82; Legón, *op. cit.*, pp. 249-50.

5. Ayarragaray, *op. cit.*, pp. 175-76.

The capture of Lima by San Martín, Bolívar's victory at Carabobo, and the Treaty of Córdova between Iturbide and O'Donojú convinced the pope that the colonies were irrevocably lost to Spain and that the exercise of the *real patronato* was impossible. Continued noncommunication with Rome meant paralysis of the ecclesiastical organization in Spanish America. Unless he listened to American pleas the pope would be confronted with the very unpleasant prospect of a serious schism, or the breakup of the Catholic Church in America.[6] The Holy Father was faced with a dilemma. It was his duty to see that the faithful in America were provided with adequate spiritual leaders. To supply them by means of Spanish presentation would be regarded as an insult in America. Yet, the reverse, i.e., recognition of national patronage or even the ignoring of the royal patronage, would be regarded by Spain as political recognition of the new states and justification for a break.

At the precise moment when Rome altered its attitude because the loss of the Spanish colonies appeared to be a certainty, the Liberal constitutional government in Spain, set up as a result of the Revolt of 1820, proceeded to antagonize the pope and impel him along a new road. The anticlerical measures of the Madrid government, which culminated in the expulsion of the nuncio from Madrid in January, 1823, filled the pope with apprehension for the Church not only in Spain but also in America. He began to question why he should now lend his moral support to a government, which, if its authority were reëstablished in America, would cause irreparable damage to the Church in the New World. In fine, the unsympathetic attitude of the Liberals toward the ancient privileges of the Church in Spain made the pope lukewarm in his championship of the old ecclesiastical rights of the Spanish government in America.

The Spanish Cortes, anticlerical and liberal though it may have been, was essentially nationalistic and therefore just as determined as Ferdinand had been not to recognize Spanish-American independence. On February 22, 1822, the Spanish ministry issued a circular to the European governments supplicating them not to put obstacles in the way of the reëstablishment of Spanish rights in America "which had never been renounced." The pope, when given the circular, was asked to promise in writing not to recognize American independence before Spain did. Pius VII refused to comply with the request and declared his adherence to the principle of neutrality. Such a declaration was indeed a departure from the old policy, for, as has been seen, the pope was willing to issue an encyclical in 1816 urging the American clergy to support the

6. Leturia, *op. cit.*, pp. 12, 39.

Spanish cause. A renewed demand by the Madrid government in June, 1822, elicited the response that the pope "could be severely censured, and with good reason, if he supported in writing, because of political reasons, a policy which would prolong transcendental spiritual ills."[7] In view of the fact that the pope, only two years later, when absolutism was reëstablished in Spain, was willing to issue another encyclical urging the American clergy to support Ferdinand VII, one cannot avoid the conclusion that the Holy Father was not averse to using his office for political purposes if the government he supported adhered to political principles in harmony with his own. Yet, it cannot be denied that throughout this period no matter whether the Spanish government was liberal or absolutist, the papacy was sincerely endeavoring to find a way to heal the spiritual ills of America.

The period 1820-23 was the psychological time for the rebel governments to approach Rome and present their cases. During those years, Pius VII was in a receptive mood, and undoubtedly, if the Spanish-Americans had been fully aware of their opportunity and had hastened to take advantage of it, they would have been able to secure real concessions from him. Unfortunately the American governments generally were slow in acting, or, if prompt action was taken, the ecclesiastical business was entrusted to political agents who neglected or totally ignored their spiritual instructions. When special ecclesiastical missions with definite instructions were finally sent to Rome, absolutism had been reëstablished in Spain, and the propitious moment had passed.

As early as 1819, Simón Bolívar considered seriously the problem of negotiating an agreement with Rome which would give to Colombia the right of patronage as exercised by the Spanish kings in the colonies. Due to his influence, the Congress of Angostura (1819) decided to entrust to a political mission ordered to England the additional duty of securing from Pius VII the preconization of bishops for vacant sees. Fernando Peñalver and José Vergara were entrusted with the politico-religious mission. Their instructions, issued by the Congress on July 7, 1819, ordered them to negotiate with the pope "as head of the Catholic Church, and not as the temporal lord of the Legations." They were to tell the Holy Father that the people of New Granada and Venezuela were loyal Catholics who refused to believe that the oppressive and tyrannical Spanish government was being supported against them by the successor of St. Peter. Finally, they were to prepare the way for the negotiation of a concordat. On January 3, 1820, the Congress passed a law which

7. *Ibid.*, pp. 185-87.

provided that until a concordat could be arranged the vice-president should approve those nominated for the lower ecclesiastical offices.[8]

Peñalver and Vergara arrived in London on September 20, 1819. The refusal of Foreign Secretary Castlereagh to meet them meant failure as far as the political objective of the mission was concerned. Peñalver determined to return to Venezuela to report on the situation, but before embarking he and Vergara disposed of their ecclesiastical business by forwarding a memorial to the pope through the nuncio at Paris. This was a statement of ecclesiastical conditions in America, and it concluded with a petition that the pope confirm as bishops those persons proposed by the American governments. Cardinal Consalvi, the papal Secretary of State, rejected the proposal that the pope confirm proprietary bishops for America, for that would have amounted to recognition, which was not to be considered. It must be remembered that at that time not a single foreign government had bestowed recognition on the rebel states, and it was therefore unwise to ask Rome to take that step.[9]

Francisco Antonio Zea was the next agent sent to Europe by Bolívar (June, 1820). His instructions, drawn up by the Liberator himself, dealt primarily with political matters, but he was also charged to negotiate with the pope for a nuncio or extraordinary delegate with ample powers to examine the real state of affairs in America and propose a remedy. It was unfortunate that Zea did not take advantage of the favorable situation created by the Liberal Revolt, in 1820, to go to Rome and negotiate directly with the pope. But he was principally concerned with the larger question of independence and had no time to devote to the religious problems entrusted to him. Finally on April 8, 1822, Zea addressed to the pope through the nuncio at Paris a note demanding immediate recognition of the Colombian government. The nuncio on the advice of the representatives of the Holy Allies in Paris returned the note to Zea with the explanation that he had no authority to send it to Rome. Cardinal Consalvi, in writing to the nuncio concerning the incident, said that, while he did not disapprove of the nuncio's action, it should be remembered that since Colombia was a Catholic country the position of the Holy See was very difficult, and it must treat the Americans with some consideration. "I do not intend by this," he said, "that we should adopt a conduct different from that of all the other countries and ministries in Europe, but I only remark that the double character of the office of the Holy Father—political and spiritual—places him, on

---

8. Villanueva, *La Santa Alianza*, p. 202; Leturia, *op. cit.*, pp. 91-92.

9. Ayarragaray, *op. cit.*, pp. 209-10; "Texto original latino del informe de Peñalver y Vergara," in Leturia, *op. cit.*, pp. 294-97.

the religious side, in a more delicate and embarrassed position than that of all other sovereigns, because of the injury which anger aroused by a rebuff could cause religion."[10]

From 1814 to 1833, the chief obstacle to the establishment of direct relations between Spanish America and Rome was the Spanish embassy in the Eternal City. Antonio Vargas y Laguna, the Spanish ambassador after 1814, was called the "Marquis de Constancia" because of his personal loyalty to absolutism and legitimacy and his never failing efforts to combat the representation of the American governments in the Roman Curia. Narrow, intransigent, fanatical, he organized a veritable camarilla against the American agents. When constitutional government was established in Madrid, Vargas refused to support it and was removed from his post on May 21, 1820. José Aparicio, who succeeded as chargé of the embassy until the return of Vargas in 1824, was equally tireless in his efforts to prevent American agents from gaining audience with the pope.[11]

Two high ecclesiastics of Colombia, Bishops Lasso de la Vega of Mérida and Salvador Jiménez of Popayán, coöperated with Bolívar in attempting to secure papal intervention. Both bishops were appointees of Ferdinand VII and were loyal to the Spanish cause up to the time of the establishment of constitutional government in Spain. The Bishop of Mérida was the first to abandon his allegiance to Spain and embrace the republican cause. On the occasion of the installation of the Congress of Cúcuta (1821), he published a pastoral encouraging the people to obedience to the national representative authority. General Santander said of him, "The bishop is more patriotic than Bolívar." The Liberator himself wrote of Lasso, "He is a holy man full of eminent qualities, who abhors the Liberals of Spain even more than the patriots, because they have declared against the ecclesiastical institutions, whereas we protect them." When Lasso told Bolívar that he would have no difficulty communicating with Rome, the Liberator urged him to do so. Consequently, on October 20, 1821, the Bishop wrote a letter to Pius VII, in which he justified American independence, presented a picture of ecclesiastical conditions in Colombia, and touched upon certain grave problems confronting the Church. The letter, which was significant as being the first one written by an American bishop in support of

10. Leturia, *op. cit.*, pp. 104-6.

11. Because of the refusal of the pope to accept as Spanish ambassador the Jansenist Joaquín Lorenzo Villanueva, the liberal government of Madrid expelled the papal nuncio and reduced Aparicio, in charge of the post at Rome, to a mere agent. When the absolutist régime was reëstablished in Spain, Aparicio left Rome hurriedly. Yet he returned in 1827 as *chargé*, and, in 1834, he became ambassador for Queen Christina. (Ayarragaray, *op. cit.*, pp. 208-9.)

emancipation, was unaccountably delayed and was not received by the pontiff until September, 1822. The pope, now inclining to a free America, welcomed the letter and replied immediately. He refrained from discussing politics, saying that he was anxious to avoid being enmeshed in the political question, but desired to remedy the religious situation and requested more information.

The pope's reply was received with great acclaim in America (Bishop Lasso had it published broadcast), for his adoption of a neutral attitude was interpreted to mean that he was not opposed to American independence. This was assuredly a far cry from the encyclical of 1816. Lasso's second letter, with the detailed information requested by the pope, was dispatched March 19, 1823. In this letter he said of the Colombian government: "I have no hesitation in affirming that its dispositions with respect to religion are most favorable and satisfactory." He suggested as a temporary remedy for the spiritual ills of Colombia the appointment of auxiliary bishops for the vacant sees. Lasso's report was accompanied by a letter from Vice-President Santander to the pope. Pius VII died before an answer could be prepared to Lasso's letter, but his successor, Leo XII, wrote the Bishop on November 19, 1823. The new pontiff promised to study the problem carefully and decide "soon" on a policy. In the meantime, he suggested that they appeal to Muzi, the apostolic vicar then being sent to Chile, for he had been given the powers necessary to handle such a situation. The failure of Muzi's mission in Chile prevented his doing anything for Colombia.[12]

Bishop Jiménez of Popayán also wrote the pope (April 19, 1823), beseeching him to stay the disintegration of the Church in America. Bishop Jiménez, an obstinate royalist, had been on the point of abandoning his diocese and returning to Spain, when a remarkable letter written to him by Bolívar induced him to remain with his flock and recognize the Republic. The Liberator stated as his conviction that politics were one thing and religion another, and if the Bishop left his post he would be abandoning his divinely appointed mission, not for religious, but for political reasons. "I wish to believe," he wrote, "that you are swayed by firm and powerful reasons to consider abandoning your gentle lambs of Popayán. But I do not believe that you can be deaf to the cries of those afflicted sheep, and to the voice of the government of Colombia which entreats you to be one of the leaders on the road to Heaven. Think of the great number of faithful Christians and tender innocents prevented from receiving the sacrament of confirmation because of your absence;

12. Leturia, *op. cit.*, pp. 130-39, 247-53, 271-76; "S. Bolívar al Ill. señor Obispo de Mérida, Guayaquil, 14 de junio de 1823," in Vicente Lecuna (ed.), *Cartas del Libertador* (Caracas, 1929-30), III, 206.

how many students of divinity will be unable to receive the august character of minister of Christ, because you will not consecrate their vocation at the altar, and in the profession of holy truth. You know that the people of Colombia need priests and that the war has deprived them of divine aid because of the scarcity of priests. The responsibility of a possible disintegration of the Church in America falls squarely upon those who could maintain unity of the Catholic Church." Bolívar's arguments, seemingly, were unanswerable, for the Bishop decided to remain in Colombia and justified his decision by citing the anti-religious revolt of 1820 in Spain and the actual emancipation of Colombia, in fact, if not in law. The long-delayed reply of Leo XII (June 5, 1824) to the letter of Bishop Jiménez, contained only words of praise for his loyalty to the papacy in remaining in America. Thus no change was effected in the diplomatic or political realms by the letters of the two bishops of Colombia.[13]

When Santander was installed in Bogotá as vice-president of Great Colombia, he determined to use the powers granted him by the Congress of Cúcuta to enter into negotiations with the papacy. He began by avoiding the errors of prior missions, like those of Peñalver, Vergara, and Zea, of entrusting the agent with mixed political and ecclesiastical business. José Echeverría, who was at that time in Spain, was appointed minister plenipotentiary to Rome (July 12, 1822). He was instructed to work for the recognition of Colombian independence and national patronage. The mission did not materialize, for in September, 1822, Echeverría died in Dieppe while preparing to go to Rome. Augustín Gutiérrez Moreno, then in Chile, was appointed by General Santander to succeed Echeverría, but he was unable to accept, and Dr. Ignacio Sánchez de Tejada, then living in London, was appointed in June, 1823, as Colombian minister to the Holy See.[14] Before Tejada could reach his post important events in Madrid and Rome had transpired, with consequent alteration of papal policy. The psychological moment for rapprochement between Rome and America had passed. Before entering upon a narration of Tejada's mission it is necessary to discuss the efforts of La Plata and Chile to enter into an understanding with the Holy See.

Since noncommunication between La Plata and Rome had been of longer duration than that of any other part of Spanish America, the ecclesiastical situation by 1820 was consequently most distressing in the Platine provinces. The inability of the revolutionary government to

13. Leturia, *op. cit.*, 130-278.
14. Pedro A. Zubieta, *Apuntaciones sobre las Primeras Misiones Diplomáticas de Colombia* (Bogotá, 1924), pp. 575-76.

secure papal consecration of bishops led inevitably to the consideration of radical plans to meet the emergency. One was to ignore the pope and consecrate bishops without his consent. Since this plan would amount to the establishment of a national church, it scandalized the loyal adherents of papal supremacy, particularly a Franciscan friar named Pedro Pacheco, a teacher of philosophy at the University of Córdova and a staunch supporter of independence. The friar was a curious personality; he was suspected of being a royalist by the revolutionaries and of being a revolutionary by the royalists. As a matter of fact, he was an active agent of the revolutionary cause. Pacheco, after visiting Spain and Italy, suddenly appeared in Buenos Aires declaring that the pope and the king of Spain had appointed him bishop of Salta. When asked to show his papers, he refused and left for Rio de Janeiro with the intention of being consecrated there. The willingness of the friar to accept nomination at the hands of the king of Spain was severely condemned by the government of Buenos Aires, for it was felt that such an action would compromise their independence. Dean Funes, the most prominent of the Argentinian ecclesiastics, also condemned Pacheco, for he felt that the king of Spain had no power to nominate bishops in that country and to receive an appointment from him was tantamount to treason.[15]

Pacheco did not go to Rio de Janeiro but sailed for Rome instead. He arrived in the Eternal City, via Gibraltar, on September 3, 1821. The object of his personally appointed mission to the pope has been a subject of mystery to historians. His enemies declared that he "fled from Argentina overcome with the mania of being consecrated bishop of Salta." His defenders declared that he "undertook the long and perilous journey to inform the Holy Father of the condition of the Church and to implore his aid in finding a remedy." Perhaps Pacheco's real purpose was to be consecrated bishop of Salta and by this act renew the extinguished hierarchy in Argentina.[16]

Although the objects of the friar's mission were nebulous, he caused the Spanish government serious concern. The Spanish Minister of State ordered Chargé Aparicio to learn if Pacheco was instructed to work for the recognition of the independence of La Plata. Aparicio thereupon conducted a most artful campaign against him. Notwithstanding Spanish opposition, the friar was received twice in secret audience by Pius VII, but he was not presented at the Vatican as a political agent either for or against Spanish-American independence.

15. Legón, *op. cit.*, p. 481; Leturia, *op. cit.*, pp. 45-46, 58.
16. Leturia, *op. cit.*, p. 59.

He presented several memorials to Cardinal Consalvi in which were described the irreligious spirit of the Argentinian revolt, the persecution and extinction of bishoprics, and the failure of the attempted approach to Rome by the mission of Valentín Gómez. He came to Rome, he said, to ask aid to save the Church in its present crisis. Pacheco proposed a remedy for the problem; it was to send to La Plata an apostolic vicar with archiepiscopal dignity and provided with ample powers. Also, two or three bishops *in partibus* should be sent.[17]

Pacheco's proposal was both sound and practical. To send to Argentina a nuncio with diplomatic character would be premature and would involve political recognition. On the other hand, a vicar or apostolic delegate without diplomatic character could not arouse Spanish protests for the nomination of bishops *in partibus* had never been a matter subject to the patronage and objection to the naming of proprietary bishops would thereby be avoided. Thus the spiritual necessities of America would be served without precipitating a break with Spain. The pope declined to act on Pacheco's proposal, for he undoubtedly realized that the government of Buenos Aires would refuse to accept an apostolic delegate considering the manner in which his appointment had been petitioned.

Yet, the very plan that was suggested by Pacheco was adopted by Pius VII, in 1823, with reference to Chile. In Chile, as in other parts of Spanish America, the episcopacy was thoroughly disorganized because of the revolution. Bishop José Rodríguez Zorrilla of Santiago had been deprived of his ecclesiastical authority and exiled by order of the Dictator. In 1821 he was allowed to return to Chile, but not to resume his office. This circumstance made Catholic reorganization of Chile a difficult matter. Dictator O'Higgins decided, with the advice of the governor of the bishopric, the presbyter José Ignacio Cienfuegos, who was a liberal creole ecclesiastic and ardent supporter of independence, to send an official delegation to Rome. Cienfuegos himself was appointed chief of the mission. His instructions, drawn up by O'Higgins, were partly as follows: "Declare our filial and religious obedience to the Holy

17. Both residential and titular bishops receive on consecration the episcopal power; they are really bishops. The difference is this: the residential bishops are ordinary and immediate administrators of a diocese of which they take possession. The titular bishops do not take possession of any diocese; it is the custom to grant them nevertheless the archiepiscopal or episcopal title of primitive or extinct dioceses or those fallen into the hands of the infidel (*in partibus infidelium*). The pope employs the titular bishops in the government of the Church either as nuncios, extraordinary administrators of constituted dioceses, coadjutors or auxiliaries of proprietary bishops, and ecclesiastical governors of territory not constituted a diocese. The *patronato de Indias* did not cover these offices and thus the creation of titular bishops as delegates, apostolic vicars, or auxiliary bishops was the most sensible provisional solution of the matter of the patronage.

See, protesting our faith, belief, union and communion with the head of the Church. Request of him an apostolic nuncio who may be either a citizen of this country or any other when His Holiness may wish to appoint; petition a declaration conceding to the Chilean nation the patronage granted the kings of Spain by Julius II; request the erection of cathedrals in Cochimbo, Talca, and Chiloé, in addition to Osorno and Valdívia, and that this capital (Santiago) be made a metropolitan see; ask of him that, at least in the interim, he send to Chile auxiliary bishops to take the places of the proprietary bishops."[18]

Cienfuegos, accompanied by five companions, sailed from Valparaiso, January 25, 1822, and arrived in Genoa on June 19. He immediately wrote the Cardinal-Secretary announcing that the Chilean government had sent him to swear obedience to the pope and to report to him on the spiritual necessities of his people. When the Spanish chargé Aparicio requested that Cienfuegos be refused entry into Rome, Cardinal Consalvi replied (July 6, 1822), "Having been informed that Archdeacon Cienfuegos came to Rome to explain to the pope the spiritual necessities of his people, the Holy Father believed that as common father of the faithful he could not refuse to listen to whatever news they brought from America touching on the state of religion, although without entering into any political relations that could offend the rights of the legitimate sovereign. Not long ago there came to Rome from Buenos Aires an ecclesiastic [Fray Pedro Pacheco] to lay before His Holiness the necessities of those faithful, and His Holiness, because of his apostolic ministry, listened to him, without injuring in this way any of the rights of His Catholic Majesty. Thus the Holy Father and his government will absolutely abstain from recognizing and treating Cienfuegos as a minister of the Chilean government."[19]

On August 6, Cienfuegos was granted an audience with the pope. After he described the necessities of the Chilean Church, he suggested as a temporary measure that an apostolic vicar be sent to Chile. This suggestion was submitted to a congregation of six cardinals. Among these was Della Genga, the later Leo XII. After a lengthy discussion in the congregation, the proposal of Cienfuegos was approved in April, 1823, by the cardinals, and Mgr. Ostini was named Vicar Apostolic of Chile. But since he was unable to accept, Mgr. Juan Muzi was appointed. Muzi was consecrated Archbishop of Filipos *in partibus infidelium* and Vicar Apostolic. Because of the insistence of Friar Pacheco, who was then in Rome, that La Plata was in even greater need of a

18. Luis Galdames, *Estudio de la Historia de Chile* (Santiago, 1911), p. 309; Leturia, *op. cit.*, p. 178.

19. Leturia, *op. cit.*, pp. 188-89.

vicar apostolic than Chile, the congregation enlarged Muzi's jurisdiction to include all of America. He was empowered to consecrate titular bishops and to repair as soon as possible the injuries caused by the struggle over investiture. He was advised to be cautious in the exercise of his powers and to abstain from the use of his authority in any colony where Spanish authority existed or where there was a probability of its being reëstablished.[20]

As was to be expected, Spain protested the pope's appointment of a vicar apostolic. Pius VII justified his decision by declaring that his action was made necessary because of his pastoral obligations and that it was merely a provisional action which would not disparage Spain's rights in any way. Cardinal Consalvi reiterated on several occasions that Muzi's mission had no political meaning and would in no way injure the *real patronato*.

Apostolic Vicar Muzi, accompanied by his secretary José Sallusti, and the canon, Conti Mastai (the later Pius IX)[21] sailed from Genoa on October 4, 1823. The death of Pius VII, which occurred shortly after Muzi's departure, did not interrupt the mission. The Apostolic Vicar received confirmatory papers from the new pope, Leo XII, shortly after his arrival in Buenos Aires. The papal delegate was given an enthusiastic reception by the populace of Buenos Aires, and General San Martín visited him twice to welcome him. The authorities, however, were very reserved in presenting themselves, and they even prohibited Muzi from exercising his ministry. When the provisor of the vacant bishopric, Señor Zavalleta, requested instructions on the attitude he should assume toward the pontifical representative, Rivadavia replied that he "did not recognize any character in that individual." The newspapers adopted an antagonistic attitude toward the Vicar and accused him of being the envoy of the Holy Alliance. Furthermore his sale of vast quantities of bulls and relics which he had brought over with him was criticized as being mercenary. Using the pretext that the presence of Muzi threatened a revolt, Rivadavia ordered him to leave the country immediately.[22] Thus ended in rancor and disappointment the attempt of Cardinal Consalvi to bring Argentina back into the fold.

The Apostolic Vicar arrived in Santiago de Chile in March, 1824. He was received with enthusiasm by the populace, and with pomp and veneration as the nuncio of the pope by General Ramón Freire, who

20. José Sallusti, *Historia de las Misiones Apostólicas de Monseñor Juan Muzi en el Estado de Chile* (Santiago, 1906), pp. 7-8.
21. For an account of the rôle played in the mission by the later Pius IX, see J. J. Shea, *The Life of Pope Pius IX* (New York, 1877), pp. 32-40.
22. Sallusti, *op. cit.*, pp. 227-28; Legón, *op. cit.*, p. 490.

had succeeded O'Higgins as dictator of Chile. Muzi delivered to Director Freire a letter addressed to him by Leo XII. This letter was notable as being the first one written by the pope to a political chieftain in America. In March, 1824, the Apostolic Vicar was voted a monthly subsistence of five hundred pesos by the Chilean Congress.[23] On July 13, 1824, Simón Bolívar wrote from Peru complimenting Muzi on his arrival in America. He expressed hope that arrangements could be made for the conclusion of a concordat with Colombia.[24]

Muzi's mission to Chile resulted in disastrous failure when the Apostolic Vicar ran afoul of the *patronato nacional*. The papal representative resolutely refused to accept the government's nominees for ecclesiastical positions. For this conflict Cienfuegos was partly responsible, since he, when the mission had been approved by Pius VII, wrote O'Higgins telling him that the Chilean government had been conceded the right of presentation to benefices and the administration of the tithes, and that the Vicar was to consecrate those persons nominated for vacant episcopacies by the government. All this practically amounted, he said, to a recognition of Chilean independence. This was untrue and was flatly contradicted by the new Cardinal-Secretary, Della Somaglia. Cienfuegos, therefore, led the Chilean government to believe that the right of national patronage had been confirmed. Muzi, on the other hand, could not acknowledge the right of the Chilean government to make ecclesiastical appointments. The difficulty of his position was increased because in Chile, as in Buenos Aires, he was regarded as being an agent of the Holy Alliance. Muzi, recognizing the impossibility of conciliating the irreconcilable, asked for his passports.[25]

The Vicar sailed from Valparaiso for Montevideo via Cape Horn on October 30, 1824. While in the capital of the Banda Oriental he published an apostolic letter in which he defended his actions.[26] He sailed from Montevideo for Europe and arrived in Rome on June 18,

23. Ricardo Anguita (ed.), *Leyes promulgadas en Chile desde 1810 hasta el 1º de Junio de 1913* (Santiago, 1913), I, 150.

24. "José Sánchez Carrion al Illmo. Señor don Juan Muzi, Arzobispo Filipense, Vicario Apostólico en la República de Chile, Huanuco, 13 de Julio de 1824," in *Cartas del Libertador*, IV, 114; Sallusti, *op. cit.*, p. 237.

25. Sallusti, *op. cit.*, p. 146; Galdames, *op. cit.*, pp. 317-18. According to Riva Palacio (*op. cit.*, IV, 151) Muzi was sent to America to combat the independence movement, but when he started to work for Ferdinand VII he was dismissed from Chile. There is no foundation for this assertion.

26. The minister of Chile to London, Mariano Egaña, told the Mexican agent, Vázquez, that the treatment of Muzi by Chile was a national disgrace. The actions of the Vicar, said Egaña, had been correct and disinterested, and his intentions the most honorable; he did not in the least fail to perform his duty. If he refused to consecrate two candidates proposed to him by the government he had excellent reasons for refusal. (Antonio de la Peña y Reyes, *León XII y Los Países Hispano-Americanos*, Mexico, 1924, p. 67.)

1825. The fundamental cause of the failure of the mission was misunderstanding for which Cienfuegos was responsible, and the Chileans' lack of confidence in the Vatican because of its acts in support of conservative and royalist tendencies. The intervention of the Holy Father, far from being beneficial in the dioceses of La Plata and Chile, left a very bad impression and an antagonistic attitude toward the papacy. On the other hand, the mission of Muzi was significant because it was the beginning of a *modus vivendi* with the American governments. In spite of Spanish protests a relationship of a kind was established between Rome and America. Later events proved this to be the logical steppingstone to recognition.

In 1824, the history of Papal-American relations assumed a different character. The change was due to the accession of a new pope, Leo XII, the restoration of Ferdinand VII to his absolute authority, the appearance of Mexico as a prominent supplicant at the Vatican, and the presence in Rome of a great diplomat, Ignacio de Tejada of Colombia.

When Leo XII ascended the throne of Peter, the aged Cardinal Consalvi, although no longer Cardinal-Secretary, summarized for the new pontiff his handling of the delicate ecclesiastical relations with Hispanic-America. He said, "What position ought we to take towards the Catholics in South America? Last year I treated the Spanish Cortes with forbearance with a view to obtaining, in case they should remain in power for a lengthy period, the right of appointing bishops to the vacant sees in distant lands. The legitimate Spanish monarch has no authority over these provinces, each of which is like a kingdom. I have allowed Spain more than fifteen years in which to work for the establishment of its sovereignty, but whether it is due to ingratitude or to infirmity, Spain has used our silence as a weapon against the rebels. If Spain had granted us permission to appoint bishops in Colombia, Mexico, and wherever we demanded it, we would have granted the legitimate monarch a respite of thirty years in which to get firmly into the saddle; but the time might easily come when Spain, without having regained its power, would say to us: 'I must resign my sovereignty; save your dogmas as well as you can.' It would then be too late for Rome. If we had waited so long, our apostolic vicar might have found the country filled with Methodists, Presbyterians, and even sunworshippers. I have therefore maintained friendly relations between Rome and those who so violently and with such a well-founded hope of success have refused obedience to the *juntas* and to Ferdinand VII."[27]

Ferdinand VII, having resumed the full enjoyment of his absolute

27. Artaud de Montor, *Histoire du Pape León XII* (Paris, 1843), I, 166 ff.

power, thanks to the Holy Allies, and France in particular, was anxious to be restored to his authority in America as well. His one remaining hope in America was the clergy who had always loyally supported the royal cause. He hoped that they, being convinced of the evils of republican government which was in direct opposition to their own interests, would decide to organize their forces to destroy the new political system. Ambassador Vargas, who had been restored to the Roman embassy, was ordered to request Leo XII to issue an encyclical to the prelates of America exhorting them to preach obedience to the legitimate authority of the Spanish king. A subtle argument used by Vargas to influence Cardinal Somaglia was somewhat as follows: the Americans were opposed to the establishment of legitimate government; this could be equally applied to apostolic authority; the only way to keep them in the Roman faith was to oblige their submission to the legitimate political authority; otherwise, the result would be serious schism, or, at least, indifference on the subject of religion.[28]

On September 24, 1824, the pope issued his celebrated encyclical to the archbishops and bishops of America, asking them to support the cause of "our very dear son Ferdinand, Catholic King of Spain, whose sublime and solid virtues cause him to place before the splendor of his greatness the luster of religion and the happiness of his subjects."[29] The publication of this document created a sensation throughout the length and breadth of America. American confidence, won by Pius VII after years of effort, was lost at a stroke. The suspicion that Leo XII was in league with the Holy Allies was now confirmed. A positive result produced by the encyclical was that of strengthening the Americans in their determination to protect their independence. An intense love of the national state was professed by all classes, including the ecclesiastics. According to Riva Palacio, "The encyclical, since it praised the virtues (?) of Ferdinand VII, and advocated a return to the colonial system (i.e., slavery), alienated many loyal Catholics in America."[30] In view of the fact that it was recognized by all, save Ferdinand VII, that the colonies were irrevocably lost, the action of the pope in issuing the encyclical was unintelligible. Indeed, because of the very absurdity of the action, the encyclical was declared by some to be apocryphal. They point to the singular circumstances under which it first appeared, i.e., in the *Gaceta de Madrid*, six months after the date of its purported signature by the pope. Yet, to refute all this, the Cardinal-Secretary when questioned

28. Ayarragaray, *op. cit.*, pp. 185, 234-35.
29. Peña y Reyes, *op. cit.*, p. iii.
30. Riva Palacio, *op. cit.*, IV, 139.

did not deny the authenticity of the encyclical.[31] But whatever the reason for its issuance, its publication certainly did not facilitate the establishment of a working agreement between Rome and America.

Within a year, however, the attitude of the pope changed and he agreed to receive American agents charged with negotiating on ecclesiastical matters. But he was still unwilling to discuss political subjects. The person most responsible for the modification of papal policy was Ignacio de Tejada, the Colombian representative at Rome. Tejada stands out among the several American agents who were sent to Rome as the most capable and the most successful. Undoubtedly the prestige of Great Colombia, the best organized government in South America, with the great Liberator at its head, tended to lend considerable support to Tejada. Nevertheless, his ability, discretion, energy, patience, and perseverance were qualities which contributed in even greater measure to the success of his long mission in Rome. He became the veritable head of the different American agencies accredited to the pope, and on numerous occasions he was entrusted with the business of the other republics. Indeed, he came to be regarded as the *agente privado* of all America before the pope. Tejada, like the majority of diplomatic agents sent to Rome, was a cleric. It was thought that ecclesiastics would have a better chance of success, for if the Spanish ambassador protested their missions, they could claim that they were concerned only with spiritual matters and that they did not come to Caesar but to the vicar of Christ. Tejada was instructed to negotiate for: the immediate provision of all vacant bishoprics; authority to bishops to secularize the regulars; appointment by the pope of a legate authorized to negotiate a concordat which would allow the primate of Colombia to erect or divide dioceses in accordance with the needs of the population, and to confer canonical institution on the bishops presented by the government; and the confirmation in the government of Great Colombia of the patronage which the kings of Spain had exercised.[32]

Tejada arrived in Rome in September, 1824, and took up his residence in an obscure pension near the Plaza de Popolo. Although Ambassador Vargas, who was now reinstated in his old post in Rome, was unsuccessful in his efforts to prevent Tejada's entry, he continued to intrigue against the American agent. Twice the Colombian's residence was entered by the spies of the Spanish Ambassador. Notwithstanding the

31. See Ayarragaray, *op. cit.*, pp. 184-88, 199-203, for proof of the authenticity of the encyclical. See also, Peña y Reyes, *op. cit.*, p. 49; Cuevas, *op. cit.*, V, 165-70; and Joaquín Ramírez Cabañas, *Las Relaciones entre México y el Vaticano* (Mexico, 1928), pp. 14-22.

32. Zubieta, *op. cit.*, p. 580.

protests of Vargas, who was supported by the Austrian ambassador, Tejada was received privately by the Cardinal-Secretary of State, Della Somaglia. His mission, he declared, was not political, but merely spiritual. He only came to enlighten the pope on the state of the Church in Colombia, where, after fourteen years of noncommunication with the papacy, all but two of the episcopal sees were vacant. These two bishops, he said, had to administer to three million people scattered over a country as large as France and Spain combined. He also described the menace of Protestantism in Colombia. The English, Dutch, Swiss, and other Protestants were coming to America in great numbers, and the Bible Society of England was scattering its doctrine and missions in profusion. He concluded by expressing the confidence of the people of Colombia that their petitions would be speedily granted since they only asked for a satisfactory settlement of matters in the purely spiritual order. Cardinal Somaglia listened attentively but would not commit himself beyond promising that the matter would be studied. He counseled Tejada not to pose as a diplomatic or public character for he would not be received as one. Furthermore, it was the pope's desire, he said, that the Colombian retire to Bologna to avoid the criticism of the Spanish ambassador. Tejada acceded, saying that he was still hopeful for the success of his mission. Vargas, however, was dissatisfied with Tejada's residence in Bologna, and as a result of his continued protestations, the Colombian agent was ordered, in November, 1824, to leave the Papal States. He then took up his residence in Florence. The expulsion of her minister was regarded by Colombia as an affront, and Tejada was ordered to abandon his mission if the papacy did not raise the ban against him. The agent, however, understood that success depended on patience, and he was content to bide his time. His perseverance was rewarded, for within a year he was allowed to take up his residence in Civita Vecchia, and in the following year, 1826, he was invited to return to Rome as "Diputado para los negocios eclesiásticos de Colombia en Roma."[33]

Rome's new policy, to receive American representatives as ecclesiastical delegates, but on the express condition that this action did not imply political recognition, was adopted as an immediate reaction to the news that Mexico was sending a notable mission to the papacy headed by the presbyter Francisco Pablo Vázquez.

After 1824 the problem of the Mexican Church was added to that of Colombia, Argentina, and Chile, to plague the Holy Father. Although

33. *Ibid.*, pp. 567-81; Ayarragaray, *op. cit.*, p. 228; Gil Fortoul, *op. cit.*, I, 381.

Mexican independence had been achieved in 1821 and patronage was declared terminated by the Regency, the rapid political changes accompanying the rise and fall of the Empire prevented the dispatch of a mission to Rome. The necessity of appealing to the Vatican for a restoration of ecclesiastical relations was apparent to all from the beginning, and with the passage of time the need of a solution became more pressing because Mexico was feeling the disastrous effects of noncommunication with Rome. By 1825 the metropolitan and five suffragan sees were vacant. The only bishops were those of Puebla, Oaxaca, and Yucatán, and, by 1829, when Antonio Pérez, Bishop of Puebla, died, Mexico had not a single bishop. There was also an alarming decline in the number of secular clergy.[34]

After the establishment of the Republic, the Congress turned to a consideration of the ecclesiastical situation. The debates over patronage, concordats, and like subjects were so protracted that the government decided to lose no more valuable time but to send an agent to Rome at once. Therefore, while the Congress was still debating on the nature of the envoy's instructions, Francisco Vázquez departed for Europe. He arrived in England on July 25, 1825.[35] News that Mexico was sending a mission to Rome interested Leo XII greatly, for the condition of the Church in Mexico, particularly the alleged Protestant propaganda from the United States, troubled the pope. He was inclined to admit Vázquez to Rome and grant him an audience. But the Spanish ambassador presented the usual protests. The assurance of Cardinal Somaglia that Rome did not intend to recognize any legation from a rebellious colony of Spain, but was only disposed to receive the Mexicans in his capacity as head of the Church, had no effect upon Spain. "The Spanish government," reported the papal nuncio in Madrid to the Cardinal-Secretary, "in spite of its absolute impotence, is determined to continue the unequal struggle which it has been prosecuting for so long with its rebellious colonies. It conforms in this with the national character not to accept any workable or intelligent proposal; and consequently proceeds to lose the little influence that it retains.... For this fatal obstinacy the Holy Alliance bears responsibility since its representa-

34. Lorenzo de Zavala, *Ensayo Histórico de las Revoluciones de México* (Mexico, 1845), II, 170; Cabañas, *op. cit.*, pp. LXI-XV.

35. *Ibid.*, I, 292-93. Father Cuevas (*op. cit.*, V, 157-58) discusses the mission of a secret agent who was sent to Rome soon after the overthrow of Iturbide. This man, Father José María Marchena, was instructed to learn what the Roman Curia thought of Mexican independence, and whether it was willing to enter into a concordat with the republic. Marchena, quite irresponsible and incompetent, was, of course, unable to accomplish anything. Cuevas believes he caused more harm than good.

tives in Madrid and in Paris do not cease to encourage Spain to defend at all cost her rights in America, and prevent the triumph of the rebel demagogues."[36]

The pope then sought the good offices of France to aid him in breaking down the opposition of Ferdinand VII. The French government accepted, seeing in this an opportunity to play the rôle of protector of the Catholic Church in Spanish America, which could be used to counteract the commercial influence of England over the new nations. Consequently a conference attended by the papal nuncio, the ambassadors of Russia and Austria, the minister of Prussia, and the French minister Baron de Damás, met in Paris on October 7, 1825. The nuncio explained the situation created by the Mexican mission and requested the members of the Holy Alliance to persuade the Spanish king to cease his opposition. The conference advised the pope to receive the Mexican envoys only as delegates in purely spiritual matters, and they agreed to invite their representatives at Madrid to convert Ferdinand VII to their point of view. But when approached the Spanish sovereign refused positively to heed the advice of the Holy Allies. In commenting on Spanish intransigence the papal nuncio at Madrid wrote, "The obstacles put in the way of the ecclesiastical authority in America should be enough to drive out of those lands all principles of canonical jurisprudence, and to introduce in Spain a species of Anglican supremacy." Notwithstanding the objections of Spain, Leo XII was not to be deterred. Tejada and Vázquez were both invited to come to Rome, but only as ecclesiastical agents. The Colombian representative consented. Vázquez, unfortunately, since the *sine qua non* of his instructions was that he be received as a diplomatic envoy, had to refuse. The papal nuncio in Paris tried in vain to convince the Mexican Minister of Foreign Affairs of the impossibility of the Holy See receiving Vázquez in a diplomatic character. "Señor Tejada, the Colombian agent," he said, "does not bear any title except that of deputy for the ecclesiastical business of Colombia, and he is content with this. Why should Mexico wish for more with things in their present state?"[37] Personally Vázquez was inclined to favor a compromise, and in a letter to Ramos Arizpe, the Mexican Minister of State, he wrote that he was convinced that Rome was inclined to do anything short of recognition. The pope was really desirous of meeting their spiritual necessities but without compromising himself with the Spanish government. As for political recog-

36. Leturia, *op. cit.*, p. 7.
37. Villanueva, *op. cit.*, pp. 27, n. 47, 204-7.

nition, it was certain that Rome would wait upon the European powers.[38] The result was that Vázquez did not go to Rome; at least not until 1830.

Leo XII did not stop with receiving ecclesiastical agents from the Spanish-American republics. He decided to disregard the ancient right of royal patronage, and in the celebrated consistory of May 21, 1827, he preconized candidates presented by the government of Colombia as proprietary bishops for six vacant seats in Colombia. The following were confirmed at that time: Fernando Caicedo y Flórez as archbishop of Bogotá, Ignacio Méndez as archbishop of Caracas, Félix Calixto Miranda as bishop of Cuenca, José María Estévez as bishop of Santa Marta, Manuel Santos Escobar as bishop of Quito, and Mariano Garnica as bishop of Antioquia. In a letter to the pope Bolívar expressed great pleasure that the ecclesiastical vacancies had been filled. He also announced that the government of Great Colombia had assumed the right of patronage.[39] This act deprived *real patronato* of that which constituted its chief value, i.e., the privilege of royal presentation. It is not surprising then that Ferdinand VII regarded the pope's action in preconizing bishops without royal presentation as a violation of the Spanish patronage. The act was condemned as giving aid and comfort to the rebels, for since the independence movement centered about the native ecclesiastics, said Ferdinand, the new bishops would be the most bitter enemies of the Spanish régime. In other words the pope's action made independence more certain. Ferdinand VII demanded that in the future the pope wait upon him for nominations. The assurance of the nuncio in Madrid that the bulls of confirmation sent to the Colombian bishops did not contain any expression which could be construed by the government of Colombia as granting it the right of presentation did not satisfy Ferdinand. Nor was he moved by a personal letter written to him, on July 4, 1827, by Leo XII, which contained assurances that the pope did not intend to depart from his policy to refuse political recognition to the new states in America. "But when we were solicited," wrote Leo XII, "for purely spiritual purposes to remedy an unhappy religious situation which threatened to destroy the Church completely, after announcing that we would perform this election of our own free will (*de motu proprio*), how could we refuse to give spiritual aid and render an account to God? . . . If we had questioned your Majesty on these candidates, we would surely have run the risk of having the Americans refuse them."[40]

The next move of Leo XII was to send a new nuncio to Madrid to seek an understanding with Ferdinand. The king, although not aiming at an actual termination of relations with the Vatican, ordered the nuncio stopped at Irún and refused to allow him to enter Spain. The breach between Rome and Madrid was soon healed when Ferdinand's anger cooled and he wrote the pope a conciliatory letter. His conduct, he said, was dictated by necessity and not by choice. But since he was anxious to give proof of his affection for the Holy Father, he was sending an ambassador to Rome to settle the difficulty. Don Pedro Gómez Labrador, a councillor of state of wide experience, was appointed ambassador to Rome on this difficult mission. Labrador, mentally and temperamentally very much like Vargas, entered into his negotiations with the Holy See by demanding in a highhanded manner that the patronal rights of his sovereign be recognized to the limit. Furthermore, since there was a widespread belief that the bulls of investiture of the Colombian bishops had been issued after presentation by Bolívar, he requested that the pope publish in the newspapers a notice to the effect that "in the nomination of bishops, he did not act on the proposal of any rebel chief." The Cardinal-Secretary finally consented and inserted a short notice in the papers to this effect. But when Labrador tried to prevent the pope from receiving agents from America he was met with refusal. Also, when the ambassador proposed that the pope should observe previous presentation by the Spanish king "since His Catholic Majesty had not renounced the prerogatives of sovereignty as founder of the Church in the rebellious colonies," Cardinal Somaglia countered with the statement that "the privileges conceded by the Holy See to the Catholic Sovereigns cease to have value when they would be injurious to the Church."[41]

In the midst of the negotiations the pope announced that he planned at the next consistory to be held in September, 1828, to preconize more bishops for America. To avoid a new conflict with Spain he proposed to name only titular bishops, "concerning whose nomination the patronal monarch has confessed he has no rights," he said. Still Labrador protested, and then Leo XII, with great emotion, exclaimed that he would give his blood for the king, but that he could never give him his soul. The September consistory had to be postponed, but on December 22, 1828, the pope preconized several apostolic vicars with episcopal char-

40. Ayarragaray, *op. cit.*, pp. 259-68; Villanueva, *op. cit.*, pp. 208-9; Zubieta, *op. cit.*, p. 581.

41. Ayarragaray, *op. cit.*, pp. 269-71, 278-81.

acter, among these being Dean Cienfuegos of Santiago, Chile, and Friar Justo Santa María de Oro of Cuyo.[42]

Leo XII died on March 31, 1829, and was succeeded in the Vatican by Pius VIII. The new pope was firm in his refusal to recognize national patronage. He refused to consecrate bishops, not only for Colombia, but for Mexico and the other American states. The reason advanced for his refusal was that, as regarded Mexico, the internal disorders presaged the extinction of the national state, and, as for Great Colombia, the disintegration of the federal state was imminent. The efforts of Pius VIII to harmonize his policy with that of the Spanish king were met with the usual rebuff. The pope, therefore, in spite of his natural reserve, had to yield to the pressure of facts. The impending ruin of the Church in America and the demoralization of the clergy, for now there was scarcely a bishop in all America, compelled the pope to consider measures to remedy the evils. Therefore, in spite of his favorable attitude toward Spain, he notified the Spanish ambassador of his intention to consecrate bishops for America at the Christmas consistory (1830). Labrador was thoroughly discouraged and wrote his government that in his judgment it was useless to object further.[43]

It was about this time (1830) that the Mexican envoy, Francisco Vázquez, finally entered Rome. Because of the pope's refusal to treat him as the diplomatic representative of an independent nation, Vázquez had been detained for three years in Brussels, Paris, and London. In the summer of 1830, accompanied by a numerous retinue, Vázquez went to Rome to present a virtual ultimatum to the pope. He was instructed by his government to negotiate a concordat in which the *conditio sine qua non* was the nomination of proprietary bishops. In the name of his government he was to declare that in the future Mexico would not receive apostolic vicars, but only proprietary bishops. Vázquez presented a list of persons whom the Mexican government wished to have confirmed in the vacant sees. When the Cardinal-Secretary attempted to induce Vázquez to accept as a temporary measure the naming of titular bishops, he flatly refused to negotiate, saying that he was bound by a limited and express mandate.[44]

42. Legón, *op. cit.*, p. 492.

43. Ayarragaray, *op. cit.*, pp. 288-90; Zubieta, *op. cit.*, p. 588.

44. Ayarragaray, *op. cit.*, pp. 294-95. Zavala's (*op. cit.*, II, 172-73) account of Vázquez's mission disagrees with the above. According to Zavala, Vázquez consented to go to Rome as a simple ecclesiastic. There, without mentioning the Mexican government, he requested that the pope *motu proprio* (that is, without consideration of national rights) appoint bishops for America. The action of Vázquez, says Zavala, was an insult to the Mexican nation. See Luis Medina Ascensio, *La Santa sede y la emancipación Mexicana* (Guadalajara, 1946).

Death saved Pius VIII from the radical action of confirming proprietary bishops for America. Gregory XVI, who was elected to the see of Peter on February 2, 1831, was the pope who first recognized the independence of the Spanish-American republics. When Gregory became pope, the atmosphere in the Vatican was charged with a bitter resentment for the Spanish king because of his intransigence. Since the restoration of Spanish power in America was now an absolute impossibility, the high ecclesiastics advised the pope to restore normal ecclesiastical relations with America. Gregory heeded the advice and lost no time in adopting a definite policy. The new course was stated in the bull *Sollicitudo Ecclesiarum* (August, 1831), which referred particularly to the Portuguese situation,[45] but which could be extended to all Spanish America. In this bull the pope declared his intention to exercise freely his rights and his spiritual functions. If he treated of ecclesiastical affairs with temporal governments, it was not to be regarded as political recognition, but only recognition of the existence of the said government for the carrying on of ecclesiastical affairs. Finally, he declared his intention to establish relations with *de facto* governments when they gave indication of stability. When the Spanish ambassador inquired if, as one would deduce from the bull, the pope intended to recognize the Spanish-American republics, he was put off with the reply, "Almost none of the new states can present circumstances similar to those of Portugal. Thus the Spanish ambassador can imply that the moment is not so imminent when the Holy See would recognize any of them."[46] Notwithstanding this explanation, it was well understood that papal recognition of America was not far distant.

Beginning with the consistory of 1831, Gregory XVI proceeded boldly to preconize proprietary bishops for America. In Mexico seven sees were filled: Puebla, Chiapas, Linares, Guadalajara, Durango, Michoacán, and Monterrey. Francisco Vázquez was consecrated by the pope Bishop of Puebla, and he in turn consecrated the other Mexican bishops. More Mexican sees were filled in 1834 and in 1836. By 1838 only the archdiocese of Mexico and the see of Oaxaca were vacant due

45. Dom Miguel, son of John VI and brother of Pedro I of Brazil, after the death of his father and during the minority of his niece, María de Gloria, was regent. Supported by absolutists he tried to retain the throne for himself. A struggle ensued in which both factions tried to secure from the pope the provision of bishops for vacant sees. Finally Gregory XVI decided to preconize the candidates presented by Dom Miguel. To explain his policy he issued the bull. (Ayarragaray, *op. cit.*, p. 306.)

46. *Ibid.*, pp. 304-10; Zubieta, *op. cit.*, pp. 589-91; Pedro Leturia, "Gregorio XVI y la emancipación de la América Española," *Revista de Historia de América*, Instituto Panamericano de Geografía é Historia, Mexico D.F., No. 26 (Dic., 1948), 309-77.

to the voluntary exile of their prelates. The archiepiscopal see of Mexico was not filled until 1840.[47]

In 1832 titular bishops for vacant sees in Argentina and Chile were appointed by the pope. It was not until the next year, 1833, that Tejada, now the agent for New Granada only, since the dissolution of Great Colombia, secured the preconization of bishops for Antioquia, Santa Marta, and Popayán and for an archbishop for Bogotá. In none of these cases did the pope formally recognize the right of presentation in the American governments, although he was often willing to accept names suggested to him.

In an encyclical to the bishops of America Gregory XVI expressly ordered them to refuse to recognize patronage, and in the oaths of obedience demanded of the bishops, the same denial was implied.[48] It is noteworthy that to the present day the papacy has never recognized patronage as being an inherent right in sovereignty.

It might be thought that Gregory XVI would not recognize the political independence of the Spanish-American republics without first arriving at a settlement regarding the patronage. He, however, prudently made the act a political one only, leaving the problem of national patronage for later study and solution. He realized that if recognition waited upon a settlement of the religious issue, it might never come. The death of Ferdinand VII in 1833 facilitated a solution of the problem. Out of consideration for Ferdinand himself, who chose to regard recognition as a very personal affront, the pope had refrained from political action. With that obstacle now removed and the Spanish government distraught by civil strife, the opportune moment had arrived for decisive action. On November 26, 1835, Gregory XVI formally recognized the independence of the Republic of New Granada. On December 14, 1835, Ignacio Tejada's long years of patient, tactful diplomacy were rewarded when he was received in papal audience as the *chargé* of the Republic of New Granada. When the pope manifested a desire to send a nuncio to New Granada, Tejada was instructed to oppose this because the Holy Father wanted the Republic to bear the expenses and because it was feared that the papal representative would exercise an ultramontane influence which would be dangerous to the infant State. Tejada, however, was not able to halt the pope, for, on May 18, 1836, Mgr. Baluffi was named internuncio extraordinary to New

47. Riva Palacio, *op. cit.*, IV, pp. 29, 284, 454.

48. Zubieta, *op. cit.*, p. 598. Pope Pius IX, in allocution *numquam fore* (December 15, 1856) energetically denied the legitimacy of national patronage as a right inherited from the kings of Spain. Also, the right of secular presentation was condemned as an error in the *Syllabus*. (Zamora, *Patronato Español é Indiano*, pp. 245-46.) .

Granada. He was the first nuncio accredited to a Spanish-American republic.[49]

The recognition of New Granada marked the end of the American problem as far as political recognition and Spanish opposition were concerned. Thereafter the pope's dealings with Spanish America were direct and unhampered by considerations for Spanish susceptibilities. When Rome became satisfied as to the political stability of the new governments set up in America and as to their friendliness toward the principle of papal supremacy, recognition was bestowed. The problem of the patronage, however, remained to complicate and strain Papal-American relations for many years to come.

49. "Ignacio Tejada á Santander, Roma, 18 de Diciembre de 1835," in *Archivo Santander* (Bogotá, 1924-25), XXI, 372-73; Zubieta, *op. cit.*, pp. 597-98.

Chapter IV

Church and State in Venezuela

For nearly a decade after the achievement of independence the political fortunes of Venezuela, Colombia, and Ecuador were merged in a single republic, Great Colombia. This remarkable State, the handiwork of Simón Bolívar, had its genesis in the Congress of Angostura, which had been convened by the Liberator following the inauguration of his third, and eventually successful, attempt to liberate the Spanish colonies of northern South America. On August 15, 1819, the legislators of Angostura, representing Venezuela and New Granada, signed a provisional constitution which embodied with slight change, a constitutional project submitted by Bolívar. Neither in the project nor in the adopted instrument was there any reference to religion. Bolívar was of the opinion, and the constituents evidently concurred, that the constitutional guarantee of civil liberty comprehended religious liberty and should not be a subject of special legislation because it belonged exclusively to individual conscience.[1]

The act of December 17, 1819, which constituted the republic of Great Colombia, provided that a congress should meet at Rosario de Cúcuta to draw up a constitution.[2] In evidence of the fact that the Colombian clergy favored independence and union with Venezuela, the ecclesiastical *cabildo* of Bogotá, shortly after the battle of Boyacá, paid

1. The most novel feature of Bolívar's project, that having to do with the organization of the "Moral Power," a great institution of censorship and supervision of education and public morality, was rejected by the Congress. For the text of the Moral Power, see "El Poder Moral Propuesto por Bolívar en Angostura," in Gil Fortoul, *Historia Constitucional de Venezuela*, pp. 545-51. For Church and State in the Bolivarian era, see Mary Watters, *A History of the Church in Venezuela, 1810-1930* (Chapel Hill, 1933), pp. 71-124.

2. Daniel F. O'Leary, *Bolívar y la Emancipación de Sur-América* (Madrid, 1915), II, 24; "S. Bolívar al Excmo. señor Vicepresidente de Cundinamarca, Angostura, 20 de diciembre de 1819," in *Cartas de Bolívar*, II, 125.

to the government a considerable part of the tithes, despite its poverty.[3] Following Bolívar's decisive victory at Carabobo (June 24, 1821), which assured the independence from Spain of northern South America, a constituent congress composed of representatives from New Granada and Venezuela convened at Cúcuta. The Constitution of Angostura, which, as we have seen, contained no article on religion, was used by the constituents as the basis for their deliberations. Some of them wished to insert an article making Catholicism the religion of the State, but the majority opposed, and, after a noisy scene, the constitution was approved without any reference to an official religion or even to religious toleration.[4] This was in accordance with the wishes of Bolívar, for, as the Liberator explained later, "When the Constitution of Colombia was drawn up, knowing that tolerance of any religion other than the Catholic would not be permitted, I was careful that nothing should be said (in the constitution) about religion, so that, since there was no clause which prescribed the form of cult, aliens could adore God as they pleased. The people of Colombia were not yet prepared for any change in the matter of religion. The priests exercised a great influence over the ignorant masses. Religious liberty ought to be the consequence of free institutions and a system of general education."[5]

It is not true, as is commonly asserted, that the Constitution of Cúcuta contained no reference whatsoever to religion. The preamble read: "In the name of God, Author and Legislator of the Universe." But more important was the prologue or introductory statement. In presenting the constitution to the people the framers wrote: "That which your representatives have always had in view, and that which has been the object of their most serious meditations, is that these laws should conform entirely to the maxims and dogmas of the Roman Catholic Apostolic religion which all of us profess and which we glory in professing. It has been the religion of our fathers, and it is and will be the religion of the State; its ministers are the only ones who enjoy the free exercise of their functions, and the government authorizes necessary contributions for the Sacred Cult."[6] The fact that the Catholic religion was not established, in the body of the constitution, itself, as the State

---

3. Henao y Arrubla, *Historia de Colombia*, II, 425.
4. "Constitución de la República de Colombia, Rosario de Cúcuta, 1821," in Manuel Antonio Pombo y José Joaquín Guerra, *Constituciones de Colombia* (Bogotá, 1911), I, 717-59. The representatives of the Department of Venezuela were most antagonistic toward the Church. Mary Watters, "The Present Status of the Church in Venezuela," in *The Hispanic American Historical Review*, XIII, No. 1 (February, 1933), p. 24.
5. Gil Fortoul, *op. cit.*, I, 318.
6. Pombo y Guerra, *op. cit.*, p. 720.

religion, was due not to atheistic or Masonic opposition to the principle, but only to the inexperience of the constitution makers. It was taken for granted that the old religious status would continue (as witness the preamble quoted above), and that it would be regulated by ordinary legislation.

The legislative Congress of Cúcuta was very active, as a matter of fact, in determining by special laws the ecclesiastical jurisdiction. A law of August 22, 1821, abolished the Inquisition and appropriated its properties for the public treasury. It provided that archbishops and bishops "reassume the ecclesiastical and purely spiritual jurisdiction, of which they had been deprived by the establishment of the Inquisition, hear causes of faith according to the canons and common ecclesiastical law, and impose on the guilty penalties established by the power of the Church." To remove obstacles to foreign immigration, the law added, "The hearing of such causes of faith will affect only the Roman Catholics born in Colombia, their children, and those who, having come from other countries, have been inscribed in the parochial registers as Catholics. Aliens or their dependents cannot be molested in their beliefs, providing they do not show disrespect for the Catholic faith." Likewise, by the same law, full episcopal jurisdiction was guaranteed over purely spiritual matters, but all causes relating to the external discipline of the Church, like the prohibition of books, were left to the civil power. It was also provided that Colombian bishops were to be limited to the native-born.[7] After prohibiting the publication of sacred books without license of the ecclesiastical ordinary, the law of September 14, 1821, classified as punishable writings those contrary to the dogmas of the Roman Catholic faith. Vice President Santander interpreted this law very liberally, for he authorized the publication of the works of Voltaire, Rousseau, and Diderot, which had been on the Index.[8]

In sponsoring a law which declared that the supreme government was the protector of the Catholic Church in Colombia, Bolívar revealed himself as a truly great statesman. Although he opposed the establishment of a State-Church, on the other hand he opposed absolute separation such as obtained in the United States. Since the Catholic Church was not only dominant, but universal, in Colombia, he felt that the government was morally bound to protect it and maintain it in all its purity. Thus we see Bolívar, personally a free-thinker, *as president* attend mass regularly on Sunday, endow convents and other ecclesiastical

7. *Ibid.*, I, 319; Leturia, *La Acción Diplomática*, pp. 137-38.
8. A. Berthe, *García Moreno, Président de L'Equateur* (Paris, 1887), p. 37.

institutions with public funds, honor bishops officially, and seek contact with the Holy See.[9]

General Santander, the head of the Colombian government on the numerous occasions when Bolívar was campaigning in Quito, Peru, and Charcas, was more insistent than the Liberator that the State should dominate the Church. He demanded that restrictions be placed upon the political activities of the clerics; by such means, he argued, not only would the security of republican principles be enhanced, but the status of religion would be improved. Santander, a prominent Mason, has been accused of encouraging Masonic anti-Catholic propaganda.[10] This assertion is subject to some doubt, yet it is true that Santander's extreme regalistic attitude evoked the severe criticism of Bolívar.[11]

Although the Congress of Cúcuta tried to avoid the patronal problem, that difficult and delicate question could not be successfully side-tracked. When the republican army occupied Popayán, in 1819, Bishop Salvador Jiménez de Encina, a Spaniard, abandoned his diocese and threatened to excommunicate anyone who should attempt to assume his office. The republican authorities, accustomed as they were to royal interference in such a situation, felt constrained to intervene. The chapter was ordered to name a diocesan governor. This was done, and the capitular action was ratified by the government (April, 1821). By convincing Bishop Jiménez that republican principles were not contrary to the Church, Bolívar induced him to return to his diocese. By decree of July 28, 1823, the bishop was restored to his post.[12] Thus it is seen that the Congress proceeded on the assumption that it had inherited the patronal authority.

The question of the tithes also brought up the problem of patronage. On September 15, 1821, Bishop Lasso de la Vega of Mérida addressed a memorial to Vice-President Santander on the subject of the tithes. He declared that since the tithes had been granted by Pope Alexander VI to the kings of Spain, it was evident that, with the founding of the republic, they reverted to the Church and belonged to her alone. Santander replied that the republican government had inherited the sovereignty of the Spanish kings and all that belonged to it, particularly the tithes. As for bestowing the tithes upon the Church, Santander said, "Your worship [Lasso] ought to be well informed that the government

9. Gil Fortoul, *op. cit.*, I, 435.

10. Berthe, *op. cit.*, p. 36.

11. "S. Bolívar á S. E. el General F. de P. Santander, Potosí, 21 de octubre de 1825," in *Cartas del Libertador*, V, 135-44.

12. "S. Bolívar al Illmo. señor don Salvador Jiménez, Obispo de Popayán, Popayán, 31 de enero de 1822," in *Cartas del Libertador*, III, 17; Gil Fortoul, *op. cit.*, I, 319-20.

of the republic has not failed and will not fail to do so...because it is the duty of all government to support its cult and its ministers."[13]

Bishop Lasso was puzzled by the reply of the Vice-President, for he did not understand how a government, which had just refused to recognize Catholicism as the religion of the State, could declare itself to be in possession of the patronal rights. Congress, nevertheless, declared adherence to the principle that the existing laws remained in force "until a concordat can [could] be celebrated with the Apostolic See on this grave problem." Therefore the government convoked an ecclesiastical *junta* in Bogotá to agree on the essential principles of a concordat. In the *junta*, which did not meet until March, 1823, the opinion of Bishop Lasso prevailed; that is, that the patronage had come to an end.[14]

The Congress was not disposed to accept the decision of the *junta*, for it passed a law (July 28, 1824) declaring that the right of patronage, which had been exercised by the Spanish kings, belonged to the State. Because of the importance of this law, its principal features are presented below:

> The Senate and Chamber of Representatives of the Republic of Colombia in Congress assembled:
> Decree:
> Article 1. The Republic of Colombia ought to continue in the exercise of the right of patronage which the kings of Spain had over the metropolitan churches, cathedrals, and parishes in this part of America.
> Article 2. This right is a duty of the Republic of Colombia and of its government, and it demands that the Apostolic See do not change or alter it; and the Executive Power under this principle will celebrate with His Holiness a concordat which will assure for all time, and irrevocably, this prerogative of the Republic and avoid conflicts and claims for the future.
> Article 3. The right of patronage and protection are exercised, first, by the Congress; second, by the Executive Power with the Senate; third, by the Executive Power alone; fourth, by the intendants; and fifth, by the governors.
> The High Court of the Republic, and the Superior Courts will hear cases that arise out of this matter.

The law proceeds to give in considerable detail the patronal powers and duties of the Congress, executive power, intendants, governors, High Court, and Superior Courts. These are presented in summary as follows:

13. Leturia, *op. cit.*, p. 146.

14. *Ibid.*, pp. 146-47; José Manuel Restrepo, *Historia de Colombia* (Bogotá, 1848), III, 412; Juan Pablo Restrepo, *La Iglesia y el Estado en Colombia* (London, 1881), pp 140-43.

Article 4. The Congress is empowered to:

1. Erect new dioceses or reorganize old ones, to designate their territorial limits, and assign funds to be employed in the building and repairing of metropolitan and episcopal churches.

2. Permit, or even summon, national or provincial councils or synods.

3. Permit or refuse the founding of new monasteries and hospitals, and to suppress those existing if deemed advisable, and to assume control of their property.

4. Draw up tariffs of parochial fees.

5. Regulate the administration of the tithes.

6. Grant or refuse the exequatur to bull and briefs.

7. Enact legislation deemed necessary for the vigorous maintenance of exterior discipline of the Church, and for the conservation and exercise of the ecclesiastical patronage.

8. Nominate those to be presented to His Holiness for the archiepiscopal and episcopal sees.

9. Enact legislation for the establishment, rule, and support of the missions for the Indians.

Article 6. The Executive is empowered to:

1. Present to the pope for his approval the actions of Congress on the erection of new dioceses and the alteration of old ones.

2. Present to the pope the nominees of Congress for the archiepiscopal and episcopal positions.

3. Present to the prelates and chapters for the prebendaries and canons, nominees selected jointly with the Senate.

4. Grant or refuse consent to the nominees of the prelates and chapters for provisors and capitular vicars.

5. Guard against the introduction of any novelty in the exterior discipline of the Church, and see that the ecclesiastics do not usurp the patronage of the State.

6. Grant the exequatur to briefs on matters of grace.

7. Watch over the proper supervision of the dioceses by the prelates.

8. Issue administrative decrees regulating the laws of Congress to protect religion, the public cult, and its ministers.

Article 7. The intendants are empowered to:

1. Name and present to the respective prelates the curates of the diocese included within the department.

2. Erect and fix the limits of new parishes.

3. Take care that the national patronage is observed and report on same to the Executive Power.

4. See that ecclesiastics do not usurp the civil jurisdiction.

5. Keep the Executive Power informed regarding clerics worthy of advancement.

Article 8. The governors are empowered to:

1. Name the *mayordomos de fábrica* of the cathedral and parish churches of their provinces, and to make them render an account of their management according to law.

2. Name, on the proposal of the respective municipalities, the syndics, *mayordomos,* and administrators of the hospitals of their provinces.

3. Permit or refuse the founding of chapels and churches, but not cathedrals, parochial churches, or monasteries.

4. Watch over the observance of the patronage.

5. Visit hospitals and remedy abuses in them; propose to the Executive Power, through the intendants, the reforms that should be introduced to improve those establishments.

6. Supervise *cofradías.*

7. Inform the intendants regarding the need of establishing new parishes.

8. Inform the indendants regarding ecclesiastics worthy of promotion.

Article 9. The High Court of Justice has jurisdiction over the following subjects:

1. Disloyalty of the archbishop and bishop to the republic, and violation on their part of the national patronage.

2. Controversies between two or more dioceses concerning their territorial limits.

3. Controversies arising out of concordats.

Article 10. The Superior Courts have jurisdiction over the following subjects:

1. Disloyalty to the republic, or usurpation of the patronage, by the other ecclesiastics.

2. Conflict over jurisdiction between civil and ecclesiastical courts.

The remaining articles of the *Ley de Patronato* regulate very minutely the manner of filling ecclesiastical vacancies, from the highest to the lowest. This law, substantially unchanged, is in force in Venezuela today.[15]

Papal confirmation, by concordat, of Colombia's pretentions to the patronage had been the objective of the government from the inception of the republic. Peñalver and Vergara, in 1819, and Francisco Zea, in

15. *Ley de Patronato Eclesiástico* (Caracas, 1911), pp. 4-25; for full text, see Watters, *History of the Church in Venezuela,* pp. 222-37.

1820, were instructed among other things to negotiate with the Holy See a formal recognition of the national patronage. When Dr. Ignacio Tejada was appointed Colombian minister to Rome, he was instructed to negotiate a concordat which would recognize the claims of the nation over ecclesiastical matters. In fairness to the Colombian government, it should be mentioned that its prime concern in dispatching envoys to Rome was not to secure papal recognition of national claims, but papal consent to the restoration of the hierarchy and clerical establishment in Colombia. It was most concerned, in short, with the promotion of the spiritual welfare of the people who were sadly in need of clerics, both high and low. This deplorable situation was testified to by Mgr. J. Mazio in a *relación* written at the end of 1823: "In the other dioceses of the new Republic of Colombia, very many suffer, in addition, the still greater misfortune of being deprived of their pastors, whether by emigration or by death. Among them, counting Venezuela (Caracas), Cuenca, Santa Marta, Guayana, Cartagena, Quito, and the archbishopric of Santa Fé de Bogotá, there remain only Popayán, Panamá, and Mérida which enjoy the presence of their own bishops."[16]

Despite obstacles and delays that would have taxed to the breaking point the endurance of the most patient of men, Tejada persisted in his efforts to secure favorable action by the Holy See. Colombia's first diplomatic victory in Rome occurred in 1825 when Mgr. José Buenaventura Arias was appointed Auxiliary Bishop of Mérida. He was the candidate presented by Bishop Lasso de la Vega. In 1827 Pope Leo XII confirmed in the other vacant sees the candidates presented by the government.[17]

On November 5, 1828, Bolívar wrote to Pope Leo XII expressing gratitude for the nomination by His Holiness of the first bishops of Colombian nationality, "in the absence now of the royal patronage." Bolívar was inclined to regard the law of patronage of 1824 as an idle gesture if pontifical confirmation were not secured. Therefore, he discretely explained the law to the pope and concluded with the hope that His Holiness would finally confirm it.[18]

A subject of particular interest to the Colombian government, in the exercise of its patronal prerogative, was the reform of the regular orders. In Colombia, as in other parts of Spanish America, the most numerous and flagrant instances of lax discipline and immoral practices among

16. Leturia, *op. cit.*, p. 112, n. 10.
17. Henao y Arrubla, *op. cit.*, p. 428; Zubieta, *Misiones Diplomáticas de Colombia*, p. 581.
18. "S. Bolívar á Su Santidad el Papa León XII, Bogotá, 7 de noviembre de 1828," in *Cartas del Libertador*, VIII, 105-6; José D. Monsalve, *El Ideal Político del Libertador Simón Bolívar* (Madrid, 1917), II, 398-400.

ecclesiastics were to be found in the establishments of the regulars. Since a contributing cause of this unfortunate situation was the large number of houses with a greatly depreciated membership, the Congress of Cúcuta on August 6, 1821, suppressed convents of regulars that did not have at least eight religious. The property of the suppressed convents was confiscated and applied to education and charity. On July 10, 1827, a decree was published excepting convents actually being conducted as schools and hospitals from the force of the law of 1821.

The political vicissitudes of Great Colombia convinced the Liberator more and more through the passing years that greater dependence had to be reposed in the Church as a stabilizing force. We find him actually, in his last years, becoming somewhat of a proclerical. The failure of the constituent congress of Ocaña (June 10, 1828), due to the opposition of the Santanderistas, forced Bolívar, much against his will, to assume dictatorial power. Having suspended the constitutional régime he proceeded to strengthen the position of the Church by special decree. As he wrote General Páez, he proposed to inaugurate a reform régime "on the solid basis of religion."[19]   By decree of July 11 he suspended the law of March 4, 1826, which prohibited the admission into convents of novices under the age of twenty-five years. The purpose of the Liberator was to provide more clergy to work in the missions. He also suspended the laws of August 6, 1821, and April 7, 1826, which suppressed the small regular establishments. Another decree restored in the army the positions of vicars general and chaplains.[20]   In support of religion as one of the greatest forces that can be opposed to anarchy, the Liberator recommended to General Páez friendly relations with the Archbishop of Caracas. To the Archbishop, on the other hand, Bolívar stressed the urgency of necessary reforms.[21]

On August 27, 1828, Bolívar resorted to the novel expedient of constitutionalizing the dictatorship by issuing an "organic decree of the dictatorship." In article 25, he established, for the first time, the Catholic religion on an official basis. The article read, "The government supports and protects the Roman Catholic Apostolic religion as the religion of Colombians." One of the functions of the Council of State (article 10) was, "to nominate persons for the positions of archbishop, bishop,

19. "S. Bolíviar á S. E. el General J. A. Páez, Bogotá, 30 de junio de 1828," in *Cartas del Libertador*, VII, 338.

20. Gil Fortoul, *op. cit.*, I, 434.

21. "S. Bolívar al Exmo. Señor General J. A. Páez, Bogotá, 23 de agosto de 1828," and "S. Bolívar al señor Cristóbal Mendoza, Bogotá, 22 de agosto de 1828," in *Cartas del Libertador*, III, 28-30.

dignidades, canons, *raciones, y media raciones* of the metropolitan and cathedral churches."[22]

After an unsuccessful attempt upon his life (September 25, 1828), the Liberator swung even farther to the side of the proclericals. Attributing the conspiracy to the Masonic adherents of Santander, Bolívar prohibited secret societies of all kinds. All who met in secret societies were to be judged as conspirators. Moreover he attributed the conspiracy to the radical philosophy being taught in the schools and colleges. Consequently he reorganized the general plan of studies, giving it a pronounced religious character in the hope that "the precepts of holy religion will abate the sophisms of the impious." Resorting to the methods of the Inquisition, Bolívar ordered deleted from the texts of Jeremy Bentham those parts opposed to religion, morals, and public order.[23]

Bolívar's reactionary decrees of 1828 favoring the Church aroused anticlericalism in Venezuela which was much more pronounced than in Colombia. Páez wrote the Liberator: "We have worked much to destroy the horrors of fanaticism and the influence of the priests on the people; in Venezuela they now rarely meddle with public matters in their ministry...I judge that when you tell me the government is to support religion, it will be with all the delicacy that the enlightenment of an age which prefers, in my opinion, liberty of thought to civil liberty, demands."[24]

When Bolívar resigned his dictatorial power to the constituent congress of Bogotá (January, 1830), he said, "Permit me that as my last act I recommend that you protect the holy religion which we profess; the profuse fountain of the benedictions of heaven."[25] This was the Liberator's last public act in support of the faith. Was Bolívar a Catholic? From the foregoing there should be little doubt that he was. Yet writes a notable Venezuelan authority, "Scarcely a Christian, or perhaps purely a deist, impregnated with the French philosophy of the eighteenth century against Catholic dogma, he always defended liberty of conscience, and of cults, with the exception, in the nature of a parenthesis, of the political reaction of 1828. That he confessed in his last hours proves only that now the spirit of the Liberator was no more than its shadow."[26] Just as the growing anarchy in Colombia undermined Bolívar's faith in

22. Pombo y Guerra, *op. cit.,* pp. 812-14.

23. Gil Fortoul, *op. cit.,* I, 322, 434, 443-44.

24. Simon B. O'Leary, *Memorias del General O'Leary,* II, 149-50, quoted by Watters, *op. cit.,* pp. 25-26.

25. Pombo y Guerra, *op. cit.,* p. 818.

26. Gil Fortoul, *op. cit.,* I, 495, n. 1.

the republic and inclined him to monarchy, so also the license of free-thinking convinced him of the necessity of returning to religious authority. As early as 1825 he was convinced of this for he wrote his sister that he was prepared to protect religion to the death.[27] There is little doubt that the political experiences of the Liberator converted him to Catholicism.

The constituent congress of Bogotá, to which Bolívar resigned his authority, faithfully performed its duty in drawing up an instrument of government in spite of the opposition of Venezuela and Ecuador. Under the presidency of Marshal Sucre and the vice-presidency of José María Estévez, Bishop of Santa Marta, the new constitution was signed April 29, 1830. The Roman Catholic religion was recognized as that of Colombia, and it declared that "it is the duty of the government, in the exercise of the patronage of the Colombian Church, to protect it and not to tolerate the public exercise of any other." With respect to appointment to ecclesiastical dignities the Senate was to draw up a *terna* from which the president should select the names to be proposed to the pope.[28]

Despite the mediatory efforts of Sucre and Bishop Estévez, the Venezuelan adherents of General Páez refused to accept the new constitution. Instead, Páez issued a decree ordering a Venezuelan congress to be held in Valencia on April 30. On May 31, 1830, General Juan Flores convoked a constituent congress for Ecuador to meet at Riobamba on August 10. Thus Venezuela and Ecuador seceded from Great Colombia, and the unified republic for which Bolívar had struggled so valiantly collapsed only a few days before his death (December 17, 1830).

VENEZUELA

Following Venezuelan secession from the Republic of Great Colombia, a constituent assembly convened at Valencia, in May, 1830, to recreate a separate and independent state of Venezuela. The party in control of the Congress had championed, since 1821, the federal principle and had opposed the unitary constitution of Cúcuta. The "Conservative Oligarchy," as this majority group was called, supported a liberal religious policy, and therefore, following the example of the constitutions inspired by Bolívar, inserted no special article on the subject of religious liberty in the constitution which was promulgated in September, 1830.

27. "S. Bolívar á la Señora María Antonia Bolívar, Potosí, 27 de octubre de 1825," in *Cartas del Libertador*, V, 147.
28. "Constitución de la República de Colombia, Bogotá, 1830," in Pombo y Guerra, *op. cit.*, pp. 829-68.

In imitation also of the Colombian régime, the constituent congress, by resolution, on October 14, 1830, declared that the right of patronage belonged to the nation and incorporated the *Ley de Patronato* of 1824 into its legislation.[29] In the course of its national history Venezuela has enacted twenty-six constitutions, but it has never to the present day altered the essential features of the Law of the Patronage. It has been characterized as "a classic of Venezuelan jurisprudence." Restrictions on Church influence began earlier and were carried further in Venezuela than elsewhere in Latin America. Anticlericalism, based in liberal philosophy and political design rather than the Church's behavior in the war of emancipation, was strong in the small minority which exercised leadership. Unchecked anticlericalism resulted in legislation that restricted the Church more than in any other country of the continent.

The acts of the Congress created bitter opposition in the ranks of the militarists and the clericals. The former, led by José Gregorio Monagas, proclaiming a program of Colombian federation, military *fueros*, and Roman Catholicism as the exclusive religion of the State, staged a futile revolt in 1831. Thereafter the clerical opposition was confined largely to the refusal of the prelates to swear an oath of unqualified obedience to the constitution, because of its failure to recognize explicitly Catholicism as the State religion. The government had ordered all citizens to assemble on a given day in the churches where a mass was to be celebrated and an oath of obedience sworn to the constitution. Archbishop Méndez protested the act of the government in going "outside of its civil powers to concern itself even with the liturgy of the Church," but declared he would overlook the "defect of power" to order the various acts performed.[30]

A few days later the Archbishop enumerated the articles and omissions of the constitution that alarmed his conscience. He deplored the failure of the Congress to include an article relating to religion. He protested free speech to senators and representatives if extended to religious subjects. The control of Congress over education, he con-

---

29. Gil Fortoul, *op. cit.*, II, 34; *Catholic Encyclopedia*, XI, 330. For the Church under the Conservative Oligarchy, see Watters, *History of the Church in Venezuela*, 125-62.

30. Gil Fortoul, *op. cit.*, II, 35-36, 144. Archbishop Méndez, uncle of Bolívar's faithful secretary, Briceño Méndez, was beholden to the Liberator for his elevation to the archiepiscopal see. Vice-Admiral Fleming wrote about the prelate (November 29, 1829, La Guaira): "The Archbishop is a mediocre man, ignorant, uneducated and dissolute, who has spent most of his life among the *llaneros* whose manners he has adopted. Like them he has many natural children, and I have seen him dispute and quarrel at a gambling table." (Gil Fortoul, *op. cit.*, II, 36-37). The high character and ability of the Archbishop is vigorously defended by Miss Watters. (*Status of the Church*, p. 30, n. 22.)

tended, should not include the seminaries; the constitutional guarantee of doing all which is not prohibited by law ought to comprise also the divine and ecclesiastical law; and liberty of thought ought not to apply to religion, its dogmas, morals, or discipline. Méndez then communicated to the government the following oath which he was willing to take: "In the opinion that the Roman Catholic religion will continue to be the only one in Venezuela, and on condition that the Republic will negotiate and conclude a concordat with the Holy See...and excepting always the liberty, independence, and discipline of the Church— I swear, by the Holy Gospel, to obey, sustain, and defend the constitution sanctioned by the constituent congress of the State of Venezuela on September 22, 1830."

The Council of State refused, quite obviously, to sanction a conditional oath, and the Archbishop was notified that if he persisted in his opposition he would be removed from office and banished. But the prelate remained obstinate, and was exiled to Curaçao on November 21, 1831. At the same time, and for the same reason, the bishops of Mérida and Guayana were banished also. While at Curaçao Archbishop Méndez was in communication with General Santander, to whom he complained of irreligion, immorality, and radical activities of the "Jacobins" in Venezuela.[31] Exile cooled the ardor of the prelates, and when they agreed to take the oath, they were allowed to return to Venezuela (April, 1832).[32]

Not only did the government of the "Oligarchy" force the submission of the prelates, but it adopted drastic ecclesiastical reform measures. By act of Congress (February 18, 1834) freedom of all religious sects was decreed. This action was intended primarily to encourage foreign non-Catholic immigration. In that same year there was founded in Caracas the first Protestant church—an English chapel. The Protestants were also allowed to maintain a cemetery. The impost of the tithes was suppressed and it was decreed that the Catholic Church and its ministers should be paid from the public treasury; the ecclesiastical budget was to be drawn up annually with the approval of Congress.[33] In 1836 the government ordered established, in the capital of each

---

31. "El Arzobispo de Caracas á Santander, Curazao, enero 23 de 1832," and "El Arzobispo de Caracas á Santander, Curazao, marzo 24 de 1832," in *Archivo Santander*, XIX, 181, 278.

32. Rafael María Baralt y Ramón Díaz, *Resumen de la Historia de Venezuela* (Curaçao, 1887), III, 403.

33. "A. Fortique á Santander, Paris, 9 de mayo de 1834," in *Archivo Santander*, XX, 341; Gustavo Arboleda, *Historia Contemporanea de Colombia* (Bogotá, 1918), I, 192. The abolition of the tithes was demoralizing since it made the clergy financially dependent on an unsympathetic government.

province, a main office and, in each canton, a suboffice of the civil registry for births, marriages, and deaths. This law, which would have deprived the clerics of one of their most influential functions, remained a dead letter for many years to come. Since the Venezuelan prelates had increased the number of feast days out of all reason and to the great economic detriment of the country, the government asked the pope, in 1836, to reduce them to a reasonable number. On June 20, 1837, Pope Gregory XVI published a brief fixing the number of feast days. Although the list was still too long, the Congress finally agreed to grant the *pase*. To the number of fiestas were to be added, of course, the several national holidays. In 1837 a law was passed revoking the act of the government of Great Colombia in 1828 which legalized the existence of several monasteries despite the law of suppression. The few remaining monasteries in Venezuela consequently were suppressed, and their property devoted to the purposes of public education. After 1837 there were in Venezuela only convents for nuns. These were suppressed in 1874.[34]

The Oligarchy was, furthermore, a vigilant guardian of the national patronage. Indeed, this very watchfulness has been declared to have been the means of saving the republic from clerical reactions such as occurred in other States. On March 21, 1833, in reply to a petition of the hierarchy that the *Ley de Patronato* of 1824 be suspended or reformed, the Congress declared it to be in force and ordered its observance "to avoid inconveniences to the civil authority in the exercise of its rights, and to the government as patron and protector of the Church of Venezuela."[35] In the face of the oft-repeated policy of the Republic to maintain complete the right of patronage inherited from Spain, Archbishop Méndez refused canonical institution to prebendaries presented by the government. Moreover, in opposition to the law which suppressed the tithes, he threatened in a pastoral to excommunicate all Christians who did not pay the tithes. Because of his opposition he was banished again in 1836.[36] He went to Curaçao where he lived for three years, and then to New Granada where he died in 1839.

On May 13, 1841, the Congress decreed that the exequatur of the government granted to bulls of institution issued to any Venezuelan prelate by the Supreme Pontiff should contain a clause stating that the *pase* was to be conceded only when the rights and prerogatives of the nation were preserved in their entirety. Also that the *pase* should be

34. Gil Fortoul, *op. cit.*, II, 34-35.
35. *Ley de Patronato*, pp. 3-4.
36. "J. F. Blanco á Santander, Caracas, 20 de octubre de 1836," in *Archivo Santander*, XXII, 344-45; Baralt y Díaz, *op. cit.*, III, 421.

granted only after the archbishop and bishop named in the bull of institution, should swear the following oath: "I, ——, Archbishop or Bishop
of ——, swear that never will I consider the oath of obedience to the
constitution, the laws, and the government of the republic, which I swore
to prior to my presentation to His Holiness, directly or indirectly annulled nor in any part diminished by the oath of obedience to the Apostolic See which I must take at the time of my consecration; nor by any
later act under any motive. So help me God."[37]

Also in exercise of its patronal duties the government, in 1843, under
the presidency of General Carlos Soublette, on observing the lamentable
scarcity of curates, endowed several parishes, and introduced about
one hundred Spanish priests. The Liberal opposition criticized this action
as being unwarranted and outside of the patronal obligations. In 1845
a law was passed prohibiting, without permit of the national government, the entry of foreign priests into Venezuela.[38]

The Conservative Oligarchy, triumphant in Venezuela after the dissolution of Great Colombia, retained control of the government until
1847. The policies of the dominant faction were enlightened, progressive, and moderate. Páez, Vargas, and Soublette gave Venezuela a
relatively peaceful and auspicious start along the road of political and
economic development. Their religious policy was firm yet tolerant, and
was devoid of that harshness and tactlessness, which, in other countries,
crystallized fanatical opposition and reaction. In the conflicts with
Archbishop Méndez, the government exerted itself to avoid conflict, but
so stubborn was the prelate that a reasonable understanding was impossible. With the realization that Venezuelan development was dependent on immigration, acts were passed to make the country more
inviting to non-Catholics. Yet, it is illogical to conclude from these
acts that the government was disposed to separate Church and State.
Quite to the contrary, the Conservatives were intent on maintaining
the patronal control, and in rendering the Church a more effective
instrument to perform its divine mission.

The election of José Tadeo Monagas inaugurated the Liberal Oli-
garchic régime in Venezuelan history. Elected as a Conservative,
Monagas soon deserted the "Godos," as the Conservatives were called,
and allied himself with Antonio Leocadio Guzmán, leader of the
Liberals. In February, 1849, Guzmán, as Minister of Interior and
Justice, ordered the governors of the provinces to issue more peremptory
orders not to admit into any port foreign priests who should arrive

37. *Ley de Patronato*, p. 28.
38. Gil Fortoul, *op. cit.*, II, 34-35, 276.

without the permission of the national government. In August, 1848, a similar prohibition had already been directed at the Jesuits. Guzmán, while recognizing the need of increasing the national clergy, would not consent to the immigration of foreign clerics. He also sponsored measures, which, however, were not enforced, to regulate the appointment of priests and the administration of parishes. He proposed the creation of a *junta*, to be named annually by the parish voters, which with the priest was to prepare the budget for the parish. The *junta* also was to select candidates for vacant curacies to be presented to the diocesan prelate. Guzmán also recommended as a stimulus to immigration suspension of the law which provided that the marriage ceremony could only be celebrated by Catholic priests. He advocated a prior civil ceremony. Guzmán's liberalism found little support in the program of Monagas, which was strictly personalistic. Consequently it was not long before the Liberal leader was ousted from the government.[39]

The Monagas brothers, José Tadeo and José Gregorio, alternated in control of the presidential office from 1848 to 1858. Although not as pro-clerical as at the time of the revolt of 1831, they were on the whole friendly to the Catholic Church. In 1853 a moderate increase was made in ecclesiastical appropriations. An impost of one-half per cent on imports was provided for the construction and repair of churches. In 1857 an ephemeral constitution sponsored by President José Tadeo contained a clause declaring that the State protected the Roman Catholic religion and that the government would always sustain its ministers and the cult.

When José Tadeo Monagas was overthrown in 1858 by a Conservative-Liberal coalition, his constitution of 1857 was also scrapped. In December, 1858, a new frame of government with federalistic features was promulgated. In this instrument there was a reversion to the old practice of remaining silent on the subject of religion. Yet it seemed to be understood that the laws providing for liberty of cults and the payment of ecclesiastical appropriations as a consequence of the right of patronage were still in force. There was no change wrought in the political status of the Church other than that if a subsequent congress desired it could separate Church and State by simple legislation.[40]

The establishment of federalism, instead of solving Venezuela's difficulties, merely constituted the pretext for another, and even more bloody, civil war. There soon emerged, temporarily, out of the conflict,

39. Gil Fortoul, *op. cit.*, II, 34-35, 275-78. For the Church under the Monagas regime and the civil war, 1848-70, see Watters, *History of the Church in Venezuela*, pp. 163-82.

40. Gil Fortoul, *op. cit.*, II, 353; Arosemena, *op. cit.*, II, 141-42.

General Páez as dictator. In this, his final tenure of power, Páez revealed himself quite unmistakably as a pro-clerical. In the hope of having the pope recognize by concordat those patronal prerogatives claimed and maintained up to that time by all parties, Conservative as well as Liberal, President Páez conferred credentials as a plenipotentiary on the Archbishop of Caracas, Silvestre Guevara y Lira.[41] The Archbishop, although a man of considerable political experience, was inclined to conciliation and peace; he was, it was said, *dulce y fácil* (sweet and easy). Therefore, although he was instructed to negotiate a concordat, "without losing sight of our law of patronage," he brought back to Caracas, in September, 1862, a document which convinced many that he had lost complete sight of the national claims. "In Rome," his critics declared, "he put his religious conscience before that of the State; he was the representative of the Church, and not of the Republic."

The concordat, which was signed in Rome on July 26, 1862,[42] and which aroused a perfect furore of opposition in Venezuela, is worthy of careful examination because it exhibits so well a settlement acceptable to the papacy. Article 1 provided: "The Catholic religion will continue to be that of the republic, and the government will recognize the duty of defending and conserving it effectively with all the rights and prerogatives that belong to it by the ordination of God and the canonical sanction."

Regarding public instruction the concordat provided that it should conform entirely to Catholic doctrine and that bishops should have free direction and inspection of faculties of theology, canon law, and other ecclesiastical subjects. Also, the bishops should be given the right of inspection to see that nothing contrary to Catholicism was taught. Since this would have given the prelates the right to censor books and writings of all kinds, the concordat, therefore, would have violated liberty of thought guaranteed by the constitution.

In consideration of the government's agreement to pay specified sums for the support of the cult and its ministers, the Holy See agreed to tolerate the law of 1833 which abolished the tithes. Until 1833, the ecclesiastical income had been based on the tithes. The Congress, regarding this impost as excessive and contrary to public prosperity, passed a law which abolished the tithes and provided for the support of the cult

---

41. Guevara y Lira was consecrated archbishop in 1853, having been named by the National Congress on the recommendation of President José Gregorio Monagas, who was his relative. He had considerable experience in politics, having served in the Senate and in the Council of State. (Gil Fortoul, *op. cit.*, II, 493.)

42. Angelo Mercati, ed., *Raccolta di Concordati su Materie Ecclesiastiche tra la Santa Sede e la Autorità Civili* (Rome, 1919), pp. 971-83. Cited hereinafter as *Raccolta di Concordati*.

by annual congressional appropriations. The evident intention of the papacy was to make the clergy economically independent of the Congress by itemizing fixed incomes for the clerics. The total annual appropriation amounted to 32,250 pesos.

The concordat provided that, in exchange for the obligations which the government contracted, the Holy See would concede the right of presentation. It specified the mode of procedure in selecting and making nominations, i.e., the president of the republic should propose to the pope candidates for vacancies in archiepiscopal and episcopal sees and dignities, and the pope would then give canonical institution in the accustomed form, it being agreed that the person proposed could not assume office or participate in affairs of his church until after he had received the bull of institution. The pope, in turn, agreed not to erect new dioceses except with the government's approval.

The Council of State advised ratification of the concordat, and President Páez signed it on March 6, 1863. That Páez and his councillors should have approved such a reactionary concordat can be explained only as a frantic eleventh hour effort to ward off disaster by courting the support of the clericals. A few days later, however, Páez was ousted from the government by the federalists and the National Assembly rejected the concordat. The new congress established under the Constitution of March 28, 1864, advised President Falcón to reopen negotiations with Rome "to put the concordat in harmony with the national laws and the spirit and letter of the new constitution, which, like earlier ones, guarantees religious liberty and freedom of the press." Lucio Pulido was sent to Rome in June, 1864, to negotiate, but his mission was a failure. Thus by a narrow margin Venezuela escaped falling under a clerical blight.[43]

Within ten years after the fall of Páez and the menace of clerical supremacy, another and more powerful dictator had arisen in Venezuela, and unfortunately for the Catholic Church, he pursued a religious policy antithetical to that of his predecessor. Out of the welter and turmoil of internecine warfare which followed the formation of the Venezuelan Confederation, emerged Antonio Guzmán Blanco, Liberal-Federal leader, president, dictator, and dominator of Venezuelan politics for almost two decades. Guzmán Blanco was of the same opinion as his father, Antonio Guzmán, that the political power of the Catholic Church had to be curbed. Since the clerics were the supporters of the Conservatives, or "Godos," arch-enemies of the Liberals, they were re-

43. Lisandro Alvarado, *Historia de la Revolución Federal en Venezuela* (Caracas, 1909), pp. 526-27; *Cath. Ency.*, XV, 331.

garded as serious obstacles in the path of Guzmán Blanco's ambition. In his wars upon the Godos, he was constantly confronted with the necessity of dealing with opposition clerics.[44] In commenting on clerical opposition to the federal cause, Guzmán Blanco wrote: "I desire harmony with the Church, but if the clergy persist, so unwarrantedly, in provoking a conflict, I shall suppress them. To do otherwise would make us remiss in our duties to the Revolution, the Liberal cause, and to the Republic. We can never consent that the words of clergy, in the press or in the tribune, shall be the echo of reaction."[45]

Archbishop Guevara y Lira, unfortunately for harmony between the powers, resented the demands of the Liberals that priests be appointed and removed to suit party convenience. The Archbishop's ultramontanism had been exhibited in his negotiations for a concordat in 1862. Furthermore, after the new civil code had been issued in 1867, Archbishop Guevara showed himself a vigorous defender of Catholicism in protesting against certain features in the code which he believed to be out of harmony with the laws of the Church.[46] It was inevitable that the Archbishop and Guzmán Blanco should have clashed. Consequently, when the dictator ordered *Te Deums* sung in the churches in celebration of the Liberal victory, the prelate objected and suggested that a thanksgiving mass would be more appropriate if deferred until the general amnesty offered by the president should be put into effect.[47] The suggested postponement was not acceptable to the acting chief executive in Caracas, and somewhat against the wishes of Guzmán Blanco the Archbishop was banished to the island of Trinidad. When Guzmán Blanco returned to Caracas he attempted to effect a reconciliation with the prelate but to no effect, since Guevara y Lira was obdurate in his opposition to the Liberals. From Trinidad he fomented plots against the government through his faithful clerical agents. Since the situation had become intolerable, the Congress, on June 3, 1873, decreed the vacancy of the archiepiscopal see, for Guevara y Lira was still technically the incumbent. In 1875 the difficulty was terminated when Guevara y Lira abdicated the see at the suggestion of Pius IX and through the

---

44. "Guzmán Blanco á Ciudadanos General Primer Designado y Ministro del Gobierno Nacional, Cuartel General en Valencia, 19 de setiembre de 1870," in *Memorandum del General Guzmán Blanco* (Caracas, 1876), p. 76.

45. "Guzmán Blanco á Ciudadano General Primer Designado y Ministros del Gobierno Nacional, Cuartel General in Puerto Cabello, 26 de agosto de 1870," in *Mem. del G. Blanco*, pp. 56-57.

46. Arosemena, *op. cit.*, II, 182-83.

47. "Guzmán Blanco á Ciudadano General Encargado de la Presidencia, Cuartel General en Puerto Cabello, 22 de setiembre de 1870," in *Mem. del G. Blanco*, p. 81; *Cath. Ency.*, XV, 331. For Guzmán Blanco and the Church, see Watters, *History of the Church*, pp. 183-213.

mediation of Mgr. Rocca Cocchia, the apostolic delegate. The nomination of José Ponte to the see was promptly confirmed by the pope.[48]

The clash between Archbishop Guevara y Lira and Guzmán Blanco served to break down the flood-gates which restrained the dictator's resentment for clerical influence. In 1873 he inaugurated one of the most complete and devastating attacks ever directed against the Catholic Church in Latin America. The initial act deprived the clergy of control over the civil registry; or, to be more exact, the law of 1836 was ordered enforced. The recording of births, marriages, and deaths in the parish books without a corresponding entry in the public register was prohibited. It was hoped that this would diminish clerical influence over domestic relations. Cemeteries were taken from the control of the clergy and were opened to Jews and heretics. At the same time, the civil rite of marriage was declared to be the only legal form. The civil ceremony was given precedence over the religious, and many technicalities were introduced to render the latter difficult. The attempt of the dictator to legalize the marriage of those in holy orders was prevented by an outraged public conscience. In 1874 the Congress, appealing to the law of patronage, abolished all convents, monasteries, colleges, and other religious institutions. Monastic and church property was confiscated for the benefit of the government. The customary ecclesiastical revenues were abolished and appropriations for the Church were suspended. Public education was declared to be lay, gratuitous, and obligatory; consequently, parish schools were abolished notwithstanding the fact that existing educational facilities were sadly deficient. Even ecclesiastical seminaries were suppressed, and priests were to be educated in the national university where the doctrine of infallibility was repudiated.[49] In the hope of seeing Protestantism take root and prosper in Venezuela, Guzmán Blanco offered one of the confiscated churches to the Protestants, but as there was no organization to accept the offer, it was withdrawn.[50]

In spite of the radical reform measures imposed on Venezuela by the fiat of Guzmán Blanco, Church and State, in theory at least, continued to be united. In the Constitution of May 23, 1874, religious liberty was guaranteed, but "only the Roman Catholic Apostolic religion can [could] exercise the public cult outside of churches."[51] The

48. Arosemena, *op. cit.*, II, 186-87; "Guzmán Blanco á Ciudadanos Ministros del Despacho, Valencia, 25 de febrero de 1871," in *Mem. del G. Blanco*, p. 126.

49. William E. Curtis, *Venezuela* (n.p., n.d.), pp. 204-8; Gil Fortoul, *op. cit*, II, 501; *Cath. Ency.*, XV, 331; Watters, *op. cit.*, pp. 34-35.

50. W. R. Wheeler and W. E. Browning, *Modern Missions on the Spanish Main* (Philadelphia, 1925), p. 286.

51. Art. 14, Sec. 13, Arosemena, *op. cit.*, II, 108.

Catholic Church was accorded, therefore, a privileged position which was denied to other cults. In further evidence of a continuation of a connection between Church and State, the constitution provided (Art. 98) that the right of exercising the ecclesiastical patronage belonged to the nation, and that the nature of its exercise was to be determined by law.[52]

A bold but futile attempt was made by Guzmán Blanco, at the time of his controversy with Archbishop Guevara y Lira, to nationalize the Venezuelan Church. The refusal of Guevara to resign and of the pope to compel his resignation induced Guzmán Blanco to suggest to Congress the termination of papal control over the Venezuelan Church. The servile Congress replied to the dictator: "Faithful to our duties, faithful to our convictions, and faithful to the holy dogma of the religion of Jesus Christ, of that great Being who conserved the world's freedom with his blood, we do not hesitate to emancipate the Church of Venezuela from that episcopacy which pretends, as an infallible and omnipotent power, to absorb from Rome the vitality of a free people, the beliefs of our conscience, and the noble aspirations and destinies which pertain to us as component parts of the great human family."[53]

The resultant legislation, however, did not embody the ideas of the president, for it aimed, in substance, to prohibit entry into Venezuela of foreign ecclesiastical prelates and abrogated the laws of patronage. In short, the Congress proposed to disestablish the Roman Church without substituting anything in its place, certainly not a national church such as Guzmán Blanco suggested. Fortunately, the law was not promulgated, since the controversy over the archiepiscopal see was satisfactorily settled. After that the government desisted in its attack on the Church, but it did not abrogate the laws which had been enacted. With due consideration to this fact, apparent harmonious relations existed between Church and State during the remaining years of Guzmán Blanco's dictatorship (1876-88). The dictator had been successful in destroying what influence the Church had managed to retain. The clergy became servile to a government that treated them with indignity. The Church was never able to recover its lost prestige.

After the overthrow of Guzmán Blanco in 1888, a rapprochement between Church and State developed. In spite of special laws to the contrary, various religious orders were allowed to return to Venezuela. In 1891, the government invited the Capuchins to undertake missionary work among the savages of the Orinoco. In 1894 the Salesians were

52. Arosemena, *op. cit.,* II, 121.
53. *Ibid.,* pp. 180-86; Curtis, *op. cit.,* pp. 205-6.

invited to aid in education. In 1899 and in 1903 the Augustinians and the Dominicans returned. By law of September 28, 1900, the ecclesiastical seminaries were ordered reëstablished.[54]

The return of the Church to a normal status after the reforms of Guzmán Blanco was a slow and tedious process. Many of the laws of "the Illustrious American" were continued in force because a spirit of antagonism toward the Church was pronounced among the legislators of the country. The laws of liberty of cults, the civil register, civil marriage, secularized cemeteries, prohibition of entry into Venezuela of foreign ecclesiastics of any cult, prohibition of religious ceremonies outside of church buildings, and prohibition of all regular orders were still kept on the statute books, but they were not all enforced. Under President Cipriano Castro the Civil Code was reformed by introducing a divorce law. On the other hand the Roman Catholic Apostolic religion was declared once more, in the Constitution of 1904, to be the national religion and the State contributed to its support. Likewise the State reasserted its control over the ecclesiastical patronage and declared the Law of 1824 to be in force once more. In the Constitution of 1904, for example, Article 124 read: "Since the nation is in possession of the right of ecclesiastical patronage, it will exercise it conforming to the Law of July 28, 1824."[55]

During the long dictatorship of Juan Vicente Gómez (1909-35), although many of the anticlerical measures of Guzmán Blanco still remained technically in force, President Gómez was inclined to be lenient and saw that they were not drastically applied. Many religious orders, for example, reëntered Venezuela in spite of the existence of special laws against them. This did not signify, on the other hand, that Gómez was a less zealous protector of patronal rights for quite to the contrary, he extended the scope of patronage to non-Catholic cults. By decree of October 24, 1911, it was declared: "(1) The exercise of all cults tolerated in the Republic will be regulated by the *Ley de Patronato* of 1824; (2) where the *Ley de Patronato* refers to the see of the Catholic Church, or to the pontiff, it is understood as referring, to all effects of this decree, to the superior ecclesiastical authority of each non-Catholic cult legally established in this country."[56] It is suspected that Gómez issued this decree in answer to clerical protest against foreign missionary activity. It was an effective way to attack Protestantism and at the same time adhere to the letter of the law of toleration. As can be readily appreciated, Protestantism stood small chance of propagation in Venezuela so

54. *Cath. Ency.*, XV, 331; Watters, *Status of the Church*, pp. 37-38.
55. N. Veloz Goiticoa, *Venezuela* (Caracas, 1919), pp. 75-78.
56. *Ley de Patronato*, p. 48.

long as the law prohibiting the entry into the republic of "foreigners dedicated especially to the service of any cult or religion" remained in force.

Although President Juan Vicente Gómez made certain concessions to the Church with respect to education and welfare work, the dictator's treatment of the clergy has been described as ruthless.[57] Proscriptions were not confined to members of the lower clergy, for the bishops of Valencia (1929) and Mérida (1930) suffered expulsion for venturing criticism.[58]

In the years following the Gómez dictatorship there was improvement in the status and prestige of the Church in Venezuela. Thanks to clerical accommodation to noninterference in political matters, and since the State was no longer apprehensive of ecclesiastical intrusion, Church and State relations became extremely cordial.[59] The image of the Church was improved by its stand against the dictatorship of Marcos Pérez Jiménez. In a pastoral letter of May 1, 1957, Archbishop Rafael Arias of Caracas subscribed to labor's right to freely organize and share in the country's riches. He also pointed out the many social ills which the government had ignored. He even accused the government of inequitable distribution of the oil resources.[60]

Although the prelate's letter greatly embarrassed the dictator, he feared to arrest the archbishop. Instead, he expressed his disapproval by confiscating issues of the Caracas Catholic daily *La Religion*, which contained political criticisms of the dictatorship, and by arresting clerics on charges of aiding and abetting seditious causes.[61] After the overthrow of Pérez Jiménez on January 21, 1958, the hierarchy declared its support of the new liberal government and its program of democratic social reform.

A new social consciousness on the part of the Catholic Church in Venezuela has also been responsible for its rise in prestige. Under the leadership of Archbishop Arias of Caracas and the late Cardinal Humberto Quintero, the hierarchy became increasingly less conservative and gave more attention to areas of national interest outside the realms of the strictly religious. The Church recognizes that moral and

57. José Rafael Pocaterra, *Gómez, the Shame of America* (Paris, 1929), p. 136.

58. Watters, *Status of the Church*, pp. 40-41.

59. For example, when Mgr. José Humberto Quintero, Archbishop of Caracas, was appointed Venezuela's first cardinal, President Betancourt visited and congratulated the prelate.

60. *Hispanic American Report*, X, No. 6 (July, 1957), 309.

61. *Ibid.*, XI, No. 1 (January, 1958), 30. Luis Colmenares Díaz, *La espada y el incensio: la iglesia bajo Pérez Jiménez* (Caracas, 1961), is a Marxist account of Church and State in Venezuela, 1948-57.

religious problems cannot be successfully attacked until those of a material order are resolved.

Prominent among social welfare activities initiated by Catholic clerics are *Ciudad de los Muchachos* (Boys' Town), modeled after the famous Boys' Town founded by Father Flanagan near Omaha, Nebraska, and *Fé y Alegría,* a socio-educational movement to improve the condition of orphaned and abandoned boys and girls. The movement is expanding rapidly. In 1962 it had 27 schools with an attendance of 10,000.[62]

Since 1958 the Church has been increasingly outspoken for social change, the preservation of moral and civil order, the suppression of atheistic Communism, and the support and respect of democratic institutions. Thus the State has found an ally against the social and political disorder which has intensified in recent years. Nevertheless it must be noted that the voice of the hierarchy in Venezuela does not approach the strength of that of many other Latin-American countries where the Church has greater temporal influence. Although COPEI, the Christian Democratic party, favors a more sympathetic attitude toward the Church, it cannot be regarded as an official Catholic party. The Church cannot participate in politics.

The present constitution of Venezuela, promulgated in 1961, contains but two articles touching on religion. The first (Art. 65) guarantees religious liberty under the supreme inspection of all cults by the federal executive. The second (Art. 130) declares that the republic has the right of ecclesiastical patronage. Relations between Church and State, as we have noted, had been regulated by the Law of Patronage, passed in 1824, under which the Venezuelan government exercised almost complete control over Church affairs. More recently, however, resulting from an initiative by President Rómulo Betancourt, a *Modus Vivendi* was signed with the Holy See on March 6, 1964, which entailed fundamental changes in the interpretation and practice of patronage, but not its formal abolition. According to President Betancourt he sought to adapt the letter of the constitution to the existing state of affairs.

The *Modus Vivendi* recognizes the full authority of the Church in religious matters and guarantees the freedom of Catholic teaching in Venezuela. The juridic personality of the Church is recognized in the administration of dioceses, cathedral chapters, seminaries, parishes, religious orders and congregations. It may set up new ecclesiastical jurisdictions, although the consent of the government is required. The ap-

62. *Venezuela Up-to-Date,* X, No. 1 (May, 1962), 1.

pointment of prelates will be a matter for the Holy See, which must, however, consult the government beforehand so that it may, if it wishes, file objections of a general political nature. The consent of the Congress will no longer be necessary. Archbishops and bishops must be Venezuelans by birth. These will appoint priests. Official consent will be required for the entry and residence of foreign clergy. The State will continue its subsidies to the Church within the limits of its budget. These subsidies did not amount to much in the past. Also, the Venezuelan State explicitly recognizes the right of Catholic laymen, notably *Acción Católica*, to publicly propagandize the teachings of the faith. Finally, the *Modus Vivendi* provides for the continuation of diplomatic representation between Venezuela and the Holy See. Venezuela will accredit an ambassador to the Vatican, and the Holy See will send an apostolic nuncio to Caracas where he will be dean of the diplomatic corps. No longer are papal bulls, briefs, and other communications subject to the *pase*.[63]

Despite, or perhaps because of, the *Modus Vivendi*, the political relationship which exists in Venezuela between Church and State is very intimate, and although the constitution purposely avoids the designation, the Catholic Church is the State-Church. Official Church—no! De facto—yes![64] In the national budget of 1963 slightly better than $1.5 million were designated for the Church. Appropriations for the Church are made in the budget of the Ministry of Justice. Salaries are paid to the hierarchy, also to certain lesser functionaries, and to a limited number of priests. Some funds are available for Church building repairs and also for Indian missions in rural areas. The Church possesses little property and receives only limited private contributions. Thus the political weakness of the Church is matched by economic weakness.

Under the law Catholic schools are required to observe all regulations affecting public instruction. The same textbooks, except the religious, are used. Religious instruction may be given in public schools if the parents desire it. Since the Catholic schools, with only a few exceptions, are supported by tuition fees and since the costs are high, the result is that they are accessible only to the middle and upper classes.

Under Pérez Jiménez Catholic educational institutions were given a relatively free hand with the result that there was considerable growth. The first Catholic university (Universidad Católica Ándres Bello) was founded in Caracas through the efforts of the hierarchy. Teachers from

63. For text of the *Modus Vivendi*, see *El Nacional* (Caracas), March 7, 1964.
64. Seven religious holidays are recognized by the government as official holidays.

various reactionary Spanish Catholic orders flooded the country's cultural institutions. Today many Catholic orders are well represented in Venezuelan education. Approximately 15 per cent of the school population is enrolled in the Catholic schools. Protestant schools are very few in number. The result is that the schools of Venezuela, public and private, are inadequate to meet the national needs. The lack of teachers and educational facilities is evidenced by the fact that 43 per cent of the population over 15 years of age is a conservative estimate of illiteracy in that country.[65]

Civil marriage is the only legal form in Venezuela. It is usually followed, it is true, by the religious ceremony, but the civil certificate must be produced before the priest can legally perform the ceremony. Perhaps because of the high fees charged by the clergy, or because of the unavailability of the priests in rural areas, or because of indifference, a large number of men and women dispense with lay and religious rites and live in open concubinage. The result is a record number (57 per cent) of illegitimate births.[66] The popularity of free love unions in Venezuela is not to be attributed only to the reasons enumerated above, for, as one writer says, "Frequently it is the woman who objects to being legally bound, averring that she has a stronger position when simply cohabiting with the man than if he could claim any legal rights as a husband." There is no social degradation attached to this form of concubinage.[67] Divorce and remarriage are legal in Venezuela.

The Catholic Church of Venezuela is handicapped, as it is in other Latin-American countries, because of the scarcity and inferior caliber of its priesthood. In 1963 there were 1,400 priests for a country of 7 million Catholics. The ratio was one priest to about 5,500. More than one-half of the clergy are regulars, the majority of these being foreigners, mostly Spanish. One-half of the diocesan clergy are also foreigners. The lack of vocations among the country's youth is illustrated by the fact that in 1963 only 150 seminarians were in attendance throughout the country. A national Church which depends on foreign clergy is certainly not in a healthy condition.

Those recruited to the clergy are too frequently men of low intellectual ability and too incompetent to formulate or direct programs for the people's social and spiritual welfare. The ignorance of the lowest classes is so dense that superstition plays a great part in their lives, and it is

65. Francis Houtart, *El cambio social en América Latina* (Bogotá, 1964), p. 174.
66. *Ibid.*, p. 143.
67. Charles E. Akers, *A History of South America, 1854-1904* (London, 1912), pp. 637-38; Wheeler and Browning, *op. cit.*, p. 272. The percentage of free unions is 19.24. Houtart, *op. cit.*, p. 141.

not difficult for the priesthood to instill into their minds outward respect for religious forms and dread of dire consequences for disobedience to priestly injunctions. But the people of the higher classes, particularly the men, scorn the medieval arguments and threats of the clergy and are inclined to free thought in religion. Social changes arising from rapid urbanization and industrialization seem to militate against the development of a strong spiritual life.

Protestantism has made little headway in Venezuela. In 1962 it counted only 26,042 members in the country, its appeal being restricted largely to the lower classes. A desertion of Catholicism by members of the upper classes would represent a loss of social status. In Venezuela, in contrast to Colombia, there has been little friction between the Catholic clergy and Protestant ministers and missionaries.

Despite efforts to improve religious conditions in Venezuela, it must be confessed that religion is not a strong force in the country. The status of the Catholic Church is one of comparative weakness. Of 92 per cent of the population who have been baptized in the Roman Catholic Church, not more than 25 per cent are active communicants. For most, personal commitment goes only so far as acknowledged belief. Religious obligation is felt to be little more than a minimal compliance with an outward form. A prominent North American clerical investigator lists Venezuela among those Latin-American countries where the Church appears to be losing ground.[68] The increase in the number of free-thinkers and the continued waning respect for the clergy and the Church will result, unless these tendencies are checked, in despoiling the Catholic Church of the remaining privileges which it enjoys in the Republic of Venezuela.

68. Albert J. Nevins, M.M., "How Catholic is Latin America?" *The Sign*, Vol. 36, No. 2 (September, 1956), 11-18.

Chapter V

The Religious Problem in the Constitutional History of Colombia

In Colombia, to a far more marked degree than in Venezuela, the struggle of the parties for power revolved about the religious issue. From the independence period to the present day, religious policy has ever been a prominent feature of party programs, and the recurrent alterations of the political order have always been attended by radical changes in ecclesiastical polity. No doubt the origin of this unfortunate tendency can be traced back to colonial times when the royal officials of New Granada and the prelates were accustomed to strive for political control, the latter generally being the victors. At any rate the Catholic Church has been more tenacious in its hold upon national and civil life in Colombia than in any other Latin-American country.

The Conservatives governed Colombia, then called New Granada, most of the time following the dissolution of Great Colombia in 1830 until 1849. They, like the Conservative Oligarchy in Chile, represented the permanent interests and effective powers of the country, the landowners, clericals, and the military. An essential part of their program of organization and stabilization was protection of Catholicism. When the State of New Granada was created (November 17, 1831) after the fall of Great Colombia, Roman Catholicism was declared to be the religion of the republic, the public worship of any other faith was not to be tolerated, and the government assumed the exercise of the patronage. This was in conformity with the religious provisions of the Constitution of 1830 of Great Colombia which was adopted temporarily (December 15, 1831) until a new constitution should be framed and promulgated.[1] In the convention which proclaimed the State of New Granada, two prelates, Bishop Sotomayor of Cartagena and Bishop Estévez of Santa Marta, played prominent rôles. At the head of the provisional government was Archbishop Caicedo y Flórez of Bogotá.[2]

1. Pombo y Guerra, *Constituciones de Colombia*, II, 882.
2. "Francisco Soto á Santander, Bogotá, 29 de diciembre de 1831," in *Archivo Santander*, XIX, 139-44; Arboleda, *Historia Contemporanea de Colombia*, I, 46.

In February, 1832, a new constitution for the republic of New Granada was promulgated. The loyalty of the constituents to the Catholic faith was clearly evidenced in their introduction to the constitution. It read in part as follows: "In it (the constitution) has been established ...the rigorous duty of New Granada to protect the Roman Catholic Apostolic religion; this divine and only true religion, precious cause of the good which the people of New Granada inherit from their fathers ...will be preserved pure and intact."[3] Consequently, Article 15 read, "It is the duty of the government to protect the Granadinos in the exercise of the Roman Catholic Apostolic religion."[4]

Under the new constitution General Francisco de Paula Santander was elected president, and Joaquín Mosquera was elected vice-president. Since Santander was in New York at the time and did not return to assume his office until the fall of 1832, Mosquera exercised the temporary headship of the government. Mosquera was a member of one of the most influential families of the republic and was a devoted Catholic. He retained the cabinet of Archbishop Caicedo, and, in agreement with the new constitution, designated for the Council of State, the Archbishop, Bishop Sotomayor, and Fr. Manuel Benito Revollo, a canon.[5] The new republic was inaugurated by warm friends and official members of the Roman Catholic Church.

The Granadine government entertained pretentions to a patronage more ample than that enjoyed by the king of Spain. The Law of Patronage of 1824 was regarded as continuing in full force, and many actions were taken which presumed the existence of that right, although it had never been recognized by the papacy. By decree of May 3, 1833, for example, Santander created in Casanare an auxiliary bishop of the metropolitan see of Bogotá, and Fr. José Antonio Cháves was nominated for the position. He was canonically instituted soon after as bishop *in partibus*. In April, 1834, the Congress met to elect an archbishop of Bogotá and bishops of Cartagena and Panamá. Manuel José Mosquera, a brother of the vice-president and only thirty-four years old, was elected archbishop. Thus the government of New Granada exercised the patronal right of presentation.[6] It undertook, moveover, to exercise the rights of *pase* or exequatur over pontifical communications. In the constitutional convention of 1832 the desirability of reducing the number

3. "Constitución del Estado de la Nueva Granada Dada Por La Convención Constituyente en el año de 1832, Bogotá, 1832," in Pombo y Guerra, *op. cit.*, II, 888.

4. "Florentino González á Santander, Bogotá, 31 de diciembre de 1831," in *Archivo Santander*, XIX, 144-46.

5. Arboleda, *op. cit.*, I, 47.

6. Arboleda, *op. cit.*, 181, 216-18.

of religious festival days was discussed.[7] It was decided not to constitutionalize the reform, but instead the pope was requested to publish a brief providing for a reduction of feast days. On March 28, 1835, the *pase* was given to the pontifical brief, and a few days later it was ordered executed in New Granada by legislative act.[8] Another brief on reform of the regular orders was issued by the pope in 1835. To restore discipline in the regular orders, the pope delegated to the archbishop the duties of visiting and reforming. This brief, however, was not given the governmental *pase* until May 8, 1840, and then with the following reservation, "the *pase* is conceded without prejudice to the sovereignty and prerogatives of the nation."[9] The acme of control over the patronage was reached in 1841, when a law of May 18 of that year provided that the police should keep watch over prelates, priests, and chapters to see that they "introduced no novelty in external discipline, or usurped the patronage or sovereign prerogatives of the republic."[10]

The law of April 16, 1836 established the supremacy of civil tribunals over the ecclesiastical in many matters commonly regarded as belonging exclusively to the religious and spiritual order. This was a severe blow at the ecclesiastical *fuero*, or right to maintain separate and independent courts. "The priest," said Santander, "is not removed from the jurisdiction of the civil laws and the temporal authorities in all things that have relation to society."[11] In 1835 Santander sponsored a law granting land in cemeteries for non-Catholics. When accused of being anti-Catholic because of this tolerant action, Santander said, "I love my religion because I live happily in it, and know that outside of the Catholic Church there is no eternal salvation."[12] That Santander was a friend of the Church was further evidenced by his suppression, in 1833, of a radical periodical, "El Cachaco de Bogotá," which was fighting for liberty of cults and suppression of all religious orders.[13] Yet, the religious policy of Santander was so displeasing to the clerics that many of them joined with the discontented "Bolivianos" who constituted the opposition.

The ecclesiastical policy of New Granada was not so unsatisfactory to Pope Gregory XVI but that he agreed to recognize the independence

7. "M. M. Nuñez á Santander, Cartagena, 25 de enero de 1832," in *Archivo Santander*, XIX, 191.

8. Restrepo, *La Iglesia y el Estado en Colombia*, p. 163; Arboleda, *op. cit.*, p. 252.

9. Restrepo, *La Iglesia y el Estado*, p. 164; "Ignacio Tejada á Santander, Roma, 27 de junio de 1835," in *Archivo Santander*, XXI, 265.

10. Restrepo, *op. cit.*, p. 166.

11. "F. de P. Santander á José M. Botero, Bogotá, 9 de agosto de 1835," in *Archivo Santander*, XXI, 316; Restrepo, *op. cit.*, p. 165.

12. "Santander á José M. Botero," in *Archivo Santander*, XXI, 313.

13. Arboleda, *op. cit.*, p. 192.

of the republic on November 26, 1835. This event, as has been indicated elsewhere, was due in large measure to the untiring efforts of Ignacio Tejada, who had been sent to Rome as the representative of Great Colombia and who was retained at his post as the chargé of New Granada. In receiving Tejada in public audience, the act which constituted recognition, the pontiff said that he "experienced a particular pleasure in being able to recognize a government which gave so many proofs of stability, no less than its adhesion to the Catholic religion, and of its constant veneration of the Holy See."[14]

New Granada enjoys the distinction of being the first Spanish-American republic to be recognized politically by the Holy See. Recognition was attended by a complete restoration of the hierarchy in the republic. The following prelates were preconized by the pope: José Antonio Cháves as Auxiliary Bishop of the archdiocese of Bogotá, Juan de Cruz Gómez Plata as Bishop of Antioquia, Luis José Serrano as Bishop of Santa Marta, Antonio Barbano as Bishop of Popayán, and Manuel José Mosquera as Archbishop of Bogotá. When the pope indicated his intention of sending an official representative to Bogotá, Tejada was instructed to oppose the plan for it was feared that a representative of the pope would exercise an ultramontane influence and render difficult the operation of the patronage and the inauguration of reforms. His Holiness was not to be deterred, however, for in May, 1836, Mgr. Cayetano Baluffi was sent to New Granada as internuncio extraordinary. He arrived in Bogotá on January 16, 1837, and was recognized as the diplomatic representative of the pope, but he was not permitted to exercise functions relative to ecclesiastical government and discipline. Thus inflexible were the Granadinos in the exercise of the right of patronage.[15] By law of June 12, 1840, the executive power was given the right to accord the *pase* to briefs and papal acts granting powers and instructions to envoys or internuncios to act in New Granada. After the passage of this law Baluffi was recognized in his religious functions.[16]

Santander's successor in the presidency, José Ignacio de Márquez (1837-41), was also a good Catholic but he refused to allow this to influence him in enforcing the laws. For example, when serious pressure was brought to bear on him to exclude the works of Jeremy Bentham from the schools, he pointed out that they had been sanctioned

14. "Ignacio Tejada á Santander, Roma, 27 de noviembre (and) 18 de diciembre de 1835," in *Archivo Santander*, XXI, 372-73.

15. Zubieta, *Misiones Diplomáticas de Colombia*, pp. 595-97; "J. de D. Aranzazu á Santander, Rionegro, 20 de octubre de 1836," in *Archivo Santander*, XXII, 350-52.

16. Arboleda, *op. cit.*, I, 385; Restrepo, *op. cit.*, p. 166.

by law as texts, and he refused to suspend their use.[17] Furthermore, in August, 1837, President Márquez issued a circular to the governors demanding that the law of March 4, 1826, regarding admission of novitiates be observed. It will be recalled that this law established twenty-five years as the minimum age at which novices could be admitted into convents. Flagrant and widespread disregard of the prohibition occasioned the presidential instruction.

The most serious ecclesiastical problem which confronted President Márquez was the case of the convents of Pasto. By act of Congress, June 5, 1839, the exemption enjoyed by the convents of Pasto with respect to the suppression of small or "minor convents" was removed. It was provided that the property of certain convents which were almost deserted should be applied to the support of missions and education. Although the measure had been sponsored by the bishop of Popayán, a cry went up that this was an attempt to destroy religion. Urged by local members of the clergy, the people of Pasto arose in rebellion. That the hierarchy did not condone the revolt is shown by the pastoral of Archbishop Mosquera (July 17, 1839), "In no case can we justify revolutionary acts under the pretext of religion." The provincial authorities, unable to put down the revolt by arms, signed a humiliating capitulation. President Márquez refused to recognize the capitulation and determined to enforce the law. General Pedro A. Herrán was appointed to restore order. This he accomplished, although he had to use force, to the indignation of the Santanderistas.[18] Consequently the Pasto incident was cited as additional evidence of the anti-Catholic or "liberal" policy of the President.

General Pedro Alcántara Herrán, the man who suppressed the Pasto rebellion, was elected in 1842 to succeed President Márquez. During his administration clerical influence increased considerably. The new Constitution of 1843, more conservative than that of 1832, stated in even more emphatic terms the close union which existed between Church and State. In addition to the provision (Article 15) that "it is also the duty of the government to protect the exercise of the Roman Catholic Apostolic religion for the Granadinos," there was added (Article 16), "The Roman Catholic Apostolic religion is the only cult which the Republic supports and maintains."[19] In further evidence of the increasing support given by the government to the Catholic faith, the Jesuits

17. Arboleda, *op. cit.*, I, 311.
18. Henao y Arrubla, *Historia de Colombia*, II, 487-93.
19. "Constitución Política de la República de la Nueva Granada, Reformada por el Congreso en sus sesiones de 1842 y 1843, Bogotá, 1843," in Pombo y Guerra, *op. cit.*, pp. 957-1002.

were allowed to return to New Granada to assume educational and missionary activities. The Jesuits arrived in 1844, the first to tread the soil of New Granada since their expulsion in 1767.[20]

In 1845 General Tomás Mosquera was elected president with the aid of the clergy, the militarists, and a Conservative majority. Although a Conservative, President Mosquera (1845-49) manifested liberal leanings; he abolished the tithes and diminished the fiscal protection to the Church. Yet, on the other hand, he extended the jurisdiction of the Jesuits in the missionary field, for he realized the exceptional importance of the missions in assuring to the government control of the interior.[21] When Mosquera's candidate for the presidency was defeated in 1849, the long Conservative rule came to an end, and there was inaugurated a radical régime under which the Church suffered grievously. Under the Conservatives the status accorded the Church was not what the ultramontanes desired, but notwithstanding the extreme *regalismo* of Santander and Márquez, Catholicism found constant protection and support in the Conservative presidents. Its status was a happy one compared to that of the period of the Liberal supremacy.

The Liberal party, victorious in 1849 and remaining in the ascendancy with only short interruptions until 1880, promoted a vast "democratic" program in which the Church was the principal sufferer. The first act of President José Hilario López, which ended the long peace between Church and State, was the order of May 21, 1850, which allowed the Jesuits but forty-eight hours to leave the country. The hardships of the expulsion duplicated the events of 1767. Some of the Jesuits went to Jamaica, and others found refuge in Ecuador. Shortly after (June 20) the sanctity of matrimony was attacked by the legalization of divorce. Strongly influenced by the '48 socialistic ideas, President López and his Liberal adherents in the Congress pursued their anti-ecclesiastical policy. In 1851 laws were passed annulling the tithes and setting a fixed income for the clergy, abolishing the right of asylum in Catholic churches, giving to *cabildos* the right to nominate parish curates, and extinguishing all *fueros* or ecclesiastical privilege of separate courts. The Supreme Court of the nation was given jurisdiction over cases concerning prelates regarding not only common crimes but "the improper exercise of their functions." This was an invasion of the ecclesiastical right for it delegated to the ordinary courts subjects of exclusive ecclesiastical control.[22]

In March, 1852, the State further arrogated to itself exclusively ecclesiastical rights by incorporating the conciliar seminary of the arch-

20. Henao y Arrubla, *op. cit.*, II, 506.
21. *Ibid.*, p. 529.
22. Restrepo, *op. cit.*, pp. 220-21, 510-11; Pombo y Guerra, *op. cit.*, II, 1008-10.

diocese with the national college of San Bartolomé. This act took away from the Church the right to educate its own priests. Archbishop Mosquera protested in vain.[23] In February, 1852, the government sent a circular to the prelates, asking if they did not deem it necessary and advisable to consent to the establishment of absolute separation of Church and State. The prelates, of course, refused to recognize any good in the proposal. The Archbishop stated emphatically that the union of the spiritual and temporal powers was the natural state.[24]

Notwithstanding the objections of the prelates, President López appeared before Congress as an advocate of separation. He said, "I have meditated profoundly on this troublesome matter, and I have finally decided to indicate to you the convenience of sanctioning the complete independence of the Church. The Constitution is opposed, it is true, to the adoption of this idea, but it can be amended during the coming year, and in the meantime certain dispositions in this matter can be advanced."[25] As will be indicated shortly, the suggestion of the president was enacted into constitutional law the next year.

The radical act of actual separation was not necessary to bring about a break with the hierarchy. Archbishop Mosquera had written several vigorous protests against the anti-Catholic laws passed by the Congress, and several other prelates joined him in his protests. Finally, because of the vigor of the metropolitan's opposition, a process was brought against him in the Senate. He was charged with "exciting and provoking disobedience to public authority" and "representing as contrary to religion or precepts of evangelical morality the legal operation of governmental authority." The prelate was found guilty, although it is difficult to see in what respects he erred, and he was exiled from the country. In September, 1852, he went to New York, and from there he proceeded to Europe. He was called to Rome by Pius IX, who approved his actions. He died in Marseilles, December 10, 1853. Archbishop Mosquera was unquestionably one of the outstanding prelates of Latin America, and his loss to New Granada, not alone to the Church of that republic, was irreparable. The bishops of Pamplona, Santa Marta, and Cartagena, who also protested against the anticlerical laws, were exiled. With them were included quite a number of priests.[26]

In the presidential election of 1853, the Conservatives offered no candidate and refrained from voting. Two factions of the Liberal party offered candidates. The Radicals or *Golgotas*, composed of young in-

23. Restrepo, *op. cit.*, p. 346.
24. *Ibid.*, p. 172.
25. Pombo y Guerra, *op. cit.*, II, 1011.
26. Pombo y Guerra, *op. cit.*, II, 1010; Restrepo, *op. cit.*, pp. 222-25; 231-40.

telligentsia who desired to destroy all influence of the clergy not only in politics but in "the tribunal of conscience" as well, nominated General Tomás Herrera. The *Democráticos*, or *Draconianos*, supported General José María Obando. The election (April 1, 1853) resulted in the victory of Obando. Herrera consequently became president of the Senate.[27]

One of the first acts of the new administration was to promulgate a new constitution which guaranteed to all Granadinos (Article 5) "the free profession, public or private, of their religion, providing it does not disturb the public peace, offend pure morals, nor impede the exercise of any other cult." It further provided (Article 10) that there should be no forced contribution for the support of any cult.[28] With the limitations imposed by the Constitution of 1843 removed, the Congress proceeded (June 15, 1853) to separate Church and State. This was the first act of separation in Latin-American history. According to the law, "From September first, next, all intervention of the civil, national, and municipal authorities will cease in the election and presentation of all persons whatsoever for the provision of ecclesiastical benefices, and in all and any matters relating to the exercise of the Catholic cult or any other professed by the people of New Granada." The ownership of churches was declared to be vested in the resident Catholics of the parishes and that of cathedrals in the resident Catholics of the dioceses.[29] The act of separation should have inaugurated an era of liberty for the Church, but instead it meant close surveillance verging on servitude.

Other anticlerical acts passed during the short administration of Obando (1853-54) were: marriage made an obligatory civil ceremony and the cemeteries secularized and placed under the control of the municipal authorities. Since the powers were separated it was deemed no longer necessary to maintain representation at Rome.[30]

A better understanding between Church and State became noticeable after 1855. By law of May 14 of that year, churches and congregations were given juridic personality to hold property. In the next year the repugnant divorce law was abrogated, and the law of civil marriage was tempered somewhat by providing that the religious ceremony would be accepted as valid for civil effects if the contracting parties repaired to a notary or judge immediately after the religious ceremony for the purpose of registration.[31]

27. Pombo y Guerra, *op. cit.*, pp. 1011-12; Henao y Arrubla, *op. cit.*, p. 542.
28. "Constitución Política de la Nueva Granada Expedida por el Congreso, Bogotá, 1853," in Pombo y Guerra, *op. cit.*, II, 1017-42.
29. Restrepo, *op. cit.*, p. 191, 264.
30. Pombo y Guerra, *op. cit.*, II, 1011; Henao y Arrubla, *op. cit.*, p. 545.
31. Restrepo, *op. cit.*, pp. 379, 511.

In May, 1858, to the rapidly accumulating list of Colombian constitutions another one was added. This supreme charter established a Granadine Confederation. Religious liberty was guaranteed (Article 56).[32] Since the prohibition in the constitution of 1853 against the entry of Jesuits into the country was no longer in force, President Ospina allowed them to return and put the College of San Bartolomé under their direction. Other measures of the government conciliatory toward the Catholic Church served to reëstablish a considerable measure of tranquility. But it proved to be merely the calm before the storm—the most devastating storm ever experienced by the Catholic Church in Colombia.

In 1860, General Tomás Mosquera, who had been a leader of the Conservatives, joined with the Liberals for personal reasons and became one of the most radical opponents of the Church. After a successful conflict with the army of the Confederation, Mosquera gained control of the government in July, 1861. In an effort to retain power and rule above the law, he instituted radical politico-religious reforms. In short he declared a "Kulturkampf." Because of clerical opposition, more potential than actual, the dictator decreed (July 20, 1861) that no cleric could exercise his religious functions without the authorization of the president of the republic or governor of a state. This patent denial of the independent existence of the Church, as legally established by the Law of Separation, was based on extravagant claims of the governmental right of *tuición* or protection. On July 26, once more the Jesuits were ordered out of the country, "as a police measure."[33] On September 9, a law of disamortization was passed. Property held in the dead hands of religious corporations or communities was to revert to the nation. Only buildings needed for the direct use of the cult were exempt from the decree. On November 3, all convents, monasteries, and religious houses were suppressed. By later legislation it was provided that each nun should be paid by the government 240 pesos annually. To each male religious was to be paid from 180 to 480 pesos, according to the number of years he had been in orders in 1861.[34]

It was not to be expected that the Archbishop and other prelates would supinely acquiesce in the despoliation of the Church. On the contrary, Archbishop Antonio Herrán registered such a vigorous protest

32. "Constitución Política para La Confederación Granadina. Sancionada el día 22 de mayo de 1858, Bogotá, 1858," in Pombo y Guerra, *op. cit.*, II, 1059-91.

33. Henao y Arrubla, *op. cit.*, pp. 570-71; Restrepo, *op. cit.*, p. 380, 570; Pombo y Guerra, *op. cit.*, II, 1097.

34. Henao y Arrubla, *op. cit.*, pp. 570-71; Restrepo, *op. cit.*, p. 381; Pombo y Guerra, *op. cit.*, II, 1098.

that he was charged with sedition and desire to overthrow the supreme authority of the State. Consequently, by decree of November 3, 1861, he was ordered imprisoned "until the executive power determines his term of confinement or expulsion." He was eventually confined for some time at a place on the Atlantic seacoast. Other prelates also suffered either imprisonment or exile.[35]

In disregard of the separation of the temporal and religious powers, President Mosquera interpreted the governmental right of *tuición* or protection to imply intervention in the internal affairs of the Church. "It is the duty of the government," he said, "by the right of *tuición*, which the Republic exercises, to protect the Colombians in the exercise of their religious cult, and to avoid conflicts which arise from the intervention of ecclesiastics in political subjects." Consequently the dictator decreed that no minister of any cult could exercise his ministry without having previously taken an oath to obey the constitution and the laws of the republic. Those who refused to obey were to be exiled.[36]

When his power was sufficiently consolidated Mosquera convoked a convention to reform the constitution. An amnesty was granted to political prisoners, but it is noteworthy that it did not apply to clerics. The constitutional convention, in the control of the Liberals, drew up a federal constitution in which, as was to be expected, Catholicism fared worse than ever. The free profession, public or private, of any religion was guaranteed (Article 15), but, as Rafael Núñez said, "Religious liberty was guaranteed, but not for Catholics."[37] It was Article 23, which provided that "to support national sovereignty and maintain public security and tranquility, the national government or that of the states, may exercise the right of supreme inspection over religious cults," which was contorted to deny the privilege of religious liberty.[38]

In 1866 Mosquera was "reëlected" president, and soon after he became dictator. Then, because of the opposition of certain Catholic prelates, he returned to a violent persecution of the Catholic religion. The archbishop of Bogotá and the bishops of Pasto and Santa Marta were imprisoned or exiled. This was the final furious effort of the dictator to create radical support for his personal rule.[39] He failed and was exiled (1867).

Liberal control still persisted in Colombia for the next thirteen years.

35. Restrepo, *op. cit.*, pp. 576-81.
36. *Ibid.*, pp. 582, 592.
37. Rafael Núñez, *La Reforma Política en Colombia* (Bogotá, 1886), p. 241.
38. "Constitución de los Estados Unidos de Colombia. Sancionada por la Convención Nacional el 8 de mayo de 1863, Bogotá, 1867," in Pombo y Guerra, *op. cit.*, II, 1127-64; Restrepo, *op. cit.*, p. 588.
39. Pombo y Guerra, *op. cit.*, II, 1173; Restrepo, *op. cit.*, p. 600.

The party, however, abandoned much of its original extremeness and, after 1870, no longer desired the complete separation of Church and State. But the Conservatives, who had become a clerical party, were constantly on the watch to frustrate any attempt to harm the Church further. Liberal supremacy terminated when they made the serious mistake of electing Dr. Rafael Núñez to the presidency. During the long years of Liberal ascendancy (1849-80) numerous ecclesiastical reform measures, many of which were frankly anticlerical in character, had been enacted. Some of these were revoked or altered, but nevertheless in 1880, on the eve of the era of Rafael Núñez, the legal status of Catholicism was unique for a Catholic country of that period. Church and State were separated; the ecclesiastical *fueros* were abolished; the government recognized no civil compulsion in the payment of tithes; ecclesiastical property, with the exception of the actual Church buildings and residences of the clergy, had been appropriated by the government; the religious orders were abolished; cemeteries were secularized; marriage was declared to be an obligatory civil ceremony; and in the exercise of the right of "inspection of cults" the government controlled purely spiritual matters. Such was the unhappy state of the Catholic Church in Colombia in 1880.

The Church found a savior and champion in President Rafael Núñez. Elected to the presidency as a Liberal, in 1880, Núñez, who had once been a socialistic radical, learned from governmental experience that excessive liberalism had disorganized the country. He became convinced that the cause of Colombia's travail was vain idealism, and consequently he espoused conservative, realistic policies which he hoped would bring peace and progress. The Liberal turned Conservative; but it was not until after his reëlection to the presidency in 1884 that Dr. Núñez formally inaugurated his conservative program. Restoration of the power and influence of the Catholic Church in Colombia was a cardinal feature of the new policy, as will become abundantly evident by what follows.

In 1885 President Núñez convened a national council of states to frame a new constitution. The document, which was promulgated in August, 1886, was strongly centralistic and proclerical. The preamble proclaimed God as the supreme fountain of all authority. Roman Catholicism was to be respected as an essential factor of the social order. The constitution declared, however: "It is understood that the Catholic Church is not and shall not be official and shall preserve its own independence." This independence was guaranteed further in Article 53: "The Catholic Church will be free to administer its interior affairs and to exercise acts of spiritual authority and ecclesiastical jurisdiction without necessity of authorization of the civil power. And as a juridic person represented in each diocese by the respective legitimate prelate, it can also exercise civil acts by its own law which the present constitution recognizes." The exercise of all cults not contrary to Christian morality was guaranteed, as well as freedom of the individual from molestation on account of religious opinions. Finally, the government was authorized to celebrate a concordat with the Holy See for the purpose of defining and establishing relations between the civil and ecclesiastical powers.[40]

Núñez suggested that the main object of the educational system should be the inculcation of Christian doctrine. He therefore ordered the teaching of religion in the public schools. He protected religion like Portales of Chile, said García Calderón, in order to give a disorganized nation the firm unity of a law.[41] "Fanaticism," wrote Rafael Núñez, "is not religion any more than demagogy is liberty; but between religion and morality there is an indissoluble bond." Although he was a strong believer in the moralizing office of the Church, Núñez did not fail to recognize its past abuses.[42] The Constitution of 1888, which continues to be the fundamental law under which Colombians are governed today, was significant religiously in that it recognized the primacy of the Catholic Church and symbolized the triumph of the clerical party.

The clerical reaction was climaxed by the negotiation, as authorized by the constitution, of a concordat with the papacy, which was signed on December 31, 1887, and sanctioned by Congress in 1888. This concordat, which was declared by the Archbishop of Cartagena to be "one of the best in the world"[43] and by an eminent ecclesiastical historian to be "a model of mutual relations between Church and State,"[44] has been in force in the Republic of Colombia from 1888 to the present day. Since this treaty has been acceptable to ecclesiastics the full text is presented here in order that the reader may appreciate what the Church regards as the most satisfactory agreement possible:

> In the name of the most holy and indivisible Trinity, His Holiness the Supreme Pontiff Leo XIII and the President of the Republic of Colombia, His Excellency Señor Rafael Núñez, name as plenipotentiaries respectively:

40. "The Constitution of Colombia," in J. I. Rodríguez, *American Constitutions* (Washington, 1906), II, 318-79.

41. Francisco García Calderón, *Latin America, Its Rise and Progress* (London, 1913), p. 210.

42. Núñez, *op. cit.*, pp. 539-41.

43. Archbishop of Cartagena to J. L. Mecham, Cartagena, November 7, 1927.

44. Zamora, *Patronato Español é Indiano*, p. 90.

His Holiness, the most eminent Signor Mariano Rampolla del Tindaro, cardinal presbyter of the Holy Roman Church of Santa Cecilia, and his Secretary of State, and

The President of the Republic, his excellency Señor Joaquín Fernando Vélez, Envoy Extraordinary and Minister Plenipotentiary before the Holy See:

Who, after presenting their respective credentials, have agreed to the following:

Article 1. The Roman Catholic Apostolic religion is the religion of Colombia, the public powers recognize it as an essential element of the social order, and they are bound to protect and enforce respect for it and its ministers, leaving to it at the same time the full enjoyment of its rights and prerogatives.

Article 2. The Catholic Church will enjoy complete liberty and independence of the civil power, and consequently there shall be no intervention of this power in the free exercise of its spiritual authority and ecclesiastical jurisdiction, its government and administration conforming to its own laws.

Article 3. Canonical legislation is independent of the civil law, and forms no part of it, but it will be solemnly respected by the authorities of the Republic.

Article 4. The State recognizes in the Church, represented by its legitimate hierarchial authority, true and proper juridical personality, and capacity to enjoy and exercise the rights that appertain to it.

Article 5. The Church has the right to acquire by legal title, and possess and administer freely movable and immovable property in the manner established by the common law, and its properties and foundations will be no less inviolable than those of citizens of the Republic.

Article 6. Ecclesiastical properties can be taxed in the same manner and to the same extent as private property; however, buildings destined for the use of the cult, conciliar seminaries, and episcopal and cural residences, can never be burdened with contributions nor occupied or used for other purposes.

Article 7. The members of the secular and regular clergy cannot be obliged to perform public duties incompatible with their ministry and profession, and furthermore, they will always be exempt from military service.

Article 8. The government is obliged to incorporate in its laws of criminal procedure provisions to safeguard the sacerdotal dignity, wherever, for any reason, a minister of the Church figures in a process.

Article 9. The diocesan and parochial ordinaries can collect from the faithful emoluments and ecclesiastical rents canonically and equitably established and based in either immemorial custom in each diocese, or the performance of religious services; and, in order that the acts and obligations thus originating create civil effect, and that the temporal authority shall lend its aid, the ordinaries will act in agreement with the government.

Article 10. There can be freely constituted and established in Colombia religious orders and associations of both sexes, always provided that their canonical foundation is authorized by the competent ecclesiastical authority. These will be governed by their own constitutions; and, in order to enjoy juridic personality and be under the protection of the laws, they shall submit to the civil power the canonical authorization granted by the respective superior ecclesiastical authority.

Article 11. The Holy See will accord its aid and coöperation to the government in establishing in Colombia religious institutions dedicated particularly to the exercise of charity, missions, education of the young, instruction in general, and other works of public utility and beneficence.

Article 12. In the universities, colleges, schools, and other centers of learning, education and public instruction will be organized and directed in conformity with the dogmas and morals of the Catholic religion. Religious instruction will be obligatory in such centers, and the pious practices of the Catholic religion will be observed in them.

Article 13. Consequently, in said centers of learning, the respective diocesan ordinaries, by themselves, or by special delegates, will exercise the right, respecting religion and morals, of inspection and revision of textbooks. The archbishop of Bogotá will designate the books that ought to serve as texts for religion and morals in the universities; and to the end of assuring uniformity of instruction in the indicated matters, this prelate, in agreement with the other diocesan ordinaries, will select the texts for the other schools of official instruction.[45] The government will prevent, in the conduct of literary and scientific courses, and, in general, in all branches of instruction, the propagation of ideas contrary to Catholic dogma and to the respect and veneration due the Church.

Article 14. In the event that the instruction in religion and morals, in spite of the orders and preventive measures of the government, do not conform to Catholic doctrine, the respective diocesan ordinary can restrain such professors or masters of faculty from the teaching of such subjects.

45. For example, on the title page of Carlos Alberto Lleras Acosta, *Instrucción Cívica* (Bogotá, 1926), which was used in the public schools as a textbook, appears the following: "Approved by the ecclesiastical censor Félix Restrepo, S.J. Permission to print given by the Archbishop of Bogotá."

Article 15. The right of making nominations to vacant archbishoprics and bishoprics belongs to the Holy See. The Holy Father, nevertheless, as proof of special deference, and with the intention of preserving harmonious relations between Church and State, agrees that, in the filling of archiepiscopal and episcopal sees, the wishes of the President of the Republic take precedence. Consequently, for each vacancy he will recommend directly to the Holy See the ecclesiastics who in his opinion possess the necessary gifts and qualifications for the episcopal dignity. The Holy See, on its part, before making nominations will always announce the names of the candidates it wishes to promote so that it may learn whether the President has reasons of a civil or political character to consider the said candidates as *personas non grata*. Diocesan vacancies will be filled as soon as possible, and will not last longer than six months.

Article 16. The Holy See can establish new dioceses and alter the territorial limits of those existing today when it regards this as useful and necessary for spiritual welfare, consulting the government previously and receiving any opinions from it that are just and convenient.

Article 17. The marriage ceremony celebrated according to the provisions of the Council of Trent applies to all who profess the Roman Catholic Religion and is necessary for the creation of civil effects appertaining to the persons and property of the contracting parties and their descendants. The act of the ceremony will be witnessed by the functionary determined by law for the sole object of verifying the entry of the marriage in the civil register, providing it is not a marriage in *articulo mortis*, in which case such supplementary proof may be dispensed with if it is not practical to satisfy this formality. It is the duty of the contracting parties to fulfil the requirements relative to the intervention of the civil functionary of the register, the duty of the parish priest being limited to notifying them of the obligation which the civil law imposes on them.

Article 18. Concerning marriages celebrated any time in conformity with the provisions of the Council of Trent, and which ought to have the desired civil effect, those of ecclesiastical origin should be admitted preferentially as supplementary proof.

Article 19. Causes affecting the bond of matrimony and the cohabitation of husband and wife, as well as those relating to the validity of betrothals, will be under the exclusive jurisdiction of the ecclesiastical authorities. The civil effects of matrimony will be regulated by the civil powers.

Article 20. The armies of the Republic will enjoy the exemptions and favors known as military privileges, which will be determined by the Holy Father in a separate act.

Article 21. After the divine offices, the following prayer will be recited in all the churches of the Republic: *Domine Salvam fac Praesidencius et supremas eius auctoritates.*

Article 22. The government of the Republic recognizes in perpetuity in the nature of a consolidated debt, the value of redeemed mortgages in its treasury and of disentailed properties belonging to churches, *cofradías, patronatos,* chapels, and institutions of instruction and beneficence controlled by the Church, which have been at a certain time, entered into the public debt of the nation. This recognized debt will pay without diminution the annual liquid interest of 4½ per cent, payable semi-annually.

Article 23. The income from *patronatos,* chapels, *cofradías,* and other particular foundations will be recognized and paid directly to whoever, according to the foundations, has the right of receiving it, or to their legally constituted proxies. The payment will be made without diminution, as in the preceding article, and will start after the next year of 1888. In the event of some of the indicated entities being extinguished by prior agreement between the competent ecclesiastical authorities and the government, the income will be applied to pious and beneficent uses without violating in any way the will of the founders.

Article 24. The Holy See, in recognition of the condition of the national treasury of Colombia, and of the utility which the Church derives from the convention, grants to the Republic the following concessions: (a) the disentailed property belonging in its major part to convents and religious associations already extinguished and not included in the preceding article, is not to be recognized as part of the capital amount, and (b) it is granted exemption from obligations for rents or interests due, or for any other cause, on disentailed ecclesiastical properties up to December 31, 1887.

Article 25. In return for this concession the government of Colombia pledges itself to assign in perpetuity an annual liquid sum, which, at present, is fixed at 100,000 pesos Colombian, and which will be increased when the treasury situation improves; this money will be proportionately assigned and within limits agreed on by the two supreme powers, for the support of the dioceses, chapters, seminaries, missions, and other proper works of the civilizing action of the Church.

Article 26. The surviving members of the extinguished religious communities will continue to enjoy the income which the preceding provisions have assigned to them for their maintenance and other necessities.

Article 27. If, regarding this (preceding) point, there are doubts or difficulties, the government will confer with the competent ecclesiastical authority with the object of establishing procedure.

Article 28. The government will turn over to the religious entities the disentailed properties belonging to them, which have no assigned use, and in the event that the owner does not appear or has no mission to perform, there will be applied the returns of the sale of such property or its administration to analogous beneficences and pious works according to the most pressing necessities of each diocese following the advice of the competent authority.

Article 29. The Holy See, with the object of contributing to the public tranquillity, declares, on its part, that the persons in Colombia, who, during the past vicissitudes have purchased disentailed property or redeemed mortgages in the national treasury according to the provision of the civil laws in force at that time, will not be molested at any time or in any manner by the ecclesiastical authorities; this dispensation extends not only to those executing such acts, but to those who have taken part in them as first buyers or as legitimate successors, and those who have redeemed mortgages. They will enjoy securely and peacefully possession in these properties, emoluments, and returns; (the Holy See) requiring, nevertheless, that similar abusive alienations will not be repeated in the future.

Article 30. The government of the Republic will regulate with the respective diocesan ordinaries all matters concerning the cemeteries, endeavoring to reconcile the legitimate exigencies of civil and sanitary character with the veneration due these sacred places and the ecclesiastical prescriptions; and in case of discord this matter will be the subject of a special agreement between the Holy See and the government of Colombia.

Article 31. Agreements between the Holy See and the government of Colombia for the encouragement of Catholic missions among the barbarian tribes will require no additional approval on the part of Congress.

Article 32. By the present agreement all laws, orders, and decrees, of any description, promulgated at any time, which contradict or oppose this convention, which, when signed, will have the force of law of the State, are derogated and abrogated.

Article 33. The ratification and exchange of the present convention will take place within six months of the date of signature, and sooner if possible.

In pledge of which the indicated plenipotentiaries place their signature and seal on this convention.

Done in Rome on December 31, 1887.

(Signed) Cardinal Rampolla.
Joaquín F. Vélez.[46]

---

46. *Raccolta di Concordati*, pp. 1051-61. The concordat is also found in Antonio José Uribe, *Anales Diplomáticos y Consulares de Colombia* (Bogotá, 1920), VI, 330-35.

The relations between the Colombian government and the Holy See are regulated, in addition to the Concordat of 1888, by some important supplementary conventions. On July 20, 1892, Cardinal Rampolla and Joaquín Vélez signed a *convención adicional* to the Concordat concerning the *fuero eclesiástico*, cemeteries, and the civil register. Regarding the *fuero eclesiástico*, it was agreed that: (1) civil causes of ecclesiastics and causes relating to property and temporal rights of churches and ecclesiastical foundations should be heard in civil tribunals; (2) criminal causes concerning ecclesiastics in crimes foreign to religion should also be heard in the lay courts, but these trials should not be public; (3) sentences against ecclesiastics providing for the death penalty or opprobrious punishment should not be executed until the president of the Republic reviewed the case; (4) ecclesiastics should not be sentenced to labor on public works; and (5) in the arrest, detention, and punishment of ecclesiastics all possible respect should be paid to their sacred character.

On the subject of cemeteries, the convention supplemented Article 30 of the Concordat as follows: (1) all cemeteries of the Republic, with the exception of those belonging to private individuals, should be entrusted to the ecclesiastical authority, who would administer and regulate them independently of the civil authority; (2) an exception was made to allow the government to continue its financial support of certain large cemeteries in some of the cities. With respect to these, administration was to continue in the civil authority, but the Church reserved the right of supervision; (3) cemeteries for non-Catholics were to be created with municipal funds; and (4) the Church recognized the government's right to enforce sanitary and public regulations with respect to the cemeteries.

As to the civil register the convention provided that the ecclesiastics entrusted with the records of births, marriages, and deaths should submit authentic copies to the government every six months, but these copies were not to serve as evidence except in the event of loss of the parochial books.[47] In 1898, and following at ten year intervals, supplementary conventions were negotiated establishing the amount the government should appropriate to the Church. This small appropriation was regarded as compensation for the injuries caused by confiscation of Church property during the administration of Mosquera.

A convention concerning the missions was negotiated in 1902. This treaty provided for the administrative organization of the mission work and delimitation of fields of activity. The government obligated itself to appropriate annually $75,000 for the support of the missions. To

47. *Raccolta di Concordati*, pp. 1061-69.

the mission authorities was entrusted the direction of public primary schools within the mission districts. The government, in addition, agreed to grant to the missions, out of the public domain, lands for cultivation and pasturage.[48] In commenting on governmental interest in the missions, President Nel Ospina said, "The government supports the missions with the aid of the Church, for they are not only powerful instruments of civilization and culture, but they are also a means of making effective the national action in unknown and far-off regions."[49] In 1928 an accord was entered into between Colombia and the Holy See for the purpose of organizing the religious service of the army. By this agreement the "castrensial jurisdiction" was established.[50]

The relations between Church and State in Colombia since the days of President Rafael Núñez and the negotiation of the Concordat greatly improved. This was due largely to the fact that both political parties, Conservatives and Liberals, accepted the basic position of religion as defined in the Concordat. Whereas in the nineteenth century religion had been the major issue distinguishing the two parties, after the settlement of the 1880's the religious principle was played down in party alignment.[51]

Latent Liberal hostility to the clergy flared up in the 1930's when a Liberal reform program reached high tide during the presidency of Alfonso López. One of several constitutional amendments adopted in 1936 to entrench the López program provided for freedom of religion and equality of cults, stripped the Church of control over education, and barred priests from politics.[52]

The radical López program created a reaction and was soon overturned in 1937 by a coalition of moderate Liberals and Conservatives. The Church was restored to its position of influence in education. In 1942 President Eduardo Santos, a moderate Liberal, concluded a new pact with the Vatican which modified the Concordat of 1887. It limited clerical control of education and stipulated that bishops must be Colombian citizens approved by the government. The new concordat gave the government a greater measure of control over the Catholic Church in Colombia, but in actual practice the position of the Church was little

48. *Anales Diplomáticos y Consulares,* pp. 432-36.

49. *Mensaje de Presidente de la República de Colombia al Congreso Nacional en las Sesiones de 1926* (Bogotá, 1926), p. 74.

50. *Mensaje Presidencial de 1929,* p. 28.

51. Vernon L. Fluharty, *Dance of the Millions: Military Rule and the Social Revolution in Colombia, 1930-1956* (Pittsburgh, 1957), p. 228.

52. *Ibid.,* pp. 54-55.

changed. The government's right to control educational institutions has been exercised but weakly.[53]

The return of the Conservatives to power under Ospina Pérez (1946-50) and particularly under the fanatical proclerical Laureano Gómez (1950-53) hurled the country into one of Latin America's bloodiest civil wars. The struggle developed into one of bitter reprisals between demagogic leftwing Liberals and ultra-Conservatives. Liberal leaders retired to the *llanos*, or highly inaccessible backcountry, where they set up guerrilla organizations. Eventually the struggle lost its political purpose and developed into undisguised banditry.[54] It is estimated that perhaps a quarter of a million lives were lost in this Conservative-Liberal conflict in which unfortunately the Church and religion were not able to escape involvement.

Following the assassination of the Liberal leader Jorge Eliécer Gaitán and the Bogotá riots of April, 1948 (called the Bogotazo), an anti-Church fury, probably communist inspired, spread over the country. Churches, convents, and schools were burned, and priests were seized and killed.[55] In April, 1949, Archbishop Ismael Perdomo of Bogotá issued a pastoral circular urging the clergy to avoid denunciation of Liberalism as heretical and to cease support of one party in preference to another. But in defiance of the pastoral there were prelates who forbade Catholics to vote for Liberal candidates "who wish to implant civil marriage, divorce, and coeducation which would open the doors to immorality and Communism."[56] Also, many of the fanatical clergy paid no attention to the warning of the primate but fed the hate for Liberals.

Because of the strongly religious and clerical nature of Laureano Gómez, the hate soon took on the coloration of a religious crusade. Laureano Gómez personified the clerical-authoritarian tradition of Spain. He voiced the kind of Hispanicism and Catholicism to which a considerable part of the Colombian people were attached. He restricted civil liberties and began systematically to hunt down Liberal leaders. "In essence, it [the Civil War] was the Crusades, the Inquisition, and the Castilian Reconquest of the pagan Moors, all over again in miniature."[57]

The persecution of Protestant missionaries, although unrelated to the Conservative-Liberal conflict, was a by-product of the general spirit of

53. John D. Martz, *Colombia: A Contemporary Political Survey* (Chapel Hill, 1962), pp. 25-26.

54. *Hispanic American Report*, XIII, No. 1 (January, 1960), 40.

55. Fluharty, *op. cit.*, p. 103.

56. *Hispanic American Report*, II, No. 5 (May, 1949), 12.

57. Fluharty, *op. cit.*, p. 121.

lawlessness and religious fanaticism. In such an atmosphere it was not surprising that attention was directed at alien sects that were trying to carry out religious conversions in a country that was officially Catholic and had no need for "foreign missions."

Fanatical mobs, often incited by clerical agitators, were responsible for outrages against the Protestants. Churches were burned, schools were closed, and missionaries were murdered. Data released by the Evangelical Confederation of Colombia showed that, from 1948 to 1953, 42 church buildings were destroyed by fire or dynamite, 110 Protestant primary schools were closed, 54 of them by government order, and 51 Colombian Protestants were murdered.[58] By 1959 more than 115 Protestants had been killed and 200 schools were closed. This violence was carried out in the name of religion, presumably against the will of the hierarchy to which the fanatical clergy paid no attention.[59]

There is little doubt that the Colombian governments of Laureano Gómez and Rojas Pinilla encouraged and abetted the persecution of the Protestants. A Treaty on Missions was negotiated with the Vatican which outlawed all forms of Christian activity, other than Roman Catholic, in parts of the country designated Catholic Missions Territories. These areas, comprising 331,000 square miles and having more than 1,000,000 population, were by governmental order of September 3, 1953, restricted to the exclusive missionary activity of the Roman Catholic Church. Departmental governors were instructed to take all steps to terminate religious activities of non-Catholic groups. Thus Protestants were prohibited, contrary to the guarantees of the Constitution, from working in about two-thirds of Colombian territory.[60]

Laureano Gómez placed Protestants in the same category with Communists and "revolutionary bandits." Rojas Pinilla said that Protestants were molested not because of religion but because of meddling in politics. He linked Protestantism with communism.

After the fall of Rojas Pinilla the government eased up on or ignored many restrictive decrees passed by previous anti-Protestant regimes. Following the death of Bogotá's extremely conservative Cardinal Archbishop Luque Sánchez (May, 1959), the new Archbishop Primate Mgr. Luis Concha Córdoba inaugurated a new approach to Catholic-Protestant relations. For example, in December, 1960, in a public conference in Cali, Catholic priests joined Protestant ministers in discussing the defense of Christianity against communism. The new

58. *Hispanic American Report*, VI, No. 8 (September, 1953), 25.
59. *Ibid.*, XII, No. 16 (October, 1959), 557.
60. *Christianity Today*, VII, No. 21 (July 19, 1963), 14.

Catholic strategy in combatting the "Protestant invasion" was to abandon violence in favor of an intensive program of Catholic indoctrination and education so as to render Colombian Catholics impervious to Protestant propaganda.[61]

Perhaps the threat of Protestantism was exaggerated for Protestantism had not succeeded in reaching any substantial portion of the population. Nevertheless the Protestant missionary example had stimulated activity on the part of the Catholic Church in areas where it had been most remiss: social service and efforts to raise the parishioners' standards of living. The hierarchy has increasingly expressed concern for the welfare of the mass of the population. The Church is no longer completely identified with the most conservative political elements. For example, in September, 1961, the episcopate published a collective letter on agrarian reform. The pastoral letter came to the conclusion of the absolute necessity of agrarian reform. Of course there was a violent reaction by the landowners.[62]

The new trend of ecclesiastical policy also included in Colombia reaction against dictatorships. When President Gustavo Rojas Pinilla began to withdraw support of the Catholic Church, and in June, 1956, officially proclaimed a corporative Third Force, the Church assumed a democratic attitude and tried to erase the discontent created by years of collaboration with the dictatorship. Cardinal Cristano Luque, the Primate of Colombia, denounced the Third Force as fascistic. Complaints against the dictatorship and its brutal police repression came from Catholic pulpits, and several bishops openly favored return to democracy.[63] There can be little doubt that clerical opposition to the *imposición* planned by Rojas Pinilla to perpetuate himself in power greatly aided in his overthrow in May, 1957. Following that event Church-State relations proceeded on a relatively tranquil course.

Although the dominant role of the government in education was reaffirmed by constitutional amendment in 1945, the influence of the Church remained powerful. The terms of the Concordat provide that instruction in the universities, colleges, schools, and other centers of instruction shall be "in conformity with the dogmas and morals of the Catholic religion." Religious instruction is made obligatory in all public schools, and the right is reserved to the prelates to designate textbooks

61. *Hispanic American Report*, XII, No. 10 (October, 1959), 557, XIII, No. 12 (December, 1960), 900.
62. Francisco Houtart, "El cambio social en America Latina," *FERES*, No. 18 (Bogotá, 1964), 92.
63. *Hispanic American Report*, IX, No. 8 (September, 1956), 386; *Ibid.*, X, No. 4 (May, 1957), 196.

on morals and religion. Other texts are often included. No diplomas of *bachiller* which entitles the holder to admission to the professional courses in the universities will be granted without completion of the prescribed courses in religion taught by clerics. The National High Council of Education includes some representatives of the Church.

Although the government proclaims a brave and ambitious program of free but compulsory primary education for children between the years of seven and fifteen, little is done to put it into effect. Trained teachers are lacking and buildings are scarce. In Colombia the estimated illiteracy is about 40 per cent. To this group should be added 32 per cent who have had only a year or two of elementary education and who are barely literate. To combat illiteracy the Catholic Church sponsors the *Acción Cultural Popular,* a system of radio schools to promote literacy in the rural areas. This operation, which in 1958 numbered more than 17,000 schools and 145,000 enrolled students, was initiated in 1948 by Father José Joaquín Salcedo in the village of Suatenza, Department of Cundinamarca. *Suatenza,* as the program is called, receives financial contributions from public and private sources, but above all from the Catholic Church.[64]

The Catholic educational system in Colombia is the largest in Latin America. There are more than 3,000 schools and 275,000 pupils.[65] The Church has a strong vested interest in secondary education, owning about 75 per cent of the nation's academic secondary schools. To assist in this work new teaching orders have entered the country. In 1927, by governmental decree and decision of the Council of State, a virtual monopoly of secondary education by the Jesuits was broken. On the university level the country's oldest and most highly respected institutions are under Catholic control. In 1931 Universidad Católica Javeriana reopened in Bogotá after more than 100 years of interruption.

The government of Colombia maintains a diplomatic representative before the Holy See. In 1927 the rank of this representative was raised to that of ambassador. A papal nuncio is accredited to Bogotá. A decree of November, 1958, provides that cardinals and archbishops of the Roman Catholic Church may be given diplomatic passports for their travels.

Colombia is regarded as the most Catholic of all Latin American countries. According to Father Nevins, "The Catholicism of Colombia has often been compared to that of Quebec. It is a traditional Catholic

64. *U.S. Army Area Handbook for Colombia,* Department of the Army Pamphlet, No. 550-26 (2nd ed.; Washington, G.P.O., June 22, 1964), 168.

65. John J. Considine, *New Horizons in Latin America* (New York, 1958), p. 228.

life, conservative but strong."[66] The hierarchy is impressive and the clergy is numerous. There are 3,500 priests, that is, one priest to 3,650 Catholics, one of the highest ratios in Latin America.[67]

Although almost all Colombians are regarded as Catholics, there is great ignorance of religion and great inadequacy of religious instruction. Too much emphasis seems to be given to the formal elements of religion, leaving the people without a clear understanding of doctrine. Since Catholicism is not a vital force in the life of the individual church member, it is not surprising that the percentage of "mass missers" is almost as great in Colombia as in the average Latin-American country.[68]

All who have any knowledge of the past history and present tendencies in Colombia agree that the religious question is not definitely settled in that republic. Since the clergy regard the status established by the Concordat to be a model one, for that very reason it is destined to be subjected to constant attack by the elements that refuse to accept the clerical viewpoint. Sooner or later the enemies of the Concordat will be swept into power and the inevitable reform of ecclesiastical legislation will follow.

66. Albert J. Nevins, M.M., "How Catholic is Latin America?" *The Sign*, Vol. 36, No. 2 (September, 1956), 14.
67. Considine, *op. cit.*, p. 228. There are six archbishops and twenty-two bishops.
68. Nevins, *op. cit.*, p. 13; William J. Coleman, M.M., *Latin American Catholicism: A Self-Evaluation* (Maryknoll, N.Y., 1958), p. 3.

Chapter VI

The Vicissitudes of Roman Catholicism in Ecuador

The aversion of the Latin American to compromise, or to the adoption of half-way measures in meeting problems, is clearly illustrated by the vicissitudes of the Catholic Church in the Republic of Ecuador. There, as in Colombia, religious policy has been a prominent feature of political campaigns, and, as the factions, generally calling themselves "Conservatives" and "Liberals" alternated in the control of the government, the political status of the Church changed within extreme and unreasonable limits. It is difficult to imagine a greater divergence in policies than between those advocated and translated into fact by García Moreno and Eloy Alfaro. Yet these systems, as widely separated as the poles, were foisted on the people of Ecuador because, presumably, the leaders knew better than the people what they wanted and what was good for them.

"Intolerance of cults distinct from the Catholic has been consecrated (in Ecuador), thus departing from the accepted policy of New Granada and Venezuela, and adhering to the current ideas in Peru and Bolivia." Thus wrote a political commentator in 1888 when analyzing religious policy in Ecuador.[1] This description, inapplicable to Ecuador since 1900, was nevertheless true for most of the nineteenth century. When Ecuador separated from Great Colombia, she established, in the Constitution of September 11, 1830, Roman Catholicism as the religion of the State to the exclusion of any other faith.[2] The *Ley de Patronato* of 1824 was incorporated in the Constitution. General Juan José Flores, compatriot of Bolívar and first president of Ecuador, although charged with being an atheist,[3] supported Catholicism during his first administration (1830-34) as the sole State religion. His internal policy was characterized

1. Arosemena, *Estudios Constitucionales*, I, 539.
2. Annibal Velloso Rebello, "García Moreno," in *Revista do Instituto Historico e Geographico Brasileiro* (Rio de Janeiro, 1920), CXLI, 126; Juan Ignacio Larrea, *La Iglesia y el Estado en el Ecuador* (Sevilla, 1954), p. 30; Julio Tobar Donoso, *La Iglesia Ecuatoriana en el siglo*, XIX (Quito, 1934), 110.
3. Rebello, *op. cit.*, p. 137.

by preference for the military and the clergy, but as a matter of fact President Flores, selfish and dictatorial by nature, had little respect for the Church. He supported it if it in turn consented to be subjected and reinforced his authority.

Vicente Rocafuerte, the successor of Flores to the presidency, was the official champion of the Liberals, a great intellect, and a good Catholic withal.[4] Regarded as the greatest of Ecuador's reformers, one of Rocafuerte's first acts as president was to have a new constitution drafted in the interest of greater liberalism. Remarking on the need of constitutional reform, he said, "The Constitution of 1830, which should be reformed or annulled, as is convenient, presents rare anomalies. Beside the declarations of sovereignty of the people, the creation of a legislative body, the distribution of powers, liberty of the press, and other similar subjects, which are pure democracy, are intolerance of cults other than the Roman Catholic, the recognition of *fueros*, the pupilage of the natives, and the *status quo* of the ecclesiastical and monastic establishments which had been consecrated by our colonial laws."[5] In dilating on the subject of constitutional reform, President Rocafuerte made the following pertinent remarks concerning religion: "The reform of the clergy, the purity of their customs, the dignity of the cult, the education of the priests, abolition of certain abuses, the extinction of so many feast days which retard the increase of public wealth, should engage the attention of the legislators...; religious reform should always precede the political."[6]

In spite of the recommendations of the President the constituents did not liberalize the religious clauses of the Constitution of 1835. Roman Catholicism was declared to be the religion of the republic to the exclusion of any other, and the government was specifically obligated to protect it. Since Rocafuerte felt that the religious conservatism of the great majority of Ecuadoreans hampered progress, he attempted to secularize public education. A step in this direction was the taking of the College of San Fernando from the Dominicans and combining it with the University. Also, manifesting leanings toward religious freedom, he tried to introduce Protestantism into Ecuador. But the inherent conservatism and religious attachment of the people against which Rocafuerte struggled proved to be too strong for him. For example, when a Quaker was allowed to enter Quito, and was put in charge of a

---

4. *Ibid.*
5. "El Jefe Supremo á la Convención," in Francisco Ignacio Salazár, *Actas de la Convención Nacional del Ecuador, Año de 1835* (Quito, 1891), p. CCXXXV.
6. *Ibid.*, p. CCXXXVIII.

school, the people were outraged and speedily drove him from the country.[7] Whatever of a liberalizing nature had been implanted in Ecuador during the presidency of Vicente Rocafuerte was lost during the reaction of Flores' second and third terms of office (1839-45). Ambitious and opportunistic, Flores secured the adoption of a new constitution in 1843 which lengthened the presidential term to eight years. With an air of orthodoxy the religious clause of the constitution read, "The religion of the State is the Roman Catholic Apostolic"; but, as a bid for Liberal support, it read further, "to the exclusion of the public exercise of any other cult." The freedom of private worship of non-Catholic cults aroused violent opposition, particularly in Quito and Cuenca, "where reigned a medieval fanaticism which proscribed independent thought and religious independence."[8] The clergy refused to take the oath to the constitution and accused Flores of being in league with the Masons of New Granada. When the Liberals finally mustered enough strength to revolt against the corrupt and despotic rule of Flores the clerics joined them with cries of "Viva la Religión," and "Abajo la Constitución."[9] Flores was unable to withstand the diverse forces of an outraged public conscience, and so, in 1845, he was driven into exile.

After the overthrow of Flores, Ecuador was plunged into veritable anarchy, from which condition it was not rescued until Gabriel García Moreno assumed the control of government in 1860. This most remarkable man in the history of Ecuador was a scion of one of the most aristocratic families of pure Castilian blood. Trained in the law at the University of Quito, he became well known as a publicist and writer. In the political and religious war which accomplished the overthrow of Flores, he was one of the principal actors, thereby evidencing at that early date in his career his devotion to the Roman Catholic Church. Because of the Liberal ascendancy there was no political place for García Moreno in Ecuador; consequently he went to Europe. In 1850, after six months spent in the Old World, he recrossed the sea firmly convinced by the excesses of liberalism that "Jesus Christ was the only Savior of the people, and that the State without religion was irremediably destined to the sabre of the autocrat or the poinard of the anarchist."[10] He felt that the Church should be used to restrain the nation and give it the moral discipline it so badly needed.

7. Berthe, *García Moreno*, pp. 80, 103; "J. M. Obando á Santander, Pasto, 8 de julio de 1835," in *Archivo Santander*, XXI, 275.
8. Rebello, *op. cit.*, pp. 137-38; Berthe, *op. cit.*, p. 106.
9. Berthe, *op. cit.*, pp. 106-8; Pedro Fermin Cevallos, *Historia del Ecuador* (Guayaquil, 1886-89), V, 534.
10. Berthe, *op. cit.*, p. 143.

Following his return from Europe García Moreno was instrumental in securing for the Jesuits, who had been expelled from New Granada, admission to Ecuador (1851). By law of March, 1851, the Jesuits were restored their old properties which had not been alienated. A great festival marked the opening, after eighty-three years, of the Church of Jesus in Quito. The government of New Granada protested vigorously against the admission of the Jesuits into Ecuador. The diplomatic agent of New Granada accredited to the government in Quito was guilty of the questionable diplomatic action of publishing a venomous pamphlet against the Holy Company. García Moreno assumed the rôle of defender of the Jesuits. His "Defensa de los Jesuitas" is a remarkably restrained, dignified, and scholarly treatise on the work and objects of the Society of Jesus.[11] The able support of García Moreno was of no avail, however, for, in 1852, the expulsion of the Jesuits was decreed.[12] Then the author of the celebrated "Defensa de los Jesuitas," wrote as a complement to that work a "Farewell to the Jesuits."

The attack by García Moreno, in satirical verse, on the dictatorial government of the pseudo-Liberal José Urbina brought upon him the decree of expulsion from Ecuador (1855). His experience as an exile in Europe added to his political and religious conservatism, and when he returned to his native country in 1857, he founded a political party, the National Union, to advance his reform program. After resorting to the use of arms, in traditional Ecuadorean style, to gain possession of the government, García Moreno established his authority in Quito in 1860. The next fifteen years in the Republic of the Equator was truly the "age of García Moreno." As dictator he forced acceptance by his country of his peculiar ideas on the subject of politico-ecclesiastical relationships. In brief he aimed at establishing a religious despotism in which the clergy should be supreme and the civil authority secondary thereto. The Ecuadorean State under García Moreno represented the nearest approach to a theocracy in the western world.

"The Church," said García Moreno, "should always march side by side with the civil power under conditions of real independence."[13] Therefore the Constitution of 1861, which reflected the political philosophy of the President, made a special effort to secure an exclusive position for the Catholic Church.[14] García Moreno represented all the forces of social conservatism under the tutelage of the Church. He believed that

11. Rebello, *op. cit.*, pp. 151-52; Richard Pattee, *Gabriel García Moreno y el Ecuador de su tiempo* (Quito, 1941), pp. 95-96.

12. Pattee, *op. cit.*, 101-4.

13. Rebello, *op. cit.*, p. 179.

14. Berthe, *op. cit.*, p. 297.

the Roman Catholic religion was the only national tradition in the republic, the only creative agent and instrument of unity. Faith and order were, in his estimation, inseparably linked, but the Church could only function successfully if it were free of all official tutelage. Therefore he negotiated a concordat with the papacy which authorized exceptional privileges for the Church.

Late in 1861 Ignacio Ordoñez, Archdeacon of Cuenca, was sent on mission to France to secure religious of both sexes for the primary schools. From France he was ordered to proceed to Rome to negotiate a concordat. In his instructions to Ordoñez, the President wrote, "I wish complete liberty for the church, and comprehensive reform of the secular and regular clergy." After six months of discussion the Concordat was signed, September 26, 1862, by Cardinal Antonelli and Ignacio Ordoñez. Pope Pius IX sent an apostolic delegate to Quito to exchange ratifications. García Moreno expressed satisfaction with all terms of the Concordat, but was disappointed to note that it contained nothing regarding the reform of the clergy which he had solicited. He therefore sent Ordoñez back to Rome with instructions that the Concordat would be ratified only on condition that the pope agreed to the reform. The pope finally acquiesced and decided to send an apostolic delegate to Ecuador with full powers to institute reform measures. All obstacles having been removed, the Concordat was promulgated in Ecuador on April 22, 1863. In Quito a pontifical mass celebrated the event.[15]

The Concordat entered into by Pius IX and García Moreno conveyed to the Church in Ecuador greater privileges than it had enjoyed under the Spanish régime. Since this instrument is universally regarded as one of the most notable of modern times, the text is presented as follows:

Concordat between Pius IX and the Republic of Ecuador.

September 26, 1862.

In the name of the most holy and indivisible Trinity, His Holiness the Supreme Pontiff Pius IX and the President of the Republic of Ecuador name as their respective plenipotentiaries.

His Holiness, his eminence the Sig. Jacobo Antonelli, Cardinal of the Holy Roman Church, Deacon of Santa Agata de Suburra and Secretary of State and Foreign Relations.

And His Excellency the President of the Republic, the most excellent Señor Don Ignacio Ordoñez, Archdeacon of the Cathedral Church of Cuenca in the same republic and Minister Plenipotentiary near the Holy See.

15. *Ibid.*, pp. 318-24.

Who, after having exchanged their respective plenary powers, agree on the following articles:

Article 1. The Roman Catholic Apostolic religion will continue to be the only religion of the Republic of Ecuador, and it [the State] will always protect all the rights and prerogatives which it ought to enjoy according to the laws of God and canonical dispositions. Consequently there will never be permitted in Ecuador a dissident cult or any society condemned by the Church.

Article 2. In each one of the present dioceses, and in those which will be erected later, there will be a diocesan seminary whose direction, régime, and administration belong freely and exclusively to the diocesan ordinaries according to the dispositions of the Council of Trent and of the canonical laws. Rectors, professors, and others employed in the instruction and direction of said establishments will be freely nominated and removed by the ordinaries.

Article 3. The instruction of the youth in the Universities, colleges, faculties, and public and private schools will in all things conform to the doctrine of the Catholic religion. The bishops will have the exclusive right to designate texts for instruction in ecclesiastical sciences as well as in moral and religious instruction. In addition the bishops and the ordinaries will exercise freely the right to prohibit books contrary to religion and good customs, and to see that the government adopts proper measures to prevent the importation or dissemination of said books in the Republic.

Article 4. The bishops, in accordance with the duties of their pastoral ministry, will take care that there shall be no instruction contrary to the Catholic religion and proper customs. With this aim no one can instruct in any public or private institution in the subjects of theology, catechism, or religious doctrine without having obtained the authorization of the diocesan prelate, who can revoke the permit if he deems it opportune. For the examinations (of teachers) in the primary institutions the diocesan will always name an assistant to examine in religious and moral instruction. He cannot assume the discharge of this duty without the consent of the said diocesan.

Article 5. Since by divine right the primacy of honor and jurisdiction in the Universal Church belongs to the Roman Pontiff, all bishops, as well as clergy and the faithful, will have free communication with the Holy See. Consequently no secular authority can place obstacles in the way of the full and free exercise of this right of communication by obliging the bishops, clergy, and people to submit to the government as an intermediary in their communications with the Roman See, or by subjecting bulls, briefs, and rescripts to the exequatur of the government.

Article 6. The ecclesiastical ordinaries of the Republic can govern their dioceses with full liberty, convoke and celebrate provincial and diocesan councils, and exercise the rights which belong to them by virtue of their sacred ministry and current canonical provisions approved by the Holy See, without being interfered with in the performance of their duties. Thus the government of Ecuador will dispense with its patronal power, and will assist the bishops when solicited, particularly when they are confronted with the evil works of those people who seek to pervert the spirit of the faithful and corrupt their customs.

Article 7. Appeals to the civil power (*recursos de fuerza*) are abolished, and sentences pronounced by the ordinary ecclesiastical judges can only be appealed to the superior ecclesiastical tribunals or to the Holy See, according to the discipline established by the brief *Exposcit* of the Supreme Pontiff Gregory XIII, and likewise by canonical prescriptions. Matrimonial causes in particular must conform to the prescriptions of the constitution *Dei Miseratione* of Pope Benedict XIV.... The ecclesiastical judges will pronounce their judgments, without submitting them to the prior opinion of the secular assessors, to whom nevertheless they can go for advice when they deem it opportune. The ecclesiastics who are lawyers can discharge the office of assessor in this kind of judgment.

Article 8. All ecclesiastical causes and especially those relating to faith, the sacraments (which includes matrimonial causes), customs, holy functions, sacred rights and duties whether by reason of persons or subject, excepting the major causes reserved for the Holy Pontiff . . . will be heard in the ecclesiastical tribunals. The same will be tried as civil causes of ecclesiastics, and other matters included in the penal code of the Republic will be tried as crimes. To all ecclesiastical judgments the civil authorities will lend aid and protection, so that the judges can enforce the execution of penalties and sentences pronounced by them.

Article 9. The Holy See consents that persons as well as ecclesiastical properties shall be subject to the public imposts on a par with persons and properties of other citizens. The civil authority should enter into an agreement with the ecclesiastical to obtain the corresponding authorization whenever coaction is necessary. Excepted from said imposts are seminaries, properties and things immediately destined for the cult, and charitable institutions.

Article 10. Out of respect for the majesty of God who is the King of Kings and Lord of Lords, the immunity of churches will be respected in so far as public security and the exigencies of justice permit. In such event the Holy See consents that the ecclesiastical authority, the parish priests, and prelates of the regular houses, permit the extraction of refugees on the request of the civil authorities.

Article 11. Since the income from the tithes is devoted to the support of the divine cult and its ministers, the government of Ecuador is obliged to maintain Catholic instruction in the Republic, and His Holiness consents that the government continue to receive a third part of the tithes. For the collection and administration of the tithes the two authorities, civil and ecclesiastical, will enter into an agreement.

Article 12. By virtue of the right of patronage which the Supreme Pontiff concedes to the President of Ecuador, the latter can propose for archbishops and bishops clerics, qualified in the sense of the sacred canons. Thus, immediately after an episcopal vacancy appears, the archbishop will ask the other bishops for their votes for the filling of the vacancy; if the vacancy happens to be that of the archbishop, the senior bishop will order the votes, and will present a list of three candidates to the President who will select one of these, and will propose it to the Supreme Pontiff so that he might confer canonical institution in the form prescribed by the sacred canons. In case the bishops fail to make the presentation within six months, for any cause whatever, the President of Ecuador may do it himself, and if he does not act within three months, the right of election is reserved to the Holy See, just as if it had been solicited. To facilitate this action, the government, or the ecclesiastical authority in the event of its failure to act, will notify His Holiness immediately after the designated time has elapsed. But those proposed cannot under any circumstance enter upon the performance of their duties and the administration of churches, without first receiving the bulls of canonical institution. In the erection of new bishoprics the President of the Republic will propose directly for the first time the new bishops to the Holy See.

Article 13. In the same manner His Holiness concedes to the President of the Republic the right of naming qualified ecclesiastics for prebends, dignities, and canons....

Article 14. Regarding the provision of parochial benefices, the ordinaries, complying with the prescriptions of the Holy Council of Trent, will send to the government a list of qualified ecclesiastics upon whom the parish can be conferred; and the President will directly by himself, or by means of his delegates in the provinces, elect one of them.... If it is necessary to make territorial divisions in the parishes this can be done in agreement with the ordinary and the local civil authority.

Article 15. When a vacancy occurs in an episcopal church the chapter will freely elect the capitular vicar in the time and form prescribed by the Council of Trent....

Article 16. The Holy See, in the exercise of its proper jurisdiction, will erect new dioceses and will establish new limits in those now in existence. Considering the too vast extent of the present dioceses in the Republic, as soon as this concordat is ratified, there will be conceded to a special delegate the necessary powers to proceed with the aid of the government and the respective bishops to the territorial delimitation of the dioceses that can be conveniently established, and to fix the grants and income of the church, bishops, chapters, and seminary.

Article 17. The executive decree of May 28, 1836, concerning the redemption of mortgages held in favor of pious causes remains abolished in Ecuador. The Holy See, in view of the benefits derived from the present concordat, and desirous of providing for the public tranquility, in order to remedy the evils caused by the transfer of the mortgages held by the Ecuadorean Church to the national treasury, accedes to the reiterated requests of the President; and hereby decrees and declares that those who, from the year 1836 until the present promoted such transfer, as well as the possessors of the said redeemed funds and those who by any means acquired possession of same, will not be subjected at any time or in any manner, to the slightest molestation on the part of His Holiness or of the Roman Pontiffs his successors.

Article 18. Regarding the obligations contracted by the government with its creditors on account of the transferred mortgages, the Holy See consents that by paying a tenth part to the treasury, both of the transferred capital, as well as of the suppressed rents, the government can be free of all responsibility. As security for the payment of this amount, the government assigns a fourth part of the third which it derives from the tithes, which will be put in the hands of the ordinaries so that they may be divided by them in proportional parts in favor of their legitimate creditors, taking care that the principal will be capitalized in a secure and profitable manner....

Article 19. The Church will enjoy the right to acquire property freely and by any just title, and the properties now in its possession or acquired later will be guaranteed by law. The administration of ecclesiastical properties belongs to the persons designated by the sacred canons, who alone will examine the accounts and economic regulations. The property of ecclesiastical foundations of any kind, such as hospitals and other charitable institutions, which are not administered by the ecclesiastical authority, will be transferred to it, so that it can immediately make the proper investments. Regarding the old and new ecclesiastical foundations, none can be suppressed or combined without the intervention of the authority of the Holy See, excepting the right which belongs to the bishops according to the Holy Council of Trent.

Article 20. In addition to the orders and religious congregations which now exist in the Republic of Ecuador, the diocesan ordinaries can freely and without exception admit and establish in their respective dioceses new orders or institutes approved by the Church in conformity with the necessities of the people. To facilitate this the government will lend its aid.

Article 21. After the divine offices in all the churches of the Republic of Ecuador, the following prayer will be said: *Domine salvam fac Rempublicam; Domine salvam fac Praesidium ejus.*

Article 22. The government of the Republic of Ecuador is obligated to employ all proper measures for the propagation of the faith and for the conversion of people found in that territory; and in addition, to lend all favor and aid to the establishment and progress of the holy missions, which with laudable purpose, have been undertaken under the authority of the Sacred Congregation of Propaganda.

Article 23. All other things which pertain to ecclesiastical persons and things, and concerning which nothing is provided in the articles of the present concordat, will be directed and administered according to the present canonical discipline of the Church, approved by the Holy See.

Article 24. By virtue of this concordat all contrary laws and decrees published up to the present in any manner and form in Ecuador are revoked; and the same concordat ought always to be considered as a law of the State. Therefore, each one of the contracting parties promises for himself, and for his successors, the faithful observance of all and each one of the articles which it contains. If any difficulty arises at a future date, the Holy Father and the President of Ecuador agree to settle it in an amicable manner.

Article 25. The ratification of the present concordat will take place within a year, or sooner if possible. In pledge of which the undersigned plenipotentiaries sign and seal the present convention with their respective seals.

Given in Rome on September 26, 1862.

> Jacobus Cardinal Antonelli.
> Ignacio Ordoñez.[16]

By the Concordat Ecuador definitely abandoned to the Holy See national pretentions to the exercise of the ecclesiastical patronage. Although the instrument recognized in the Catholic Church in Ecuador exceptional rights and privileges, it was not unique in this respect by any means. In fact, it was, with a few exceptions, a recapitulation of the concordats entered into by Pope Pius IX and the republics of Costa Rica and Guatemala, both on October 17, 1852. These concordats were, in a

16. *Raccolta di Concordati*, pp. 983-95. For a summary of the articles, see Larrea, *op. cit.*, pp. 34-35.

way, models for subsequent Latin-American concordats. They represented the maximum concessions the papacy was willing to make to national claims over the Church.[17] Within and without the Republic of Ecuador great dissatisfaction was expressed toward the Concordat. Liberals and Radicals determined to destroy it and several attempts were made in the Congress to modify it by law, but none of these succeeded because of the dominating influence of the President. Externally, throughout South America the Concordat was denounced as treason to South American independence, for it was claimed that by the agreement Ecuador was converted into a fief of Rome. President Mosquera of Colombia invited the Ecuadoreans to overthrow their President, and in 1863, he undertook an invasion "to liberate the brother democrats of Ecuador from the theocratic yoke of Professor Moreno." This outside interference tended, however, to strengthen the hold of the dictator who continued to bestow more and more power and privileges upon the Church.[18]

Education, as was stipulated in the Concordat, was placed under the complete control of the clergy. García Moreno, intensely interested in education, had a law passed providing for a public school system, and instruction in the schools was divided among the religious orders. Because of a dearth of competent native teaching material, foreign teaching orders were introduced, particularly from France. Since García Moreno wished to reorganize higher education on a solid base, he sought the aid of the Jesuits. The Congress consequently authorized the Jesuits to establish institutions of learning in Ecuador, with full and entire liberty to employ their traditional educational methods. The Jesuits, inured to reverses in the school of experience, stipulated in the agreement with the government, which allowed for their return to Ecuador, that "in the event altogether improbable, that the government suppresses the Company of Jesus, the members of the Society will not be deported or dispersed except after the lapse of eight months after the day of suppression. They will enjoy during this time all the constitutional and legal guarantees to arrange for their voyage and dispose of their property."[19]

The reform of the clergy, demanded by García Moreno as a prerequisite to the ratification of the Concordat, was undertaken in good faith by the pope. The papal delegate assigned to supervise this work was vigorously supported by the President. The regulars, however, presented real difficulties, and much still remained to be done when García

17. For the concordats of October 7, 1852, with Costa Rica and Guatemala, see *Raccolta di Concordati*, pp. 800-21.

18. Berthe, *op. cit.*, pp. 376-77, 393.

19. *Ibid.*, p. 583.

Moreno's term of office expired in 1865. In consequence of the Concordat, four new bishoprics were created in Ecuador. They were Cuenca, Loja, Riobamba, and Ibarra.[20]

At the expiration of his four-year term of office García Moreno gave way to another man who was expected to be his puppet. The new president, however, was quickly pushed aside, and during the absence of García Moreno in Europe on a diplomatic mission, the Radicals gained control of the government. For a brief period ensued a bitter anticlerical reaction. The execution of the Concordat was suspended and the law of patronage was restored. In vain the apostolic delegate protested and the followers of García Moreno charged the government with betrayal. Fortunately for the Church, García Moreno returned to power in January, 1869. Then for the next six years Ecuador was taken further than ever on the road to theocracy.[21]

Since García Moreno wished to increase the powers of the president he summoned a constituent convention "composed of Conservatives and good Catholics." His project for a new constitution was adopted without modification (1869). The new frame of government, which was made to conform to the principles of the *Syllabus*, was as strongly impregnated with theocracy as if it had issued from the Vatican. "The Roman Catholic religion," stipulated Article 1, "is declared to be the religion of the State, to the exclusion of any other, and it remains in possession of its inalienable rights and prerogatives which are invested in it by divine law, and canonical prescriptions; the public powers are obligated to aid and make it respected." Being a Catholic was made a requisite for citizenship, and whoever belonged to a sect condemned by the Church lost his civil rights (Article 3). Since it was impossible to keep heretics out of the country, García Moreno hoped that by depriving them of civil rights they would be discouraged from coming. The Constitution also guaranteed the right of ecclesiastics to be tried in Church courts in all civil causes except those of a financial and political character. Ecclesiastical judges in civil cases were to be guided by the civil law.[22] When García Moreno assumed the presidency under the new Constitution he swore the following oath: "I swear by God Our Lord, and by the Holy Gospel, to perform faithfully my duty as president of this republic, to profess the Roman Catholic Apostolic religion; to preserve the integrity and independence of the State; to observe and enforce the observance of this Constitution and the laws. If I am successful it is because God is my support and my defence; if not, then God

20. *Ibid.*, pp. 331-33; Rebello, *op. cit.*, p. 185.
21. Berthe, *op. cit.*, pp. 468-69, 509.
22. Rebello, *op. cit.*, pp. 200-1; Berthe, *op. cit.*, pp. 538-40.

and the *patria* will be my judges." Religion and *patria* were the dominant passions in the life of García Moreno.[23]

The governmental program of García Moreno, following the adoption of the Constitution of 1869, "read like an episcopal address." The following statements were uttered by him during this period: "Civilization, which is built on Catholicism, degenerates and debases in measure as it departs from Catholic principles," and "Religion is the sole bond which is left to us in this country, divided as it is by the interests of parties, races, and beliefs." His program was, he said: "the respect and protection of the Catholic Church, unshakable attachment to the Holy See, education based on morality and faith, and liberty for all and in everything, excepting crime and criminals."

The reform of the clergy, the preoccupation of García Moreno in his first administration, had languished during the Radical régime because of the abolition of the ecclesiastical tribunals. After the inauguration of his second term, the President appealed once more to the pope to send another delegate to resume the work of reform of the regular orders with the support and coöperation of the government and the episcopate. Pleased with the zeal of the President, the pope hastened to acquiesce. Under the impulse of García Moreno a number of provincial councils were convened to consider the reform of ecclesiastical discipline. One of the principal achievements of the provincial councils was a complete revamping of seminary curricula and discipline.[24]

The welfare of the faith outside of Ecuador was also a matter of deep concern to García Moreno, for he intervened in the domestic affairs of Colombia when a radical government was assaulting the Church. He eulogized Maximilian as the deliverer of Mexico from the "excesses of a rapacious, immoral, and turbulent demagogy." He protested to Victor Emmanuel against the taking of Rome and the absorption of the Papal States into the Kingdom of Italy. Congress was induced to make a gift of 52,000 francs to "the Prisoner of the Vatican." Finally, in 1873, in mystic ardor, García Moreno, by official decree, consecrated Ecuador to the Sacred Heart of Jesus.[25]

On August 6, 1875, President García Moreno, a religious fanatic perhaps, but nevertheless a great benefactor of Ecuador, fell in the public square of Quito at the hands of assassins. Since the assassination was thought to be a Masonic plot, the murdered president was decreed by Congress the name of "Regenerator of the *patria* and martyr of Catholic

23. Berthe, *op. cit.*, p. 529. For the Constitution of 1869, see Pattee, *op. cit.*, pp. 345-54.

24. Berthe, *op. cit.*, p. 559.

25. García Calderón, *op. cit.*, pp. 218-19; Berthe, *op. cit.*, pp. 672, 684, 691.

civilization." The Congress also ordered a statue erected with this inscription, "To the most excellent García Moreno, Ecuador's greatest son, died for religion and the *patria*." Catholics throughout the world recognized in the death of García Moreno the loss of a zealous champion of the Church. Pope Pius IX, a prisoner in the Vatican, expressed sincere sorrow over the death of a faithful son of the Church.[26] The Peruvian litterateur and publicist, Francisco García Calderón, wrote the following estimate of García Moreno: "Indefatigable, stoical, strong in decision, admirably logical in his life, García Moreno is one of the great individuals of American history. He was not a tyrant like Guzmán Blanco or Porfirio Díaz. For fifteen years, from 1859 to 1874, he completely transformed his little country in accord with a vast plan which only his death prevented from realization. Mystic in the Spanish manner, he was never satisfied with sterile contemplation; he felt the necessity of action to be an organizer and creator."[27]

After the death of García Moreno, the Congress of Ecuador sent an address to Pope Pius IX, announcing their allegiance to the Catholic principles of the martyred president. The clericals were aggressively anxious to retain as many as possible of the privileges gained during the ascendancy of "the Catholic President." But the old forces of clericalism and conservatism, without the guiding genius of García Moreno, soon aroused a powerful opposition. The Liberals and Radicals were successful, in 1877, in forcing the deposition and exile of President Borrero, "whose absurd policy," said General Ignacio Veintemilla, leader of the Radicals, "perpetuates institutions incompatible with democratic government."[28] The seizure of the presidency by General Veintemilla ushered in a short but turbulent period of anticlerical reform.

One of the first acts of the new government was to suspend the Concordat in June, 1877, as being contrary to national sovereignty. The law of patronage was restored. These acts provoked a clerical revolt, and the bishop of Riobamba went so far as to threaten excommunication of all those who refused to recognize the Concordat. Veintemilla countered with a decree which provided that all rebel prelates would be deprived of their ecclesiastical revenues. After fifteen months of dictatorship, Veintemilla convened a constituent convention to fabricate the ninth of Ecuador's constitutions. On the religious question it was suggested that the old article providing: "The Catholic religion is that

26. Berthe, *op. cit.*, pp. 63, 82, 745-46.

27. Francisco García Calderón, *Democracías Latinas de América*, quoted by Rebeilo, *op. cit.*, p. 92.

28. Berthe, *op. cit.*, p. 776; Carlos Vila Monsalve, "Relaciones entre la iglesia y el estado ecuatoriano," *Latino-America* (Mexico), Vol. 2, No. 22 (October 1, 1950), 445.

of the State to the exclusion of all others," be suppressed. But the proposal was defeated on the ground that, "The government protects the actual status which is religious unity." On the other hand an attempt of the moderates to restore the Concordat was defeated. However, in 1882, when Veintemilla's grip was weakening, to conciliate the Conservatives, he received the papal nuncio and declared his intention to defend the Holy Catholic faith. As proof of his sincerity he restored the Concordat. But these measures were satisfactory neither to the Conservatives nor the Liberals, for a temporary union of these elements accomplished the overthrow of the dictator.[29]

Again the pendulum swung to the other extreme. Once more the clericals came into power, for President José Camaño, the successor of Veintemilla, formed an intimate alliance with the clergy and the old partisans of García Moreno. On May 2, 1881, a new concordat was negotiated, substantially the same as that of 1862, with the exception that the jurisdiction of the ecclesiastical courts was somewhat restricted.[30] Once more the republic was dedicated to the Sacred Heart of Jesus, and it was decreed that a national temple should be erected and dedicated to the Sacred Heart as a perpetual monument of gratitude to God. The decree had to be ratified by the constituent convention which had just been convened to frame a constitution satisfactory to the Conservatives. The proposal to erect a national temple was approved despite the objections of some members that Quito had too many churches and could spend the money to better advantage on the Indian missions.[31]

On November 18, 1890, a special concordat was negotiated with the papacy. Its purpose was to provide a substitute for the tithes. It was agreed that in lieu of the tithes the Church should receive thirty cents per year on each hundred *sucres* collected on rural lands. This tax was to except holdings of a value not in excess of one hundred *sucres*, buildings used for residence purposes, and cacao plantations. Also, property belonging to the Church was exempt from the tax.[32]

It was stated in a bulletin published by the Bureau of American Republics in 1892, that the relations between Church and State in Ecuador had been settled satisfactorily to both parties. This optimistic declaration was soon proved to be unfounded in fact for, by 1897, another anticlerical régime was established, which, excepting minor fluctuations of control, is still dominant in the Republic of Ecuador. The Liberals

---

29. Berthe, *op. cit.*, pp. 784-93; Juan Montalvo, *Las Catilinarias* (Paris, 1925), I, 41.
30. *Raccolta di Concordati*, pp. 1001-13.
31. Berthe, *op. cit.*, pp. 794, 797; Pedro Fermin Cevallos, *Resumen de la Historia del Ecuador* (Guayaquil, 1889), p. 27; C. R. Enock, *Ecuador* (London, 1914), p. 82.
32. *Raccolta di Concordati*, pp. 1079-85.

under General Eloy Alfaro, an anticlerical who hated the corrupt and retrograde priestcraft, seized the government in 1897 and proceeded to purge Ecuador of clericalism. The reform movement was inaugurated with moderation as evidenced by the fact that the new Constitution of 1897 contained the traditional clause providing that Roman Catholicism should be the State religion to the exclusion of all other forms of religious worship. But, because of a Conservative and clerical movement against his government, President Alfaro was driven to more extreme measures against the Church. A law of patronage enacted September 11, 1899, violated numerous provisions of the Concordat; for example: (1) papal legates should not exercise jurisdiction in the Republic without the consent of the Council of State; (2) bulls and rescripts could not be published without the approval of the president; (3) revenues for the support of the Church should be raised by the State alone; (4) Congress should have the power (a) to create new parishes and determine the number of priests in cathedral churches, (b) elect archbishops and bishops, who must be native-born Ecuadoreans, and whose names should be presented to the Apostolic See by the president, (c) permit the meeting of Church councils; (5) only citizens of Ecuador should have the right to act as curates; and (6) no new religious orders should be established in the Republic.[33] These violations of the terms of the Concordat, unrecognized by the papacy, really terminated that agreement. After 1900, therefore, there was no concordat between Ecuador and the Vatican, and diplomatic relations were discontinued. Though the Catholic Church remained the State religion, it was made dependent on the civil authorities to an extreme degree.

The anticlerical policy inaugurated by Alfaro was continued by President Plaza Gutiérrez (1901-05) who effected a veritable social revolution. In 1904 a law was passed guaranteeing religious toleration and protection to ministers of dissident faiths. The establishment of new convents and monasteries was prohibited and rural land held in the dead hands of the Church was nationalized and let to the highest bidders. Another law signed by President Plaza Gutiérrez permitted civil marriage and divorce. According to this measure and subsequent modifications of it absolute divorce must be by mutual consent, but separation can be secured for cruelty, desertion, or adultery. The civil marriage is the only legal form recognized by the government.[34]

The measures of Alfaro and Plaza Gutiérrez have been characterized as "the inevitable reaction from the dogmas and oppression of papistry."

33. John Lee, *Religious Liberty in South America* (New York, 1907), pp. 234 ff.
34. Monsalve, *op. cit.*, p. 445.

But Latin-American people cannot hastily materialize their ideals without serious injury to their social state, and since the great majority of the people belong to the Catholic faith, the excessive zeal of the reformers caused the Conservatives to rush once more to the defense of religion. The Conservatives gained control of the government in 1905, but their triumph was short-lived, for the anticlerical forces were too strong. Ex-president Alfaro emerged from retirement, and in defense of "democracy and liberal principles of government," not to mention "constitutionality," ousted the Conservative incumbent and seized the reins of government—as "Supreme Dictator."[35]

In 1906 President Alfaro proclaimed a new constitution. This instrument which set a new pattern of relationship between Church and State guaranteed "liberty of conscience in all its aspects and manifestations, provided that these be not contrary to morality and public order." By this act, coupled with the unofficial nullification of the Law of Patronage of 1899,[36] Church and State were separated in Ecuador. The burdensome infringements upon the Church's freedom of action evident in the Constitution of 1897 were not contained in the Constitution of 1906. The Church henceforth could communicate with the Vatican through the papal delegate in Lima. The clericals, however, were dissatisfied with separation, which was regarded as tantamount to the creation of an irreligious state. Supported by the Conservatives the hierarchy branded Liberalism as anti-Catholic and sought a return to the undemocratic principles of García Moreno.[37]

It was a tenuous formula of separation which emerged in 1906. "Because of the shortsightedness of a nonaccommodating Church and the hasty measures enacted by fear-stricken Liberals, the possibility lessened of achieving real religious toleration and separation in an atmosphere of good will."[38] Eventually, in the decade of the 1930's, such an atmosphere developed and facilitated cordial accommodation between Church and State.

Because of public agitation resulting from a number of anti-Church acts of the Liberal Reform, particularly those relating to public instruction and the expropriation of ecclesiastical properties, President Paez asked the Holy See to send a representative to Quito to negotiate an understanding. Two pacts were signed on July 24, 1937, a *Modus Vi-*

---

35. Enock, *op. cit.*, pp. 85-86.

36. Pope Pius X nominated Bishop Feduco González Suárez, Archbishop of Quito, but President Alfaro refused to recognize the Archbishop's appointment. He tried unsuccessfully to invoke the Law of Patronage of 1899, which thereafter fell into disuse. Robert W. Bialek, *Catholic Politics: A History Based on Ecuador* (New York, 1963), p. 72.

37. *Ibid.*, pp. 74-77, 82.

38. *Ibid.*, p. 86.

vendi and a *Convención Adicional.* They reëstablished diplomatic relations, interrupted for almost half a century, and fixed the bases for a regime of understanding and collaboration.

According to the terms of the *Modus Vivendi*:[39] (1) the Equadorean government guaranteed to the Catholic Church the free exercise of its proper activities; (2) the government also guaranteed freedom of education and the right of the Church to establish an educational system; (3) the State and Church pledged their united efforts in missionary activities in the Oriente; (4) the Holy See warned clerics to abstain from political action; (5) the Church was granted juridic personality; (6) diplomatic representatives were to be exchanged, and the papal nuncio at Quito was to be dean of the diplomatic corps; and (7) the Holy See would communicate to the government of Ecuador the names of those elected to become bishops in order to avoid the naming of anyone not acceptable to the State for political reasons.

The supplementary convention provided that: (1) the proscribed "political action" mentioned in Article 4 limited the right of the clergy "to preach, expose, and defend the dogmatic and moral Catholic doctrine," (2) ecclesiastical publications and papal and episcopal documents, "not including political matters," can be freely published and circulated; and (3) for the individual pensions which the regular clergy had been receiving since 1908 because of the nationalization of their properties, there was substituted a lump payment of 1,500,000 sucres. In return for this sum the Vatican disclaimed further interest in the ecclesiastical properties nationalized during the Liberal Revolution.

The *Modus Vivendi* was a long step in working out a reconciliation between Church and State. More important than the settlement of the expropriation problem was the grant of juridic personality. This meant among other things that the Church could now hold property. By way of gifts and widows' bequests, the Church began to reacquire property holdings. Today the Church of Ecuador should be rated as wealthy.

The current constitution of Ecuador, adopted in 1946, contains just one article (Art. 168) dealing with religion. It guarantees freedom of conscience and provides that the "law shall make no discrimination for religious, ideological or racial reasons." This constitution restored "in the name of God" to the preamble. For half a century after Alfaro no mention was made of God in any of the constitutions. In 1951 an unsuccessful attempt to eliminate God provoked considerable discussion. To many of the Liberals the mere mention of God in the constitution put in jeopardy the separation of Church and State. They reasoned that

---

39. For text, see Larrea, *op. cit.,* pp. 153-57.

the reference to God means to all Conservatives nothing more nor less than the equivalent: "The Catholic God is the God of the Ecuadorean State," for so thoroughly has religion in Ecuador been identified with the Catholic Church.

The Church, which once enjoyed a monopoly of all education in Ecuador, has been forced to witness the establishment of universal, public, secular education. "The State as such," according to Constitutional Article 171, "neither teaches nor attacks any religion." No religious instruction is given in the public schools. The great inadequacy of the public school system is evidenced by Ecuador's excessively high illiteracy rate of 43.7 per cent of the population over ten years of age.[40]

Since the Constitution of 1906, and all succeeding constitutions, did not prevent the Church from maintaining an educational system of its own, it took full advantage of this liberty. Ultimately there were numerous primary schools in Ecuador conducted by the Church (estimated at 15 per cent of the number of public schools) and supported by tuition fees.[41] These schools conform their course programs to the terms of the law of public instruction. The government does not assist in the support of confessional schools.

Ecuadorean parents seem to prefer, despite conflicting ideologies, the confessional schools to the lay. The head of a *colegio* in Quito told the author, "In this school, men from all parties—Freemasons, Communists, Conservatives, Liberals—have their daughters receive their education." The same people who give a Catholic education to their children are the ones who fight and cry in Congress against religion.

The failure of the Constitution to mention Catholicism as the State religion is not to be taken to mean that there is an absolute separation of Church and State. The terms of the *Modus Vivendi* evidence the contrary. Also, the government is inextricably involved in ecclesiastical relationships because of its nationalization of Church properties. Title to Church buildings, schools, and dwellings is vested in the State, which turns them over to the Catholic Church and its ministers for use. Certain churches and ecclesiastical localities have been declared by the State to be "monuments of art." They are under the control of diocesan commissions in which the government has representation.[42] The ministry entrusted with religious matters is the *Ministerio de Gobierno, Policía, Municipalidades, y Cultos.*

40. *Statistical Abstract of Latin America, 1963*, Center of Latin American Studies, University of California (Los Angeles, 1964), p. 25.
41. Lilo Linke, *Ecuador* (London and New York, 1954), p. 98.
42. Article VIII of the *Modus Vivendi.*

Since the 1937 agreement with the Vatican, Church officials have—
nominally at least—been forbidden to participate directly in political
matters. On a number of occasions clerics have been accused of violating
this mandate, as for example, when, in 1951 the Archbishop of Quito
issued a pastoral letter reminding parents that it was forbidden to send
their children to non-Catholic (i.e. Protestant) schools, and in 1960
the Archbishop of Cuenca threatened his parishioners with excommunication if they voted for Galo Plaza whom the Archbishop termed a
Marxist and an atheist. Although the first instance was a doubtful
case of political intervention, this was not true of the second which was
a false accusation.[43] To circumvent the injunction to refrain from
political activity, the clergy have had ardent advocates not only in the
Conservative party, but also the falangist-inspired Acción Revolucionaría
Nacional Ecuatoriana (ARNE), and the Christian Democratic equivalent in Ecuador, the Movimiento Social Cristiano (MSC).[44]

Unlike most other Latin-American countries, there is no scarcity of
priests in Ecuador. At least there are more vocations for the orders
than can be "handled."[45] The clergy is almost exclusively a sierra
product. The sole seminary at Quito receives almost no recruits from
the coast, which is the stronghold of the Liberals. With the exception
of the missions only the national clergy are permitted by law. When
the law was evaded by the entry of foreign priests, the Liberals demanded that Protestants be allowed to enter also.

The efforts of foreign priests and religious orders (e.g. the Maryknoll Fathers), who seek to reform the clergy and make it more social
minded, have frequently been frustrated by the local priesthood who
want no foreign interference. Although there is considerable educational
and missionary activity carried on by the Church, the clergy have been
tardy in developing a social consciousness. There are some interesting
exceptions, however, for in some of the dioceses, such as Riobamba and
Ibarra, programs have been inaugurated by the bishops frankly aimed at
improving the living standards of the peasant families. Much work of
this nature needs to be done to correct the harsh criticism of the rural
clergy as ignorant, fanatical, and profiteers at the expense of their flocks.

Protestant missionaries first came to Ecuador soon after the Liberals
took over power in 1895, but over the years they have made comparatively little headway. Incidents between Protestants and Catholics,

---

43. *Hispanic American Report*, XIII, No. 4 (April, 1960), p. 260.

44. *Ibid.*, XV, No. 3 (March, 1962), p. 248.

45. Father Nevins (*op. cit.*, p. 67) says that a majority of the rural population is
being lost to the Church "because of the lack of priests." It is not a general lack of
priests, but a lack in the rural areas.

often provoked by antagonistic Catholic clerics, and once rather common, have become quite rare in recent years. When they do occur the government conscientiously attempts to support the constitutional guarantees and afford police protection. Despite the activities of both Catholic and Protestant missionaries, the great body of the Indians is not being reached.[46]

Protestantism certainly is not a threat to the Catholic Church in Ecuador. Nor is there today much anticlericalism in the country. The legal status of the Church is no longer a prime issue. This does not mean, however, that the prospect of further attacks on the Church-State relationship can be dismissed. Ecuadorean Liberals, ever suspicious of clerical pretensions, do not reject the possibility of a "union of Church and State and all that such a union implies."[47] Perhaps Ecuador has not outlived the Church-State conflict.

46. Nevins, *op. cit.*, p. 67.
47. Bialek, *op. cit.*, p. 93.

Chapter VII

The State-Church of Peru

That the Catholic Church is the State ecclesiastical establishment of Peru admits of no question, for, indeed, the system of interdependence of State and Church is one of the most comprehensive and absolute in Latin America. Furthermore, this ecclesiastical policy has been maintained with little or no change throughout the years. The relations between the government of Peru and the Roman Catholic Church have been both intimate and friendly from independence to the present time. Despite the fact that the Peruvian colonial background (political, economic, and ethnical) was very similar to that of Mexico, it is remarkable that the histories of the Church in the two countries have been so different. In contrast with Mexico's turbulent religious history, relations between Peru and the Vatican, once established in 1835, when the first republican archbishop was appointed, have never been interrupted and a formal *modus vivendi* amounting practically to a concordat has been established between the two authorities. The Peruvian governments have been almost uniformly friendly to the Church, the Church has never been a serious political issue, and, finally, no anticlerical campaign in Peru has gained much headway.

In Peru, as in other parts of colonial Spanish America, there existed a perfect coöperation between the religious hierarchy and the political autocracy. Since, with the exception of an abortive revolt in Cuzco in 1814, Peru was untouched by the wars for independence until invaded by the armies of San Martín and Bolívar, this alliance continued without impairment until 1821. The Church of Peru as an organized body remained loyal to the Spanish cause as long as there was any hope of its success. The hierarchy, while it existed, worked energetically for the old régime, and consequently many of the bishops were forced to abandon their sees in the face of the oncoming patriot armies. Although Archbishop Las Heras of Lima remained at his post after the advent of San Martín and even signed the declaration of independence, he and the bishop of Huamanga were expelled from the country because of their opposition to the provisional government's action in limiting the freedom which the Church had previously enjoyed.[1]

The severance of Spanish control and the interruption of papal relations contributed to the dismemberment of the hierarchy, and consequently the lower clergy were left very much to their own devices. Most of them, being natives of Peru, and often mestizos, were favorable towards independence, and the absence of hierarchial restraint afforded opportunity of which they were prompt to take advantage. Conspicuous among the pro-independence clerics was Luna Pizarro, a native of Arequipa and occupant of high positions in educational institutions and in the cathedral of Lima. Luna Pizarro was strongly imbued with the philosophy of the French Revolution.[2]

On February 12, 1821, General San Martín, shortly after his invasion of Peru, issued a *reglamento provisional*, based on his authority as "Protector" of the country. In this provisional instrument he declared that the right of national patronage was assumed by the independent government of Peru. Later, when the Protector occupied Lima, he issued an *estatuto provisional* for the governance of Peru until a permanent constitution should be adopted. The first section related to the Roman Catholic Church:

> The Apostolic Roman Catholic religion is the religion of the State; the government recognizes as one of its first duties that of maintaining and conserving it by all the means that are within the bounds of human prudence. Whoever attacks its doctrines and principles, either in public or in private, shall be severely punished in proportion to the scandal he may have caused.
>
> Others who profess the Christian religion but who dissent in some principles from the religion of the State may obtain permission from the government, with the consent of the Council of State, to make use of the right which may be theirs, provided their conduct is not prejudicial to public order.
>
> No one may hold public office who does not profess the religion of the State.[3]

San Martín, although a sincere and ardent communicant of the Catholic faith, was not religiously uncompromising, as is evidenced by the fact that he was willing to concede a limited degree of religious free-

---

1. Pérez Armendaris, Bishop of Cuzco (1809-19), openly favored the revolutionary movement of 1814 in his diocese. Francis Merriman Stanger, "Church and State in Peru," in *The Hispanic American Historical Review*, VII, No. 4 (November, 1927), p. 420.

2. *Ibid.*

3. *Ibid.*, p. 421; Juan F. Olivo, *Constituciones del Peru, 1821-1919* (Lima, 1922), p. 15.

dom. Also, when he learned that certain religious houses supported the royalist régime, he did not hesitate to suppress them, nor to expel the archbishop himself for expressions of opposition.[4]

In further evidence of San Martín's tolerance, he invited to Peru James Thomson, a Scottish Baptist minister, to undertake the direction of public instruction in the republic. Thomson had done good work setting up the Lancastrian school system in Argentina and Chile, and, in recognition of his services in the latter country he was conferred by special act the status of citizen. It is interesting to note that Thomson was enthusiastically supported in his educational work, and even in the distribution of the Bible, by Catholic priests. The lower clergy of Peru during this period were remarkably liberal and tolerant. In commenting on this tolerance, Thomson wrote several years later, after his departure from Peru, "The writer has traveled during some ten years over a great part of the new states of South America and Mexico, distributing Holy Scriptures in them in the freest and most open fashion without interruption or molestation."[5]

When, as a result of his famous interview with Simón Bolívar in Guayaquil, San Martín became convinced that no effective coöperation with the latter was possible, he decided to lay down his authority and withdraw from Peru. Accordingly, he convoked the first Peruvian Congress in Lima, and on September 20, 1822, surrendered his power as Protector into its hands. This assemblage of fifty-one delegates was composed of some twenty clerics, including the presiding officer Luna Pizarro. But, remarkably enough, the clerical members were the most liberal group in the Congress.[6]

The Congress when considering the formulation of a constitution was confronted with the problem of the legal status of religion in the State. At first it was proposed, and the proposal was supported by most of the clerical delegates, that the constitution should contain the simple clause: "The religion of the nation is the Roman Catholic." This, it was hoped, would leave the way open for religious liberty. Peru, however, was not ready for such a progressive step, for, although the proposal was approved by the Congress, on the following day (November 30, 1822), due to the presentation of a petition signed by a great number of the leading citizens of Lima, there was added to the clause: "with

4. Moses, *Background of Revolution in South America*, p. 81.

5. W. E. Browning, John Ritchie, and K. G. Grubb, *The West Coast Republics of South America* (London, 1930), p. 77.

6. Stanger, *op. cit.*, p. 421; P. Pruvonena, *Memorias y Documentos Para la Historia de la Independencia del Perú* (Paris, 1858), p. 115.

the exclusion of any other."[7]   Thus, in the Constitution of 1823 even the qualified toleration granted by the Protector came to an end.

The Constitution of 1823 did not conform with Bolívar's plan for the government of Peru.   Since the Liberator was not able to secure the acceptance of his *constitución vitalicia* until December, 1826, in the meantime he ruled without constitutional restraint as the "Supreme Political Chief of the Peruvian Nation."   During this period he was responsible for administrative regulations and reforms affecting the Church.   With the acquiescence of the ecclesiastical authorities he reduced the number of convents and dedicated their buildings and income to public use, particularly for hospitals and orphanages.   The Liberator displayed a particular solicitude for the poverty-stricken Indians, and their onerous payments to the clergy were substantially reduced.   To prevent further abuse he fixed a tariff of fees for religious services.   He also secured a reduction in the number of religious holidays.[8]

The regular orders seemed to be the particular object of Bolívar's attention since he suspected them of royalist sympathies.   Several monasteries were suppressed, and their properties confiscated and devoted to public education and charity.   In the future all regulars were to submit to diocesan authority.   Eight was established as the minimum number of inmates of a monastery, and minors were prohibited from taking the vows.[9]

The filling of ecclesiastical vacancies and the resumption of relations with Rome were other ecclesiastical problems attacked by the Liberator. By 1826 Bishop José Sebastián Goyeneche of Arequipa was the only remaining bishop in Peru.   Indeed, for a period, he was the only bishop from Ecuador to the Straits of Magellan.   Since for several years he was the sole authority for the ordination of priests, he was called "The Spiritual Father of America."   Bolívar attempted to solve the problem of filling vacancies in the prelacies by electing men who were ostensibly presented to the pope for consecration, but who, since there was no hope of securing papal institution, entered upon their official duties as bishops-elect.   This plan was so strenuously opposed by the clergy that it was applied for only a short time.   Bolívar was always hopeful that relations between Peru and the Roman Curia could be established and a concordat concluded.   Accordingly, when giving instructions to the

7. Guillermo U. Olaechea, *La Constitución del Peru* (Lima, 1922), p. xxiii; Olivo, *op. cit.*, pp. 27-70.
8. Daniel F. O'Leary, *Bolívar y la Emancipación de Sud-América* (Madrid, 1915), II, 419.
9. Stanger, *op. cit.*, p. 423; "Bolívar al Exmo. Señor Presidente del Consejo de Gobierno, D. J. Hipólito Unanué, Cuzco, 22 de julio de 1825," in *Cartas del Libertador*, V, 42.

Consejo de Gobierno preceding his departure for Bolivia, he advised that the diplomatic mission then being sent to Europe be also authorized to negotiate with the Holy See. However, no Peruvian agents ever reached Rome.[10]

The reforms of the Liberator in the ecclesiastical domain did not necessarily manifest an anticlerical attitude on his part any more than did the reform measures of San Martín. Bolívar was a firm believer in the efficacy of the Church as an aid to the political arm. He was a practical statesman and recognized the Church as a factor to be reckoned with. Accordingly, in his *constitución vitalicia* of 1826, which he proposed for Peru, Catholicism was made the religion of the State, but with no restrictions on other religions. He provided elaborate clauses for the control of the patronage by the national government.

Intense clerical opposition was aroused because of the reforms introduced by the Liberator in ecclesiastical matters. In the pulpit and in the confessional the policy of the government was branded as impious. Then the enemies of independence took advantage of the clerical discontent to intrigue for the royalist cause. In Arequipa, a hot-bed of royalism, the royalist party was headed by Bishop Goyeneche. Since he refused to heed Bolívar's entreaties to desist in his opposition, most of his authority was taken from him, although he was not removed from office. The dean of the cathedral, Dr. Córdoba, was authorized by the government to govern the diocese. This interference on the part of the civil authorities in making ecclesiastical appointments served to accentuate the opposition and Bolívar even lost the support of the National Liberal Party with Luna Pizarro at its head.[11] For religious and political reasons, the *constitución vitalicia* of Bolívar, containing the most liberal provisions on religion to appear in any Peruvian constitution until 1915, was put aside immediately after the retirement of the Liberator from Peru.

The third constitution of Peru (1828), framed after the withdrawal of Bolívar, contained the following article on religion: "The religion of the State is the Apostolic Roman Catholic; the nation protects it by all the means in keeping with the spirit of the Gospel, and will not permit the exercise of any other religion." It is to be observed that the prohibition was extended to the exercise of any dissident cult without distinguishing between public or private ceremonies. The same extreme intolerance was preserved in the next of Peru's numerous constitutions,

10. Stanger, *op. cit.*, p. 424; Leturia, *La Acción Diplomática*, p. 112; Sallusti, *Misiones Apostólicas*, p. 402; José Sánchez Carrión al Illmo. Señor don Juan Muzi, Cuartel General en Huanuco, 13 de julio de 1824," in *Cartas del Libertador*, IV, 114.

11. O'Leary, *op. cit.*, II, 543.

that of 1834. But in 1839 the severity was lessened by limiting the prohibition to the public exercise of any other cult. This was carried over into the charters of 1856 and 1860, notwithstanding the efforts of President Ramón Castilla and the so-called "Liberals" to induce Congress to amend the constitution to allow religious liberty.[12]

In the meantime, that is, in June, 1835, formal religious relations were established with Rome when the pope instituted the first republican archbishop of Peru. In phrasing the bulls of institution, however, the Holy Father carefully avoided both political recognition and the right of national presentation, although the government's nominees were accepted for preconization. These bulls of institution were given the *pase*, but the government attached to them legalizing formulas protesting against any phrasing of the document which failed to recognize the right of national patronage. President José Rufino Echenique, being hopeful that a concordat would straighten out the difficulties with the Vatican, decided to send to Rome an envoy extraordinary on special mission. Accordingly, in 1853, Dr. Bartolomé Herrera went to Rome with particular instructions on two propositions: first, "that the President of the Republic will continue to exercise the patronage like the kings of Spain were accustomed to exercise it"; and second, "Bishops-elect can govern their churches before receiving the bulls of institution."[13] The mission failed.

Although failing to establish religious toleration, Castilla and the Liberals were more successful in their efforts to abolish the *fueros* and the tithes. The former exempted clerics from the jurisdiction of the regular courts, and made the clergy a separate and privileged class, something which was thought incompatible with democracy. The Liberals hoped that this reform would not only terminate the privileged position of the clericals, but would also terminate their influence in politics. Therefore, although the ecclesiastical courts were brought under the jurisdiction of the judicial branch of the civil government in 1852, the *fueros* were abolished outright in the Constitution of 1856, an instrument dictated by the Liberals. The tithes were abolished, and, in 1859, it was provided that the archbishop, bishops, dignitaries, and canons in the service of cathedrals should be paid from the national treasury. Conciliar seminaries, colleges, and hospitals were to be given aid by the government sufficient to make up the deficit caused by the

12. R. M. Taurel, *De La Liberté Religieuse au Pérou* (Paris, 1851), p. 1. The Constitution gave to the Congress the sole right of initiating constitutional amendments; Olivo, *op. cit.*, pp. 149-88.

13. Chacaltana, *Patronato Nacional Argentino*, p. 103; Stanger, *op. cit.*, p. 426.

abolition of the tithes.[14] Other more drastic anticlerical reforms were
contemplated by the Liberals, but their program was frustrated by the
opposition of the clergy and the Conservatives. In 1860 the latter party
came into power and proceeded to amend the constitution. This Conservative, revised edition is known as the Constitution of 1860, and it
enjoyed the very long life, for Peruvian constitutions, of sixty years.

The Constitution of 1860 provided not only for the State profession
and support of the Catholic religion, but it also contained numerous
provisions respecting the exercise of the patronage and the maintenance
of relations with the Holy See.[15] With few changes the religious articles
of 1860 were incorporated into the succeeding organic laws of 1920 and
1933. Although Article 4 of the former charter declared: "The Nation
professes the Roman Catholic Apostolic religion; the State protects it
and does not permit the *public* exercise of any other," and although the
penal code (March 1, 1863) imposed a penalty of one year's imprisonment upon anyone who publicly celebrated any cult other than the
Catholic,[16] there was little interference with personal religious beliefs,
and Protestants were even allowed to maintain their own churches.
Nevertheless there occurred in 1890 an incident which illustrated how
precarious was the position of Evangelical missionaries in Peru. In
that year a certain Francisco G. Penzotti, agent of the American Bible
Society, was arrested in Callao charged with violating the fourth article
of the Constitution. A sensational trial followed, for the clergy were
determined to secure a decision favorable to their interpretation of the
Constitution. The judges of the lower courts sought evasion and the
case finally came to the Supreme Court which handed down a decision
favorable to Penzotti. This was regarded by the Protestants as a great
victory for religious liberty. At any rate it removed apprehension and
missionary enterprise was stimulated. In the next decade as many
missionaries visited Peru as during the preceding three-quarters of a
century.[17] After the Penzotti case there were some instances of missionaries being impeded in their work, but these were isolated cases.

An English traveler wrote of Peru in 1910: "Under no Latin-American government is there greater freedom for, and license to, alien religions than in Peru. This is the more remarkable since Peruvians still
maintain the most complete adhesion to Rome and in spite of the wholly

14. Villarán, *Const. Peruana*, p. 86.
15. For the Constitution of 1860, see Rodríguez, *American Constitutions*, II, 254-77.
16. Eduardo García Calderón, ed., *Constitución, Códigos, y Leyes del Peru* (Lima,
1923), Art. 100, p. 501. Mr. Stanger (*op. cit.*, p. 434) evidently overlooked the Penal
Code when he declared, "No law had ever defined offenses or established penalties."
17. *The West Coast Republics*, p. 71.

aggressive manner in which certain Protestant missionaries have come to the country to stir up revolt and rebellion among the poor and ignorant Indians against the teaching and influence of the Church."[18]

It is doubtful if the prohibitory clause in the Constitution would have been suppressed in 1915 had not the Congress become aroused because of a mob attack on a Protestant mission among the Indians. By constitutional amendment, there was struck out of Article 4 the prohibition of the public exercise of any other religious cult. The passage of the law was strongly resisted by the clergy, and even by the president, who refused to proclaim it after its adoption. Accordingly, in a tumultuous session, during which the galleries were crowded by ardent female supporters of the Church, the Congress proclaimed the law.[19]

The present constitution of Peru (promulgated April 9, 1933) retains the sense of the amendment of 1915, i.e., "Respecting the sentiments of the national majority, the State protects the Roman Catholic Apostolic religion. All other religions enjoy freedom in the exercise of their respective beliefs" (Art. 232). Also there is inserted in the bill of rights: "Freedom of conscience and belief is inviolable" (Art. 59). The Constitution thus grants full liberty of conscience and religion. There are no religious tests for exercising the suffrage or holding public office. In Peru, unlike many Latin-American countries, clerics can vote and hold office. But this is subject to the following condition: members of the clergy cannot be elected to the Senate or the Deputies or to the presidency or vice-presidency.

The Roman Catholic Church, being the only religious body recognized by law, the civil code contains provisions (Articles 83-94) covering the definition of clergymen and religious, the qualifications necessary for the profession; their exemptions from public services (army and jury); the recovery of civil rights of religious upon their being secularized, and the like.[20] As is to be expected in the case of a country having a State-Church, the crimes against the established religion and its ministers are carefully enumerated in the penal code and heavy penalties are attached.[21]

Since 1856, when the ecclesiastical *fueros* were abolished, the clergy have enjoyed no special exemption in legal trials; they are tried in public courts, civil or criminal, as the case may be. According to the organic law of the judiciary, the Supreme Court may take original cognizance

18. P. F. Martin, *Peru in the Twentieth Century* (London, 1911), p. 131.
19. Pedro Dávalos y Lissón, *La Primera Centuria* (Lima, 1919), I, 199; Stanger, *op. cit.*, p. 434.
20. García Calderón, *Constitución, Códigos y Leyes*, p. 37.
21. *Ibid.*, p. 501 (Art. 100), p. 543 (Arts. 101-106).

of cases brought against archbishops and bishops. Therefore, the practice in Peru is that archbishops and bishops are subject to the jurisdiction of the ordinary courts for common crimes but when delinquent in the exercise of their episcopal functions, they are judged by the Supreme Court.[22]

The efforts of various chief executives of Peru, beginning with Bolívar, to secure apostolic recognition of national patronage through the negotiation of a concordat have been noted. Although Pius IX refused to confirm Peru's radical pretentions to national patronage in a formal concordat, he was finally induced, in 1874, to grant by papal brief, the right of patronage, but without the concessions and obligations usually contained in a concordat. This bull, which has established a *modus vivendi* still effective today, was as follows:

> Pius—Servant of the servants of God:
> Among the notable favors which God in his boundless mercy has heaped on the Peruvian nation, the gift of the true Catholic religion, which the Peruvians have wisely cherished exactly as it was announced by the preachers of the Gospel, outshines all others. They have so wisely cultivated it that they have become heroes whom the Church judges worthy of being honored on the altars. This becomes for the said nation a real glory, since it also has never faltered in its duty to support the faith after Peru separated itself from the control of the Catholic kings of Spain. It was declared, in fact, in a solemn manner in the Constitution of the Republic, that Peru professes the Catholic religion which it protects, and does not permit the public exercise of other cults.
>
> This solicitude in maintaining Catholic unity has been responsible for other acts of a similar nature by the public authority. Such are: grants to existing dioceses or to newly created ones have been increased or liberally established; subsidies have been granted to the seminaries established for the propagation of the faith; with equal munificence provision has been made for the dissemination of the holy doctrine, that is, parishes have been founded in towns of those who have been converted to the faith; and, finally, considerable money has been expended to embellish or repair churches, to build new ones, and to favor or promote the splendor of the religious cult.
>
> All these things which were known to us, we have been reminded of and told again by our very loved son and illustrious person Pedro Gálvez, delegate of the Republic of Peru near this Apostolic See, for the purpose of obtaining from us a public and solemn testimony of the merits acquired by the said republic respecting the Catholic Church.

22. Stuart, *op. cit.*, p. 86; Chacaltana, *op. cit.*, pp. 69-70.

For this reason, being desirous of satisfying the wishes which the government of Peru has expressed to us by its representative, and following in this an example of our predecessors who desired to heap favors and grace upon those who have merited well of the Christian cause:

We have resolved, after having sought the advice of some cardinals of the Roman Church, to concede, as we in fact do concede by our apostolic authority, to the president of the Republic of Peru and to his successor *pro tempore*, the enjoyment, in the territory of the republic, of the right of patronage, such as was enjoyed by grace of the Apostolic See, by the Catholic kings of Spain before Peru was separated from their authority.

Nevertheless we impose as a condition and rule upon the concession of this privilege, that the property actually assigned to the clergy by act of gift, as well as to the sacred ministry and to the exercise of the cult in the dioceses of the territory of the Republic, will be preserved integrally and distributed with diligence and fidelity; and also, we impose as a condition that the government of Peru shall continue favoring and protecting the Catholic religion.

In observing these laws and conditions, the president of the Republic of Peru and his successors will have the right when vacancies occur in the archiepiscopal and episcopal sees to present to the Apostolic See worthy and proper ecclesiastics, in order that canonical institution shall take place according to the rules prescribed by the Church. The presentation of candidates, however, ought to be made, excepting when legitimately prevented, within one year of the time when the vacancy occurs. The candidates, thus presented, will not exercise any right, with respect to episcopal administration, before they have obtained the apostolic letters of institution....

The president of the Republic will also have the right of presenting to the bishop worthy persons to be promoted to the dignities and canoncies *de gratia* ... also, to present worthy persons for the collation of prebends of cathedral churches ... if the vacancy has been declared by the ecclesiastical authority.

The said president will also enjoy the right of presentation to canoncies *de oficio* and to parishes, always observing the canonical form of *concurso y del examen*; in exercising this examination the president will elect an ecclesiastic from among the three suggested (the best qualified having been presented to him), to the end that the said ecclesiastic will receive immediately canonical institution from the bishop.

Finally, the presidents of the Republic will enjoy in the churches of Peru the honors that were once enjoyed by the kings of Spain by virtue of the right of patronage conceded by the Holy See.

We desire, order, and establish all these things.....
Given in Rome, near St. Peters (March 3, 1874).[23]

Since the terms of the bull were regarded as being incompatible with
the prerogatives of national sovereignty, the government of Peru refused to accept it. It was not until Nicolás de Pierola became president,
or rather dictator, that the exequatur was granted on January 27, 1880.[24]
Since that date the bull has operated as a *modus vivendi* in the place of
a concordat, which evidently the Peruvian government is still hopeful of
concluding.

Somewhat in conformity with the papal grant, but not necessarily as
a consequence of the same, the present constitution of Peru provides
that the president may exercise the patronage in accordance with the
laws and existing practices. The Congress, moreover, is empowered
to make regulations necessary for the exercise of the right of patronage.
For the filling of vacancies in archbishoprics and bishoprics the president nominates Peruvian citizens by birth or naturalization whose
names are submitted to the Holy See for canonical institution. The
president also makes nominations to the bishops for the dignities and
canonries of the Cathedrals and for the curacies and other ecclesiastical
benefices.[25]

Although the law requires that the president "approve or disapprove
conciliar decrees and pontifical bulls, briefs, and rescripts with the consent of Congress, and in contentious matters only after having first been
heard by the Supreme Court of Justice,"[26] the old *regalía* of the *pase*
has fallen into disuse and it is only preserved in the institution of bishops
and the demarcation of dioceses. The clergy are accustomed to communicate freely with the Vatican, provided this is done through the
archiepiscopal chancellery, notwithstanding that the civil code provides:
"To obtain from the Roman Pontiff dispensations, indults, and other
favors, it is necessary to appeal to the Supreme Government which will
grant authorization and give the proper direction. The indults, dispensations, and favors which are consigned in any other way shall not
be issued."[27]

As has been noted, Pope Pius IX was induced to recognize the right
of patronage in Peru because of the fine Catholic spirit manifested there
in supporting the Church. Furthermore, the term of the bull was con-
ditioned on the continuance of financial support. We find therefore,

23. Olaechea, *op. cit.*, pp. 253-57.
24. *Ibid.*, pp. 257-58; Chacaltana, *op. cit.*, p. 102.
25. Constitution of 1933, Art. 154: 23-25; Art. 235.
26. Constitution of 1933, Art. 154: 26.
27. García Calderón, *Constitución, Códigos y Leyes*, p. 37.

that the government makes an annual appropriation for the salaries of certain dignitaries of the Church. When the tithes were suppressed in 1859, the nation made itself responsible to the Church for the amount the tithes had produced. Consequently, from 1859 to the present date, the general budget has carried annual appropriations for the salaries of the archbishops and bishops. The lesser clergy are paid from fees and contributions, supplemented by income from Church property. There are no subventions by the State. The tariff of parochial fees is approved by the government.

The chief sources of ecclesiastical income, aside from governmental contributions and fees, are income from Church property and gifts. The Catholic Church in colonial Peru, as in New Spain, because of the munificence of the crown, the pious grants of individuals, and the industry of the clergy, reinforced by the principle of mortmain, was by all odds the greatest property holder and the wealthiest institution in the colony. The wealth and economic influence of the Church suffered slight impairment even after the winning of independence. This was true notwithstanding an effort made in 1828 to abolish vinculation of property as well as the giving of it into mortmain.[28] Since the law was not made retroactive, the numerous pious foundations dating from distant colonial times remained untouched.

The Church today has the right of possession of its properties and juridic personality to litigate before the courts with respect to them. There is no legal restriction on its ability to receive bequests, but, until 1901, it was prohibited from receiving inheritances and real estate. The object of this was to prevent more property falling into mortmain. But on September 30, 1901, the law of free-disposition, so-called, was passed, which removed the prohibition on the Church and religious orders of the right of disposing of their property without the consent of the government. Since the passage of this law the Church may freely acquire property, although the provisions of the civil code which relate to the inheriting of real estate have not been annulled. Thus the Church in Peru, as a juridic person, can acquire and possess property of all kinds, as well as contract obligations and exercise civil actions according to the statutes of the country. Churches and all places of worship are exempt from taxation, but all revenue-yielding property of the Church pays the same imposts as private property. It is remarkable that, notwithstanding the vast ecclesiastical holdings in urban and rural real estate, this condition has not been a matter of popular concern.

28. This law was incorporated in the civil code, Article 1194. (García Calderón, *Constitución, Códigos y Leyes,* p. 148).

Unlike Mexico and other Latin-American countries, Peru has experienced no serious movement towards wholesale confiscation.[29]

As is to be expected in a country where the Catholic religion is the favored cult, it enjoys certain privileges in the realm of education. Although the Church has no authority whatever over public instruction, nevertheless, according to the *Reglamento General de Instrucción*, it is not only permitted, but is required, to give instruction in the Catholic faith in the public schools of primary and intermediate grades.[30] With respect to the general program of instruction, which applies not only to State schools, but to private schools as well, the Church has no authority. Ecclesiastics, male and female, are allowed to instruct in non-religious subjects in the public schools if they have the qualifications.

The Catholic Church maintains its own educational system. At the primary level there are only a few parochial schools, but there are many private Catholic schools staffed by orders of religious men and women. Church schools, as noted above, are controlled by an official program of instruction which is common to private and State schools without any distinction whatever.

Most of the schools are supported by tuition fees, but even when the schooling is free the expenses for uniforms and incidentals are considerable. Therefore the private Catholic schools are usually reserved for those able to afford the considerable costs. The Catholic Church in Peru educates about 150,000 children or 8 per cent of the grade school population. Catholic educational opportunities are limited because of the shortage of buildings and teachers. The government has aided by appropriating subsidies. In Peru, as in most parts of South America, a regular Catholic education exists but apparently only for the middle and upper classes—thus giving rise to the notion that the Catholic faith is linked to wealth and illiteracy.[31] The illiteracy rate in Peru is estimated at 52 per cent (over age 15 years).[32]

Since matrimony is one of the sacraments of the Catholic Church and is regarded as a peculiar subject for regulation, it was natural that its ecclesiastical monopoly should have been sanctioned by law. This, moreover, was merely confirmation of a practice which had been established during centuries of Spanish rule. The civil code prescribed that

29. Stanger, *op. cit.*, p. 437.

30. Peru is one of the six Latin-American countries that have Catholic religious and moral instruction in the public schools. The others are: Argentina, Brazil, Colombia, Costa Rica, and Haiti.

31. William J. Coleman, *Latin American Catholicism: A Self-Evaluation* (Maryknoll, N.Y., 1954), p. 53; Erik von Kuehnelt-Leddihn, "Catholics in Latin America," *The Commonweal* (June 23, 1961), p. 324.

32. Francisco Houtart, *El cambio social en América Latina* (Bogotá, 1964), p. 174.

"marriages in the republic shall be celebrated with the formalities established by the Church in the Council of Trent." The ecclesiastical ceremony until 1934 was sufficient and legal and needed only to be registered in the civil register of the district governor within eight days.

The prohibition of marriages outside of the Church, even of non-Catholics, was implied from the constitutional proscription of the public exercise of dissident faiths. Because of the great hardships and manifest injustice of this law upon non-Catholics, there was long agitation for its amendment. Finally civil marriage of non-Catholics was legalized in 1897, when a storm of public protest was aroused because a North American couple were denied legalization of their union. The refusal, or inability, of the president to come to the relief of the Americans resulted in congressional action. The law of December 23, 1897, relieved persons not of the Catholic religion, from the Church ceremony. They must appear, however, before a judicial court in order that it may be shown that they are entitled to be married under the provisions of the civil code. The ceremony is performed by the alcalde of the provincial council in the district where they are domiciled. Those to whom the Church denies license because of the difference in cults must also conform to this procedure. The clericals strongly resisted the passage of this statute, as they did the toleration law of 1915, and, in this instance likewise, the Congress passed the law over the objections of a reluctant chief executive.

Formerly, that is, prior to 1930, the laws of the Church on the indissolubility of the marriage bonds were given civil sanction. Divorce which allows remarriage is never permitted by the Catholic Church; there can only be remarriage after the death of one of the parties, or annulment of the union. Thus, in Peru, legal separation was granted after a hearing in the ecclesiastical tribunal, and after the verdict, the parties proceeded to the civil tribunal for the division of their properties and the liquidation of their conjugal society.

By decree-law of October 4, 1930, the civil marriage was made obligatory and no longer could the religious marriage produce civil effects. The decree-law of October 8, 1930, established absolute divorce, Peru thus becoming one of fifteen Latin-American countries permitting absolute divorce. Those five countries that still do not admit divorce are: Argentina, Brazil, Colombia, Chile, and Paraguay.[33]

Another practice in Peru which was sanctioned by centuries of experience under Spanish rule was the delegation to the Church of

33. Ricardo Gallardo, *Divorcio, Separación de Cuerpos y Nulidad del Matrimonio en las naciones Latino-Americanas* (Madrid, 1957), p. 13. See also, Gordon Ireland and Jesús de Galíndez, *Divorce in the Americas* (Buffalo, 1947), pp. 232-33.

control of cemeteries. Clerical control was maintained until 1869 when municipal councils were instructed to provide and maintain lay cemeteries for the burial of non-Catholics. The adoption of these laws was based on a very limited tolerance and also sanitary considerations because of the religious prejudice against the proper burial of "heretics." After 1869 there was further liberalization of practice with the result that the old clerical control of burials was broken.

The Department of Justice and Religion has charge of matters of patronage and ecclesiastical relations. These are not onerous responsibilities for usually the annual *memorias*, or reports, of the Department have very little to say about ecclesiastical affairs. The prefects of the departments have been given supervisory powers over ecclesiastical matters connected with the patronage. They are in the nature of vice-patrons. Peru maintains an embassy at the Vatican, and the Pope in return has accredited to Lima a papal nuncio who is the dean of the diplomatic corps.

The passage of the toleration act of 1915 was followed by increased Protestant missionary activity in Peru. In the decade 1915-25 a larger number of missionaries had gone to the land of the Incas than in all the preceding hundred years. In 1928 the total number of Protestant missionaries, with their native helpers, was 339. In 1960 there were 618 Protestant clergy serving a church community of 74,210 representing 0.7 per cent of the total population of the country. In contrast a Roman Catholic clergy numbering 1,740 served a Roman Catholic community of 9,423,000 comprising 89.5 per cent of the total population of 10,524,000.[34] There is no gainsaying the fact that Protestantism has made little headway in Peru.

A more far-reaching and significant result of the passage of the Act of 1915 was the reaction on Catholicism itself. Contrary to the predictions of dire disaster made by clerics in opposing the passage of the bill, it marked the beginning of a revival of the Catholic Church in Peru. The act served to awaken the hierarchy to a realization that the Church had no real hold on the hearts of the people. This awakening led to numerous measures of reform. There was a general tightening up on the part of the Church of the control of the government departments where the religious and educational interests were affected. A Catholic University was founded in Lima in 1917 "to conserve the continuity of education given in the elementary and high schools, and to train up a body of one hundred per cent Catholics." Another significant reform

34. W. Stanley Rycroft and Myrtle M. Clemmer, *A Factual Study of Latin America*, Commission on Ecumenical Mission and Relations, The United Presbyterian Church in the U.S.A. (New York, 1963). See Table No. 49, p. 234.

measure was the order of the Archbishop of Lima that ten-minute sermons in the vernacular should be delivered at all Sunday masses. A significant result of the new revival was that more men were attracted to the Church.[35]

In Peru there is a strong tradition of clerical interference in political matters. The counseling of parishioners as to how they should vote, and the influencing of legislation and governmental officers, are regarded as legitimate and necessary activities on the part of the clergy. The Church in Peru, therefore, is still accustomed to make use of its organization and discipline to apply pressure when and where it chooses. A well-organized and disciplined institution, the Church has been recognized as necessary to stable government. It is significant that the chief executive was unwilling to promulgate the anticlerical laws passed by Congress in 1897 and 1915. President Leguía, a strong conservative, and dictator for many years, bestowed signal favors on the Church. In 1923 he dedicated Peru to the Sacred Heart of Jesus. Yet, it is a notable fact that had it not been for his evasion of the laws, non-Catholic missionary enterprises could not have been carried on in Peru.

Clerical influence is, to no small degree, the result of its by no means negligible control of education. The exclusive privilege of giving religious instruction in public schools virtually assigns the youth of the land to be cast in the Catholic mould. A reverence for the Church and its dogmas, profound respect for its ministers, and a dread of disobeying its authority are cardinal aims of this ecclesiastical instruction. If these aims are attained, and no one can say that the Church has failed, then the political position of the cult is given greater security. The medium of education as a bulwark of Catholic control is reinforced by its privileged position in other matters, notably those affecting and regulating the private lives of individuals.

In regard to domestic life the dominating influence of clerical authority is most marked. The Catholic women of Peru, as of other parts of South America, are most ardent, almost fanatical, supporters of the faith and subservient followers of clerical instructions and advice: as witness, for example, female demonstrations when the Toleration Act of 1915 was passed by Congress. While the men are not so imbued with marked religious inclination, they dread disobeying the authority of the Church. Among the uneducated Indians of the sierras and coastal region, the priesthood is regarded with superstitious awe and fear. The uncivilized savages of the great Amazonian river valleys pay little attention to priests or creed.

35. *West Coast Republics*, pp. 71-72; *Christian Work in South America*, The Montevideo Congress, 1925 (New York, 1925), I, 263.

Although the Peruvian Church is strong politically, and exercises great control over domestic life, it is charged with failure in the performance of its divine mission to inculcate real spirituality among its communicants. Pedro Dávalos y Lissón has written: "The sacred word in the pulpit although it reaped regular fruit in the missions and in the *feris de cuaresma*, in general did not move the hearts to contrition. The Christian people were content to hear mass and oblige their children to confess." Furthermore, he points out, in evidence of decreased spirituality, few people accompanied the procession of *Santísimo* and even fewer those of the saints. Yet the remembrance of the old destructive earthquakes brought numerous participants to the procession of Señor de los Milagros. Needless to remark, the continued observance of this custom is based in superstition and not piety. In the provinces the cult continues in the same state as in the colonial régime. On the part of the Indians there is the same ignorance, the same superstition. There are numerous cases of "miracles" and consequent patron saints in the sierras where ignorance and fanaticism are common. But in Lima there are no saints.[36]

We quote more recent clerical critics. "We find," says a pastoral letter of the Bishop of Abancay, Peru, February, 1963, "that religion, even among the most pious, consists of vulgar external manifestations, completely unspiritual and valueless, and divorced from the practice of the simplest virtues and obedience to the law of God. We can only lament the proven existence of superstition in such worship."[37] The majority of the sacraments seem to be only for women and children, and baptism and extreme unction suffices for the men.

What does the average Catholic know of his faith? According to a report concerning the Chimbote conference of 1953—a severe self-evaluation of Latin-American Catholicism—"All that has been said about the poverty of religious instruction in Argentina must be thought of as applying in a greater degree to Peru." The report charges a lack of Christian criteria in all aspects of life. "In their religious life they practice mostly a traditional routine of external acts and devotions."[38] According to Father Nevins, Catholicism in Peru is stagnant.

The failure of the Catholic Church in Peru to prevent religious indifference and to inculcate a spiritual appreciation can be attributed in no small degree to the very unsatisfactory caliber of clerical personnel. Since the modern Church lacks the prestige which it enjoyed in the past, it no longer attracts to the priesthood and regular orders the sons of

36. Dávalos y Lissón, I, 202-5.
37. *Christianity Today*, VII, No. 21 (July 19, 1963), p. 15.
38. Coleman, *op. cit.*, pp. 28-29.

aristocratic Catholic families or even those of modest and middle circumstances. The clerical career, instead of being looked up to with awe and reverence, is scorned today with slighting remarks. Thus, whereas in prior times the persons of both sexes in the convents and monasteries mounted into the thousands, now in Peru very few wish to serve God in the priesthood. So few are the qualified for the higher ecclesiastical positions that the government often has difficulty in selecting nominees for the election of a bishop. Because of the serious scarcity of priests it has been necessary to provide curacies and chaplaincies with foreign priests—mostly Spanish. And although these foreigners were almost always sent with guarantees of rectitude and culture, too many of them sought only to enrich themselves.

The bishops cannot be held to too strict responsibility for the curates, careless of instruction in the catechism and lacking in abnegation and the necessary dedication to social and moral reform. Their hands are tied. The scarcity of priests makes discipline impossible. Certainly removal from office could not be used as a disciplinary measure, for the bishops feel that nonadministration of the sacraments would be an even greater evil. Of course the exceptions among the curates are numerous; there are many men who labor and perform good work in the face of many difficulties.

Peru is a priest-starved country. The ratio of priests to Catholic population is approximately one to 6,000. With a population of over 10 million there are 800 foreign priests and only about 700 native priests. In the hinterlands parishes of 40 to 50 thousand souls are not uncommon. Small bands of missionaries like the Maryknoll Fathers are trying to do a job too big for them.[39] In response to a plea by Pope John XXIII to rush help to the beleaguered area, hundreds of diocesan clergy from the United States, Canada, and Ireland have volunteered to work in Latin America. Many of these "Papal Volunteers" are working in Peru. To illustrate the dire need, in Lima alone 10 to 15 new parishes a year are needed to keep abreast of the population growth.

Although the scarcity of priests in Peru is a most important problem in the religious category, an equally important one is the adaptation of the mentality and deportment of the clerics to a socio-cultural change which is sweeping the continent. It will take more than teaching doctrine and the administration of the sacraments to help build a strong Christian community. The clergy are being called upon by their hierarchy to help provide the people with programs of social action that are commensurate with their needs. The Peruvian bishops' pastoral

39. Nevins, *op. cit.*, p. 69.

letter on politics and social reform of May 1, 1963, was a call for reform in housing, sanitation, education, and particularly agrarian reform.[40] Clerical opposition to conservative and reactionary elements—former allies—has developed. Father Nevins quotes a Peruvian priest: "Our best Church-goers are the leading oppressors of the poor. Their wealth gives them power to silence anyone who opposes them. The encyclicals should be our most potent weapon to win back the masses. But our wealthy Catholics prefer a sentimental Catholicism to a dynamic one."[41]

Undoubtedly the new approach to modernizing the Church in Peru and making it an instrument of social and economic reform has been responsible for some modest advance. Nevertheless, the clerics, ignoring their own lack of success in the economic sphere, are attempting to provide a blueprint for the economic reconstruction of the whole nation. It is argued that the Church can make a more telling contribution to economic advance and the growth of spiritual strength by concentrating its actions within its unique and proper field of endeavor.[42] The Catholic Church in Peru is not restricted by need or opportunity to improve the discharge of its proper spiritual obligations to the faithful.

The separation of Church and State although freely predicted has not been popular in Peru. Yet, there is a definite anticlerical movement which aims at disestablishment. These modern anticlericals are not to be confused with the Liberals who were responsible for such religious reform as abolition of *fueros* and tithes, legalization of civil marriage, and religious toleration. The Liberals of the earlier years were nominally Catholics who protested their loyalty to the Church while they fought its control in politics. The antagonists of the Peruvian Church today are not even nominal Catholics. They are frankly, even boastingly, irreligious; they see no need for either Church or religion.[43] There appears to be small likelihood that iconoclastic and skeptical arguments will accomplish a separation of Church and State. The separation will come peacefully and automatically when the State and the Church become convinced that they are both prepared for it and their individual interests will be best served thereby. A hastening of disestablishment and the adoption of drastic and coercive measures could result only in violence and a generally unsatisfactory situation.

---

40. *Recent Church Documents from Latin America*, Center of Intercultural Formation, Monograph No. 2 (Cuernavaca, Mexico, 1962-63), p. 41.

41. Nevins, *op. cit.*, p. 14.

42. Frederick B. Pike, "The Modernized Church in Peru: Two Aspects," *The Review of Politics*, Vol. 26, No. 3 (July, 1964), pp. 307-18.

43. The "master" of skeptical Peruvian youths is Manuel Gonzáles Prada (1848-1918). It is said that the influence of this famous iconoclast in shaping the religious philosophy of Peruvian youths has been greater than that of any other person. Stanger, *op. cit.*, p. 433.

Chapter VIII

The Established Cult in the Mid-Continintal Republics of Bolivia and Paraguay

BOLIVIA

Alto Perú, Bolivia today, did not break away from Spanish authority until August 6, 1825, following the liberation of Peru at the battle of Ayacucho. Prior to the definitive establishment of her independence, Bolivia, after an ineffective creole revolt in Chuquisaca and La Paz in 1809, was continuously under Spanish control, notwithstanding determined efforts of the patriots of La Plata to liberate the province. An effective force in prolonging the rule of Spain in the Audiencia of Charcas was the Roman Catholic hierarchy which was unswerving in its loyalty. Archbishop Moxó of Chuquisaca and Bishop La Santa of La Paz lent invaluable support to José Goyeneche, the royalist commander, in suppressing separatist and liberal tendencies within the province, and in preventing their introduction from La Plata. Bishop La Santa, in addition to fulminating excommunications, even organized armies against the patriots. Since the population of *Alto Perú* was nearly 90 per cent Indian, ignorant and superstitiously attached to the Roman Catholic Church, the influence of the Church in the cause of Spain was incalculable. Not all the clergy, however, were affiliated with the Spanish cause, for the leader of the uprising in La Paz was José Medina, a curate. And a guerrilla leader who harassed the loyalists for several years was Muñecas, also a cleric. Furthermore, the unwelcome (although needed) reform measures instituted by Archbishop Moxó, a strict disciplinarian, caused many curates to league against him, and this league served to aid the cause of independence.[1]

There was nothing in the history of Bolivia, either before or during the wars for independence, to indicate religious dissent or desire for a change in the political status of the Catholic Church. The disposition

1. Alcides Arguedas, *Historia General de Bolivia* (La Paz, 1922), pp. 5-6; José María Camacho, *Compendio de la Historia de Bolivia* (La Paz, 1927), pp. 126-28, 159-60.

of the subject of religion in the model constitution submitted by the Liberator to the republic which bore his name was therefore at variance with the popular demands of the new state. At the beginning of 1826, the Liberator sent to Bolivia from Lima his project of a constitution. Bolívar recognized the Church as a factor to be reckoned with and provided in his constitution for the national control of the ecclesiastical patronage. Thus, to the Senate he delegated power (1) to make *reglamentos eclesiásticos*; (2) to propose in triple lists (*en terna*) to the Chamber of Censors names of those to be presented for archbishops, bishops, dignitaries, canons, and prebends of cathedrals; (3) to make rules for the exercise of the patronage and issue laws on all ecclesiastical subjects which had any relation to the government; and (4) to examine and approve or disapprove conciliar decrees, bulls, briefs, and pontifical rescripts. To the president he gave the power to present to the ecclesiastical government one of the candidates proposed on triple lists by the electoral body for curates or vicars in the provinces. Bolívar carefully avoided any mention, however, in his list of constitutional guarantees or elsewhere in his constitution, of religion, either as to proscription or as to privilege.[2]

In explaining his omission of an article on religion, the Liberator, in a statement to the Bolivian Assembly which accompanied the proposed constitution, said:

"I will mention one article which my conscience has forced me to omit. In a political constitution no religion should be prescribed, because, according to the best doctrines on fundamental laws, these are the guarantees of political and civil rights, and, as religion does not pertain to either of these rights, it is of an indefinable nature in the social order and belongs to the moral and intellectual. Religion governs man in his home, in his office, within himself; it alone has the right to examine his intimate conscience. Laws, on the contrary, look on the surface of things; they do not govern except outside the house of the citizen. Applying these considerations, can a State govern the consciences of its subjects, watch over the fulfilment of religious laws, and reward or punish, when the tribunals are in Heaven and when God is the judge? The Inquisition alone would be capable of replacing such courts in this world. Shall the Inquisition return with its fiery torches? Religion is the law of the conscience. All law over it annuls it, for by imposing necessity for duty, there is destroyed the merit of faith which is the basis of religion. The sacred precepts and dogmas are useful, luminous, and

2. *Proyecto de Constitución para la República de Bolivia y Discurso del Libertador* (Buenos Aires, 1826), pp. 12-13, 15, 21.

of metaphysical evidence; all of us ought to profess them, but this is a moral and not a political duty."[3]

Notwithstanding the eloquent plea of the Liberator for religious toleration and the separation of Church and State, the Bolivian Constituent Assembly added to the constitution the following article: "The Roman Catholic Apostolic religion is the religion of the Republic to the exclusion of all other public cults. The government protects it and insures it respect, recognizing the principle that there is no human power over conscience." The final contradictory statement in the article was evidently the result of a desire on the part of the framers of the constitution to appease Bolívar. At the same time a more compelling force, a desire to satisfy Bolivians and recognize their religious demands, was responsible for the constitutional law of exclusion. Considering the religious background of Bolivia, the break suggested by Bolívar was too precipitous and unwarranted. The Assembly also stipulated in the new constitution that the president must profess the religion of the republic. But the provisions suggested by Bolívar regarding the national control of patronage were left untouched.[4]

The wisdom of the framers of the Constitution of 1826 in providing for a civil-ecclesiastical relationship conformable to the actual demands and limited attainments of the overwhelming majority of the population has been justified by the subsequent history of the cult in Bolivia. The privileged position enjoyed by the Catholic Church has caused very little dissatisfaction of any consequence.[5] Indeed, it has never constituted a problem, and today, after more than a hundred years of trial, the political status of the Catholic Church is very much what it was in 1826.

In Bolivia's numerous constitutions, culminating in the Constitution of 1961, the articles relating to the Roman Catholic religion have, with only a few exceptions, been very slightly changed.[6] In 1871 the article prohibiting the public exercise of non-Catholic cults was amended to read "except in the colonies where it is tolerated." The object of the exception was to attract foreign immigration which might be restrained because of the prohibition of the exercise of other cults. In 1905 the same article was amended again to permit the public exercise, throughout the republic, of all cults. Thus religious toleration, legally at least,

---

3. *Ibid.,* pp. 14-15.

4. Jenaro Sanjinés, *Las Constituciones de Bolivia* (La Paz, 1906), pp. 2, 13-15, 41, 74.

5. "Bolivia has been less influenced by religious discussion than other countries [in Latin America]." Chacaltana, *Patronato Nacional Argentino,* p. 104.

6. The constitutional status herein described is that of the Constitution of 1961 which was suspended following the overthrow of President Paz Estenssoro in 1964. The status of the Church remained unchanged.

was not introduced into Bolivia until that date. The act of 1905 is called "the Magna Carta of the missions in Bolivia," for few or no Protestant missions existed in Bolivia prior to the enactment of the law.[7]

Not only are liberty of conscience and religious toleration guaranteed, but practically all religious tests for the exercise of political rights have been abolished. There are no restrictions on the exercise of the suffrage, and no religious tests for holding public office. No longer, for example, is it stipulated that the president of the republic must be a Roman Catholic, although it is true that members of the clergy are not eligible for election to the presidency, vice-presidency or to the Congress.

The constitutions of Bolivia prior to 1961 listed among the powers of the president: (1) exercise of the right of patronage in the churches and over ecclesiastical persons and benefices; (2) nomination of archbishops and bishops, selecting them from among the names submitted—three for each place—by the Senate; (3) appointment of canons, prebendaries, and other Church dignitaries, selecting the names from those suggested by the cathedral chapters; and (4) the grant or refusal, with the advice of the Senate, of acceptance of the decrees of councils, or the briefs, bulls, and rescripts of the supreme pontiff. Because of these provisions, the system which existed in Bolivia was that of national patronage, but it was exercised mildly on the part of the government.[8] For example, in practice the exequatur was only required on bulls of institution of residential prelates. With respect to all the remaining papal documents full liberty of entry was accorded. Communication between the Bolivian hierarchy and the papacy was free and unhampered. Bolivia and the Vatican exchange diplomatic representatives; since 1917 the Holy See has sent an apostolic nuncio to La Paz.

In an effort to have the State's interpretation of the patronage accepted by the pope, General Santa Cruz was sent to Rome to conclude a concordat. On May 29, 1851, the Bolivian delegate and the Cardinal-Secretary of State signed an agreement designed to serve as a norm for the relations of Church and State in Bolivia. In this pact the pontiff conceded to the president of Bolivia the patronage or privilege of presenting for any vacancy in archiepiscopal or episcopal churches or for ecclesiastical dignities. The president was also conceded the right to nominate six prebends for each chapter. The pope also agreed that personal causes of ecclesiastics in civil matters should be referred to lay tribunals. All criminal causes, of course, were to be strictly reserved

---

7. *The West Coast Republics*, p. 126.

8. Mgr. Augusto Sieffert, Bishop of La Paz, to J. L. Mecham, La Paz, December 29, 1927.

for the ecclesiastical tribunals. Because the pope "arrogantly conceded" patronage, instead of recognizing its inherency in national sovereignty, the Bolivian Congress refused to approve the concordat.[9]

Three times during the history of Bolivia negotiations were initiated to arrange a concordat with the Vatican, but with no result. The reason for failure was that the Constitution of Bolivia attributed to the nation the right of patronage which could only be conceded by virtue of a concordat. In Bolivia, as in several other Latin-American countries where concordats have not been concluded, the pope never recognized *patronato nacional*, but tolerated it. A sort of working agreement existed between the Republic and the Vatican, with the latter accepting, but not recognizing the validity of the national pretentions. Thus, "the Church is living," said Bishop Sieffert, "with more or less liberty according to *la manía* [whim] of each government."[10]

The Constitution of 1961 introduced a major innovation—it eliminated the articles dealing with *patronato nacional*. The government no longer reserved the right to select high Church officials nor to approve documents emanating from the papacy. Bolivia thus took a long step in the direction of the separation of Church and State but the Catholic Church continued in fact to be the official and favored cult. The Constitution said (Art. 3) that "the State recognizes and upholds the Roman Catholic Apostolic Religion," though it "guarantees the public exercise of any other worship." Looking forward to an accommodation with the Vatican, the same article read: "Relations with the Church shall be regulated by agreements between the Bolivian State and the Holy See." High ranking members of the hierarchy are usually present and officiate at important governmental functions.

When the tithes and primacies were supplanted by a land tax in 1880, the Republic recognized the obligation of paying from the rural land tax a subsidy for the support of the cult. For many years the national budget provided for the appropriation of this money, and every year a competence was paid to parish priests. Later, however, these payments were stricken from the budget, and only prelates and chapters of cathedral churches were made an assignment from the national budget. The Catholic Church, after 1961, continued to receive modest financial support from the government through the Ministry of Education and Fine Arts and the Ministry of Foreign Affairs and Worship. Most of the funds were for subsidies for Catholic schools

9. Chacaltana, *op. cit.*, p. 104; *West Coast Republics*, p. 122.
10. Bishop Sieffert to J. L. Mecham.

and for salaries of high-ranking prelates. In the 1961 budget these sums totaled $72,000.[11]

According to the Constitution (Art. 24), "The property of the Church, of religious orders and congregations, and of institutions engaged in educational, welfare, and charitable pursuits shall enjoy the same rights and guarantees as private individuals." This suggests a further inquiry into the nature of the financial support of the Church and its clergy.

The principal sources of ecclesiastical income are donations, collections, fees, income from properties held, and governmental subsidy. The chief means of support is the charity of the faithful. This is expressed principally in the regular collections and occasional gifts and endowments both in money and in property. There are no legal restrictions in Bolivia on the right of the Church to receive entailments. The money received from fees is not inconsiderable and constitutes the chief means of support of those lesser ecclesiastics who do not enjoy a salary paid by the government. In each diocese there is a published tariff of rates called an *arancel*, in which is listed the amounts the faithful ought to pay for the performance of various religious services. For example, in the *Arancel Eclesiástico* of 1927 for the diocese of La Paz, it was stipulated that the fee for baptisms *de primera*, that is, at the altar and with candles, music, and bells, was six *bolivianos*; baptisms *de segunda*, that is, minus the accessories, was, for whites, one *boliviano* and, for Indians, one-half *boliviano*. The fees for performing a simple marriage ceremony in church or at home ranged from twelve and fifteen *bolivianos* for Indians and mestizos to twenty-five for whites. A *matrimonio pomposo*, which includes decorating the Church, cost fifty *bolivianos*. Burial fees were quoted at one to twenty *bolivianos* for infants and fourteen to thirty-five for adults; the inclusion or omission of items like vigil, mass, and singing accounted for the different rates. The fees for a great variety of special masses ranged from three *bolivianos* for the most simple mass (*misa rezada sencilla*) to 150 *bolivianos* for an elaborate *misa gregoriana*. In the *arancel* it was stipulated that priests perform services gratuitously for the poor; by way of illustration, the priests were ordered to give the poor decent funerals and burials without cost. They were ordered not to make changes in the rates and to keep a careful record of all fees received.[12]

It is impossible to ascertain the extent of real property belonging to

11. *U.S. Army Area Handbook for Bolivia.* Prepared by Foreign Areas Studies Division (Washington: August, 1963), p. 262.

12. *Arancel Eclesiástico de la Diócesis de La Paz* (La Paz, 1927), pp. 3-26. In 1927, the *boliviano* was worth $0.389 in U.S. currency.

the Church in addition to the buildings actually used for religious purposes, but apparently it is not large. The income from the revenue producing properties, which, incidentally, are not tax exempt and enjoy no advantage over private property, is an important item in the support of the Church. By law of July 17, 1880, all ecclesiastical buildings belonging to both the secular and regular clergy are exempt from the property tax. Yet in practice this law has not saved the Church from the payment of various municipal imposts. It has legal title and possession of its properties, under the administration of the bishop. He names as his agents the curates of the parishes, whose bookkeeping he audits each year. The regular establishments have their own administrators named by the bishop. To alienate ecclesiastical property it used to be necessary to secure permission from the *Patronato Nacional*, that is, the government.[13]

The law does not recognize any authority of the Church over the public schools, although religious instruction outside of regular hours is permitted. Instead of there being ecclesiastical control of public education, there is governmental supervision over Catholic schools. The Ministry of Education exercises supervision over courses, degrees, and hours of study and prescribes regulations governing all these matters.

In Bolivia, the public schools of primary grade far outnumber the Church schools, because instruction up to the *cursos facultados* is free. In 1960 there were 360,000 pupils in the public primary schools and 43,000 in the private institutions.[14] Governmental support of education is woefully inadequate. It is not surprising therefore that the percentage of illiteracy in the nation, over 15 years of age, is estimated to be in excess of sixty-five.[15]

The Catholic schools must be supported by fees and donations, although on occasion the government pays them a small subvention. In the secondary educational field the Church schools are more numerous and are preferred for their superior excellence. Several schools and colleges for young men are conducted by the Jesuits, Franciscans, and Christian Brothers. Most of those for girls are maintained by the Christian Sisters and Daughters of Santa Ana. In Sucre, La Paz, and Cochabamba, there are diocesan seminaries. To the credit of the Catholic prelates in Bolivia, they have called attention to the government's neglect of the problem of Indian education. Of an estimated population of about 3 million, 63 per cent are Indians and practically the

13. Bishop Sieffert to J. L. Mecham.
14. *Statistical Abstract of Latin America* (1963), pp. 22-28.
15. Francisco Houtart, *El cambio social en América Latina* (Bogotá, 1964), p. 174.

total number is to be classified as illiterate. In the interest of the greatly abused and downtrodden Indian the Church launched a "Pro-Indio Crusade." Remarkably enough, liberal elements like the Student Federation attacked the crusade because of their anticlericalism and fear of a general Indian uprising.[16]

The Protestants in Bolivia have confined their educational efforts almost entirely to missionary schools for the Indians. In La Paz and Cochabamba there are Methodist colleges called *El Instituto Americano*. They are supposed to be of a purely educational and non-sectarian nature, but have been accused of engaging in Protestant propaganda. The Protestant schools in Bolivia are very few, says Archbishop Pierini, "because, happily, Protestantism among us, as a religion, is an exotic plant, and this despite the fact that for some years the emissaries of Protestantism have made supreme efforts to establish a foot-hold in this country."[17]

In 1960 the Protestant community in Bolivia totaled 34,219 or one per cent of the population of the country. The number of Protestant clergy was listed as 569. Although most of the population of the country, 3,316,000, was claimed by the Catholic Church, the total number of Catholic clergy was only 694.[18]

The Protestant movement in Bolivia has not gained many followers due largely to the strongly entrenched Catholic tradition. The Catholic Church nevertheless has displayed a degree of concern about Protestantism out of proportion to its actual progress. Significant activities of Protestant missionaries in the fields of education, medicine, and social work have gained the respect of the populace. The largest Protestant denominations are the Seventh Day Adventists and the Pentecostals.

In Bolivia, as in other Latin-American countries, the ancient exclusive control of the Church over the institution of matrimony has been broken. Prior to 1911 the law sanctioned and recognized as binding and exclusive the formalities regulating matrimony as ruled by the Council of Trent. However, on October 11, 1911, a new law was enacted by the Bolivian Congress to the following effect: "The law only recognizes the civil marriage, after which there can be performed the canonical or religious ceremony, but it will not satisfy the legal requirements of the civil ceremony." In 1920 an exception was made in favor of the Indians, allowing them to fulfill the requirements of civil matrimony by celebrating the canonical. This law was deemed advisable because of the

16. Marsh, *op. cit.*, pp. 28-29; *Christian Work in South America*, I, 126-27.
17. For an account of the feeble efforts of Protestantism in Bolivia, see *West Coast Republics*, pp. 125-36.
18. W. Stanley Rycroft and Myrtle M. Clemmer, *A Factual Study of Latin America*, United Presbyterian Church in the U.S.A. (New York, 1963), p. 234.

fanatical attachment of the ignorant Indians to the priests, and their inability to regard anything other than the religious ceremony as being binding. In an effort to curb the numerous illegal unions among the Indians, therefore, the civil law was amended as noted.

Bolivian law until 1932 did not recognize absolute divorce permitting remarriage. It only recognized separation of bodies and goods. All questions arising between husband and wife were decided by the ecclesiastical tribunals. In 1926 a law was introduced in the Congress to legalize absolute divorce and to allow remarriage. Public opinion was strongly opposed to the measure, and it was defeated. Shortly after, on April 15, 1932, a law was passed permitting absolute divorce. This law is now in force.[19]

Until October 7, 1908, cemeteries in Bolivia were under the direction and government of the ecclesiastics. On that date they were entrusted to municipal authorities and free burials were provided. Outside of La Paz there are no sectarian burial grounds. In commenting on the municipal control of the cemeteries, Bishop Sieffert says, "There has been established the greatest confusion in the administration of the cemeteries, which are perfect images of disorder and lack of care. At the same time there do not exist complete registers of deaths in La Paz."[20]

The contemporary situation of the Catholic Church in Bolivia is a logical consequence of the nature of its membership—the illiterate natives and half-breeds who constitute nearly 90 per cent of the population of the country. Considering its *milieu* the unhealthful condition of Church and religion in the Andean republic is not surprising. The descendants of the Aymaras and Quichuas of *Alto Perú* are nominally Catholics. They receive the sacrament of baptism; most of them are married by the Church; and they attend all imaginable kinds of ceremonies which occur with an unfortunate rapidity of succession, from an economic and social standpoint. They show outward reverence for Church ritual, but their general ignorance on all subjects beyond their limited domestic life renders it unlikely that they hold any religious convictions. As for precepts of religion and prescriptions of its commandments, they know not a word. There is a great proportion of paganism in their faith, and the Catholic rites are merged in others inherited from the days of the Incas. In commenting on the mixture of primitive and Christian worship which he detected among the Indians of Bolivia, an American scholar says, "The old rites of the Indians are

19. Ricardo Gallardo, *Divorcio, Separación de Cuerpos y Nulidad del Matrimonio en las Naciones Latino-Americanos* (Madrid, 1957), pp. 80-81.

20. Bishop Sieffert to J. L. Mecham, La Paz, October 6, 1927.

grafted upon a new principle, often with but a change in name and not in symbol. The spirit of the old prayers for abundant rivers and rich harvests breathes through the new devotions, and the quaint melancholy songs of the ancient Quichua or Aymara tribes often follow upon a fiesta in which the rites of the Christian religion are but new form for an old and pathetically simple speech. The rivers and the harvests are the forms in which they understand the Deity. It is hard to teach men new faiths or religious or moral niceties whose first and only prayer has always been for the daily bread fairly wrung from a stubborn earth."[21] "To see and hear the Indians during a religious festival," writes a European visitor in the same vein, "one might well take them for idolators accomplishing the ceremonies of the ancient cult of the sun, followed by a Roman saturnalia, but never for Christians celebrating Easter or the Feast of the Trinity."[22]

This very ignorance of the Indians strengthens the influence of the clergy, for the priesthood is regarded with awe and is accorded servile obedience. The willingness of the Indians to be exploited has undoubtedly influenced many of the less scrupulous curates to requite the faith and trust of their charges with extortionate demands. Serious accusations, exaggerated it is true, but legitimately based, have been brought against the venality and perverted morals of the Bolivian clergy, particularly those curates entrusted with parishes remote from the diocesan capitals. The rural clergy of Bolivia, like that of Peru, is sadly deficient. Recruited from the half-breeds and Indians, raised amid the most humble surroundings, and given a superficial training, these country priests are impossible moral mentors of their parishioners. The indictment penned by a distinguished Bolivian historian half a century ago is still applicable to the rural clerics of Bolivia. He wrote: "Unfortunately, with rare exceptions, the priest in the canton is dissolute, avaricious, full of vices, and incapable of commanding respect; he receives money for masses he never says, at least when and where he should, and he is content to say one mass for many individuals when he has been paid for several; he loans money with interest and makes a fortune."[23]

The problem confronting the hierarchy in Bolivia is identical with that of Peru, i.e., the difficulty of procuring worthy candidates for service in the Church. Praiseworthy desires of the bishops to replace bad priests are constantly balked by the scarcity of material. In Bolivia,

21. Isaiah Bowman, "Regional Population Groups of Atacama," in *Bulletin*, American Geographical Society, XLI, 1909, p. 211.
22. Paul Walle, *Bolivia* (London, 1914), p. 145.
23. Alcides Arguedas, *Pueblo Enfermo* (2nd ed.; Barcelona, 1910), p. 43.

as we have noted, there are scarcely more Catholic clergy than Protestant ministers, and fully half of the clergy are foreigners. Almost all of the regulars who are fulfilling the functions of priests are foreigners, mostly Spanish. Even the hierarchy is dominated by foreigners, for one of the two archbishops, two of the five bishops, and all of the apostolic vicars are foreigners.[24] A partial, but completely inadequate, answer to the scarcity of clergy in Bolivia, is the work of lay apostolic groups such as Catholic Action. Bolivia has been recognized as strictly a mission country, a fact dramatized by the presence of not only Protestant but foreign Catholic missionaries.[25]

The Catholic Church in Bolivia, in both the religious and non-religious spheres, is weak. Although most Bolivians are rated Roman Catholics, only a small minority have more than a rudimentary background in doctrine and dogma. Religious education is grossly inadequate. Most Bolivian Catholics, like Latin-American Catholics in general, are quite lax in religious practices. The general neglect of religious duties is usually met with a considerable degree of tolerance. Women are more conscientious in religious practice, which is considered more properly a feminine sphere of activity.

During the last decade the Church has demonstrated an awareness of its own weakness and has sought to strengthen its role in society. It has instituted or is expanding programs designed to stimulate greater spirituality among the faithful and to broaden its own activities in the social sphere. Social action was stimulated, no doubt, by the growing social consciousness encouraged by the MNR (Movimiento Nacionalista Revolutionario) since its rise to power in 1952. This new approach by the Church was illustrated by an invitation, through the initiative of the papal nuncio, to a team of Canadian Oblate missionaries, well trained in social action, to take up work among the Bolivian miners at Catavi.[26] The progress of Catholic social action in Bolivia has not been on a large scale because of lack of funds, personnel, and experience. Despite its good intentions the Church cannot be expected to compete with government action in scope and popularity.

Although the Church supported the social reforms of the government, including the nationalization of the tin mines, it was critical of the leftist tendencies of the MNR. The archbishop of La Paz, in

24. *Army Area Handbook for Bolivia, op. cit.*, p. 264.
25. Nevins, *op. cit.*, pp. 14, 67.
26. *Army Area Handbook for Bolivia, op. cit.*, p. 256. In March, 1964, an agreement was entered into between the Bolivian government and the Episcopal Conference of Bolivia providing for the exemption from import duties of all goods and articles needed by the Church for its social aid action.

November, 1959, criticized the government's toleration of communism, claiming that pro-Catholics were frequently arrested and communist elements were seldom prosecuted. In June, 1960, the archbishop issued a circular stating that the people should not vote for those who denied God. They should repudiate the "red peace of Communism."[27]

The position of the Church, generally, is noninterference in politics and relative isolation from crucial national problems. The government therefore has made no especially strong campaign against the status and position of the Church. Nevertheless there is still a religious question in Bolivia, and we can state confidently that there will be further changes in Church-State relationships. It would be idle however, to indulge in specifics.

PARAGUAY

The Catholic Church in Paraguay, like the Paraguayans themselves, was the victim of heartless oppression during a large part of the nineteenth century. From the time when the Spanish authority was cast aside in 1811, and the *real patronato*, consequently, was disavowed, until the death of Francisco Solano López in 1870, the Church was in fact not a Roman but a Paraguayan Catholic Church. Under the dictators Francia and the López, the clergy plumbed the lowest depths of degradation, insult, and servility. The curse of the dictators not only retarded the political and economic development of the republic, but the moral and the spiritual likewise, because of the unnatural channels into which religious endeavor and precepts were forcibly diverted.

Unfortunately the Church itself was indirectly responsible in a small way for the tyrannical rules imposed upon the hapless country. "In the state in which Paraguay was after the revolution," says an American writer of Paraguayan history, "it required neither superior talent nor education to lead the simple people whose ignorance was their inheritance from the Jesuit fathers."[28] The Jesuit plan of training and evangelization resulted, whether they intentionally desired it or

27. *Hispanic American Report*, XII, No. 11 (November, 1959), p. 620, XIII, No. 6 (June, 1960), p. 403.

28. Charles A. Washburn, *A History of Paraguay* (Boston, 1871), I, 163. Washburn was American Minister to Paraguay during the Paraguayan War. His two volume history of Paraguay, although suffering in balanced judgment according to the modern canons of historical criticism, is nevertheless the best history of the country. His adverse criticism of the Jesuits is too severe and causes one to question his impartiality. For a sympathetic treatment of the "Jesuit Republic," see R. B. Cunningham Graham, *A Vanished Arcadia* (New York, 1901).

not, in keeping the Indians as ignorant as possible of every duty but that of unquestioning, passive obedience. Although the Jesuit control came to an end, in theory, a half century before independence, nevertheless their lessons in complete and abject submission to the clerical will continued to be taught by their successors, the Franciscans. Thus, when the time came for the Paraguayans to assume control of their own political destinies, they were the least fit for the task of all the peoples of Spanish America. How natural was it, then, that they should bow submissively to the absolute will of a domineering personality.

Dr. José Gaspar Rodríguez Francia, *El Supremo*, seized control of the Paraguayan government soon after its declaration of independence, and for the next thirty years he ruled the inland republic with a despotic fiendishness unparalleled in the history of America.[29] Although Christian belief rested lightly upon the conscience of the dictator, he being in reality an infidel notwithstanding the fact that he received a degree of doctor of theology in the University of Córdova; and although he entertained contempt for the gross ignorance and scandalous lives of the lazy and dissolute priests, it was not for these reasons that Francia hated them. It was because the priests exercised great influence over the lower classes and because a Church government with authority independent of the civil power was inconsistent with absolute rule. Since Francia proposed to brook not even a shadow of authority other than his own, the Church, the only institution likely to rival his influence, was forced to bow to his will. To obviate all possibility of danger from that institution, Francia took all its property into his own hands, deprived it of all ceremonials which were wont to impress the populace, caused the priests to become his passive agents by making them report to him, and in the end made himself the head of the Church after the example of Henry VIII of England. When the bishop, because of insults and persecution suffered at the hands of the tyrant, became insane, Francia appointed to the headship of the diocese a creature of his own whom he called a vicar-general. The priests were so persecuted that they scarcely ventured to exercise any of their functions except receive death-bed confessions and administer extreme unction. As for confessions, the dictator did not object to people confessing to the priests, but the priests had to confess to him. Naturally all relations with Rome were suspended, for in closing the ports to the ingress of foreigners, Francia made no exception in favor of papal nuncios or agents. However, it was

29. Dr. P. H. Box in *The Origins of the Paraguayan War* (Urbana, Ill., 1929), p. 11, qualifies the harshness of Francia's rule. He writes: "He ruled with the consent of the Paraguayan people."

scarcely likely that the Holy See would countenance the high-handed measures of *El Supremo.*[30]

The treatment of the Church by Francia's successor, Carlos Antonio López, was a slight improvement (it could scarcely have been worse), but still the troubles of the ecclesiastics were not over by any means. In 1844 López gave Paraguay a constitution carefully designed by himself to preserve the supreme authority in his own hands. This constitution contained the customary provisions regarding the nation's right to control the ecclesiastical patronage. For example, the president exercised the patronage of the churches, the livings, and ecclesiastical persons according to the laws; he could name the bishop and the members of the ecclesiastical senate; he could celebrate concordats with the Holy Apostolic See, concede or refuse his approval to the decrees of ecclesiastical councils, and give or deny the exequatur to the pontifical bulls or briefs, without which requisite nobody should enforce them.

The dictator subjected the Church to the iron control of classic regalism, for he would brook no authority but his own. To reduce the prestige and respect for bishops he enacted a law in November, 1845, entitled "Reform of the Privileges of the Reverend Bishops." It abolished the ringing of church bells in honor of bishops and public kneeling when a bishop passed. Also, no bishop should use a throne or robe either in or out of the church.[31]

In an endeavor to renew relations with the pope, which had been entirely suspended during Francia's time, López made overtures while he was consul, asking for the appointment of a bishop. In accordance with the national pretension to patronage, he recommended for the episcopal office his brother, Basilio López. The nomination was accepted by the pope and thus relations were restored.

Carlos López, however, was the real head of the Paraguayan Church, for Basilio, an eccentric, good-natured individual, thoroughly devoid of ambition or avarice, exercised no authority or power which was not conceded to him by his brother the president. The dictator, like Dr. Francia, had been educated in theology, but in later life was a scoffer at religion, howbeit he observed the outward forms. And although he entertained no greater fondness for the clergy than did *El Supremo*, he found that he could put priests to better use than did Francia. That is, he determined not to suppress them, but to make them the auxiliaries

30. Washburn, *op. cit.*, I, 166-70, 213; W. H. Koebel, *Paraguay* (London, 1917), pp. 174-75; Julio César Chaves, *El supremo dictador: biografía de José Gaspar de Francia* (3rd ed.; Buenos Aires, 1958), pp. 303-12.

31. R. B. Cunningham Graham, *Portrait of a Dictator: Francisco Solano López* (London, 1933), p. 65.

to his power. He restored parishes throughout the country and in many cases gave the priests civil authority in addition to their spiritual functions. But, like Francia, he required them to report to him, and the secrets of the confessional all came to his knowledge.[32]

Bishop Basilio López died in 1859, and the pope was requested to appoint another bishop. The Holy Father, however, demanded: first, a restoration of Church property that had been withheld for nearly fifty years, and second, the right of appointing a bishop, not a Paraguayan, who should be responsible to him, and not to the president of the republic. López, naturally, refused to consent to either demand and resolved, in an extremity, to assume the headship of the Church himself. When the pope threatened to place an interdict over Paraguay, López defended his stand by declaring that divided authority was not compatible with peace and order, and therefore he could not yield. Pius IX finally agreed, in 1860, to invest Bishop Juan Gregorio Urbieta, López' nominee. Bishop Urbieta was an old, infirm, and inoffensive person who never pretended to question the right of the government to render his spiritual functions entirely subordinate to the temporal authority. The actual diocesan administrator was Manuel Antonio Palacios, who was appointed auxiliary bishop in 1862 with the right of succession when a vacancy should occur. Palacios had been recommended by Carlos López at the solicitation of his son Francisco Solano López, presumably because Palacios was an abject, servile flatterer of the dictator's heir apparent.[33]

Francisco Solano López followed the examples of his father and Dr. Francia in refusing to tolerate any authority apart from his own in Paraguay. Since he considered the Church as the most formidable of his potential rivals, he used Bishop Palacios as a willing tool to subordinate the complete ecclesiastical organization to his will. The shameful subservience of the Bishop to the Dictator is reported by a foreign observer, a certain Mr. Thompson: "The Bishop used to go and wait in López' corridor with his hat in his hand. When López came out, the Bishop shuffled up towards him with a deprecating look, and made a deep bow, to which López would return a nod, without touching his cap."[34]

All the clergy from the Bishop down were converted into an active instrument of espionage, systematized into complete subordination. The greatest service the Bishop and the clergy performed for the tyrant was that of instructing the populace in their duties to a divinely appointed

32. Washburn, *op. cit.*, I, 465-67, 477.
33. *Ibid.*, I, 463, II, 54-55; Graham, *Portrait of a Dictator*, pp. 113-15.
34. Koebel, *op. cit.*, p. 188.

ruler. From the pulpit López was proclaimed as the anointed of the Lord, and it was consequently the duty of the people to devote their lives, labor, and fortunes to him, and to count nothing a sacrifice which he might demand. To question the legitimacy of his acts was both treason and heresy. A catechism, originally prepared by a bishop of Tucumán in 1784 to instruct the people in the principal obligations that the vassal owes to his king and lord as the divinely appointed ruler, was adapted by Palacios, with slight changes, to inspire in the people their proper duty to López.[35]

The responsibility of the Bishop for changing a peace-loving people into fanatically aggressive warriors is evidenced by a letter which he wrote to López in 1865: "It has been with no small difficulty, excellent sir, that we have labored with a people so unwarlike as ours, but happily this difficulty we have now overcome, and made to almost disappear by the words of evangelical truth, and by means of the confessional, in which daily we are engaged confessing hundreds of soldiers, disposing and fortifying them for the struggle and making them to understand with the greatest clearness, that those who give their lives in the combat for their country will be recompensed and eternally rewarded by the Eternal Creator."[36]

Thus, a Catholic prelate was responsible in no small measure for "the tragedy of Paraguay." The decimation of the Paraguayan race, the awful result of blind, fanatical allegiance sworn to an insane ruler, was only made possible because of clerical teaching of religious duty to the "divinely appointed president."

After Paraguay had been liberated by the allied arms of Argentina, Brazil, and Uruguay from the tyranny of Francisco Solano López, it was necessary to overhaul the government. Unfortunately the tendency of the framers of the new constitution (promulgated, 1870), was to follow too closely foreign, particularly Argentinian, practices and accord little attention to the peculiar needs of Paraguay. As one writer stated, "If we had to express in a few words the result of a comparison between the two constitutions which Paraguay has had up to now, we would say that the first was too Paraguayan, and the second too Argentinian."[37] Yet, if the Argentinian example was followed in framing the religious clauses of the constitution, regarding which there is no evidence, then, fortunately for Paraguay, the Argentinian policy with respect to the Catholic Church was remarkably well adapted to the

35. Washburn, *op. cit.*, II, 56.
36. *Ibid.*, II, 57-58.
37. Justo Arosemena, *Estudios Constitucionales sobre los gobiernos de la América Latina*, 2 vols. (Paris, 1888), I, 291-92.

religious requirements of the Paraguayans. The Constitution of 1870, in fact, involved a very slight departure from the principles theoretically proclaimed and guaranteed in the Constitution of 1844, but it differed from the earlier instrument in that the actual ecclesiastical policy of the government harmonized with the constitutional requirements.

The Roman Catholic Apostolic religion was declared to be that of the State. Nevertheless toleration was protected by the denial to Congress of the power to forbid the free exercise of any other religion within the territory of the republic and in the guarantee to all inhabitants of the right of professing freely their cult. And, in order to encourage immigration, of which Paraguay was in great need, the Constitution guaranteed to aliens the right to freely profess their religion. This inducement, however, did not attract Protestants, for the great majority of the few immigrants to Paraguay were Italians and Argentinians who already professed the Catholic faith. Although Protestant immigration was negligible, a rather notable exception was the Mennonite community. In 1927 the Mennonites abandoned their colony in Canada and settled in Paraguay in the Gran Chaco on a vast tract of land given them by the government. To facilitate the immigration of the Mennonites the Paraguayan Congress granted them a charter containing exemptions which they were not able to secure elsewhere. Since the founding of the Mennonite colony "represents one of the most ideal-impelled migrations on record," the main clauses of the charter deserve to be mentioned. They were:

> Article 1. Members of the community known as Mennonites who come to the country as components of a colonization enterprise, and their descendants, shall enjoy the following rights and privileges:
>
> a. To practice their religion and to worship with absolute liberty without any restriction and consequently, to make affirmation by a simple "Yes" or "No" in courts of justice, instead of by oath; and to be exempt from obligatory service either as combatants or non-combatants, both in times of peace and during war.
>
> b. To establish, maintain, and administer schools and establishments of learning, and to teach and learn their language, which is German, without any restriction.
>
> Article 2. The sale of alcoholic or intoxicating beverages is prohibited within a zone of five kilometres from the properties belonging to the Mennonite colonies, unless the competent authorities of these colonies request that the government permit such sale and the government accedes to the request.

Article 3. The following concessions are granted to the Mennonite colonies for a period of ten years from the arrival of the first colonists:

a. The free entry of furniture, machinery, utensils, drugs, seeds, animals, implements, and, in general, of everything that may be necessary for the installation and development of the colonies.

b. Exemption from all classes of national and municipal taxes.

Article 4. No immigration law, or law of any other character, existing or that may be passed in future, shall impede the entrance of Mennonite immigrants into the country because of age or physical or mental incapacity.[38]

According to the terms of the above contract, five thousand Mennonites established a colony on a tract of land some 3,000,000 acres in extent on the eastern slope of the Andes and along the Paraguay River west of Puerto Casado. The Mennonite enterprise was not missionary in any sense of the term. Although greatly hampered by nature and the Paraguayan-Bolivian conflict in the Gran Chaco, the Mennonites demonstrated that men could farm successfully in a hitherto neglected area.[39]

The Catholic clergy, like the other elements of the Paraguayan nation, had been reduced almost to the point of extinction by Francisco Solano López's disastrous war. Thus for several generations there was only a very limited clerical personnel with which to carry on. In addition, following the turn of the century, the Liberals made bitter onslaughts against the Church. Bishop Bagarin described the situation: "With political opposition as it existed in Paraguay the union of Church and State proved a tragedy; the enemies of religion used government interference to block everything that might strengthen Christian life." For example, it took proclerical demonstrations and days of wrangling to secure passage of a bill approving the increase of the number of dioceses in Paraguay from one to three.[40]

According to the present constitution of Paraguay, which was adopted in 1940, "The Roman Catholic Apostolic Religion is the state religion, but other cults not opposed to morality and public order are tolerated. The head of the Paraguayan Church and the bishops must be native citizens" (Article 3). The President, who must "follow the

38. Quoted in Webster E. Browning, *The River Plate Republics* (London, 1928), pp. 59-61.

39. For the Mennonite colony, see Harris Gaylord Warren, *Paraguay, An Informal History* (Norman, Oklahoma, 1949), pp. 274-75.

40. John J. Considine, *New Horizons in Latin America* (New York, 1958), pp. 119-20.

Roman Catholic Apostolic faith," "exercises the rights of National Patronage of the Republic in the presentation of archbishops and bishops, proposed in a list of three by the Council of State, in agreement with the Ecclesiastical Senate or the national clergy assembled." The President, in agreement with the Council of State and the unicameral legislature, approves or withholds conciliar decrees and pontifical bulls, briefs, and rescripts (Article 51:8). He is also empowered to sign concordats; however, none has been concluded because of papal refusal to recognize the national patronage. The Vatican acquiesces nevertheless in the nation's exercise of the patronage. The Ministry of Education and Worship is in charge of the relations of the State with the Church. The Archbishop of Asunción is constitutionally assigned membership in the Council of State. In further evidence of the official and privileged status of the Catholic Church in Paraguay, religious holidays are also official holidays and the Republic sends an ambassador to the Holy See and receives an apostolic nuncio at Asunción.

The Paraguayan government pays the salaries of the archbishop and bishops, the personnel of the curias, professors of seminaries, as well as scholarship aid to seminarians. The governmental subsidy is so small that the State certainly does not lay itself open to the charge of lavishing financial favors on the Church, and moreover it is so insignificant that the Church must come to feel in time that its connection with the State is unprofitable. For support the clergy are dependent almost exclusively upon such sources of income as gifts, bequests, fees, and rents. Although there are no limitations on the right of the Church to hold property the extent of real ecclesiastical holdings is not great, and compared with other South American countries the Catholic Church in Paraguay is poor.

Marriage has been declared a civil contract, and although the Roman Catholic and other religious marriage rites are permitted they can be performed only after the civil ceremony. The law is sometimes disregarded and the civil ceremony omitted. For the legitimization of children and in matters of inheritances, only the civil ceremony is legally taken into account. About 50 per cent of the births in Paraguay are illegitimate, despite the fact that the percentage of free unions (concubinage), 14.69 per cent, is slightly less than the Latin-American average. The greatest incidence of free unions and illegitimacy is in the rural regions, where there is the greatest absence of clergy.[41]

41. Francisco Houtart, *El cambio social en América Latina* (Bogotá, 1964), pp. 141, 143.

Divorce and remarriage are not allowed, although legal separation was sanctioned in 1891.[42] Whenever a divorce project is introduced in the legislature, the Church opposes it very strenuously since it represents a dangerous break from authority. The cemeteries belong to the State and are open to all irrespective of creed. Any religious group, however, may maintain its own burial grounds.

Public education is free, compulsory, and lay; religious instruction is not allowed in the public schools as a part of the regular curriculum. Most of the public educational work of whatever grade is confined to the cities and towns; consequently the great majority of the children of Paraguay, living in rural communities, are denied all educational facilities. Private primary instruction, in charge of religious as well as secular entities, is on the increase. A few private schools are subsidized by the government. Both Catholic and Protestant missionaries are extending educational facilities but it must be admitted they are lamentably inadequate to cope with their great problem. In so far as facilities for secondary education exist, they are afforded by the religious schools. Although instruction in the private schools is under the general supervision of the government, the administration of their internal affairs is untrammeled. These schools are free to teach religion as a special subject. Regarding education in Paraguay, it can be fairly concluded that neither the State nor private agencies have more than scratched the surface of appalling illiteracy.[43]

Paraguay, with an area larger than California, and a population of 1,718,000 in 1960, had only 313 priests, more than half of whom were engaged in nonparochial work. Thus the number of inhabitants per diocesan priest was about one to ten thousand.[44] In Paraguay it is much the same story as in other Latin-American countries: "Priests are scarce and vocations are few."[45]

The episcopal diocese of Asunción, which up to 1929 had been a suffragan of the Archbishop of Buenos Aires, was raised to metropolitan rank and new dioceses of Concepción and Encarnación were created. The Church, through the episcopate, the clergy, and organizations of the faithful, is starting to take an interest in the improvement of conditions for the economic, moral, and spiritual progress of the people.

42. Ricardo Gallardo, *Divorcio, Separación de Cuerpos y Nulidad de Matrimonio en las Naciones Latino-Américanos* (Madrid, 1957), p. 13.

43. According to Father Houtart (*op. cit.*, p. 174), illiteracy, over 15 years of age, is 30 per cent. Father John J. Considine in *New Horizons in Latin America* (New York, 1958), p. 122, rates illiteracy at 75 per cent.

44. *Statistical Abstract of Latin America, 1963*, p. 22.

45. Nevins, *op. cit.*, p. 67.

Good work being done by Catholic Action, the lay apostolate, and Pax Romana, the university student movement, should be mentioned.[46]

In 1958 the Archbishop of Asunción mustered enough courage to criticize the government of the current dictator and recommend popular participation in the renovation of the political health of the nation.[47] But when a young priest, Father Ramón Talavera, was so strongly critical of the policies of President Stroessner and consequently was forced to flee to Montevideo, the Archbishop was forced to reiterate the Church's stand against political activities and condemn the "malicious and irresponsible" acts of the priest. This statement was interpreted as demonstrating how far the Church would go in avoiding a clash with the dictator. In April, 1962, the Archbishop commended Stroessner for his collaboration with the Church in its work for "the moral and spiritual elevation of the people."[48]

The missionary needs and opportunities in Paraguay are great. In a region once the stronghold of the Jesuits, the Catholic Church is now relatively weaker in leadership, membership, influence, and enterprise than in any other South American republic. The failure of Catholicism in Paraguay should be to the advantage of Protestantism, yet with the exception of Ecuador, it is the most neglected of South American republics by the Evangelical missionaries. To aid Evangelical missionary work, the Paraguayan government passed a law in 1909 to facilitate the establishment of Protestant missions to convert the Indian tribes. By virtue of this act the president of the republic was authorized to grant public lands in parcels not exceeding 7,500 hectares (18,750 acres) to individuals or companies organized for the purpose of converting the Indians. On each of these concessions was to be established a "reduction," with the necessary churches, houses, and schools. Although the act failed to stimulate missionary activity, the Christianizing and civilizing of the Indians has remained a major consideration of the Paraguayan government and it wisely refrained from discriminating against any Christian cult.[49]

In 1960 the Protestant community of Paraguay numbered 11,173 or 0.7 per cent of the total population of the country. The Protestant clergy, who confined their activities almost exclusively to Asunción, numbered 165.[50] The sects represented in Paraguay are: (1) the

46. Considine, *op. cit.*, pp. 120-21.
47. *Hispanic American Report*, XI, No. 3 (March, 1958), 170.
48. *Ibid.*, XII, No. 12 (December, 1958), 696, XV, No. 4 (April, 1962), 1160.
49. Koebel, *op. cit.*, pp. 218-19.
50. W. Stanley Rycroft and Myrtle M. Clemmer, *A Factual Study of Latin America*, United Presbyterian Church in the U.S.A. (New York, 1963), p. 234.

older ones: Anglicans, Baptists, Lutherans and Methodists; and (2) the newer and more active ones: Mormons, Jehovah's Witnesses, and Adventists. The ministry is almost exclusively foreign.

In Paraguay there is no organized anticlerical group, but merely a widespread passivity or actual disdain for the Church. This is particularly true on the part of the men. It is more a case of contempt for individual priests than a generalized anticlericalism.[51] A campaign has been waged for separation of Church and State by the young intelligentsia, but the movement does not appear to be strong or destined to achieve success in the near future. It is the policy of the politicians—and dictators—to let the Church alone so long as it does not interfere in matters of State. But changes have been accomplished in other countries with such unexpected suddenness, that it would be foolhardy to declare the improbability of similar action in Paraguay.

51. Elman R. Service and Helen S. Service, *Tobatí: Paraguayan Town* (Chicago, 1954), 238-40.

Chapter IX

The Religious Question in Chile

The separation of Church from State occurred in Chile in 1925. The religious question had occupied a most prominent position in the history of that country, and great difficulty was experienced in finding a satisfactory solution of the problem. But after inaugurating her independent career as one of the most intolerant of the Catholic governments of South America, Chile became one of the most liberal nations in matters of religion.

From the outbreak of the struggle for independence until 1833, proclamations, provisional statutes, and organic laws proclaimed the Catholic religion as that of Chileans to the exclusion of all other faiths. In explaining this exclusive policy the great liberal, Balmaceda, said, "The revolution of independence was waged by valorous, patriotic men imbued with a love of Chilean nationality; but they were under the influence of Church customs, beliefs, and superstitions even, of the colonial period. It is not strange, then, that in the different constitutions and constitutional projects from 1810 to 1833 they stipulated privileges in favor of the Catholic Church and frankly refused liberty of conscience."[1] In support of the denial of freedom of worship, Juan de Egaña, a revolutionary patriot, wrote a treatise (1820) on religious liberty entitled *Memoria política sobre si conviene en Chile la libertad de cultos.* The propositions emphasized by him were: (1) a number of cults within a single State conduces to irreligion; (2) the existence of two or more religions side by side will tend to inevitable conflict which will destroy the State; and (3) religious uniformity is the most effective means of establishing tranquillity in the affairs of the nation.[2] The views of Egaña found general acceptance, not only in post-revolutionary Chile, but throughout Spanish America.

1. Julio Bañados Espinosa, *Balmacada, su Gobierno, y la Revolución de 1891* (Paris, 1894), pp. 32-33.
2. Bernard Moses, *The Intellectual Background of Revolution in South America, 1810-1824* (New York, 1926), pp. 67-68.

The Constitution of 1818, the first fundamental law designed to guide the course of the infant republic after its independence had been definitely secured, denied freedom of worship to any faith other than the Roman Catholic, which was put under the protection and control of the new government. The article pertinent to this subject read: "The Roman Catholic Apostolic religion is the sole and exclusive faith of the State of Chile. Its protection, conservation, purity, and inviolability will be one of the duties of the chiefs of society who will never permit another public cult or doctrine contrary to that of Jesus Christ."[3] The republic also declared its right to assume the patronal authority once exercised over the Catholic Church in Chile by the kings of Spain. Only Chilean citizens resident in the State could be appointed to ecclesiastical benefices.[4] As has been noted elsewhere, national patronage could only exist when there was a formal or tacit agreement by the papacy. This acquiescence on the part of Rome was not forthcoming for several years. In the meantime the governmental authorities undertook to act in the emergency. On January 4, 1819, a decree was published providing rules for the better government and control of the mendicant orders and for an improvement of the morals of the regulars.[5] The relations between dictator Bernardo O'Higgins and the Church dignitaries and clergy were relatively cordial. "But," declares a Chilean historian, "enemies of emancipation as these dignitaries had been, if they tolerated the dictatorship of O'Higgins, they did not accept it in good faith."[6] The majority of the high Church officials were native Spaniards, and, as neither Spain nor the papacy had as yet recognized the independence of Chile, it is not surprising that the Spanish clergy were in secret sympathy with the mother country.

The intransigent royalism of the higher ecclesiastics was most pronounced in Bishop Rodríguez Zorrilla of Santiago. Although a creole, he had been nominated for the vacant see of Santiago by Ferdinand VII, and, in 1815, the pope issued a bull for his institution. Bishop Rodríguez, a narrow, dogmatic pedant, was a notorious opponent of the Revolution. In his first episcopal letter he condemned the revolt. To him the rebellion was the greatest of crimes, and he predicted that it would result in opening the door to irreligion. To his clergy he represented the Revolution as an impious schism and its leaders as "impenitent Voltaireans." In legitimate defense, O'Higgins, after failing to quiet the Bishop by

3. Ricardo Anguita (ed.), *Leyes Promulgadas en Chile desde 1810 hasta el 10 de junio de 1913* (Santiago, 1913), I, 53.

4. *Ibid.*, I, 55.

5. *Ibid.*, I, 64-65.

6. Luis Galdames, *Estudio de la Historia de Chile* (Santiago, 1911), p. 309.

gentle means, was forced to exile him to San Luis in the province of Cuyo. Besides Bishop Rodríguez, three other ecclesiastics were expelled from the country. O'Higgins, because of his desire to placate the clericals, and because, as a good son of the Church himself he was confident that it would put no obstacles in his way if it realized that he had no ulterior motives, allowed Bishop Rodríguez to return to Chile in 1821.[7]

Since the other Chilean bishopric, Concepción,[8] was vacant, O'Higgins was confronted with the ticklish problem of filling it. Although the right of national patronage had been asserted in the Constitution, he realized that it would be futile to make nominations until the pope should consent to recognize them. O'Higgins decided, therefore, with the advice of the acting governor of the diocese of Santiago (the patriot canon José Ignacio Cienfuegos), to send an official delegation to Rome to negotiate the restoration of religious relations with the papacy. Cienfuegos was induced by the dictator to head the mission, and was successful, as has been seen, in persuading the pope to agree to a temporary arrangement by sending an apostolic vicar to Chile. The mission of Juan Muzi was a failure because of the demand of the Chilean government that national patronage be recognized. This, Rome would not concede.

Notwithstanding the generally cordial feeling that existed between O'Higgins and the Church, on occasion their *entente* became strained. When, for example, the dictator favored the founding of a theatre in Santiago to stimulate interest in the drama, he was criticized by the clergy who regarded theatrical presentations as immoral.[9] Likewise, when O'Higgins, as a service to the large foreign population of Valparaiso and because of his desire to encourage immigration, even of communicants of other faiths, ordered the establishment in Valparaiso of a cemetery for dissidents, a storm of clerical protest was aroused.[10]

The creation of a quasi-liberal government under the headship of General Ramón Freire, after the deposition of dictator O'Higgins, was followed by legislative enactments which were branded by the clergy as being anticlerical. Because of his financial needs, as well as his con-

7. Ayarragaray, *La Iglesia en América*, pp. 239-41; Leturia, *La Acción Diplomática*, p. 176.

8. In the colonial period there were two bishoprics in Chile, Santiago and Concepción, suffragans of the archbishop of Lima. Pope Gregory XVI in 1840 elevated the see of Santiago to archiepiscopal dignity, and created two new dioceses, La Serena and Ancúd. The first bishop of Santiago was Manuel Vicuña. He died May 3, 1843. (Francisco V. Vergara, *Historia de Chile*, Valparaiso, 1898, p. 254.)

9. Galdames, *op. cit.*, pp. 307-8.

10. Henry Clay Evans, *Chile and its Relations with the United States* (Durham, 1927), p. 36.

viction that the clergy needed reform, Freire suppressed some of the religious houses and confiscated their property. Several of the orders were dispossessed of their convents in order to give James Thomson, agent of the British and Foreign Bible Society, room for his schools established on the Lancastrian plan.[11] The tithes were abolished and regular salaries were fixed for the clergy to be paid by the government. The bishop of Santiago, for example, was paid two thousand *escudos* (gold crowns) a year, in addition to four thousand paid by the diocese.[12] This attack on the Church was also a direct consequence of the support given by the clergy to the centralistic-conservative forces known as the *Pelucones,* who were opposed to the *Pípolos,* or federal-liberals who were in control of the government almost continuously from 1823 to 1830.

The determination of the Freire administration to assert national patronage, plus its anticlerical legislative program, doomed to failure the mission of Juan Muzi. The withdrawal of the papal vicar amid conditions which Nicolás Bravo branded as a national disgrace and Muzi's subsequent defense proclamation, issued at Montevideo, in which he attacked the good faith of the Chilean government, strained the relations between the clericals and the civil authorities almost to the breaking point. Under these conditions Bishop Rodríguez renewed his criticism of the republic. Since the Bishop refused to refrain from his attacks, Freire was forced to remove him from office. Later, on December 22, 1825, Supreme Director Blanco Encalada banished the militant bishop from the territory of the republic. From Valparaiso Rodríguez sailed to Acapulco, where he arrived sick and sad of heart, but regretting that he had not made an even more strenuous fight. He passed the remainder of his days in Spain, supported by a small pension granted him by Ferdinand VII.[13] When Bishop Rodríguez was removed from his see, the cathedral chapter met, and in accordance with custom, nominated as capitular vicar Archdeacon Cienfuegos whose candidature Blanco Encalada had presented. When Cienfuegos resigned, in 1825, another governmental nominee, Canon Diego Antonio Elizondo, was installed in the administration of the diocese. In 1832 the vacancy in the

11. W. E. Browning, John Richie, and K. G. Grubb, *The West Coast Republics of South America* (London, 1930), p. 77.

12. Sallusti, *Misiones Apostólicas de Monseñor Juan Muzi,* p. 439. According to Galdames (Luis Galdames, *Historia de Chile; La Evolución Constitucional, 1810-1925,* Santiago, 1926, I, 947) the confiscation of the property of the regulars was applied on a small scale and did not continue for long.

13. Galdames, *op. cit.,* p. 317; Vergara, *op. cit.,* pp. 253-54; Ayarragaray, *op. cit.,* pp. 241-42, 246.

see came to an end when Cienfuegos was appointed titular bishop of Santiago.[14]

During the decade of the 1820's Chile was afflicted with several constitutions. These elaborate, but short-lived, fundamental laws, although differing as to idealistic principles of government, were all in agreement in assigning to Catholicism a favored legal position. The Constitution of 1822, which was published by O'Higgins in a futile eleventh hour effort to prevent his overthrow, contained the religious articles of the Constitution of 1818, with this addition: "The inhabitants of the territory shall pay it (Roman Catholic Church) the greatest respect and veneration, whatever might be their private opinions.... Article 11. All violations of the preceding article will be a crime against the fundamental laws of the land."[15]

The Constitution of 1823, which was framed by Juan de Egaña for General Freire, declared the Roman faith to be the religion of the State and prohibited the public or private exercise of other cults. Citizenship was confined to Roman Catholics. The president was given the right of ecclesiastical presentation and control of the *pase*. Moreover the Constitution provided that each year a senator should undertake an investigation tour of the provinces to examine the status of religious and moral conditions.[16] When enabling legislation was being enacted to enforce the judicial clauses of the Constitution an attempt was made to suppress the ecclesiastical *fuero*. The reform was frustrated, however, as being too impolitic.[17] Highlights in the ensuing near-anarchic political situation in Chile were: (1) the derogation of the Constitution of 1823 by General Freire in January, 1825; (2) the declaration of federalism in 1826; (3) the assuming by Freire, in 1827, of the position of *jefe político y militar* (a dictatorship); and (4) the promulgation of a most liberal constitution in 1828.[18] During these chaotic times there was no abatement in the exercise of the patronage. In 1827 Freire decreed that he would name to the lesser benefices only those nominated to him by the ecclesiastical *cabildos*. Time was also found to undertake a further reform of the regulars. In 1826 properties belonging to some of the regular communities were confiscated and sold. The realization from the sales was devoted "to the support of the cult and the number of regulars deemed convenient." This reform therefore had as its prime

14. Ayarragaray, *op. cit.*, pp. 241-44.
15. "Constitución Política de 1822," Art. 11, in Anguita, *op. cit.*, I, 102-13.
16. "Constitución Política de 1823," in Anguita, *op. cit.*, I, 126-43.
17. Galdames, *Evolución Constitucional*, I, 947.
18. Anguita, *op. cit.*, I, 165, 168, 174.

motive curtailment of the number of the too-numerous regulars.[19] The Constitution of 1828 was more liberal religiously than the preceding instruments in that it sanctioned the private worship of dissidents and declared that no one could be persecuted or molested for his private opinions. The executive power was given the control of the *pase*, the power to negotiate concordats, and the exercise of the patronage with this limitation, i.e., bishops could not be presented without the consent of the Deputies. A retrogressive step was taken in 1828, when a law concerning abuses of the liberty of the press was enacted. By this act all published attacks on the dogma of the Roman Catholic Church were defined as blasphemy and punishable as same.[20]

Not until 1833 did political and social conditions become composed in Chile. The preceding decade was indeed a period of trial and tribulation, yet it is important to note that throughout the political vicissitudes of Chile little was done by legislation or governmental action to destroy or curtail the rights of particular interests. The Church emerged practically unscathed in fortune and privilege.[21]

The Constitution of 1833, which represented a thorough remodeling of that of 1828 after the decisive victory of the Conservatives at the battle of Lircai, was in force in Chile until 1925, a longer period than enjoyed by any other Latin-American constitution. No attempt was made in that notable document to reduce the severity of Chile's religious policy. This was not to be expected, since the staunchest allies of the clericals were in control of the government. The constitutional provisions relating to the Church and religion were the following: (1) the religion of the republic was Roman Catholic, and the public exercise of any other faith was prohibited; (2) the president in taking his oath of office was to swear to observe and protect the Catholic religion; (3) the president was empowered (a) to nominate, subject to approval by the Senate, archbishops, bishops, canons, and prebends of cathedrals, selecting from lists of three names for each office prepared by the Council of State, (b) to exercise the right of patronage with respect to churches, benefices, and ecclesiastical persons, (c) to grant or refuse, with the consent of the Council of State, admission to decrees of councils, papal bulls, briefs, and rescripts; and (d) to maintain diplomatic relations with the Vatican and conclude concordats with it; and (4) the Council of State, of which a Church dignitary must be a member, was to have cognizance over all matters of ecclesiastical patronage that might be subject to litigation.[22]

19. *Ibid.*, I, 171, 177.
20. "Constitución Política de 1828," in *ibid.*, I, 180-89, 193.
21. Galdames, *Evolución Constitucional*, I, 947.
22. "Constitución Política de 1833," in Anguita, *op. cit.*, I, 214-26.

According to Galdames, "The Constitution of 1833 corresponded perfectly to the social condition of that time. Thus, the establishment of the Catholic religion as that of the State was simply due to the fact that all were Catholics."[23] It is true indeed that the prohibition of the public exercise of dissident faiths in Chile was due to the effect of the historical traditions of the country and the collective thought that the one true faith was the Catholic.[24]

The constitutional exclusion of the public exercise of other cults was never completely enforced. The first Anglican chaplain assigned to Chile reached Valparaiso in 1837 and remained there two years. In 1847, Rev. David Trumbull organized a Protestant Union church in Valparaiso, and in 1856 this congregation erected its own building, the first Protestant church edifice to be erected on the west coast of South America.[25] Soon afterward a second church was built. Services were held regularly and openly and the authorities did not interfere. The constitutional phrase "public exercise" was generally regarded as not prohibiting religious worship of non-Catholics *inside* buildings. This interpretation, fortified by thirty years of practice, was incorporated into law in 1865, when the so-called *Ley Interpretativa* was passed by the Congress. This law declared that the prohibition, in Article 5, of the public exercise of dissident faiths did not refer to religious services indoors. Not only were Protestants permitted to conduct services inside private buildings belonging to them, but they were permitted to establish and support schools for the instruction of their children in the doctrines of their respective religions.[26] As a result of the *Ley Interpretativa* of

23. Galdames, *op. cit.*, p. 333.

24. Dr. Jorge Huneeus, the notable Chilean writer on constitutional and legal subjects, in commenting (*Obras de Don Jorge Huneeus*, Santiago, 1890, I, 68) on Article 5, declared that literally interpreted, it was intended as a recognition of the existing religious status, and should have read, for purposes of clarity, that the Roman Catholic religion was the religion of the majority of Chileans. But, says Huneeus, constitutions do not have as their purpose the recognition of status; and therefore, being superfluous, Article 5 should have been suppressed for it was certainly not the intention of the framers of the constitution to impose on the State a determined religion. This is artful and subtle reasoning, which, nevertheless, reflects no credit on Huneeus. The framers of the Constitution of 1833 certainly *did* intend to impose on the State a determined religion, and a cursory examination of the conditions under which the constitution was framed will substantiate this contention.

25. *West Coast Republics*, pp. 28-29.

26. The text of the famous *Ley Interpretativa* was the following:

Interpretative Law of Article 5,
Santiago de Chile, July 27, 1865.

The National Congress has discussed and approved the following project of law:

Article 1. It is declared that by Article 5 of the Constitution those who do not profess the Roman Catholic Apostolic religion are permitted to practice their cult inside private buildings.

1865, which legalized religious toleration, numerous Protestant churches were erected throughout the country. Yet it must be admitted that the establishment in fact of liberty of cults in Chile was realized only by violation of constitutional principle.[27]

In 1836 legislation was enacted which created two new bishoprics, Coquimbo and Chiloé. These with the bishopric of Concepción were made suffragans of the new archiepiscopal see of Santiago. In 1842 the University of Chile was recreated by law. It comprised five faculties, one of which was in theology. In 1846 another law on abuses of the liberty of the press was published which prescribed heavy penalties of fine and imprisonment for published attacks upon the religion of the State.[28] The above facts, somewhat isolated it is true, are presented to evidence the satisfactory status enjoyed by the Church under the régime of the Conservative Oligarchy. Yet the clericals were not allowed free rein to their ambitious pretensions as evidenced by the following facts. The *Ley sobre Matrimonio de Disidentes* (1844) freed non-Catholics from the obligation of celebrating nuptials according to the Catholic rites. The *Ley sobre el Patronato Civil* conceded to the executive authority of the government the right of watching over curates to see that they fulfilled their duties. The *Ley sobre Profesión Religiosa* required twenty-five years as the minimum age for receiving major orders.[29] These acts caused considerable discussion and dissension in the clerical ranks and disrupted the long standing harmonious relations that existed between the Church and the temporal authorities. So opposed was Archbishop Eyzaguirre to the "aggressions of the government" that he resigned in 1845, after having held his position for but two years. His successor, Rafael Valdivieso, continued to resist the so-called "regalistic prerogatives" for the balance of the term of President Bulnes (1841-51).

Protestant ideas were being widely disseminated during this period and there began to develop an element which was unfriendly to the religion of the State. This culminated in the founding in Santiago of a periodical, *El Mercurio*, dedicated to religious toleration. The leading

---

Article 2. Dissidents are permitted to establish and support private schools for the instruction of their children in the doctrine of their religion.

Approved and sanctioned by the Council of State and promulgated as law.

Juan Joaquín Pérez,
Federico Errázuriz.

(*Constitución y Leyes Políticas de la República de Chile Vigente en 1881*, Santiago, 1881, p. 48.)

27. José Guillermo Guerra, *La Constitución de 1925* (Santiago, 1929), p. 39.

28. Anguita, *op. cit.*, I, 262, 392, 395, 478.

29. Galdames, *op. cit.*, pp. 376-77; Anguita, *op. cit.*, I, 436-37; Guerra, *op. cit.*, pp. 38-39.

lights of Chilean letters, Bilbao and Lastarria, also began at this time to attack the Conservative order and its various props, particularly the clergy. The Church was stimulated to action, and under the protection of the Archbishop, *La Revista Católica* was founded in 1843 to check the subversive teachings that "threatened to corrupt the intellectual youth of Chile." The Jesuits, who had recently been permitted to return to Chile, lent the Archbishop their able assistance. It appears, however, that notwithstanding clerical resistance, the domination of the Church and the religious spirit of Chileans were gradually waning. For instance, no longer was "Ave María Purísima" added to the cries of the hours or weather conditions by the *serenos*, or night-watchmen. Also, the practice of dipping the banners of the battalions when a priest passed with the host in the procession of the *Corpus* was abolished. These changes were trivial, but they indicated in which direction public opinion was shifting.[30]

The attitude taken by the State as well as by the Church toward the intermarriage of Protestants and Catholics contributed to an acrimonious dispute between Archbishop Valdivieso and United States Minister to Chile, Seth Barton. Mr. Barton, a divorced Protestant, married a prominent Chilean señorita. The Archbishop condemned the marriage and beseeched the bride to leave the man to whom she was not married according to the rites of the Catholic Church. Barton's violent reaction was not confined to the prelate but included the Chilean government as well. The result was demand for his recall. The incident was not helpful to the position of Americans in Chile.[31]

During the first term of President Montt (1851-56), cordial relations existed between the spiritual and temporal orders. The governmental budget for the State cult was increased annually after 1853, and the condition of the Church continued to improve. In 1853 the republic pledged itself to support the Church out of the national treasury. The tithes, which were still collected even after the reforms of Freire, were abolished. The Archbishop of Santiago was authorized by the pope to agree to this arrangement.[32] In the civil code, promulgated on January 1, 1857, the State confirmed strict religious exclusion by entrusting the register to the clergy. On the subject of matrimony the code contained the following provisions: (1) marriage between Catholic persons shall be celebrated with the solemnities established by the Church and shall comply with ecclesiastical authority; (2) those who profess a different religion and wish to contract marriage can do so by

30. Galdames, *op. cit.*, p. 376.
31. Evans, *op. cit.*, pp. 122-26.
32. Bravo, *Estudios Constitucionales*, p. 26, n. 1.

having the ceremony performed by a priest in the presence of two witnesses; and (3) marriage is dissolved only by the death of one of the parties.[33] It was during the second term of President Montt (1857-61), when a younger and more liberal element gained control of the government, that there developed a growing coolness between Church and State. The particular incident which terminated the old-time harmony was rather insignificant. Two canons who were expelled from the cathedral chapter because of lack of respect for their superiors appealed to the Supreme Court which revoked the sentence of the chapter. The archbishop protested vigorously, alleging unwarranted interference on the part of the civil authorities. A protracted discussion between the metropolitan and the Minister of Cult was terminated by the submission of the canons, through the mediation of the government, to the will of the Church. The incident, although closed, left bitter memories which rankled in the breasts of clericals and nonclericals alike, and any future harmonious understanding became impossible.[34] Although the clergy and the old aristocracy opposed the so-called irreligious government and its liberal tendencies, they were forced to give way before a changing order in Chile. The bigotry and intransigence of an earlier time was being replaced by a temperate tolerance. Therefore, in spite of frenzied clerical opposition, the *Ley Interpretativa* legalizing religious freedom was passed. The *Ley* was not a constitutional amendment, but only a congressional law. Therefore, since it appeared to many to run counter to the constitutional proscription of religious freedom, an attempt was made to guarantee the liberty of cults by constitutional amendment. The effort was defeated. A second attempt was made in 1874. At that time a constitutional amendment providing for "religious freedom" was adopted by the Congress, but since it failed of ratification by the next Congress it did not become an amendment to the Constitution.[35]

During the administration of President Errázuriz (1871-76) the control of the government passed out of the hands of the old Conservative party and into the control of the Liberals and Radicals who were frankly opposed to the pretensions of the Catholic Church. At the beginning of Errázuriz's administration the government was composed of a Conservative-Liberal coalition. The futility of such a combination soon became apparent when dissension arose over the educational program. The Conservative members of the coalition government disapproved the

33. Galdames, *Historia de Chile*, p. 334; Anguita, *op. cit.*, I.

34. Diego Barros Arana, *Un decenio de la historia de Chile.* 2 vols. (Santiago, 1906), I, 318.

35. Alcibiades Roldán, *Elementos de Derecho Constitucional de Chile* (Santiago, 1917), p. 222; Guerra, *op. cit.*, p. 42.

measure sponsored by the Liberals which granted preference to the natural sciences in the State schools. This they declared to be prejudicial to religion and dangerous to private morals. A decree was issued which declared that religious instruction was not obligatory in State colleges, but was available for students whose parents demanded it. The so-called "theological questions" were the rock upon which the coalition government foundered in 1873. These questions were: (1) suppression of the *fuero eclesiástico*; (2) secularization of cemeteries;[36] (3) civil marriage; and (4) separation of Church and State. An irreconcilable difference of opinion in the cabinet precipitated a crisis which resulted in the dissolution of the coalition and the ousting of the Conservatives. Although the Liberal-Radical bloc was triumphant, it was not able or willing to enact far-reaching clerical reform. Nevertheless the *fuero eclesiástico* was abolished for all civil and criminal causes, and the penal code, promulgated in 1874, enumerated penalties for priests, without distinction to cults, who preached doctrines subversive of public order and contrary to the Constitution and the laws of the republic. Regarding the use and control of cemeteries, it was provided that Protestants might be buried in designated portions of Catholic cemeteries. Finally, the tithes were abolished and were replaced by a tax. Nothing was done at this time about civil marriage and the separation of Church and State.[37]

The clergy, naturally, offered violent opposition to the reform measures. "The political struggle," says Galdames, "became a religious fight and the Conservative party became a clerical or ultramontane party."[38] The fight was led by the aged Archbishop of Santiago, Rafael Valentín Valdivieso, who even proceeded to the limit of excommunicating those who had supported the laws. His fulminations and bans were not sufficient, however, to alter the course of the government. The Archbishop, an energetic defender of the prerogatives of the Church, never ceased to protest the exercise of *patronato* by the government. The election of a successor to Archbishop Valdivieso, who died in 1878 after having been primate for thirty years, led to the renewal of an even more determined governmental assault upon the exclusive privileges and prerogatives of the Catholic Church. President Pinto (1876-81), a Liberal, in endeavoring to insure the establishment of harmonious relations between the government and the Church, proposed as candidate for the see of Santi-

36. Old colonial decrees regulating the control of cemeteries were still in force. The clergy could refuse to bury persons who had died without fulfilling the precepts of Catholicism.

37. Galdames, *op. cit.*, pp. 410-13; Bravo, *op. cit.*, p. 64.

38. Galdames, *Historia de Chile*, p. 412.

ago, Francisco de Paula Taforo, canon of the cathedral of Santiago and a man of pronounced liberal leanings. Due to the objections of the Chilean clergy the pope refused to install the government's nominee, and thus there was created a conflict over the right to exercise the national patronage.[39] Notwithstanding protracted negotiations, both the Vatican and the Chilean government were obdurate, and in the meantime the archiepiscopal see remained vacant. Finally, in response to a request of President Santa María (1881-86), an apostolic delegate was sent to Chile. Mgr. Celestino del Frate, the pope's envoy, after a careful study of the problem, became convinced that it was inadvisable to confirm Taforo's nomination, and counseled the pope against it. President Santa María then decided that the time for a break with the Vatican had arrived and gave the Apostolic Delegate his passports. Before withdrawing from Chile, Del Frate publicly announced that the pretense to national patronage by Chile was without foundation or sanction. Although this statement was made in a tactless manner, nevertheless it was literally true. There had never been a concordat between Chile and the papacy. The *entente* was not one of law, but only of convenience. "The failure of the negotiations," writes a constitutionalist authority, "made the Chilean regalists realize that patronage was not an inherent right of the national sovereignty, because the political power lacked adequate means to enforce it; and the Roman Curia, in spite of threats and violence, possessed sufficient strength to resist the exercise of this pretended right when it saw the peace of the Church compromised. Nevertheless, there emerged from the conflict profound modifications of the union of Church and State, proceeding on the road to its complete liquidation."[40]

The pretext sought by Santa María to inaugurate the reforms demanded by the *partidos de libertad* was furnished by the unfortunate outcome of Del Frate's mission. The dismissal of the Apostolic Delegate was followed by the passage of notable ecclesiastical reform laws. On June 1, 1883, the president in his message to Congress declared that the time had arrived for the realization of the oldest and dearest aspirations of the liberal thinkers of Chile; i.e., common cemeteries, civil matrimony, civil register, and liberty of conscience. The Congress, composed almost exclusively of Liberals, Radicals, and Nationalists, was thoroughly in accord with the administration's program. More influential than the President himself in the passage of the reform laws was the Minister of Interior, José Manuel Balmaceda. Balmaceda had studied for the priesthood in the Seminario de Santiago, but constant reading of philosophical

39. *Ibid.*, pp. 436-37.
40. Bravo, *op. cit.*, p. 65.

and scientific works had shaken his faith, and he sought refuge first in agriculture and later in politics. As a member of the Congress in 1874 he supported the constitutional amendment to disestablish the Church. As Minister of Interior in the cabinet of President Santa María, José Balmaceda was the man most responsible for the *reformas teológicas*. He regarded the power of the Church as an iron despotism which seized a person at birth and controlled his most serious acts up to and even after death. "The Church marches, in a sense, against the liberal current of the century," he said.[41] He proposed to check the invading pretensions of the Church against the independence of the State, the individual, and civil society. He did not delude himself into believing that the solution of the problem of Church-State relationships was simple, for he realized that it required laborious and prudent governmental action. Galdames describes Balmaceda as "liberal, reformista, pensador, laico, casi ateo."[42]

The first of the *leyes reformas teológicas*, the *Ley de Cemeterios Laicos*, released the cemeteries from the control of the Church and provided for their free use by all religious communions. The law was passed by a large majority. The capitular vicar of Santiago condemned it and prohibited the exercise of the cult within the State cemeteries and chapels annexed thereto. The government replied by closing Catholic cemeteries and prohibiting burials within churches. On January 16, 1884, the law of civil marriage was passed, which legalized and made compulsory the civil ceremony conducted by the official in charge of the civil register. Although marriages without the participation of Catholic priests were now valid, those desiring the religious ceremony either before or after the civil act were at liberty to have it performed. According to the new legislation questions of divorce and nullity belonged to the civil jurisdiction, and not to the ecclesiastical courts as in the past. Divorce, however, was declared to be only suspension and not dissolution of the married state.[43] Thus the Church was deprived of its old prerogative of legally constituting the family, and very naturally the passage of the civil marriage law caused the clergy to cry to high heaven. They protested, threatened, and even went to the extreme of attempting to prevent the marriage of anyone who voted for the measure. So much opposition was aroused by the clergy against this "sacrilegious law" that the country seemed to be on the verge of revolution.[44]

41. Espinosa, *op. cit.*, pp. 35, 47-48.
42. Galdames, *op. cit.*, p. 439.
43. Eulojio Rojas Mery (ed.), *Códigos de Chile* (Santiago, 1893), pp. 577-83; Anguita, *op. cit.*, II, 592-95; Luis F. Borja, *Estudios sobre el Código Civil Chileno* (Paris, 1901-8), III, 50.
44. Espinosa, *op. cit.*, pp. 38-44.

On July 17, 1884, the Law of the Civil Register was enacted.[45] The records of births, marriages, and deaths had been kept by the parish priests, not to aid the State in the discharge of administration, but because the Church thought this was the logical complement of its right to preside over the most solemn events in the lives of the people. The keeping of the register, claimed the Liberals, was not a religious but essentially an administrative act and should be entrusted to the civil authorities. Furthermore, because of the great importance of these documentary proofs in matters of litigation, inheritance for example, the custody of the records should constitute a public service where responsibility could not be affected by religious ideas, and where they would be administered with greater efficiency, for rarely indeed were the parochial registers free of omissions and errors.[46] For these reasons, then, the Church was deprived of its administration of the records of vital statistics.

Liberty of conscience was another important item in the program of the Liberal administration. The *Ley Interpretativa* of 1865, although professing to guarantee religious liberty, was nevertheless unconstitutional, and, as has been noted above, an unsuccessful attempt was made in 1874 to provide for religious toleration by constitutional amendment. In November, 1884, the Congress again approved the suppression of Article 5, but the succeeding Congress allowed the required period of time to pass without ratifying the reform. But notwithstanding the failure of the amendment religious freedom had been recognized and continued to be recognized in Chile.[47] By way of pertinent illustration: in 1885 the government granted an unusually liberal charter to a Protestant group, whereby "Those who profess the Reformed Church religion according to the doctrines of Holy Scriptures, may promote primary and secondary instruction according to modern methods and practice, and propagate the worship of their belief obedient to the law of the land."[48]

The hardest battle was fought over the question of the separation of Church and State. Three possible systems of Church-State relationships

45. Mery, *Códigos de Chile*, pp. 584-92; Anguita, *op. cit.*, II, 606-9.
46. *Ibid.*, p. 42. Maladministration of the civil register was not uncommon during the colonial period, for witness the plaint of a viceroy: "Experience has shown that the clergy do not keep this register and these lists accurate, but (with a pious falsehood) certify that some have died—in which they are in collusion with the governors and principal Indians—pocketing the tribute themselves and benefitting to the prejudice of the royal treasury." ("Instrucción Para el Virrey...Marqués de Amarillas," in *Instrucciones Reservadas que los Virreyes de Nueva España Dejaron á sus Sucesores*, Mexico, 1867, p. 81).
47. Guerra, *op. cit.*, p. 42; Anguita, *op. cit.*, II, 632-33.
48. *West Coast Republics*, p. 29.

were championed: (1) the union of Church and State without patronage and without liberty of cults (the ideal of the Church); (2) the union of Church and State, the patronage, and freedom of cults (the proposal of the administration); and (3) absolute separation of Church and State, and the reduction of the Church to the status of a simple institution of private law (championed by the Radicals). When he was a deputy in 1874, Balmaceda had supported a measure designed to separate Church and State, but which reserved to the Church a status in public law and supported it by a State subsidy. Nevertheless, for politic reasons, he and President Santa María supported plan number two above. They realized that the storm aroused because of the religious laws was carrying the country to the brink of revolution, and it would be foolhardy to invite additional trouble. Immense proclerical parades, pilgrimages, and meetings proclaimed revolt, and priests from the pulpits added fuel to the fire. In the interest of expediency, the union of Church and State was not abolished, but, said Balmaceda, "Between the partisans of definite and immediate separation of Church and State, and the partisans of gradual and progressive separation, there is no difference of doctrine. There's only a difference in procedure. We will advance step by step with perfect security and we propose to arrive at the same goal."[49] The *reformas teológicas* seriously weakened the Chilean Church; in a formal encounter it had been defeated and humiliated; its prestige was shaken and thereafter it was placed on the defensive.

When Balmaceda succeeded his old chief to the presidency in 1886, he tried, in the interest of peace and harmony, to conciliate the clericals by settling in accord with their views the old question of the vacant archbishopric. Accordingly, relations were reëstablished with the Vatican and Mariano Casanova was preconized Archbishop of Santiago (1887). The restoration of contact with the papacy inaugurated a quarter century or more of satisfactory Church-State relations. Archbishop Casanova and his successor in 1911, Juan Ignacio González Eyzaguirre, were both able and tactful men, zealous of the rights of the Church, but wise in avoiding violent conflicts such as had embittered relations under Archbishop Valdivieso. In 1895 Archbishop Casanova summoned a diocesan synod which thoroughly reorganized the internal régime of the Church. In 1905 he convened a solemn Eucharistic Congress. A Catholic University in Santiago and numerous schools and colleges connected with conciliar seminaries were founded. And finally, an appeal was made to workmen to attach themselves to Catholic labor associations which were under the direction of priests. As a result of its intensive propa-

49. Espinosa, *op. cit.*, p. 48.

ganda campaign, the Catholic Church in Chile enjoyed a remarkable renaissance. Its prestige and influence were supported and advanced in no small way by its great wealth. So vast were the holdings of the Church and so great its income that it was seldom necessary for the government to appropriate more than a million dollars annually for its support.[50]

In its struggle for rehabilitation, the Church was consistently supported by the Conservative party which regarded it as the staunchest champion of order and authority. The Conservatives, in league with some Liberals, withstood successfully the attempt of the Radical party in 1906 to bring about complete separation of Church and State. The question of education was always conducive to conflict in the Congress. There were numerous schools of all grades conducted by the Church within the republic. In them religious instruction was an essential part of the curriculum. Concerning this there was no argument. In the public schools religious instruction was compulsory. The Conservatives thought that the State should concern itself with education as little as possible, leaving this matter to private individuals and institutions. The Radicals, on the other hand, contended that the State should be the only educator, and its instruction ought to be free, obligatory, and laical. It was impossible, obviously, to reconcile such extreme viewpoints.

The Treaty of Ancón, which ended the War of the Pacific, contributed in addition to the well-known territorial problem between Chile and Peru, a serious religious difficulty which reached a crisis in 1910. The ecclesiastical conflict originated in the omission of any clause in the Treaty of Ancón concerning the ecclesiastical jurisdiction of the territory which changed hands. Although deprived of political jurisdiction over the provinces, Peru attempted to retain moral control through the clergy who were under the diocesan authority of Arequipa. The clergy, violently patriotic, responded nobly, and kept their flocks permanently attached to the Peruvian cause. The diocese of Arequipa embraced not only the provinces of Tacna and Arica, but Tarapacá as well. It was in the latter province where the religious difficulty appeared first. When Tarapacá was occupied by Chile during the war most of the Peruvian priests withdrew and it became the duty of the Chilean government to fill the vacancies. Since military chaplains could not administer to the spiritual needs of people not a part of the army, the pope was persuaded, April 6, 1882, to make an exception to the law by granting parochial jurisdiction over Tarapacá to a military chaplain. Shortly after, the apostolic vicarates of Tarapacá and Antofagasta were created under Chilean control.

50. Charles E. Akers, *A History of South America, 1854-1904* (London, 1912).

As for the provinces of Tacna and Arica, there the ecclesiastical control of the Peruvian Church was complete, and for several years the Chilean government seemed to be unconcerned. After 1900, however, the matter became too prominent to be disregarded. The bishop of Arequipa refused to grant licenses to Chilean priests, and Peruvian priests refused to officiate at Chilean festivals. Also, and most serious, the Peruvian clergy were redoubling their efforts to incite greater resistance to the Chileans. Chile appealed, May 15, 1908, to the pope to create an apostolic vicarate for Tacna dependent only on Rome and governed by a foreign functionary, neither Peruvian nor Chilean. The pope, striving to avoid any semblance of political intervention, refused to act.

Since it was recognized by Chile that the dispute could not be settled by the pope, she decided to resort to direct and severe measures with Peru and abandon useless discussions. Consequently, on February 17, 1910, an order was issued expelling all Peruvian priests from Tacna and Arica. As a result all religious services in the provinces were suspended and diplomatic relations between Peru and Chile were broken off. The religious crisis compelled the pope to abandon his attitude of noninterference, and, on April 15, 1910, he agreed to name, in conjunction with the Chilean government, a military vicar general for the two provinces. In 1915 the pope elevated the military vicar general to the position of bishop auxiliary of the diocese of Santiago, and thus the parishes were restored to their normal ecclesiastical status. When Church and State were separated in Chile in 1925, the clergy of the provinces were freed of governmental control, as were the clergy of the rest of the republic. The return of Tacna to Peru, under the agreement of 1929, meant that the Church in that province was absorbed into the Church-State system of Peru.[51]

Separation of Church and State was a cherished political ideal of advanced thinkers in Chile. Many times in the history of the republic they had attempted to abolish what they regarded as an antiquated civil-ecclesiastical union. Their efforts resulted invariably in failure; yet, with the passage of time the prospects of ultimate success became brighter. Several factors contributed to the eventual peaceful and eminently satisfactory dissolution of the Church-State bonds.

After, and even before, World War I, a great change in religious attitude came over Chileans. Writing in 1911, Galdames said, "There is to be noted in the entire country a marked religious evolution. It is not that the people are separating from the Church, for at least three-

51. The above account is based on José Luis Fermandoiz, *El Conflicto Eclesiástico de Tacna* (Santiago, 1923).

quarters of the population continue to be sincere Catholics. Nor is it due to hostility of Protestantism. The free-thinkers do not constitute an organized nucleus against the Church. It is simple tolerance and religious indifference."[52] In evidence of this increased tolerance, Chileans no longer regarded it as a stamp of honor for a believer to abominate another cult than his own, and in judging an individual, no longer was it the practice, as of old, to inquire into his religious beliefs. As for increased religious indifference, this was evidenced by the astonishing scarcity of men at mass and the general laxity in the observance of fasting and confession. Chileans were becoming mentally prepared for the separation. This applied to the thinker as well as to the religious laggard. The former, with his developing tolerance, was becoming convinced that neither Church nor State could gain anything through a continuance of the union. As for the latter, he was no longer a serious factor, except that he could not be relied upon by the Church to support it in a struggle.

Another event which contributed immediately to dissolution was the victory of the Radical and Democratic parties at the polls in 1920. In the elections of that year the candidate of the dominant political Oligarchy, supported by the Conservatives and a large section of the Liberals, was defeated by Señor Arturo Alessandri, who became Chile's first "middle-class president." Now that the Radicals were in power it was a foregone conclusion that they would make another attempt to abolish the union between the Church and State. It was not unexpected, therefore, when President Alessandri proposed to the Congress, June 1, 1923, the advisability of amending the fundamental law to free the Church of all governmental connections. He wished the State, he said, to be the neutral and impartial protector of the rights of all. It was not proper therefore that a particular cult should be privileged above others. Moreover it was injurious to the Church, for it became inextricably involved in politics. On the dangers of this position, President Alessandri quoted Bishop Valdivieso (April 30, 1859), "When ministers become affiliated with political groups, they compromise the sacred interests of their charge. The future of the Church, the most precious interests of religion, are then tied up to the fortunes of a party."[53]

There was dissent on the part of the hierarchy at first, but once convinced that the movement was sincere and had no ulterior motives, the clergy, led by the octogenarian primate Mgr. Crescente Errázuriz, agreed that both Church and State would profit by the disestablishment.

52. Galdames, *Historia de Chile*, p. 493.
53. *Mensaje Leido por S. E. el Presidente de la República* (Santiago, June 1, 1923), pp. 28-31.

The ecclesiastical and governmental officials therefore entered into a friendly, businesslike agreement, the former promising no resistance to separation, the latter guaranteeing to the Church title to its vast properties, the right to conduct its own schools, and financial aid over a brief transitional period. Consequently there was little opposition to the incorporation in the new constitution of Chile, which was promulgated on September 18, 1925, of a clause which definitely terminated the ancient system of a State-Church. This step was made possible, not only because of the ascendancy of the Radical opponents of the patronal system, but also because the other elements of society, even including the clergy, realized, either that this was a logical and beneficial action, or else that it would be futile to attempt opposition. Chile thus earned the enviable distinction of being one of the few Latin-American nations that solved this delicate problem, not only without bloodshed, but in a spirit of good fellowship and hearty coöperation on both sides. "The dissolution was not accomplished," said one of the constituents, "by repudiation, but by divorce through mutual consent."[54]

The Constitution of 1925, which is still in force in Chile, contains the following provisions touching on religion:

> Article 10. The Constitution insures to all the inhabitants of the Republic:
> Practice of all beliefs, liberty of conscience and the free exercise of all religions that may not be contrary to morality, good usage and public order. Therefore, the respective religious bodies have the right to erect and maintain houses of worship and accessory property under the conditions of security and hygiene as fixed by the laws and regulations.
> The churches, creeds, and religious institutions of any ritual shall have those rights in respect to their property as the law now in force may stipulate or recognize; but they will be subject, under the guarantees of this constitution, to common law in the exercise of ownership of their future acquired property.
> Churches and accessory property intended for the service of any religious sect are exempt from taxation.[55]

The first of the transitory provisions of the Constitution declares abolished all laws concerning the interrelations of Church and State, appointment to ecclesiastical positions, presentation to benefices, authori-

54. Guerra, *op. cit.*, p. 49.

55. For the religious question in the convention, see *Ministerio del Interior, Actas Oficiales de las Sesiones celebrados por la Comisión y Subcomisiones encargadas del estudio del Proyecto de Nueva Constitución Política de la República* (Santiago, 1925), pp. 397, 471.

zation of papal communications, and related subjects. Also, it was provided that, to facilitate the transition of the Catholic Church from a protected organization into an independent entity, the government should appropriate it the sum of 2,500,000 pesos annually for a period of five years.

In commenting on the act of separation, President Alessandri said, "There has been established the principle of liberty and conscience in respectful form without wounding the sensibilities of anyone, and thus there has been consecrated the principle of absolute separation of the temporal and spiritual orders."[56] On September 20, 1925, in referring to the termination of the union of Church and State, Mgr. Crescente Errázuriz, the venerable Archbishop of Santiago, said in his pastoral: "It is just to note that the authorities of Chile, in establishing this separation, have not been actuated by the spirit of persecution which characterizes other countries where Catholicism has been attacked. By the sacrifice of separation, the Church acquires, at least, the liberty which divine law accords it; and, finally, the State is separated from the Church; but the Church is not separated from the State, and will always be ready to serve it."[57]

The actual régime of religious cults in Chile is that of separation from the State. Liberty of conscience and freedom of worship are guaranteed so long as they are are not opposed to morals, good customs, and public order. There are no religious tests for the exercise of the suffrage or for holding public office. The Church enjoys juridical personality for legal and constitutional effects.[58] Separation did not mean official ignorance of the fact that the great majority of the Chileans are counted as Catholics, Chile continues to accredit a diplomatic representative to the Vatican, and the Vatican in turn accredits an apostolic nuncio to Santiago. The department of government in Chile which looks after ecclesiastical affairs is the Ministry of Foreign Relations. Having renounced all patronal claims the government obviously has no present rights in the election of ecclesiastical officers, and the Chilean clergy are free to communicate at will with the Vatican.

Title to the large ecclesiastical holdings valued at millions of dollars was handed over to the Church without any restrictions whatever. It was recognized as independent possessor and administrator of its revenue producing properties, as well as churches, monasteries and convents,

56. Arturo Alessandri, *Reformas Constitucionales* (Santiago, 1925), p. 56.

57. *Informativo Postal N. 38*, Ministerio de Relaciones Exteriores, República de Chile (to J. L. Mecham).

58. For the legal position of the Roman Catholic Church under the 1833 and 1925 constitutions, see Gerardo Infante Vial, *Personalidad jurídica de la Iglesia en Chile* (Santiago, 1962).

primary and secondary schools, seminaries, hospitals, and the Universities of Santiago and Valparaiso, the former being almost as large and influential academically as the University of Chile. The Church property which is used exclusively for religious purposes is tax exempt. This, of course, applies to all cults. When the property is devoted to commercial purposes, however, and incidentally the Catholic Church is one of the largest landowners in Chile, it is assessed the same tax as that of private individuals. No restrictions are placed upon the Church to receive entailments, bequests, and the like. The chief sources of income are revenues from properties, and donations and subscriptions of the faithful. The people have taken up the chief burden of supporting the Church by voluntary contribution without a protest.

The Church exercises no control over public education. On the other hand it is not prevented from maintaining a complete educational system, under limited governmental supervision, from the primary grades to the university. In the public schools there are classes in religion, but these are elective. There are in Chile, out of a total of 4,200 schools and colleges, 600 private schools, and of the latter, 500 are maintained by the Catholic Church. The majority of the remaining private schools are supported by Protestant sects. The Catholic schools, primary as well as secondary, usually require no tuition fees and are maintained by money from members of the Church and from the bishopric subsidies. A few receive funds from the government.[59] Members of the priesthood are not allowed to teach in public schools.

The *teológicas reformas* of Santa María relating to matrimony and the control of cemeteries are still in force in Chile. The only legal form of marriage is the civil marriage according to the law of 1884. The religious ceremony may be performed when desired, but for several years it has been the law that the civil rites must be celebrated first.[60] Everyone goes through the form of civil marriage obediently, but no Catholic considers himself married until after the ceremony has been performed by the Church. The priests coöperate with the government and refuse to marry a couple until the civil marriage certificate is produced. Chile does not permit divorce. There may be legal separation, but this does not allow for remarriage. Only when civil nullity has been proclaimed may individuals again marry.

59. "Since 1951 there has existed a relatively generous system of State aid to private and Church-related schools." William J. Coleman, *Latin American Catholicism: A Self-Evaluation* (Maryknoll, N.Y., 1958), p. 53.

60. The marriage of President Ibañez was an exception to this rule. After the religious ceremony, which occurred in a church in the presence of a notable assemblage, the bridal couple did not present themselves until several hours later before the civil officials for the performance of the civil ceremony. (*La Prensa*, New York, December 4, 1927.)

There are public, or general, and private cemeteries in Chile. The general cemeteries, of which there are several in Santiago, are under the charge of the Charity Council under the direction of the Minister of Interior. Funds for their maintenance are derived from rents or sales of plots, and from governmental and public subscriptions. In Santiago there are Catholic and Protestant cemeteries. There are likewise private cemeteries scattered throughout Chile. The public has exercised the right since 1884 of electing cemeteries for their deceased. Since that date the Catholic Church has been forced to abandon its onetime right of exclusive jurisdiction over interments.

Following the disestablishment of the Catholic Church in Chile in 1925, religion, contrary to the dire predictions of Conservative and clerical opponents of separation, did not decline. There was perfect cordiality between Church and State, and in this atmosphere of reverence and confidence the Church grew in prestige and influence. Although no longer the troublesome political factor that it was in the past, the Catholic Church became, nevertheless, a powerful force in the body politic. It seems that, as the political activities of the clergy decreased, their moral influence increased.

The clergy of Chile, well-educated, widely traveled, alert and broad-minded, rank high among Latin-American ecclesiastics. Most of the prelates, 6 archbishops and 27 bishops, including the renowned socially conscious Bishop Larraín of Talca, have been recruited from the hundred or more families of the aristocracy which ruled Chile in the past. With one priest to 2,750 Catholics, the Chilean ratio of priests (2,300) to communicants (6,477,000) is the lowest of all Latin America. Of a total population of 7,465,000 in 1960, 86.8 per cent are regarded as Catholics.[61] The average 10 per cent Sunday mass attendance, (13 per cent women and 7 per cent men) means that the percentage of "mass missers" is quite as large in Chile as in other Latin-American countries.

The tolerance of Chileans and the constitutional guarantees of freedom of religion have been favorable to the Evangelical movement. In 1960 there were in Chile 510 Protestant clergy and 803,140 Protestant communicants representing 10.8 per cent of the total population. This is the largest percentage for all Latin America.[62] The largest sect is the Pentecostal which numbers more than 600,000. There is some validity in Chile for the clerical warning of a "Protestant threat."[63]

There is today neither a clerical nor an anticlerical party in Chile. The Conservatives, the traditional party of the Roman Catholic Church,

61. *Statistical Abstract of Latin America, 1963*, p. 22; W. Stanley Rycroft and Myrtle M. Clemmer, *A Factual Study of Latin America* (New York, 1963), p. 235.

62. Rycroft and Clemmer, *op. cit.*, p. 234.

63. See Ignacio Vergara, *El Protestantismo en Chile* (Santiago de Chile, 1962).

have experienced defections as the Christian Democrats (PDC) have become representative of a more liberal Catholicism. The Liberals, also friendly to the Catholic Church, have suffered defections to the PDC. The Marxism of the Socialists and the anticlericalism of the Radicals cause them to be frowned upon by the Church, which is unalterably opposed to communism.[64]

The hierarchy does not regard it as political intervention to urge the faithful to vote for those parties friendly to the Church. Cardinal Caro Rodríguez, when pleading for moderation in the election of 1958, said that the Catholic Church favored electoral peace but no particular candidate.[65]

Organized in 1937 by young liberal Catholics concerned with Catholic oriented reform, the National Falange changed its name in 1957 to the Chilean Democratic party (PDC). It regarded moral problems and political democracy as essential goals. The two pillars of the PDC's program are: (1) concern for the dignity of man and the improvement of his condition as urged in Papal encyclicals from *Rerum Novarum* to *Mater et Magistra*, and (2) a technical approach to economic problems. While the PDC is non-confessional, its leadership is predominantly Catholic.[66] The PDC came to power in Chile in 1964 with the election of Eduardo Frei to the national presidency. The victory of this relatively new party, although not necessarily a result of Church action, was nevertheless in harmony with a new trend in Catholic policy in Chile.

There probably was an earlier and more conscientious effort on the part of the Chilean hierarchy and clergy to implement the papal social encyclicals than was true of the Church in the other Latin-American countries. Archbishop Crescente Errázuriz was one of the first to encourage a greater social consciousness among the clergy. He was a zealous exponent of the social principles of Pope Leo XIII and supported President Arturo Alessandri's labor laws.[67] His successor Archbishop José Caro Rodríguez, who became cardinal in 1946, was also active in revitalizing the Church. Most credit however, for the social action movement in the Catholic Church in Chile, and in other parts of Latin America, belongs to Mgr. Manuel Larraín, Bishop of Talca.

When he was vice-rector of the Catholic University of Santiago, Mgr. Larraín told his students: "Because you are Catholic you must

64. Ricardo Fuentes Castellano, "El Partido Demócrata Cristiano y el Comunismo en Chile," in *Estudios Centroamericanos*, Vol. 17, No. 170 (May, 1962), 136-39.

65. *Hispanic American Report*, XI, No. 6 (June, 1958), 333.

66. Frederick B. Pike, *Chile and the United States, 1880-1962* (Notre Dame, Ind., 1963), pp. 259-61.

67. See Fidel Araneda Bravo, *El Arzobispo Errázuriz y la evolución política y social en Chile* (Santiago, 1956).

think with a social mind." Some of his students, including Eduardo Frei, organized the Falanga Social Cristiana. When he became Bishop of Talca he began vigorously to implement the encyclicals. He was the first prelate to transfer title to ecclesiastical lands to tenants. For this he was accused of being a Red. In fact his activities in organizing Catholic action for a program of social reform caused ultra Conservatives to label his activities "Black Communism."[68] As president of the Latin American Bishops Council (CELAM) the Bishop of Talca is promoting Catholic action for social reform throughout Latin America.

In the fall of 1961 the Chilean bishops announced that 13,200 acres of land belonging to the Church would be divided and sold to several families. They organized an Institute for Agricultural Development to coördinate the transfer and see that the lands were put to the best use. The release of Church lands was done at no little sacrifice to the Church for it was a source of needed income to carry on charitable work.[69]

The Chilean bishops were not content with land reform only but set about to work for national reform. Poor housing, unemployment, low wages, illiteracy, bad diet and governmental inefficiency were cited as "a distressing and anti-Christian state of affairs."

On September 26, 1962, Cardinal Raúl Silva Henriquez and twenty archbishops and bishops published a Chilean Bishops' Pastoral Letter on Social Problems. This has been described as "an attack on Chile's sociological realities." Poverty and maldistribution of wealth were condemned as "anti-Christian reality." "It is essential," said the pastoral, "to promote in every way possible the study of social problems in the light of the doctrine of the Church, because it forms an integral part of the Christian concept of life." This was an exhortation for Catholic action and a condemnation of the abuses of liberal capitalism. The pastoral also warned against communism and collaboration with communism as a solution for Chile's problems.[70]

When the Catholic Church in Chile ceased to be a formidable deterrent to change, the Conservatives ceased to regard union of Church and State as essential. The more recent efforts of the Church on behalf of social justice have contributed to a further alienation of the former traditional bulwarks of the Church.

68. Albert J. Nevins, "How Catholic is Latin America?" *The Sign*, Vol. 36, No. 2 (September, 1956), 13-14.

69. "La iglesia y el problema del campesinado Chileano," *Finis Terrae*, IX (1st quarter, 1962), 71-88; *Our Sunday Visitor*, LII, No. 38 (January 19, 1964), 1.

70. *Recent Church Documents from Latin America*, Center of Inter-cultural Formation, Monograph No. 2, 1962-63 (Fordham University, New York), pp. 1, 24, 32-33; *Hispanic American Reports*, XV, No. 9 (September, 1962), 840.

Chapter X

The State-Church in Argentina

In the Argentine republic there has been steady adherence to a religious policy determined in the earliest days of the struggle for independence. The most successful of the Spanish colonies in maintaining without interruption their political independence after the home authority was discarded in 1810, the provinces of La Plata made no attempt to reduce the Church from the high position it enjoyed in the colonial system. The Constitution of April 22, 1819, the first formal one of the Argentine Nation, then known as the United Provinces of La Plata, sanctioned the traditional principle of the religion of the State. "The government owes to religion," it declared, "the most efficacious and powerful protection, and the inhabitants of all the territory respect it, whatever might be their private opinions."[1] The right to exercise the patronal privilege of presentation was affirmed. It provided that the executive should select from triple lists of names (*ternas*) prepared by the Senate, nominees for vacant archiepiscopal and episcopal sees. Nominations for other benefices and dignities were vested in the executive alone. To the Church was accorded the privilege of permanent representation in the Senate, in the persons of a bishop and three lesser ecclesiastics. On the other hand, archbishops and bishops were placed on a par with the highest civil functionaries, such as ministers of state, and, like them, were subject to accusation in the Senate by the Chamber of Representatives, "for the crimes of treason, collusion, misappropriation of the public funds, violation of the Constitution" and other crimes. In subjecting ecclesiastics to trial before the Senate, the privilege of the ecclesiastical *fuero* was denied. In order that there should be no doubt as to the intent of the Constitution to consider prelates supported by the State as public employees, it required that "no political, civil, military, or *ecclesiastical employee* can [could] continue in his office without taking oath to observe and support

---

1. Agustín de Vedia, *Constitución Argentina* (Buenos Aires, 1907), p. 100. See Rómulo Carbia, *La Revolución de Mayo y la iglesia* (Buenos Aires, 1945).

the Constitution."[2] A notable feature of this, as well as of other constitutions of La Plata, was that it guaranteed liberty of conscience. In the constituent assembly which framed the Constitution of 1819 were nine clerics, and the presiding officer of the convention was the distinguished liberal canon Dr. Gregorio Funes.[3]

The kaleidoscopic political changes in La Plata did not permit the application of the new constitution, for there ensued a ten-year period of near-anarchy during which the only semblance of order appeared in the province of Buenos Aires under the governorship of Martín Rodríguez. The Church had been, since 1810, independent of papal control; and when the hierarchy became extinct, the clergy, free of all restraint, fell into corrupt ways. By 1820 the situation became intolerable and it was necessary for Bernardino Rivadavia, principal minister of Governor Rodríguez and one of Latin America's greatest statesmen, to include the Church in his reform program. "It would be puerile," says an Argentinian authority, "to stop and discourse on doctrinaire questions, when all who have investigated the events know the truth: the immediate object of the reform was to correct the habits of an undisciplined and licentious clergy.... The corruption of the monastic orders was great, and their reform was hoped for and desired by Catholics themselves."[4] Under the guidance of Rivadavia the Congress passed an ecclesiastical reform law on December 21, 1822. It abolished the tithes and the ecclesiastical *fuero*. Rules of discipline were prescribed for religious orders, the membership of ecclesiastical houses was limited to a minimum of sixteen and a maximum of thirty, and no one was allowed to enter orders until he was twenty-five years old. Some regular orders, like the Bethlehemites, were suppressed and their property confiscated by the State. The goods and rents of houses not suppressed were administered by the prelates, but in conformity with the law which required an annual accounting of the administration to the government. Also, cathedral churches and all buildings, lands, and other properties not appertaining to the immediate service of the cult were put under the exclusive control of the government. By decrees of January 4 and 17, 1823, provision was made to support the Church from the public treasury and control the construction of churches in the province.[5]

2. Cesáreo Chalcatana, *Patronato Nacional Argentino* (Buenos Aires, 1885), p. 70.

3. Augustín Piaggio, *La Influencia del Clero en la Independencia Argentina, 1810-1820* (Barcelona, 1912), p. 240; J. Francisco Silva, *El Libertador Bolívar y el Deán Funes en la Política Argentina* (Madrid, 1918), pp. 106-14.

4. José Ingenieros, *La Evolución de las Ideas Argentinas* (Buenos Aires, 1920), I, 440-41.

5. *Ibid.*, I, 492-95; Mariano de Vedia y Mitre, *De Rivadavia á Rosas* (Buenos Aires, 1930), pp. 51-52. For a temperate discussion of the ill-advised reform policy of Rivadavia, see José Manuel Estrada, *La Iglesia y el Estado* (Buenos Aires, 1929), pp. 35-37.

It was during the ascendancy of Rivadavia that Vicar Apostolic Mgr. Juan Muzi arrived in Buenos Aires. The political functionaries, regarding Muzi as a diplomatic agent not accredited to the government of La Plata, refused to allow him to perform any official act prior to papal recognition of Argentine independence and ordered him to leave the country. Following his arrival in Santiago, Chile, on March 6, 1824, Muzi issued a pastoral to Chileans and, indirectly, to all Americans. He pointed out the necessity of maintaining relations with Rome and combatting those who with "the false and specious name of reformers treat like a purely human work the divine constitution of the Church and of its supreme head, pretending to form a National Church separated from the Universal Church and its head." There is little doubt that the Apostolic Vicar was alluding to the reforms of Rivadavia. When Muzi stopped at Montevideo, on his return to Italy, he secretly named Mariano Medrano apostolic delegate with all the rights and powers enjoyed by a capitular vicar in a vacant episcopal see. Medrano had distinguished himself, as will be noted shortly, by opposing the ecclesiastical reform.[6]

The reforms of Rivadavia, which strongly smacked of doctrinaire regalism and which, although well-intentioned, were in many cases anticanonical, aroused a storm of protest on the part of the so-called *apostólicos* or ultramontanes. The officers of the government were called "the libertines of Buenos Aires" and were charged with license, apostasy, and impiety. Some of the more fanatical of the *apostólicos*, under the leadership of a certain Gregorio Tagle, with the cry of "religión ó muerte" on their lips, even resorted to violence. Dr. Mariano Medrano, provisor of the bishopric of Buenos Aires, *en sede vacante*, objected strenuously and appealed to the Chamber of Representatives to affirm the incompetence of the civil power to legislate in ecclesiastical matters. Rivadavia countered by requesting the removal of Medrano from his position as provisor. The Chamber approved the removal and notified the cathedral chapter, which took action in 1822. The chapter thereupon, with the approval of Rivadavia, elected Mariano Zavaleta as provisor of the diocese.[7]

Notwithstanding violent protests on the part of the *apostólicos*, the ecclesiastical reform was well received in Buenos Aires, even by the clergy. Dean Funes favored it and publicly refuted the arguments of Juan Muzi, who condemned the reform and national patronage.[8]

6. Ingenieros, *op. cit.*, II, 518.

7. Faustino J. Legón, *Doctrina y Ejercicio del Patronato Nacional* (Buenos Aires, 1920), pp. 473-75.

8. For the attitude of Dean Funes on ecclesiastical polity, see Silva, *Bolívar y Deán Funes*, p. 111.

Rivadavia's attack was not directed at religion in general, nor at the dogmas of the Catholic Church in particular, but only at the external control of that organization. He preferred a concordat which would convey to the government most of the authority that had been exercised in political affairs by the kings of Spain, but since an agreement with the pope was impossible at that time, he reiterated the intention of the government to retain the prerogatives of the Spanish monarchs and establish a national church. Thus, on September 3, 1821, Rivadavia declared that while the Holy See withheld recognition, and until a concordat should be concluded, the Argentinian government would deny to Rome any control over the Church in Argentina. "Neither Rivadavia nor the clerics who assisted him in his reforms were Masons," said Rómulo Carbia, "nor was the reform, even in its most advanced stages, other than the consequence of a clear regalism, executed imprudently, with a well-defined object and a clear orientation.... In no case was the reform a Voltairean campaign against the Church."[9]

In 1826 the provinces of La Plata made another essay at union with a centralistic constitution and under the presidency of Bernardino Rivadavia. This constitution reproduced most of the provisions of the law of 1819 regarding religion, but in spirit it tended to even greater tolerance. This spirit of tolerance was reflected in the treaty of amity and commerce with Great Britain, concluded in 1825. It guaranteed to British subjects perfect liberty of conscience and the right to worship inside their houses and churches. The first Protestant church was built in Buenos Aires in 1829. The Protestants were also given the right to maintain and control their own cemeteries. As in the earlier constitution, that of 1826 gave the president the right to nominate archbishops and bishops from triple lists prepared by the Senate. A new element of control was introduced by the provision which gave to the Supreme Court the power of exequatur with respect to all papal bulls and encyclicals, for it was to recommend to the president whether or not such documents should be admitted into the country.[10]

Mariano Medrano, secretly appointed apostolic delegate by Juan Muzi in 1825, did not dare, because of the circumstances of his appointment, to assert the prerogatives of his position while the government was under the control of Rivadavia. The resignation of that great statesman on June 27, 1827, did not improve conditions, for his successors exercised to the full the patronal rights over the national Church. It

9. Rómulo D. Carbia, "La Revolución de Mayo y la Iglesia," in *Anales de la Facultad de Derecho* (Buenos Aires, 1915), p. 271.

10. Vedia, *op. cit.*, p. 100; L. S. Rowe, *The Federal System of the Argentine Republic* (Washington, 1921), p. 128.

was not until the ascendancy, in 1829, of Viamonte, a puppet of Juan Manuel de Rosas, who was already preparing the stage for his dictatorship, that the Conservatives came into their own and official relations with the Holy See entered a new phase. Until 1829 noncommunication with Rome was virtually complete. Not since the unsuccessful mission of Valentín Gómez had a government in Buenos Aires attempted to negotiate with Rome, and, on the other hand, overtures by the pope, notably the Muzi mission, had been emphatically rejected. Yet it is true that, during this period, unofficial overtures were made by men like Friar Pacheco, and some priests of the interior provinces received bulls from Rome. Often these papal documents were sent in response to official provincial solicitation. For example, on December 22, 1825, Pope Leo XII, in answer to a petition of the government of San Juan, named Fray Justo Santa María de Oro, bishop *in partibus* and vicar apostolic of Cuyo.[11]

When Viamonte assumed control of the government, the *apostólica camarilla*, headed by Mariano Medrano, Gregorio Tagle, and Tomás Manuel de Anchorena, induced him to appeal to the pope for the nomination of a bishop of Buenos Aires. On October 8, 1829, Governor Viamonte, through his minister Tomás Guido, wrote to the pope asking that he name a proprietary bishop, or one *in partibus*, for Buenos Aires, in order to provide for the spiritual necessities of the country, "so long as this should not be in contradiction of the existing laws of the land." This exception, referring to the laws of Rivadavia, indicates clearly that the right of national patronage had not been renounced, but, on the contrary, was reinforced by the government's presentation of the names of Diego Estanislao Zavaleta and Mariano Medrano for episcopal institution.[12] Over the protests of the Spanish ambassador, Labrador, Pope Pius VIII responded on March 13, 1830, that he had anticipated the Argentinian supplication by appointing, on October 7, 1829, Mariano Medrano as Bishop of Aulón, *in partibus*, and Vicar Apostolic with authority to occupy the vacant see.[13] Medrano, leaving his bull with the government for the exequatur, went to Rio de Janeiro in September, 1830, for his consecration. The *fiscal* Agrelo now entered the lists as a staunch champion of national patronage. He requested that the commission and instructions to the Vicar Apostolic, mentioned in the bull

---

11. In 1834 Pope Gregory XVI created the diocese of Cuyo and named Santa María de Oro the first bishop. The dismemberment of the Córdoban diocese, to which Cuyo belonged, created an irregular situation and a consequent serious ecclesiastical conflict which was finally settled by the government of the Confederation. (Legón, *op. cit.*, p. 492.)

12. P. Leturia, "Alusiones en la Cámara Argentina al origen histórico del Patronato de Indias," in *Razón y Fé* (1927), Vol. 78, 334.

13. Ingenieros, *op. cit.*, II, 411.

but not presented to the government, be submitted likewise for the exequatur. Medrano refused to accede, saying that they related to spiritual subjects. Fortunately for Medrano and the *apostólicos*, Tomás Manuel de Anchorena occupied the influential position of Minister of Cult. It would suffice, he declared, for Medrano to swear a solemn oath to observe and comply with the laws of the province. This Medrano did on January 31, 1831. The cathedral chapter, while recognizing Medrano as Vicar Apostolic, refused to concede that this title enabled him to assume control of the diocese. To end the controversy, Rosas signed a decree on March 23, 1831, to the effect that "it being absolutely necessary to end this controversy and avoid doubts and discussions that might cause disorders prejudicial to the ministers of the gospel, the government determines to recognize in all this province, Mariano Medrano, Bishop of Aulón, as Vicar Apostolic of this diocese of Buenos Aires with all and each of the rights with which he is authorized, and which a capitular vicar in a vacant episcopal see should enjoy." Due to Rosas' absence from the capital on a campaign, the chapter persisted in its opposition, and Medrano was unable to take possession of his see until August 3, 1831, when he was given governmental aid.[14]

Anchorena, the *apostólico* minister who frankly questioned the validity of national patronage, was responsible for numerous acts of intolerance and religious persecution. For example, one of his decrees was aimed at the importation and reading of books "which manifestly tended to attack the moral teachings of the Gospels, the truth and sanctity of the religion of the State, and the divinity of Jesus Christ, its founder." Anchorena governed the Church and the clergy with such vigor that he was called Torquemada and his ministry, the Inquisition. When Anchorena resigned on January 30, 1832, the increasing power of the *apostólicos* suffered a temporary decline.[15]

The controversy over the appointment of Mariano Medrano as Vicar Apostolic proved to be only a prelude to a more serious crisis resulting from his appointment as proprietary bishop. On July 2, 1832, Pope Gregory XVI, *motu proprio*, named Mariano Medrano Bishop of Buenos Aires. On the same day the Pope named Mariano Escalada, the provisor, Bishop of Aulón, *in partibus*, and Vicar Apostolic with authority to act as auxiliary of the diocese. Due to the fact that the government was at that time in the control of enemies of the *apostólicos*, Medrano and Escalada withheld presentation of their bulls, but finally, in August, 1833, they were forced to turn them over to the *fiscal*.

14. Legón, *op. cit.*, pp. 493-94.
15. Ingenieros, *op. cit.*, II, 425.

Once more Agrelo rushed to the defense of Argentine patronage against the pretentions of the Roman Curia. Because of his objection to the use in the bull of the term *motu proprio*, which was interpreted to mean that the Pope disregarded the government's right of presentation, Medrano's bull was denied the *pase* or exequatur (December 19, 1833). The bull of Mariano Escalada was also retained by the government.[16]

To put an end to the ever-recurring disputes and disagreements over the nature and extent of national patronage, the government, acting on the proposal of Agrelo, appointed a special committee of thirty-nine theologians and jurists to pass judgment upon fourteen propositions, which, in the opinion of the government, ought to be accepted as basic principles of the *patronato nacional*. Some of these were as follows: (1) included in sovereignty, which is vested in the people, is the right of ecclesiastical patronage; (2) the nation has the right, under sovereignty, to grant or refuse the exequatur to all papal documents and communications; (3) the government has the right of presentation to ecclesiastical offices and benefices; (4) the government has the right to alter the limits of ecclesiastical jurisdictions; (5) the pope cannot reserve to himself the right to appoint to vacant sees or alter the territorial limits of dioceses; (6) the oath demanded by bishops should in no way operate to diminish their obligations to the State; (7) bishops should, on taking oath, recognize the *patronato nacional* and swear fidelity and respect to the government; (8) all citizens should submit to the government for the exequatur any bull or communication of whatever description received from the Roman Curia; and (9) noncommunication will continue until the papacy recognizes national rights in a concordat.[17]

The committee, with the exception of only two members, Anchorena and Felipe Arana, approved the fourteen propositions. These principles, together with the written opinions of the individual members of the committee, were published by Agrelo and became famous as the *Memorial Ajustado de 1834*. This document thereafter constituted a pattern for ecclesiastical policy in Argentina.

Agrelo, having the opinions of the members of the committee, consented, on March 24, 1834, to recognize Medrano as Bishop of Buenos Aires, since his name had in fact been presented to the pope in 1829. If there were no disposition to interpret the papal use of *motu proprio* too strictly, Medrano's appointment could be regarded as conforming to the national pretensions. Escalada, however, having never been nominated by the government, was refused recognition as bishop aux-

16. Adolfo Saldías, *Historia de la Confederación Argentina* (Buenos Aires, 1911), V, 115-16.

17. Chacaltana, *op. cit.*, pp. 115-18; Saldías, *op. cit.*, II, 197-99.

iliary. His bull was withheld until April 23, 1835, when Rosas, ten days after assuming dictatorial control over the government, ordered the exequatur.[18]

Under the dictatorship of Juan Manuel de Rosas (1835-52) the Catholic Church was converted into a servile instrument of the tyranny. Although he was personally indifferent to religious matters, Rosas nevertheless understood that the Church could be used as a most efficacious instrument of his absolutism. His policy, therefore, was to protect the Church, even to the extent of being the persecutor of its political adversaries, but on condition that it should submit to his personal power. He cherished the *patronato*, but in the same spirit as he regarded his control of the civil government, i.e., he conceived it as being something personal, illimitable, and without legal checks. If the government were to function properly, no one should oppose his will.[19]

The Church allied itself with the tyranny at the start, and in the end was hopelessly subjected by it. Because Rosas was kindly disposed toward the ecclesiastical interests it was natural that, in the beginning, all elements adverse to the reforms of Rivadavia should adhere to his policy. For instance, many of the houses of the regulars, disestablished by Rivadavia, were restored and the Jesuits were allowed to return to the country. For obvious reasons the regulars supported the tyrant. But once enrolled in the service of the "Santa Causa de la Federación," and after the absolutism of the tyranny was converted into a regalistic absolutism of the worst kind, the clergy were unable to extricate themselves. Rosas began by assisting ecclesiastical interests and ended by persecuting the clergy. But Bishop Medrano, it appears, was a willing, abject supporter of Rosas; he was a sort of *mayordomo* to a feudal lord. "In the persons of Rosas and Medrano," says Ingenieros, "was realized the union of throne and altar."[20]

Rosas, realizing the necessity of discipline and morality in the lower clergy, was responsible for numerous decrees and orders which suspended, removed, or jailed priests for immoral conduct. He induced Medrano to consent to a diminution in the number of religious festival days. The ecclesiastical tribunals were also reformed. In 1847 the Jesuits were expelled by order of Rosas on the charge of sedition.[21]

Rosas' insistence on the observance of the patronage was inflexible

18. Ingenieros, *op. cit.*, II, 519; Saldías, *op. cit.*, p. 117.

19. Saldías (*op. cit.*, p. 115) defends Rosas as a good Catholic and a zealous protector of the patronage. He insists that Rosas did not promote antagonisms. His conclusions have not been accepted by the present writer.

20. *Ibid.*, II, 520.

21. Sarsfield, *Relaciones del Estado con la Iglesia*, p. 147; Saldías, *op. cit.*, V, 117.

and brooked no violation. He declared that he would regard as invalid any bull, brief, or rescript which appeared to have emanated from the Roman Curia after May 25, 1810, and which had not received the exequatur of the Minister of Foreign Affairs. This invalidation was specifically extended to the bulls of bishops *in partibus infidelium.* Any violator of the decree was subject to punishment "as a disturber of the public order and an assailant of the sovereignty and independence of the republic."[22]

Of course the patronage was used abusively—outside of all civil and ecclesiastical limitations. The Church, unable to protect itself, was forced to depart from its spiritual mission and support some of the most ignominious acts of the terror. On December 7, 1836, a note was sent to Bishop Medrano commanding him to order the clergy, in all discourses of whatever nature, to counsel obedience to the Federal cause and condemn that of the Unitarians. When the bull of the Bishop of Cuyo was granted the *pase* in October, 1839, the Bishop had to swear to defend and sustain, in sermons, confessions, and conversations, the liberty and independence of the republic *under the Federal régime.* Thus, in place of an Argentine clergy, we have a Federal clergy. Indeed, the use of the Federal red in altar decorations was made compulsory, and the faithful in Buenos Aires saw, on the very altars, the picture of Rosas the "Restorer of the Laws." Clerical humiliation and degradation reached their climax when, with Christ and the Virgin, the pictures and images of the heroes of the "Santa Causa de la Federación" were adored. Thus was established the cult of the tyrant and his political system.[23]

The overthrow of Rosas on the battlefield of Caseros by General Justo José de Urquiza and his Uruguayan and Brazilian allies necessitated a complete reorganization of the government of Argentina. With that end in view, Urquiza, who bore the title of "Provisional Director of the Argentine Confederation," convened a Constituent Assembly at Santa Fé in November, 1852. All the provinces, with the exception of Buenos Aires, were represented. Since the convention drew heavily upon a notable treatise called "Bases and Suggestions for the Political Organization of the Argentine Republic," written for the guidance of the constituents by the distinguished publicist Juan Bautista Alberdi, it is appropriate to examine his suggestions regarding the proper legal relationship that should obtain between Church and State. According to Alberdi, solicitude for religion should be the first object of the fundamental law, for, he said, "it is for the complexion of peoples what pure blood is for the

22. Chacaltana, *op. cit.,* pp. 72-74; Saldías, *op. cit.,* V, 115.
23. Ricardo Levene, *Lecciones de Historia Argentina* (Buenos Aires, 1919), II, 365; Ingenieros, *op. cit.,* II, 488 ff.

health of the individual." Yet, argued Alberdi, the ecclesiastical policy of Argentina should be dictated by reason, and thus the logical policy for Argentina should be religious toleration. Immigrants must be attracted, not discouraged, as would certainly be the case if religious exclusion were adopted. "Religious liberty," he said, "is the means of populating the country." Alberdi's motto was: "To govern is to populate." Consequently, Article 3 of his project read: "The Confederation adopts and sustains the Catholic faith and guarantees liberty for all other faiths." With respect to the patronage he suggested that the president be given the power: (1) to select for archbishops, bishops, dignitaries, and prebends of cathedral churches, from triple lists of names prepared by the Senate; (2) to exercise the right of national patronage with respect to churches, benefices, and ecclesiastical persons; and (3) to grant or refuse the *pase* to bulls, briefs, and papal documents with the consent of the Senate.[24]

While accepting without question and little debate Alberdi's proposal on the patronage, some of the members of the Convention desired a less tolerant religious policy than he advocated. They wanted the constitution to declare that Catholicism was the religion of the State, and "the only true one." But this was opposed on the ground that the State represented the collectivity of people and it could not profess an intimate belief which was not that of all the inhabitants. Nevertheless, since all accepted the proposition that Catholicism was the religion of the majority, this gave the federal government the right to intervene in the cult. Therefore the final formula: the government *supports* the cult. That the suggestions of Alberdi, relating to religion, were adopted by the Convention of Santa Fé can be evidenced by an examination of the Constitution of 1853. The principal religious clauses in that instrument were the following: (1) the federal government supports the Roman Catholic religion; (2) all inhabitants shall enjoy, subject to the laws regulating their exercise, the right freely to profess their religion; (3) aliens may practice freely their religion; (4) no member of the religious orders shall be elected to Congress; (5) Congress shall have the power: (a) to promote the conversion of the Indians on the frontiers; (b) to approve or reject concordats entered into with the Apostolic See, and to make rules for the exercise of the ecclesiastical patronage throughout the nation; (c) to admit into the territory of the nation religious orders in addition to those now existing; (6) the president, who must be a Roman Catholic, is given the following powers: (a) he shall exercise the

24. Juan B. Alberdi, *Bases y Puntos de Partida para la Organización de la República Argentina* (Buenos Aires, 1914), pp. 109-11, 285, 307, 308.

right of national ecclesiastical patronage by nominating bishops for cathedral churches, selected from the three names proposed to him by the Senate; (b) he shall, with the advice of the Supreme Court, grant or refuse passage to the decrees of councils, and bulls, briefs, and rescripts of the supreme pontiff of Rome, but said grant or refusal shall be made law whenever such ecclesiastical enactments contain provisions of a general or permanent character; and (c) he shall conclude and sign agreements with the pope.[25]

Unlike the earlier constitutions, that of 1853 did not declare Catholicism to be the faith of the State, but provided rather: "The federal government supports the Roman Catholic religion." This, it is contended, means that the Catholic religion is not the State religion in Argentina. Some see in it the *modus operandi* of a State-Church; others see in it the reverse. Some contend that "support" refers to financial aid, but they disagree greatly as to what should constitute a proper subsidy. It is argued by others that, if the framers of the Constitution wished to establish a State-Church they would have reproduced articles from earlier constitutions, instead of using the term "support," which only means "protect." Here is evidence, it is argued, that the Catholic religion is not the State religion.[26] But surely, if a faith is financially supported by the State, if some of its personnel is subject to governmental nomination, if the president of the republic must belong to that faith, if all religious ceremonies in which the State participates are conducted by that faith, and if pontifical documents issued for the governance of that faith are subject to governmental scrutiny, it is certainly the State religion quite as much as is the Established Church of England.

In August, 1856, the Congress of the Confederation, in enacting legislation for the organization of the ministries, incorporated Justice, Cult, and Public Instruction in one department. The jurisdiction of the division relating to Cult was defined as follows:

1. All that concerns the cult and the exercise of the national patronage.
2. All matters relating to the religious orders.
3. The issuance, according to the law, of the *pase*, or the retention of conciliar decrees, pontifical bulls, rescripts, and briefs of any ecclesiastical authority.
4. The examination of all appeals to the Holy See, or to any ecclesiastical authority outside of the territory of the Confederation.

25. Constitution of Argentina, Articles 2, 14, 20, 65, 67, 86. For the sessions of the Constituent Convention of 1853, see *Documentos relativos á la organización constitucional de la República Argentina* (Buenos Aires, 1911), III.

26. Vedia, *op. cit.*, p. 42.

5. Matters relating to the creation of dioceses, the territorial limits of same, and creation of parishes.
6. Establishment, direction, control, and support of ecclesiastical seminaries.
7. Matters relating to missions and the catechising of Indians.[27]

The national administration and control of matters relating to the Church remained in the Ministry of Justice, Cult, and Public Instruction until 1898 when the *Ministerio de Relaciones Exteriores y Culto* was organized.[28]

Not until 1860 did the Province of Buenos Aires become a member of the new federal union under the Constitution of 1853. The political schism in La Plata served to complicate the ecclesiastical problem, for in the city of Buenos Aires resided the prelate to whom was entrusted the pastoral cares of all the littoral which had entered the confederation. When the aged Bishop of Buenos Aires, Mariano Medrano, died, Auxiliary Bishop Mgr. Escalada was presented for the vacancy by the government of the province in March, 1854. The pope preconized Escalada *motu proprio*, and thus when the bull of institution was presented to the governor for his *pase*, he was hesitant because he regarded the subject as of "a delicate nature." He therefore appointed a special committee to advise him on the matter. The committee, after due deliberation, recommended that, "since Escalada had been proposed by the government and had taken the oath," he should grant the exequatur. This was done on September 10, 1855. Immediately after assuming possession of the diocese, Escalada notified President Urquiza that he was to be regarded as ecclesiastical head of the littoral.

President Urquiza, in the meantime, had taken steps to remedy the abnormal ecclesiastical situation by sending emissaries to Rome to negotiate the reëstablishment of religious relations. His first agent was Salvador Jiménez. Jiménez was instructed to petition for the creation of a littoral diocese free of Buenos Aires and to negotiate for a concordat. Very little is known about this mission, which was secretly conducted, other than that Jiménez was unable to accomplish anything, for the bases of a concordat suggested by the Cardinal-Secretary were incompatible with the Argentine Constitution.[29]

In 1855 the Congress of the Confederation, exercising its professed prerogative of national patronage, created a "Diocesis litoral" composed

27. *Colección Completa de Leyes Nacionales* (Buenos Aires, 1918), I, 233-34.
28. *Recopilación de Leyes Usuales de la República Argentina* (Buenos Aires, 1927), p. 24.
29. Legón, *op. cit.*, pp. 507-8, 512.

of the provinces of Santa Fé, Corrientes, and Entre Rios.[30] Since this action had to be confirmed by the pope, it was decided to send another emissary to Rome to point out the anomalous situation of dependent provinces of the see of Buenos Aires being separated politically from it, and to entreat the pope for a bull of erection. Juan B. Alberdi was chosen to represent Argentina before the Holy See, to recommend the creation of a bishopric of the littoral and also the provision of the vacant dioceses of Salta, Córdoba, and Cuyo. In exercising its right of patronage, the government presented names for the vacancies. Shortly after he initiated negotiations in Rome, Alberdi moved to Spain and the post at the Vatican was assumed by Benito Filippiani (1857). What Alberdi accomplished and the reason for his retirement are shrouded in mystery. It appears, however, that he opened negotiations for a concordat, for he said in a memorandum presented to the Holy See, "The Argentine government desires to celebrate a concordat with the Holy See. The Constitution (Article 27) authorizes it to enter into treaties with friendly nations; Rome is more than friendly to us; it is our spiritual capital." President Urquiza did not attempt to conceal his desire to negotiate a concordat, for, in a message to Congress in 1857, he said, "In spite of the unquestionable legitimacy of the rights attaching to national patronage in our churches, I do not question that the conclusion of a concordat will remove all doubt and all reason for scruples of conscience, and for that reason I have resorted to the Supreme Pontiff to conclude one."[31]

Filippiani secured the canonical institution of the three bishops who had been presented for the vacancies in Salta, Córdoba, and Cuyo, and he was probably responsible for the appointment by Pius IX of Mgr. Marino Marini, Archbishop of Palmyra *in partibus*, as Apostolic Delegate to the Confederation. In September, 1858, Juan del Campillo replaced Filippiani as official representative at Rome. Del Campillo secured papal consent to a reduction in the number of religious holidays in Argentina and to the erection of a bishopric of the littoral. In July, 1859, Mgr. Segura was granted a bull of institution as bishop of the new diocese. But the negotiations over a concordat resulted in an impasse. Although the Cardinal-Secretary agreed to recognize national patronage as it related to presentation to archbishoprics and bishoprics, he positively refused to recognize the exercise of the exequatur with respect to all

---

30. *Leyes Nacionales*, I, 176. For more legislation illustrative of the exercise of the patronage by the government of the Confederation, see *Leyes Nacionales*, I, 244 (scale of salaries for ecclesiastics); p. 274 (appropriation to defray the expenses from Europe of Capuchins to work in the missions); p. 343 (the President instructed to negotiate with pope for diminution in number of feast days); and pp. 352-53 (endowment of conciliar seminaries).

31. Legón, *op. cit.*, pp. 512-14.

briefs and bulls. This was something that the papacy had never conceded to any country. Thus, the concordat, the principal object of Del Campillo's mission, was not concluded.[32]

A curious incident cropped up in 1860 as a result of the treaty which Alberdi concluded with Spain. In that treaty the Spanish crown transferred its privileges of all kinds in La Plata to the Confederation. When he heard of this provision the nuncio in Madrid demanded a written statement that "these privileges" did not include patronage. Said Alberdi, "This resistance reveals the persuasion of the Holy See that the right of patronage is included among these things which the treaty confers on us, for on the other hand it would not have displayed such resistance."[33] Notwithstanding this apparent admission, the Vatican has never agreed that patronage is something which can be transferred as an element of sovereignty.

Technically all of the dioceses of Argentina were under the control of the Archbishop of Charcas. Such was the status on the eve of independence, and such it remained, in theory at least, after that event. Apostolic Delegate Marini, appreciating the need of freeing Argentina from dependence on a foreign archbishop, supported the movement to elevate the see of Buenos Aires into an archbishopric. After the reincorporation of Buenos Aires into the union, the solution of the problem was easy. In 1865 Buenos Aires was created a metropolitan see and Escalada was made the first archbishop.[34]

The government of the consolidated nation accentuated still more the regalism supported in Paraná, the capital of the Confederation. An incident which occurred shortly after the creation of the complete union evidenced this marked regalistic attitude. When Bishop Segura of Paraná, diocese of the littoral, died, the ecclesiastical chapter proceeded to elect the dean, Miguel Vidal, as capitular vicar. This fact was communicated to the national government. The *fiscal*, Ferrería, characterized the action of the chapter as "very strange," and declared that it could not function without governmental approval. The election was patently illegal, declared the *fiscal*, but since the chapter did not act in a spirit of resistance to the government, nor refuse recognition of national patronage, he advised that the matter should be overlooked and the election confirmed. A circular was sent to all bishops acquainting them of the incident and recommending strict adherence to the laws in the future. Bishop Escalada of Buenos Aires, however, declared that he did not think it was the duty of the chapter to ask governmental

32. *Ibid.*, p. 516; Chacaltana, *op. cit.*, p. 291.
33. Legón, *op. cit.*, pp. 517-18.
34. *Leyes Nacionales*, II, 213-14; Hernáez, *Colección de Bulas*, II, 309-15.

permission to name a capitular vicar. He contended that, as long as the pope did not recognize the patronage, the prelates owed him obedience as the spiritual head. Ferrería countered with the statement that so long as no concordat was concluded the Constitution should be obeyed to the letter. When the Apostolic Delegate insisted on the right of the Church itself to provide for vacant dioceses, the *fiscal* proceeded to examine the credentials of the papal representative himself. Ferrería went so far as to issue a decree denying recognition of the title "apostolic delegate" since it was not recognized in public ecclesiastical law. Therefore, in spite of the fact that, several years before, the government of Paraná had officially received the Apostolic Delegate, now, in 1863, his briefs were sent to the Supreme Court for study. In response to a protest by Marini, President Mitre intervened to assure him that whatever might be the decision of the Court, the government did not propose to alter the position which he occupied in the republic.[35]

Another and much more serious controversy regarding the patronage was created when the capitular vicar of the diocese of Córdoba (*en sede vacante*) Dr. Jerónimo Clara declared in a pastoral on April 25, 1884, that no Catholic parent could legitimately send his daughters to a certain normal school for girls which was directed by Protestant women teachers. The government of Córdoba notified the national Minister of Cult, Eduardo Wilde, regarding the pastoral and declared it to be subversive of the social order and opposed to the national authority. Wilde condemned the pastoral and ordered the cathedral chapter to take proper measures. The canons replied that they had no jurisdiction and furthermore agreed with the Vicar that it was illicit for Catholic children to attend such schools. Since the chapter refused to act, the Vicar, Dr. Jerónimo Clara, was suspended from office. But neither he nor the chapter would recognize the validity of the government's action. In the national Congress the pros and cons of the case were argued with great vehemence, but with opinion somewhat evenly divided as to the legal authority of the government to remove a prelate from office. Fortunately the government was not compelled to resort to force, for, at this juncture the new diocesan, Mgr. Tissera, took charge of the see and Clara was thus relieved of his authority.[36]

The controversy did not terminate by any means with the supplanting of the Vicar. On September 13, 1884, Bishop Buenaventura Risso Patrón published a pastoral on the subject of the schools of his own diocese of Salta. He approved the stand of Vicar Clara and contended that what applied to Córdoba applied to Salta. Children could not be sent to

35. Legón, *op. cit.*, pp. 522-24.
36. *Ibid.*, pp. 527-29.

schools directed by heretics, he said, without the parents incurring the penalty of being deprived of the sacraments. The vicars of Santiago del Estero and Jujuy joined Risso Patrón in defending Clara's stand. Since the national government regarded the tone of these declarations as being even more offensive than that of Clara himself, the three prelates were declared suspended by decree of November 3, 1884. The sudden death of Bishop Risso Patrón terminated his "case," but the question of the right of the government to remove the two vicars from office contributed to a bitter controversy of which once more there were repercussions in the Congress. The metropolitan and other bishops declared that the decree of November 3 was invalid, for the authority to remove bishops and prelates belonged to the pope.[37]

Then the Apostolic Delegate, Mgr. Matera, became involved in the controversy. In September, 1884, Matera went to Córdoba, and while there he was privately interviewed by Miss Frances Armstrong, director of the normal school that had been denounced by Clara. She evidently appealed to the Delegate to raise the anathema which hung over the school. Enemies of Matera charged that the Delegate consented to raise the ban on condition that the government accede to certain demands. Matera himself declared that he regarded his conversation with Miss Armstrong as a purely private and unofficial matter, and that he was thoroughly within his rights in advising her to announce that it was not her intention to proselyte in the school for the Protestant faith, and that, on the contrary, she would place no obstacle in the way of instruction in the Catholic catechism in the school. He particularly counseled her to direct her requests by petition to the government.

When Matera's conversation with Miss Armstrong was reported to the Minister of Cult, Eduardo Wilde, he became greatly aroused and declared that Matera was interfering in affairs over which he had no authority. The Minister of Foreign Relations requested the Apostolic Delegate to explain his conduct. Matera, in his reply, explained that the affair was no more than a private conversation and far from interfering he recommended that the legal course of petition be resorted to. But because of the peremptory demands of the government for an explanation, Matera lost control of his better reason and allowed certain damaging expressions to creep into his reply. The result was that, on October 14, the Apostolic Delegate was given his passports and allowed twenty-four hours to leave the country. The government of Argentina, although legally within its rights, was much too precipitate and harsh. It certainly should have been considerate enough of the pope to allow

37. *Ibid.*, pp. 533-35.

him to recall his representative. Naturally, the Catholics protested the expulsion of the Delegate and from high and low places the incident was branded as a breach of diplomatic usage and a crowning national disgrace. The incident, at all events, emphasized the necessity of determining exactly the character and position of the papal representative. A doctrinal question which related to the rights of papal representatives in purely religious subjects was latent in the conflict. The attorney-general contended that neither prelates nor chapters had the right to enter into direct relations with the diplomatic representative of the pope. The pope's representative, said Vélez Sarsfield, ought to be considered only as envoy of the sovereign of the Papal States.[38]

President Roca, immediately after the expulsion of Matera, accredited Mariano Balcarce, Argentinian minister to France, as envoy extraordinary and minister plenipotentiary on special mission to the Vatican, to explain to the pope why the conduct of the Delegate was unacceptable and to protest the loyalty and love of the Argentine Nation for the Holy See. Cardinal Jacobini, Secretary of State, far from reproving the acts of Matera, refused to censure him. He declared that Argentina's actions were contrary to all diplomatic practice. As long as Cardinal Jacobini was in charge of papal relations he refused to send a representative to Buenos Aires. When Cardinal Rampolla became Secretary of State, Argentina decided to appeal to the Vatican once more. In 1892, shortly before relinquishing office, President Pellegrini despatched Vicente G. Quesada to Rome on special mission to heal the breach. He was instructed "to defend the right of patronage inherent in national sovereignty and to facilitate the regular procedure for its exercise in the provision of the first dignities of the Argentine Church." He was to refuse to consider a concordat and the possible suggestion that a permanent nuncio be sent to Buenos Aires. According to Quesada it seemed that the instructions were entirely too rigid and severe and calculated to perpetuate the break. Nevertheless, he and Cardinal Rampolla negotiated in fine spirit and the preconization of Mgr. Pablo Padilla as Bishop of Salta was secured.

When Dr. Luis Saénz Peña became president, his foreign minister, Tomás Anchorena, instructed Quesada confidentially to terminate the negotiations as based on the instructions of the prior administration. They were ill-conceived, he felt, and any attempt to abide by them would merely serve to perpetuate strained relations. "The Holy See," he said, "by celebrating a concordat, no doubt would recognize patronage in the

38. Sarsfield, *op. cit.*, pp. 133-34; Legón, *op. cit.*, pp. 536-39.

national government or certain rights of patronage in ecclesiastical subjects such as are now more or less in vogue. But it will never recognize that patronage or those rights are inherent in sovereignty, for to no government, absolutely none, has it been conceded in that form."[39]

The opinion of Anchorena was sound and has been justified by subsequent history. Never has a concordat been concluded by Argentina with Rome, but practically all that would have been guaranteed by a concordat has been secured by tacit agreement. The pope theoretically reserves the right to appoint bishops, but, actually, when a vacancy occurs, the federal Senate exercises the right of sending three names to the president who transmits one to the pontiff who has the choice of accepting or rejecting it. The pope's acquiescence in this procedure is a fact, but he has never ceased to argue that it is in no way to be regarded as a recognition of the inherence of patronage in sovereignty. Nor are the government's nominees always accepted as a matter of course, as for example in 1923, when the pope refused to confirm Mgr. Miguel de Andrea, the republic's nominee for the archiepiscopal see of Buenos Aires.[40] The government for some time refused to make another nomination, and thus for over two years during the Alvear administration the controversy between Argentina and the Vatican made the relations of Church and State an acute political problem. Throughout the controversy the government was very insistent that its patronal right should be protected to the limit. In his message to Congress the President said, "The Executive will admit no discussion over the right of patronage determined by the Constitution."[41] Finally, in the latter part of 1926, President Alvear suggested to the Vatican the appointment of Mgr. José María Bottaro as Archbishop of Buenos Aires. Papal confirmation was accorded and the crisis was passed.[42]

The right of presentation in Argentina applies only to the first dignities of the Church, i.e., the archbishop and bishops. There is omission, in the Constitution, of the customary phrase that the government "exercises the powers of patronage respecting churches, benefices, and ecclesiastical persons." Thus it is presumable that the framers of the Constitution wished to leave the greatest liberty to the Church. The question as to whether or not the patronage applied to auxiliary bishops was settled in 1919 by the Supreme Court. The opinion of the Court

39. Legón, *op. cit.*, p. 545.
40. *Ministerio de Relaciones Exteriores y Culto, Circular Informativa Mensual* (Buenos Aires, 1924), pp. 313-14.
41. *Ministerio de Relaciones Exteriores y Culto, Circular Informativa Mensual* (Buenos Aires, 1925), pp. 1071-72.
42. *Current History*, December, 1926, pp. 439-40.

was that the government had the right to nominate auxiliary bishops.[43] Yet the age-old question regarding the nature of the patronage is periodically argued in the Argentine press and in Congress.

While the scope of the patronage is more restricted in Argentina than in many countries where the Catholic cult is the established religion, and notwithstanding the fact that there are no religious tests for exercising the suffrage or holding public office,[44] nevertheless the national government occupies an exceptional position in its relations to the Roman Catholic Church, as has already been noted. Furthermore, the Holy See is represented at Buenos Aires by an apostolic nuncio, and the Argentine Nation has an accredited diplomatic representative at the Vatican. In 1927 this representative was raised to the rank of ambassador. In the Ministry of Foreign Affairs and Cult, there is a Subsecretary of Worship in charge of ecclesiastical matters as they relate to the government.

Although the clergy are allowed to communicate freely with Rome, a situation unknown under the *real patronato de Indias*, this does not apply to the admission of pontifical decrees. It is interesting to note that in those countries where Church and State are separate the government does not undertake to pass upon the admission of papal documents. On the other hand it rarely happens that the right of the *pase* is not based on the patronage.

The relation of the provincial governments to the Roman Catholic Church calls for brief explanation. That there is no agreement on what is the legal relationship is evidenced by the fact that prominent constitutional authorities have given affirmative answers to each of the following questions: Does the province exercise the patronage of the Catholic Church within its territory to the extent permitted by the National Constitution? Does the province exercise the vice-patronage as agent of the federal power exclusively? Does not the patronage belong exclusively to the federal government which does not admit of any delegation of power whatever to the governors of the provinces?

The numerous political changes through which the provinces passed before a permanent Argentine Union was formed adds to the difficulty of arriving at a correct answer to the problem. When La Plata disintegrated in 1820, each province, on assuming the plenitude of sovereignty, claimed that it inherited the exercise of the ecclesiastical patronage. In

---

43. José N. Matienzo, *Cuestiones de Derecho Público Argentino* (Buenos Aires, 1924), pp. 97-101.

44. The president and vice-president are the only officials of whom the Constitution demands a religious belief. Priests living in religious communities are not allowed the suffrage.

the Constitution of Corrientes of 1821, for example, the provincial governor was delegated all those powers relating to presentation, exequatur, and negotiation of a concordat that had been given to the president of the defunct United Provinces by the Constitution of 1819. The same attitude toward the patronage was manifested in the succession of provincial constitutions down to the completion of the national union in 1860. Then the Constitution of Corrientes of 1864 provided that (1) the government was obliged to support the Catholic cult in those matters that properly belonged to it, and to promote its aggrandizement and progress; (2) the provincial legislature had the power to regulate the civil, judicial, and ecclesiastical division of the province, and to make rules for the exercise of the patronage in those matters not delegated to the president of the republic; and (3) the executive power had the right to exercise the patronage in those matters not delegated to the president.[45]

Although succeeding constitutions of Corrientes did not contain a word on the subject of patronage, it is contended that their silence did not mean a renunciation of the right. The provinces accordingly can still exercise the patronage regarding those matters not specifically granted to the central authority. By virtue of their residual patronal rights, they can determine and regulate Church fees for marriages, baptisms, and other religious ceremonies. Also they can intervene in regulating the selection and tenure of parish priests. These are powers possessed although not always exercised.

Passing from matters relating to the political status of the Church, under the current Constitution of 1853, attention will be directed to its support, its property rights, and its relation to education, marriage, and the like. The support of the cult is regarded as an obligation based upon the enjoyment of the patronage. The government is required to make annual appropriations for the hierarchy, cathedral chapters, seminaries, and Indian missions. This subvention is not large. The lower clergy of parochial churches and charitable institutions receive no aid from the State, but depend on fees and contributions of the faithful. Only the priests attached to cathedrals are paid salaries, and consequently are regarded as government employees. Considerable revenue is derived by the Church from its properties. Since no restriction has ever been placed upon the ability of the Church to receive entailments and bequests, its real properties and other possessions are of great value. Church holdings have not been nationalized, with the exception of cathedrals. The other churches and buildings belong to their respective

45. Hernán F. Gómez, *Instituciones de la Provincia de Corrientes* (Buenos Aires, 1922), pp. 236-59.

congregations. Cathedrals are exempt from taxation but other ecclesiastical edifices are assessed certain municipal imposts.

The public schools in the Argentine republic, as in the United States, are absolutely secular. The Church exercises no control over public education. A statute of 1884 provided that no religious instruction could be given in public schools during regular hours. But the federal school law of 1888 provided that "after official hours, religious instruction [Catholic and otherwise] may be given to the children who voluntarily remain in the schools for the purpose of receiving it. This religious instruction in the public schools shall be given only by authorized ministers of the different persuasions, before or after school hours." A law of 1904 made it a punishable offense to give religious instruction to children whose parents did not previously request it.[46]

That there should be no teaching of religion in public educational institutions was taken for granted by virtually everyone. In the succeeding decades clericalism and anticlericalism were hardly a serious factor in Argentine politics. But all this was changed when, in December, 1943, a decree-law of the new Ramírez administration, which inaugurated the Perón era in Argentina, reintroduced religious instruction into the regular schedules of all federally supported schools. The children of parents who did not desire this instruction were to be given "moral instruction."[47]

Although it was never proved that this was "the coin in which the Roman Catholic hierarchy was paid for its support of the revolutionary government," as was alleged, and that the bishops were ready to coöperate with an antidemocratic program to gain advantage for their creed, it was true nevertheless that the decree-law was hailed by the clerics with enthusiasm.[48] When the decree-law was validated by the Congress in 1947, the Argentine Cardinals Luis Copello and Antonio Caggiano and the archbishops formally called on Perón and thanked him for sustaining the decree.[49] Immediately following the overthrow of Perón in 1955 the statute of 1947 was repealed and religious instruction was removed from the classrooms of the public schools.

About one-third of the educational institutions of the country depend on charitable and religious organizations for their support. The great majority of these are conducted by Catholic societies, charitable organi-

46. Leyes Nacionales, VI, 34-35; Angel V. Andrada (ed.), *Leyes Nacionales, Decretos demas Resoluciones de la República Argentina* (Buenos Aires, 1927), II, 243-54.

47. John J. Kennedy, *Catholicism, Nationalism, and Democracy in Argentina* (Notre Dame, Ind., 1958), p. 196.

48. *Ibid.*, pp. 187, 196-97.

49. L. Edward Shuck, Jr., "Church and State in Argentina," *Western Political Quarterly*, II, No. 4 (December, 1949), 533.

zations, and orders, for the diocesan Church itself does not maintain parochial schools. It is estimated that the Church controls about 5 per cent of the total school enrollment. In 1959 the number of Catholic schools totaled 1,177 and students enrolled totaled 338,305.[50]

The Catholics, in recent years, have spared no effort to strengthen their educational work. Their schools are generally housed in adequate, modern, and often impressive buildings, and the quality of instruction is excellent. Some of the largest secondary educational institutions are maintained by the Roman Church, and the grade of instruction rivals that of the government schools. Recently a system of Catholic universities was established.

Protestant schools are not numerous. No religious school can operate without an official permit, and the courses of study must be the same as prescribed by the government for the public schools. In general, all private educational institutions are subject to such governmental supervision as will ensure a general uniformity of instruction throughout the republic in order that the status of the graduates of secondary public, private, and religious schools will be the same for the purpose of classification upon their application for entrance into the universities or other higher educational institutions. The Catholic schools generally charge no tuition fees. In some cases the national government and the respective municipalities contribute to their support. Diocesan seminaries are supported outright by annual federal appropriations.[51]

On November 2, 1888, a civil marriage law was passed and is still in force. This law grants validity only to marriages publicly solemnized in the office of the functionary in charge of the civil register.[52] Any priest who violates the law by performing the marriage ceremony before the civil act is subject to heavy penalty. In December, 1954, the Perón-controlled Congress legalized absolute divorce. This law was revoked March 1, 1956. Since that date Argentina has been one of the five Latin-American countries that does not sanction divorce which allows for remarriage.

No longer are all cemeteries controlled by the Church, as was the case under the Spanish régime and in the early days of independence. Catholics are allowed to maintain separate cemeteries, but they are subject, of course, as are those municipally controlled, to governmental supervision, sanitary control, and the like. Thus, although Argentina is a Catholic country and the Catholic Church is a State establishment,

---

50. *Statistical Abstract of Latin America, 1963*, p. 22.

51. *The Catholic World*, Vol. 116, p. 676.

52. The Law of the Civil Register was enacted October 31, 1884. (*Recop. de Leyes Usuales*, 1927, pp. 501-9.)

one encounters there lay primary education, civil marriage, and purely municipal cemeteries. The Church has been deprived of its traditional control of certain vital matters affecting the private lives of the inhabitants.

Unlike most of the Latin-American countries Argentina was the scene of only mild manifestations of anticlericalism and these occurred in the nineteenth century. After the passage of lay education and civil marriage laws in the 1880's religion ceased to be a political issue. The two principal parties, the Conservatives (National Democrats) and the Liberals or "Radicals" (Radical Civic Union) were not disposed to disturb the placid waters, but not so the Socialists who advocated separation of Church and State. The Socialists, however, never threatened to become a majority party. The Conservative party, that of the landowning aristocracy, was consistently backed by the Church. The Conservatives managed by fair means and foul to maintain control over the national government, with the exception of the period 1916-30, until the military coup in 1943.

With the military revolution of 1943 and the ascendancy of Juan D. Perón, the new régime, to strengthen its position, sought an effective alliance with the clergy. The government decree of December, 1943, which made religious instruction compulsory in state schools, was an overture for clerical support which the hierarchy accepted eagerly. Only a few of the clergy and prelates, like Bishop Miguel de Andrea,[53] recognized the danger of close association with an antidemocratic régime. In fact clerical approval of the religious instruction decree and other Perón favors lent color to the charge that Argentine Catholicism was antidemocratic.[54]

In the election campaign of 1945-46 the hierarchy publicly urged the faithful not to vote for a party (Perón's opposition: the Democratic Union) which advocated separation of Church and State, the abolition of religious instruction, and legalization of divorce. With Catholic support Perón was victorious. In the congressional campaign of 1947-48 the hierarchy once again urged the faithful not to vote for those regarded as enemies of the Church.[55] The clerics in gratitude to Perón for his favors represented his cause as a fulfillment of the social program of the Church as set forth in the encyclicals *Rerum Novarum* and *Quadragesimo Anno.* Perónism was attractive to many Catholics because it seemed to offer support for such moral objectives as protection of the family and

53. George I. Blanksten, *Perón's Argentina* (Chicago, 1953), pp. 231-32.
54. Kennedy, *op. cit.*, p. 186.
55. *La Prensa*, Buenos Aires, November 17, 1945 and December 31, 1947.

ethical conduct as defined by the Church.[56] Perón, as a matter of fact, said in 1945: "My social policy will be inspired by the Papal encyclicals."[57] The Constitution of 1949 did not change the legal relationship of Church and State, except that perhaps it favored the Church more than the Constitution of 1853.

The apparent *entente* between the Church and Perón aroused feelings of anticlericalism which had been dormant for many years. The Radicals now included the Catholic Church in their attacks against the régime.

The pro-Perón policy of the Roman Catholic hierarchy greatly bothered Catholic apologists,[58] and well it might, for the evidences of clerical coöperation with the totalitarian régime were too patent to be denied. This does not ignore the fact that large numbers of clerics were unhappy about the situation. Fortunately, Perón's breaking of the *entente* afforded the Argentine clergy opportunity to recover some dignity and prestige. "What a stain it would have been on the pages of history," says Father Considine, "if Perón had come and gone and the Church was recorded as having bowed in subjection to the blandishments of the dictator."[59]

It evidently was not any conscious effort on the part of the Church which brought about a decision by Perón to alter his policy. Since the Church was the only major organization, group, or institution in Argentina not fully subjected to Peronista control, its influence and power had to be destroyed. For example, Perón, witnessing the increase of Church influence in Argentine labor unions, condemned this "meddling" and warned that labor had nothing to do with religion. The dictator was fearful of a resurgent Church which he believed was playing politics and renewing its old alliance with the oligarchy, or Conservative privileged class, which was one of the principal targets of his social revolution. Perón's movement contained many adherents who considered that Catholicism was an anachronism in a syndicatist, industrialized state. They demanded social reforms which were unacceptable to the Church.[60]

It was in November, 1954, when Perón evidently came to a decision that he would never again be able to rely on the backing of the Church and therefore decided to crush Catholic dissidents before they

56. Frederick B. Pike, ed., *Freedom and Reform in Latin America* (Notre Dame, Ind., 1959), p. 130.

57. Pablo Marsal S., *Perón y la Iglesia* (Buenos Aires, 1955), p. 146.

58. Peter M. Dunne, "Church and State in Argentina," in *Review of Politics*, Vol. 7, No. 4 (October, 1945), pp. 395-417, explains why so many churchmen in Argentina, *but not all*, approved the Perón régime. Also, see Kennedy, *op. cit.*, pp. 185-86.

59. John J. Considine, *New Horizons in Latin America* (New York, 1958), p. viii.

60. *Hispanic American Report*, VII, No. 11 (December, 1954), 33-34.

became a threat to his authority. A speech on November 10, 1954, was a veritable declaration of war against the Church. Charging that the Church was making an effort to undermine the government, Perón condemned "evil shepherds" and "bad priests." In particular, he accused three bishops of being enemies of the government and a number of priests of "illicit activities." These opening charges were soon translated into action.[61]

A number of priests were imprisoned for having meddled in politics and for having tried to suborn the trade unions. Catholic newspapers were closed, religious processions were prohibited, religious festivals were removed from the calendar of public holidays, and Catholic students' clubs were raided. In December, 1954, the rubber-stamp Congress legalized divorce. At the same time Perón authorized provincial governments to legalize prostitution, which, as a result of Catholic action, had been banned in 1937. In April, 1955, the teaching of religion and morals, which had been obligatory in all state schools, was abandoned. State aid to Catholic schools was cut off and some religious schools were closed for "abusing Argentine law and the Constitution." There was a purge of clerical and proclerical teachers, and many priests were arrested for "disrespect." The government justified its actions as "not against the Church but against those who use it as a means to attack us."[62] Inevitably the assault resulted in the call by the Congress, in May, 1955, for a constitutional convention to disestablish the Church.[63] The Perón regime was overthrown before the separation of Church and State could be formalized.

This aggressive anti-Catholic campaign was a political blunder for it aroused much more widespread opposition than he had expected. The Church, which had earlier inclined to Perónism, not for political but for socio-economic reasons, was later driven to defend itself when denied all possibilities in the spiritual order. Argentine Catholicism proved its vitality when it finally faced up to the menace of the dictator.

In response to Perón's provocative speech of November 10, 1954, the Argentine hierarchy issued a pastoral signed by all the members of the episcopacy which made clear that the Church was prepared to defend its right to guide the moral affairs of the nation. On many succeeding

61. "Church and State in Argentina: Factors in Perón's Downfall," *The World Today* (Chatham House, Royal Institute of International Affairs), XII, No. 2 (February, 1956), 58-66. Also see, Arthur P. Whitaker, *Argentine Upheaval: Perón's Fall and the New Regime* (New York, 1956), p. 1.

62. *Boletín Oficial* (Buenos Aires), Leyes de mayo 21 and 23, 1955; *Hispanic American Report*, VIII, No. 2 (March, 1955), 85; No. 3 (April, 1955), 131; and No. 4 (May, 1955), 181-84.

63. *Hispanic American Report*, VIII, No. 5 (June, 1955), 232.

occasions the Church leaders, with the support of the Vatican, spoke out against the anti-Catholic attack. Following Perón's expulsion of two Catholic prelates, on June 16, 1955, Pope Pius XII excommunicated all governmental authorities who had "trampled on the rights of the Church."[64]

Catholic reaction against Perónism reached its height in June, 1955. Catholic Action, a militant lay organization, marshalled anti-Peronista demonstrations. Perón's efforts to placate the Church and get the pope to lift the ban of excommunication came too late, for the Argentine military, in a movement in which the clericals were not associated, overthrew the dictatorship on September 23, 1955. Undoubtedly Perón's attack on the Church must be regarded as a contributing cause of his downfall.[65] The Church emerged from its shame with greatly increased prestige.

After the fall of Perón most of his anti-Catholic measures were revoked and the Church was restored to the *status quo ante* 1943. The so-called *ley desacato* which punished disrespectful words and actions against government officials was repealed. Tax exemptions on both Roman Catholic and Protestant churches were restored, and the law legalizing prostitution was repealed. A governmental decree of March 1, 1956, which suspended the divorce law of 1947 was later ratified by the Congress. Argentina is one of the five Latin-American countries which does not allow absolute divorce. There was a reappearance of religious holidays on the national calendar.[66]

In March, 1956, the prohibition of religious instruction in public schools was repealed. At the same time the government authorized by decree-law the establishment of Catholic universities qualified to grant degrees and professional titles. Whereas the hierarchy and Catholic leaders favored a system of private Catholic universities to break the principle of lay education, this move was regarded by others as an attempt to undermine the traditional monopoly by the State of higher education. The decree-law was later ratified by the Congress.[67]

Hopes entertained by Argentine clericals for a concordat with the Vatican never materialized. The Holy See seemed content, for the moment, with the reëstablishment of the pre-1943 constitutional status of the Argentine Church. Accordingly *patronato nacional* operated as

64. *Ibid.*, No. 6 (July, 1955), 284.
65. Chatham House, *The World Today, op. cit.*, pp. 65-66.
66. *Hispanic American Report*, VIII, No. 9 (October, 1955), 434; No. 12 (January, 1956), 579; *Boletín Oficial* (Buenos Aires), Decree 4070, March 1, 1956.
67. *Hispanic American Report*, IX, No. 5 (June, 1956), 256; No. 6 (July, 1956), 308; XI, No. 9 (September, 1958), 516.

before. For example, in 1957, and again in 1961, as a result of negotiations with the Vatican, new dioceses and archdioceses were created by Congressional legislation. For the installation of the new prelates, approved by the Vatican, the government voted increased appropriations. By the end of 1963 Argentina had twelve archdioceses and thirty-seven dioceses.[68]

The creation of new dioceses meant of course the creation of new parishes and an increase in the number of priests. Still, there is a scarcity of clergy in Argentina, for in 1960 there were 4,859 priests or 4,100 Catholics per priest.[69] A Catholic report described the condition of the Catholic Church in Argentina in 1958 as discouraging and enumerated the following six causes of the sad situation: (1) scarcity of clergy; (2) extensive parishes and dioceses, making pastoral visits impossible; (3) scarcity of leaders and Catholics capable of becoming leaders; (4) lack of apostolic responsibility through faulty forms of education; (5) self-complacency of the nominal Catholics; and (6) lack of responsibility and generosity on the part of those who practice the faith. On the other hand this discouraging appraisal was compensated by the admission of an improvement in the quality of religious instruction and an awakening of a true apostolic spirit among the young.[70] There has also been an awakening among many of the churchmen of a sensitivity to social trends. But "social Catholicism," dedicated to improve welfare legislation, has produced no spectacular results.[71]

The status of the Catholic Church in Argentina is still largely defined by the Constitution of 1853. The cult occupies a somewhat anomalous middle ground between the position of a full-fledged state church and separation. Although from the point of view of the Church this is far from an ideal arrangement, it cherishes nevertheless the principle of union and condemns separation as a denial of the divine mission of the Church.

68. *Ibid.*, IX, No. 12 (January, 1957), 602; XIV, No. 4 (April, 1961), 357; XVI, No. 8 (August, 1963), 813.

69. W. Stanley Rycroft and Myrtle M. Clemmer, *A Factual Study of Latin America* (New York, 1963), p. 235.

70. William J. Coleman, *Latin American Catholicism: A Self-Evaluation* (Maryknoll, N.Y., 1958), p. 26.

71. For Catholic Action in Argentina, see Kennedy, *op. cit.*, pp. 180-81.

Chapter XI

Separation in Uruguay

In 1919 the Oriental Republic of Uruguay cut asunder the bonds which once tied the religious establishment to the political power. And, as in Brazil and Chile, separation in Uruguay has been attended by satisfying and hopeful results. The progressive Spanish-American republic, which has been called the political and sociological laboratory of South America, dared to experiment in a new religious policy. The subsequent experiences proved the success of the experiment.

In embarking upon an independent career Uruguay adopted as its religious policy that of its mentor and guardian, Argentina. The long-lived Constitution of 1830, which was drafted by a convention including five clerics, provided for the Catholic religion as that of the State, but it did not prohibit the exercise of dissident faiths. The guarantee of toleration of cults as early as 1830 was exceptional in Latin America. But, in laying claim to the exercise of the ecclesiastical patronage, Uruguay merely adopted the practice of the other Latin-American states. Thus, the Constitution provided that the president should exercise the right of patronage; that he, with the advice of the Senate, should grant or refuse the exequatur to pontifical bulls.[1]

Prior to the establishment of Uruguayan independence, ecclesiastical jurisdiction in the Banda Oriental was subordinate to the diocesan of Buenos Aires. This situation, which continued after the creation of the independent republic, was repugnant to the national sensibilities of Uruguayans. Consequently, Congress on July 17, 1830, ordered the president to petition the Holy See to create a separate diocese in the republic. The legislators went on record as being willing to defray the expenses of an episcopal see, but stipulated that the incumbent should be a citizen of the State.[2] The aspiration at the establishment of a national

1. Justo Arosemena, *Estudias Constitucionales sobre los gobiernos de la América Latina*, 2 vols. (Paris, 1888), I, 213-34, Arts. 5 and 81.

2. P. V. Goyena (ed.), *La Legislación Vigente de la República Oriental del Uruguay* (Montevideo, 1874), II, 464.

diocese was not satisfied for many years to come. Uruguay was constituted an apostolic vicarate, and not until 1878 was the diocese of Montevideo created.[3] Preliminary to the establishment of the diocese, the Apostolic Delegate to Argentina, Marino Marini, on February 24, 1863, conferred on the Vicar General of Uruguay the episcopal power of administering the sacrament of confirmation.[4]

Despite the fact that the Uruguayan Church continued to be under foreign ecclesiastical jurisdiction, the government claimed its constitutional right of ecclesiastical patronage. In the law of July 17, 1830, the Congress stipulated that the new bishop whenever created should be proposed as constitutionally required. In 1835, by act of Congress, the President was empowered to enter into an agreement with the apostolic vicar providing for the organizing of tribunals to hear ecclesiastical causes. The government, also, was very jealous of its right over the *pase* required of pontifical documents. For example, the brief of Marino Marini mentioned above was refused publication in Uruguay until the consent of the Tribunal of Justice was secured.[5]

For nearly one hundred years, despite the perpetual political turmoil incident to the ups and downs of the factions known as *Blancos* and *Colorados*, the provisions in the Constitution of 1830 on the subject of religion were never altered. Yet, during these years the Church was subjected to attack, never as violent or devastating as in Mexico, but nevertheless unremitting and effective. The result was that the privileged position of the Church was undermined and the so-called union of Church and State became more fiction than fact. Under these circumstances, therefore, little opposition would be raised to absolute separation.

The bitter rivalry between the two traditional parties, the *Colorados* and the *Blancos*, has been a dominant factor in the history of the Uruguayan republic. But, as to professing distinctive policies, they differed very slightly, the principal aims of both parties being to capture office and retain it; one represented the "ins" and the other the "outs." To a certain extent, however, the *Blancos* "were the partisans of absolutism, nationalists, and Catholics, and intolerant toward foreign cults. The *Colorados* were liberals and enemies of the Church."[6] But notwithstanding this difference, religion of itself was never a contributing cause of civil war in Uruguay. This, however, did not prevent the *Colorados*, during their tenures of office, from enacting various ec-

3. *Cath. Ency.*, XV, 231.
4. Goyena, *op. cit.*, II, 468.
5. *Ibid.*, II, 468, 491-92.
6. García Calderón, *Latin America*, pp. 131-32.

clesiastical reform measures, which the *Blancos*, presumably because of their lack of interest, never attempted to revoke. The *Colorados*, as a general rule, were mild and unaggressive anticlericals, and the *Blancos* were supine and lukewarm defenders of the State-Church. Under such a situation the power and prestige of the Church declined.

Although more far-reaching reform directed at the temporal prerogatives of the Church was not forthcoming until after 1880, certain incidents and acts occurring in the preceding years may be mentioned to illustrate the unstable political status of the Church. In evidence of the liberal attitude of the government under President Fructuoso Rivera, provision was made in 1837 for the legalization of the civil marriage ceremony for the benefit of non-Catholics. According to existing law, the Catholic Church was given exclusive control over matrimony and no marriage was recognized by the law if not performed by a priest. This was a manifest injustice to non-Catholics, and thus the decree provided that non-Catholics were free to be married by the justices of the peace. Foreign consuls retained the right until 1878 to perform the marriage ceremony for their nationals.[7]

In 1838 President Rivera suppressed the Franciscan convents and took their property for public use. "When there is not the required number of conventual inmates," read the presidential decree, "there should be no convents." There was considerable resentment in Uruguay, as in Brazil and other parts of Latin America, toward the too numerous religious of both sexes in a young undeveloped land whose principal problem was population. It was regarded as manifestly unfair to the nation and economically unwise that able bodied men and women should abstain from their natural function of race reproduction. The opposition to the conventual life was not based, consequently, in antireligious motives.[8]

In the late 1850's political elements somewhat antagonistic to the Church secured control of the government. The Jesuits who had been readmitted into the country a few years before were expelled in 1859. The vicissitudes suffered by the Company in other parts of Latin America were not escaped in the Oriental Republic. In 1861, public cemeteries were removed from ecclesiastical control and put under the direction and administration of *juntas económicas* of the respective departments. Soon, however, the political scales tipped to the other side, and in 1865, under President Venacio Flores, a *Colorado*, religious congregations

7. Goyena, *op. cit.*, I, 369; *Leyes, Decretos y Reglamentos Vigentes en 1920* (Montevideo, 1920), p. 77.

8. Goyena, *op. cit.*, II, 469.

dedicated to educational work were permitted reëntry into the country. By the terms of this decree the Jesuits returned to Uruguay.[9]

In the decade of the 1880's several important anticlerical measures were adopted. Incidentally, it is interesting to note in this connection that more anticlerical legislation was adopted throughout Latin America in this decade than in any other equal space of time. By law of June 1, 1880, the *Registro del Estado Civil* was established. This act entrusted to the justices of the peace the exclusive right of registering vital statistics, a task hitherto monopolized by the clergy. By the terms of this law the Church was deprived of its one-time exclusive control over marriages, legitimization of births, and control of cemeteries. A law of May 22, 1885, made the civil marriage compulsory and the only legal form. The civil ceremony was required to precede the religious and no ceremony should be regarded as binding in law which did not comply with the laws of the civil register. This means that a child born of a Church marriage alone is regarded by the State as being illegitimate.[10] Although the religious ceremony satisfies no legal requirement, it is generally performed for Catholics after the celebration of the civil act. Approximately one-half of the civil ceremonies receive religious consecration. The law of 1885 is in force today, substantially unchanged, with the exception that absolute divorce is permitted. Remarriage is permitted after a lapse of one year from the time of the granting of the decree. All cases relating to divorce, dissolution, or nullity of marriages are heard exclusively by the civil courts. Since divorce has been made easy there has been a steady increase yearly.

Governmental aid to the Catholic Church was constantly curtailed until, in 1892, it amounted to only $19,712 per annum. The Church, therefore, as the State-Church, enjoyed little or no pecuniary advantage. The clergy and the various necessary ecclesiastical activities had to be supported by contributions of the faithful, bequests, fees, and income from real property. Separation, certainly, would impose no financial hardship upon the Church. It is important to note that the Catholic Church, as the State-Church, continued to enjoy, until 1919, when separation occurred, a peculiar advantage with respect to education. Instruction in the Catholic faith was included in the general program of studies laid down for the schools operated by the State. In 1909 the teaching of religion in the public schools was prohibited. Later, coeducation was accepted. Everything relating to the exercise of the na-

9. *Ibid.*, II, 470.

10. *Leyes, Decretos y Reglamentos Vigentes del Registro del Estado Civil* (Montevideo, 1921), Articles 83 and 91.

tional patronage and the religion of the State was entrusted to the *Departamento de Fomento, Cultos é Instrucción Público.* Of course the conduct of negotiations with the Holy See, with which official diplomatic relations were maintained until 1919, continued to be exercised by the Department of Foreign Relations.

José Batlle y Ordóñez, the great liberal statesman who wrought a socio-politico transformation of Uruguay in the first decades of the twentieth century, was responsible, more than any other individual, for the separation of Church and State in that country. An atheist, or at least a free-thinker, he early adopted a skeptical and questioning attitude toward the Roman Catholic Church from which evolved a firm belief that the ecclesiastical and political institutions must be separate. "His magnetism and force of personality were sufficient to transmit the stamp of his ideas on religion to the dominant batllista wing of the Colorado party."[11]

The Church was disestablished in Uruguay when the republic adopted a new constitution on March 1, 1919. Considering the feeble ties which had joined Church and State, prior to the adoption of the Constitution of 1919, the act of separation cannot be regarded as a radical step. Nor, indeed, did the reform encounter serious opposition in any quarter. The opinion that absolute separation would be of mutual advantage to the temporal and spiritual orders seemed to be rather general. The severing of the traditional ties was accomplished, therefore, with a minimum of rancor and hard feeling.

In the Constitutional Convention (1916-17) projects were introduced by the various parties and individual delegates for the guidance of the committee entrusted with the framing of a new constitution. In these projects appeared proposals for the separation of Church and State. With the exception of the project of the Unión Cívica, the Catholic party, all of the model constitutions provided for separation. Excepting the extreme Catholics, there seemed to be unanimity on separation, but considerable difference of opinion as to the disposal of Church property. But on this point, the moderate and controlling elements of the two traditional parties agreed that the Catholic Church should be recognized as the legal owner of all edifices which had been constructed in whole or in part with funds from the national treasury. The agreement of the dominant parties on the issues of separation and disposition of Church buildings really relegated the whole matter to a position of secondary importance in the Convention. It is true that extremists aired their

11. Russell H. Fitzgibbon, *Uruguay, Portrait of a Democracy* (New Brunswick, N.J., 1954), p. 232.

views in considerable volume, but their proposals were refused by the Convention.[12]

The general committee appointed to draft a constitution reported, on August 10, 1917, the following article on the subject of religion: "All religious cults are free in Uruguay. The State does not recognize any religion. It recognizes in the Catholic Church ownership of all temples which have been in whole or in part constructed with funds from the national treasury, excepting only the chapels destined to the service of asylums, hospitals, jails, and other public establishments. It also declares exempt from all kinds of imposts churches consecrated to the actual use of diverse cults.[13]

The introduction of the committee's recommendation was the occasion for general debate on the subject of separation. Señor Secco Illa, representing the Unión Cívica, attacked the report. Basing his argument primarily on the fact that Uruguay was 61 per cent Catholic, he advocated no change in the ecclesiastical policy of the Republic. Dr. Juan B. Rocca, however, speaking for the Constitutional Nationalists, declared that religious sentiment would gain in prestige when the Catholic Church was freed absolutely from the influence of the State. The spirit of Article 5 of the Constitution of 1830 was profoundly altered during the years, he declared. For some time the State had no religion, and protection to the Roman Catholic Church was more nominal than effective, more apparent than real. Protection was offered in word, but denied in fact. Abolish this legal fiction, he demanded. The Socialists were conspicuous during the debates as caustic interrogators of the spokesmen of the Unión Cívica. The discussions on the whole, however, were remarkably good natured and were participated in by relatively few members. Quite evidently the Convention did not regard the question as being one of paramount importance. On August 30, 1917, the report of the committee was accepted without amendment.[14]

Under her new constitution, promulgated June 1, 1919, Uruguay enjoyed complete separation of Church and State. The legal status of the Catholic Church and its members was little different from that of religious cults in the United States. Religious toleration was guaranteed by the Constitution. The State did not contribute to the support of any cult, nor could any religion be discriminated against. The Catholic Church held title to its property, which, acquired prior to 1919, was free

12. *Diario de Sesiones de la H. Convención N. Constituyente de la República Oriental del Uruguay* (Montevideo, 1918), I, 181, 285-86; 460; Mariano de Vedia y Mitre, *El Gobierno del Uruguay* (Buenos Aires, 1919), p. 40.

13. *Diario de la Convención*, IV, 11.

14. *Ibid.*, I, 185-286; IV, 11 ff.

from taxation. The Church was recognized in law as a juridic personality with no restrictions on its power to receive bequests of entailments.[15] The hierarchy was entirely free of governmental dictation and interference. Consequently the power to make ecclesiastical appointments belonged to the ecclesiastical prelates, and free and unimpeded communication was allowed between the Uruguayan clergy and the papacy. Diplomatic relations with the Holy See were discontinued. In short, Uruguay abandoned all pretensions to the control of ecclesiastical patronage. Public education became entirely secular, for no longer could Catholic dogma be taught in schools supported by the government. Private schools of all grades were permitted and consequently the Catholic Church maintained a complete educational system in which religious instruction occupied an important position.[16]

The separation of the Church from the State in Uruguay seemed to be a great success. As was predicted, the Church reassumed its legitimate position as a spiritual and social leader. There was manifested a marked revival of loyalty to the dominant faith, which was given tangible evidence by the raising of a popular endowment fund of $1,000,000 to compensate for the government support which was withdrawn in 1919. Since the Roman Catholic organization in Uruguay is not extensive, its financial needs are not great. In 1924 there were in the Republic only eighty-five churches and chapels. There were 200 clergy, regular and secular, and 150 nuns. The national episcopacy was comprised of one archbishop and two bishops.[17]

The constitutions of 1934 and 1951 did not alter in the slightest way the provisions of 1919 concerning religion. The guarantees that all religions are free, that the Catholic Church retains ownership of Church property, and that all buildings dedicated to religious purposes are exempt from taxes, are all retained in the present organic instrument.

Since the adoption of the principle of separation there has been a remarkable absence of any issue to becloud Church-State relations. There has developed, however, what has been called a "de-Christianizing" of public life. The government goes to absurd lengths in avoiding any religious recognition. The principle of separation of Church and State is given most rigid and uncompromising interpretation. Religious holidays such as Christmas and Holy Week are recognized as official holidays but with different designations: "Family Day" and "Tourist Week." When "God Bless America" was introduced into the schools of Uruguay

15. *Constitución de la República Oriental del Uruguay* (Montevideo, 1919), Capitulo III; *Leyes, Decretos y Reglamentos de 1920*, p. 13.
16. *Christian Work in South America*, I, 264-66; *Anuario Estadístico de 1923*, p. 115.
17. *Christian Work in South America*, I, 114-15.

the name of the Deity was removed and it became "Oh, Bless America." In the public schools anything savoring of religion must be avoided. There must be no reading of the Bible or comments on religion.

The government's control of the public school system is the key to its implementation of the policy of separation of Church and State. To compensate for the exclusion of religious instruction in the public schools, the Constitution (Art. 71) provides: "In all educational institutions special attention shall be paid to the formation of the moral and civic character of students." In recognition of the "social utility" of private educational institutions those which "give free classes to a number of students in accordance with regulations which the law shall provide" are exempt from national and municipal taxes "as a subsidy for their services" (Art. 69). Most of the more than 160 Catholic private schools in Uruguay qualify for exemption. Uruguay ranks next to Argentina with the smallest number of illiterates. Based on the 1950 census, the percentage of illiterates in the population aged ten years and over was fifteen to twenty.[18]

The declared Catholic party of Uruguay, the Unión Cívica, an offshoot of the *Blancos*, is distinctly a minority group. It has never polled more than about 5 per cent of the total vote. This party, which has always opposed separation of Church and State, proclaims adherence to the principles of "Religion, Fatherhood, Family, and Property," and rejects the statism of "*Colorado* Socialism." The *Blancos* is traditionally the party of the strongly conservative landowners and their gaucho followers. Formerly strong supporters of the Church, the *Blancos* have become more or less neutral on the religious issue. They believe that religion is a matter of "private conscience." The *Colorados*, the city-dwellers, still influenced by the anticlericalism of Batlle y Ordóñez, are staunch supporters of separation of Church and State.[19] They are generally unsympathetic toward Catholicism and other denominations as well. They incorporate most of the freethinkers of whom there are a large number in Uruguay. *El Día*, which was founded by José Batlle, and which is one of the great atheistic newspapers of the world, has long made a practice of spelling *Dios* with a lower-case *d*.

Of the 2,700,000 total population of Uruguay in 1960, 2,517,000 were regarded as members of the Roman Catholic community. There were 688 priests, 477 churches, 237 schools, and 45 charitable institutions.[20]

18. *Statistical Abstract of Latin America* (Los Angeles, 1963), p. 25. In 1963, the population of Uruguay was 2,846,000, and that of Montevideo, in 1960, was 950,000.

19. Fitzgibbon, *op. cit.*, p. 238.

20. W. Stanley Rycroft and Myrtle M. Clemmer, *A Factual Study of Latin America* (New York, 1963), p. 235. This chart is based on Catholic statistics.

The number of Catholics per priest was 3,650, but this ratio is too small since there are only about 250 secular priests in the country. Uruguay, like the other Latin-American countries, suffers from lack of Catholic clergy.

Uruguay is a Catholic country, nominally, but the Uruguayans are not a religious people. In fact there is probably more general religious indifference than in any other country in Latin America. The practicing Catholics, mostly women, are few in number and generally live the Catholic life within the family circle. In Montevideo the Church has strength, but like elsewhere in Latin America the poorer hinterlands are neglected. "There are few churches in the interior of the country, and none in the more distant villages."[21]

Although Protestantism has been quite vigorous in Uruguay it has not been able to fill the void left by decreased Catholic membership. In addition to its more conventional proselytizing activities, the Evangelical sects have been active in educational and social work. These undoubtedly have a leavening social and intellectual influence greater than the restricted number of the Protestants would indicate. In 1960 the Protestant community in Uruguay numbered 42,772 or 1.6 per cent of the total population. Protestant church membership was 17,649 and the number of Protestant clergy was 152.[22] Protestant inroads have certainly not been responsible for the decline of the Catholic Church in Uruguay.

Like the hierarchies in other Latin-American countries, that of the Catholic Church in Uruguay has encouraged programs of revitalization or "new animation." There has been considerable Catholic activity in the promotion of youth movements, labor unions, and workers' groups implementing the social philosophy embodied in the papal encyclicals.[23] Much needs to be done, not to restore the old dominance of the Roman Catholic Church, but to restore its prestige and ability to instill a religious influence in the lives of the populace. There is need of a great moral force to halt the march of secularism in the Oriental Republic of Uruguay.

21. William J. Coleman, *Latin American Catholicism: A Self-Evaluation* (Maryknoll, N.Y., 1958), p. 31. For the weakening of religious feeling in Uruguay, see Fitzgibbon, *op. cit.*, p. 234.
22. Rycroft and Clemmer, *op. cit.*, p. 234.
23. Fitzgibbon, *op. cit.*, pp. 239-40.

Chapter XII

The Catholic Church in Brazil

Those who argue that it would be impolitic for Latin-American governments to bestow upon the Catholic Church free and unhampered autonomy stand refuted by the example of Brazil. The workability of the Brazilian policy of a free Church in a free State is an incontestable fact which should be invited to the attention of those anticlerical reformers of Spanish-American republics who insist that the best safeguard against usurping clericalism is repression and surveillance.

In refreshing contrast to the tendency in so many of the Spanish-American republics, there has been manifested throughout the history of independent Brazil a fine spirit of toleration, existent in practice as well as in the letter of the law. Religion as a political issue has been a subject of very minor importance, and the country has been spared the political machinations and bloody encounters of the pro and anticlerical forces.

The transition of the Brazilian Church from patronal dependency on the Portuguese crown[1] to patronal control exercised by an independent government was as gradual and free from violence as was the political metamorphosis of Brazil itself. The cutting of the political ties with the mother country was not, thanks to the establishment of a monarchy, regarded as so radical or revolutionary a step as the creation of republics on the ruins of the Spanish colonial empire. It was so much easier for the conservative elements, including the clergy, to stomach a Brazilian Empire, particularly since the hereditary emperor was a member of the old Portuguese ruling house of Braganza. With a Braganza continuing at the head of the government in Brazil, the revolutionary movement assumed a very conservative aspect. The clergy, therefore, could and did support the independence cause.

---

1. "There was never in colonial Brazil a really powerful Church or a strong clergy; nor were there domineering bishops." Gilberto Freyre, *Brazil, An Interpretation* (New York, 1945), p. 39.

Even in the abortive liberal republican revolt in Pernambuco, in 1817, so numerous and influential were the clerics that Oliveira Lima calls it "the revolution of the padres." The so-called spiritual precursor of this revolt was Bishop Azevedo Coutinho, founder of the Seminario de Olinda and instructor of the "liberals of 1817." Although the hierarchy condemned the revolt as being an heretical enterprise, Dean Bernardo Ferreira Portugal did not hesitate to publish a pastoral "to disabuse scrupulous souls." The revolution, he declared, was not contrary to the Gospel. In illustration of the prominent rôle played by the clergy in this fruitless stroke at independence, fifty-seven priests, almost all of whom were affiliated with Masonry, were numbered among those patriots who were imprisoned after the suppression of the revolt.[2]

The great majority of the clerics who were favorable to the cause of independence were opposed to the republican form of government. It was fortunate for the independence movement that there was available in Brazil, in the person of Regent Pedro, the logical head of an independent monarchial state, for here was one who could command the support of the Church. When the Portuguese Cortes attempted to return Brazil to its old colonial status, the prelates joined the popular clamor that Pedro proclaim Brazilian independence.[3] And when the Regent declared independence at Ypiranga on September 7, 1822, he was attended by several clerics, and to one of these who cried "Viva o primerio rei do Brasil" belongs the honor of being the first to proclaim Pedro king of Brazil.[4]

A National Constituent Assembly, under the presidency of José Caetano da Silva Coutinho, Bishop of Rio de Janeiro, met in Rio on April 17, 1823. In the Assembly were fifteen members of the clergy. A committee, headed by Antonio Carlos and composed of José Bonifacio de Andrada and other leaders, was entrusted with the task of drafting a project of a constitution. The draft as submitted by Antonio Carlos and as adopted by the Assembly on August 30, 1823, contained the following religious clauses: (1) guarantee of religious liberty to all Christian communities; non-Christian religions to be tolerated, but their communicants to be excluded from the exercise of political rights; (2) the Roman Catholic religion to be that of the State above all others and the only one maintained by it; (3) the exercise of the patronage, as

2. *Diccionario Historico, Geographico e Ethnographico do Brasil* (Rio de Janeiro, 1922), I, 1264-65; Eugenio Vilhena de Moraes, "O Patriotismo e o Clero No Brasil," in *Revista do Instituto Historico e Geographico Brasileiro* (Rio de Janeiro, 1925), Tomo Especial, p. 126.

3. "Representação do Bispo de S. Paulo, do 1° de Janeiro de 1822," in J. I. de Abreu e Lima, *Compendio da Historia do Brasil* (Rio de Janeiro, 1843), II, Appendix, pp. 24-25.

4. *Dic. Hist. Geog.*, I, 1277.

to the nomination for ecclesiastical benefices, vested in the emperor; (4) the right of conceding or denying the *pase*, to pontifical documents vested in the emperor; and (5) grant to the bishops of the right of censorship, with government aid, of publications on dogma and morals. An effort on the part of the Masons in the Constituent Assembly to use in the preamble "Supreme Being" instead of "Holy Trinity" was defeated. With the exception that Protestants were not excluded from the exercise of political rights, the clergy could find very little to complain about in this constitution.[5]

The Emperor, however, was so dissatisfied with the "Constitution of 1823" that he arbitrarily dissolved the Assembly, set aside the constitution, and selected a commission to frame a new fundamental law for the Empire. On March 25, 1824, an organic charter framed by Pedro's hand-picked committee was proclaimed. Under this instrument, known as the "Imperial Constitution of 1824," Brazil was governed until 1889.

Few changes were made by Pedro in the religious provisions of the constitution. "The Roman Catholic Apostolic religion," read the law, "will continue being the religion of the empire. All other religions will be permitted, with their domestic and private observance, in houses destined for that purpose, without any exterior form like a church." The guarantee of the private exercise of other cults was a long step in advance. The Constitution of 1824 conferred upon all naturalized foreigners, whatever their religion, the civil and political rights of Brazilian citizens. Yet in effect the full accord of political rights was restricted because of religious reasons. For example, members of the clergy and religious orders were denied the privilege of voting in parochial assemblies and non-Catholics were ineligible to election as deputies.[6] Religious toleration as guaranteed in Article 5 did not connote religious equality or even full religious liberty. With the Catholic Church established as the privileged faith there was a frank and legitimate disavowal of religious equality.

It surely was not a serious derogation of religious liberty to require the emperor to "swear to maintain the Roman Catholic Apostolic religion," to prevent the external ceremonies of nonofficial religions, or to prohibit non-Catholics from giving their meeting places the external appearance of a church. (By judicial interpretation it was only a belfry and a bell which gave the building "the external appearance

5. *Camara dos Deputados, Exposição Commemorativa do Centenario de la Constituinte do Brasil* (Rio de Janeiro, 1923); *Annaes do Parlamento Brasileiro, Assemblea Constituinte, 1823* (Rio de Janeiro, 1876-84), I, 46-48; Moraes, *op. cit.*, 138-42.
6. Constitution of the Empire of Brazil, in H. G. James, *The Constitutional System of Brazil* (Washington, 1923), Appendix No. 2, Arts. 5, 6, 92, 95, 179.

of a church."[7]) There was no justification, however, for prohibiting the election of a non-Catholic as a deputy. This prohibition was particularly odious, since it applied only to deputies, and not, perhaps due to oversight, to senators, councillors, ministers, regents, and the monarch himself. In the last days of the Empire, however, naturalized Brazilians and non-Catholics were eligible to election as senators and deputies. Considering the religious fanaticism of the peoples of Southern Europe, especially of the Iberian Peninsula, we must look upon Article 5 of the Imperial Constitution as a long step in the direction of tolerance. Finally, the emperor was given the right to appoint bishops to ecclesiastical benefices, and to grant or withhold the exequatur to conciliar decrees, papal letters, and other ecclesiastical legislation.[8]

As a natural concomitant of the union of religion and politics in the Empire the clergy were supported out of the public treasury. This practice had colonial antecedents. The pope and the king of Portugal had entered into an agreement whereby the whole of the tithes was to go to the government on condition that the crown supported the clergy. The government therefore paid the ecclesiastics a regular stipend, which, during the last days of Portuguese rule in Brazil, was very meager. Consequently the clergy lived in a state of poverty. The imperial government continued to pay on an economical plane. Even the prelates were forced to live in moderation and simplicity. The economic status of the lay clergy furnished a marked contrast with that of the regulars who lived in opulence.[9] Also, in consequence of the Church-State union, public instruction was entrusted to the Catholic Church, and the cemeteries belonged to and were administered by the Church. Civil marriage was not recognized. A decree of November 3, 1827, provided for the effective observance of the dispositions of the Council of Trent on the subject of matrimony and created a Tribunal of Ecclesiastical Relations at Bahia.[10] Although the external ceremonies of nonofficial cults were made dependent on the consent of the law, this consent was never given during the life of the empire. But notwithstanding the above the constitutional grant of religious toleration was fully tested and found to be a living letter.[11]

7. James C. Fletcher and D. P. Kidder, *Brazil and the Brazilians* (Boston, 1866), p. 140. In 1888 legislation was enacted suppressing the constitutional requirement that non-Catholic religious edifices should not have the external appearance of a church. (Benjamin Mossé, *Dom Pedro II*, Paris, 1889, p. 58.)

8. *Constitution of the Empire*, Article 102; J. Burnichon, *Le Brésil d'aujourd 'hui* (Paris, 1910), p. 180.

9. R. Walsh, *Notices of Brazil in 1828 and 1829* (Boston, 1831), I, 200-1.

10. Basilio de Magalhães, "D. Pedro II e a Egreja," in *Rev. do Inst. Hist.*, Vol. 152, 386.

11. Agenor de Roure, *A Constituinte Republicana* (Rio de Janeiro, 1920), p. 450.

There was a brief suspension of papal relations following the declaration of Brazilian independence. In August, 1824, the Emperor sent Francisco Correa Vidigal, a cleric, on special diplomatic mission to the Vatican to conclude a concordat and dispose of outstanding matters affecting the relations between Church and State. In particular he was instructed not to permit papal intervention in matters of State jurisdiction; to obtain an order to the effect that religious orders were no longer subject to superiors resident in Portugal, and to urge upon the pope the necessity of reforming the regular orders, of prohibiting the establishment of new convents, and of prohibiting the admission of foreign friars.[12] No immediate results were accomplished by Vidigal's mission, for the pope withheld recognition of Brazil until Portugal should recognize the Empire. But shortly after that event, the pope issued a bull, in 1827, which conceded to the crown the same rights which had formerly been exercised by the king of Portugal as secular patron and Grand Master of the Order of Christ. The attempt of the pope to concede to the Emperor prerogatives which the constitutional law had already conferred on him was repugnant. Consequently the exequatur was denied to the bull. On the ecclesiastical affairs committee of the Chamber of Deputies which recommended this drastic action were a number of priests who did not hesitate to characterize the pope's action as presumptive in the extreme. The controversy was settled in the following year (1828) by the inauguration of a *modus vivendi* by which the pope tolerated, but did not recognize, the right of patronage in the Brazilian government.[13] To free the Brazilian Church from dependence on Portuguese prelates the pope ordered, in 1828, the dioceses of Pará and Maranhão freed from the see of Lisbon and made suffragans of the archbishop of Bahia.

Regalism was dominant in Brazil in the early days of the Empire, and, in fact, it continued to be strong throughout the imperial period. Since the time of Pombal, and due largely to the great influence of that minister, the Portuguese and Brazilian churches manifested pronounced Gallican tendencies. After independence in Brazil "the virus of Jansenist and Gallican heresy" persisted. If the Emperor and his imperial officials sought to make the State preponderant over the Church, they did not lack support from the Brazilian prelates and clergy. In the first legislative assembly (1826-29) were twenty-two ecclesiastics openly committed to *regalismo*. Their concurrence in advising denial of the exequatur

12. Moraes, *op. cit.*, p. 146; Magalhães, *op. cit.*, pp. 386-87.
13. Magalhães, *op. cit.*, pp. 386-387; P. A. Martin, "Causes of the Collapse of the Brazilian Empire," in *The Hispanic American Historical Review*, IV, No. 1 (February, 1921), 10.

to the bull of 1827 has been noted. Furthermore the leading prelates were defenders of the prerogatives of the State against the direct pretensions of the Holy See.[14] Father Diogo Antonio Feijó, later regent of the Empire, was also a vigorous defender of regalism. The Church was under the tutelage of the State. Numerous laws and decrees, many of them petty and vexatious, were issued providing for the constant intervention of the State in religious matters. Yet, despite the irritating supervision of State over Church, the clergy were so acquiescent that no serious opposition was aroused for almost half a century.

Not only were the clergy of the early Empire essentially Gallican, but they were also marked by their liberalism. It is a matter of record that the clerics in the Constituent Assembly were more liberal than the laymen. Since most of them were Masons, this liberal attitude was partially due to Masonic influence.[15] Bishop José Caetano da Silva Coutinho, who presided over the Assembly, was a most enlightened individual, tolerant to every sect. He was Bishop of Rio de Janeiro when Lord Strangford negotiated a treaty, in 1810, which gave to the English the right to build a chapel for divine services, provided it was not erected as a public edifice, but as a private house, and did not use bells to assemble the congregation. The pope's nuncio protested this concession, but Bishop Silva Coutinho favored granting to the English the right to build a chapel. "The English," said he, "have really no religion; but they are a proud and obstinate people. If you oppose them, they will persist, and make it an affair of infinite importance; but if you concede to their wishes, the chapel will be built, and nobody will ever go near it." The bishop's prophecy proved to be true, for in 1828, the English church, with a potential capacity of 600-700, was attended by a scant thirty or forty.[16]

As indicated by one of the subjects upon which Vidigal, special envoy to Rome, was particularly instructed, the regular orders were the objects of attack in Brazil. Not the government and people alone, but the lay clerics as well, were hostile to monastic institutions. The regulars were not numerous, but in comparison with the secular clergy, they were very wealthy. This disparity in economic status probably accounted in part for the opposition of the seculars. The regulars, moreover, were ultramontane in sympathy and foreign in composition and control. In

14. Statesmen, and even the foremost clergymen, fought for the alleged rights of the State against Rome. Mary Crescentia Thornton, *The Church and Freemasonry in Brazil, 1872-1875* (Washington, D.C., 1948), pp. 51, 68-69.

15. *Assemblea Constituinte 1823*, I, 48; Moraes, *op. cit.*, p. 145; "A. Maçonaria e a Independencia," in *Documentos para a Historia da Independencia* (Rio de Janeiro, 1923), I, 394-99.

16. Walsh, *op. cit.*, I, 181-85, 205.

short, they were branded as being antinationalist. Another cause of discontent with the regular orders was popular disapproval of the withdrawal from the worldly life, and reproduction, of so many males and females. It constituted an impediment in the way of populating a sparsely settled country. The secular clergy did not escape the same criticism. Senhor Feijó, a priest and member of the ecclesiastical committee of the Deputies proposed "that it would be proper to apply to the pope to relieve the clergy from the penalty annexed to marrying."[17] Abolition of ecclesiastical celibacy was also advocated as a measure of moral reform, for a goodly number of priests kept concubines.[18]

During the reign of Pedro I and under the Regency several acts were passed directed at the regular orders. The law of 1828 (1) prohibited entry and residence of foreign friars in the empire; (2) prohibited creation of new orders or religious associations of both sexes; and (3) expelled from the country friars and congregations who obeyed superiors resident outside Brazil.[19] The Benedictines and Carmelites were prohibited from taking novices, a measure designed to bring about the total extinction of the orders. As congregations became extinct their property was incorporated in the national patrimony.[20] To escape confiscation of their property, the orders resorted to alienation, but a law of December 9, 1830, declared null all alienations made by religious orders without governmental license. In 1831, under the inspiration of Feijó as Minister of Justice, the government undertook a reform of the religious orders in full accord with the papal internuncio at Rio de Janeiro. So bitter was the opposition to reform raised by the monks that a measure was introduced (1833) in the Parliament, providing for the secularization of all property of the regulars. It did not pass, but twenty years later it was again proposed by Nabuco de Araujo.[21] The suppression of numerous convents was not an unmixed blessing. Indispensable charitable work was performed by the orders. In all of the principal cities the convents were crowded with the lame, halt, and blind. In Rio, it was said, the whole mendicity was supported at the convents. The closing of some of the convents necessitated governmental assuming of control of the eleemosynary institutions or their transfer to the lay orders. This was attended by confusion and considerable hardship for the poor.[22]

17. *Ibid.,* I, 201.
18. The Minister of Justice said, in 1834, that the government should abolish clerical celibacy which "does not exist anyway." C. H. Haring, *Empire in Brazil* (Cambridge, Mass., 1958), p. 114.
19. Magalhães, *op. cit.,* p. 388.
20. Walsh, *op. cit.,* I, 201-8.
21. Magalhães, *op. cit.,* 388-89.
22. Walsh, *op. cit.,* I, 202.

In 1834 the question of abolition of ecclesiastical celibacy was again revived. The provincial council of São Paulo adopted the following resolution: (1) the bishops in the dioceses have the same rights as the pope over the Catholic Church; (2) the law of celibacy is simply disciplinary. In February, 1834, the Foreign Minister wrote a remarkable letter to the papal internuncio on the subject. He said that the imperial government believed that, in accordance with the São Paulo resolution, the matter of celibacy of curates was a matter of discipline which should be left to the sovereign determination of the State. Knowing that celibacy did not exist in fact, this situation made for great public immorality. The government desired, consequently, that energetic measures be adopted. He concluded by stating that he did not wish to have the opinion of the government made public.[23] Suffice it to say that ecclesiastical celibacy was not abolished, and that immorality among the clergy continued to be pronounced throughout the imperial period.

Archbishop Pietro Ostini, named papal nuncio to Brazil, arrived in Rio de Janeiro in June, 1830. He was the first diplomatic representative sent by the Holy See to any of the new states in Latin America. Ostini was vested with a two-fold character: (1) as nuncio to the imperial court of Dom Pedro I, and (2) as apostolic delegate to "South America and the Provinces of Mexico." It was hoped that the apostolic delegation attached to the nunciature could inaugurate a new system of papal relations with the former Spanish colonies. Although there was exchange of correspondence between Rio and the various capitals of Latin America during the decade 1830-40, the efforts of the nunciature failed of concrete achievements.[24]

Because of the extreme regalistic attitude of Father Diogo Antonio Feijó, who has been described as "the bitterest foe of papal supremacy ever produced by the Brazilian Church,"[25] an issue developed between the Regency and the Vatican over the exercise of patronage. In March, 1833, the Regency nominated to the vacant see of Rio de Janeiro, Antonio Maria de Moura, who had been active in politics and had supported radical proposals such as abolition of celibacy and divorce for adultery. Pope Gregory XVI refused to confirm. In addition to his suspicions concerning the purity of the nominee's doctrines, the Pope questioned the validity of Moura's ordination as bishop since he was a bastard son. The Regency persisted and even hinted at establishing a national church.

23. Magalhães, *op. cit.*, pp. 389-90.
24. See William J. Coleman, *The First Apostolic Delegation in Rio de Janeiro and its Influence in Spanish America: A Study in Papal Policy, 1830-1840* (Washington, D.C., 1950).
25. Manoel Cardozo, "The Holy See and the Question of the Bishop-Elect of Rio, 1833-1839," in *The Americas*, X, No. 1 (July, 1953), 16.

But there was a change of heart with a change of the Regency in 1837, with the result that a new archbishop was preconized by the Pope.[26]

State supervision over the Church continued to develop and increase during the reign of Pedro II. The Emperor's attitude toward the Catholic faith has been greatly misunderstood. He has been charged with being a Voltairean, an evolutionist, and an atheist. As a matter of fact he subscribed to the dogmas of the Church, and, as one writer says, "Nothing said or written would have put him in the clutches of the Inquisition."[27] A liberal thinker, in matters of religion, he has been called, quite aptly "a *limited* Catholic." In sponsoring ecclesiastical reform, and in strengthening royal control over the Church, the Emperor was not actuated by anticlerical motives. His campaign against the religious orders, inaugurated in 1854,[28] had the full support of the papal internuncio and the bishops of Brazil. The need of reform of the decadent religious orders was recognized as being urgent and necessary by all good Catholics. In 1854 the Emperor, in an *aviso*, declared that to him belonged the power of nominating to all benefices and dignities, independent of the advice and counsel of the prelates, as was the custom before. This was carrying regalism to an extreme, and there was considerable truth in the allegation of the prelates, set forth in the *Pastoral Collectiva* of March 19, 1890, that their tutelage to the Empire was a form of servitude.[29] Yet the regalistic policy of the Emperor was not in any sense antireligious.

A faithful and trustworthy description of religious conditions in Brazil in the first half of the reign of Pedro II has been left us by two Protestant missionaries, Rev. James C. Fletcher and Rev. D. P. Kidder. "It is my firm conviction," said Mr. Fletcher in 1845, "that there is not a Roman Catholic country on the globe where there prevails a greater degree of toleration or a greater liberality of feeling toward Protestants. I will here state, that in all my residence and travels in Brazil in the character of a Protestant missionary, I never received the slightest opposition or indignity from the people. As might have been expected, a few of the priests made all the opposition they could; but the circumstance that these were unable to excite the people showed how little

26. *Ibid.*, pp. 3-16.

27. Magalhães de Azeredo, "Dom Pedro II, Traços da Sua Physionomia Moral," in *Rev. Do Inst. Hist. e Geog.*, Tomo Especial, 1925, p. 969.

28. The law of 1855 declared that henceforth no religious orders could open seminaries in Brazil. It was held that the real intention was to weaken the importance of the religious orders—a bulwark of the Church's independence in its apostolic duties. Frederick B. Pike, *Freedom and Reform in Latin America* (Notre Dame, Ind., 1959), pp. 295-96.

29. Padre Julio Maria, "A religião," in *O Livro do Centenario* (Rio de Janeiro, 1901), I, 60.

influence they possessed. On the other hand, perhaps quite as many of the clergy, and those of the most respectable in the empire, manifested toward us and our work both favor and friendship. From them, as well as from the intelligent laity, did we often hear the severest reprehension of abuses that were tolerated in the religious system and practices of the country, and sincere regrets that no more spirituality pervaded the public mind."[30]

In rather unpleasant contrast to the agreeable pictures of religious toleration described by Fletcher and Kidder were their accusations of clerical corruption in imperial Brazil. The lives and practices of the priests were notoriously corrupt, contended the missionaries, and they cited several examples which fell under their personal observation. The messages of the Minister of Justice annually alluded to this state of affairs. Finally, a foreign naturalist, who visited Brazil between the years 1836 and 1841, was quoted as follows: "The present clergy of Brazil are more debased and immoral than any other class of men." A consequence of the shameful immorality of the clergy was a loss of influence over the people.[31]

It was inevitable that the Emperor's lukewarm attitude on religion, his liberalism, and, above all, his fostering of an extreme regalism would eventually arouse the opposition of the ultramontanists. The tranquil relations which had existed for so many years between Church and State were disturbed in 1873 by the so-called *questão religiosa*. This was a repercussion of the current ultramontane tendencies of the time, and it assumed the form in Brazil of an assault upon Freemasonry.

Since 1807, when the first lodge was founded in Bahia, Masonry had flourished in Brazil. In the last days of the colonial era the Masonic lodges were forces for the propagation of republican-democratic ideas. Their influence was felt in the Revolution of Pernambuco in 1817, and after the failure of that revolt the lodges continued to propagate liberal principles.[32] Under the Empire Masonry gathered into its membership numerous ecclesiastics. High officials of the Empire including Pedro II and his prime minister, Baron Rio Branco, were Masons. Furthermore, in illustration of the harmonious relations which existed between the Brazilian Church and Masonry, Masons were admitted freely into the *irmandades* or religious and benevolent associations. These brotherhoods, composed almost exclusively of laymen, were conducted under Church auspices and were supposed to be amenable to Church discipline.

30. Fletcher and Kidder, *op. cit.*, p. 143.
31. *Ibid.*, pp. 140-42.
32. Felisbello Freire, *Historia Constitucional da Republica dos Estados do Brasil* (Rio de Janeiro, 1893), I, 42-43.

This liberal interrelationship between Church and Masonry continued in Brazil even after the publication of the *Syllabus* of Pius IX, which anathematized Masonry. The encyclical *Quanta Cura*, of which the *Syllabus* was an *addenda*, had never been approved by Pedro II. The government refused to accord the exequatur. Technically, therefore, the pope's opposition to Freemasonry had never been officially communicated to the Brazilian clergy.[33] Certain prelates, however, took it upon themselves to observe the commands of the Vatican and precipitated thereby the one serious religious conflict in the history of the Empire.

The initial event of the "religious question" was the act of Bishop Pedro Maria de Lacerda of Rio de Janeiro in ordering (March 3, 1872) the suspension of a priest who delivered a sermon in a Masonic lodge. The priest was ordered to abjure Masonry but refused.[34] The incident caused the smouldering fires of opposition between ultramontanists and Masonry to break into open flame. Under the presidency of Baron Rio Branco, Grand Master of the Masons, a great session was held in Rio de Janeiro on April 16, 1872. A resolution was adopted pledging the lodges to attack the episcopacy in the press and to invite all Masons of Brazil to take part in the battle against the Church. Although Masonry, in the early period of the Empire, manifested no antagonism toward the Church, such was no longer the case. Many critics of Catholicism had been gathered into the membership of the lodges, and eventually they succeeded in identifying Masonry with their own hostility to the Church. Whether the lodges sponsored this policy, as charged by the clergy, it is difficult to state. At any rate there were numerous recriminations and counter-recriminations.[35]

Bishop Lacerda became so frightened because of the furore he aroused that he hastened to reverse his position. The new Bishop of Olinda, on the contrary, determined with the reckless enthusiasm of youth, for he was but twenty-eight years of age, to seize the opportunity for initiating a reform designed to restore papal control over the Brazilian Church. On May 24, 1872, Vital María Gonçalves de Oliveira, a Capuchin and ardent ultramontanist, became bishop of the diocese of Olinda. He was considered by the Masons as a dangerous man and they did not delay putting him to the test. On June 27, 1872, the press announced that the Masonic lodge of Recife would commemorate the anniversary of its foundation by celebrating a mass. Bishop Vital ordered the clergy not to participate in any ceremony announced as

33. Magalhães, *op. cit.*, p. 397; Martin, *op. cit.*, p. 11.

34. A. O. Viveiros de Castro, "Contribuiçoes Para A Biographia De D. Pedro II," in *Rev. do Inst. Hist. e Geog.*, Tomo Especial, 1925, pp. 477-79; Magalhães, *op. cit.*, p. 397.

35. *Dic. Hist. Geog.*, II, 229; Castro, *op. cit.*, pp. 477-78.

Masonry, and all Catholic societies were ordered to expel such members as belonged to Masonic lodges. Interdicts were laid upon the churches that disobeyed the order.[36]

Lodges and brotherhoods appealed to the Emperor for relief. The government then sought the intervention of the papal internuncio. The internuncio counseled the bishop against doing anything which would antagonize the government. Seeing that the papal representative would do nothing for him, Vital wrote to the pope. In his reply, May 29, 1873, Pius IX praised the zeal of the Bishop and gave him full power to work with all rigor against the Masonic brotherhoods. Vital was ordered to convey this communication to all the bishops of Brazil in order that they might do likewise in their dioceses.[37] In attempting to enforce this papal order, which never received the imperial exequatur, Bishop Vital made himself liable for violating the constitutional law.

Of the twelve prelates of the Empire, only one, Bishop Macedo Costa of Pará joined Vital's crusade. The others observed a discrete silence. On March 25, 1873, the Bishop of Pará issued a pastoral combatting Masonry. He ordered all Masonic members of *irmandades* to renounce Masonry or withdraw from the associations. Those that refused to expel their Masonic members were suspended.[38] As in Pernambuco churches and chapels were put under the interdict in Pará.

In August, 1873, Pedro II sent the Baron de Penedo to the Vatican on special mission to urge papal intervention in bringing the recalcitrant prelates to reason. The mission was a complete success, for Pope Pius IX, through his Secretary of State Cardinal Antonelli, wrote to the Bishop of Olinda on December 18, 1873, formally disapproving of his conduct and ordering the restoration of the brotherhoods to their old status. The about face in papal position was taken only after the Brazilian envoy assured His Holiness that the government would not take drastic action against the bishops.[39]

The government should have been satisfied with the pope's condemnation of the bishops, for it had won a complete victory, and, in the words of Bishop Macedo Costa, "Masonry was left all the honors of a triumph." But unfortunately, in a vengeful spirit, it decided to prosecute the prelates of Pará and Olinda. On the advice of the Council of

---

36. Castro, *op. cit.*, pp. 479-80; Magalhães, *op. cit.*, p. 398.

37. Castro, *op. cit.*, pp. 485-90; Magalhães, *op. cit.*, p. 399.

38. Castro, *op. cit.*, pp. 480-81; Magalhães, *op. cit.*, pp. 398-99; Martin, *op. cit.*, p. 13.

39. It is a moot question whether the pope really censured Bishop Vital. See Castro, *op. cit.*, pp. 508-12; Padre Julio Maria, *op. cit.*, I, 91 ff.; Dr. Alexandre José Barboza Lima, "Um Grande Brasileiro, Frei Vital," in *Rev. do Inst. Hist. e Geog.*, LXXI, Parte II, 147. On May 3, 1876, Bishop Vital received a reassuring message from Pius IX: "I approve, as long ago I approved, all that you have done." Thornton, *op. cit.*, p. 248.

State,[40] Pedro II ordered the bishops to withdraw the interdicts within fifteen days. Following their refusal to revoke the interdicts, their arrest was ordered on November 7, 1873.

In separate trials (February and June, 1874) before the Supreme Tribunal of Justice, the two bishops were convicted on the identical charges of violating Article 96 of the Criminal Code, to wit: "to seek to impede in any manner the will of the executive and moderative power, conforming to the constitution and the laws."[41] They were assessed the "intermediate" penalty of four years imprisonment at hard labor. The Emperor commuted the sentences to simple imprisonment. The two prelates were men of great scholarly attainments and virtue and enjoyed the affectionate regard of their flocks. To subject them to penal servitude, notwithstanding the seriousness of their offense, was impolitic because of the scandal and indignation this produced among the clergy and the faithful. Furthermore it was an act unworthy of the benevolent Emperor. Eventually, after the mischief was done, on September 17, 1875, due to the intercession of Princess Isabella, Pedro II granted amnesty to the prelates.[42]

The "religious question" is considered one of the major causes that contributed to the downfall of the Brazilian Empire in 1889.[43] It seriously weakened the prestige of the Empire and proved, in the words of Oliveira Lima, that "the monarchy which acted in this fashion was not clerical."[44] The bishops were regarded as martyrs and the clergy claimed that they were attacked in their essential liberties. The vigilant action of the State was an offense which the Church considered as an expression of despotism. A fundamental issue, at the base of the conflict, was the resolution of the Church to operate as a free institution in opposition to the determination of the State to be supreme arbiter in religious matters.[45] The Bishop of Pará declared, "Give liberty to the Church of Jesus Christ.... Leave her to be governed according to her own laws."[46] So dissatisfied were the clergy with the pretended partner-

40. Joaquin Nabuco opposed prosecution of the two bishops for, (1) it would affect the dignity and moral force of the episcopacy, and (2) imprisonment of the bishops would cause more trouble and stimulate a religious war. (Castro, *op. cit.*, pp. 496-97.)

41. *Ibid.*, p. 506.

42. *Ibid.*, pp. 505-6; *Dic. Hist. Geog.*, II, 229. For the best discussion of the question of the bishops, see J. Dornas Filho, *O Padroado e a igreja brasileira* (São Paulo, 1938).

43. See Percy A. Martin, "Cause of the Collapse of the Brazilian Empire," in *Hisp. Am. Hist. Rev.*, IV (February, 1921), 4-48.

44. Manuel Oliveira Lima, *Formation Historique de la Nationalité Braziliene* (Paris, 1911), pp. 259-60.

45. Thornton, *op. cit.*, p. 216.

46. Oliveira Lima, *op. cit.*, p. 260.

ship of Church and Empire that they were unwilling to defend this status with vigor when the crisis came.

There were other elements in Brazil, however, that were campaigning for the dissolution of the Church-State connection. The most active of these were the Republicans, Socialists, and Positivists. They felt that, since the Church exercised a great influence in all matters relating to education and the social life of the people, no sweeping reform could be effected until its domination had been broken. The extreme liberalism of Pedro II invited the introduction and spread of radical political, social, and religious propaganda. This movement became so pronounced after about 1870 that that date is said to mark the intellectual emancipation of the country.[47] Since the various "isms," among them republicanism, socialism, Haeckelism, and Positivism, advocated a break with the past, the Catholic Church, the institution which was most closely associated with the past, was attacked with vigor. An uninviting prospect, which tended to consolidate liberal opposition to the dynasty, was the ardent devotion to the Church of the heiress apparent, the Princess Isabella.[48] When Isabella acted as regent, during Pedro's absence in the United States and Europe, she showed herself to be swayed by Church influence in political questions. It was partly because of this fear of clericalism that the Empire was finally abolished.

Positivism, or the *Systema de Philosophia Positiva*, as it was known in Brazil, was propagated in that country by Benjamin Constant and Miguel Lemos.[49] The Positivists exercised an influence in the evolution of democracy in Brazil, far out of proportion to their restricted numbers. In defense of individual liberty they championed the abolition of Negro slavery and the separation of the temporal from the spiritual authority. The divorce of religion from all political connection was regarded by the Positivists as an essential of spiritual liberty. In a letter written by the *Centro Positivista do Brasil* to the Bishop of Pará in 1888, an attempt was made to convince the prelate that all interests, including the clerical,

47. Freire, *op. cit.*, I, 402; Oliveira Vianna, "A Queda Do Imperio," in *Rev. do Inst. Hist. e Geog.*, Tomo Especial, 1925, pp. 838-39.

48. The Princess was accused of being instrumental in bringing about the defeat, in the Deputies, of a bill to free Protestants from certain legal disabilities. (Martin, *op. cit.*, p. 23, n. 41.)

49. Positivism as developed by August Comte is both a philosophical and a religious system. As a philosophy it denies the validity of metaphysical speculations, and maintains that sense experience is the supreme criterion of human knowledge. As a religious system Positivism denies the existence of a personal God and takes humanity, the Great Being, as the object of its veneration. Positivism has a cult, sacraments, and ceremonies. The Positivists erected a Temple of Humanity in Rio de Janeiro in 1891.

would be best served by the overthrow of the Empire. The letter ended by predicting the fall of the Empire after the abolition of slavery.[50]

The prophecy of the *Centro Positivista* was correct; the abolition of slavery in Brazil was followed almost immediately by the overthrow of the Empire and the establishment of a federal republic. Since one of the demands of the anti-imperial forces was separation of Church and State, this reform was carried through with dispatch and thoroughness by the provisional government which exercised control from November 15, 1889 to February 25, 1891. By decree, dated January 7, 1890, Church and State were separated and the patronage was abolished. Freedom of worship was guaranteed and the federal and state authorities were prohibited from subsidizing any religion, or making any distinction between the inhabitants of the country based on religious or philosophical beliefs or opinions. Public officers were forbidden to interfere in any way with the formation of religious societies and it was declared to be unlawful to stir up religious dissension among the people. Religious corporations were granted juridic personality to acquire property and were recognized as valid owners of properties actually held by them. The salaries of those in the service of the Church were ordered to be discontinued at the expiration of a year. Thus, by the decree of separation the Catholic Church retained possession of its communicants, buildings, lands, incomes, and hierarchical organization.[51]

Another decree of the provisional government, also dated January 7, 1890, abolished the existing religious holidays, except Sunday, and established nine new holidays commemorating secular events. On January 24, compulsory civil marriage was decreed, and, on January 26, Church nuptials, prior to the civil, were prohibited. On September 27, 1890, the existing cemeteries were secularized and put under the control of the municipalities. Religious bodies were allowed, in the future, to provide separate burial places, although always subject to the laws.[52]

That the disestablishment of the Church was not unwelcome to the hierarchy was evidenced by the Collective Pastoral published on March 19, 1890. The bishops noted that the Church had secured "a certain sum of liberties which she had never succeeded in obtaining during the time of the monarchy," when it felt "suffocated."[53]

50. Freire, *op. cit.*, I, 410-11.

51. *Constituição do Republica dos Estados Unidos do Brasil. Acompanhada das Leis Organicas Publicadas desde 15 de Novembra de 1889* (Rio de Janeiro, 1891), p. 49; James, *op. cit.*, p. 140.

52. *Constituição do Republica ... Acompanhada das Leis*, p. 50.

53. Thales de Azevedo, *O Catolicismo no Brasil* (Rio de Janeiro, 1955), p. 20.

The definitive status of the Roman Catholic Church in republican Brazil was worked out in the Constituent Congress which met in Rio de Janeiro on November 15, 1890. The provisional government sought to facilitate, and perhaps control, its deliberations by submitting to it a model constitution. The decrees of 1890 separating Church and State were incorporated into this draft. The following additional items were included: exclusion of the Jesuits, prohibition of the founding of new convents or monastic orders, denial of political rights to clerics, and imposing upon religious associations in their property rights the limitations of the laws of mortmain.

The religious clauses of the project were subjected to careful scrutiny and extended debate in the Convention, which revealed itself as being less radical than the provisional government on the religious issues. Many members of the Assembly were of the same opinion as Shr. Coelho e Campos, who said that he favored Cavour's formula, "a free Church in a free State," and therefore he could not accept several of the religious provisions of the project. The exclusion of the Jesuits from the country aroused protests. More than one delegate defended the great work of the Society of Jesus in transplanting European civilization to the wilderness of Brazil, and they mentioned in particular the names of Fathers Nobrega and Anchieta. The majority, being of the opinion that the exclusion of the Jesuits would not be worthy of a liberal constitution, voted to strike out of the project the clause relating to the order, but the prohibition of new convents and monastic orders was allowed to stand.[54]

The denial to clerics of all political rights also aroused opposition. This clause was amended to provide that no one could be declared incapable of holding office because he was a religious, excepting members of monastic orders subject to a vow of obedience. The reëstablishment of the laws of mortmain which had been enacted during the colonial period was also combatted successfully. Religious corporations were allowed to acquire property "according to the dispositions of the common law." A slight amendment to the provision legalizing civil marriage was also adopted by the Congress. To the words "The republic recognizes only civil marriage," were added, "which celebration is gratuitous."[55] At the present date, according to constitutional law, the civil marriage is free, but in reality revenue stamps are required. Since the constitutional project did not refer to divorce, but declared that civil marriage was indissoluble, certain members of the Congress at-

54. Roure, *op. cit.*, pp. 472-73.
55. *Ibid.*, p. 497.

tempted to have absolute divorce adopted. Their efforts ended in failure, as have all similar attempts to date.

According to the Federal Republican Constitution promulgated on February 24, 1891, the separation of Church and State in Brazil was complete. Fortunate indeed was the Republic that the majority of the members of the Constituent Congress were men of forbearance and tolerance. There were no constitutional restrictions upon the liberty of conscience and religion; no tests for exercising the suffrage or holding office. All political connections between Church and State were severed. Although the diplomatic corps at Rio de Janeiro enjoyed the presence of a papal nuncio as one of its members, and Brazil accredited an ambassador to the Vatican, this adherence to tradition had no political significance. All pretensions to national patronage were abolished in 1890. The government took no part in the naming of prelates, or in granting the *pase* to pontifical documents.

A wise action of the fathers of the Republic was the bestowal on the Church of title to its properties. Nationalization of ecclesiastical holdings would have led inevitably to future conflicts between the temporal and spiritual organizations. All buildings used exclusively for religious purposes were exempt from taxation, but other realty owned by the Church was not. The government would not pay the salaries of those who entered the priesthood since the date of separation, nor contribute to the support of the Church in any other way, with the exception of making contributions to the missions which were regarded as aid to national material progress.[56]

The disestablishment of the Church in Brazil also meant the breaking of the hold of the clergy upon the educational system of the country. Under the Constitution public instruction was to be laical. Religious instruction could be given in the public schools but the government did not pay the teachers and the instruction had to be after school hours. The Church, being deprived of its ancient control over public education, could maintain its own system of elementary and secondary schools. The Catholic Church could also support hospitals and asylums.

The status of a free Church in a free State, constitutionalized in 1891, was preserved, although slightly changed, by Brazil's next constitutions: 1934, 1937, and 1946. The present Constitution of 1946, after invoking "the protection of God" in the preamble, touches on religion and matters relating to it, as follows: the federal, state, and municipal

56. Mgr. Joaquin Nabuco, Archbishop of Rio de Janeiro, to J. L. Mecham, Rio de Janeiro, January 8, 1928.

governments are forbidden to levy taxes on "places of worship of any sect" (Art. 31, V, b); "Freedom of conscience and belief is inviolable, and the free exercise of religious sects is assured, as long as they are not contrary to public order or good morals. Religious associations shall acquire juridical personality according to civil law. No one shall be deprived of his rights by reason of religious, philosophic, or political convictions.... Without restraint of the ones favored, religious ministration to the Armed Forces shall be offered by a Brazilian...; cemeteries shall be secular in character and shall be administered by the municipal authority. All religious confessions shall be permitted to practice their rites therein. Religious associations may maintain private cemeteries, according to law" (Art. 141: 7, 8, 9, 10); marriage, which cannot be dissolved, shall be civil and its celebration free of charge. Religious marriage shall be equivalent to civil marriage, and shall have civil effects, if performed according to law and recorded in the public registry (Art. 163: 1, 2); and Article 168 provides that teaching legislation shall adopt the following principle: "Religious instruction shall be a part of the teaching schedule of public schools, matriculation therein shall be optional, and the instruction shall be provided in accordance with the religious confession of the pupil."

The reference to God in the preamble, and the provisions relating to marriage and religious education, were expressive of the new position of the State in relation to the spiritual bases of nationality. Whereas the Constitution of 1891 had aimed at a total indifference and neutrality of the State toward religious faiths, the Constitution of 1946 reflected awareness of the religious belief of the majority of the people.[57] This fact has been attested in many ways extraconstitutionally.

Many informal ties between the religious and governmental powers and authorities survived legal separation. Frequently federal and state governmental appropriations for education, health, and other social welfare services are administered through the Church and religious organizations. Also, the aid of the prelacy is often solicited in support of important legislative or executive policy. Though the Church usually refrains from supporting specific candidates in elections, it feels free to make recommendations and formulate programs on matters of national or regional concern such as economic development, agrarian reform, education, labor legislation, and taxation. Most presidents and high officials of Brazil—including the pro-Communist João Goulart—have

57. The Constitution conferred on members of monastic orders the right to vote, which had been denied by the Constitution of 1891. Priests were not prohibited from holding office, although the Church itself decided in 1949 that the clergy should not be candidates for public office.

recognized the advantages of consultation with the prelacy and well-publicized appearances at religious ceremonies.

In a sense the Catholic Church in Brazil is "official" because Brazilians are Catholic, but its influence is not overriding. In fact Brazilian Catholics have been notoriously disregardful of clerical advice concerning their exercise of the suffrage. For example, in the presidential campaign of 1950, the efforts of the Catholic Electoral League to prevent the election of João Café Filho as vice-president because of his anti-clerical views were defeated. Also, in 1955, the election of Kubitschek and Goulart was a defeat for the Church, since Cardinal Câmara had urged Catholic votes in favor of the opposition. Later the Church threw its support behind Kubitschek; and still later, at the time of the critical issue over Goulart's succession to the presidency, the prelates made a forthright appeal for respect of the Constitution and the legal succession. When Goulart was inaugurated he invited members of the Catholic hierarchy to a luncheon at the presidential palace in Brasilia.[58]

The Catholic Church in Brazil has been an important factor in the struggle against communism. The hierarchy has generally taken a strong anti-Communist position. In the election of 1955 Cardinal Câmara urged the voters not to aid the Communists. In September, 1958, Cardinal Augusto Alvaro da Silva, Archbishop of Bahia, stated in one interview that "Catholics who ally themselves with the Communist Party are selling out their country and renouncing their faith." On the other hand, Cardinal Vasconcellos da Mota of São Paulo announced that Goulart, head of the Communist-supported Brazilian Labor Party, "inspires the Church with the greatest confidence." This was the same prelate who, in 1955, issued a pastoral attacking United States liberalism and declaring United States-supported Protestantism to be as dangerous an imperialism as communism.[59] No measure of the Church's effectiveness against communism seems to be available.

Brazil has been described as the "most Catholic nation of our times." Certainly there are more Catholics in Brazil than in any other country, since it counts well over 90 per cent of its population of 63,666,000 (1960 statistics) as affiliated with the Roman Catholic Church. The Brazilian Church holds third place in size of episcopal hierarchy—after Italy and the United States—with 3 cardinals, 31 archbishops, and 107 bishops. It had, in 1960, 10,616 priests, or 5,550 Catholics per priest.[60]

58. *Hispanic American Report*, VIII, No. 9 (October, 1955), 438-39; X, No. 7 (August, 1957), 387; J. A. Camacho, *Brazil: An Interim Assessment* (London, 1952), p. 88.

59. *Hispanic American Report*, VIII, No. 9 (October, 1955), 442; XI, No. 9 (September, 1958), 523.

60. W. Stanley Rycroft and Myrtle M. Clemmer, *A Factual Study of Latin America* (New York, 1963), p. 235.

The vast majority of Brazilians consider themselves Catholic, however superficially they may observe their religious duties and however much they may ignore the advice of the Church on political affairs. They are Catholics by tradition rather than by strong faith. "Indifference and a tendency towards compromise are perhaps the most characteristic features of these attitudes. This is why adherence to the Church is merely nominal for a vast majority of the population."[61]

In 1956 a Maryknoll Father wrote that Catholicism is dying in Brazil as a consequence of acute numerical deficiency of the clergy. This gloomy prospect was repeated by a clerical sociologist who wrote in 1957: "If preventive measures are not taken in due time, the Brazilian Church shall have to endure great if not irretrievable losses, and most of Brazil may perhaps be lost to Catholicism."[62] The status of the Church in Brazil has further deteriorated since these two clerical writers sounded their warning.

There is without doubt a great scarcity of Catholic clergy in Brazil. Since few Brazilians seek the Church as a career, the production of the seminaries is small. Thus there has been need to resort to foreign priests who now number about one-half of the total number of clergy in Brazil. This accretion, however, does not match the growth of population but lags far behind it.[63]

There seems to be much validity to the criticism that had there been a truly religious spirit in Brazil she would not have had to borrow priests from abroad. Brazil suffers, particularly in the rural areas, from a lack of religious supervision and leadership. The parish priests have little prestige and are given inadequate financial support. According to a general Catholic survey, 90 per cent of Brazil's Catholics are badly instructed and poorly trained. Only 10 per cent assist more or less regularly at mass. The result is that Brazil has come to be regarded as a major missionary area for foreign-based religious orders, Protestant and Catholic.[64]

Reaction to the relatively weak influence of the Church over the Brazilian people has taken various forms, traditional African fetish cults, spiritualism, Protestantism, and secularism.

The Catholic-Afro-Brazilian fetish cult seems to be rapidly spreading, particularly in northeastern Brazil and along the coast, the areas of heaviest Negro concentration. Brought to Brazil by the slaves, the

61. Thales de Azevedo, *Social Change in Brazil* (Gainesville, Fla., 1963), p. 65.
62. *Ibid.*, p. 62.
63. *Ibid.*, p. 61.
64. William J. Coleman, *Latin American Catholicism: A Self-Evaluation* (Maryknoll, N.Y., 1958), p. 31.

traditional fetish cults have become fused with Catholicism. According to Gilberto Freyre, Afro-Brazilian pagan idols have been "acculturated" into Catholic saints. The ceremonies are something like voodoo. Many have the idea that they can remain Catholics and follow these cults as well. The Church does not excommunicate them but consents to their receiving the sacraments. A student of religious conditions in Brazil says: "Brazilian black magic of syncretic Catholic-Afro-Brazilian type has been rapidly spreading, to the distress of Catholic priests and Protestant pastors."[65]

Spiritualism, or invocation of the souls of the dead, has become, according to some estimates, the second religion in Brazil, claiming as much as 20 per cent of the population in some areas. In large cities spiritualist centers are numerous. Many spiritualists believe that they can be Catholic and follow the cult as well. While disapproving, the Church does not disavow these "hybrid Catholics."[66]

Keeping pace with the growth of spiritualism and other cults in Brazil, there has been a phenomenal Protestant development. Since no country in Latin America has been as tolerant and hospitable to foreign ideas as Brazil, it is not surprising therefore that Evangelical Christianity has reached its highest development in that country.

For many years there had been considerable proselytizing by several Protestant sects in Brazil, particularly the Methodist Episcopal, South, which was assigned the Brazilian missionary field. The foreign colonies, the German, English, and American, practiced their own faiths freely in their own churches. The most numerous were: Methodists, Baptists, Lutherans, Anglicans, and Presbyterians. Most of the pastors were foreigners. Protestants were particularly active in Brazil in fostering education. In addition to German Lutheran parochial schools in southern Brazil, the Protestant sects maintained schools at various levels throughout Brazil. The most notable Protestant school in South America is Mackenzie College of São Paulo, a Presbyterian institution. Another great Protestant college is the Isabella Hendrix, located in Bello Horizonte (capital of Minas Gerais). This college for girls is maintained by the Methodists.

At the end of World War II there was an influx of new Protestant groups: Mormons, Pentecostals, Jehovah's Witnesses, and adherents of

65. Quoted by W. Stanley Rycroft, *Religion and Faith in Latin America* (Philadelphia, 1958), p. 137. Also see John J. Considine, *New Horizons in Latin America* (New York, 1958), pp. 36-52.

66. Charles Wagley in *An Introduction to Brazil* (New York, 1963), p. 244, estimated the number of spiritualists as "over" one million. W. Stanley Rycroft in *Religion and Faith in Latin America*, p. 137, estimates that "there are ten million spiritualist members in Brazil."

the Four Square Gospel. Their methods of direct appeal by lay ministers have had remarkable success, particularly the Pentecostals, whose members are said to equal one-half of all Protestants in Brazil. A characteristic feature of the Pentecostal sect—and to a lesser degree of the other sects—is that it is nationalized, that is, the ministers as well as the communicants are Brazilian. It escapes the "foreign influence" taint. The Protestant seminaries in Brazil are said to produce more ministers than the number of priests produced by the Catholic seminaries. Of the older Protestant sects the Baptists claimed in 1960 to be one of the fastest-growing denominations in Brazil with 165,000 members.[67]

Even Catholic leaders in Brazil acknowledged that the rise of Protestantism, and the other non-Catholic cults, as well as the general trend to religious indifference was a result of the weakness of the Church and called for a strengthening of Catholicism. Without neglecting the spiritual and intellectual aspects of a program of Catholic renewal, the counterattack of the Church has taken the form principally of a new social consciousness.

Of the several examples of Catholic social action in Brazil, one of the most notable was the "Natal movement" which was started in 1954 by Bishop Eugenio de Araujo Salas. Natal was an archdiocese of 565,000 Catholics with only 62 priests. The area in northeast Brazil was notoriously poverty and disease stricken and Communist infected. The Bishop with his own funds initiated evangelization and social action which required the collaboration of bishops, diocesan and regular clergy, Brothers, Sisters and laymen. Better living conditions were sought through over-all social action of Catholic inspiration. The Communists were met and defeated for the control of labor unions by offering hope of better conditions.[68] This does not mean that the socioeconomic problems of northeast Brazil have been solved; the surface of the problem has barely been scratched. Not only does its magnitude exceed the limited resources of the Catholic Church, but taxes those of the Brazilian government supplemented with foreign assistance.[69]

A National Conference of Bishops of Brazil (1960) mapped out a program that included mass education by radio, unionization of rural workers, agrarian reform, and the elaboration of social legislation adapted to the rural milieu. Agrarian reform was urged as an alternative to revolution.[70]

67. *Hispanic American Report*, XIII, No. 1 (November, 1960), 838.

68. Rev. Tiago G. Gloin, "The Natal movement in Brazil," *Conference for Religious*, April 13-17, 1962, Maastricht, Holland.

69. For United States help to SUDENE (Development Agency for Northeast Brazil), see Department of State *Bulletin*, XLV, No. 1153 (July 31, 1961), 196-97.

70. *Hispanic American Report*, XIII, No. 12 (December, 1960), 929.

On April 30, 1963, the Brazilian hierarchy, headed by the three cardinals, issued a pastoral letter on social reform. It was entitled, "For an Authentic Christian Reform of Brazilian Social Structures." In light of Pope John's encyclical *Pacem in Terris* the Roman Catholic hierarchy made an analysis of conditions in Brazil. Their message stated that Brazil is "an underdeveloped country, where the masses do not share in the progress of the country and where poverty and premature death exist on a large scale and where the impact between rural and urban realities generates very grave consequencs of loss of individuality. Recalling that the peace advocated by the encyclical is based on order, the pastoral says concerning Brazilian conditions: "It is an order of things where a minority disposing of resources has full access to culture, health, comfort and luxury while a majority deprived of resources is denied the exercise of many of the fundamental and natural rights enumerated in *Pacem in Terris*, such as the right to existence and to a decent standard of living... in short, to rights that are intrinsic to man's life in society." The pastoral then called for extensive reforms in land ownership, private enterprise, taxes, administration, elections and education.[71]

In Brazil there is no problem of Church-State relations unless it be matters occasionally raised such as the legalization of divorce or religious instruction in the schools. The separation of Church and State ceased long ago to be an issue; anticlericalism, insofar as it exists in Brazil, has little to feed on. The concern of the Church, the largest organizationally and in membership in Latin America, is, paradoxically, the halting of a fast-diminishing influence and prestige. To accomplish this objective the Brazilian hierarchy, with the aid and encouragement of the Vatican, has embarked on a program of modernization and revitalization. Its outcome will determine the future status of the Catholic Church in Brazil.

71. *Recent Documents from Latin America*, Monograph No. 2, 1962-63, The Center of Intercultural Formation, Cuernavaca, Mexico, pp. 14-35; *Brazilian Bulletin*, Brazilian Government Trade Bureau (New York, June 1, 1963), p. 3.

Chapter XIII

Church and State in the Republics of the Caribbean

HAITI

The island of Santo Domingo, originally called Española, was the first seat of Catholicism in America. From the seed planted by Father Boyl and the missionaries brought to America by Columbus and Ovando grew with amazing rapidity the towering and sheltering tree of Christianity. So rapid was the growth of the Catholic faith that Pope Julius II promulgated a bull in 1504, at the request of Queen Isabella, creating an archbishopric and two bishoprics in the island of Española. But since the rights of royal patronage were not recognized by the pope, King Ferdinand refused to consent to the creation of the sees. Finally the pope capitulated, and by the bull *Universalis Ecclesiae* (July 28, 1508) provided for the establishment of the archbishopric of Ayguacen and the bishoprics of Maguen and Bayunen, all in the island of Española. These three sees were never actually founded, for by 1510 the population of the island had declined so alarmingly as to make an elaborate ecclesiastical hierarchy superfluous. Ferdinand accordingly asked the pope to suppress the dioceses and create only one bishopric in Española and another in Porto Rico, both to be dependent on the archbishop of Seville. This was done by the bull *Romanus Pontifex*, August 8, 1511. In 1547 the see of Santo Domingo was raised to the rank of an archbishopric.

When Spain lost to France (1697) her political control over the western part of the island, the *real patronato* over the Catholic Church in that region was terminated. For over a hundred years the patronal control of the Catholic Church in Haiti was exercised by the French crown with prerogatives not greatly dissimilar from, but by no means as comprehensive as, those possessed by the Spanish kings. In the meantime thousands of Negro slaves were brought into the island,

and eventually they outnumbered the whites several times to one.[1] Feeble efforts were exerted by the clergy, exclusively white, to convey the mysteries of Christianity to the blacks so recently wrested from the wilds of Africa. The clergy existed primarily for the service of the white population; the blacks were objects of secondary importance. Little wonder then that the slaves acquired only a very thin and impermanent veneer of Christianity. The failure of the French clergy and missionaries to effect a permanent Christianization of the Negro slaves is evidenced by the persistence to the present day of African religious rites called voodooism. Indeed, after the termination of the French domination, the practice of voodooism became almost universal, and the work of Christianization had to be undertaken anew in the nineteenth century.

From 1803, when the French withdrew from Haiti, until 1860, when a concordat was signed, the ecclesiastical system was in a semi-disorganized state, and the clergy were said to have been *sans foi ni loi*.[2] The Haitians, having none of their race trained for the priesthood, had perforce to rely on the white clergy for the administration of the sacraments and the government of the Catholic Church.

The constitution of Toussaint L'Ouverture, in 1801, although it recognized liberty of conscience, decreed that the Apostolic Roman Catholic religion was the only one to be professed in public. The termination of French rule meant also a virtual cessation of relations with the papacy. The Holy See desired to control the Church in Haiti without any interference on the part of the temporal power, but the Haitian government, on the other hand, like the Spanish-American republics, advanced unacceptable pretensions to the exercise of the patronage. Under these conditions the clergy decreased in numbers and the influence of the Church waned. Had it not been for the Haitian annexation of Santo Domingo, the Spanish part of the island, in 1822, the prelacies in Haiti would have become extinct. As it was, the canonically instituted archbishop of Santo Domingo aided in continuing the recognized ecclesiastical succession in the island.

With few exceptions the Haitian rulers were harsh, if not oppressive, towards the Catholic Church. The following description of religious and social conditions in the island in 1826 occurs in the report of the British Consul-General in Haiti: "The Government has appropriated

1. In 1788 there were in Haiti 28,000 whites, 22,000 free colored, and 405,000 Negro slaves. Lathrop Stoddard, *The French Revolution in San Domingo* (New York, 1914), p. 9.

2. "Hearings before a Select Committee on Haiti and Santo Domingo," United States Senate. Sen. Res. 112, 67 Cong. (Washington, 1922), p. 1285.

all the Church property to its own use. The clergy rely wholly on the fees, two-thirds of which they are obliged to pay into the treasury.... It is not a subject of surprise that morality should be on as low a stage ... marriage is scarcely thought of...."[3]   In 1828 there were in the island only about forty priests, and it was the professed determination of President Boyer not to increase this number, because the poverty-stricken government required the Church revenues for its own uses.   Finally, in 1830, President Boyer expelled the archbishop of Santo Domingo and the bishop of Port-au-Prince, for political reasons.   This act severed all connection with the papacy.[4]

In an effort to settle the dispute with Haiti, John England, Bishop of Charleston, was sent to Port-au-Prince, in 1834, in the capacity of a legate.   Bishop England, being unable to reconcile the views of the pope and President Boyer, left Haiti, but he returned in 1836 to sign a concordat.   He took this treaty with him to Rome hoping to have it ratified, but Gregory XII refused.   Instead, Bishop England was sent back to Haiti with the title of "Vicar Apostolic, Administrator of the Church of Haiti."   Boyer refused to receive him as the pope's agent in such a capacity.   Thus, for a time, the diplomatic *pourparlers* were ended.[5]

In 1842 negotiations were resumed by Rome with the dispatch of Joseph Rosati, Bishop of St. Louis (Missouri), to Port-au-Prince as papal legate.   On February 17, 1842, Bishop Rosati signed a concordat with the Haitian government.   This treaty was not ratified because of internal disturbances in Haiti.[6]

In 1860 President Geffrard reopened the parleys with the Vatican concerning the situation of the Catholic clergy in Haiti.   When the Holy See abandoned its efforts to force on the Negro republic high central control of the Church, the conclusion of a concordat was no longer a difficult matter.   On March 28, 1860, a treaty which still regulates the relations of Haiti with the Holy See was signed at Rome by Cardinal Antonelli and M. Piérre Faubert for Haiti.   This concordat secured full and special protection for the Roman Catholic Church in Haiti.   "The Roman Catholic Apostolic religion," read Article I, "which is the religion of the great majority of Haitians, will be specially protected, as well as its ministers, in the Republic of Haiti, and it will enjoy the rights and attributes which are proper to it."   The Concordat insured the dispatch

3. Quoted in Sumner Welles, *Naboth's Vineyard, The Dominican Republic, 1844-1924* (New York, 1928), I, 35.

4. *Ibid.*, p. 186; James Franklin, *The Present State of Haiti* (London, 1822), pp. 393-94.

5. J. N. Léger, *Haiti, Her History and Her Detractors* (New York, 1907), p. 187; Hernáez, *Colección de Bulas*, II, 30.

6. Léger, *op. cit.*, p. 187, n. 5; Hernáez, *op. cit.*, II, 32.

to the island, for the first time since independence, of a recognized and responsible priesthood. The Church undertook to establish parishes and missions, and, in the words of the Concordat, "those orders and institutions which are approved by the Catholic Church," including schools, hospitals, asylums, and orphanages. The instrument provided for the establishment of an archbishopric at Port-au-Prince, and dependent bishoprics elsewhere. The prelates, who were to be paid by the State, were to be nominated by the president of the Republic and approved by the pope. All were required to take an oath of fealty to the government. Provision was also made for the establishment and maintenance of cathedral chapters and seminaries. The priests were to be nominated by the bishops, but the nominations had to be approved by the government. In addition to the stipends which the clergy were to receive from the State, they were allowed to exact certain fees for the performance of special services like baptisms, marriages, and masses.[7] Two additional conventions entered into in 1861 and 1862 and a statute known as the *Loi des Fabriques* provided for the carrying out of the terms of the concordat.[8]

The Concordat opened the way to the Vatican to establish an ecclesiastical organization in Haiti, and soon the Church was put on a regular footing which has ever since been maintained. In December, 1860, an apostolic delegate was sent to Haiti and, on October 3, 1861, the hierarchy composed of an archdiocese and four dioceses was established.[9] In conformity with an understanding between the papacy and the Haitian government French clerics and nuns were brought into the country in 1864 to assume the exclusive administration of the Church in its spiritual, charitable, and educational activities. The seminary of Saint Jacques in Quimper, France, was designated the particular one for the training of the Haitian priesthood. The Haitian government maintains scholarships in this seminary.[10] At Port-au-Prince there is a seminary for the training of Haitian priests. In 1930 there were but eight native priests in the whole republic, but in 1960 there were about one hundred. The French priests, Brothers of Christian Instruction, and nuns, who number approximately seven hundred, are widely distributed over the country and are doing good work in charge of parishes, active mission work, education, and the charities.

7. *Raccolta di Concordati*, pp. 929-34; Emily G. Balch (ed.), *Occupied Haiti* (New York, 1927), p. 5; Hernáez, *op. cit.*, II, 30.

8. *Report of the President's Commission for the Study and Review of Conditions in the Republic of Haiti, March 26, 1930* (Washington, 1930), p. 15.

9. In 1930 an apostolic nunciature was established. The hierarchy is still composed today of an archdiocese and four dioceses.

10. *Livre Bleu D'Haiti* (Port-au-Prince, 1920), p. 141; Léger, *op. cit.*, p. 270.

From 1860 to 1957, relations between the Catholic Church and the Haitian government were most cordial. Barring a controversy in 1880, caused by clerical opposition to the civil marriage law, there was little or no friction between the lay and ecclesiastical orders. Both parties exhibited remarkable good faith in living up to the terms of the Concordat, which is the legal basis of the relationship which exists between the Catholic Church and the Haitian government. The only statement contained in the present Constitution of 1957 on the subject of religion (Art. 20) provides: "All religions and all sects recognized in Haiti are free. Everyone has the right to profess his religion and to engage in his own religious practices, provided that he does not disturb the public peace. The Catholic religion, professed by the majority of Haitians, enjoys a special situation by virtue of the Concordat." All of Haiti's constitutions guaranteed freedom of conscience and religion for there has been a marked spirit of tolerance since the country won its independence.

In conformity with the Concordat, the Republic provides salaries for the archbishop, bishops, and priests. Each annual budget contains items for religious purposes, but not all of these appropriations are intended for the State-Church alone. Approximately 10 per cent of the total amount is destined for the uses of the Protestant churches, for the government aids and encourages the spread of the Christian religion of all denominations. The budget of 1963-64 provided a total of 1,337,000 gourdes[11] for religion, and 1,152,341 gourdes for the Roman Catholic Church. For the Church the appropriation provided 941,681 gourdes for clerical personnel, including the apostolic representative, and 194,000 gourdes for upkeep of buildings.[12] Since Church property has been nationalized the construction of new buildings and the repair of old ones is a government responsibility. The Ministry of Foreign Affairs and Worship is vested with the management of religious matters.

A large share of the burden of education in Haiti has been assumed by the Catholic Church. This state of affairs is not the consequence exactly of the existence of a privileged religion. Although the Roman Church receives governmental aid in supporting its schools, subsidies are also given Protestant educational enterprises. The commanding position of the Catholic Church in education is the result therefore, not of special privilege, but of the superiority of numbers enjoyed by that faith as the nominal faith of the great majority of the people.

Despite attempts of Haitian administrators to give more attention

---

11. The ratio of the gourde to the dollar is about five to one.
12. Figures supplied by Haitian Embassy, Washington, D.C.

to public education, the Church continues to be the "right arm" of the Department of Public Instruction. The schools supported by public money, or receiving subventions, are the national "presbyterial" and "congregational" schools. In the national, or State schools, religious instruction is part of the curriculum. The presbyterial, or priests' schools, and the congregational, or schools conducted by teaching orders, are of course, Catholic. There were in 1960, 513 Catholic schools in Haiti.[13] The teachers in the Catholic educational institutions are French men and women, members of religious orders. The most prominent male teaching order is the Brothers of Christian Instruction, while the Sisters of St. Joseph de Cluny and Les Filles de la Sagesse are the most important of the female orders.

Only a few natives are used as subordinate teachers in the schools. Some Haitians complain that the Church teaching does not give a sufficiently "patriotic" education and overemphasizes religion. Whatever might be the truth of this criticism there is little doubt that the type of instruction in the Church schools is vastly superior to that of the public schools. In addition to the Catholic educational work some teaching is being done by Protestant missionaries. A small government subsidy is enjoyed by certain Protestant educational undertakings.[14]

At the beginning of her national independence Haiti deprived the Church of its ancient control over marriage. The civil marriage was made the only legal form, but this did not prevent the religious ceremony from following the civil. The ministers of all creeds were forbidden to celebrate nuptials without requesting the presentation of the certificate of the civil marriage. After the conclusion of the Concordat the clergy were inclined to disregard this requirement and eventually they contended that they had the right to perform religious marriages without taking any notice of the civil ceremony. Because of the clerical opposition, the House of Representatives, in 1879, passed a resolution requesting the president to denounce the Concordat of 1860. When President Salomon prepared to carry out the wishes of the Congress the clergy decided that their opposition had gone too far, and consequently they promised to obey the civil marriage law. Since then there has been no friction over its observance. Unlike most of the countries where the Catholic Church is the State-Church, absolute divorce is legalized in Haiti. Divorce is granted for adultery and grave abuses, and when one of the parties is sentenced to *peines afflictives et infamantes*. Remar-

13. W. Stanley Rycroft and Myrtle M. Clemmer, *A Factual Study of Latin America* (New York, 1963), Table No. 50, p. 235, based on *Basic Ecclesiastical Statistics for Latin America* 1960, edited by William J. Gibbons, et al.

14. Balch, *op. cit.*, pp. 96-98; *Livre Bleu*, pp. 141-43; *Senate Hearings*, p. 1349.

riage is allowed after the lapse of one year, but a divorced person is not allowed to remarry a former spouse.[15]

According to the foregoing it will be observed that the status of the Catholic Church in Haiti presents certain marked contrasts from that in other Latin-American countries where it enjoys the privileged position of a State establishment. In the first place, an alien clergy administers the Church in Haiti; the hierarchy and the lowly priests, the teaching brothers, and the nuns are foreigners. This situation arises from easily understood causes, but nevertheless it is interesting. A contrast is also found in rights of ownership in ecclesiastical property, for in Haiti, unlike other countries with a State-Church, the property is nationalized. Divorce is absolute, while in other countries it is conditional or prohibited. Finally, the Church, which is supported by the State, does not enjoy a monopoly of governmental subsidies for religious purposes.

What is the hold of Catholicism upon the inhabitants of Haiti today? Although generally regarded as a preponderatingly Catholic country, this is not true. In all but the highest circles the real religion of the people is of African origin, with a veneer of Christianity. These African rites are called generically voodooism; the different tribes had originally different religious ceremonies, but as no tribal distinctions have survived in Haiti, the result is a blend of the old superstitious practices. Voodooism is based upon fear, the propitiation of the deities being very important. Priests and teachers have tried for centuries to root out the superstitious practices, but they have scarcely made an impression. Several attempts have been made by the Haitian government to suppress voodooism, but it dares not be too stringent. Some of the presidents of Haiti, even, have been voodoo priests. It is contended that approximately 90 per cent of the Haitians are believers in voodoo and presumably good Catholics will attend the rites of the cult. Christian celebrations, like Easter, have a strong African infusion. This situation is analogous to that of numerous Latin-American countries where pagan rites of the Indians persisted and became fused with Roman Catholicism. Catholic priests and Protestant missionaries are making a fine fight to eradicate paganism in Haiti—much has been accomplished, but much more remains to be done. Haiti is, therefore, above all else a great missionary challenge.

The relatively tranquil relations between the Catholic Church and the Haitian government deteriorated greatly after 1957 when Dr. François Duvalier ("Papa Doc") came into power, and thereafter consolidated one of the most tyrannical dictatorships in the history of a country not

15. Civil Code of Haiti, Articles 213-19, 283-84; Léger, *op. cit.*, p. 283.

unacquainted with tyranny. It was Duvalier's hypersensitivity concerning actual and potential opposition to his personalistic rule which led to conflict with the hierarchy and clergy of the Catholic Church.

Most of Haiti's priests were white French-born who were intimately associated with the mulatto upper class which had controlled Haiti socially and politically until 1946. The advent of black rule at that time stimulated nationalism—called Haitianization—the desire to free Haiti from French influence and emphasize Haiti's African heritage. The French clergy—predominately ultraconservative Bretons—were accused of trying for decades to meddle in politics to maintain the "spiritual colonization" of Haiti.

Thus, when Dr. Duvalier, an ebony black, became president, he not only suspected the clergy of alliance with the mulatto opposition, but he also regarded them as agents of a foreign power. In other words the foreign clergy were socially and politically subversive. The solution was the Haitianization of the clergy—a native clergy that could be controlled. Although the Duvalier government had appointed two successive Haitian-born priests to the position of Education Minister, it continued to be suspicious of French-born priests. Duvalier himself, a nominal Catholic who occasionally attended church, was accused—probably correctly—of being a practicing voodoo priest.

"Papa Doc" Duvalier's feud with the Catholic Church began in August, 1959, when two French Roman Catholic priests were expelled from the country for "security reasons." An assembly of Catholics gathered in the cathedral of Port-au-Prince in silent protest against the government's action was broken up by club-wielding police who invaded the place of worship. When Archbishop François Poisier criticized the expulsion of the priests and the violation of the cathedral, he was ordered arrested because he had violated the penal code which prohibited religious authorities to censure or criticize the acts of public authority. The warrant for the arrest of the prelate, however, was suspended.[16]

This did not restore harmonious relations for Duvalier continued to be irritated because of the preponderance of French-born priests among the clergy. Although three of the four bishops were French, the native-origins of the clerical personnel had greatly changed, for in 1959, a Church source reported that the number of Haitian priests had risen to 110, compared with 180 Frenchmen. In addition there were 40 Oblate Fathers from Canada and the United States and 20 Belgian priests who had been recently expelled from Red China.[17] Their presence should

16. *Hispanic American Report*, XII, No. 9 (September, 1959), 490.
17. *New York Times*, August 24, 1959.

have served to dilute Duvalier's resentment against the French priests. This was not the case for the dictator's objective was a native clergy subservient to him.

The threat to arrest the Archbishop and the deportation of the two priests led to the publication in the Catholic daily, *La Phalange*, of a letter by five priests accusing the government of resorting to "totalitarianism" in its campaign against the Church. The government, said the priests, was trying to force the Church to pledge "absolute obedience." The priests rejected the charges of clerical involvement in antigovernment activities.[18]

A little more than a year later, on March 24, 1960, Archbishop Poisier was summarily expelled from the country on the charge of encouraging student strikes and of giving monetary aid to "subversive" students to overthrow the regime. The Vatican announced the appointment of Bishop Rémy Augustine, a native-born Haitian and the first Negro to hold the office of bishop, to take over Poisier's duties with the title of Apostolic Administrator for Haiti. The Haitian government refused to recognize Bishop Rémy's appointment, and on January 10, 1961, ordered the expulsion of the Bishop and four priests on charges of social and political subversion. The Catholic newspaper, *La Phalange*, was seized by the government, and an unknown number of priests and nuns—probably as many as 130—were arrested. On January 12, the Consistorial Congregation of the Vatican automatically excommunicated everyone having anything to do with the expulsion of the bishops. President François Duvalier, a Roman Catholic, was then thought to be among those put under the ban.[19]

The purge of the Roman Catholic hierarchy cost Duvalier excommunication but little else. In fact, his inauguration on May 22, 1961, was celebrated by a *Te Deum* mass in the cathedral of Port-au-Prince. Duvalier continued to maintain a public position of respect for the Vatican, while insisting that he was opposed only to "bad priests" and not the Roman Catholic Church. He accepted the papal appointment of Claudius Angenor, a Haitian, as acting administrator of the Port-au-Prince archdiocese.[20] The stands of both Duvalier and the Vatican seemed to be equivocal.

The expulsion of prelates and clergy did not cease. In November, 1962, Mgr. Paul Jean Maria Robert, the French-born bishop of Gonaïves, together with four French priests, were expelled. The Bishop was

18. *Ibid.*, August 29, 1959.

19. *Ibid.*, November 25, 27, 29, 1960; January 11, 13, 1961; *Hispanic American Report*, XIV, No. 1 (January, 1961), 37.

20. *New York Times*, February 2, 1961.

charged with heading a crusade against the government's policy of encouraging voodoo. At this point the Vatican recalled the papal nuncio and abandoned a rural school building program. A 1958 agreement, under which the Jesuits operated in Haiti, was terminated in January, 1964, with the expulsion of eighteen Canadian Jesuit missionaries. The Jesuit-staffed seminary at Port-au-Prince was closed.[21]

With only two of the five prelates remaining, and the dioceses greatly bereft of priests, the Catholic Church in Haiti absorbed the insults and attacks of "Papa Doc" hoping for the better day which is usually expected to follow the inevitable end of dictatorship.

THE DOMINICAN REPUBLIC

The Roman Catholic religion has been the State religion of the Dominican Republic since that country won its independence from Haiti in 1844. This is in recognition, according to early constitutions, of the fact that the majority of the Dominicans profess the Catholic religion.[22] Separation from the hateful Haitian domination had as one of its prime objects the reëstablishment of the traditional religion of the Dominicans. The cry set up by the conspirators who inaugurated the revolt was "God, Country, and Liberty,"[23] and when the independent republic was established the national motto became, "Dios, Patria, Libertad."

The ecclesiastical schism forced upon the Dominican people because of the actions of the Haitian government came to an end with the reëstablishment of the hierarchy by the pope in 1848.[24] Don Tomás de Portes é Infante was created archbishop of the ancient metropolitan see of Santo Domingo. Soon the Archbishop became involved in difficulties with President Santana (1853) because of his pro-Spanish sympathies and intervention in political matters. When the Spanish historian Don Mariano Torrente was sent to the Republic as special agent the chapter of the cathedral with the Archbishop at its head publicly welcomed him. Moreover, upon pointing out to the visitor the Spanish arms still fixed above the High Altar, the Archbishop said, "There we keep it as a reminder of better days and as a symbol of our hope for a happier and more tranquil future." Santana accused the aged Archbishop

21. *Hispanic American Report*, XVII, No. 2 (February, 1964), 134.

22. "The relations of Church and State shall continue as at present, since the Roman Catholic Apostolic religion is that professed by a majority of the Dominicans." Constitution of the Dominican Republic, 1925, Pan American Union (Washington, D.C., 1925), Art. 92.

23. Sumner Welles, *Naboth's Vineyard, The Dominican Republic, 1844-1944* (New York, 1928), I, 59.

24. Otto Schoenrich, *Santo Domingo* (New York, 1918), p. 186.

of fostering dissatisfaction among the people and ordered him to take an oath of allegiance to the Constitution. Portes é Infante at first refused, but gave in at length and took the required oath. His troubles however caused him to lose his mind. Other prelates who refused to obey the orders of the President were exiled. By these summary methods Santana obtained a submissive clergy.[25]

The restoration of Spanish rule in Santo Domingo (1861), although welcomed by the clergy, did not prove to be an unmixed blessing. The new Spanish Archbishop, Don Bienvenido Monzón y Martín, aroused indignation in the native clergy by replacing Dominicans with Spanish priests in the most important posts, and by attempting to reform their lives, which, it must be admitted, were notoriously lax. But most resented of all was his action in forcing the native priests to abandon fees for their parochial services and content themselves with a meager monthly stipend.[26] The Dominican clergy, consequently, were not greatly exercised when Spain abandoned Santo Domingo in 1865.

From 1865 to the present date the history of the Church in the Dominican Republic has been devoid of important incident, excepting the elevation of two of the prelates to the position of president of the Republic. In 1880 Padre Fernando Arturo de Meriño, a man of extraordinary force of personality, eloquence, and presence, was elected president of the Dominican Republic. He was a complete success as an administrator, for, says Welles, "No more vigorous rule, no more decisive sway had ever previously been exercised by any Dominican President."[27] After his retirement from the presidency, Don Meriño won even greater fame as Archbishop of Santo Domingo.

In 1912, in an effort to ward off intervention by appeasing the United States, the Dominican Congress elected Adolfo A. Nouel, Archbishop of Santo Domingo, as Provisional President for a period of two years. Unlike his illustrious clerical predecessor in the presidency, Archbishop Nouel had neither the liking nor the talents for the Chief Magistracy of the Dominican Republic. He was glad therefore to relinquish his office before the expiration of the two year term. In 1922 another cleric, Canon Armando Lamarche Marchena, failed of being elected to the presidency by a narrow margin.[28] The incidents mentioned were illustrative not only of the political activities of Dominican prelates and clerics, but also of the great confidence which they inspired, in a political manner, in the inhabitants of the island republic.

25. Welles, *op. cit.*, I, 126, 131-32.
26. *Ibid.*, I, 240-41.
27. *Ibid.*, I, 439-41.
28. *Ibid.*, II, 699-708, 873.

Although prior to 1954 no concordat had been concluded between the Dominican Republic and the Vatican, friendly relations existed with the papacy. Diplomatic intercourse was cared for by the interchange of fully accredited representatives. In 1884 the Dominican government entered into a sort of working agreement with the Holy See, according to the terms of which the archbishop of Santo Domingo was to be appointed by the pope from a list of three names, native Dominicans or residents of the Republic, submitted by the Dominican Congress. The State agreed to pay the salaries of the archbishop and certain other ecclesiastical officials.[29]

Prior to the adoption of the Constitution of 1955, all of the earlier organic charters of the Republic contained only one general article which indirectly recognized Roman Catholicism as the State religion. For example, Article 93 of the Constitution of 1947 read: "The relations of the Church and State shall continue as at present, inasmuch as the Apostolic Roman Catholic Religion is that which the majority of Dominicans profess." This meant that all legislation governing the relations between Church and State, including patronage, was recognized by this Constitution.

Many years of friendly relations between the Dominican Church and President Rafael Leonidas Trujillo Molina, the "Benefactor of the Fatherland," paved the way for the negotiation in 1954 of a Concordat with the papacy. Generally the Concordat only meant a formalizing of the relations in actual practice between Church and State, although in some respects there were reciprocal concessions notably in the areas of marital relations and education.[30] Legislation was immediately enacted to implement the terms of the Concordat.

Following the adoption of the Concordat, the Constitution of 1955, and also the present Constitution of 1962, disposed of the whole subject of Church-State relations with one Article (11), which reads: "Relations between the Church and the State are regulated by the Concordat between the Holy See and the Dominican Republic, in accordance with the law of God and the Catholic tradition of the Dominican Republic." In another article (8:5) there is the guarantee of "Freedom of conscience and of worship, subject to respect for the public order and good customs."

According to the Concordat the government appropriates for the support of the Church, but, since the subsidy is small, the clergy, having no other sources of income, are dependent on the contributions of the faithful. In 1845 all mortgages and perpetual rents established in favor

29. Schoenrich, *op. cit.*, p. 186.
30. *Resol.* 3874 (July 10, 1954), *Gaceta Oficial*, Cuidad Trujillo, July 21, 1954.

of the Church had been abolished. There was dispute, however, whether the churches, which were built with public funds and were tax exempt, were not the property of the State. Pursuant to the Concordat, the Dominican government granted corporate or legal personalty to the Church and made provision for its ownership of property. The same law (September 30, 1954) exempted the clerical personnel from the payment of taxes and charges on personal and movable property. Also they were granted franking privileges in postal and telegraphic services.[31]

The Catholic Church exercises no control of an administrative nature over public education, although, according to the Concordat, "public instruction shall be based on principles of Catholic doctrine and morals." Religious instruction may be given in the public schools at the request of parents and members of the clergy may teach in them. The Church maintains private schools of a primary and secondary character. In 1960 there were 69 such schools. These received no aid from the government, although a Catholic seminary did receive an official subsidy. The Catholic and Protestant schools (there are only a few of the latter) must follow the general plan of instruction in the public schools. In accordance with the Concordat, degrees and diplomas issued by Catholic schools have the same validity as the secular, without supervision by civil authorities.[32]

The Church is no longer in exclusive control of the institution of matrimony in the Dominican Republic, for the civil marriage is recognized. By law of 1924 ecclesiastics were empowered to perform marriages having civil and religious force providing the act is inscribed in the civil register. The Dominican Republic is listed among the Latin-American countries sanctioning absolute divorce,[33] but this is qualified, for, although the civil law recognizes divorce and remarriage, this applies only to non-Catholic marriages. Law 3932 of September 14, 1954, provides that the Catholic religious marriage ceremony indicates intention on the part of the contracting parties to renounce divorce, and accordingly the civil courts will not be open to such appeals. The law provides not only for the registration of Catholic marriages, but the tariff of fees to be charged for such ceremonies.[34]

There are no restrictions on liberty of conscience and religion in the

31. *Ley* 3928 (September 20, 1954), *Gaceta Oficial*, Ciudad Trujillo, September 25, 1954.

32. *Ley* 3936 (September 20, 1954), *Gaceta Oficial*, Ciudad Trujillo, September 25, 1954.

33. See Ricardo Gallardo, *Divorcio, Separación de Cuerpos y Nulidad del Matrimonio en las Naciones Latino-Americanos* (Madrid, 1957).

34. *Ley* 3932 (September 14, 1954), *Gaceta Oficial*, September 25, 1954; *Ley* 4166 (June 2, 1955), *Gaceta Oficial*, June 8, 1955.

Republic. Indeed, Dominican Catholicism is characterized by a marked tolerance for other sects. Yet, it is to be noted that Protestantism in the Dominican Republic is negligible, for its churches are few and feeble. In 1960 the total Protestant community numbered 42,030 or 1.5 per cent of the total population; Protestant Church membership was 16,595, and the number of Protestant clergy was 236. In 1957 a law prohibited the activities of the Jehovah's Witnesses, but in 1960 the law was repealed.[35] A number of denominations maintain missions and schools in the island republic; these include: Seventh Day Adventists, Assembly of God, Anglican Episcopal, and Dominican Evangelical Church. Most of the Protestants are Negroes from the British West Indies and Virgin Islands. For these are the Wesleyan Methodist Church of England and the African Methodist Church. Except among immigrants from Haiti, there is slight trace of the voodooism so prevalent in the black republic.

There are no religious tests for the exercise of the suffrage or for holding office. In the past members of the clergy frequently participated in politics and often were officeholders. After the inauguration of the Trujillo regime however, the clergy lost its stomach for politics and endeavored to avoid involvement. This was regarded by many as Church acquiescence, if not sanction, of the dictatorship.

With the exception of a few friars brought over from France and Spain, the Dominican clergy is native and has been trained in the seminary in Santo Domingo. In 1960 there were 310 priests, not all diocesan, serving a Catholic population of 2,673,000, or 8,600 Catholics per priest.[36] The priests, as a body, are not respected by foreigners and educated natives, although they are held in superstitious veneration by the ignorant masses. The black sheep among the Dominican clergy are all too numerous; no inconsiderable number live openly with their women, and drunkenness is frequent. The French priests of Haiti, models of moral rectitude, are disgusted with their fellow clerics in the eastern part of the island.[37]

The last years of the Trujillo dictatorship were marked by estrangement between the former obsequious clergy and the "Benefactor of the Fatherland." The Church opposition in the Dominican Republic, unlike that of recent years against other dictators in Latin America, was not due to any anticlerical initiative taken by Trujillo. It was simply a case of the Church no longer being able to remain silent in face of

35. Rycroft and Clemmer, *op. cit.*, pp. 234-35.

36. *Ibid.*, p. 235. In 1957 there were in the Dominican Republic two archbishops and three bishops. John J. Considine, *New Horizons in Latin America* (New York, 1958), p. 333.

37. Schoenrich, *op. cit.*, pp. 188-90.

the mounting violence and cynicism of the dictatorship. The consciences of the ecclesiastics could no longer be restrained.

In January, 1960, a pastoral of the hierarchy asked for the grant of individual freedom. The bishops demanded the rights of privacy of home and family, of emigration, freedom of conscience, and freedom of press and assembly. These rights, they said, had been denied for thirty years. They declared that the Catholic Church must defend the rights of the individual against the State, and that the suppression of individual rights was "a grave offense against God."³⁸ Trujillo countered this unprecedented action by the clergy by calling attention to his staunch support of the Church. Thereupon, President Balaguer and his cabinet sent a letter to the bishops asking that they confer on Trujillo the title "Benefactor of the Catholic Church in the Dominican Republic." This, said Balaguer, would demonstrate solidarity between Church and State. The Church however, had come to believe that further demonstrations of solidarity with the dictatorship would not be healthful. Trujillo was denied the title, for the prelates declared that it was not in their power to bestow it—the power belonged to the Holy See. In an effort to appease, they said: "While reiterating our gratitude and recognizing the limits of our power, we are sure in our hearts that God, the infallible recompenser, will not let merit go unrewarded."³⁹

The dictator, angered at the outspoken opposition of the Church, instituted terrorist tactics against both native and foreign priests. United States and Canadian clerics were expelled as "undesirable aliens." The assassination of Trujillo on May 30, 1961, called a halt to the widening breach between Church and State. The Church came out enthusiastically in favor of democracy, but disapproved the leftist democracy of President Juan Bosch who was quickly ousted from power.

Although the State-Church in the Dominican Republic encounters practically no opposition from Protestantism and almost monopolizes the religious field, it nevertheless is losing its hold upon a large number of the 90 per cent of the population counted as "Catholic." There is general religious indifference and laxity on the part of the laity. A clerical observer writing ten years ago said that the Catholic Church in the Dominican Republic was "going backward."⁴⁰ Since then the

38. *Hispanic American Report*, XIII, No. 1 (January 1960), 29; No. 2 (February, 1960), 104.

39. *Ibid.*, XIV, No. 2 (February, 1961), 132.

40. Albert J. Nevins, "How Catholic is Latin America?" *The Sign*, Vol. 36, No. 2 (September, 1956), p. 67. For the political role of the Church in the aftermath of the Trujillo dictatorship, see Howard J. Wiarda, "The Changing Political Orientation of the Catholic Church in the Dominican Republic," *A Journal of Church and State*, VII, No. 2 (Spring, 1965), 238-54.

situation has not improved. The Church is failing in its mission but whether or not this is due to its union with the State is doubtful. The State is not a burden upon the Church and does not impose restrictions on its activities. The terms of the Concordat are generally favorable to the Church.

With or without union, the Catholic Church in the Dominican Republic cannot prosper with its present clergy. It has been demonstrated that the native priests are incompetent and that the hierarchy is unwilling or unable to control them. A partial remedy for the ills of Catholicism in the island republic would be the introduction of more foreign priests to serve as models for the elevation of the standards of the native clerics.

CUBA

When Cuba severed her political connection with Spain, she also terminated the ancient union of the civil and ecclesiastical orders. Since the Roman Catholic religion continued after independence to be virtually the only one of any standing in the island, the disestablishment of the Church was a phenomenon difficult for Americans to understand. Yet, the Catholic Church of Spanish Cuba was really a Spanish institution; all the bishops as well as most of the priests were appointed from Madrid. The churchmen, therefore, during the rebellion, quite generally espoused the cause of Spain. The separation, consequently, was a national act of revenge in retaliation for the pro-Spanish activities of the clericals. Furthermore, it was felt that an institution which had been a bulwark of royalism and conservatism had to be deprived of political influence in the future, as a security measure for the republic. The opposition was to the Church as an institution quite apart from its dogma. This same kind of opposition is to be found throughout Latin America, but in it there is little encouragement for Protestantism.

When General John R. Brooke assumed authority, on January 1, 1899, as military governor of Cuba, he issued a proclamation declaring that the laws of the country were to continue in force and that they would be modified in the manner that necessity might advise. To aid him in consolidating peace, he named a Council of Secretaries, composed of natives. These Cuban secretaries immediately undertook to put through some measures against the Catholic Church. General Brooke was induced to enact a law establishing civil marriage as the only legally binding ceremony. A fee of one dollar was fixed by the measure. The Church objected to the law but without effect.[41]

When General Leonard Wood became Military Governor-General of Cuba, he was confronted with serious Church questions. The principal problems at issue were: (1) establishment of civil marriage; (2) confiscation of Church property; and (3) secularization of the cemeteries. In 1900 General Wood amended the civil marriage law so that a Church marriage, by any lawful sect, or a civil marriage should be equally valid. Divorce and nullification of marriages, however, were transferred from the ecclesiastical to the civil courts. In the interest of sanitary protection and equality of treatment, civil cemeteries were established. The Church was allowed to retain control over the cemeteries already in its possession, but they were subject to state regulation.[42]

The knotty question involving the Church property which had been confiscated was also brought to Governor Wood for settlement. The problem dated from 1837-41, when Spain secularized a great portion of the property belonging to the religious orders. This act of seizure aroused protracted controversy with the Holy See and was not settled until the conclusion of the Concordat of 1861. By the terms of that instrument Spain agreed to pay to the Church an annual rental for the properties which had been put to secular uses by the government. This amounted to an allowance for the maintenance of worship. After the American intervention in Cuba the payments to the Church for the use of the properties ceased. The Church therefore demanded that the rent be paid or the properties returned. In finding a solution for this problem, as for other religious problems as well, Leonard Wood was guided by sound common sense and recognized fundamental principles of justice. Unhampered by prejudice he decided that the claims of the Church were just and reasonable, and so he agreed with the Bishop of Havana that the State should be granted an option to buy the property in question at an agreed valuation within five years from date. Until the date of purchase the State should pay an annual rental of 5 per cent of the accepted value.[43] In reporting on the settlement of the Church property controversy, General Wood said, "I consider this settlement of

41. Eric F. Wood, *Leonard Wood* (New York, 1920), p. 159; Charles E. Chapman, *A History of the Cuban Republic* (New York, 1927), p. 119.

42. Wood, *op. cit.*, pp. 159-60. John G. Holme, *The Life of Leonard Wood* (New York, 1920), p. 101.

43. Wood, *op. cit.*, pp. 161-62. Although President Estrada Palma called the attention of the Cuban Congress to the obligation to purchase the property, the Congress failed to act. The problem was not settled until the second American occupation. Charles E. Magoon, *Republic of Cuba: Report of the Provisional Administration* (Havana, 1908), pp. 80-82.

the question of the Church property as most important, and one which will remove from the coming Cuban government a great and fruitful source of annoyance."[44]

In the Constitutional Convention of 1900-1 the Catholic Church was subjected to vigorous attack. So radical were some of the members on the question of religion that one, Salvador Cisneros, former revolutionary president of Cuba, proposed to strike out of the preamble the phrase, "invoking the favor of God." After an animated debate over the religious article of the Constitution, the following was adopted: "The profession of all religions is free, as well as the exercise of all cults without limitation, except that they must respect Christian morality and public order. The Church will be separated from the State, and in no case will it subsidize any cult."[45]

"By definitely pronouncing for a separation of Church and State," says Professor Chapman, "the Cubans rid themselves of an issue that has disturbed the politics of their sister republics to the south."[46] On the other hand, it is very doubtful whether the subsequent harmonious relations between the Catholic Church and the State could have been possible had it not been for the restraining hand of General Wood, who prevented confiscation of Church properties. It was fortunate for the Church that an American, and a non-Catholic, had the authority to check a ruthless attack on the Church. If the same wise restraint had been applied in other Latin-American countries, vexatious religious problems would never have arisen.

The constitutional status of the Roman Catholic Church in Cuba was established by the two organic charters of 1901 and 1940. The articles dealing with religion were almost identical in both instruments. The Constitution of 1940, which in the preamble invokes "the favor of God," provides in Article 35 that "The profession of all religions is free, as well as the exercise of all kinds of worship, without other limitation than respect for Christian morality and public order. The Church shall be separated from the State, which shall not grant a subvention to any religion." Article 55, which deals with education, says: "Official instruction shall be laic. Centers of private instruction shall be subject to regulation and inspection by the State; however, in all cases the right shall be preserved of imparting, separate from technical instruction, the religious education that may be desired." Since profound changes affecting the Roman Catholic Church and religion in general

44. Wood, *op. cit.*, p. 162.
45. *Constitución de la República de Cuba* (Havana, 1910), Art. 26; Howard B. Grose, *Advance in the Antilles* (New York, 1910), p. 43.
46. Chapman, *op. cit.*, p. 134.

were instituted in Cuba after 1959, the nature and extent of these changes will be more apparent if we describe first the legal position and actual condition of the Church on the eve of the establishment of the Fidel Castro régime.

The legal status of the Catholic Church in Cuba in 1958, under the Constitution of 1940, was practically the same as in the United States. There were no restrictions on liberty of conscience and religion and no religious tests for exercising suffrage or holding office. In an effort to be strictly nonpartisan in religious matters, the government did not allow chapels in prisons. The Church was entirely independent of the State, and no rights were enjoyed by the government in the election of ecclesiastical officers. Also, the government was enjoined from subsidizing any religion. Although no concordat was ever concluded between the Republic and the Holy See, Cuba and the Vatican exchanged diplomatic representatives.

Title to ecclesiastical property was vested in the Church. When Cuba threw off the Spanish yoke the Catholic Church narrowly escaped confiscation of its property by the State, thanks to the opposition of General Wood. In 1958 the Church was the holder of extensive revenue producing properties. Upon these properties it paid taxes, but edifices and places of worship were exempt. No restrictions were placed upon the ability of the Church to receive entailments. Wills and inheritances, as they affected the Church, were subject only to the civil law.

Religion and religious sects were entirely divorced from public instruction in Cuba. No religious instruction was allowed in the public schools, and ecclesiastics could not be employed in them. There were self-supporting Church schools, in which, of course, religious instruction could be given. Nevertheless they were supervised by the Department of Public Instruction which required them to conform to the public school laws. The children of the State schools received religious instruction at the option of the parents, in what are known as *doctrinas*. These were classes conducted by the parish priests, on Church property, which met on Saturdays. Most of the 339 Catholic schools were for secondary and higher education. In 1946 the University of St. Thomas of Villanueva was founded in Havana. This was the only nongovernment institution offering instruction at the university level. There were 86 primary and 10 secondary Evangelical schools in Cuba.[47]

In 1899 the control of the institution of matrimony was wrested from the Church. At that time the civil ceremony was made the only legal

47. Considine, *op. cit.*, pp. 330, 333; Rycroft and Clemmer, *op. cit.*, p. 234; Wyatt MacGaffey and Clifford R. Barnett, *Cuba: its people, its society, its culture* (New Haven, Conn., 1962), p. 201.

form. The next year, however, as has been noted above, General Wood succeeded in having the law changed to make either the civil or the religious marriage legal and binding. Divorce was not recognized. But by the law of July 29, 1918, the civil ceremony was made once more the only legal form. The religious act is valid only when it complies with the requirements of the civil code. The same law recognized absolute divorce. Remarriage is allowed one year after the granting of the divorce decree.[48]

In 1957, when the population of Cuba was 6,166,000, the Catholic population was 5,620,000. There were two archbishops, five bishops, and 690 priests. The ratio of communicants to priests was 8,145 to one. The nuns who worked in schools, hospitals, and charitable institutions numbered 2,408.[49]

Most of the priests and nuns were foreigners, the great majority being Spaniards.[50] But of the hierarchy only one of the prelates was a foreigner. Most of the Cubans were found in the secular clergy, for few of the foreign clergy were engaged in parochial work. The Catholic schools were usually owned, directed, and staffed by foreign regulars. The domination of the Cuban Church by the Spanish clergy had for many years stimulated hopes for a native clergy which never materialized. According to a critical but reliable Canadian clerical authority on the Church in Cuba: "The Spanishness of the Cuban clergy and hierarchy is one of the factors that must be understood if one is to approach the concept of State-Church relations that the Cuban Church tended to regard as an ideal."[51]

Belated efforts by Catholic Action to associate the Church with the life and interests of the lower class showed few results by 1959. The Church continued to be associated with the governing circles and imperialism. According to Dewart's further indictment of the Cuban Church, the hierarchy was reluctant to publish Pope John XXIII's *Pacem in Terris* and considered the Pope to be semi-Communist.[52] The reputation of the Church for corruption and antipopular policies made it one of the principal targets of leaders of revolutionary movements.

48. Article 43 of the Constitution of 1946 reads: "Only marriages authorized by officials having legal capacity to effect them are valid. Civil marriage is gratuitous and shall be recognized by the law. Marriage may be dissolved by agreement of the husband and wife, or in the petition of either of the two for the reasons and in the form established by the law."

49. Considine, *op. cit.*, pp. 330, 333.

50. According to MacGaffey and Barnett, *op. cit.*, p. 203, only one-fifth of the total religious were Cuban.

51. Leslie Dewart, *Christianity and Revolution* (New York, 1963), p. 93.

52. Dewart's article in *Continuum* (Winter, 1964), cited by John A. Mackay, "A Fresh Look at Cuba," *The Christian Century*, LXXXI, No. 32 (August 5, 1964), 986.

The condition of Roman Catholicism in Cuba on the eve of the Castro take-over was not encouraging. Of a nominal Catholic population of over five million, scarcely 10 per cent practiced the Catholic religion to any extent. The Church, which had never been as influential in the national life in Cuba as in other Latin-American countries, was so powerless that active anticlericalism was not and never had been a problem. Opposition to it was collectivist and atheist—such as in Freemasonry, communism, and Protestantism—rather than libertarian and direct. After the wars of independence, to which the lodges contributed, Masonry continued to denounce the Church as a suppressor of liberty.[53] Concerning the threat of atheistic communism the Church was acutely aware and endeavored to combat it, as we shall see. As for Protestantism, the Evangelical Church attained a relatively high degree of strength and influence in Cuba. That Evangelical pastors almost equaled, with 609, the 723 Catholic priests, and that Evangelical churches and schools were numerous, must be tempered by the fact that the Protestant community of 208,584 represented only 3.2 per cent of the population.[54] A far greater threat to the Catholic Church than that presented by Masonry, communism, or Protestantism was the inability of the Church to combat general apathy and indifference and thus retain a hold on its own "nominal" communicants. The greater danger to the Church, therefore, was not enemies from without, but weakness within the Church. It was at such a time of crisis in the life of the Cuban Church that its problems were multiplied by Fidel Castro's seizure of the government on January 1, 1959.

Since the Church had tried to abstain from politics—except for occasional warnings to the faithful not to vote for Communists—it remained silent concerning the Batista dictatorship. But as Batista's power waned the conservatively minded people looked more and more to the Church for leadership and thus forced a political role on it. In July, 1957, the Church, after a meeting of the hierarchy, announced a middle-of-the-road compromise policy, saying that the Church was "outside and above all political parties."[55] The insensitivity of the Cuban Catholic elite to the injustices of the prerevolutionary social situation, and the determination of the hierarchy to remain silent, provoked criticism and even division in the Catholic camp. The leading dissident was the Archbishop of Santiago, Msgr. Enrique Pérez Serrantes, who had consistently opposed Batista. In 1953 he had intervened to save Fidel Castro from death after the failure of the 26 of July, 1953, attack on the

53. MacGaffey and Barnett, *op. cit.*, p. 199.
54. Rycroft and Clemmer, *op. cit.*, p. 234.
55. *Hispanic American Report*, X, No. 6 (July, 1957), 301.

Moncada Army Barracks. In 1957 Archbishop Serrantes in a pastoral letter urged a peaceful solution of the crisis, and in 1958 he led the movement to ask Batista to resign.[56]

It is significant that while the Church was anti-Batista in the last days of his regime, it was not pro-Castro. Nevertheless after Castro took over, many clerics and members of the Catholic laity, seemed to favor coexistence with the revolution which in its early days appeared to be concerned primarily with social justice. Thus, the land reform law of May 17, 1959, was defended by Archbishop Pérez Serrantes and Bishop Evelío Díaz, and also by numerous lay Catholic organizations, as being in line with the papal encyclicals.[57]

If, at the time of his triumph, Fidel Castro appeared to be satisfied with Catholic coöperation, this did not restrain him, a year later, from instituting policies and measures most injurious to the Church and religion. On January 20, 1960, Castro brought the religious question out into the open. He referred to reactionary and counterrevolutionary elements in the clergy and requested the bishops to stop further possible subversive activities.[58] Shortly thereafter the Cuban Catholic Church began to react against the excesses of the revolutionary government. It first manifested its alarm when in May, 1960, Archbishop Enrique Pérez Serrantes of Santiago, the prelate who had regarded Castro as a social reformer, published a pastoral letter expressing concern over the inroads of communism in Cuba and deploring the encouragement of the class struggle. He warned, "The enemy (Communism)...is within the gates (of Cuba) speaking loudly as though on its own property." As Castro turned from liberator to dictator the Archbishop acknowledged his error quickly.[59]

On August 7, the Cuban hierarchy released a pastoral letter condemning Communist influences in the Castro regime. The Vatican envoy, Rev. Father Luis G. Losada Rodríguez, joined in the condemnation of Communist inroads. He said: "The Fidelistas have cleverly masked their Leninist program. The leaders in the Sierra Maestra decided upon it during the early months of their insurrection."[60]

In a television appearance on August 11, 1960, Castro responded to these accusations. He denounced the "fascist" elements of the Church and charged that the Spanish priests—who comprised more than two-

56. MacGaffey and Barnett, *op. cit.*, p. 202; Mackay, *op. cit.*, p. 985.
57. Dewart, *op. cit.*, p. 148.
58. *Ibid.*, p. 155.
59. Irving P. Pflaum, "Trends in the Cuban Revolution," *American Universities Field Service Reports Service*, V, No. 4 (Cuba, August, 1960), 2.
60. *Ibid.*, p. 3.

thirds of the Cuban priesthood—were responsible for antirevolutionary sentiment of the Church. He accused the hierarchy of "systematic provocations against the revolution."[61] Since the clerical attacks did not cease, Castro took measures, by the end of 1960, to make it impossible for the Church to speak publicly again. Also, clerical newspapers were liquidated.

The Bay of Pigs invasion fiasco of April 19, 1961, produced repercussions injurious to the Catholic Church in Cuba. In a speech on May 1, 1961, Castro announced retaliatory measures against counterrevolutionaries, particularly the Spanish "curas falangistas." Alien resident and visitor's visas of all foreign priests would be revoked. In September, 1961, following anti-Communist demonstrations in front of the Havana Cathedral, there was a massive expulsion of Spanish priests. Auxiliary Bishop Eduardo Boza Masvidal, charged with fomenting the demonstrations and plotting against the Revolution, was arrested and deported, although he was a Cuban.[62]

Many Cuban priests also left the country. The papal nuncio opposed the voluntary exodus of the clergy and supported the Cuban government's request that nuns in particular stay at their posts in hospitals, orphanages, and old peoples' homes. The request was in vain for more than four-fifths of the nuns left, and about 400 priests went into exile. In March, 1964, it was reported that of the 700 priests before the revolution, less than 200 remained.[63]

In his speech of May 1, 1961, Fidel Castro also announced that all private schools would be nationalized, without compensation, because of the teaching of counterrevolution. He accused the clergy of poisoning the minds of children. Thus the schools of all sects, including the Catholic schools from the nursery level to the Catholic University of Santo Tomás de Villaneuva, were seized.[64] Religious instruction is now prohibited in public schools, but Marxism-Leninism is taught. Although all Catholic school property has been seized by the Cuban government, it has refrained from nationalizing Church edifices.

Since the flight from Cuba of some 300,000 people, including a majority of the churchgoing Roman Catholics, and most of the clergy and prelates, those church members who remained assumed the task of keeping the organization and the faith alive. The Church policy was to absorb the buffeting and hope for better days. Interestingly, Cuba

---

61. *Hispanic American Report*, XIII, No. 8 (August, 1960), 525.
62. *Hispanic American Report*, XIV, No. 9 (September, 1961), 790; Dewart, *op. cit.*, p. 175.
63. *New York Times*, March 29, 1964.
64. *Ibid.*

maintained diplomatic relations with the Vatican. Although Castro and Cuban officials who had restrained and arrested Catholic bishops had incurred automatic excommunication, there was no formal statement from the Vatican. On the contrary, President Dorticós, in February, 1963, received a medal from Pope John XXIII indicative of improved relations.[65]

It is quite true that among the Church members who remained in Cuba there was a new interest in faith and practice. The old casual attitude toward religious observances was replaced by conscientious observance. In Roman Catholic parishes, despite the loss of communicants, the number of persons attending mass was as great as before the revolution. Catholic Action emphasized teaching the catechism and preparing children for first communion since the private schools were no longer available for this service.

Fidel Castro's measures affecting religion were also imposed on the Protestant churches. They included: all educational institutions taken over by the State; street meetings prohibited; and all social work taken away. Although expulsion edicts did not apply to Protestants, a large number of pastors and other Protestants were part of the exodus after the Bay of Pigs. But despite these losses and reverses, Protestantism under Fidel Castro has been described as "not only holding up but moving up."[66] In fact, the Evangelical Church in Cuba is said to be growing rapidly in membership, zeal, and devotion.

It is the contention of a prominent Protestant spokesman, Dr. John A. Mackay, that "in Cuba today there is basic freedom for all religious faiths." He notes that in Cuba the churches continue to own their own places of worship and that members of the clergy are not discriminated against as such, "so long as they are willing to live within the existing social order." The Mexican government of the early 1930's, says Dr. Mackay, was far more antireligious than the government of Cuba; also, Protestants in Cuba "have immeasurably more freedom to work and witness than do their counterparts in Franco Spain."[67]

There are widely divergent views, however, concerning the existence of religious freedom in Cuba where the regime professes atheistic communism. If freedom is one and indivisible, can we say that there is religious freedom without cultural, social, and political freedom?

65. *Hispanic American Report*, XVI, No. 3 (February, 1963), 129.
66. *Christianity Today*, VII, No. 21 (July 19, 1963), 13.
67. Mackay, *op. cit.*, p. 985.

Chapter XIV

State Church and Free Church in the Republics of Central America

Religion has been one of the most disturbing factors in the history of the republics of Central America. The Catholic Church in two of the republics, Guatemala and El Salvador, undoubtedly suffered more vicissitudes in its fortunes than in other Latin-American countries, with the possible exception of Mexico. Yet, the aggravated nature of the problem was in no sense the result of exaggerated clerical abuses peculiar to Central America. Although it would be futile to deny the existence of clerical predominance in the spiritual, social, and even in the economic and political spheres of these countries, there was no marked difference in this respect from other parts of Spanish America. The bitter, devastating, politico-ecclesiastic conflicts were the result rather of attempts to enforce unwise policies, pro and anticlerical. The extremists among the clericals and antireligionists alternated in control of the governments and, with a vindictiveness common to bigots, insisted on forcing their remedies down the throats of their adversaries. There was no compromise on religious policy. The inevitable result was revolution and counterrevolution, repressive measures and retaliatory measures.

When reports of the Mexican declaration of independence, the *Plan de Iguala*, were received in Guatemala, the captain-general summoned an extraordinary council to decide upon a course of action. On September 15, 1821, the ecclesiastical and civil leaders met in a *Junta Consultativa*. The Archbishop of Guatemala, D. Fray Ramón Casáus, and other ecclesiastics opposed an immediate declaration of independence and counseled delay until they should receive more news from Mexico. The majority of the *junta*, however, voted in favor of an immediate declaration of independence.[1] The rights of religion were amply guar-

---

1. Alejandro Marure, *Bosquejo Histórico de las Revoluciones de Centro-América* (Guatemala, 1877), p. 23; Floyd Cramer, *Our Neighbor Nicaragua* (New York, 1929), p. 45.

anteed by the *junta* which was controlled by the aristocratic class, reinforced by a liberal representation of the clergy. The action of the extraordinary council which met in Guatemala City was supposed to apply to the whole of the captaincy-general, yet the provinces were disposed to act individually. As a matter of fact, the province of Chiapas in a *cabildo abierto*, or town meeting, at Ciudad Real, anticipated the action of Guatemala by declaring independence on September 3, 1821. On the same date Chiapas voted for annexation to the Mexican Empire of Iturbide. The clergy were prominently active in the secession movement in Chiapas, and the oaths of allegiance to the Empire were taken before the ecclesiastical authorities. The clergy, being hostile to the reforms of the liberal government in Spain respecting the Church, looked upon Iturbide as the savior of their ancient prerogatives and monopolies. He was called the "padre salvador de la religión y de la patria." On September 28, 1821, the province of Honduras declared independence of the motherland with the precise stipulation that the religion which all the inhabitants should recognize was the Roman Catholic Apostolic. On October 11, 1821, independence was declared in León, Nicaragua, and on October 29, 1821, in Cartago, Costa Rica. In the *Junta Superior Gubernativa*, the provisional governing body in Costa Rica, four of the twelve members were clerics.[2]

All the provinces of Central America with the exception of El Salvador consented to annexation to Mexico. This action was sponsored by the Central American clergy because of the ascendancy enjoyed by the clericals in the Empire. In the short period that Central America was an appendage of the Empire of Iturbide, no change took place in the relations of Church and State. When the Central Americans, after the downfall of Augustín I, determined to establish their political independence under republican institutions, a National Constituent Assembly met in Guatemala City on June 24, 1823. The president of the Assembly was José Matías Delgado, a cleric, of whom more later. On July 1, the Assembly proclaimed independence from Mexico and the establishment of a confederation of the provinces. In this proclamation the Catholic religion was declared to be that of the State. In the words of the proclamation it was "recognized as a public duty, that the only religion of the Federation should be the Catholic Apostolic Roman."[3]

2. Francisco Montero Barrantes, *Elementos de Historia de Costa Rica* (San José de Costa Rica, 1892), pp. 174, 187; Félix Salgado, *Elementos de Historia de Honduras* (Tegucigalpa, 1927), p. 26.

3. Barrantes, *op. cit.*, p. 204. Chiapas was not represented in the Assembly, since that province continued attached to Mexico. The Mexican Republic recognized the Federation of Central America on August 20, 1824.

The withdrawal of the Mexican troops under General Filisola, on August 3, 1823, removed a considerable restraint upon the Liberals, and they were at greater liberty to carry out their plans. The membership of the Assembly was sharply divided into two groups. The Conservative or Moderate party, called contemptuously the "Serviles" by their opponents, was favorable to the centralistic form of government and Church retention of its *fueros*. The Liberals or Radicals were federalists and desired to see the abolition of unjust privileges. They were anxious for clerical reform. This party alignment, which appeared for the first time in the Constituent Assembly of 1823, was destined to perpetuation through most of the histories of the Central American republics. The Serviles, although in the majority in the Assembly, had to give way to the more aggressive, impetuous, and better organized Liberals. Thus the Serviles were not able to prevent the passage, in 1824, of certain anticlerical laws. One of these subjected episcopal pastorals to the control of the government. In short, pastorals had to receive the *pase* like papal bulls. The immediate occasion for this law was the issuance of antirepublican pastorals by Archbishop Casáus. Another act provided that appointments of parish priests by the archbishop should be previously submitted for confirmation by the chief of state. A third law deprived the clergy of their privilege to import goods into the country free of duties.[4] On November 22, 1824, after seventeen months' deliberation, a constitution was finally proclaimed for the Federal Republic of Central America. Article 11 declared Roman Catholicism to be the religion of the State to the exclusion of the public exercise of any other. With the exception of the additional contradictory guarantee of toleration the Federal Constitution avoided the subject of religion. This omission contributed to subsequent acrimonious arguments as to whether the Federal or State governments controlled patronage. The clerics were by no means satisfied with the Constitution, because they felt that it did not accord them sufficient guarantees. Accordingly, many of them refused to swear an oath of allegiance to the Federation. In the end the clergy submitted and swore the necessary oaths.[5]

The Constitutional Congress of the "Estados Federados de Centro América" was installed (February 6, 1825) under Liberal control. On April 21, 1825, the Congress chose Manuel José Arce, presumed to be a Liberal, as the president of the Federation. Before being made president Arce had attacked clerical abuses, particularly in the regular

4. Marure, *op. cit.*, pp. 111, 160; H. H. Bancroft, *History of Central America* (San Francisco, 1887), III, 70-71, 628.

5. Augusto C. Coello, *El Digesto Constitucional de Honduras* (Tegucigalpa, 1923), p. 14; Marure, *op. cit.*, p. 120.

orders. With the government in their control the Liberals decided that the time had arrived to do away with clerical privileges and bring the Church under the subjection of the civil authorities.

During the short-lived Liberal ascendancy, several laws were passed in 1826 against the Church. The tithes were reduced one-half; prelates of regular orders were forbidden to recognize their respective generals in Spain; and twenty-three years was established as the minimum age for entry into any convent. The anticlerical laws of 1826 aroused the ire of the clergy and serious troubles ensued. The clericals, seizing this opportunity to destroy the opposition, gave utterance to most fanatical language and sowed alarm among the people. Even liberal-minded men, opposed to the too precipitate action of the extremists, took up the cause of the Church. By 1827 the Liberal control had been broken and once more the Conservatives were in the saddle.[6]

In the meantime, the States of the Federation were organizing governments under constitutions adopted in the following order: El Salvador, June 12, 1824; Costa Rica, January 21, 1825; Guatemala, October 11, 1825; Honduras, December 11, 1825; and Nicaragua, April 8, 1826. In these constitutions the Roman Catholic faith was declared to be the religion of the State. A serious and troublesome question over the control of ecclesiastical patronage confronted the government of the Federation immediately after its creation.

For many years, dating back into the Spanish colonial period, the people of Costa Rica and El Salvador had desired the establishment of separate and independent dioceses for the provinces, but their petitions were repulsed with exasperating regularity. When independence was won, the Salvadoreños, led by the independentist cleric D. Matías Delgado, who was ambitious to be the first bishop, endeavored to influence the National Constituent Assembly to establish a bishopric in El Salvador. But the Assembly decided "that without prior and express accord with the papacy, no one could or ought to be presented for election to the prelacies." This did not balk Delgado, for he influenced the Constituent Congress of El Salvador ("less circumspect than the national representation") to erect a diocese in the State. The parish of San Salvador was converted into a diocese and Delgado was appointed the first bishop. The archbishop of Guatemala, D. Ramón Casáus, published an edict, June 21, 1824, declaring null and void the action of the Congress of Salvador. Delgado refused to resign and acted as bishop, though without papal confirmation, for about four years. El Salvador sent a representative to Rome to solicit the confirmation of Delgado by

6. Bancroft, *op. cit.*, III, 628; Marure, *op. cit.*, p. 160.

the pope. The pontiff refused to accede, and instead, on December 1, 1826, he issued a brief to the metropolitan of Guatemala declaring the acts of El Salvador illegitimate and contrary to the rights of the Holy See. All acts of Delgado were null and void and he was given fifty days to renounce his office under pain of being branded a schismatic.[7]

The controversy concerning the diocese of San Salvador had a deep influence on the politics of all Central America. The Liberals supported Delgado, the Serviles supported the Archbishop of Guatemala. The National Constituent Assembly finally concerned itself with the question and appointed a committee to study the nature of patronage, particularly as it related to the establishment of dioceses. The patronage committee, or *Comisión de Negocios Eclesiásticos*, reported September 2, 1824, that (1) the Nation did not enjoy the right of patronage; (2) if it did, it would be simple patronage, or the right of presentation to a bishopric and not for the erection of an episcopal see; and (3) granted it acquired the patronage, it would be national in scope and could not be exercised by individual states. The committee also reported that El Salvador did not have the right to erect a bishopric because only the pope possessed this power.

The National Assembly accepted the report of the committee and declared, by decree of July 18, 1825, that the acts of the government of El Salvador were illegal. It was hoped that this action would calm the Archbishop. Then, to satisfy the populace, the Congress proceeded to create a bishopric for El Salvador. This pretended assumption of the right of patronage by the Federal Congress was distasteful to both the clergy and the people. The federal action, therefore, was generally ignored. Even the president refused to comply with the law.

The inhabitants of Costa Rica had also been desirous for many years to have a bishopric of their own, which should be independent of the episcopal see of León, Nicaragua. After the establishment of an independent State, the Assembly of Costa Rica was unwilling to remain dependent any longer on Nicaragua in ecclesiastical matters. Accordingly, on September 29, 1825, a decree was issued establishing the bishopric of San José with limits to be the same as those of the State. Fray Luis Barcía was named bishop and the chapter of León was requested to delegate his functions to him. The chapter, regarding the action as uncanonical, appealed to the Assembly of Costa Rica to revoke the act in order to avoid a schism as in El Salvador. Fortunately Fray Luis García refused to accept the episcopal dignity and thus saved Costa

---

7. Marure, *op. cit.*, pp. 129-35; Manuel Montúfar, *Memorias para la Historia de la Revolución de Centro-América* (Jalapa, 1832), p. 34.

Rica from serious consequences. The Costa Ricans were not so obdurate as the Salvadoreños and they decided to let the matter drop.[8]

Arce's election to the presidency, on April 21, 1825, was the result of a compromise between the parties. He pledged himself to remain neutral on certain matters, one of these being the question of the bishopric. He promised to leave the decision as to the creation of the see of San Salvador to the next Congress. But, as has been noted, its action was unsatisfactory to the President, espousing as he did the cause of the Serviles who wished to abolish the bishopric of El Salvador. The anticlerical laws of 1826 were also displeasing to him, for he greatly desired not to alienate the Serviles. In the end, Arce, once a Liberal, became the head of the Serviles, and in league with the Archbishop, who had once preached against him, and with the friars who had called him a heretic, he supported the very opinions he had once combatted. But there was no hypocrisy or selfishness in the about-face made by Arce, for he acted on pure and upright motives. He did not accept the presidency as a partisan, but rather as the representative of all the people. Sincerely desirous of abolishing factionalism and establishing peace and harmony, he saw in the Liberal anticlerical program disruptive factors which had to be curbed.

For about two years (1827-28) the Serviles were in the ascendancy. The reaction was carried to limits repugnant to Arce, but over which he had no control. Guatemala in particular was, in the opinion of a Liberal critic, under the domination of "the *togados* and *tonsurados*, who promulgated laws fit for the middle ages."[9] Repression and reaction begot the inevitable—revolution. The Liberals took up arms and found an able leader in Francisco Morazán, a man of exceptional talents. Arce presented a weak opposition to the victorious march of the Liberals, perhaps because of his disgust with all extremists. At any rate, Morazán captured Guatemala City and Arce withdrew from the country. From April 13, 1829, when Morazán occupied the plaza of Guatemala City, until April 13, 1839, when General Carrera occupied it, the history of Central America was marked by an incessant struggle between the Serviles and the Liberals, with the latter in control of the government throughout this period.[10]

8. *Revista de Costa Rica en el Siglo XIX* (San José de Costa Rica, 1902), pp. 309-11; Barrantes, *op. cit.*, p. 217.

9. Raúl Aguero, *Guatemala, La Revolución Liberal de 1871* (San José de Costa Rica, 1914), p. 8.

10. Mary W. Williams, "The Ecclesiastical Policy of Francisco Morazán and the Other Central American Liberals," in the *Hispanic American Historical Review*, III, No. 2 (May, 1920), 128.

After seizing control of the Federal government the Liberals instituted measures against their real or supposed enemies. The stage was thus set for the inauguration of an anticlerical reform, the most drastic in all of Latin America up to that date. The Liberals struck first at the Archbishop. Ramón Casáus y Torres, Spanish-born and a Dominican friar, had been nominated for the archiepiscopal see of Guatemala by the Spanish Council of the Regency on March 30, 1811. Shortly after he assumed office (although it is to be noted that the papal bull of his confirmation was not issued until 1815), he took a very active part in suppressing the independentist revolt in Granada. He published an edict declaring the rebels of 1811 to be monsters; the names "heretics" and "friends of independence" were synonymous to him. After the declaration of Central American independence, the Archbishop continued to be an inveterate enemy of republican and liberal institutions. The government was forced, because of the antirepublican propaganda of the prelate, to restrict his activities by subjecting his pastorals to the rule of the *pase*. President José Francisco Barrundia, a puppet of Morazán, preferred a charge that the Archbishop was plotting against the government and ordered his expulsion from the country. Franciscans, Dominicans, and Recollet friars were also accused of plotting and their banishment was ordered. On the night of July 10-11, 1829, armed forces, acting under orders of the president, seized the metropolitan and the friars, 289 in number, escorted them to the Atlantic Coast and embarked them for Havana. Archbishop Casáus accepted a pension from the Spanish government in Cuba, and later was appointed administrator of the vacant see of Havana. He held this office until his death and persistently refused to return to Guatemala although a decree which declared him a traitor had been revoked in 1839.[11]

On July 28, 1829, monastic orders were abolished by Congress and their property confiscated. On September 7, 1829, another law prohibited the entry into the Federation of members of any religious order. On June 13, 1830, the Congress confirmed the banishment of the Archbishop. He was formally charged with opposing independence, inciting rebellion, and receiving a subsidy from the Spanish king. The see of Guatemala was declared vacant, and until it would be canonically filled, its income was to go to the national treasury. The chapter was to name, with the approval of the government, a vicar and governor.[12] The cathedral chapter named a vicar, but Casáus resisted the legality of this action and named a vicar on his own account. The whole situation

11. Bancroft, *op. cit.*, III, 30, 103-4, 628; Marure, *op. cit.*, p. 111; Montúfar, *Memorias*, p. 170; Williams, *Morazán*, pp. 129-33.

12. Lorenzo Montúfar, *El General Francisco Morazán* (Guatemala, 1896), pp. 154-59.

remained in suspension until Pope Gregory XVI declared the capitular vicar to be the legal administrator.

On May 2, 1832, the Federal Congress proclaimed religious toleration. It decreed that all inhabitants of the Republic were free to adore God according to their beliefs and that the national government protected the exercise of this liberty. Later, Congress declared marriage to be a civil contract, and the religious ceremony was not necessary for the satisfaction of legal requirements. Also, the right of appointing to ecclesiastical dignities belonged to the nation and was to be exercised by the president.[13]

The state governments were also under the control of the reformers during this period (1829-39), and by state legislation the federal anticlerical program was reinforced. The *jefe de estado*, or governor, of the State of Guatemala was Mariano Gálvez, the right-hand man of General Morazán. Gálvez secularized the cemeteries, reduced the number of Church holidays, allowed nuns to leave convents and take their dowries, declared marriage a civil contract, and provided for absolute divorce. The marriage and divorce laws were not favorably received by the people. He had overstepped the bounds of prudence and provoked a revolt. The Serviles and clerics fanned the flames of discontent by branding him a heretic and a tyrant. In 1838 Gálvez fell, "a victim of the fanatics and hypocrites," says an admirer. After the overthrow of the reformer all his laws against the Church were suspended, the ecclesiastical *fueros* were restored, and the Roman Catholic faith was reaffirmed as the religion of the State of Guatemala.[14]

In Costa Rica, the *jefe de estado*, Braulio Carrillo, also reduced the number of religious feast days. He defended his action by saying that the too numerous festivals were injurious to public morals and the prosperity of the State. On March 31, 1835, the Assembly of Costa Rica decreed the abolition of the tithes. The government's treasury assumed the obligations met in the past by the tithes. Their abolition resulted in a rebellion in which many clerics were implicated. As a result, one was executed, several were banished, and many more were fined.[15]

The constitution of the State of Honduras, although recognizing the Roman Catholic faith as the State religion to the exclusion of the public exercise of any other, gave to the executive authority the right to approve titles for prelacies and other ecclesiastical benefices. An amendment, adopted in February, 1835, guaranteed religious toleration and

13. *Ibid.*, pp. 17-19; Bancroft, *op. cit.*, III, 629.
14. Rafael Aguirre Cinta, *Lecciones de Historia General de Guatemala* (Guatemala, 1899), pp. 106-7; Montúfar, *Morazán*, pp. 15-17.
15. Barrantes, *op. cit.*, pp. 228-32.

"the maintenance of all cults in harmony with the laws." Other acts were passed affecting the clergy, among these being one legalizing the marriage of secular priests.

The ascendancy of Morazán, Gálvez, and the Liberals was terminated in 1839 when the forces of localism and religious fanaticism proved to be too strong for them. The immediate cause of the reactionary revolt was the belief of the fanatical Indians, encouraged by the priests, that the poisoning of the wells by the Liberals was the cause of a cholera scourge. The leader of the Indians was Rafael Carrera, a young, illiterate, mountaineer mestizo. A mere tool of the priests, Carrera declared a prime object of the Servile revolt to be the complete restoration to the clergy of their *fueros*. In March, 1839, Morazán was defeated and exiled and the Federation of Central America was dissolved.[16]

THE REPUBLICS OF CENTRAL AMERICA

Guatemala

One of the first acts of the Constitutional Assembly of Guatemala, which was summoned by Carrera to frame a new constitution for the republic, was the abrogation of the reform laws of the Liberals and the restoration of the ecclesiastical *fueros*. The Serviles undid what their opponents had done. Once more the pendulum swung to the other extreme, and for many years, particularly in Guatemala, the Serviles had their inning and made the most of it. From 1839 to 1865 General Rafael Carrera, dictator of Guatemala and recognized leader of the Serviles, dominated nearly all of Central America. He was a tower of strength to the Catholic Church.

Not only were the *fueros* restored to the clergy of Guatemala, but the monastic orders were reëstablished and the exiled friars allowed to return. Guatemala was the only one of the Central American republics which revoked the ban against the regulars. Clerical exiles like Archbishop Casáus were invited to return, but since the metropolitan refused, Archbishop Coadjutor Francisco de Paula García Pelaez took charge of the see. In 1843 the Jesuits, who had been excluded since the expulsion of 1767, were allowed into the country. With the passage of the years the union of Church and State became more and more intimate. In the Constitution of 1851 the Church was granted representation in the Congress, the chapter being given two deputies. The next year, on October 7, 1852, the Cardinal-Secretary Antonelli and D. Fernando de Lorenzana for Guatemala, signed a concordat, which was ratified by President

16. Coello, *op. cit.*, pp. 69, 85; Williams, *Morazán*, p. 142.

Carrera. By this agreement, which is notable as being the first concordat concluded with any Latin-American country, the republic recognized the Roman Catholic religion as the sole and exclusive religion of the State; promised to preserve the tithes and pay to the Church in addition a fixed sum from the national treasury; granted the clerics all kinds of privileges including that of control of education and the censorship of books. In return for these concessions the president of the republic received from the pope the right of the patronage, i.e., presentation.[17] The relations between Carrera and the Vatican, as can be imagined, were very close. In 1853, Carrera was decorated by the Holy Father with the Grand Cross of the Order of Saint Gregory the Great, of the military class. This was a reward for his encouragement of Catholicism, and truly he merited recognition as a staunch and uncompromising supporter of the faith.[18]

After the death of Carrera, in 1865, Vicente Cerna became president of Guatemala. Cerna, a Conservative, was also a warm friend of the Church. In fact, he was charged with being a too warm friend of the Jesuits. Although Cerna was reëlected to the presidency in 1869, the election was closely contested by the Liberals led by Miguel García Granados, a deputy. The rapid increase of Liberal strength, particularly in the middle classes of the towns and in the army, was an omen of impending change in the political situation. But true to tradition, the Liberals, now strong in the Congress, were unwilling to abide by the decision of the polls. In 1870, Granados headed an armed revolt. The uprising proved to be abortive and Granados sought safety in flight across the Mexican border. The overthrow of Dueñas, Servile dictator of El Salvador, by the Liberals of El Salvador and Honduras early in 1871, was a blow to conservatism throughout Central America, and revived the hopes of the Liberals of Guatemala. Granados organized a new expedition in Chiapas and invaded Guatemala. The final victory of the Liberals and the overthrow of Cerna were accomplished on June 29, 1871. Until a constitution could be framed and a regular government organized, García Granados governed as provisional president.[19]

The inevitable complement of Liberal political ascendancy was another anticlerical reform more radical than any of the past. The first decree of the revolutionary government, dated May 24, 1871, expelled the Jesuits from the republic as obstacles to liberal ideas. Seventy-three Jesuits, most of them foreigners, were bundled aboard a steamer and shipped out of the country. They first went to El Salvador where they

17. *Raccolta di Concordati*, pp. 810-21.
18. Cinta, *op. cit.*, pp. 121, 139-43.
19. Bancroft, *op. cit.*, III, 415, 424-25.

fared no better. The property of the Jesuits was confiscated. The tithes were suppressed and the government agreed to defray any deficit incurred in consequence by the diocese. The extinction of all male religious orders was next decreed. The native friars were permitted to remain in the country and were given monthly allowances for their support, but they were forbidden to show themselves in public with their clerical garbs. The property of the regulars was ordered confiscated. The State also absorbed properties held in mortmain. In the last months of the provisional presidency of García Granados the *fuero eclesiástico* in both civil and criminal causes was abolished, and the freedom of worship was decreed. These acts meant the destruction of the Concordat.[20]

According to Bancroft, when García Granados revolted he had at first no intention of attacking the Church. He denied that his government had ever contemplated wounding the religious feelings of the nation. The resolve of the new régime "to cut loose of the ecclesiastical incubus, and to establish the supremacy of the civil authority in the State on a strong basis," was forced, says Bancroft, by "the priests who would not rest contented with the loss of their former high standing."[21] The statement is deficient in that it fails to acknowledge an uncompromising spirit on both sides. The Liberals were not inclined to tolerate the perpetuation of clerical privileges granted by Carrera, and, on the other hand, the clergy, very logically, were disposed to defend their rights. In October, 1871, Archbishop Bernardo Piñol and Mariano Ortiz Urruela, Bishop of Teya *in partibus infidelium*, were ordered to leave the country because of their activities in promoting resistance to the reform. Papal relations were temporarily broken.

Justo R. Barrios succeeded García Granados to the presidency in June, 1873. Granados as an executive had not been a success; he was unable to rule with the necessary firmness and as a result the reactionaries kept the country in turmoil. Barrios, on the contrary, ruled with a hand of iron; he tolerated no opposition. Under his dictatorship the forces of conservatism were well-nigh annihilated. Numerous acts of despotism and brutality were attributed to him by his clerical enemies, and impartial judgment agrees that these stories were basically true. The anticlerical policy adopted by Barrios has been compared with that of Morazán. He extended the prohibition of religious orders to the nunneries, confiscated their properties, and allowed each ex-nun a life pension of twelve dollars per month. All religious communities of either sex were forbidden in Guatemala. The disamortized capital was ordered

20. *Ibid.*, III, 425-27; Cinta, *op. cit.*, pp. 196-201.
21. Bancroft, *op. cit.*, III, 425.

to be devoted to the aid of commerce and agriculture. The Church buildings were used for educational purposes. Civil marriage was declared legal, cemeteries were secularized, and ecclesiastics were forbidden to appear outside of the churches with their frocks or other official insignia.[22] The anticlerical reform measures of Granados and Barrios were given permanency by being incorporated into a new constitution. This document, adopted in December, 1879, and modified later, was the instrument under which Guatemala was governed until 1945. According to its terms, the Church was denied juridic personality, could own no property, not even its temples of worship, and was prohibited from participating in political discussion. Also, the Constitution provided for suppression of monasteries, secularization of public education, and complete separation of Church and State. The power of the Church had been definitely destroyed.

In 1884 the breach in Church and State relations was partially healed by the signing of a new concordat. By the terms of the new treaty Guatemala abandoned its rights to national patronage and the papacy renounced claims to a privileged position for the Church in Guatemala. The principal provisions of the Concordat were as follows:

1. The Roman Pontiff was guaranteed the right of free communication with the prelates, clergy, and people of Guatemala.
2. The right of governing the clergy, the Church, and maintaining discipline was vested in the ordinary.
3. The diocesan seminary of Guatemala was to be reëstablished and its administration and control were to vest in the diocesan prelate.
4. Occupants of the metropolitan see were to be appointed by the pope *motu proprio.*
5. When a vacancy should occur in the metropolitan see, the chapter should proceed freely to elect a capitular vicar.
6. The clergy were exempt from military service.
7. In compensation for properties of the Church which were confiscated by the State, the government of Guatemala assumed the obligation of paying to the Church annually 30,000 pesos.
8. The pope acquiesced in the confiscations, and agreed never to molest the holders of properties of which the Church had been deprived.[23]

Apparently both Church and State in Guatemala had abandoned pretentions to privilege in each others' domain. Yet, the formal separation of Church and State was only theoretical, for in fact, the Church remained very much under temporal restraint. Although the govern-

22. *Ibid.,* III, 427, 432-33; Cinta, *op. cit.,* p. 201.
23. *Raccolta di Concordati,* pp. 1018-20.

ment retained no rights of nomination to the metropolitan see or its administration, it continued to interfere, endeavoring in this way to enjoy the privileges of patronage without assuming its responsibilities. Evidence of its interference was the fact that most of the archbishops suffered exile by the government.

The otherthrow of the Jorge Ubico dictatorship was followed in 1945 by the adoption of a new constitution notable for its advanced socio-economic features. This constitution, drafted by a body in which an anticlerical majority prevailed, did not alter the anticlerical legislation despite Catholic endeavors to mitigate its rigors. In Article 29 the Constitution provided: "The profession of all religions is free, as well as the practice of all cults, without any preference and *in the interior of churches* (i.e., toleration inside of churches alone). Religious societies and groups or their members as such, and ministers of cults, may not intervene in politics or in questions related to the organization of labor." Article 32 provided: "The establishment of conventual congregations and of all kinds of monastic institutions or associations . . . is prohibited." A slight concession to Catholics was the grant, under the right of assembly, of "religious demonstrations outside of churches."

A decade later, in 1955, Guatemalans were again engaged in drafting a constitution. This followed the overthrow of the pro-Communist government of Jacobo Arbenz by Carlos Castillo Armas. Another prominent opponent of the Moscow-oriented Arbenz regime was the Archbishop of Guatemala, Mariano Rossell y Arellano. On April 9, 1964, the Archbishop published a pastoral letter calling attention of all Catholics to the presence of communism in Guatemala and demanding that the people "rise as a single man against this enemy of God and country."[24]

The Constituent Assembly which convened in September, 1955, was composed largely of conservative Catholics. Efforts of the clericals to restore the established Church were defeated by Castillo Armas and his majority in the Assembly.[25] The Church, however, was not denied important concessions. It was granted juridic personality and allowed to acquire and possess real estate provided that it be used for religious, social welfare, or educational purposes. Since this was not retroactive the properties confiscated in the past were not restored. The old ban

24. *Carta Pastoral sobre el Communismo Ateo en Guatemala, Abril de 1954* (Tegucigalpa, Honduras, 1954). In recognition of his anti-Communist services Archbishop Rossell y Arellano was decorated by Castillo Armas with the Order of Liberation.

25. *Hispanic American Report*, VIII, No. 5 (June, 1955), 205-6; No. 9 (October, 1955), 406. Archbishop Rossell y Arellano demanded that the Constituent Assembly give the Roman Catholic Church "a pre-eminent position over other religions and the establishment of complete Catholic instruction in all schools."

on conventual establishments was removed, and, although religious associations and ministers of all faiths were forbidden to intervene in political affairs, the old prohibition of clerical participation in labor questions was rescinded. The Church also won a concession pertaining to education. The new constitution provided: "The law will regulate the teaching of religion in public schools. The state will not give this education and it will be optional." Thus, the door was opened to the teaching of Catholicism in government schools by clericals or religious on an optional basis.[26] The exchange of diplomatic representation with the Vatican was continued.

The Constitution did not alter the denial of validity to religious wedding services. Since 1879 civil marriage had been the only legal form in Guatemala. A ceremony by a priest could follow the civil rites and generally did, but this did not satisfy legal requirements. In 1959 a law permitted clergymen to perform the civil marriages. Thus, in a broad sense the religious ceremony became legal. After one year of married life absolute divorce is legal on application by mutual consent, or on grounds of a determined cause.[27]

There are few Catholic schools in Guatemala, only 77 in 1960, whereas before 1871 they were to be found in all of the villages of the republic. Today most of the Catholic schools cater to the children of middle and upper class families. The Jesuits appear most active, but Franciscans, Augustinians, and Maryknollers[28] are also prominent. The Rafael Landívar Catholic University in Guatemala City is a new institution which opened its doors in February, 1962. Its second year enrollment was only about 325 students, but it projects an enrollment in 1966 of about 2,000. It remains for the future to determine the influence of Rafael Landívar on Catholic education in Guatemala. The illiteracy rate is estimated at about 70 per cent.

The Catholic Church in Guatemala suffers from the same illness which plagues the Church throughout Latin America, i.e., a shortage of priests. Serving a nominal Catholic population of about three million there are only 279 (1960 census) priests, or a ratio of 11,100 Catholics per priest.[29] One archbishop and seven bishops comprise the hierarchy.

As for religious practices, Guatemala is notorious for the intermingling of pagan and Christian rites in the ceremonies of the Indians. According to Whetten, "There is a general but usually vague belief in

26. *Ibid.*, VIII, No. 6 (July, 1955), 257.
27. Civil Code of Guatemala, Articles 123 and 182 (MS).
28. A goal of the Maryknoll schools is the formation of an indigenous clergy. They present to the Indians the religious vocation as a possibility.
29. *Statistical Abstract of Latin America, 1963*, p. 22.

God and Christ, who are thought to be all powerful and preëminent but are too distant from man to exert influence on him directly. Prayers are therefore commonly offered to lesser deities in the hope that they will intercede."[30] Although most of the Indians have been baptized, they persist in idol worship. The Church has few illusions as to the depth of the Indians' faith.

Next to the shortage of priests, responsibility for the failures of the Catholic Church in Guatemala has been attributed by Archbishop Rossell y Arellano to the increased activities of Protestant missionaries. In this instance the prelate did not exaggerate the Protestant "threat" as have the clergy in other Latin American countries. Of a total population of 3,546,000, the Protestant community was, in 1960, 106,884. The Protestant clergy was 337 in contrast to 279 Catholic clergy.[31]

Most of the Protestant missionaries are engaged in educational, health, and welfare work, in addition to their regular religious activities. Small Evangelical congregations can now be found in the larger towns throughout the country. In addition to any religious appeal which Protestantism might offer, it is attractive to some Indians and *ladinos* because of the practical nature of missionary activities related to the improvement of life in this world. The principal Protestant groups operating in the country are: Presbyterians (the largest), Baptists, Methodists, Nazarenes, Seventh Day Adventists, Quakers, and Mormons.[32]

Since the general attitude of the Catholic clergy is that the Evangelicals are interlopers trying to win converts from an already established Christian cult, the Protestant missionaries are regarded with suspicion and resentment. The priests have charged, with considerable truth, that the anticlerical laws were more rigidly enforced against Catholics than against Protestants. On the other hand the missionaries are often unsparing in their denunciation of priests for neglecting to improve the moral and physical well-being of their parishioners. According to a Protestant minister, "the priest is only one step removed from the witch-doctor—he is an agent of ignorance, idolatry and reaction."[33]

The legal status of the Catholic Church in Guatemala is much improved since 1954. It is no longer denied its freedom, and so is un-

---

30. Nathan L. Whetten, *Guatemala, the land and the people* (New Haven, Conn., 1961), p. 289. Also see Mary P. Holleran, *Church and State in Guatemala* (New York, 1949), pp. 223-35.

31. W. Stanley Rycroft and Myrtle M. Clemmer, *A Factual Study of Latin America* (New York, 1963), p. 234.

32. Whetten, *op. cit.*, pp. 308-9.

33. Holleran, *op. cit.*, pp. 251-52.

hampered by the government to perform its spiritual mission.[34] It is apparent however, that the work of "re-Christianizing" the nation is beyond the capacity of the Church, and consequently this task must be shared with other cults. It would appear that there is ample opportunity for all who wish to promote the spiritual, moral, social, and economic welfare of the Guatemalan people.

El Salvador

Guatemala's little neighbor, El Salvador, experienced an almost identical history of ecclesiastical relationships. This was the inevitable result of the all-too-common practice by the Central American republics of interfering in the internal affairs of each other. Yet, fortunate for the historian, this interrelationship made for a certain continuity and harmony of development in all of the republics.

After the overthrow of Morazán, the Conservatives in El Salvador set up an independent republic under a constitution (1841) which recognized only the Roman Catholic religion. Then Dr. Jorge Viteri y Ungo was sent to Rome to petition the pope to create a bishopric of San Salvador. The petition was granted. On September 28, 1842, Pope Gregory XVI signed a bull creating the episcopal see, and in October of the same year Viteri assumed the episcopal dignity as the first Bishop of San Salvador. Viteri's episcopal reign was short and stormy. Although he directed his clergy to refrain from interfering in political affairs, he forced the retirement of President Guzmán and established his puppet, Malespín, in the presidency (February, 1844). For a time the Bishop was dominant, but eventually his arrogance turned public opinion against him. In 1847 President Aguilar issued a decree to enforce the article of the penal code which condemned the practice of ecclesiastics making use of their spiritual offices to promote political disturbances. The Bishop was ordered out of Salvador and went to reside in Nicaragua. He was later transferred by the pope to the diocese of León.[35]

At the request of the government of El Salvador, the pope preconized Tomás Miguel Piñeda y Zaldana as administrator of the diocese with the right of succession. When Viteri was moved to the see of Nicaragua, Piñeda became the second bishop of San Salvador. But he also had his troubles with temporal authorities. The government, at that time in control of the Liberals, required the clergy to take an oath of allegiance.

34. The suspension of the Constitution of 1956 by the military coup of March, 1963, did not alter the laws concerning religion.

35. *Revista de Costa Rica en Siglo XIX*, p. 312; Bancroft, *op cit.*, III, 289-94; Hernáez, *Colección de Bulas*, II, 110.

This they refused to do, and Bishop Piñeda and numerous clerics fled to Guatemala, where they were kindly received by Carrera. When a change of government occurred in El Salvador, Bishop Piñeda returned and ruled until his death in 1875.[36] On June 10, 1862, President Barrios ratified a concordat which had been negotiated with Cardinal Antonelli by Fernando de Lorenzana. The terms of the instrument followed the same lines as those set down in 1852 in the concordats of Guatemala and Costa Rica.[37]

The Conservative president of El Salvador who welcomed the return of exiled Bishop Piñeda was Francisco Dueñas, an ardent defender of the clerical interests. Dueñas at one time had taken the vows as a Dominican, but when the convents were closed in 1829, he left the cloister and secured a papal dispensation. During the presidency of Dueñas (1863-71) the clerical party was in the ascendancy and El Salvador experienced a far-reaching Conservative reaction. The privileged clerical status was constitutionalized in 1864.

The Conservative régime was terminated in 1871 by a combined attack upon Dueñas by the Liberals of Honduras and El Salvador. After 1871 the histories of the ecclesiastical reform movements in El Salvador and Guatemala were almost identical. Liberal governments established in both republics simultaneously instituted the same reforms and then, about the same time gave permanence to these reforms in constitutions. Prior to the Liberal revolution of 1871 no other faith than the Catholic was tolerated in El Salvador. But as a result of the revolt, freedom of thought and religion was proclaimed, the cemeteries were removed from clerical control, civil marriage was legalized, education was made non-clerical, and monastic orders were abolished.[38] All of these changes were embodied in El Salvador's many constitutions preceding that of 1962, which removed many of the old restrictions on the Catholic Church.

Under the régime of the Constitution of 1962, Church and State in El Salvador are separated. Nearly all of the anticlerical laws of previous years are retained. The government does not enjoy rights in the election of ecclesiastical officers, nor does it contribute in any way to the support of religion. The Constitution guarantees the free exercise of all faiths and provides that no religious act shall serve to establish the civil status of persons.[39] Monastic orders are prohibited. When Church

36. Bancroft, *op. cit.*, III, 303, 632.
37. *Raccolta di Concordati*, pp. 960-70.
38. Bancroft, *op. cit.*, III, 392; Robertson, *op. cit.*, p. 452; International Bureau of American Republics, Bulletin No. 58, *The Republic of Salvador* (Washington, 1892), p. 33; *Constitución Política de la República de El Salvador* (San Salvador, 1914).
39. The civil marriage is the only legal ceremony.

and State were separated in 1871, the Salvadoreños showed restraint in foregoing the nationalization of Church properties such as ecclesiastical edifices, schools, and dwellings. But, although the juridic personality of the Church was recognized, it was prohibited from acquiring real estate except for the actual services of the respective corporation. No restriction was placed upon its ability to receive bequests, providing they were not in real estate. The Constitution of 1962 removed the restriction on the acquisition of real property.

The position of the Church with reference to education has been no different in El Salvador from that in Guatemala. After 1871 public education was divorced from all religious instruction. Nor were clerics allowed to teach in the public schools. Article 200 of the Constitution of 1962, however, allows religious instruction in public schools at the option of parents. In 1960 there were 88 Catholic schools in El Salvador serving about one-fifth of the total school population. It is interesting that the religious sisters enrolled about 70 per cent of all girls in their grade and high schools.[40]

There is no concordat between El Salvador and the Vatican. Official diplomatic representatives, nevertheless, are exchanged. Following early friction and bitterness, amicable relations have existed in recent years between El Salvador and the papacy. This was evidenced by the elevation, in 1929, of the see of San Salvador to the archiepiscopal rank. In addition to the archbishop, there are five bishops, and 277 priests. Of the 2,520,000 people representing the total population, 2,108,000 or 83.7 per cent are rated as members of the Catholic community. There are 7,600 Catholics per priest.[41] The Catholic Church in El Salvador also suffers from a priest shortage.

In a critical appraisal of the status of Roman Catholicism in El Salvador, a Maryknoll Father reported in 1958 that 80 per cent of 2,000,000 inhabitants live in rural areas where Catholicism can hardly be expected to be outstanding. A deficiency in the knowledge of doctrine allowed superstitions to replace true Catholic teachings. The social environment was described as "not Christian but pagan." Catholicism was practiced only occasionally.[42] Another Maryknoll writer struck a more optimistic note. Viewing the scene in 1956, he wrote: "El Salvador is rapidly moving into a position where it must soon be classified with those countries where the Church is strong and vital. Traveling priests

40. Frederick B. Pike, "The Catholic Church in Central America," *The Review of Politics*, Vol. 21, No. 1 (January, 1959), 103-4.

41. Rycroft and Clemmer, *op. cit.*, p. 235.

42. William J. Coleman, *Latin American Catholicism, A Self-Evaluation* (Maryknoll, N.Y., 1958), p. 30.

were bringing religion to the former abandoned areas of the country. Although there was still a need of priests, the Church had developed a strong nucleus of seminarians."[43]   They numbered 53 in 1957.

In 1960 there was a Protestant community in El Salvador totaling 54,918 or 2.2 per cent of the total population. They were served by 293 ministers—a formidable number considering that the total number of Catholic priests was 277. It is not Protestantism, however, which is the greatest threat to Catholicism, but rather the omnipresent religious indifference and apathy which prevails throughout Latin America.

Honduras

The fortunes of Catholicism in Honduras were closely linked with those of the faith in Guatemala. The ecclesiastical histories of Honduras and Guatemala dovetail in many places, but not to the remarkable extent noted as between El Salvador and Guatemala.

The Republic, after the dissolution of the Federation, was inaugurated under a Conservative régime. On January 11, 1840, the Congress was installed with ceremonies more religious than political. Forty-four *Te Deum* masses were sung on that day, and President Ferrera was "be-smoked with incense in the cathedral." The next year the see of Honduras which had been vacant since 1819 was filled. At first the pope named the presbyter Dr. José Trinidad Reyes for bishop, but the government was displeased with the nomination. The Vatican was notified that the bishop-elect had died, which was false. Gregory XVI then named Francisco de Paula Compoy, who had been recommended by the government.[44]

During the greater part of the period 1840 to 1880, administrations friendly to the clerical interests were in power. The constitutions of 1848, 1865, and 1873 established Roman Catholicism as the State religion to the exclusion of the public exercise of any other. Religious toleration was guaranteed in these words: "The high powers will protect it [the Roman Catholic Church] with wise laws, but neither these nor any other authority will intervene in the private exercise of any other cult that may be established in the country if these do not disturb public order." In 1861 a concordat was concluded with the papacy by President Guardiola. This agreement was almost identical, article for article, with the one negotiated with Guatemala in 1852.[45]

43. Albert J. Nevins, "How Catholic is Latin America?" *The Sign*, Vol. 36, No. 2 (September, 1956), 67.
44. Bancroft, *op. cit.*, III, 310; Salgado, *op. cit.*, p. 39.
45. Coello, *op. cit.*, pp. 100, 118.

President Guardiola, a satellite of Carrera, and a staunch Servile, had the novel experience of being excommunicated. Miguel del Cid, capitular vicar of the vacant see of Honduras, opposed the granting of religious toleration to the inhabitants of the islands in the Bay of Bahía as provided by treaty with Great Britain. The vicar, angry because President Guardiola would not recommend him to the pope for the espiscopal dignity, took the granting of religious toleration in the islands as a pretext to excommunicate the president whom he accused of persecuting the Church. The government forbade the publication of the decree and expelled the vicar. A special envoy secured papal approval of the conduct of President Guardiola. Pius IX ordered the excommunication raised and the vicar removed from his office.[46]

After the obstinate resistance of President Medina, leader of the reactionary elements, was broken down, a liberal anti-Church reform was instituted in Honduras contemporary with the reform in Guatemala and El Salvador. The Constitution of November 1, 1880, consolidated these reforms. Subsequent fundamental charters of government, promulgated in 1894, 1906, 1924, and 1936 extended even further the scope of the attack on the privileges and prerogatives of the Church.

The Constitution of 1936, which was in force until 1957, preserved most of the anticlerical provisions of the law of 1880, with the addition of the grant of juridical personality to religious associations in 1912. It provided for separation of Church and State, the free exercise of all religions, no governmental subsidies to religious denominations, the prohibition of monastic orders, and no religious instruction in public schools.

After about 1950 there was a relaxation of anticlerical severity toward the Church in Honduras, as there was in other parts of Central America. This developing friendly attitude toward religion culminated in concessions when a new constitution was drafted in 1957. When the Constituent Assembly convened, the Archbishop of Tegucigalpa inaugurated the opening session with a solemn invocation. This was significant because it was "the first time in over a century that an act strictly official in nature had received the benediction of a priest."[47]

In the Constitution which emerged from this Assembly the name of God was once more mentioned in the preamble. This constitution, which is still the fundamental law of the country, departed from the earlier charters in the following respects: it removed the prohibitions on religious instruction in the public schools, monastic orders, and government subsidies to religious educational activities. It did, however, con-

46. Salgado *op. cit.*, pp. 50-51.
47. Pike, *op. cit.*, p. 96.

tinue to recognize only the civil marriage, absolute divorce, and the prohibition of political activities by the religious. Separation of Church and State and the other anticlerical laws remained unaffected by the new constitution.

The separation of Church and State in Honduras dates from 1880 when President Marco Aurelio Soto revoked the concordat. Since then no new concordat has been negotiated, although relations with the Vatican have been generally friendly. A diplomatic representative has been accredited to the Holy See. The Church is free and independent of the State. The government as a rule does not interfere in the filling of ecclesiastical vacancies. The State inspects and controls all creeds, according to the law and police regulations concerning their external ceremonies. The exercise of all religions not in opposition to the laws of the country is guaranteed by the Constitution, yet the Catholic sympathies of the population react against all professors of dissident faiths.

The Church in Honduras owns its temples, residences, and schools upon which it does not pay taxes. Many years ago its real property was absorbed by the State. Denied revenue property and receiving no financial aid from the government (the tithes were abolished in 1871) the priests are very poor, depending entirely on fees and contributions for their support.

The private educational facilities afforded by the Church are meager. There are only 34 schools of all grades. Most of the teachers are foreign priests or brothers and nuns whose coming into the country in recent years helped to alleviate a distressing educational situation.[48] The number of Protestant schools in Honduras is also very meager.

The laws of Honduras establish the civil marriage ceremony as the only legal form. A Church marriage must not be performed prior to the civil. Divorce and separation are legalized. The cemeteries, as in El Salvador and Guatemala, have been secularized and are controlled entirely by the municipalities.

According to the census of 1960, the population of Honduras was 1,887,000, and of these 1,553,000 or 82.3 per cent were counted as Catholics. Serving these "Catholics" were only 156 priests, making a ratio of 9,950 to each priest.[49] One archbishop and four bishops comprised the hierarchy.

The Protestant community of Honduras, in 1960, was 28,593. The Protestant clergy numbered 209, a figure considerably in excess of Catholic priests, but not indicative of Protestant strength in the country.

48. *Ibid.*, pp. 104-5.
49. Rycroft and Clemmer, *op. cit.*, pp. 234-35.

Religious conditions in Honduras call for a general program of re-Christianization. The Central American country has been described as almost entirely non-Christian with little morality, social or private. Catholicism has made little appeal as a religious or social force. While most Hondurans profess a belief in God and have their children baptized, there is no Christian family life. Indeed this is not surprising since the percentage of illegitimate births in relation to live births is 65 per cent.[50] The native clergy who are poorly trained in the local seminaries, reflect too often in their own lives the general low moral standards. Thus, in Honduras, where, next to Haiti, the religious conditions appear the worst in Latin America, the plight of the Church reflects not internal weaknesses alone but the poverty and backwardness of the republic itself.

Nicaragua

The Catholic Church in Nicaragua has not suffered the vicissitudes it encountered in the republics of Guatemala, El Salvador, and Honduras. Also the Church enjoys a more favored legal status in Nicaragua today than it does in the other republics. In 1862 a Concordat was signed with the Vatican defining the relations between Church and State. Since then dissensions have occurred, but the controversies have been amicably settled. The principal features of the Concordat were the papal recognition of the national right of presentation and the government's assuming of the obligation to support the Church. The tithes were abolished in the same year.[51]

In witness of the strength of clericalism in Nicaragua, in 1871 when the rest of Central America was in revolt against the Church, the government gave shelter to the Jesuits who had been expelled from Guatemala. There was some slight opposition to this action, but it was easily overcome. But fears that the Jesuits would cause trouble were realized in May, 1881. A Spanish professor made a speech at the opening of the Instituto de Occidente, an educational institution under special government protection, in which he said that liberty of conscience and speech were necessary for the perfect education of free men. The Jesuits of León aroused the fanatical rabble by saying that the religion of their fathers was imperilled by the propaganda of the free-thinkers of the Instituto. They demanded prompt action on the part of Bishop Ulloa y Larrios, but the prelate refused to support them. Riots instigated by the

50. Francisco Houtart, *El cambio social en América Latina* (Bogotá, 1964), p. 143. Guatemala rates highest in illegitimate births at 73 per cent.

51. *Raccolta di Concordati*, pp. 948-59.

Jesuits were suppressed by the government and the members of the order were expelled from Nicaraguan soil. This episode is not to be regarded as a counterpart of the Liberal movement in the neighboring republics, for the government which acted against the Jesuits was friendly to the Church, but obviously could not tolerate subversive acts.[52]

The delayed Liberal anticlerical attack in Nicaragua occurred after 1894, during the dictatorial régime of Santos Zelaya. Legislation violative of the Concordat terminated that agreement and really dissolved the union of Church and State. Because of his opposition, Bishop Ulloa y Larrios was banished to Panama. Until his death in 1908 his coadjutor, Bishop Simeone Pereira, succeeded him in the administration of the diocese of León. After the overthrow of Zelaya the Church found sympathetic support in the Conservative party, which alternated in power with the Liberals, but the anticlerical legislation dating back to 1894 was not revoked. Nicaragua's several constitutions ending with the current instrument of 1950 all contained remarkably similar provisions on the subject of religion.

The Constitution of 1950, which invokes God in the preamble—contrary to the preceding charters—declares that the State has no official religion. It guarantees religious freedom and forbids any legislation protecting or restraining any particular faith. The juridic personality of religious associations and denominations is recognized, and thus the Church has the right to own and acquire real property. The "buildings and their dependencies, devoted exclusively to the use of religious faiths are exempt from taxation." Public elementary education is laic. Cemeteries are secular. The Constitution contains no provisions enjoining clerics from political expression, nor does it prohibit monastic orders.

Church and State are legally separated but the Catholic faith is regarded as the *de facto* official religion. The Constitution of 1911, while declaring separation, reads: "The majority of the Nicaraguan people profess the Catholic Apostolic Roman religion. The State guarantees the free exercise of this cult; and also all others so long as they do not oppose Christian morality and public order. The State is prohibited from issuing laws to protect or restrain particular cults." Although the Constitution no longer mentions the Roman Catholic religion by name, the government "recognizes" the cult in practice, and grants it many privileges. Official diplomatic relations are maintained with the Vatican. The Church receives no subsidy from the government, except money for the upkeep of old churches that are considered national monuments.

The constitutional mandate that public education be laic has been

52. Bancroft, *op. cit.*, III, 476, 484, 633-34.

modified slightly to allow voluntary catechists to enter the public schools one day a week for religious instruction to students whose parents so opt.

The 95 Catholic schools in Nicaragua are well-attended and are the best in the country. Unfortunately, however, most of them cater only to the children of middle and upper class families, although many provide scholarships for children of lesser means. Also, there are some schools for the poor conducted by religious orders from the profits of their richer schools. All of the teaching orders labor under government restrictions more or less severe that require private schools to conform to public school programs. The Jesuits recently established at Managua a "Central American University," projected to serve the higher educational needs for the Catholics of all of Central America.[53]

Catholic statistics, as of 1960, for Nicaragua were as follows: population of the Roman Catholic community 1,012,000 or 71 per cent of the total population of 1,424,000, and the Roman Catholic clergy 222. Thus, the ratio of Catholics to each priest is 4,550 to 1.[54] One archbishop and five bishops comprise the hierarchy.

The Protestant community numbers 64,383 or 4.5 per cent of the total population. There are 169 members of the Protestant clergy. The principal denominations are Jehovah's Witnesses, Mormons, Baptists, and Adventists. Protestantism seems to be very strong in some places, and if the sects could consolidate their strength they might expect considerable success in the future. The weakness of the Catholic Church and failure of Catholicism to appeal as a religious or social force in Nicaragua has created a vacuum favorable to non-Catholic sects. Whether the situation will be fully exploited remains for the future to disclose.

Costa Rica

Being further removed from the storm-center of Central America (Guatemala), Costa Rica was less influenced than her northern neighbors in the politico-ecclesiastical turmoils in that republic. In November, 1838, Costa Rica proclaimed her separation from the Federation of Central America. A Conservative régime, friendly to the Church, was set up under President Braulio Carrillo, but he proved to be so dictatorial that he was overthrown, and a Liberal government under Francisco Morazán, recently returned from exile in Peru, was established early in 1842. Morazán's tenure as president of Costa Rica was brief, for, in September, 1842, he was overthrown and executed by the Conservatives. The prospect of being ruled by the "anarchist" Morazán was revolting

53. Pike, *op. cit.*, p. 104.
54. Rycroft and Clemmer, *op. cit.*, pp. 234-35.

to the majority of Costa Ricans who were pronouncedly Conservative in opinion.[55]

From 1842 to 1883 very little occurred to disturb the placid waters of State-Church harmony. The several constitutions that were promulgated during this period were uniformly most friendly toward the Catholic Church which was declared to be the State-Church. The instruments of 1844, 1847, and 1859 declared that Roman Catholicism was the only religion to be tolerated. In 1860, however, a more liberal note was introduced into the constitutional law when it was provided that Roman Catholicism should be the State religion, but other denominations should be tolerated. The next constitution, that of 1871, which was in force until 1949, continued the principle of religious toleration.[56]

The independent bishopric which the people of Costa Rica had solicited for nearly three centuries was finally created (February 28, 1850), by bull of Pope Pius IX. This freed the Church in Costa Rica from ecclesiastical control resident in another State, the Bishop of León in Nicaragua. Anselmo Llorente y Lafuente, a native of Cartago, was consecrated first Bishop of Costa Rica on November 7, 1851. After the creation of the bishopric, the people of Costa Rica wanted their own seminary, for candidates for the priesthood still had to go to León for training. A seminary was not founded in Costa Rica, however, until 1878.

In 1852 a concordat was negotiated with the papacy by Fernando de Lorenzana and was signed on the same date (October 7) as was the concordat with Guatemala. The terms differed but slightly from the Guatemalan concordat. By the terms of the Costa Rican instrument the jurisdiction previously exercised by the ecclesiastical authorities in litigations involving Church possessions or its temporal rights was transferred to the civil tribunals, but it was stipulated at the same time that, in courts of second and third instance, legal trial of criminal cases involving priests required the assistance of ecclesiastics nominated by the bishop, as judicial assessors. Today the jurisdiction of the Church court, or *Juzgado Eclesiástico*, extends over causes of discipline and moral conduct of the clergy, marriage as it refers to the sacraments, and causes of faith.[57]

Bishop Llorente, like the first Bishop of San Salvador, tasted the bitterness of exile. When he refused to pay, or allow his clergy to pay, an equitable tax decreed by Congress on September 29, 1858, for the sup-

55. William S. Robertson, *History of the Latin American Nations* (New York, 1925), p. 449.

56. Barrantes, *op. cit.*, II, 93.

57. *Raccolta di Concordati*, pp. 800-10; *Costa Rica en Siglo XIX*, pp. 297, 301, 316; Hernáez, *Colección de Bulas*, II, 114.

port of the hospitals, he was expelled from Costa Rica by President Mora. The Bishop sought refuge in Nicaragua and remained there until August, 1859, when he returned to his see after the fall of his adversary. The overthrow of Mora, who, on the whole, had been friendly towards clerical interests, was due in no small degree to public indignation because of his banishment of the Bishop. One of the first acts of the new government was to recall Llorente, who ruled his diocese until his death in 1871. The government then proposed a successor who was not approved by the Roman Curia. Consequently a capitular vicar administered the diocese for almost ten years. Finally, in February, 1880, the pope confirmed the government's nominee, Bernard August Thiel.[58]

Bishop Thiel, like his predecessor, soon ran afoul of the government. In 1883 a decree was published forbidding the entry into the Republic of members of the Society of Jesus, although a few were allowed to remain in their college at Cartago. This act seemed to support the suspicion that President Fernández and his adherents were antagonistic to the Church. At least the Jesuits began to agitate and fanned the fires of intolerance and fanaticism in the ignorant masses. At first the Bishop refused to join in the attack on "the government which intended to destroy the religion of the majority," and he ordered his clergy to desist. But later compromised himself, and, in July, 1884, suffered expulsion along with the Jesuits.[59] Fernández forthwith instituted anticlerical measures. By decree the law of December 2, 1852, approving the Concordat, was derogated. Thus diplomatic relations with the papacy were broken. Then the cemeteries were secularized. Writes a partisan regarding this measure: "On that day came to an end the inhuman management of the cemeteries, by means of which the penalties of the Church persecuted human beings after death." Another decree prohibited the establishment of monastic orders or religious communities. Vicar Antonio Zamora, who administered the diocese during the absence of Bishop Thiel, was able to restore friendly relations with the government, so that, after the death of President Fernández, Thiel was allowed to return, upon promising to observe the laws and not interfere in public affairs.[60]

Since 1886 harmonious relations have prevailed between Church and State in Costa Rica, due perhaps to the abstention of the clergy from intervention in political affairs. This did not mean, however, that the Church had to remain silent when an issue arose closely affecting its interests. Such a situation arose in 1949 when a Constituent Assembly

58. *Costa Rica en Siglo XIX*, p. 350.
59. The ban on the Jesuits remained in effect until 1943.
60. Barrantes, *op. cit.*, II, 260-64, 300.

convened to draft a new constitution. Some evidence of anticlericalism was present when it was proposed that priests be barred from holding public office and that education be declared an essential function of the State. Archbishop Víctor Manuel Sanabria y Martínez and the clergy aroused public opinion and induced the delegates to abandon the proposals.[61]

According to constitutional law the Catholic Church has always been the State-Church of Costa Rica. The Constitution of 1949, after "invoking the name of God" in the preamble, provides (Article 76): "The Apostolic Roman Catholic Religion is that of the State, which contributes to its maintenance, without impeding the free exercise in the Republic of other worship that is not opposed to universal morality or good customs." In matters of internal government the Church is free of governmental control, although "no political propaganda may be carried on in any way by clericals or secular persons invoking religious motives or making use of religious beliefs" (Article 27).

Although there is no concordat, the Roman Catholic Church in Costa Rica could not reasonably desire a more satisfactory legal status—barring the free exercise of other cults. The government contributes one per cent of the annual budget for the support of the Catholic Church. This subsidy, however, is small, with the result that the Church is greatly handicapped because of the lack of financial resources. With respect to the civil registration of births and marriages the religious certificates are accepted as legal, a practice at variance with the other Central American republics. Divorce is legal, practically at the will of the parties.[62]

From the Constitutional clause: "The Roman Catholic Apostolic Religion is that of the State" is derived the argument that "religious education is an obligation of the State."[63] To a certain extent the argument has been sustained by the fact that religious education is obligatory in all public grade schools. Only students whose parents present a written excuse can be exempted. There is no government subvention to religious education. Nevertheless, the State stresses the importance of adequate religious training for the formation of the whole personality. There is close coöperation between the Church hierarchy

61. Pike, *op. cit.*, p. 94. The Archbishop of San José held that priests could not be denied their canonical function of teaching in private schools and from the pulpit. *Hispanic America Report*, II, No. 10 (October, 1949), 14.

62. Pike, *op. cit.*, p. 108. See John and Mavis Biesanz, *Costa Rican Life* (New York, 1944), pp. 202-24.

63. For a study of the antecedents and consequences of Art. 76 of the Constitution of 1949, see Un Circulo de Abogados de la Liga Espiritual de Profesionales Católicos, *Costa Rica un Estado Católico* (San José, C.R., 1955).

and the Ministry of Public Education.[64] In 1960 it was reported that there were 39 Catholic schools in Costa Rica. The Church schools, whose curricula must conform to official programs, except for religious courses, are generally rated superior in quality to the public schools.

The government department entrusted with the supervision of ecclesiastical relations is the Ministerio de Relaciones Exteriores y Culto. Since 1908 the Vatican and Costa Rica have exchanged diplomatic representatives. The papal internuncio accredited to Costa Rica is also the papal representative to other Central American republics. In further evidence of State preference to the Catholic Church, a decree of May 27, 1956, exempted bishops and archbishops of the Roman Catholic Church from having to use passports or visas to enter or leave Costa Rica "if in the exercise of their function in the Central American region." The government recognized religious holidays, notably the Feast of Our Lady of the Angels, the patroness of Costa Rica.

The hierarchy of the Catholic Church in Costa Rica is comprised of one archbishop and two bishops. According to the 1960 census, out of a total population of 1,099,962, 1,037,000, or 94.3 per cent, were Catholics —real and nominal. There were 246 priests. The number of Catholics per individual priest was 4,200, a rather low ratio for Latin America.[65]

By way of contrast, 267 Evangelical clergy ministered to a Protestant community of 47,361. Most of the Protestant converts come from the lower classes, for those of upper classes, more prestige conscious, believe that "if one is not a Catholic he will fare better, from the standpoint of worldly expediency, by not affiliating himself with any religion than he would by turning to Protestantism." Not satisfied with this advantage, the Catholic Church has protested Protestant activities. For example, paid advertising by a Baptist group was protested, but the government refused to take action on the ground that its intervention would be a violation of the freedom of the press. Also when the government authorized the Asociación Luterana Evangélica to establish schools, hospitals, and orphans' homes, and Catholic organizations protested, the State stood its ground, holding that it had granted juridic personality to a nonreligious organization. On the other hand, in May, 1961, the Supreme Court sustained a government decision to revoke a parade permit granted a Protestant organization. The Court upheld the power of the president to grant or revoke permits for public demonstrations. Since the Catholic Church is a *national one*, said the Court, the govern-

64. Biesanz, *op. cit.*, p. 207; Pike, *op. cit.*, p. 103.
65. Rycroft and Clemmer, *op. cit.*, pp. 234-35.

ment would not sanction a public demonstration by another faith considered a "religious procession."[66]

Protestants are charged with being the advance-guard of American imperialism, who operate with immense reserves of United States gold. The United States thus is identified with Protestantism and is attacked along with it. After Costa Rica entered World War II on the side of the United States, Archbishop Víctor Manuel Sanabria y Martínez lamented: "Proselyting Protestant propaganda is an instrument of subjection and imperialism.... If the North American political protectorate is injurious to our Hispanic and Latin political tradition, the religious protectorate is doubly injurious."[67]

Although the attitude of Archbishop Sanabria toward the war and the United States left much to be desired, he was active in promoting the social welfare activities of the Church consonant with the encyclicals *Rerum Novarum* and *Quadragisimo Anno*. He helped organize *Rerum Novarum*, a Catholic workers' union or association, dedicated to the improvement of economic, social, and moral conditions of laborers. It has ever since played an important role in trade unionism. The social reform work of Archbishop Sanabria was continued by his successor, Archbishop Rubén Odio Herrera.[68] Because of the leadership of these two prelates Catholic influence has greatly increased in the social and moral life of the nation. In fact the Roman Catholic Church in Costa Rica has been cited as a model for many other lands. It is a leader in implementing the social doctrine of the Church. Although it has problems—needing priests and educational opportunities—the Church in Costa Rica is progressive and respected.[69]

Panama

The Catholic Church in Panama, until the separation from Colombia, was closely united with the latter State. The Concordat of 1886 regulated the State-Church relations on the Isthmus, but when the independent Republic of Panama was established in 1903, the ecclesiastical and temporal powers were separated. This was due to the fact that liberal opinion which had insisted on separation was strong in Panama.

66. *Hispanic American Report*, V, No. 6 (July, 1952), 14; XIV, No. 5 (May, 1961), 40; XVI, No. 1 (March, 1963), 28.

67. Biesanz, *op. cit.*, p. 222.

68. Pike, *op. cit.*, p. 108.

69. Nevins, *op. cit.*, p. 14. Also see Víctor Brenes, "La Iglesia Católica en Costa Rica," *Mundo Hispánico* (Madrid), 12 (141), (December, 1958), pp. 33-34.

The Constitution of 1904, while recognizing[70] that the Roman Catholic religion was that of the majority of the Republic's inhabitants, bestowed no special privileges on the Church. It was affirmation of a fact which could well have been omitted. The free operation of all religions and cults was guaranteed. No religious tests were required to hold office or to exercise the full rights of a citizen. The government had no privileges in the election of ecclesiastical officers, and, not until 1929, did it have an envoy accredited to the Vatican. But on the other hand, while the government did not contribute to the support of the Catholic Church, it assumed the responsibility for encouraging and aiding Catholic missionary activities among the Indian tribes and for providing religious instruction for those who wanted it in the public schools. There were no special restrictions on Church properties or its right to conduct unhampered its internal religious and economic affairs.

In 1925, Pope Pius XI made the Church in Panama independent of the Archdiocese of Cartagena by creation of the Archdiocese of Panama. Within the archdiocese are two dioceses. To relieve the shortage of priests, and to increase dependence on foreign priests, a Catholic seminary was opened for the training of young native priests.

The Constitution of 1946, the current *magna carta* of the isthmian republic made no significant change concerning the Church and religion. It provides that:

> The profession of all religions is free, as is the practice of all forms of worship, without any limitation other than respect for Christian morality and public order. (Art. 35)
>
> It is recognized that the Catholic religion is that of the majority of Panamanians. It will be taught in the public schools, but learning it and attending acts of religious worship shall not be compulsory for pupils when so requested by their parents or guardians. The law shall provide what assistance should be given to this religion for missions to native tribes and for similar purposes. (Art. 36)
>
> Religious organizations have juridical capacity and they manage and administer their property within the limits prescribed by law, the same as other juridical persons. (Art. 37)
>
> Ministers of religious faiths may not hold civil or military public posts, except those relating to social welfare or public instruction. (Art. 43)

70. "Recognition" seems to mean that the position of the Church is favorable. William W. Pierson and Federico G. Gil, *Governments of Latin America* (New York, 1957), p. 445.

Article 103 prohibits the formation of political parties on the basis of sex, race, or *religion*. And finally, Article 141 provides that: "A citizen who has no religious beliefs may dispense with the invocation to God in the oath."[71]

In Panama, Church property has not been nationalized, nor are there restrictions on the ability of the Church to receive entailments and bequests. The income of the Church is meager and restricts its activities.

Although the Constitution provides for the teaching of the catechism in primary and secondary schools, parents may have their children exempted from religious instruction. Religious orders operate private schools. In 1960 they numbered 31. They receive no subventions from the government, but on the contrary must pay taxes. In general, the caliber of the Catholic schools is considered superior to the public schools.

The Church, of course, has no control over the civil register, although prior to 1917, when the public control was established, the Church registry of baptisms was accepted as legal proof of date of birth. Either the civil or the religious marriage ceremony is now regarded as legal provided it is registered with the civil authorities. Despite the efforts of the Church to encourage religious marriages, Panama, with 30 per cent free unions (concubinage), rates third highest in Latin America, after Guatemala (41 per cent), and Haiti (39 per cent). Illegitimate births in relation to live births is 46 per cent.[72] Absolute divorce is legal. Since 1910 the Church has been deprived of its administration of cemeteries. The municipalities have assumed this control.

The population of the Republic of Panama (1960 census) was 1,066,122. Of these, 893,000, or 83.8 per cent, were counted as Catholics on the basis presumably of their baptism. Serving this "Catholic" population were 171 priests, making a ratio of 5,200 Catholics to each priest.[73] A shortage of priests is regarded as one of the greatest handicaps facing the Catholic Church in Panama. This deficiency is not being solved by the Catholic seminary, for the vocations are few among young native Panamanians.

Faced by widespread religious indifference the Panamanian Church has embarked on programs to halt the secular trend. Catholic Action, the lay organization dedicated to the re-Christianization of society, has

71. For a general discussion of "Religion" in Panama, see *Special Warfare Area Handbook for Panama*, Special Operations Research Office, The American University (Washington, D.C.: March, 1962), pp. 83-92.

72. Francisco Houtart, *El cambio social en América Latina* (Bogotá, 1964), pp. 141-43.

73. Rycroft and Clemmer, *op. cit.*, pp. 234-35. In 1960 there were 81,306 Protestants in Panama, served by 176 ministers.

campaigned since the 1940's against materialism, religious indifference, and moral laxity. Working closely with the hierarchy and the clergy, it has sought to give examples of Christian practice, but unfortunately, the sum total of its efforts have been inadequate to confront the great problems of the country.

Belatedly the Church in Panama seems to have overcome a former passivity with respect to social welfare activities. Great stimulation came undoubtedly from the papal encyclicals and a Roman Catholic Conference on Rural Life, held in Panama in 1955, in which 19 Latin-American delegations participated. Catholic doctrine on social justice was focused on the methods and means of improving land tenure.[74]

Due perhaps to the presence of the United States in the Canal Zone, and to the confusion of nationalities in the republic, Panama developed a religious policy which, while recognizing Catholicism as the predominant religion of the country, guarantees freedom of religious practice and non-governmental interference in religious activities. On the other hand, the people of Panama seem to prefer ecclesiastical abstinence from interference in political affairs. The Church acquiesced, with the result that it acquired a reputation of aloofness from the problems and needs of the country. It is an image which the Church is now attempting to erase.

74. *Hispanic American Report*, VII, No. 4 (May, 1955), 162.

Chapter XV

Church and State Conflict in Mexico:
1821-1910

The independence of Mexico, which the prelates of the Catholic Church had condemned as heresy, was finally achieved in 1821 under most exceptional circumstances. "It [independence] was the natural result," says Lucas Alamán, "of a simple change of front by the army, instigated by the higher clergy who were antagonistic to the Spanish Cortes.... Independence was achieved by the very ones who had opposed it."[1] The restoration of the Spanish liberal Constitution of 1812, the confiscation of part of the Church's property, the abolition of the Inquisition, the establishment of a free press, and the seizure of the tithes of the clergy produced greater discontent in Mexico than in Spain, for, again quoting Alamán, "In Mexico those offended by the measures were the most influential and the most elevated." The menace of the extension to Mexico of the restrictions on clerical privileges, as well as the actual property losses (for there part of the Church's wealth had been seized arbitrarily by Spanish officials to combat revolt), forced the clergy to the conclusion that absolute separation from Spain and its radicalism was necessary. Priests declared from their pulpits that the preservation of Catholicism demanded freedom from Spain. It is undoubtedly true that anxiety over the preservation of their civil and political rights was the compelling factor in causing the clergy to cast their lot for independence, but it should also be recorded, in justice to the numerous less selfishly-minded clerics, that they conscientiously interpreted the acts of the Spanish Cortes as an attack on dogmatic religion itself. The course of revolution tended to atheism; such was the lesson of the French Revolution.

Having decided on independence, a meeting of conservative leaders, prominent among whom were several clerics, was held in the oratorio of the church of San Felipe Neri in Mexico City. It was decided to

1. Vicente Riva Ralacio, ed., *México á Través de los Siglos* (5 vols., Mexico, 1888-89), III, 657. See W. Eugene Shiels, "Church and State in the First Decade of Mexican Independence," in *Catholic Historical Review*, XXVIII (July, 1942), 206-28.

compromise with the rebels who were in the field continuing the struggle initiated by Hidalgo and, when control should be established over the independence movement, to create a monarchy with a Spanish *infante* at the head. The conspirators were careful not to mention constitutional institutions.[2] The plans of the conservative rebels were translated into acts without the slightest hitch. On February 24, 1821, Agustín de Iturbide, leader of the royalist forces and co-conspirator, and Vicente Guerrero, leader of the liberal rebels, proclaimed the famous *Plan de Iguala.* "The *Plan* provided a scheme whereby all the inhabitants of New Spain could unite, on the basis of mutual toleration, in establishing the political independence of the country."[3] Its principal provisions were: (1) the preservation of the Roman Catholic religion and clerical privileges; (2) independence; and (3) equality of creoles and Europeans in the government.[4] So universal was the appeal of the *Plan* to all classes that nothing could stop the triumphant march of Iturbide and the Army of the Three Guarantees. On September 27, "El Libertador," as the mestizo turn-coat was called by an adoring populace, occupied Mexico City. The definitive separation of Mexico had been accomplished under terms satisfactory to the ecclesiastics. Only the Roman Catholic religion was to be tolerated and the members of the regular and secular clergy were to be protected in all their rights and properties. In other words the ecclesiastical *fueros* were guaranteed.

It was necessary, however, to incorporate these guarantees into constitutional law and establish a capable government willing to insure their observance. On February 4, 1822, a Constituent Congress in which the clergy were well represented, was convoked. Before organizing for business the deputies, accompanied by the *Junta* and the Regency, went to the cathedral and heard mass. There all took an oath to support the Roman Catholic religion to the exclusion of all others. "This religious ceremony," says a Mexican historian, "indicates the supremacy of the clergy, without whose intervention in matters of policy, acts would have been illegal and all authority would have been insecure and weak."[5]

For nine months the Constituent Congress, divided into irreconcilable monarchist and republican groups, sat without doing anything constructive on the constitution. Finally Iturbide took matters into his own

2. Riva Palacio, *op. cit.*, III, 662-63; Tiburio Catalán to Gen. Vicente Guerrero, Chilapa, April 8, 1822. Riva Palacio Papers in the García Collection, University of Texas Library.

3. Herbert Ingram Priestley, *The Mexican Nation, A History* (New York, 1923), p. 247.

4. José M. Gamboa, *Leyes Constitucionales de México Durante el Siglo XIX* (Mexico, 1901), pp. 282-85.

5. Riva Palacio, *op. cit.*, IV, 16, 18, 54-55; *Colección de los Decretos y Ordenes del Soberano Congreso Mexicano* (Mexico, 1825), p. 39.

hands and forced the Congress to choose him as emperor. Since the
clericals feared that the majority of the deputies were inclining toward a
republic, the very idea of which was repulsive to them, they hastened to
the support of Iturbide and the Empire. On July 25, 1822, Agustín I
was crowned as Emperor in a stately ceremony in which several ecclesiastical prelates officiated. "The Mexicans, struggling for a liberal
independence, had been tricked into a conservative one by Iturbide and
the Church."[6]

Agustín I desired to appear as the recognized champion of the
Church. He declared that the faith of his Empire should be Catholic,
Apostolic, and Roman, without toleration of any other; and that the
secular and regular clergy should be protected in their *fueros* and
preëminences. The "Spanish priests," who had held themselves aloof
at the time of Iturbide's elevation, for they wanted a Bourbon on the
throne, gradually accommodated themselves to the new régime. But
not so Archbishop Fonte. A peninsular, he regarded independence as
treason and abandoned his metropolitan see after the creation of the
Empire and returned to Spain. When the Mexican government wished
to declare the see vacant it received a rebuff from the pope. Bishops
Bergosa of Oaxaca and Cabañas of Guadalajara were also seriously compromised because of their vehement polemics against independence.[7]

Despite clerical support, the Empire was overthrown within a year
after its creation. It was not true that the Empire was attacked because
of the clerical domination. Despite the fact that there was a rising opposition to the ecclesiastical *fuero*, Iturbide was dethroned not because
of the nature of his following, but because of his political blunders.
Indeed, these very mistakes weakened his clerical support, and when
the crisis arrived the clergy were not willing to assume a determined
stand on his behalf. In other words, opposition to the Church was a
minor factor in contributing to the downfall of the Empire.

Although the clerics had not been backward in assuming management of governmental affairs, they refused to concede to the State any
control over the Church. They revealed the goal of their ambitions in
the discussions relating to the patronage. On October 19, 1821, Iturbide,
as president of the Regency, requested Archbishop Fonte to state what
policy the government should pursue in the matter of filling the ever-
increasing ecclesiastical vacancies. He consulted his chapter and a
junta of bishops. The prelates announced as their opinion that (1) with
the winning of independence the patronage which had been conceded

6. Priestley, *op. cit.*, p. 261.
7. Riva Palacio, *op. cit.*, III, 356.

by the pope to the kings of Spain came to an end; (2) to exercise the patronage, it was necessary for the Mexican government to receive the same concession from the pope; and (3) in the meantime the provision of ecclesiastical places belonged by right of devolution in each diocese to the respective ordinary acting with the canons.[8] The report of the *junta* of prelates, as communicated to the Regency by Archbishop Fonte, seemed to support the charge that the Mexican clergy felt that the hour had arrived to liberate themselves from dependence on the civil power.

The Minister of Justice and Ecclesiastical Affairs and the patronage committees of the Congress failed to agree with the *junta* of bishops. They held that the right of the patronage belonged to the nation and that the providing of vacant archbishoprics and bishoprics should be postponed until a concordat could be concluded.[9]

The advisability of negotiating an agreement with the Vatican was generally recognized in Mexico soon after separation from the motherland. Due to clerical pressure, the Congress authorized the Regency to send an envoy to Rome, but the departure of the envoy was indefinitely postponed for various reasons. Finally, after a long delay, Francisco Pablo Vázquez went to Europe as the Mexican envoy to the pope.[10]

After the overthrow of Iturbide a call was issued for a Constituent Congress to take up once more the task of framing a fundamental charter. The Congress met on November 7, 1823. The republicans enjoyed an overwhelming majority, but they were divided into factions favoring either the centralist or the federalist form of government. The clerics, discomfited by the imperial *débâcle*, were tardy in adopting a policy to meet the new situation, with the result that the Congress was remarkably free of Church influence. Yet, numerous religious were included in the membership of the Congress, and two of these, Miguel Ramos Arizpe and Servando Mier, were the leaders, respectively, of the Federalist and Centralist groups.

Since it was imperative that a permanent government be established with the least possible delay, the Congress promulgated the *Acta Constitutiva* (January 31, 1824) which was to serve as the constitution until a detailed federal republican instrument could be framed. The *Acta*, for which Ramos Arizpe was principally responsible, provided in Article 4 that: "The religion of the Mexican nation is and shall be perpetually the Roman Catholic Apostolic. The nation will protect it by wise and

---

8. *Dictamen de la Comisión de Patronato, June 21, 1823* (Mexico, 1823), pp. 3-5; *Colección Eclesiástica Mejicana* (Mexico, 1834), I, 10-14.

9. *Dictamen de Patronato*, pp. 5-6, 11-18.

10. Juan A. Mateos, *Historia Parlamentaria de los Congresos Mexicanos de 1821 á 1857* (Mexico, 1877), I, 404; II, 269-73.

just laws and prohibits the exercise of any other." In the debates on the *Acta*, Article 4 was approved without much opposition.[11]

In the Federal Constitution which was finally adopted on October 4, 1824, Article 4 of the *Acta* was retained without change, but there were numerous additions defining the status of the State-Church. The most important of these were the power of the State to conclude concordats, grant or refuse the exequatur to all pontifical documents, and make rules for the exercise of the patronage. The preservation of the ecclesiastical *fueros* was guaranteed.[12] The disposition of the religious question by the Congress of 1824 was significant for at least two reasons. In the first place, the constituents took a definite stand in favor of national patronage. There was almost unanimous agreement that the Church was not to be freed from all governmental control. Secondly, it was demonstrated that the Mexican nation approved the retention of Catholicism as the State religion and opposed toleration toward other sects.

There should be no occasion for mystification that, immediately after the Catholic Church was established by unanimous consent as the State-Church, it was subjected to attack. The cause of complaint was not the exclusive privileges enjoyed by the Church in the purely religious sphere (very little was thought about religious freedom in Mexico in 1824), but rather its economic domination. About one-fourth of the nation's wealth belonged to the Church. "Due to the decline in the number of ecclesiastics while the quantity of Church property was increasing, there developed a condition of absentee landlordism or the latifundia evil." Independence under creole leadership only served to aggrandize the Church in wealth and prestige. During the next thirty years its strength and riches continued to increase until it became the most powerful institutionalized force in the country.[13]

The revolutionary hero Guadalupe Victoria was elected first president of Mexico under the Constitution of 1824. Like Washington, he attempted to remain neutral in political matters and selected his advisers from the rival political parties. The so-called political parties which Victoria tried unsuccessfully to reconcile were the Conservatives and the Liberals. The former recruited most of their members from the landed

11. *Ibid.*, II, 610-12; Gamboa, *op. cit.*, p. 303.
12. Mateos, *op. cit.*, II, 806-14, 855-77; Gamboa, *op. cit.*, 237-83.
13. Wilfred H. Callcott, *Church and State in Mexico, 1822-1857* (Durham, N.C., 1926), p. 66. Father Mariano Cuevas, on checking over Dr. Callcott's references, especially Mariano Otero, *Ensayo sobre la Cuestión Social* (Mexico, 1842), pointed out to the writer certain indisputable exaggerations in Callcott's figures. It is practically impossible to arrive at the exact sums, nor is it necessary for the purposes of this study, for, as any fair-minded historian of Mexico would admit, the Church in Mexico was very wealthy, and that situation constituted a problem.

aristocracy, the military, and the clergy. These were the classes which zealously guarded their privileges or *fueros*. Most of the old adherents of monarchy and centralism supported this party. The Liberals were largely creole and mestizo professional people and intellectuals, who were without special privilege; consequently they were democrats, for to them democracy meant equality of all peoples. They also supported federalism, which was understood to guarantee individual freedom. The most important groups within the two parties were the two branches of Masonry—the *Escoceses* or Scottish Rite Masons, in the Conservative party, and the *Yorkinos*, or the York Rite Masons, in the Liberal party.[14]

The *Escoceses* had long been active in the political life of Mexico. As ardent partisans of Spain they had opposed Iturbide and contributed materially to the accomplishment of his overthrow. Although a Federal Republic was established on the ruins of the Empire, the *Escoceses* continued to champion the principle of centralism, and the more reactionary members supported monarchism, or even a restoration of Spanish authority under a liberal constitution. The York Rite lodge was not organized in Mexico until after the establishment of the Republic. The idea of organizing the Masonic branch to counteract the centralistic and antirepublican propaganda of the *Escoceses* was conceived by two curates, José María Alpuche and Ramos Arizpe. After five lodges had been formed, the American Minister Joel Poinsett was asked to secure in the United States letters patent to install the grand lodge. This was Poinsett's only activity in the organization of the *Yorkinos*.[15] He was criticized, however, as acting with deliberate purpose to destroy the Conservative influence in the country, particularly the ecclesiastical. Yet the division of contending political aspirants into Centralists and Federalists, Scottish and York Rite Masons, is deceptive. "These were ephemeral alignments," says Gruening, "for a massed assault on the treasury." There was no loyalty to any other idea. "The political history of Mexico from 1825 to 1850," says the same writer, "is primarily the history of the army which noisily occupied the foreground; the Church filled the background and pulled the strings of its marionettes."[16]

Several attempts were made in the administration of President Victoria to establish relations with the papacy. After his election to the presidency Guadalupe Victoria wrote to Leo XII, naïvely expecting that he would be recognized by a simple notification. But recognition was not forthcoming. Instead, the pope sent an encyclical to the American clergy urging them to aid the king of Spain. The publication of the

14. José María Luis Mora, *Obras Sueltas* (Paris, 1847), I, viii.
15. Callcott, *op. cit.*, p. 56.
16. Ernest Gruening, *Mexico and its Heritage* (New York, 1928), p. 51.

encyclical created intense indignation among all classes in Mexico; chapters and prelates joined in the national protest against the papal proposal that allegiance to the detested Ferdinand be restored. Ramos Arizpe, Minister of Justice and Ecclesiastical Affairs, instructed Francisco Vázquez, recently dispatched to Rome as the Mexican representative, to register a protest against the encyclical "which seemed so foreign to the head of the Church." From Brussels Vázquez wrote the Cardinal-Secretary. Assuming that the pope's ill-advised action was the result of misinformation, Vázquez attempted to present a true account of Mexico's loyalty to the Church and the impossibility of a restoration of Spanish rule. Cardinal Somaglia responded almost immediately requesting that Vázquez proceed to Rome. The Cardinal, however, discretely avoided any mention of the encyclical and referred to the President of Mexico as "Sua Eccellenza il Signore Comandante Generale, Dr. Guadalupe Vittoria."[17]

Since the Constitution of 1824 provided for the national exercise of the patronage, the Republic was anxious that it should receive papal approval without delay because of the imperative need of filling ecclesiastical vacancies, for after 1821 the number of clerics had diminished considerably. It is said that by 1830 the total had been reduced by one-third. The reasons for the marked decrease were natural death, flight, and difficulty of ordination due to the lack of bishops. The last-named cause was the principal one. Some of the bishops, like Abad y Queipo, left the country even before the consummation of independence. Others like Archbishop Fonte left later. At the end of 1821 there were five bishops in Mexico, but in 1827 not a single one remained.[18] Despite the imperative need of remedying the distressing scarcity of prelates and clergy, the Congress was not disposed to secure the filling of the vacancies by sacrificing national claims to the patronage. The deputies were willing, however, to waste much valuable time in discussing its nature.[19]

After years of fruitless discussion the Congress finally agreed, October 13, 1827, on a set of instructions to guide the negotiations of the Mexican agent to the pope. Vázquez, it will be recalled, had been in Brussels for over two years awaiting these orders. Numerous members of the Mexican clergy expressed considerable alarm because the instructions contained a demand that the pope authorize in the Mexican nation the exercise of the patronage. The clergy were very unwilling, it was evident, to abandon their efforts to be free of temporal control. As for the

17. Joaquín Ramírez Cabañas (ed.), *Las Relaciones entre México y el Vaticano* (Mexico, 1928), pp. 14-27.
18. Col. Vázquez Medía to Guadalupe Victoria, Cempoala, July 16, 1828. Riva Palacio Papers.
19. Lorenzo de Zavala, *Ensayo Histórico de las Revoluciones de México* (Paris, 1831-32), II, 199.

history of Vázquez's mission after he was conveyed the long-delayed instructions, a discussion is unnecessary here, since the details were narrated elsewhere.[20]

The presidential candidates to succeed Guadalupe Victoria were Manuel Gómez Pedraza, a conservative *Yorkino*, and Vicente Guerrero, grand master of the *Yorkinos*. Although Gómez Pedraza was the undoubted legal victor at the polls in the presidential election of 1829, Guerrero possessed himself of the presidency by resorting to arms. The Congress confirmed his "election," and named Anastasio Bustamante as vice-president. But Guerrero's tenure in the office of the chief executive was short-lived. A new Conservative party made up of the clergy, army, *hacendados* (or property holders), and the remnants of the *Escoceses* and better born *Yorkinos*, coöperated under the leadership of Vice-President Bustamante to overthrow Guerrero. Bustamante then "succeeded" to the presidency (February, 1830).[21]

The conservative administration of Anastasio Bustamante was very friendly to the Catholic Church and aided in restoring its former influence. Liberal and heretical ideas were vigorously stamped out, and tolerance was condemned as the promotion of schism. The ultramontane sympathies of Bustamante and his Foreign Minister, Lucas Alamán, were shown by their willingness to abandon the right of patronal presentation. With congressional authorization Alamán sent to Vázquez for submission to the pope the names of candidates selected by the ecclesiastical chapters for appointment to the vacant benefices. The pope was asked to institute, not on the presentation of a civil sovereign, but simply *de motu proprio*. There was to be no mention of any government, republic, or state, said Zavala, but the question was to be submitted solely as one relating to "some regions called Mexican."[22] But for reasons noted elsewhere the pope was not ready to nominate the individuals whose names were given to him by the Mexican agent. The pontiff's offer to name apostolic vicars or bishops *in partibus* was refused by Vázquez. But when Gregory XVI became pope, Vázquez secured the desired nominations of bishops for the vacant sees. In the Consistory of 1831, Gregory XVI preconized *motu proprio* proprietary bishops for the sees of Puebla, Chiapas, Linares, Guadalajara, Durango, and Michoacán. Having abandoned the right of presentation to bishoprics, the government of Bustamante enacted a law, May 16, 1831, granting to the clergy the free election of canons. These acts clearly implied abandonment of all pretension to the patronage. It was a great triumph

20. Supra, pp. 79-82, 84.
21. Callcott, *op. cit.*, pp. 68-69.
22. Zavala, *op. cit.*, II, 230-31.

for clericalism.[23] The harmony established between the clergy and the government was rudely destroyed two years later when an ephemeral Liberal government was established.

To understand the "Reform of 1833" it is necessary to analyze its causes. On this subject writers have advanced the widest possible variety of explanations. In the opinion of Bancroft, the political activities of the Church were thought to be an obstacle to the development of Mexican democracy.[24] It would be well if he had explained the meaning of "democracy" as understood by the Liberals. Lorenzo de Zavala, caustic critic of the Catholic Church, and an actor in the drama he describes, was of the opinion that the overwhelming wealth and power of the Church made it a menace to the State. He wrote, "The ecclesiastical hierarchy, with its rents, its *fueros*, and its power, is of such a nature that it is not possible to preserve it in a popular government without destroying at the same time the public peace and the principle of equality. He who sanctions its existence sanctions perpetual discord."[25] Many writers saw pronounced social abuses, in addition to the political and economic, as causes of the Liberal reaction of 1833. In their opinion Gómez Farías assaulted the privileged orders because he was the champion of the rights of the masses.[26]

Ecclesiastical historians, like Father Mariano Cuevas, on the other hand, denied that Gómez Farías and the Liberals were actuated by deep-seated political, social, and economic motives. To them the whole affair was simply an atheistic movement aimed at religion itself. Gómez Farías and his followers were all disciples of the devil.[27]

It is the opinion of the present writer that Gómez Farías did not attack Catholicism as a religion. He was no Luther with a program of dogmatic reform, nor was he a Voltaire impatient of all dogma, for he wrote concerning the education of his children, "Keep the Sabbath holy, hear mass on appointed days in church, and observe Christian practices."[28] An analysis of his reform measures fails to reveal any indication of an organized assault on the tenets of Catholicism. On the other hand, further examination of the reform laws fails to prove the existence of a class movement. The "Liberals of 1833," politicians, intellectuals,

---

23. Zubieta, *Misiones Diplomáticas de Colombia,* 589; Riva Palacio, *op. cit.,* IV, 284.
24. H. H. Bancroft, *History of Mexico* (San Francisco, 1888), VI, 583.
25. Zavala, *op. cit.,* II, 237.
26. Alfonso Toro, *La Iglesia y El Estado en México* (Mexico, 1927), p. 100.
27. Mariano Cuevas, *Historia de la Iglesia en México* (5 vols.; Mexico, El Paso, 1921-28), V, 196.
28. "Reglas que deberán observar mis hijos." Undated MS, Gómez Farías Papers, García Collection. See Ricardo Delgado Román, *Valentín Gómez Farías: ideario reformista* (Guadalajara, 1958).

and professional people, have been unwarrantedly credited with championing the rights of the downtrodden masses. If so, why was not legislation enacted to benefit the lowest classes? If it was a social movement, why the absence of social legislation? The truth is that the "masses" were entirely outside the picture and were of little concern to either party. Bancroft came the closest to the truth when he said that Gómez Farías "labored to crush the politico-theocratic power." The political alliance of the clergy and the other elements composing the Conservative party had to be broken up by destroying the ecclesiastical *fueros*. And why the attack? It was in order that the Liberals might seize control of the government and force the adoption of their *political* program which was intended to make Mexico safe for democracy, that is, for the Liberals.

Following the overthrow of the Conservative régime of Bustamante, a new president and vice-president were elected. The victorious candidates were Antonio López de Santa Anna and Gómez Farías. If Santa Anna belonged to any party, which was doubtful, he was, like his vice-president, a Liberal. At least he had been fairly consistent up to 1833 in supporting liberal principles. A new Congress was also elected when the Liberal flood was at its crest. The result was "the reddest" Congress Mexico had had up to that time. The radical deputies were not inclined to forget the indignities and injuries they had suffered at the hands of the Conservatives, particularly in the States where there had been numerous bitter struggles for the possession of local government.[29] Thus the Congress convened in an atmosphere charged with a spirit of intolerance and vengeance.

From April 1, 1833, to April 24, 1834, with only a few short interruptions, Santa Anna allowed Gómez Farías to exercise the executive control. The reason for this peculiar procedure on the part of the President has been the cause of considerable bewilderment to historians. Some explain that Santa Anna was never in earnest as a Liberal, but simply wished to use Gómez Farías as a foil to test public sentiment on a progressive program. Others explain that Santa Anna was really sincere when he declared that ill-health kept him on his estate, "Manga de Clavo."[30] "It would seem," says Callcott, "that he was just about neutral in the whole matter, and was carefully watching the signs of the times."[31]

With the alacrity of an impractical idealist and a novice in govern-

29. Riva Palacio, *op. cit.*, IV, 306.
30. In a letter to Gómez Farías, dated Manga de Clavo, March 16, 1833, Santa Anna explained that ill-health made it impossible for him to go to the Capital. Gómez Farías Papers.
31. Callcott, *op. cit.*, p. 100.

ment, Farías seized the opportunity afforded him by the wily Santa Anna to plunge Mexico into an orgy of reform.

The opening gun of the Liberal attack was aimed at the ecclesiastical temporalities. The objectives of the assault were two-fold, that is, it was hoped that by depriving the Church of its wealth not only would it be rendered politically impotent, but the financial straits of the government would be relieved. The opulence of the Church contrasted with the empty public treasury and more than once the authorities were moved to tap the clerical coffers. On August 17, Congress secularized the missions of Alta and Baja, California. The rule of the mission fathers, dating from the days of Junípero Serra, was terminated by the establishment, in the erstwhile mission districts, of parishes with secular clergy. Fifteen hundred *pesos* annually were assigned to meet the expenses of each parish. The mission lands and buildings were confiscated and divided among the settlers and natives. Unfortunately the Indians were defrauded of their lands and the greater part of the old mission estates fell into the hands of political grafters. To defray the expenses assumed in supporting the Church in the Californias, the government drew upon the pious fund of the California missions which had also been confiscated.[32] The California missions were selected as the first object of Liberal attack for economic and political reasons. The pious fund and the rich mission lands tempted the impecunious Liberals who were sadly in need of funds to prosecute their program. In addition, it was felt that the mission control of California savored too much of a theocracy which stifled colonization and should therefore be abolished. Later the hospitals, real estate, and other property belonging to the Philippines missions were confiscated. This was in line with the policy to nationalize all pious funds whose revenue went out of the country. On April 16, 1834, all the missions of the republic were ordered secularized and their properties nationalized.[33] Since the economic situation of the government continued to be most precarious, Lorenzo de Zavala presented a proposition in the Chamber of Deputies for the settlement of the public debt. He suggested as the only possible solution of the national financial problem the confiscation of all properties held in mortmain. He estimated that the ecclesiastical resources were sufficient to pay off the national debt and support the Church if the latter were under government control.[34] His plan was not adopted, but it was an

32. Manuel Dublán y José María Lozano (eds.), *Legislación Mexicana* (Mexico, 1876-1904), II, 603.

33. *Ibid.*, II, 689.

34. Francisco Bulnes, *Juárez y las Revoluciones de Ayutla y de la Reforma* (Mexico, 1905), p. 90.

unmistakable harbinger of future disaster for the clericals. Therefore, many of the religious orders, to defend themselves against impending confiscation, either sold or transferred their properties. These subterfuges were halted by act of Congress which declared the illegality of sale or alienation in any manner of property and capital held in mortmain.[35]

The ecclesiastical monopoly of public education was also attacked because the reformers felt that the Church was using the schools to inculcate its political propaganda in the minds of the tender youths of the country. No other act of Gómez Farías and the Liberals more exactly illustrates their lack of practical sense than their promulgation of a law which completely secularized public education. That the government was totally unprepared to assume this burden seemed to be an inconsequential detail. Better that the children of Mexico should be without schools of any description, thought the Liberal reformers, than that the public Catholic schools should be allowed to train future champions of the clerical cause. Even the venerable old University of Mexico was suppressed because its faculty was composed of priests.[36]

The Liberals were moving inevitably toward the separation of Church and State. The next step taken in that direction was the passage of a decree (October 27) which freed the citizens of the civil responsibility of paying the tithes. Prior to this it had been the custom, dating from colonial times, for the government to enforce payment. So pronounced did clerical opposition become that it was necessary for the Minister of Justice, Andrés Quintana Roo, to issue a circular to the state authorities recommending that they prevent priests from discussing political questions from the pulpits. He declared that the priests should be made to understand that they were subjects of the temporal authority, and that "the president has [had] taken as an invariable rule of conduct the separation of interests of religion from those of the government."[37]

The clerical conscience was scandalized by the passage of another law (November 6) which repealed all laws imposing any kind of compulsion, direct or indirect, on the fulfillment of monastic vows. The religious of both sexes were accorded absolute freedom to forswear their vows and reënter secular life. "This was a blow at the very heart of the Church system," says Callcott. "For a young girl who had taken vows as a 'bride of Christ' to forswear those vows and enter into family life

35. Riva Palacio, *op. cit.*, IV, 334-35.
36. *Ibid.*, IV, 332.
37. Riva Palacio, *op. cit.*, IV, 333.

as a wife and mother was not only indecent; it was repulsive and sacrilegious in the extreme."[38]

The recently won independence of the Church, acquired by Bustamante's renunciation of the national patronage, was terminated when the government assumed, as repository of the exercise of sovereignty, the appointment of the officers of the Church. On November 3 Quintana Roo issued a decree revoking the law of May 16, 1831, which gave to the clergy the free election of canons. On December 17 the government commanded that vacant curacies be filled as provided by the laws of the Indies. The president of the republic and the governors of the states were to exercise the patronal powers formerly possessed by the viceroys, presidents of audiencias, and governors. The restoration of the national patronage, with its implication of the subordination of the Church to the State, was so repugnant to the prelates that they resolved to suffer martyrdom even before obeying the law. On April 22, 1834, the prelates were granted a thirty-day extension, under penalty of exile, to fulfill the law of December 17. Several preferred exile to submission.[39]

The religious reform had been carried forward too far and too rapidly. A general outcry was raised against the Liberal idealists who had thought it easy to reform society profoundly by laws and decrees. Their fallacious reasoning was revealed by the overwhelming opposition which they aroused and the suddenness with which they were ousted from control. A simultaneous attack on the military *fueros* caused the militarists to ally themselves with the clericals under the *Plan de Cuernavaca* to destroy all principles of the Reform and restore the *fueros* in all their purity. Their battle-cry became "Religión y Fueros." The fanatical masses were easily rallied to the support of the Church for it was not difficult for the clergy to convince the people that their sacred religion was being attacked. The Liberals should have realized the nature of the opposition and proceeded slowly. Valentín Gómez Farías, however, was not a man who, having gained power, would be willing to temporize merely to retain control, for power was to him only a more efficacious means of expediting the Reform. "He loved his country," said Bulnes, "like the biblical patriarch Abraham loved his son, with dagger upraised over his heart, ready to kill if liberty, the god of his tabernacle, so willed it."[40]

When Santa Anna had definitely decided in which direction the opinion of the influential tended, he determined to abandon his retreat

---

38. Callcott, *op. cit.*, pp. 92-93; Dublán y Lozano, *op. cit.*, II, 580.
39. Riva Palacio, *op. cit.*, IV, 334-37.
40. Bulnes, *Júarez y las Revoluciones de Ayutla*, p. 87.

in his hacienda and assume the leadership of the Conservative reaction—whatever might have been his opinions in the past. He revealed himself, thereby, to be an astute politician who follows public opinion and not a statesman who moulds it. Santa Anna returned to the capital, says Alamán, "as the supporter of the discontented and the hope of the persecuted and the plaintful." The aristrocrats and the high officers of the Church who had looked upon him with disdain, now appealed to him to save them from the reformists.[41]

The trust of the clericals was not misplaced, for Santa Anna proved to be the savior of the Church. He immediately dissolved the Congress and issued a series of executive decrees suspending the various anti-religious laws, "until a general Congress should meet." Needless to say he was in no hurry about convoking another Congress. To satisfy the clergy he named as Minister of Justice and Ecclesiastical Affairs, Bishop Juan Cayetano Portugal of Michoacán. *Te Deums* were sung in praise of Santa Anna, "El Salvador." The clergy were commanded by the metropolitan chapter to say prayers for "the great and virtuous chief Don Antonio López de Santa Anna, restorer of the liberty of the Church."[42] "Viva la Religión y el ilustre Santa Anna," shouted the masses. The Liberals were denounced as heretics and dangerous citizens, and Gómez Farías had to bear the brunt of the attack. He was finally forced to leave the country amid cries of "arch-fiend" and "Judas."

The delayed election of a new Congress was held in December, 1834. As was to be expected, the military-clerical coalition emerged victorious. On January 4, 1835, the Congress assembled in Mexico City, determined to translate the *Plan de Cuernavaca* into legal action. This meant the abrogation of the various reforms of the Liberal régime (for they had only been suspended by Santa Anna).

One of the first acts of the reactionary Congress was to declare the office of the vice-presidency legally vacant. Gómez Farías had been living in exile for nearly six months. The University of Mexico was reëstablished and a committee was organized to formulate a plan of public instruction. This action constituted recognition, by the Conservatives, that the old school system as controlled by the Church was defective and needed reform. Other measures of the Liberals which were revoked were the secularization of the California missions and the depriving of the religious communities of the free right to dispose of their properties.[43]

When Santa Anna betrayed a tendency to vacillate in his support

41. Riva Palacio, *op. cit.*, IV, 338.
42. *Ibid.*, IV, 345-46.
43. Dublán y Lozano, *op. cit.*, III, 39-40, 96.

of the *Plan de Cuernavaca*, he was subjected to such severe criticism and opposition that he preferred to retire to his hacienda. On January 28, 1835, General Miguel Barragán was named president *ad interim*. It seemed impossible now that anything could disturb the triumph of the clericals. Yet trouble started almost immediately when the Minister of Justice and Ecclesiastical Affairs, Joaquín de Iturbide,[44] incorporated in his departmental report a defense of national patronage. This statement created a furore among the clergy. They were temporarily successful in their opposition, for the various laws that established national patronage were revoked.

The old privileged status of the Catholic Church having been restored, the Assembly turned to the fulfillment of another pledge: the establishment of a centralistic government. By decree of October 3, 1835, centralism was proclaimed, and on December 30, 1836, a centralistic constitution was promulgated. This constitution, known as *Las Siete Leyes*, contained substantially the same provisions regarding the Church as the Constitution of 1824. But this was very displeasing to the clergy, for they hoped to establish their complete independence of the temporal authorities. The incorporation into the fundamental charter of clauses providing for the *pase* for all pontifical communications and the assuming by the government, until the conclusion of a concordat, of the right of presentation were vigorously opposed by the clergy but to no effect.[45]

Notwithstanding the failure of the clergy to force upon the Assembly all of the constitutional guarantees they wished, they were able, after the promulgation of that instrument, to remain in the political ascendancy for quite a time. In illustration of the extent of the clerical reaction: when the pope issued a brief (1836) authorizing a reduction in the number of religious feast days, the Chamber of Deputies, which was made up of priests and their partisans, refused admission to the brief because of the injury this would cause the clergy, who derived financial profit from the fiestas. Little consideration was given to the economic advantage to the country at large that would result from a decrease in the number of days of idleness. It would appear, then, that the Mexican Conservatives were more clerical than the pope. It was not until 1839 that the *pase* was granted to the brief of Gregory XVI.[46]

Since ecclesiastical affairs were so satisfactorily settled for the Church, it was but natural that the pope should accord political recognition to

---

44. Bishop Portugal had resigned from the Ministry of State as a protest against Santa Anna's inclination to favor national patronage. (Toro, *op. cit.*, p. 120.)

45. Riva Palacio, *op. cit.*, IV, 386.

46. Toro, *op. cit.*, p. 126.

the Mexican Republic. In November, 1836, Manuel Díaz de Bonilla was received as the official Mexican representative and the pope dispatched an internuncio to Mexico. Since papal funds were low it was agreed that the internuncio was to be supported by the Mexican government. This illustrates the extent of the reaction under President Anastacio Bustamante, who, under clerical auspices, had assumed the presidency in 1837. Bishop Vázquez of Puebla received a papal commission to institute canonical processes for the filling of vacant bishoprics. Accordingly several sees were filled, including that of Mexico which had become vacant when Archbishop Fonte died after living for many years in exile. By brief of April 25, 1837, the diocese of Chiapas was detached from the archdiocese of Guatemala and united to that of Mexico. The Holy See, however, displayed reluctance to negotiate a concordat with Mexico.[47] The pope evidently was unwilling, as were the Mexican prelates, to recognize national patronage.

President Bustamante, champion of the Church though he was, again aroused clerical opposition. The perennial financial embarrassments of the government necessitated numerous plans to raise money, none of which availed. Since no one but the clergy had money, the popular demand was that Church properties should be mortgaged. Bustamante, seeing no other escape, invited the clericals to make a loan. The metropolitan chapter acceded, but limited the loan to 750,000 *pesos*. Fears that this was but a prelude to a wholesale confiscation of Church properties and wealth caused the clericals to withdraw their support from Bustamante. The Liberals, witnessing this division in the ranks of their enemies, took courage, and labored for a return to power.

A revolt against Bustamante occurred in 1840, but the time for the reëstablishment of Liberalism had not arrived. Instead, as a result of bewildering military plots and counterplots, the irrepressible Santa Anna was restored to supremacy with a program of "personalistic centralism." Santa Anna was felicitated by the clergy on the triumph of the revolution, but not so enthusiastically as in 1834. Before long it became alarmingly apparent to the clergy that they had erred grievously in deserting Bustamante for the wily lord of Manga de Clavo. The latter was more aggressive than his predecessor in reminding the ecclesiastics of their duty as citizens to contribute to the common expenses of the government. The pious fund of the California missions was again nationalized, silver plate deposited in the cathedral of Puebla was confiscated, religious orders were forced to make contributions, and the Archbishop of Mexico was obliged to accept drafts up to 170,000 *pesos*. Santa Anna was not

47. Cabañas, *op. cit.*, pp. LXX-LXXII.

unfriendly or antagonistic toward the Church, for witness his decree allowing the Jesuits and members of monastic orders to reënter the country. He merely refused to countenance the clerical habit of looking upon all governments as if they were the servants of the Church and, on the other hand, of never wishing to spend a cent for their support.[48]

The Congress, assembled on June 10, 1842, to produce a new constitution, in accordance with the *Plan de Tacubaya,* proved to be liberal and federalistic. Since the deputies would not acquiesce in the wishes of Santa Anna, who wanted centralism with himself as the center, he retired in a huff to his hacienda and left the constituents to draft a liberal, federal instrument of government. The new project, while still in the embryonic stage, was criticized by the reactionary press as an attack on the Catholic faith and the honor and dignity of the army.

Santa Anna's henchmen easily accomplished the dissolution of the federalist Congress, and a "safe" *Junta* of Notables was convened to produce a "satisfactory" fundamental charter. On June 13, 1843, the *Bases Orgánicas,* the third of Mexico's national constitutions, was adopted. This instrument declared that the nation professed and protected the Roman Catholic religion to the exclusion of any other. Also, the military and ecclesiastical *fueros* were recognized. In this constitution were to be found the customary features regarding the negotiation of concordats and the admission of pontifical communications.[49]

The Church was powerful in official councils at the beginning of the war with the United States. In January, 1846, General Paredes, at the head of a coalition of ecclesiastical, military, and monarchial groups, seized control of the government. This general, who had shamefully diverted his army which had been organized at great national sacrifice to oppose the impending invasion by the United States, was "elected" president of the Republic by a *Junta* presided over by Archbishop Posada. Paredes was entirely clerical and ultramontane in his sympathies. He chose the Bishop of Chiapas as his Minister of Justice and Ecclesiastical Affairs, and in his summons for an extraordinary Congress he assigned twenty of the seats to the ecclesiastical prelates.[50]

Paredes, however, needed money to prosecute the war. In April he called on the Church to contribute 200,000 *pesos* per month for the support of the government. The clergy protested and the Archbishop declared that the share assigned to the archiepiscopal see, 98,000 *pesos,* was more than its total revenue. Paredes' tenure of power was of short duration, for in August, 1846, he was overthrown by Santa Anna and

48. Dublán y Lozano, *op. cit.,* IV, 111, 301-2, 363; Toro, *op. cit.,* pp. 134, 141-42.
49. For the *Leyes Bases Orgánicas de 1843,* see Gamboa, *op. cit.,* pp. 428-82.
50. Dublán y Lozano, *op. cit.,* V, 105-20.

Gómez Farías, the former now posing as a federalist and champion of the Constitution of 1824. General Salas, puppet of Santa Anna, acted as provisional president while his master assumed control of the army. To aid Santa Anna in organizing the military resources, General Salas ordered all property owners, civilian and ecclesiastical, to pay to the government a sum equal to one month's rent. Since this expedient was a failure, the provisional president ordered the issuance of letters of credit charged to the secular and regular clergy and guaranteed by designated Church properties. In order that there should be no evasion, the clergy were prohibited from alienating property.[51]

Late in December, Santa Anna and Gómez Farías were elected president and vice-president respectively. Once more Santa Anna refrained from assuming the executive control but instead led an army against the invading Americans and left Gómez Farías at the capital in control of the government. The Vice-President was no longer a zealous reformer, for years spent in exile had cooled his idealistic ardor. There was no danger, then, of a renewal of his old reform program, but necessity compelled him to seek clerical aid to finance the war. The condition of the public finances was distressing; the treasury was completely exhausted, and the Congress was at its wit's end to meet the urgent pleas of Santa Anna for food, clothing, and munitions for his troops. With affairs in this critical state, Santa Anna wrote Gómez Farías confidentially suggesting that he have the Congress authorize a loan secured by a mortgage of Church property. The bill was passed after a stormy session on January 10, 1847. The archiepiscopal chapter of Mexico filed a protest, declaring that the Church would not observe it. Furthermore, anyone who should attempt to enforce the law would be excommunicated. Despite the clerical protest Gómez Farías issued an executive decree providing that the government should raise 15,000,000 *pesos* by mortgaging or selling ecclesiastical property held in mortmain, excepting that of educational and charitable institutions.[52]

The clergy complained bitterly and many churches were closed in protest; but the government ordered them reopened. Although Santa Anna had written Gómez Farías congratulating him on the passage of the law, he unexpectedly altered his attitude and deserted his vice-president. On March 29, 1847, he issued a decree revoking the law of January 10, in return for a large cash payment by the clergy. In short, he accepted a bribe to restrain the attack on the clerical temporalities. A second time Gómez Farías was disgraced and forced out of office because of his crafty, treacherous colleague. Since Gómez Farías would not

51. *Ibid.*, V, 211-17; Riva Palacio, *op. cit.*, IV, 592, 598.
52. *Ibid.*, IV, 589-608; Dublán y Lozano, V, 246-48.

resign, the Congress proceeded to abolish the office of the vice-presidency. Once more the Church had successfully withstood a determined effort to destroy its temporalities.

Under President José Joaquín Herrera (1848-51), who enjoyed the distinction of being the first president since Guadalupe Victoria to serve out his full term of office, the Church gained in wealth and influence. It became the dominant factor in Mexican politico-economic affairs. Because of his desire to see the great number of ecclesiastical vacancies in Mexico filled, President Herrera secured the passage of a temporary law providing for appointments until a concordat should be concluded. This law required the chapters of vacant sees to present to the government a list of at least three names from which one was to be selected to be presented to the pope. The clergy opposed the law because of their desire to be free of all dependence on the civil power. Nevertheless they acquiesced and submitted the lists. The names of those selected by the government for the vacancies were then sent to the pope by a special envoy who was instructed to request that in the bulls of institution the clause *motu proprio* be omitted. The pope consented and preconized those presented by the Mexican government.[53]

After the retirement of Herrera, a feeble and corrupt Liberal régime was terminated in short order by a Conservative revolt initiated under the *Plan de Hospicio* (July, 1852). There had been many *pronunciamientos* of the military in Mexico, but this was the first proclaimed by the clericals. The plan was formulated in the cathedral chapter of Guadalajara. The revolt resulted in the recall of Santa Anna from his most recent "perpetual exile" to run as the Conservative candidate for the presidency. Santa Anna, while in exile, had been in correspondence with Lucas Alamán, spokesman of the Conservatives, and he returned with the understanding that he would be supported if he agreed to a program of cessation of political activity against the Church and security for the holders of large propertied interests.[54]

On March 17, 1853, Santa Anna was elected president, and Lucas Alamán was made his Minister of Foreign Relations. The staunch old clerical and monarchial champion died in June, but the President, not unmindful of his obligations to the clericals, made an effort to continue the policies initiated by Alamán. The Mexican minister at Rome was ordered to reopen the subject of a concordat. By 1854 the negotiations had proceeded to the working out of details, but the Revolution of Ayutla broke them off. The Jesuits were reintroduced into Mexico to assist in the education of the poorer classes and much of their property

53. Cuevas, *op. cit.*, V, 269-70.
54. Toro, *op. cit.*, pp. 205, 209.

was restored to them. Also, Santa Anna revoked the decree of November 6, 1833, which denied protection of the laws for the fulfillment of monastic vows.

Popular fear of the over-ambitious dictator, whose full official title was "Benemérito de la patria, General de División, Gran Maestre de la Nacional y distinguida Orden de Guadalupe, Gran Cruz de la Real y distinguida Orden española de Carlos III, y Presidente de la República Mexicana," finally accomplished his overthrow. "The discovery of the monarchist intrigue, the sale of La Mesilla, the declaration of the perpetual dictatorship, the despoiliations of the *camarilla* of Santa Anna, which caused a deficit of more than 20,000,000 *pesos* annually, the hateful, ridiculous, and ruinous contributions that were invented to cover it, killed the patience of the people and provoked a real revolution, the most sanguinary that had been seen in Mexico since the wars for independence."[55] The Liberal *Plan de Ayutla* (March 1, 1854) not only initiated a revolt which accomplished the definitive extrusion of Santa Anna from the political stage of Mexico, but inaugurated the most bitter and devastating attack which the Catholic Church had ever experienced in the land of the Aztecs.

In its inception the Revolution of Ayutla was hardly more than a national protest against a man who, consumed by ambition, aspired to the establishment of absolutism. Santa Anna taxed to the limit the patience of civilized society, says Bulnes, and therefore he was rejected by "a formidable and tacit coalition of all the sensible political elements of the nation."[56] After the flight of Santa Anna, however, each faction tried to perpetuate its interests and make the revolution its own. The reactionaries were determined to establish guarantees for the clerical and military privileges and secure the ascendancy of the great landlords. They hoped to turn back the clock to the good old colonial times of special privilege. Modernism should not be tolerated in Mexico. The Liberal group, composed of class-conscious mestizos and Indians, and a few creoles, "aimed at the emancipation of the country from ecclesiastical domination, and at the release of the government from military adventurers who dominated through identity of interest with the Church."[57] They proposed to make the revolution a real one and create a society based on modern principles. This conflict of economic, racial, and social interests made for civil war, which in turn opened the way for the first serious effort in Mexican history to create a democratic and constitutional government. Unlike the innumerable praetorian revolts which had

55. *Ibid.*, p. 231.
56. Bulnes, *op. cit.*, p. 117.
57. Priestly, *op. cit.*, p. 317.

distracted Mexico during the first quarter-century of her independence, the conflict which raged after the overthrow of Santa Anna was Mexico's first really popular revolution—and for that reason it triumphed.

A Liberal revolutionary *junta* which met in Cuernavaca on October 4, 1855, and which was presided over by the old Liberal reformer Valentín Gómez Farías, elected Juan Álvarez provisional president of Mexico. Álvarez appointed as his ministers Ignacio Comonfort (War), Melchor Ocampo (State), Guillermo Prieto (Treasury), Benito Juárez (Justice and Ecclesiastical Affairs), and Miguel Lerdo de Tejada (Public Works). Álvarez and Juárez were full-blooded Indians, a clear indication that a new class was coming to the front in Mexico. All members of the cabinet were Masons, and, with the possible exception of Comonfort, they were anticlericals, a situation which boded ill for the Catholic Church.[58]

On November 23, 1855, the Minister of Justice and Ecclesiastical Affairs led the initial assault on the breastworks of intrenched privilege when he issued a decree which popularly bears his name, *Ley Juárez*. This decree suppressed all special courts except the military and the ecclesiastical; and, as for these, they were deprived of all jurisdiction in civil suits. The military courts were to have jurisdiction only in cases arising from military crimes. The ecclesiastical tribunals were to hear common crimes of the members of their *fuero*, but it was provided that even the *fuero eclesiástico* was renunciable in common crimes. An accused religious could choose a civil or ecclesiastical court at will.[59]

As was to be expected immediate and vehement clerical opposition was aroused by the decree which reorganized the judicial administration. The archbishop of Mexico wrote Juárez a protest. Juárez replied that the measure did not touch religion in any way, and that the sole purpose of promulgating the decree was to establish social equality.[60] The clergy were ordered by the archbishop not to renounce their *fueros* under pain of drastic ecclesiastical penalties.

Since the *Ley Juárez* also struck at the privileges of the military, once more the Church and army united in defense of their *fueros*. Again the battle-cry was *Religión y Fueros!* The opposition to the government, both from without and within, forced Álverez to relinquish the presidency to Comonfort (December 12, 1855). This political shift signified a temporary swing of influence to the side of the Moderates. Ignacio Comonfort, a semi-Conservative and "friend at court for the

---

58. Callcott, *op. cit.*, pp. 235-36; Cuevas, *op. cit.*, V, 285.
59. Dublán y Lozano, *op. cit.*, VII, 598.
60. Fortino Hipólito Vera (ed.), *Colección de Documentos Eclesiásticos de México* (Amecameca, 1887), II, 91; Dublán y Lozano, *op. cit.*, VII, 614.

clergy," selected for his cabinet men of only moderately liberal ideas, and there was not a Mason among them. It is not to be presumed, however, that Comonfort was a tool of the clericals.

The Constituent Congress, which had been called by President Álvarez, as provided by the *Plan de Ayutla*, was formally convened on February 18, 1856. The session was opened with cries of "Viva el Congreso Constituyente! Viva Comonfort! Viva la libertad! Mueran los reaccionarios!" The delegates had been elected by a complicated, indirect method, and no ecclesiastic was allowed to vote or be voted for. There was frank and deliberate design on the part of the Liberals to secure complete control of the Congress. The great Conservative leaders, and naturally the clerics, were not present and even the moderates were only partially represented. If the Constituent Congresses of 1856 and 1916 had been really popular representative bodies, the Constitutions of 1857 and 1917 would have been more generally acceptable. The great majority of the constituents of 1856 were lawyers. The rest were militarists and employees of the Federal and State governments. The industrial, commercial, and laboring elements were not represented in the personnel of the Convention; the majority of the delegates were political theorists more interested in theory than in economic matters. Such was the personnel of the Convention, which, in open session, set itself to the task of formulating a new democratic constitution for Mexico. A committee composed of seven members was appointed on February 21 to prepare the draft of a constitution. The committee's project was not reported to the Convention until June 16. After that date it was debated article by article. Until the Congress should conclude its labors, Comonfort promulgated a temporary plan of government known as the *Estatuto Orgánico Provisional*. By this instrument the clergy were denied the right of citizenship.[61]

Since the *Ley Juárez* was only an executive decree of the provisional government, it was deemed advisable to secure its ratification by the Constituent Congress. Therefore it was submitted for the approval of the Congress, and, after a two days' debate, it was adopted by a vote of 82 to 1. Zarco, the historian of the Convention, after recording the passage of the law, writes with enthusiasm: "No more *fueros!* No more privileges! No more exceptions! Equality for all citizens! Perfect sovereignty of the temporal power! Justice for all!"[62]

61. Francisco Zarco, *Historia del Congreso Extraordinario Constituyente de 1856 y 1857* (Mexico, 1857), I, 61, 306-26, 467-87. See Walter V. Scholes, "Church and State at the Mexican Constitutional Convention, 1856-1857," in *The Américas*, IV, No. 2 (October, 1947), 151-74.
62. Zarco, *op. cit.*, I, 166-82.

On June 25, 1856, the second notable anticlerical reform measure was promulgated. This decree, named the *Ley Lerdo* from its author Lerdo de Tejada, Minister of the Treasury, provided that no corporation, civil or ecclesiastical, would be permitted to acquire or own real property, except that which was directly used for the purposes of worship. The properties then owned by such corporations would be sold at a price which at 6 per cent would yield the rent actually being charged. Tenants were to be given first choice to purchase, but if they did not take proper steps to secure their rights within three months, the property would be offered for public sale at the same price. Properties not rented or leased would be sold at public auction. All sales were subject to the payment of the *alcabala*, or sales tax, at 5 per cent. The law did not confiscate property; it decreed the necessity of alienating Church realty held in mortmain and turning back the proceeds to the Church.

The purpose of the *Ley Lerdo* was explained in a circular which accompanied the decree. The object of the measure, according to Lerdo de Tejada, was to make all large property-holders disgorge and sell to the middle and poor classes, thereby making real property more mobile and conducing to its improvement and development. It would tend to equalize the taxation of all real estate and increase the revenue of the government by the receipts from the *alcabala* and other forms of taxation.[63] It is to be noted that Lerdo de Tejada emphasized only the economic advantages of the measure. He remained silent on the political aspects of the law which were extremely important, for it was hoped that the disamortization of Church properties would destroy the political influence of the Church. The decree of disamortization was submitted to the Congress for its approval on June 28, 1856. Rules of procedure were set aside and all efforts of the opposition to block the measure were futile. After a short debate, the decree was approved on the same day by a vote of 84 to 8.[64]

On the eve of the Reform the Church was said to own over one-third of the land in Mexico. It is not possible, nor indeed is it necessary, to give in exact figures the amount of clerical capital, for there is little disagreement that the Church was unbelievably rich, controlling all agricultural activity by means of heavy mortgages and enjoying an enormous revenue. This concentration of wealth, for obvious reasons, was economically bad, but it was made doubly so since it was used to control public opinion for the support of the reactionary clerical program. Since the political aim of the Mexican Church was a reversion

63. Dublán y Lozano, *op. cit.*, VIII, 197-201.
64. *Ibid.*, VIII, 202; Zarco, *op. cit.*, I, 593-605.

to the medieval theocratic State, it was best for Mexico that the reaction be halted at any cost—even at the expense of depriving the Church of its temporalities.

The promulgation of the disamortization law stirred up a veritable hornets' nest of clerical and Conservative opposition. The attack on its property was regarded as a sword's thrust at the very heart of the Church. Archbishop Garza immediately (July 7, 1856) penned a vigorous protest to the government. He declared that the government had no jurisdiction over the Church, even as to its property rights, and he would defend the position of the Church until the Holy See had approved the law.[65] Bishop Labastida of Puebla was so violent in his protests that President Comonfort was forced to exile him. Bishop Clemente de Jesús Munguía called the *Ley Lerdo "cisomática, anárquica, impolítica y estéril."* All tenants of clerical lands were threatened with dire consequences if they dared to denounce the properties occupied by them.

In a papal allocution, Pope Pius IX condemned the reform decrees and "whatever else the civil authority has put into effect with such contempt of ecclesiastical authority and this Apostolic See."[66]

The envenomed fierceness with which the clergy resisted provoked new reform measures, some of which really did assault the purely spiritual dominion of the Church. Decrees were issued allowing those who had taken religious vows to forswear them, and once more the Jesuits, who had been readmitted into Mexico by Santa Anna, were expelled from the country. The University of Mexico was closed on the charge that it was a source of pernicious doctrine and a center of clerical propaganda. The control of the cemeteries which had been wholly vested in the Church was taken from it and given to the Department of Public Hygiene. Another law provided for the civil registration of vital statistics.[67]

On April 11, 1857, Comonfort signed a decree of Minister Iglesias (hence the name of the law *Ley Iglesias*) which prohibited coaction of the government in the collection of parochial subventions and limited the fees for the performance of religious ceremonies. If the recipient of the religious service was not earning a living wage, the clergy were required to perform their duties for charity. Although this law was very clearly of a retaliatory, as well as of a reformist nature, clerical abuses legitimized

65. Vera, *op. cit.*, III, 201 ff.
66. *Ibid.*, I, 585-89.
67. Dublán y Lozano, *op. cit.*, VII, 266-67; VIII, 154; Riva Palacio, *op. cit.*, V, 770. "The friars of the convent of San Francisco in Mexico City were caught red-handed fomenting a revolt. President Comonfort, thereupon, ordered the suppression of the convent, the nationalization of its property, and the opening of a street through the premises of the convent." Dublán y Lozano, *op. cit.*, VIII, 244-45.

its promulgation. The fees were numerous and heavy and often the priests were heartless in squeezing the *centavos* from their poverty-stricken parishioners.

The Constitution of 1857 embodied the religious policy of the Liberals. Thus, public education was declared to be free (Article 3). This article was put into the Constitution despite arguments of its opponents who contended that freedom of education would give complete license for charlatans to prey upon the public. Article 5 nullified the compulsory observance of religious vows. Although this provision did not abolish the monastic orders, it contained the germ of their suppression.[68] The *Ley Juárez* was constitutionalized as Article 13, which prohibited *fueros*, or special tribunals. Likewise, Article 27, which prohibited religious corporations from acquiring and administering real estate except that destined immediately and directly for the purposes of worship, was in reality the *Ley Lerdo*. This article was regarded by the clergy as being the most drastic of all, for, it has been remarked, "If the Constitution provided the cause of the Three Years War, it was because it included Article 27—the law of June 25."[69]

In order to circumvent more effectively the political activities of the clergy, the Constitution provided (Articles 56 and 77) that they were ineligible to election as president of the Republic or as national representatives. The right of the suffrage, however, was restored to the ecclesiastics. The Federal government (Article 123) was given the right to intervene "in matters of religious worship and outward ecclesiastical forms" only as the laws might designate. The nature and extent of governmental intervention was not defined and could only be determined by actual practice. There was no reference in the Constitution to ecclesiastical patronage, nor indeed was there any mention of the Roman Catholic religion as the religion of the State. The Constitution was also silent on the subject of religious liberty.[70]

Such were the religious clauses of the Constitution of 1857. A small and unrepresentative group of revolutionaries had resolved to free the nation forcibly and somewhat against its will from clerical domination. To accomplish this end an attempt was made to shatter the material power of the Church. These visionaries thought that a people profoundly submerged in Catholicism for three hundred years and fondly attached to the ecclesiastical authority could be forced to repudiate the

68. For the Constitution of 1857, see Gamboa, *op. cit.*, pp. 528-89.

69. Andrés Molina Enríquez, *La Reforma y Juárez* (Mexico, 1906), p. 71.

70. Article 15 of the constitutional project provided for religious freedom. After weeks of debate the question was referred back to the committee where it continued to repose until the end of the session.

past by a decree. That this was not possible, the subsequent history of the religious question in Mexico bears emphatic testimony.

The new Constitution was published on February 12, 1857, and a decree was issued by Comonfort ordering all public officials to swear an oath of allegiance to it. But the clergy forbade government officials on pain of deprivation of the sacraments to take the oath of allegiance or to purchase property in mortmain. They even went to the extent of denying burial to those who had sworn to observe the Constitution.[71] Archbishop Garza addressed a circular to all the bishops declaring that no faithful Catholic could swear allegiance to it. Bishop Munguía of Michoacán declared that he was opposed to the constitutional articles which provided for liberty of instruction, thought, press, and association; those that prohibited religious vows, titles of nobility, and honorary titles; and those abolishing the *fueros* and prohibiting the acquisition by religious corporations of real property. He also protested against the articles which defined obligations of citizenship, created a national guard, and declared that sovereignty resided in the people. The clergy wrote an infinite number of pamphlets and volumes on the question of the relations of Church and State. One of these by Bishop Munguía, containing nearly a thousand pages, urged rebellion and disobedience to the government. On the other hand the Bishop of Oaxaca was conspicuous among the prelates because of his acceptance of the Constitution. He ordered a *Te Deum* mass sung in its honor. Many priests, also, refused to obey the strict orders of the hierarchy regarding the nonobservance of the Constitution.[72]

The Constitution of 1857 was inaugurated under unsympathetic auspices. Comonfort, elected constitutional president, was of the opinion that the new "Magna Charta" was too radical and that it was not representative of the majority public opinion. Furthermore he was timorous of clerical opposition. He therefore was an advocate of thoroughgoing amendment. Of the 155 deputies elected to the National Federal Congress only twenty-one had served in the Constituent Congress. Bulnes professed to see in this meager representation of ex-constituents disapproval of the Constitution and repudiation of the reformists.[73] On December 19, 1857, the military-clerical alliance under the leadership of General Félix Zuloaga declared war upon the Constitution. Their *plan*, issued in Tacubaya, called for: (1) inviolability of Church property and revenues and reëstablishment of former exactions; (2)

71. Vera, *op. cit.*, I, 21.

72. Toro, *op. cit.*, pp. 258-60; Vicente Riva Palacio to Mariano Riva Palacio, Mexico, January 29, 1857. Riva Palacio Papers.

73. Bulnes, *op. cit.*, pp. 247-48.

reëstablishment of the *fueros*; (3) censorship of the press; (4) the Roman Catholic religion as the sole and exclusive religion of Mexico; (5) immigrants to come only from Catholic countries; (6) overthrow of the Constitution of 1857 and use of a dictatorship subservient to Church only; (7) a monarchy to be established if possible, and if not, a European protectorate; and (8) high tariff, internal duties, and use of monopolies.[74] In short, the Conservatives offered the people of Mexico militarism and the religion of the middle ages.

Comonfort accepted the *Plan de Tacubaya* and made a faltering attempt to assume leadership of the reaction, but his vacillation caused his repudiation by all parties. After his ignominious flight from the country, the reactionary army took Mexico City and General Zuloaga was proclaimed president. Comonfort's betrayed Liberal colleagues rushed to arms in defense of the Constitution, and Benito Juárez, legal successor to the presidency, was proclaimed constitutional president of Mexico. The Liberals set up a government in Vera Cruz, whereas the Conservatives retained possession of the capital. Thus was initiated a war to the death between the military-clerical alliance and the defenders of liberal ideas. The War of the Reform was essentially a religious conflict, and for that reason, perhaps, it was characterized by excessive plunder, rapine, brutal reprisals, and a general spirit of extermination. Prisoners were slaughtered in cold blood, doctors and nurses were killed, and churches were sacked. The clergy made it a holy war. They supported it financially, and the Conservative soldiers carried crosses, rosaries, and pictures of saints. "On the liberal side it was a struggle for freedom of thought and speech, for the extinction of clerical participation in affairs of state, for the nationalization of great areas of land held by the Church, for the normal participation of laymen in government, for complete equality of all citizens before the law, for intellectual progress and modernity. On the conservative side the ideal was Church and Army control, with a foreign constitutional monarchy in the background. All the old Spanish abuses based on the colonial conception of political society were to be perpetuated: special privileges, absence of liberty of conscience, class domination."[75]

After the triumph of the praetorian movement which accomplished the extrusion of Comonfort, General Zuloaga annulled the Liberal reform legislation and restored the special privileges to the army and clergy. His program, according to Bulnes, was that of intimate union of Church and State—an intolerant Church privileged as it was in the

74. Callcott, *op. cit.*, p. 315.
75. Priestley, *op. cit.*, p. 337.

eleventh century, opulent as an Asiatic monarchy over black social misery; and science on its knees before theology, with *fueros* as justice.[76]

Shortly after his assuming of the presidency Zuloaga wrote to Pius IX assuring him of the piety and devotion of the Mexican nation. The Pope replied immediately expressing great satisfaction because of the happy turn of Mexican affairs. By decree of March 1, 1858, much of the Church property was ordered restored to it. But when Zuloaga tried to restore ecclesiastical lands alienated under the *Ley Lerdo* he came into conflict with foreign nations whose citizens had bought these lands. His attempt to impose forced loans on aliens also involved him in foreign complications. The incapacity of Zuloaga finally necessitated his being pushed aside and General Miramón, who had been the real prop of the Conservative government, assumed the presidency on December 30, 1858. Miramón offered to preserve the independence and prerogatives of the clergy and the *fueros* of the army. Although he recognized the necessity of certain ecclesiastical reforms, he preferred to undertake them in coöperation with the prelates.[77]

From his temporary capital in Vera Cruz President Juárez issued a manifesto declaring his intention to make war measures of the reform legislation. The government was disposed, he said, to maintain the Constitution and to abolish despotism, hypocrisy, immorality, and disorder. To accomplish this it was necessary to end the fratricidal war initiated by the clergy and to deprive them of all the means of further resistance. To bring this about, declared Juárez, it was necessary to carry the Reform to its logical conclusion, i.e., separation of Church and State, suppression of convents, extinction of all religious congregations, liberty of conscience, and nationalization of Church property. In fulfillment of his promise, Juárez, during the course of the War of the Reform, released an avalanche of anticlerical laws upon the Church. These laws, as was frankly confessed, were military measures designed rather for moral effect than practical execution; as a challenge rather than a definite piece of legislation; for they were promulgated when the Liberals controlled only a part of Mexico. These laws, which constituted an undisguised attack on the spiritual domain of the Catholic Church, seemed to aim at the destruction of the Church itself.

The ecclesiastical temporalities were made the first object of special Liberal attention, because it was felt that if the civil war were to be ended, it could only be by depriving the Church of its revenues. On December 7, 1858, a loan of 2,500,000 *pesos* was imposed on the clergy.

76. Bulnes, *op. cit.*, p. 330.
77. Gen. Miguel Miramón to Gen. Manuel María Calvo, San Luis Potosí, July 16, 1858. Comonfort Papers, García Collection; Riva Palacio, *op. cit.*, V, 281-82.

This exaction was described as an "equivalent" of the loan made a short time before to the Conservative government. On July 12, 1859, Juárez issued an executive decree nationalizing ecclesiastical holdings. All property of the regular and secular clergy, whether rural or urban, real estate, stocks, or shares, was declared as coming under the dominion of the nation. Such Church buildings and residences of the secular clergy as should be designated by the state governors to be adequate for public worship were to be excepted from the nationalization law.[78]

The nationalization law was actual confiscation of Church properties and not a purchase. It was an extreme measure and under ordinary conditions could never have been condoned. The clergy, however, were in open rebellion against the constitutional government and were devoting the funds of the faithful to war purposes. It was therefore a proper war measure to deprive the Conservative enemy of its principal source of income. It was indeed unfortunate that the Mexican Church should have been deprived of income adequate to carry on necessary ecclesiastical activities, but such was the consequence of stubborn resistance to inevitable reform.

The law of July 12, the most important of the so-called "Laws of the Reform," also provided for separation of Church and State; the free performance of religious services by priests; suppression of all *cofradías* and of religious communities for men; and the transfer of antiques, works of art, and books from the suppressed convents to the national museums and libraries. The law also provided for a partial suppression of nunneries. Novitiates were closed and nuns were encouraged to leave the cloisters. Other laws which followed in rapid succession proclaimed religious toleration, reduced the number of religious feast days, secularized cemeteries, and established the civil register for vital statistics. Marriage was made a civil contract, and although legal separation was recognized, absolute divorce was prohibited. Because Article 3 of the law of July 12 established "perfect independence of Church and State," the Mexican legation in Rome was withdrawn. On December 4, 1860, another law was passed containing several provisions to make effective the separation of Church and State. These were: (1) protection by law of all religious beliefs on a plane of perfect equality; (2) independence of all cults in purely spiritual matters; (3) abolition of the religious oath and substitution of the simple promise to tell the truth; (4) no religious ceremonies outside of churches; (5) use of church bells subject to police regulation; (6) abolition of the right of asylum; (7) pontifical communications of a spiritual nature no longer subject to the exequatur;

78. Dublán y Lozano, *op. cit.*, VIII, 657-61, 675-88; W. H. Callcott, *Liberalism in Mexico, 1857-1929* (Stanford University, 1931), pp. 22-23.

and (8) public officials prohibited from aiding or officiating in acts of religion. All of these measures were promulgated in the name of "God, Liberty, and Reform."[79]

Following the final constitutionalist victory at the battle of Calpulalpam, the Liberal army entered Mexico City on December 27, 1860. Juárez lost no time in wreaking vengeance upon his defeated clerical adversaries and in carrying on to even more extreme limits the anticlerical reform. Because of the alliance of the prelates with the erstwhile Conservative government, Juárez ordered the expulsion from the Republic of the apostolic delegate, Archbishop Garza, and four of the bishops. All Cathedral chapters were suppressed with the exception of that of Guadalajara, which had protested against the French intervention.[80]

The decree of nationalization of Church properties was promptly put into effect after the occupation of the capital city. Those properties that had enjoyed the protection of Zuloaga and Miramón now fell into the control of the constitutional government. Furthermore hospitals and charitable institutions that had been administered by the ecclesiastics were secularized. Finally all nuns were excloistered, their dowries were returned, and their properties were confiscated. "The number of landholders must have increased by many thousands," says McBride, "the fruits of the nationalization of Church lands falling mainly into the hands of the mestizos."[81] Forty thousand transfers of property are said to have taken place. Yet the attempt to replenish the bankrupt national treasury by expropriation and nationalization ended in failure. Although it is claimed that the nationalizing operations produced for the treasury from two to six million dollars, it was necessary for Juárez to declare a moratorium, which in turn brought about the allied intervention.

The clergy were the real authors of the French intervention. Having been conquered completely on the field of battle by the constitutionalist forces, they turned to intrigue and worked for the founding of a monarchy under European protection. To preserve their privileges the Mexican clergy had renounced their legitimate sovereign in 1821; to save the Church from serious injury at the hands of the Liberal reformers, the clericals were willing, in 1861, to compromise the independence of their country. Mexican history shows that, on the part of the ecclesiastics, sentiments of national fealty were secondary to loyalty to the Church. Notwithstanding the naïve protestation of the Mexican prelates

79. Dublán y Lozano, *op. cit.*, VIII, 688-95, 705, 762-66; Toro, *op. cit.*, pp. 280-86.
80. Dublán y Lozano, *op. cit.*, IX, 12-13, 524-25, 321-22.
81. George McCutchen McBride, *The Land Systems of Mexico* (New York, 1923), p. 71.

at the time of the Intervention that they did not interfere in political matters, the apostolic nuncio informed the Empress Carlota that "the clergy had made the empire." And Father Cuevas, whose narrow prejudice in favor of the clerical cause admits of no question, proudly confesses, "To their honor, the conservatives and the Mexican bishops wished and procured a liberating intervention and a Mexican Empire."[82]

The invading French, who were received with *Te Deum* masses along the line of march to Mexico City, forced Juárez to evacuate the capital in May, 1863. General Forey, the French commander, thereupon set up a Regency, composed of Mexican monarchists and clericals, to act as a temporary governing body. The president of the Regency was General Juan Almonte, recently returned from the court of Napoleon III where he had earnestly advocated the establishment of monarchy in Mexico under French protection. Another member of the Regency was the recently exiled Archbishop Labastida. The clergy, who fondly hoped that their every wish would be granted by the French, received a rude awakening immediately after General Forey's arrival in Mexico City. In pursuance of Napoleon's orders his general issued a proclamation announcing that the proprietors of nationalized ecclesiastical property which had been regularly and legally adjudicated to them would not be disturbed in their peaceful possession, and only fraudulent sales would be subject to revision. "The Catholic religion," he announced, "will be protected and the bishops will be placed anew in their dioceses. I believe it is possible to add that the Emperor will view with pleasure the proclamation of liberty of cults by the government." Since the Regency wished to initiate a real clerical reaction, a breach with the French began to appear at a very early date. Forey wrote Napoleon, "I believe in honoring religion and its ministers, although these in this country are not always very honorable; but it is to be feared that they are going far to put the country at the feet of the clergy."[83]

Archbishop Labastida, "scheming and unprincipled churchman," was so uncompromising in his demands for a restoration of all clerical properties that Marshal Bazaine, successor to General Forey, removed him from the Regency.[84] It became abundantly evident, even in the early days of the Intervention, that the clergy would be satisfied with nothing less than a complete restoration of their old-time status.

82. Cuevas, *op. cit.*, V, 340. See Jesús García Gutiérrez, *La Iglesia Mejicana en el segundo imperio* (Mexico, 1955).

83. Toro, *op. cit.*, pp. 308-12; F. Boquet to Marshal Bazaine, Paris, July 18, 1862, in *Archivo Bazaine*, I, 6.

84. Percy F. Martin, *Maximilian in Mexico* (New York, 1914), p. 133; Riva Palacio, *op. cit.*, V, 623.

In July, 1863, an "Assembly of Notables," carefully selected by the French, proclaimed the establishment of a monarchy under a moderate, hereditary, Catholic prince with the title of Emperor of Mexico. The imperial crown was to be offered to Archduke Maximilian of Austria, and, in the event of his refusal, Napoleon III was to be asked to choose another Catholic prince for Mexico. But it was not necessary to call upon Napoleon for additional aid, since the young Archduke and particularly his brilliant and ambitious wife, Carlota, were willing to undertake the Mexican adventure. When Maximilian accepted the Mexican throne he went to Rome to see the pope, for he somewhat faintly recognized the importance of finding a solution for the religious problem in the Aztec State. When the pope said that though the rights of nations were great and must be satisfied, but those of the Church were greater, Maximilian should have gained an intimation of what the future had in store for him. Unfortunately he failed to come to a clear understanding with the pope. All he did was to request that a papal nuncio be sent to Mexico where everything could be settled later. Napoleon himself had advised Maximilian to settle all complications affecting Church affairs before accepting the Mexican throne. The failure of the prince to come to an understanding before leaving Europe was a blunder for which he paid with his life.[85]

On the very day that Emperor Maximilian and Empress Carlota entered Mexico City (June 12, 1864), a pastoral was published by the Mexican prelates. They declared that they, in fulfillment of their sacred ministry, had remained aloof from political questions and strife of parties, and that the revolution was the result of sin. The faithful were exhorted to observe their religious duties and masses were ordered celebrated *pro electo Imperatore*. This pastoral was a covert threat that the very existence of the imperial government depended on what solution the Emperor would give to the problem of the Church.

Maximilian, essentially a liberal, was determined not to head a blind reaction. He was convinced that it was impossible and impracticable to initiate a counterrevolution and restore to the clergy all of their old privileges and particularly their property. He thought, in his innocence, not knowing the Mexican clergy, that the Church question could be settled in an entirely Catholic and equitable manner through the celebration of a concordat. The Emperor therefore impatiently awaited the arrival of the nuncio, but months passed before Pius IX fulfilled his promise. Maximilian repeatedly urged the pope, through the Mexican agent in Rome, to hasten the departure of his representative and to

85. Egan Caesar Count Corti, *Maximilian and Charlotte of Mexico* (New York, 1928), II, 409-10; Martin, *op. cit.*, p. 257.

instruct him not to support the extravagant demands of the Mexican clergy.[86]

The Pope's ambassador, Mgr. Meglia, finally arrived in Mexico on December 10, 1864. That the Holy Father refused to acquiesce in Maximilian's request that he do not support the extravagant pretensions of the Mexican clergy was clearly evidenced by a letter which the Nuncio conveyed to Maximilian from the pope. The principles upon which an agreement was to be based, said Pius IX, were: (1) annulment of all the reform laws; (2) establishment of the Catholic faith to the exclusion of all other creeds; (3) entire freedom of the bishops in the exercise of their ecclesiastical functions; (4) restoration of the religious orders; (5) placing of both public and private instruction under clerical supervision; and (6) removal of all restrictions which kept the Church in dependence upon the State.[87]

Although Maximilian was stunned by the uncompromising nature of the papal demands, he communicated to the Nuncio a counterproposal of nine points which constituted his idea of a fair and equitable understanding. The liberal and enlightened Emperor proposed as the basis of a concordat: (1) toleration for all cults, but protection for the Roman Catholic religion as the religion of the State; (2) support of the Catholic cult and its ministers from the public treasury; (3) performance of all religious services by priests to be gratuitous; (4) cession to the Mexican government of all rights respecting the ecclesiastical properties which had been nationalized; (5) the emperor to have the same rights over the Church as were once possessed by the kings of Spain; (6) reëstablishment, by agreement between the pope and the emperor, of *some* of the religious orders; (7) *fueros* (agreement to be worked out); (8) the civil register to be entrusted, wherever convenient, to parish priests to perform the duties of the civil functionaries; and (9) cemeteries (agreement to be worked out).[88]

The Nuncio, after being delivered Maximilian's counterproposals, went into conference with Archbishop Labastida and other prelates. The decision was that the Emperor's proposals were unacceptable. The Nuncio then announced that his instructions did not allow him to negotiate on the basis of the Emperor's demands. This was a blow to Maximilian for he realized then that the pope had abandoned him, and his hopes for a satisfactory settlement of the Church question were

86. Toro, *op. cit.*, pp. 323-25.

87. E. Léfèvre, *Historia de la Intervención Francesa en Méjico* (Brussels and London, 1869), II, 17; Bazaine to the Minister of War (France), December 10, 1864, in *Archivo Bazaine*, XI, 2045.

88. Toro, *op. cit.*, p. 326.

doomed. The Empress asked for a conference with Mgr. Meglia, and it was on that occasion that he told her it was the clergy who had made the Empire. It was quite evident to all that Archbishop Labastida had poisoned the ear of the Nuncio, for immediately after his arrival in Mexico he had given every indication of being willing to compromise. "It is evident enough," wrote Carlota to Empress Eugenie, "that behind all the doings of the nuncio, who is a mere puppet, is concealed the figure of Mgr. Labastida, whose bad Italian I know so well that I can recognize it in every line."[89] When the Nuncio's obstinacy exasperated her beyond endurance, Carlota suggested to Bazaine that he should be thrown from the window. The mission of Mgr. Meglia came to an unfortunate end in April, 1865, when he left Mexico suddenly and in great rage because of a rebuff he had received from the Minister of Foreign Affairs. This was induced because of an insulting letter addressed to the Emperor after the promulgation of a decree which recognized the legal rights of purchasers of nationalized ecclesiastical property.[90]

Since negotiations with the Nuncio had failed, Maximilian sent a commission to Rome to appeal directly to Pius IX. However, they were told that the pope would never consent to a diminution of the rights of the clergy. When notified that the pontiff had branded his government as being anti-Catholic, Maximilian declared that the Mexican archbishop and bishops did not understand the modern age or real Catholicism; they lacked Christian hearts. If the pope excommunicated him, he said, he would be the fourth archduke of Austria who had been excommunicated.[91]

Maximilian, thoroughly disgusted with the Mexican prelates, the nuncio, and the pope, threatened to ratify the laws of Juárez. He ordered the Minister of Justice (December 27, 1864) to confirm all legitimate acquisitions of clerical property by the law of amortization. A special office was created to review titles of property previously expropriated. By the same decree it was provided that all clerics were to be paid salaries by the State. This decree aroused a storm of protest and caused an open breach between the Emperor and the clericals. Putting the clergy on a salary basis was condemned as a measure designed to deprive them of their independence. "A salary from the State," said the Empress, "would never bring them in so much, and while we are struggling here to establish the Church's position, it is their ideal to live in Europe on their money." Other decrees of a reformist nature guaranteed re-

89. Corti, *op. cit.*, II, 456; Bazaine to the Minister of War (France), December 27, 1864, in *Archivo Bazaine*, XI, 2078.

90. Martin, *op. cit.*, p. 261.

91. Toro, *op. cit.*, p. 342.

ligious toleration, opened the cemeteries to persons of all creeds, enforced the law of Juárez suppressing ecclesiastical *fueros*, and provided for the imperial exequatur of all pontifical communications.[92] The decrees of Maximilian affecting the Church justified the reforms of Juárez and the Liberals. It is contended that Maximilian supported some of the reformist measures of Juárez in an effort to win the good will of the Liberals. This was true, but, notwithstanding, the Emperor's actions were based in sincere and conscientious conviction.

The plan of Maximilian to reconcile the conflicting factions by a partial recognition of the Juárez program failed to secure the adherence of the Liberals and served to alienate the churchmen. When the clergy saw that their monarchial choice would not be their docile instrument, and that their position under the monarchy was no better than it had been under the republic, they turned on Maximilian with incredible venom. The very expectation that the Emperor would be a placid and amenable tool in the hands of the clerics was what caused them to work so persistently for a monarchial government. The awakening therefore was a severe blow.

The withdrawal of the French and the callous indifference of Pius IX to Maximilian and his cause sealed the fate of the unfortunate monarch. Retribution was at hand because of his failure to study the ecclesiastical question thoroughly before leaving Europe. A more critical and less trusting individual would have discerned the hidden dangers which imperiled the monarchial enterprise from the beginning.

After the unfortunate and impolitic execution of Maximilian, the Liberals were given an opportunity to require general enforcement and observance of the Reform Laws. The clerical party was completely shattered, and the Church was required to give absolute obedience to the existing laws. The restored Liberal government issued a circular to the governors of the states (July 20, 1868) urging upon them the enforcement of the Reform Laws. The preface to the circular read, "Since the law of July 12, 1859, declared that there existed a perfect independence between the Church and State, the government has been careful not to intervene in any of the purely ecclesiastical subjects, guaranteeing to the clergy the most ample liberty in the exercise of their spiritual functions."[93] This statement, as an example of ingenuous denial of the actual situation, deserves to be classed with the declaration of the prelates that they did not interfere in politics.

In an effort to facilitate the liquidation of Church properties, Juárez established the "Administration of Nationalized Property," and offered

92. Toro, *op. cit.*, pp. 339-40; Corti, *op. cit.*, II, 469.
93. Dublán y Lozano, *op. cit.*, X, 396.

liberal rewards to those who would denounce property concealed by the clericals. The net financial result of the whole process of expropriation until 1892, when nationalized ecclesiastical property was declared free from further claims by the treasury, was that $100,000,000 of Church property was acquired by private owners and the government realized a few millions in revenue. The principal purpose of the Reform, the destruction of the economic power of the clergy, was not completely achieved, since much of the Church's property was still held for it by proxies and large sums were paid to the clergy by the new proprietors in return for declarations that the Church renounced all rights of ownership of the particular property.[94]

After the death of Juárez (1872) the clergy began to agitate anew for the abrogation of the Reform Laws. They hoped that President Lerdo de Tejada would be more favorable; but they were disappointed. After assuming the presidency Lerdo issued a manifesto declaring his intention to insist on a strict observance of the Laws of the Reform. Indeed, the President facilitated the incorporation of the Reform Laws into the Constitution. On October 5, 1873, certain "additions and reforms of the Federal Constitution" were promulgated. Those Laws of the Reform which were constitutionalized were: (1) the separation of Church and State; (2) civil marriage; (3) prohibition to religious institutions of the right to require real estate or imposts on it; (4) substitution of a simple promise to tell the truth in place of the religious oath; and (5) illegality of monastic vows.[95]

On December 14, 1874, enabling legislation was passed by the Congress to facilitate the operation of the recently constitutionalized Laws of the Reform. Into this law was gathered much of the radical legislation of the previous twenty years. For example, under the subject of separation of Church and State, it was provided that no religious instruction was to be given in any public institution, no religious act could be performed outside of churches, clerics could not wear distinctive garbs outside of ecclesiastical premises, and church bells were to be used only as a summons to religious services. Infractions of the sections relating to the separation of Church and State, the acquisition of real estate, and prohibition of monastic orders were declared to be federal offenses and subject to trial in the federal courts. Cases arising under violation of the legal provisions relating to the simple promise to tell the truth and civil matrimony were placed under the jurisdiction of the local courts.[96]

The anti-Church reform movement initiated by Gómez Farías and

94. Phipps, *The Agrarian Question in Mexico*, pp. 90-93.
95. Dublán y Lozano, *op. cit.*, XII, 502-4; Callcott, *Liberalism in Mexico*, pp. 92-93.
96. Dublán y Lozano, *op. cit.*, XII, 683-88.

resumed by Benito Juárez had seemingly attained its goal by 1874. The victory, however, proved to be illusory and temporary, for during the long dictatorship of Porfirio Díaz, who began as a liberal and became a conservative, a policy of "conciliation," i.e., ignoring the Reform, was adopted.[97] Without abrogation of any of them, he allowed the laws to fall into disuse. Thus, with the tacit consent of Díaz there was a rebirth of ecclesiastical influence which provided fuel for the flames of revolt which broke out in 1910.

In seeking relief from the radicalism of Juárez and Lerdo de Tejada the clericals aided Díaz in his several attempts to seize control of the government. It is asserted that the clergy gave considerable financial support to the furtherance of the final successful *coup* of 1876. It is also charged that "the hero of Puebla" agreed in return for clerical support to make a concordat with the pope and derogate the Laws of Reform. Whatever may have been the truth of these charges, it is nevertheless a fact that "Porfirio Díaz attached the clerical party to his triumphal chariot with promises which he amply fulfilled."[98]

Díaz was quite aware of the continued power of the clergy in Catholic Mexico, notwithstanding the recent attacks. He aimed therefore, as a matter of policy and despite the fact that he was a grand master of Freemasonry, to consolidate and perpetuate his authority by obtaining first the sympathy and confidence and later the frank and active coöperation of the ecclesiastics. He conciliated the wishes of the bishops.

Although Porfirio Díaz made no attempt to have the Laws of Reform removed from the statute books, for it is thought he wished to have the written law serve as a potential menace should the clergy get out of hand, he nevertheless left the discretional application of the laws to the officials of each locality. The degree of enforcement, for this reason, varied greatly in different parts of Mexico. This accounts, then, for the contradictory assertions of writers that the Reform Laws were or were not enforced during the Díaz régime.[99]

In circulars issued by the Ministry of Interior on April 12, 1881, March 27, 1885, and September 11, 1889, one can detect relaxation on the part of the State authorities in the enforcement of the religious laws.

97. Karl M. Schmitt, "The Díaz Conciliation Policy on State and Local Levels, 1876-1911," in *The Hispanic American Historical Review*, Vol. 40, No. 4 (November, 1960), 513-32.

98. Edmundo González-Blanco, *Carranza y la Revolución de México* (Madrid, 1916), p. 339; Francisco Bulnes, *El Verdadero Díaz* (Mexico, 1920), p. 90.

99. Karl M. Schmitt, "Catholic Adjustment to the Secular State: The Case of Mexico, 1867-1911," in *Catholic Historical Review*, XLVIII, No. 2 (July, 1962), 182-204.

The Minister charged that, in violation of the Constitution, priests were wearing distinctive garbs in the streets, religious processions and services were being performed outside of the churches, priests were discoursing in the pulpits on political subjects, and monastic orders were known to exist clandestinely. The governors were urged to see that the laws were enforced.[100]

Thanks to *la política de conciliación*, the Church recovered much of its lost fortune. In addition to sums saved from the ruin wrought by the Reform and the conservation of property through the acts of intermediaries in agreement with the clergy, the Church received handsome gifts and bequests, for it was impossible to distinguish between gifts for current expenses and gifts that would render the parishes wealthy. Even the tithes were surreptitiously reëstablished, for almoners went soliciting from house to house, and those who refused to pay were ostracized. "The economic recovery of the Church progressed so far under Díaz that it was charged as late as 1916 that ten per cent of the capital of the country belonged to the clergy, who loaned money in the name of European bankers."[101] It is estimated that, from 1874 to 1910, the value of ecclesiastical property increased from 50,000,000 *pesos* to double that amount. Priests once more became landlords, money lenders, and business men. Many church edifices that had been retired from the cult were restored and many new churches were constructed. In 1907 there were over 8,765 churches and chapels in Mexico and 1,350 vicarages. A foreign observer wrote at that time: "The hold which the Church has upon the affections of the common people is in no way shaken, and there are probably more places of religious worship in the Republic of Mexico than in any Roman Catholic country in the world, not excepting either Spain or Italy."[102]

In education also the prime position of the Church was reëstablished. Under Díaz very little was done by the government for general education, and the burden which was once more put upon the clergy was taken up with alacrity. A number of new Catholic colleges were opened and a new system of elementary schools was built up. In 1885 there were 276 Catholic schools in Mexico and in 1905 there were 593. During these "years of reconstruction," as Cuevas calls the Díaz period, new convents were clandestinely founded in agreement with the authorities, and many of the religious orders were restored. The country again abounded with convents for monks and nuns founded under

100. Dublán y Lozano, *Legislación Mexicana*, XIV, 738-39, XVII, 151-52, XIX, 550-51.
101. Phipps, *op. cit.*, pp. 94-95.
102. Percy F. Martin, *Mexico of the Twentieth Century* (London, 1907), p. 93.

pretext of being schools and charitable institutions. The black *soutanos* of the clergy again became a familiar sight in the streets. Public religious acts also became common. Sumptuous *fiestas* like the Coronation of the Virgin of Guadalupe and other celebrated images, Eucharistic congresses, and golden anniversaries of prelates were celebrated in public.[103]

Such was the remarkable development and prosperity of the Church during the Díaz dictatorship that five new archbishoprics (Durango, Linares, Oaxaca, Puebla, and Yucatán) and eight new bishoprics (Cuernavaca, Chihuahua, Saltillo, Tepic, Tehuantepec, Aguascalientes, Tabasco, and Campeche) were created. More dioceses were erected during the Díaz period, says Cuevas, then in the time of Philip II.

For several years the dictator acted covertly and cautiously in the execution of his policy toward the Church, for he realized the danger of attempting a too sudden and public renunciation of the anticlerical laws. It was not until after 1890 that his "policy of conciliation" became sufficiently noticeable to be discussed in the press. By that time, however, his dictatorship had been firmly established and most of the old Liberal warriors of the Reform had passed from the stage of Mexican politics. Therefore, there was less need for dissimulation. In 1904 the pope sent a special delegate, Mgr. Serafini, Archbishop of Spoleto, to see if it were possible to renew the old associations of Church and State and reëstablish diplomatic relations with Mexico. But Serafini, like other papal emissaries to Mexico, failed. Even the attempted bribe of creating a Mexican cardinal would not budge the President from his determination not to restore Mexican representation at the Vatican.[104] In reality, however, Díaz maintained almost official relations with the resident apostolic delegates. He even intervened to suggest to the Vatican who should be named as bishops. "It was public and notorious besides," writes an historian of this period, "that the Mexican consul in Rome, an Italian named Angelini, was a real confidential diplomatic agent of the Mexican government to the Holy See."[105]

In view of the many favors received from the dictator, the Mexican clergy, essentially partners of the Díaz system, had little occasion to exhibit their former rebelliousness. There was consequently a cessation of clerical intrigues and political machinations. Although there was realization that the existence of the Reform Laws was a sword of Damocles

103. Cuevas, *La Iglesia en México*, V, 409; Rodolfo Menéndez Mena, *The Work of the Clergy and the Religious Persecution in Mexico* (New York, 1916), p. 18; Carleton Beals, *Porfirio Díaz* (Philadelphia and London, 1932), pp. 341-42.

104. Martin, *op. cit.*, pp. 93-94.

105. Toro, *op. cit.*, p. 359.

which constantly menaced the extralegal position of the Church, it was feared that agitation for an amendment of the Constitution would stir up a latent, but powerful opposition. In addition, it did not conform to "Porfirian policy" to release clerical dependence by the reëstablishment of ecclesiastical privileges. Thus, since the "understanding" between Díaz and the clergy depended on the continuance of the dictatorship, he had in the Church his most faithful ally. It should be no occasion for surprise, therefore, that the ecclesiastics opposed the Madero movement.

Chapter XVI

Church and State Conflict in Mexico:
1910-1965

When the Revolution of 1910 broke out the clergy in all the pulpits of the land combatted it; Madero's motives were decried and his policy was censured. Although Madero's *Plan de San Luis Potosí* contained no allusion to religious reform, there nevertheless was much in the program which alarmed the clericals. The promise of agrarian reform alarmed because it was feared that the despoiling of the great estates would affect the holdings which had been acquired or retained clandestinely. Furthermore, the promise of educational reform caused the clericals to fear for the educational facilities which they had established throughout Mexico with the acquiescence of the Díaz administration. Consequently, a "National Catholic Party" was organized under the patronage of the prelates for the ostensible purpose of combatting the impending social and economic reform.[1] In the campaign which preceded the elections held in October, 1911, the clerical partisans worked energetically for the defeat of Madero and the capture of the government. Ambassador Henry Lane Wilson reported to the Secretary of State on July 11, 1911, "The Roman Catholic Church and the party which takes its name have become violently antagonistic to Madero, and are busily engaged throughout the Republic in aspersing his motives, decrying his policies, and censuring the weakness and vacillation which is supposed to characterize his direction of affairs."[2] Notwithstanding the violent clerical opposition, Francisco I. Madero was nearly unanimously elected in what has been declared to have been the only real election that Mexico had had up to that time. The clerical attempt to halt the Revolution failed. Although Madero initiated no policy of an anticlerical nature, his overthrow by Victoriano Huerta was hailed with delight by the ecclesiastics, for it was hoped that Huerta, professed champion of the "Porfirian

1. Pérez Lugo, *La Cuestión Religiosa en México*, p. 32; Pedro González-Blanco, *De Porfirio Díaz á Carranza* (Madrid, 1916), p. 340.
2. Quoted in Gruening, *Mexico and Its Heritage*, p. 212, n. 2.

system," would also support the Díaz ecclesiastical policy of conciliation. The reëntry of the Church into the political arena was most ill-advised, for, says Gruening, "When the clergy, as of old, supported the coup d'état against the elected government and its survivors gathering to recapture control, it sowed the wind. When Huerta, despite his ruthless butchery of political opponents, was overthrown, it reaped the whirlwind."[3]

The leader of the revolt against the Huerta-Catholic-aristocratic reaction was Venustiano Carranza, Governor of the State of Coahuila. The revolution was prefaced with the customary "plan," this one being known as the *Plan de Guadalupe* (March 26, 1913). The *pronunciamiento* was brief; it announced refusal of its signatories to recognize Victoriano Huerta as constitutional president of Mexico. Carranza was proclaimed First Chief of the Constitutionalist Army, and it was provided that he should, after the occupation of Mexico City, exercise the Executive Power until a general election should be convoked.[4] The immediate object of the revolution was purely political, i.e., restoration of constitutional government. But as the civil war was protracted and it became necessary to conciliate or punish factions, social and economic reform was incorporated into the Constitutionalists' program. Thus, because of clerical support of Huerta, the Church was once more subjected to an embittered assault. But clerical opposition to liberalism, as represented by the Constitutionalist forces, was not the sole cause of the anti-Church attack. The revolutionaries also feared, not the actual but the potential, and somewhat imaginary, opposition of the clergy to a comprehensive reform program. Memory of the Church as the traditional arch-opponent of democracy and liberalism persisted in their minds, and it became very necessary, therefore, to anticipate the inevitable clerical reaction. In short, anticlericalism had become a tradition in liberalism. It can hardly be denied, furthermore, that the Church and its clergy were assaulted because a goodly number of the so-called "Constitutionalists" had repudiated the tenets of Catholicism. Those who attacked the Catholic clergy because of their political activities, marched side by side in the Constitutionalist Army with the opponents of Catholicism as a religion. But, although it is undeniable that atheism was partly responsible for the anticlerical attack which was initiated by Carranza, there seems to be no reason to reject the protestations of Mexican officials that the reform was not aimed at the Church in its spiritual sphere, but at the clergy in their temporal activities.

3. *Ibid.*, p. 213.
4. *Codificación de los Decretos del C. Venustiano Carranza* (Mexico, 1915), p. 7.

The outrages committed on the clergy and the Church during the struggle against Huerta and after his overthrow were revolting. They were made to pay dearly for their support of the reaction. In explanation of the wanton desecration of churches and holy objects, one of the Constitutionalist generals, Salvador Alvarado, said: "It was for the deliberate purpose of showing the Indians that the lightning would not strike— that the Constitutionalists were not the enemies of God as the priests had told them, that generals rode their horses into churches and publicly smashed the statues of the venerated saints."[5] It can hardly be doubted that these generals had little respect for the faith, quite aside from their lack of respect for the clergy. Some partisans, although admitting the occurrence of acts of violence, sought to exonerate Carranza and the "respectable revolutionaries" by charging that the worst crimes were committed by Francisco Villa and his followers, "who exaggerated the just resentment of the Constitutionalist party against the members of the Catholic clergy."[6] But that the First Chief was in accord with Pancho Villa in sanctioning the outrages admits of little doubt. On July 8, 1914, the two leaders defined the objects of the Revolution in a formal agreement:

> The present conflict being a struggle of the impecunious against the abuses of the powerful, and understanding that the causes of the evils that bear down the country spring from pretorianism, plutocracy, and clericalism, the Divisions of the North and of the Northeast solemnly pledge themselves to fight until complete banishment of the ex-Federal army, which shall be superseded by the Constitutional Army, to set up democratic institutions in our country, to bring welfare to labor, financial emancipation to the peasant by an equitable apportionment of land, and other means tending to solve the agrarian question, to correct, chastise, and hold to their responsibilities such members of the Roman Catholic clergy as may have lent moral or physical support to the usurper, Victoriano Huerta.[7]

On July 29, 1914, General Villa telegraphed General Villareal, Governor of Nuevo León, who had restricted the exercise of the Catholic cult and even prohibited the confession:

> I sincerely and enthusiastically felicitate you on the decree which you have just published imposing restrictions on the clergy in the State which you govern with such dignity. I also am inclined to follow your wise example because I, like you, think the greatest enemy

5. Guening, *op. cit.*, p. 214.
6. González-Blanco, *op. cit.*, p. 135.
7. Gruening, *op. cit.*, p. 98.

to our progress and liberty is the corrupting clergy, who for so long have dominated our country. (Signed) Francisco Villa.[8]

After his break with Carranza, Villa, in making a bid for conservative support, publicly charged Carranza with violating the guarantee of liberty of conscience by permitting the governors to take vengeance on the clergy for their support of the conservatives. He also accused Don Venustiano "of having profoundly offended the religious sentiments of the people by acts condemned by civilization and natural law." The First Chief replied, "General Villa, who now seeks a reconciliation with the clergy, showing himself so respectful to religion and its practices, expelled the clerics, closed the churches, and prohibited all kinds of religious acts in the places occupied during the campaign."[9] This undoubted lack of sincerity on the part of so many of the revolutionary leaders increases the difficulty of analyzing and evaluating motives and acts.

As early as October 17, 1913, it was clear that Venustiano Carranza contemplated enforcement of the Laws of Reform. In a decree published on that date, which provided for the organization of the provisional national administration, he created eight secretariats, and to one of these, the Ministry of Interior, was entrusted "Liberty of cults and supervision of this branch." There was evidently intention here to enforce strictly the laws relating to religious liberty and its corollary, the separation of Church and State. There was no occasion for surprise, therefore, particularly in view of the acts of violence committed by the Constitutionalists upon the clergy, that Carranza's declaration of Constitutional aims, published in Vera Cruz on December 12, 1914, contained a guarantee of strict enforcement of the Laws of Reform. He also promised an amendment to the laws relating to marriage and the civil state of persons. In fulfillment of his promise to change the marriage laws, the First Chief decreed, on December 29, 1914, the legalization of divorce.[10]

On June 11, 1915, Carranza announced the reform program of the Constitutionalists in the most comprehensive statement issued up to that date. On religious policy he said: "The constitutional laws of Mexico known under the name of Laws of Reform, which established the separation of the Church and State and which guarantee to the individual the right of worship in accordance with his own conscience and without offending public order, shall be strictly observed; therefore, no one shall

8. González-Blanco, *Carranza y la Revolución*, pp. 345-46.
9. González-Blanco, *De Porfirio Díaz á Carranza*, p. 135.
10. *Decretos de Carranza*, pp. 29, 136, 147, 168.

suffer in his life, freedom, and property because of his religious beliefs. Temples shall continue to be the property of the nation according to the laws in force, and the Constitutionalist Government shall again cede for the purposes of worship those which may be necessary."[11] That the policy and activities of the First Chief amounted to a denial of religious liberty was the interpretation of the American Government. President Wilson demanded as one of his conditions of recognition that religious freedom be guaranteed—not only for Americans, but for Mexicans as well.[12]

In pursuance of the declaration that the churches were the property of the nation and that the government would turn over for the purposes of worship those edifices deemed necessary, a law was passed (August 22, 1916) creating machinery to make the status effective.[13] This law removed any doubt, if indeed any existed, that it was Carranza's intention to subordinate the Church to the strictest governmental control. By the time the Constitutionalists had achieved victory and were ready to convene in a constituent convention they were rampantly anticlerical and anxious to increase the severity of the Laws of Reform.

In fulfillment of the oft-repeated assurance that when order should be established a properly elected constituent congress would be convoked to elevate to constitutional status the numerous reform-decrees published during the course of the civil war, Carranza issued a call for the election in September, 1916. The delegates were to be "popularly" elected, subject to their taking an oath of loyalty to the *Plan de Guadalupe*. In other words only Constitutionalists were eligible to election as delegates; those who supported in any way the governments or factions hostile to the Constitutionalist cause were barred from the polls. The elections resulted, then, in a Constitutionalist party convention, and it was this body which proceeded to give the Mexican nation an instrument of government "representative of the popular will." The deputies were divided into two major groups, one extremely radical, the other moderately radical. The first group, which found its principal support, on the outside, in General Álvaro Obregón, has been called the "Jacobinos Obregonistas." They, counting forty-five generals in their number, constituted the majority. The second group less radically inclined, supported Carranza's program which was surprisingly moderate. They have been called the "Liberales Carrancistas."[14]

11. *Ibid.*, p. 220.
12. Gruening, *op. cit.*, p. 587.
13. *Diario Oficial* (Mexico City), September 9, 1916.
14. *Diario de los Debates del Congreso Constituyente* (Mexico, 1917), I, 71; L. Melgarejo Randolf y J. Fernández Rojas, *El Congreso Constituyente de 1917* (Mexico, 1917), pp. 124, 749-50.

The inaugural session of the Constituent Congress was held in the Teatro Iturbide, in Querétaro, on December 1, 1916. Venustiano Carranza presided at the opening session and presented to the Convention a model constitution which was to serve as the basis of its discussions. The proposed constitution proved to be more conservative than that of 1857. It contained no labor code or provision for the nationalization of land or subsoil. The religious clauses likewise were mild when compared with the provisions eventually adopted.[15] It should be noted, however, that Carranza accepted the Constitution of 1917 without protest. His failure therefore to include in his project certain articles which were adopted did not necessarily mean that he was opposed to them.

The relation of the Church to education elicited greater interest and discussion than perhaps any other subject before the Convention. This was due not only to the recognized importance of education in itself, but since this was the first subject introduced to the Convention affecting the status of the Church, the opportunity was seized on that occasion to debate the religious question in general. Later there was little or no debate on any of the other religious articles. On the subject of education the Constitution of 1857 (Article 3) read: "Instruction is free." Carranza suggested as an amendment to this article: "There will be complete liberty of instruction; but that given in official educational institutions will be laical, and primary, elementary, and superior instruction in the said establishments will be free."[16]

The committee on the constitution, reported unfavorably on Article 3 of Carranza's project and suggested as a substitute: "There will be liberty of education, but that given in official educational institutions will be laical, the same as in the private primary, elementary, and superior schools. No religious corporation, minister of any cult, or person belonging to any similar association can establish or direct schools of primary grade, nor instruct personally in any college. The private primary schools can only be established subject to governmental vigilance. Primary instruction is obligatory for all Mexicans and instruction will be free in all official establishments." Thus the committee went considerably farther than Carranza and suggested that all education of a primary and secondary nature, public and private, be purged of religious instruction, and that religious schools of a primary nature be abolished.[17]

15. For the project, see *Diario de Debates*, I, 260-70.
16. *Ibid.*, I, 341. Article 4 of the Laws of Reform prohibited religious education in public schools. See E. V. Niemeyer, "Anticlericalism in the Mexican Constitutional Convention, 1916-1917," in *The Americas*, Vol. II, No. 1 (July, 1954), 31-49.
17. *Diario de Debates*, I, 471, 448-50.

On December 16, 1916, by a vote of 99 to 54, the committee's report on Article 3 was accepted with only one amendment. The introductory words, "There will be liberty of education," were stricken from the article, thereby evidencing frank confession on the part of the constituents that they were not guaranteeing educational liberty in Mexico. The announcement of the vote on the article was greeted by cries of "Viva la Revolución! Viva el C. Primer Jefe! La Patria se ha salvado!"[18] The vote on this, the first religious article submitted for the consideration of the Convention, showed clearly that the "Jacobins" or extreme radicals were in control and that the religious clauses of the new constitution would be the most drastic in the entire history of the Republic.

Carranza's proposal that the establishment of monastic orders be prohibited, as provided in the old constitution, was approved by the Convention (Article 5). Likewise, the proposal of the First Chief that religious liberty be guaranteed was approved and incorporated in Article 24, which read:

> Every one is free to embrace the religion of his choice and to practice all ceremonies, devotions, or observances of his respective creed, either in places of public worship or at home, provided they do not constitute an offense punishable by law.
>
> Every religious act of public worship shall be performed strictly within the places of public worship, which shall be at all times under governmental supervision.

These were drawn largely from the Leyes de Reforma of December 14, 1874.

With respect to the property rights of religious institutions, the First Chief proposed substantially the adoption of Article 27 of the Constitution of 1857. According to this Article, as amended May 14, 1901, no religious institution had the legal capacity to acquire or administer real property other than the buildings immediately and directly destined to the services of the cult. Nor did they have the legal capacity to acquire loans or administer loans made on such real property. In addition, Carranza proposed that charitable institutions belonging to or administered by religious corporations be denied the right to acquire real estate except that destined for the direct and immediate use of these institutions. It is indeed surprising that Carranza, in view of prior acts and declarations should have excepted church buildings necessary for the cult from the nationalization edict, but such was the case.

The Convention, however, went beyond Carranza's proposal and de-

18. *Ibid.*, I, 530; Randolf y Rojas, *op. cit.*, p. 445.

clared that even the church buildings required for the immediate uses of the cult belonged to the nation, and all religious charitable enterprises were abolished. The religious sections of Article 27, into which these provisions were incorporated, read as follows:

II. The religious institutions known as Churches, irrespective of creed, shall in no case have legal capacity to acquire, hold, or administer real property or loans made on such real property; all such real property or loans as may be at present held by the said religious institutions, either on their own behalf or through third parties, shall vest in the Nation, and any one shall have the right to denounce property so held. Presumptive proof shall be sufficient to declare the denunciation well-founded. Places of public worship are the property of the Nation as represented by the Federal government, which shall determine which of them may continue to be devoted to their present purposes. Episcopal residences, rectories, seminaries, orphan asylums or collegiate establishments of religious institutions, convents or any other buildings, built or designed for the administration, propaganda, or teaching of the tenets of any religious creed shall forthwith vest, as of full right, directly in the Nation, to be used exclusively for the public services of the Federation or of the States, within their respective jurisdiction. All places of public worship which shall later be erected shall be the property of the Nation.

III. Public and private charitable institutions for the sick and needy, for scientific research, or for the diffusion of knowledge, mutual aid societies or organizations formed for any lawful purpose shall in no case acquire, hold, or administer loans made on real property, unless the mortgage terms do not exceed ten years. In no case shall institutions of this character be under the patronage, direction, administration, charge, or supervision of religious corporations or institutions, nor of ministers of any religious creed or of their dependents, even though either the former or the latter shall not be in active service.[19]

Most of the religious innovations, constitutionally speaking, were incorporated in Article 130. This article, although it included, as suggested by Carranza, provisions prohibiting to Congress the power to enact any law establishing or forbidding any religion; establishing marriage as a civil contract; and prohibiting the religious oath, went far beyond any proposal made by the First Chief. The principal additional features were: (1) the law recognizes no juridic personality in religious institutions known as churches, and ministers of creeds shall be con-

19. Randolf y Rojas, *op. cit.*, p. 301. Clauses II and III of the 1917 text are partly taken from the Laws of Reform.

sidered as persons exercising a profession; (2) the state legislatures shall have the exclusive power of determining the maximum number of ministers of religious creeds according to the needs of each locality; (3) only Mexicans by birth may be ministers of any religious creed in Mexico; (4) no minister shall either publicly or privately (either in public or private meetings or in acts of worship) criticize the fundamental laws of the country, or the authorities; (5) members of the clergy shall have no vote, nor be eligible to office, nor be allowed to assemble for political purposes; (6) new temples shall not be dedicated without the permission of the Department of Interior; (7) every place of worship shall have a caretaker who shall be legally responsible for the faithful performance of the laws within the said place of worship, and for all the objects used for purposes of worship; (8) the municipal authorities, under penalty of fine and dismissal, shall keep a register of the churches and of their caretakers, and shall report to the Department of Interior through the State governor any permission to open to the public use a new place of worship, as well as any change in the caretakers; (9) studies carried on in ecclesiastical seminaries shall not be accredited in any official institution; (10) no periodical publication of a religious nature shall comment upon political affairs of the nation, nor give any information regarding the acts of officials or of private individuals in so far as the latter have to do with public affairs; (11) political associations bearing any indication by their name to any religious belief are prohibited; (12) no assemblies of any political character shall be held within places of worship; (13) no ministers shall inherit, either personally or indirectly, any real property possessed by a religious association, or any property of other ministers of the same creed or, private individuals to whom he is not related by blood within the fourth degree; and (14) no trial by jury shall ever be granted for the infraction of any of the preceding provisions.

Some of the provisions of Article 130 were taken from the constitutional amendment of 1873 (Article 123) and the Laws of Reform (1874). Most of them, however, were original with the constituents and exceeded in severity all prior legislation on ecclesiastical matters. The denial of juridic personality to the Church, the prohibition of foreign clergy of all creeds, the limitation on the number of ministers, and additional limitations on the political and property rights of individual members of the clergy were the "Jacobin" contribution to the body of Mexican anticlerical legislation. The denial of the right of trial by jury to violators of the religious clauses of the Constitution was recognition by the constituents of the unpopular nature of their reforms.

After the debates on Article 3, the other religious clauses of the Constitution were adopted with little or no discussion. The vote of December 16 was accepted as meaning that the extreme radicals were to have their way, and thereafter no attempt was made to block them. Very often votes on separate articles were dispensed with and they were accepted *en masse*. For example, Article 5, having to do with monastic vows, was unanimously approved in combination with the labor article.[20] Article 27 did not come before the Convention until the final days of the session, and then evidently the members were anxious to adjourn, for the measure was adopted hurriedly and with no attention devoted to its religious clauses. The Constituent Convention closed its session on January 31, 1917, and on February 5, the result of its labors was promulgated by Carranza. The Constitution became effective on May 1, 1917.

The evident intention of the "Jacobins of Querétaro" was to drive the Church out of politics, to destroy its social influence, and to confine it strictly to the field of religion. To accomplish this they contradicted the guarantee of religious freedom and put the Church under the domination of the State. The Constitution of 1917 went far beyond that of 1857 in its curtailment of clerical power—indeed, if strictly executed, the very existence of the Church would have been threatened.

The religious clauses, however, were not enforced, either by Carranza or by Obregón. Because of their desire to consolidate their political positions they refrained from stirring up additional opposition by seeking a strict enforcement of Article 130. For nearly eight years, so far as interference with the Church was concerned, the new Constitution might as well have been nonexistent. Although ecclesiastical primary schools were forbidden a great number continued to be operated with governmental consent. In commenting on this tolerance toward religious schools, President Obregón said, "We are not unaware of the menace of these Catholic schools whose aim is to inculcate anti-government and anti-revolutionary propaganda. But at present there is not money enough nor facilities for the government to teach all Mexican children. It is preferable that they receive any instruction rather than grow illiterate."[21]

The constitutional prohibition of religious orders, male and female,

---

20. *Diario de Debates*, I, 553. Some radical proposals made by the Yucatán delegation, which fortunately were not accepted by the Convention, were: (1) abolition of auricular confession; (2) denial to priests of the right to hold real estate; (3) the Church to pay rent for the use of edifices; (4) official commissioners to administer the donations of the faithful; and (5) no priest to be less than fifty years old.

21. Gruening, *op. cit.*, p. 220.

was also disregarded. The nuns particularly were active in hospital and other charitable work. The foreign clergy, too, had not been bothered. Also the law against public religious ceremonials and demonstrations was violated with impunity. During the presidency of Obregón numerous "coronations" of the Virgin were celebrated in various parts of Mexico. These ceremonies in which a concourse of prelates officiated were generally accompanied by processions or other manifestations outside of the churches. When the first bishop of Tacambaro was instituted (July, 1921), several acts of a religious character were performed outside of the churches.

Notwithstanding the uneasiness of the clergy because of the menace of "reglamentation" and enforcement of the Constitution, the Church prospered during the Obregón administration. New dioceses were created, other dioceses forcibly abandoned during the Revolution were reoccupied, and Church councils and Eucharistic congresses were held. The remarkable progress made by the clergy in restoring the prestige of the Church was undoubtedly responsible for the "Cubilete" episode. On January 11, 1923, on the summit of Cubilete Mountain in Guanajuato and in the presence of a vast gathering of people and eleven prelates, Apostolic Delegate Mgr. Philippi placed the first stone on the monument to "Christ the King." The ceremony, undoubtedly religious, and described as solemn and imposing, evoked governmental action. On January 13, Obregón announced the expulsion of the Apostolic Delegate because of his participation in an illegal public religious ceremony. The pope requested the government to suspend the expulsion of Mgr. Philippi, but he was not heeded, and the Delegate left Mexico. The Mexican prelates who participated in the affair were not bothered, yet it was undoubtedly the intention of Obregón that they should take warning and he chose to issue it in a dramatic manner.[22]

Although some of the State governments enacted anticlerical legislation, the National government itself, during the administrations of Carranza and Obregón, made little or no attempt to enforce the constitutional articles defining the status of religious sects. It was not until President Plutarco Elías Calles assumed control of the Mexican government nearly nine years after the promulgation of the Constitution of 1917 that those articles were converted into a living reality. The intention of the Calles administration to enforce the religious provisions of the Constitution was first made known on February 11, 1926. On that date was published the first of a series of increasingly drastic laws and

22. Luis C. Balderrama, *El Clero y el Gobierno de México* (Mexico, 1927), I, 156-59.

regulations, which culminated in a few months in the suspension of all
religious exercises in the Catholic churches in Mexico.

What caused the sword of Damocles to descend upon the heads of
the Mexican clergy? The immediate cause, asserted President Calles
in an interview which was printed in the *New York Herald Tribune*
on February 24, 1926, was the public display of disobedience on the part
of the Catholic organizations, the Mexican Episcopacy, and even the
head of the Mexican Catholic Church. On February 4, 1926, there appeared in *El Universal*, one of the leading newspapers in Mexico, an interview with Archbishop Mora y del Río. The article read in part as
follows:

> The most illustrious Señor Archbishop of Mexico was pleased
> to give to our reporter, Señor Ignacio Monroy, the following state-
> ment dictated by him: "The doctrine of the Church is unvariable,
> because it is the divinely revealed truth. The protest which we
> Mexican prelates formulated against the Constitution of 1917 re-
> specting the articles which are opposed to religious liberty and
> dogmas is maintained firmly. It has not been modified but strength-
> ened because it is derived from the doctrine of the Church. The
> information which "El Universal" published on January 27 to the
> effect that there would be inaugurated a campaign against the laws,
> unjust and contrary to natural right, is perfectly true. The Epis-
> copacy, clergy, and Catholics do not recognize and combat Articles
> 3, 5, 27, and 130 of the existing constitution. This decision we
> cannot by any motive alter without being traitors to our faith and
> our religion.

The Secretary of Interior, Adalberto Tejeda, took immediate cognizance of the statement of the Archbishop, which he regarded as being
seditious. "The State permits to the Catholic Church," he said, "the
exercise of its functions up to a point where it does not constitute an
obstacle to progress and the development of the people; but it cannot,
nor ought not to tolerate [a declaration] that the constitutional laws
are not recognized and are combatted, as was declared in the mentioned
statement." Since the government's duty is to see that the laws are
respected, said Señor Tejeda, he was presenting the facts, fully documented, to the Attorney General. The Archbishop asked for an immediate hearing and was accommodated. The reporter insisted that his
account was correct, for, he contended, Archbishop Mora read it to him
from a prepared copy. The attorney for the Archbishop, however,
denied that the prelate was correctly quoted. Since this, whether true
or not, meant retraction by the prelate, the government was willing to

dismiss the charge.[23] The issue, however, was not settled, for, on February 8, 1926, the Mexican Episcopacy endorsed the attitude of the Primate by publishing "La Protesta Colectiva del Episcopado." This document, signed by Mora y del Río and all the archbishops and bishops, proclaimed the principles of the Constitution to be contrary to the most sacred rights of the Church, Mexican society, and Christians. "It tears up by the roots," declared the prelates, "the few rights which the Constitution of 1857 (admitted *in its essential principles*, as the fundamental law by all Mexicans) guarantees to the Church as a society and to Catholics as individuals.... Not intending to meddle in political questions, but to defend in a manner which is possible to us, religious liberty of Christian people in view of the rude attack which had been made on religion, we limit ourselves to protest against the attempt energetically and decorously." Disclaiming any seditious motives, but a duty to defend the rights of the Church, the prelates enumerated those parts of the Constitution which they opposed and which made religious liberty illusory.[24]

What caused the Mexican Episcopacy to invite disaster by publicly repudiating the Constitution? The national government had not, up to February, 1926, taken any steps to enforce the religious clauses. Yet it was generally understood that President Calles was intent on enforcing the Constitution as a whole and to the letter. He, unlike his predecessor in the presidential office, was a man with an essentially one-track mind; tenacious, stubborn, uncompromising, once he embarked upon a given course, nothing could swerve him. Having determined to enforce the constitutional law the President would let no consideration deter him, and whatever might be the consequences he insisted that the commands of the fundamental charter be observed. That the prelates were encouraged in their opposition by the pope himself appears to have substantiation. Following the return from Rome of Archbishop González of Durango and Bishop Mora of San Luis Potosí, an assembly of the National Episcopacy was held in which it was agreed to combat articles 3, 5, 24, 27, and 130 of the Constitution. The prelates of Durango and San Luis delivered to the assembly a letter (dated February 2) from the pope which undoubtedly influenced the action of the prelates. This letter denounced in strong, bitter terms the Mexican government, the statute laws, and the Constitution. It said:

> It is scarcely necessary for us to tell you how wicked are the regulations and laws invoked against the Catholic citizens of

23. Balderrama, *op. cit.*, I, 39, 42; *Excelsior*, February 5, 1926.
24. *El Universal*, February 8, 1926; Toro, *op. cit.*, p. 464.

Mexico which have been sanctioned by officials hostile to the Church, and which by their enforcement long have oppressed you. You are fully aware that these laws are far from being reasonable laws, nor are they useful and necessary for the common good as assuredly all laws should be. On the contrary, they do not seem to merit the name of laws. Indeed, we are moved all the more insistently to utter this public protest and condemnation of such laws, seeing that day after day the warfare against the Catholic religion is being waged more bitterly by the rulers of the Republic.

A significant part of the letter advised and commanded the bishops to develop "united Catholic action," although admonishing the clergy against violation of the Constitution.[25]

Whatever may have decided the Mexican Episcopacy to voice public repudiation of the obnoxious religious articles there is no doubt that it was this call to the faithful to disobey the law which caused President Calles to make effective at once the constitutional prescriptions which up to that time had been latent. On February 11, 1926, the Attorney General announced that all Church property not already in the possession of the nation had been nationalized, and that orders had been issued for the arrest and deportation of all foreign priests. On the next day another order was issued for the closing of all schools, asylums, and convents where religious instruction was given. On February 13, the Minister of Interior telegraphed all the state governors calling their attention to the necessity of enforcing articles 3, 5, and 130 of the Federal Constitution. They were urged to introduce these subjects, with the least possible delay, to the State legislatures.[26]

The arrest of foreign priests for the purpose of deportation was begun without warning on the night of February 10. By September, 183 foreign-born clericals had been expelled. The great majority of these were Spaniards. Considerable protest and some violence attended the expulsion of the foreign priests. As for foreign Protestant ministers they also were not allowed to function, for, said President Calles, "The law clearly states that all priests of all cults must be of Mexican nationality. Actually the Protestant ministers are working in Mexico without harming anyone for they have always adjusted themselves to the law."[27] Minister Tejeda issued a warning statement (May 22) that all foreign Protestant ministers who failed to comply with the law would be deported.

According to a statement of the Minister of Interior (February 18)

25. Balderrama, *op. cit.*, I, 38; *New York Times*, April 20, 1926.
26. *Current History*, April, 1926, p. 116; Balderrama, *op. cit.*, I, 49.
27. *Excelsior* (Mexico City), August 10, 1926; Toro, *op. cit.*, pp. 425, 454.

investigation had disclosed that many convents existed under pretext of being Catholic colleges. Against these the government proceeded, but "with the greatest moderation." By September, 73 convents, 129 schools attached to convents, and 118 orphan asylums under religious control had been closed.[28] In some instances the closing was attended by rioting. French and Spanish nuns engaged in teaching in such institutions were deported.

On February 26 the Secretary of Public Instruction directed all private schools to register with the Ministry of Public Instruction within sixty days or be closed. Private primary schools were forbidden to teach religious subjects, or to have any connection with churches or ecclesiastical corporations. Ministers of any creed and members of religious orders were forbidden to serve as teachers. New rules were issued by the Ministry of Public Instruction for private schools. They were prohibited from using pictures, paintings, or anything that would indicate religious ideas. The mere mention of anything religious, including the names of saints, was interdicted, and the schools were to have no communication with any buildings dedicated to religious purposes.[29]

The request of President Calles that the state governments proceed to immediate "reglamentation" of the religious laws met with a ready response, at least with respect to the determination of the number of priests who could legally function. By September, 1926, the following quotas had been established:[30]

Aguascalientes	One minister for each 5,000 inhabitants.
Tamaulipas	Twelve ministers for all the state.
Nayarit	Forty for all the state.
Colima	One for each 5,000 inhabitants in the capital and one for each municipality.
Coahuila	Twelve for Saltillo, five for Torreón, and three each for the following municipalities: Piedras Negras, Monclova, Parras, and San Pedro de las Colonias; two for Matamoros, and one for each of the remaining settlements in the state.
San Luis Potosí	One for each municipality, two for Matehuala, Río Verde, and Santa María del Río, and ten for the capital.
Michoacán	Ten for Morelia, four for Pátzcuaro and five more municipalities, three in Zinapecuaro and seven more municipalities, two in Indaparapeo and seventeen more municipalities, and one each in the remaining municipalities.

28. *Memoria de la Secretaría de Gobernación, 1925 á 1926*, in Toro, *op. cit.*, pp. 455-58.
29. *El Universal*, February 26 and April 24, 1926; J. M. Puig Casauranc, *La cuestión religiosa en relación con la educación pública en México* (Mexico, 1928), pp. 10-26.
30. *Memoria de Secretaría de Gobernación, 1925 á 1926*, pp. 459-60.

Sonora	One for each 10,000 inhabitants.
Durango	Twenty-five for each cult in all the state.
Chihuahua	One for each 9,000 inhabitants.
Yucatán	Forty for all the state.
Jalisco	Two hundred and fifty for all the state.
Puebla	One for each 4,000 inhabitants.
Tabasco	Six for all the state.
Vera Cruz	One for 10,000 inhabitants; two for 30,000, four for 60,000, and beyond that number, six for each cult.
Campeche	Five for all the state.

Restriction of the Catholic clergy, as in the State of Campeche to five priests, and in the State of Sonora to one priest to each 10,000 inhabitants, the majority of whom were Catholics, was oppressive, intolerant, and violative of the principle of religious liberty. Of this there could be little argument. The restrictions also were discriminatory in that non-Catholic cults, despite their meager numbers, were often given the same number of ministers as were allowed the Catholic Church. The enemies of Catholicism were legislating it out of existence in Mexico.

The offensive of the Federal and State governments against the Catholic Church aroused a storm of protests and indignation in Mexico and in foreign countries, particularly in the United States. On March 9, Ambassador Sheffield presented a note to the Foreign Minister expressing the hope that American citizens would not be obliged to undergo actual hardship or injury in Mexico because of their religious beliefs and practices. This was as far as the government of the United States was willing to proceed in spite of the urgent demands of American Catholic prelates and laymen. Not even the expulsion in May of Mgr. George Caruana, Bishop of Porto Rico and an American citizen, who went to Mexico as papal delegate, would cause President Coolidge or Secretary Kellogg to alter their attitude.[31]

So vehement and injudicious were the protests of some of the Mexican prelates against the intolerable legislation that they soon found themselves in the toils of the law. When Archbishop Mora y del Río in a letter to President Calles attempted to justify the actions of the rebellious clerics, the President declared that the religious laws would be maintained and any act of rebellion or lack of respect would be punished. "I wish you to understand now and always," he said, "that agitation

---

31. *Current History* (July, 1926), p. 615; Callcott, *Liberalism in Mexico*, pp. 370-72. See Elizabeth A. Rice, *The Diplomatic Relations Between the United States and Mexico, as Affected by the Struggle for Religious Liberty in Mexico, 1925-1929* (Washington, D.C., 1959).

within and without this country will not alter the purpose of this government."[32]

On July 21, 1926, President Calles issued a decree, to become effective August 1, providing for the reform of the penal code in the Federal District and the Territories in matters relating to religious offenses. A detailed scale of fines and punishments was worked out to cover every possible infringement of the religious clauses of the Constitution. But beyond the provision for the registration of all ministers of any religious creed before the civil authorities, this decree was merely a recapitulation of the various constitutional clauses and existing statutes relating to religion and education. Specific instructions were given to municipal officials who were charged with putting the decree into effect and penalties were prescribed for those failing to do so.[33] On July 23, President Calles issued supplementary regulations giving effect more specifically to the constitutional prohibition of religious teaching in private schools. By these regulations no minister or any religious cult could act as the director or teacher in such schools.

Since the Catholic prelates of Mexico felt that it was impossible to practice their sacred ministry under the conditions imposed by Calles' decree, particularly the requirement that all priests be registered, they agreed, with papal approval, to withdraw the priests from all the churches in the Republic. The momentous decision to suspend all religious services was made public on July 25 in a pastoral letter signed by eight archbishops and twenty-nine bishops. "We order that," read the pastoral, "after July 31 until we order otherwise all religious services requiring the intervention of priests shall be suspended in all the churches of the country." The edifices were not to be closed but were to be entrusted to the care of the worshippers. Denying that their conduct constituted rebellion the prelates declared that they were employing "the only way open to manifest nonconformance with the anti-religious laws of the Constitution."[34]

The government would not countenance the proposal of the Episcopate that the abandoned churches be turned over to committees or individuals named by the priests but insisted that the civil authorities should assume immediate control. The municipal authorities were then to appoint committees of honorable residents who should be responsible for the churches, and keep them open for public use. President Calles refused to grant that he had added in any way to the severity of the re-

32. Balderrama, *op. cit.*, I, 51-53; *Current History* (August, 1926), p. 783.
33. "Reformas al Código Penal," in Pérez Lugo, *op. cit.*, pp. 258-63.
34. *El Universal*, July 25, 1926. See Aquílas P. Moctezuma, *El conflicto religioso de 1926; sus orígines, su desarrollo, su solución* (2nd ed.; Mexico, 1960).

ligious clauses of the Constitution. This in fact was true, with the exception of the registration requirement. The object of the register, said the President, was to enable the government to know who were entrusted with the churches and who were responsible for what went on inside of them. The Catholic hierarchy alleged, however, that registration would give the State unlimited control over the clergy and would enable it to license a priest who had not been designated by his bishop.[35]

The final religious services were held on July 30. On the following day the priests made inventories of the contents of the churches and removed their personal belongings before the formal delivery to the civil committees on August 1. The withdrawal of the priests from the churches, denoting as it did the suspension of the administration of the sacraments in a country composed of approximately 80 to 90 per cent Catholics, was a drastic action which was confidently expected in many quarters to create serious disturbances in Mexico. However, the transfer of the churches to the government was accomplished without serious disorder.

The drastic and unprecedented action on the part of the Mexican Catholic prelates in ordering the suspension of all religious exercises attracted once more the eyes of the Catholic world to the Mexican situation. Pastorals condemning the Mexican rulers were issued in the United States by Cardinals Mundelein and Hayes, and by prelates in Latin America. *L'Osservatore Romano*, official Vatican publication, attacked President Calles with considerable fury. *La Tribuna*, semi-official paper of Mussolini, accused international Masonry as being the inspirer of the Mexican laws.[36]

On August 3, President Leguía of Peru telegraphed President Calles urging him "to use his powerful influence in reëstablishing harmonious relations with the Church." President Calles, in his reply of August 4, told the dictator of Peru that he was willing to regard the message as merely a personal expression and in no wise official. "The Constitution of Mexico is not a special law," he explained to President Leguía, "but a general and fundamental code which I am obliged and am decided to enforce without fear of interdicts or supernatural punishment."

The appeal of the Knights of Columbus to Secretary Kellogg to intervene in the religious conflict was met with the usual refusal. The policy of the Coolidge government was that unless American lives and property rights were placed in jeopardy the Church-State conflict was an internal problem of the Republic of Mexico. Efforts in and out of Mexico to bring about American intervention were disapproved by the

35. *El Universal*, July 29, 1926.
36. Balderrama, *op. cit.*, I, 110-14.

pope. He saw in this a great danger to Catholics of Mexico, for it presented them as antipatriots and it excited resentment against them and against the United States.[37]

On the other hand the Mexican government was not without words of encouragement and approval. Thousands of messages of support were sent to President Calles from deputies, senators, political associations, and workers' organizations. Former President Obregón's message was of inestimable value because it meant that the armed forces, over which Obregón exercised dominant control, were behind the government and made resistance impossible. The Regional Confederation of Mexican Workers, called the *Crom*, stood solidly behind the President throughout the crisis.

On August 19, Archbishop Leopoldo Ruíz and Bishop Pascual Díaz, acting for the Episcopacy, and invoking their constitutional guarantee of the right of petition, solicited of President Calles the following liberties: conscience, thought, religion, instruction, association, and the press. The President, after acknowledging the propriety of the action of the Episcopate in petitioning him as one of the authorities vested with the power of initiating legislation, replied that, since his philosophical and political convictions rendered him thoroughly in accord with the legislation in question, he found himself unable to acquiesce in their requests.

Having been refused succor by President Calles, the Episcopate turned next to the Congress. On September 7, 1926, a petition was presented asking for modifications in the religious legislation. "There is no tyranny worse than that of bad laws," read the petition. "It is the strict duty of the Catholics to procure the abrogation of the bad laws before they annihilate religious liberty in Mexico.... What is it that we ask? Neither tolerance, nor complacency, much less prerogatives or laws. We demand liberty. We do not demand anything except liberty and for all religions."[38] Conditions had indeed changed in Mexico. The Catholic clergy were now earnestly begging for mere tolerance which they a hundred years before had been unwilling to accord to other sects. The petition received short shrift in the Chamber of Deputies, for, on September 23, 1926, a resolution was adopted by vote of 171 to 1, declaring that, since petitions could only be presented by citizens, and since by their public declarations not to observe the Constitution the heads of the Catholic Church had lost their citizenship, therefore the Chamber of Deputies could not legally listen to the petition.[39]

37. *Ibid.*, I, 123.
38. Toro, *op. cit.*, pp. 434-40.
39. Balderrama, *op. cit.*, I, 196-97.

It is not necessary to examine the legal or moral justification of this ingenious maneuver on the part of Congress, nor to stress the fact that the President and the Deputies interpreted the right of petition in different lights. The attitude of the legislators was such that, even had the petition been received, they would have refused to amend the legislation in any way. In reply to the adverse action of the Chamber, the Episcopate issued a long statement urging the Catholics not to give up the fight for amendment of the laws.

The stern intent of the Mexican government not to abate its policy was evidenced by the publication on October 16 of a presidential regulation limiting the number of Catholic priests and ministers of every denomination to 90 for each in the Federal District, 18 in the Territory of Lower California, and 3 in the Territory of Quintana Roo. Prior to the suspension of services there were 136 churches in the Federal District, cared for by 289 priests. The presidential regulation required every priest to register with the president of the municipality. On November 25, a new bill of religious regulations, based on Article 130 of the Constitution, was passed by the Congress. This bill proposed to make more rigid in many respects the prior presidential regulations. Its declared intention was to seal every loophole making evasion possible and to prepare the way for complete and absolute enforcement.[40]

Catholic organizations and individuals, even including some priests, resorted to armed violence. The principal scenes of revolutionary movements were the states of Jalisco, Guerrero, Michoacán, Colima, Guanajuato, Querétaro, Puebla, and Vera Cruz. The "Cristero" revolt continued in the State of Jalisco until July, 1929. The League for the Defense of Religious Liberty, after the resumption of religious services, admitted that it had supported the religious rebels in their resort to arms against the government since 1926. It denied, however, that the Mexican Episcopate or the Vatican had supported the armed conflict in any way.[41] The government, however, confident that the clergy were responsible for the revolutionary movements, issued an order, January 30, 1927, requiring all Catholic priests in Mexico to report to the Minister of Interior before February 10, under penalty of being declared outlaws. Later a regulation required priests and prelates to appear daily at the Ministry of Interior to sign the register. Bishop Pascual Díaz, spokesman of the Episcopate, was deported on January 12 on the charge of being the intellectual leader of the Catholic rebellion.[42]

40. *Ibid.*, II, 145-47; *Current History* (December, 1926), pp. 410, 437.
41. *Current History* (September, 1929), p. 1137; Callcott, *Liberalism in Mexico*, pp. 367-68, 379-80.
42. *Memoria de la Secretaría de Gobernación* (Mexico, 1927), Sec. *Cultos.*

The increasing violence of the revolt culminated, on April 21, 1927, in the arraignment before Minister Tejeda of several of the leading prelates on the charge of inciting to revolt. In refuting the charge Archbishop Mora y del Río told Minister Tejeda: "We have aided no revolution. We have plotted no revolution, but we do claim that the Catholics of Mexico have the right to fight for their rights by peaceful means first and with arms in an extremity." Because of this statement the Archbishop and five other prelates were ordered deported from Mexico immediately. They entered the United States at Laredo, Texas, on April 23. The deportation of other prelates followed.[43]

In explaining the status of the religious situation, President Calles reported in his message to Congress on September 1, 1927: "The religious law has been strictly enforced, and it can be said that the religious conflict caused by the rebellious clergy now has practically concluded for the laws have been complied with despite the futile resistance of the clergy. The Mexican people have shown themselves indifferent to the suspension of services. Some church edifices have been dedicated by the government to public uses. Priests who have shown willingness to obey the laws have been permitted to exercise their ministry."[44] It should be noted, however, that very few priests consented without the permission of their superiors to register. Those who registered were regarded as schismatics.

Due to the efforts of Ambassador Morrow, who was working for a settlement of the Church-State controversy, a secret meeting occurred in Vera Cruz, April 4, 1928, between Father J. J. Burke, C.S.P., General Secretary of the Catholic Welfare Conference, and President Calles. The meeting resulted in a tentative understanding substantially the same as the one adopted in June, 1929.[45]

It was reported in June, 1928, that the pope had submitted to the Congregation on Extraordinary Ecclesiastical Affairs the determination of the conditions under which the Mexican clergy should return to the churches and it was hoped that some adjustment might be effected. At this juncture President-elect Obregón was assassinated on July 17, 1928. Notwithstanding Obregón's pre-election declaration that there would be no change in the governmental attitude on the Catholic question, it had been persistently reported that he was anxious to end the conflict. President Calles' statement that Obregón was the victim of "direct clerical action" was premature, untrue, ill-considered, and seriously retarded a

43. *El Universal*, April 22 and 23, 1927.
44. *Excelsior*, September 2, 1927.
45. Walter Lippmann, "Church and State in Mexico: The American Mediation," in *Foreign Affairs*, VIII, No. 2 (January, 1930), 186.

rapprochement with the papacy. The murder was the work of a religious fanatic, instigated by a nun who acted independently of the Catholic clergy or organizations.[46]

It is interesting to note that during the religious crisis, when political revolutions occurred in Mexico, the Catholics resolutely refused to be identified with these movements, notwithstanding repeated bids made for their support. Generals Gómez and Serrano, in revolting against the Calles-Obregón machine in October, 1927, invoked Catholic aid in vain. In March, 1929, during his rebellion against the Federal government, General Escobar proclaimed religious liberty and the abrogation of the antireligious laws. Again the Catholics refused to take the bait. Perhaps they recalled that this same Escobar, two years before, in enforcing the Calles' decrees had directed the arrest of thousands of Catholics and had executed priests. Escobar's about-face on religious policy was very reminiscent of Pancho Villa's action.[47]

A partial settlement of the religious difficulty and the resumption of services in the Catholic churches of Mexico followed soon upon the heels of the inauguration of President Emilio Portes Gil. In outlining his religious policy, the new President said on May 1, 1929: "No religion will be persecuted, nor is the government guilty of any persecution of any sect. Liberty of conscience will be respected as heretofore. The Catholic clergy, when they wish, may renew the exercise of their rites with only one obligation, that they respect the laws of the land as the ministers of other denominations are doing."[48]

Archbishop Ruíz y Flores, senior prelate of Mexico, then in the United States, detected a tone of conciliation in the President's statement and said that the Catholic Church and its ministers were prepared to coöperate with the Mexican government in every proper and moral effort for the benefit of the Mexican people. Portes Gil thereupon expressed his willingness to discuss the problem with the Archbishop. Having received permission from the pope to undertake negotiations, Archbishop Ruíz and Bishop Pascual Díaz returned to Mexico. Several conferences occurred between the Mexican President and the prelates. Ambassador Morrow of the United States has been credited with contributing to the successful outcome of the conferences. On June 17 the basis for a settlement was approved, and on June 21 the pope signified his acceptance.

46. *Current History* (September, 1928), pp. 1026-27; Callcott, *Liberalism in Mexico*, p. 377.

47. Lippmann, *op. cit.*, p. 203.

48. *New York Times*, May 2, 1929. See L. Elthan Ellis, "Dwight Morrow and the Church-State Controversy in Mexico," in *Hisp. Am. Hist. Rev.*, Vol. 38, No. 4 (November, 1958), 482-505.

The understanding between President Portes Gil and the Mexican prelates was not a formal, signed contract or treaty, but merely a verbal "gentleman's agreement." The only authentic, published statement on the nature of the agreement was the signed statement of the President which was given to the press on June 21, 1929. He said:

> I take advantage of this opportunity to declare publicly and with all clarity that it is not the spirit of the Constitution, nor of the laws, nor of the government of the Republic to destroy the identity of the Catholic Church, nor of any other cult, nor to intervene in any manner in its spiritual functions. According to the oath which I took when I assumed the Provisional Government of Mexico to obey and cause to be obeyed the Constitution of the Republic and its laws, my purpose has been at all times to comply honestly with this oath and to see that the laws are applied without sectarian tendency and without injury to anyone.... With reference to certain articles of the law which have not been clearly understood, I take advantage of this opportunity to declare:
>
> I. The provision of the law which required the registration of ministers does not mean that the government can register those who have not been named by a hierarchial superior of the religious creed in question or in accordance with its regulations.
>
> II. With regard to religious instruction, the constitution and laws in force definitely prohibit it in primary or higher schools, whether public or private, but this does not prevent ministers of any religion from imparting its doctrines within the church confines to adults and their children, who may attend for that purpose.
>
> III. The Constitution as well as the laws of the country guarantee to all residents of the republic the right of petition, and therefore the members of any church may apply to the appropriate authorities for amendment, repeal or passage of any law.[49]

Superficially it would appear that the Church received little or no concession from the State, and that the *modus vivendi* marked a complete backdown on the part of the former. Such in fact was not the case, for the agreement in the matter of registration of ministers was all-important. There was tacit acknowledgment of the right of the hierarchy to designate priests who were to register. This amounted to a virtual acknowledgment of the corporate rights of the Church and the authority of the bishop of the diocese, the constitutional denial of juridic personality to religious institutions to the contrary notwithstanding. Thus the means of fortifying the principle of authority for which the Mexican clergy had contended and in defense of which they sus-

49. *New York Times*, June 22, 1929; *Excelsior*, June 22, 1929.

pended religious exercises was recognized and guaranteed by the State. This was a real victory for the clergy.

The declaration of Portes Gil that it was not the purpose of the State to interfere in any way with the spiritual functions of the Catholic Church was interpreted by Archbishop Ruíz to mean that "the laws will not be applied in a spirit of passion and sectarianism, but, on the contrary, in a spirit compatible with the existence of the Church's liberty." In other words there was guaranteed assurance that the government would put aside the utterly ruthless and vindicative methods of the Calles administration.   In pursuance of this guarantee the central government, to curb extreme local anticlerical legislation, ordered all governors, state legislatures, and municipal authorities to recognize the Federal government's supremacy and authority in questions relating to religious worship, and its exclusive right to allocate churches.   The Church was assured immunity against local radicalism.

On June 27, 1929, masses were celebrated in Mexico for the first time since July 30, 1926.   On September 17, 1929, Mgr. Pascual Díaz was formally installed as Archbishop of Mexico in the Basilica of Guadalupe. The return of the priests to the ministration of their flocks was attended by great rejoicing and the voicing of fervent prayers of public thanksgiving.   The report was widely circulated that the religious question in Mexico had been "settled."

Yet, the National League for the Defense of Religious Liberty, quite correctly, as later events proved, branded the accord of June 21 as merely "a sort of armistice." A warning was issued that much remained to be settled apart from the resumption of Catholic services in Mexico. The extremists were not averse to the use of arms to recover "the legitimate rights of the Church." The opponents of the agreement became so menacing that Mgr. Ruíz y Flores, Apostolic Delegate, and Archbishop Díaz rushed to the press in its defense. They denied that the Church had accepted the religious laws of the Calles régime. The accord was merely the basis for reaching a more complete understanding. It was not the time, said the Apostolic Delegate, to discuss, but to obey. This was counseled by the pope himself. There is little doubt that the prelates were sincerely laboring in support of a policy of conciliation and coöperation.[50]

Once again, without there being the slightest alteration of the laws, the Church blithely stepped out of the catacombs, just as if nothing

50. Abbé Alphonse Lugan, "Church and State in Mexico," in *Current History* (February, 1931), pp. 672-75.

had happened, and as if Mexico were the freest country in the world. A program known as "Catholic Action" was instituted, which had as its object the bringing of the laity into the work of re-Christianizing the nation. There were study clubs, night schools, religious prize contests, and parochial, diocesan, and national conventions. In a short time religious instruction was being imparted by catechists of Catholic Action to an average of 300,000 children. The program was just as ambitious as if the Church enjoyed the fullest freedom. "In fact that was the slogan: act, as if there were no restricting laws in force."[51]

The new resurgence of the Church reached its height in the elaborate celebration (December 1, 1931) of the four hundredth anniversary of the Virgin of Guadalupe. Twenty-seven archbishops and bishops and nearly two hundred priests officiated at the services, and over half a million people visited the famous Basilica of Guadalupe.[52]

It proved to be most imprudent for the Church to flaunt itself in the face of a sullen government and an actively hostile political party just after it had won a grudging license to exist. The Church presumed too much on the *modus vivendi*. Moreover, anticlerical legislation in some of the states should have been a warning to go slow. In June, 1931, Governor Adelberto Tejeda of Vera Cruz, ex-Minister of *Gobernación* and a fanatical anticlerical, signed a law limiting the number of priests in the state to one to every 100,000 inhabitants. This would permit only eleven priests to function in the state. Chiapas, with a population of 350,000, restricted the clergy to nine; Yucatán, with 400,000, to nine; and Tabasco went the limit by prohibiting any priests from officiating in religious ceremonies.[53] These actions were all taken in the fall of 1931.

On December 30, immediately following the Guadalupe celebration, the Congress passed a law limiting the number of priests in the Federal District and the Territory of Lower California, to one for every 50,000 inhabitants. This meant that the number of priests for the Federal District was fixed at twenty-five. Most of the states followed suit with most drastic limitations on the number of clergy; for example: Chihuahua, 1 to 9,000; Guanajuato, 1 to 25,000; Durango, 25 for the state; Chiapas, 4 for the state; and Mexico, 34 for the state. Eventually, in some of the states, e.g., Vera Cruz and Chiapas, religious services were suspended altogether. By 1935 there were considerably fewer than 500 priests for all of Mexico. In half of the states no priests were allowed

51. Wilfrid Parsons, *Mexican Martyrdom* (New York, 1936), pp. 145-46.
52. *New York Times*, December 13, 1931.
53. *Current History* (November, 1931), p. 270.

to function at all,[54] although the practice of religion was guaranteed by the Constitution.

Incidental to this anti-Church outburst many of the prelates again went into exile. In October, 1932, Archbishop Ruíz y Flores, the Apostolic Delegate, was deported as an "undesirable alien." Although a native of Mexico, he was declared a foreigner because he "owed allegiance to a foreign sovereign"—the pope. Although the Archbishop of Mexico was disposed to refuse permission to priests to register with the government, the pope accepted the laws restricting the number of clergy as a lesser evil, for it was better to have some churches open and some priests ministering to the people than none at all. The pope had earlier instructed the Apostolic Delegate, Archbishop Ruíz y Flores, to inform the people that they were not to offer armed resistance, certainly not in the name of the Catholic Church.

Profiting from their past sad experiences, the clergy and their followers refrained from armed violence and sought by legal means to secure an amelioration of the laws' severity, meantime not disdaining clandestine evasions. Petitions were presented to the courts asking *amparos* to restrain enforcement of the legislation limiting the number of clergy as being violative of the constitutional guarantee of religious liberty. These petitions were uniformly rejected by the politically controlled courts on the ground that the jurists could discover no impairment of the religious liberty of Catholics.[55]

Application of the educational philosophy of revolutionary extremists was another source of conflict which disrupted the *modus vivendi* of 1929. The opposed positions taken by Church and State on the problem of education were always pronounced. According to Article 3 of the Constitution of 1917, primary education is secular, and "no religious corporation nor minister of any religious creed shall establish or direct schools of primary instruction." From the point of view of the State the prohibition of religious schools was a part of the general campaign to destroy the temporal influence of the Church. The Church, on its part, insisted that this jeopardized the very existence of the cult. Unless children were trained in Catholic schools, they would be deprived of spiritual guidance and instruction essential for the preservation of their faith and the salvation of their souls. Laicism in the public schools was represented as being not only unreligious, but antireligious education.

In 1934 Article 3 was amended in such a fashion as to lend con-

---

54. Charles S. Macfarland, *Chaos in Mexico: The Conflict of Church and State* (New York, 1935), pp. 70-71; William F. Montavon, *The Church in Mexico Protests* (Washington, D.C., 1934), p. 14.

55. *El Universal* (Mexico), January 23, 1932.

siderable support to the clerical contention that the government's educational aims were antireligious. From the original Liberal idea that the role of sectarian schools was to raise the social and economic level of communities, there evolved the idea that schools should become "active forces in moulding public opinion towards a better understanding and an acceptance of the ideals of socialistic government."[56] If the Revolution were to be permanent it had to capture the schools.

General Plutarco Calles was one of the originators of the new educational plan to curb intellectual opposition to the Revolution. In July, 1934, he said, "It is necessary that we enter into a new phase of the Revolution which I shall call the psychological revolutionary period; we must enter into and take possession of the minds of children, the consciences of the young, because they do belong and should belong to the Revolution.... It is absolutely necessary to drive the enemy out of that entrenchment where the clergy has been, where the Conservatives have been—I refer to Education."[57] The Six Year Plan, drafted by the National Revolutionary Party (P.N.R.), but largely the work of Calles, declared for State control over all primary and secondary education, from which all religious instruction was excluded and whose programs were based on "the orientation and postulates of the Socialistic doctrine of the Mexican Revolution."[58] On the basis of the principles laid down in the Six Year Plan, Article 3 of the Constitution was amended, November 28, 1934, to read as follows:

> Education imparted by the State shall be socialistic, and in addition to excluding all religious doctrine shall combat fanaticism and prejudices, for which purpose the school shall organize its teachings and activities in a manner to permit the creation of a rational and exact concept of the universe and social life in the mind of the youth.
>
> Only the State—the Federation, the States and Municipalities—shall impart primary, secondary, and normal education.[59]

Under the terms of this amendment, no religious cult could maintain schools of any grade. This prohibition even included seminaries for the training of priests. Since foreign clergy could not function, and since training for the ministry was prohibited, the destruction of all organized religion in Mexico seemed to be the objective. However, seminaries were clandestinely operated, and priests continued to be trained, although under most difficult and dangerous circumstances. Later, pro-

56. George I. Sánchez, *Mexico, A Revolution by Education* (New York, 1936), p. 101.
57. *El Nacional* (Mexico), July 21, 1934.
58. *Plan sexenal de Gobierno del Partido Nacional Revolucionario, 1934-1939*, p. 85.
59. *Diario Oficial* (Mexico), December 13, 1934.

vision was made for the training of Mexican priests in American Catholic seminaries, notably one at El Paso, Texas.

Although Protestants submitted to the law and consented to the closing of numerous mission schools, the Catholic clergy branded socialistic education as antireligious and counseled Catholic parents not to send their children to public schools. The clergy held, with considerable justification, that "fanaticism" and "superstition" for most Mexican radicals, was synonymous with Catholicism. Therefore the eradication of fanaticism was merely another way of destroying the Catholic Church.

As for the meaning of "socialistic education," the term was impossible of exact definition. Even in high governmental places there was remarkable lack of agreement. Although there were many who subscribed to the Marxist doctrine, the majority of the Revolutionaries, including President Cárdenas himself, adhered to a strictly Mexican variety of socialism which emphasized economic nationalism, social justice in the framework of capitalism, redistribution of the land, improvement of the legal status of labor, and anticlericalism. It is significant that, whereas there was much difference of opinion regarding the components of Mexican socialism, there was near unanimous agreement that anticlericalism was a principal ingredient. The Church had good reason, therefore, to regard the adoption of the amendment to Article 3 as the signal for another attack against it.

Because there was no accepted definition of socialism, it should occasion no surprise that there was remarkable lack of uniformity in its instruction in the schools. There were as many explanations of its meaning as there were school directors. In practice it ranged all the way from Marxism unalloyed to a mild social reform theory. Whether so intended by the Revolutionary high command, to many of the school administrators socialistic education meant materialism in moral life, atheism in religion, and communism in economics and government. For example, in some of the states, including Yucatán, Hidalgo, Michoacán, and Guanajuato, the teachers were required to make an "Ideological Declaration," sponsored by the Federal Department of Education, as follows:

> In the presence of the Federal Board of Education, I———, declare that I unconditionally accept the program of the socialistic school and that I will make it known and will defend it;
>
> I declare that I am an atheist, an irreconcilable enemy of the Catholic, Apostolic, Roman religion, that I will endeavor to destroy it, detaching consciences from the bonds of any religious worship, and that I am ready to fight against the clergy anywhere and wherever it may be necessary.[60]

60. Macfarland, *op. cit.*, p. 101.

Textbooks were introduced which were violently antireligious and designed to set class against class. The purpose of these "socialistic" texts seems to have been to arouse hatred for religion, and make it appear that the Church was against the poor. It may well be that these examples of antireligion in the schools were the exception rather than the rule. Nevertheless it is difficult to escape the conclusion that the instances of "over zealous" application of atheistic doctrine received encouragement from high governmental places.

Archbishop Leopoldo Ruíz y Flores, then living in exile in the United States, expressed his concern over the establishment of socialistic education and urged on the Mexican hierarchy a course of united action in dealing with this menace. Clerical protests elicited the usual governmental retort that there was no religious persecution in Mexico. On January 16, 1936, a pastoral letter signed by Archbishop Pascual Díaz, eight other archbishops, and thirty bishops was made public. Referring to the inalienable rights of the Church, the hierarchy admonished Catholic parents, under pain of committing mortal sin, not to enroll their children in schools where socialism might be taught.[61]

Home schools established in private houses and taught by former public school teachers or laicized sisters sprang up all over the country. Since it was a penal offense to conduct private schools without permission, the owners of the houses ran the risk of having their property confiscated. Indeed, there were numerous confiscations and arrests. But on the other hand the teaching of socialism involved risks too, for many teachers in the rural districts were either murdered or had their ears cut off.

A decree on the nationalization of Church property (1935) provided that every building that was used for the administration, propaganda, or teaching of a religious cult became the property of the government. This included private homes if used for religious services or for schools. Any house having a chapel was presumed a place of worship. Even bookstores were regarded as propaganda centers. Another decree of 1935 prohibited the use of the mails for publications containing religious information.[62]

A Protestant worker in Mexico, very sympathetic toward the general social and economic program of the Mexican government, described the status of affairs in 1935 as follows:

> It was a critical hour, for Communism was sweeping over the land. The aggressive atheism which streamed daily over radio channels was blasphemous and deadly in its purpose. The whole

61. *Mexican Bishops' Pastoral: Liberty for the Church* (Washington, D.C., 1935).
62. *Diario Oficial*, February 12 and August 31, 1935.

educational system of the country was being revamped for the purpose of propagating atheistic Communism. School teachers, agents of the government, were being murdered in every state by the rebellious "plebe." Children in public schools were being taught to march to the tune of "Uno, dos, no hay Dios"—(one, two, there is no God). One was almost afraid to mention the name of Jesus. Mission schools were closed. All roads were leading to Russia.[63]

When the religious persecution was at its height, a modification of governmental severity became apparent. This seems to have dated from February 16, 1936, when President Cárdenas delivered an address containing the suggestion of conciliation. He attempted to distinguish between attacking religious beliefs and combatting fanaticism. It is not the attribute of government, he said, to combat the beliefs or creed of any religion.[64] About a month later the President declared that it was the duty of his administration to foster the social and economic program of the Revolution and not to promote antireligious campaigns. He said, "The Government will not commit the error of previous administrations by considering the religious question as a problem preëminent to other issues involved in the national program. Antireligious campaigns would only result in further resistance and definitely postpone economic revival."[65] There is no doubt that this was the reason for President Cárdenas' decision to temper the severity of the anticlerical, and even antireligious, assault.

The declaration of the President was followed by a statement by the Secretary of *Gobernación*, Silvano Barba González, to the effect that, although the religious laws would continue to be enforced, the rights of Catholics under these laws would be fully respected, the federal government would not provoke difficulties with the Catholic Church or allow it to be persecuted, and there would be respect for liberty of conscience.[66] The administrations of state governments, in response to federal promptings, began to ease restrictions on the number of priests permitted. Impetus to the return of priests and reopening of churches was given by a Supreme Court decision that state authorities could not limit the number of priests so much as to be arbitrary.[67]

The trend of the government to a more conciliatory policy was matched by a healthful personnel change in the Church hierarchy. On

63. "The Wind Shifts in Mexico," in *The Missionary Review of the World*, Vol. 61 (March, 1938), 123.

64. *El Nacional*, February 17, 1936.

65. *New York Times*, March 6, 1936.

66. *Ibid.*, March 31, 1936.

67. *Ibid.*, August 2, 1937.

February 20, 1937, following the death of Archbishop Díaz and the resignation of Archbishop Ruíz y Flores as Apostolic Delegate—both committed to resistance short of resort to arms—Luis María Martínez was appointed Archbishop of Mexico. The new primate, who also assumed the temporary position of Apostolic Delegate, was a realist who believed in moderation in the defense of the Church's rights and interests. He offered no criticism of governmental policy and no condemnation of constitutional provisions. Almost immediately there was a steady improvement in relations between the Cárdenas administration and the Church.

On March 28, 1937, Pope Pius XI issued an encyclical concerning Mexico. All Mexican clergy were urged to assume responsibilities in the field of social service; to concern themselves with the conditions of the poor "who too easily become prey of de-Christianizing propaganda, with the mirage of economic advantages presented to them as a reward for their apostasy from God and from His Church."[68] The Pope emphasized particularly the advantages of a Catholic Action program over the use of violence as a means of defending Catholic rights in Mexico. "Thus Mexican priests," says Dr. Lyle C. Brown, "were instructed to evidence concern for the socio-economic welfare of the masses and to develop Christian laymen who would protect the interests of the Church in the political field. As a general guideline, it appeared that Rome was calling for a policy of flexibility instead of the traditional doctrinaire rigidity with which Mexico's clergy previously had approached the problem of Church-State relations."[69]

When the Mexican petroleum industry was nationalized in March, 1938, and the Cárdenas administration was faced with diplomatic and financial crisis, all classes of Mexicans, including Catholic prelates and laity, supported the government in its hour of need. This did not pass unnoticed by President Cárdenas, for he publicly stated that for the first time the government was getting coöperation from Catholics.[70] This demonstration of solidarity did much to improve Church-State relations for the balance of the Cárdenas administration.

The trend toward more amicable Church-State relations received a substantial boost when Cárdenas' successor, President Ávila Camacho, declared publicly in 1940: "I am a believer" (*soy creyente*). The confession of his Catholicism by the President of the Republic, and nominal

68. Pope Pius XI, *On the Religious Situation in Mexico* (Washington, D.C., 1937), p. 12.

69. Lyle C. Brown, "Mexican Church-State Relations, 1933-1940," in *A Journal of Church and State* (Baylor University), VI, No. 2 (Spring, 1964), 220.

70. *New York Times*, April 28, 1938.

head of the Revolutionary party, was an historic event for it inaugurated an unprecedented era of compatibility between a new generation of clerical and official leaders. The Church-State conflict seemed to melt away.

President Ávila Camacho frowned upon all kinds of religious persecution, but he, like his successors in the presidency, made no attempt to repeal the anticlerical laws; best not to arouse the revolutionary extremists, and also, the Church should be kept on probation to insure its avoidance of interference in Mexican politics. A swing away from anticlericalism became a fixed policy of the PRI (Party of the Institutional Revolution). The most notable change was another amendment of constitutional Article 3 to eliminate "socialistic" education. The amended article prohibits religious elementary, secondary, and normal education, but not theological seminaries or universities. To protect religion against assault in the public schools the article says that "Freedom of religious beliefs being guaranteed by Article 24, the standard which shall guide such education shall be maintained entirely apart from any religious doctrine and, based on the results of scientific progress, shall strive against ignorance and its effects, servitudes, fanaticism, and prejudices."

Excepting this formal change of the constitution, the laws governing the Church remained essentially unaltered—but they were not enforced. The Church ordinarily was free to hold public pageants, and religious garb appeared on the streets throughout the nation. Catholic schools ceased to function secretly and operated openly "though they have been named after Mexican patriots rather than saints." Members of the radical revolutionary wing never tired of calling attention to these legal evasions,[71] but no longer did the national administration respond with enforcement measures. A sign of the times was when López Mateos as presidential candidate appeared and spoke from the same platform with a Catholic priest, both speaking as "Mexicans anxious for social justice." Said the PRI nominee: "I am a Catholic and we (Catholics) are voting for the Revolution."[72] In further evidence of the continued official trend away from the traditional anticlericalism of the Mexican Revolution, President López Mateos said that "having religious ideas does not mean being an enemy of the Revolution." The Archbishop Primate Miguel Darío Miranda expressed satisfaction with the President's statement.[73]

71. For example, in April, 1965, the youth wing of PRI, meeting in Guanajuato, urged that laws prohibiting Church schools be enforced, saying it would be better for children not to go to school at all than to receive education from priests and nuns. *The News* (Mexico City), April 10, 1965.

72. *Hispanic American Report*, XI, No. 6 (June, 1958), 304.

73. *Ibid.*, XII, No. 12 (December, 1959), 649.

When the Archbishop and the other members of the hierarchy signed a pastoral, in November, 1956, advising Catholics to exercise their civic duties, and to support political candidates favoring the greatest degree of good to the Church and nation, the PRI decided that this was not Church interference in politics—but others regarded the declaration as clerical intermeddling.

There is no Catholic party in Mexico. In fact, such is constitutionally prohibited. The *Partido de Acción Nacional* (PAN), the most influential opposition party in Mexico, has had over the years a pronounced Catholic orientation. In many of the campaigns it has been openly pro-Catholic, calling for the establishment of religious schools and the freeing of the Church from governmental controls. The Catholic clergy have usually been circumspect in avoiding identification with PAN.[74]

The clerics have also tried to avoid involvement with the *Unión Nacional de Sinarquistas* and its political branch, the *Fuerza Popular*. *Sinarquismo* was organized in 1937 by devout Catholics "to restore the Christian social order and oppose the Mexican Revolution, Fascism, Nazism, Communism, Liberal Democracy, and the values of United States culture." In other words, the *Sinarquistas* envisaged an authoritarian Utopia with the Roman Catholic faith installed as the official religion. In the 1930's and 1940's *Sinarquismo* enjoyed considerable success among youth groups, peasants, and others disillusioned by the excesses of the Mexican Revolution. The Catholic clergy encouraged it, though no priests were permitted by the hierarchy to belong to its organization. When political criticism descended to incitement to subversion the government was finally forced to take severe repressive measures. By the early 1950's *Sinarquismo* had lost most of its appeal.[75]

To correct a possible false impression that there has been no interruption in amicable Church-State relations since 1940, the textbook issue is here cited. Not only must the public schools—including some 30,000 Church schools—conform their programs of study to those provided by the Ministry of Public Education, but since 1960, standard texts have been provided, free of charge and compulsory, for all elementary schools, public and private. Until then pupils had to buy their own books.

All textbooks must be submitted for approval to the Permanent Committee on Textbooks (*Comisión Permanente de Libros de Texto*) of the Ministry of Public Education. The charge has been made, with

74. For example, when, in the presidential campaign of 1958, the PAN candidate became too pro-clerical, "the Church disavowed its connections with PAN." Howard F. Cline, *Mexico, Revolution to Evolution* (New York, 1963), p. 169.

75. See Frederick B. Pike, ed., *Freedom and Reform in Latin America* (Notre Dame, Ind., 1959), pp. 128-29; also, Joaquín Márquez Montiel, *La iglesia y el estado en México. La iglesia y la Constitución Mexicana.* (2nd ed.; Chihuahua, 1950), p. 56.

considerable basis of truth, that "on questions of religion one would search in vain for a textbook which would present a balanced view of these subjects. Mexican children today are not receiving an unbiased treatment of religious matters in their history classes."[76]

The texts were first distributed to schools in the Mexico City area without organized protests, but as they reached the provincial cities of northern Mexico they began to run into organized opposition, beginning with a big rally in Monterrey in 1962. Parent-teacher groups in several of the states opposed the compulsory texts as leftist and anticlerical. Charges were made that the Ministry of Education was filled with Communist sympathizers who would convert the schools into centers of Marxist propaganda. Catholic priests, parents, and business men organized campaigns against the *texto único*. It was called "a shame for Mexico." President López Mateos was provoked into branding the reactionary Catholics as the "forces of darkness."[77] Although the free textbooks continued to be distributed in all of the schools, their acceptance was made more palatable by the introduction of more tolerance in their selection.

Not only through textbooks is government control over Church schools growing, but the overwhelming majority of its teachers are turned out by the normal schools which are under government control. Also, religious instruction is very light, due to the heavy schedule imposed by government regulations. The number of students in Church schools is said to have increased tenfold from 1954 to 1960. In 1960 there were 2,259 Catholic schools with a total student enrollment of 446,682.[78]

The census of 1960 recorded 30,202,000 Catholics, in a total population of 34,625,000. There were 6,290 priests: diocesan and religious. The hierarchy of eleven archbishops and 57 bishops is constantly being enlarged in evidence of the phenomenal development of the Catholic Church in Mexico.

According to Cardinal José Garibi Rivera[79] Mexico faces twin menaces in communism and Protestantism, which, as we have noted, are also viewed by prelates in other Latin-American countries as major obstacles to the progress of Catholicism. As for communism, the

76. Richard B. McCormack, "Attitude Towards Religious Matters in Mexican School History Textbooks," in *The Americas*, Vol. 15, No. 3 (January, 1959), 235-47.

77. *Christian Science Monitor*, March 2, 1963; *Hispanic American Report*, XVI, No. 1 (March, 1963), 19-20.

78. *Statistical Abstract of Latin America, 1963* (UCLA), p. 22.

79. When Pope John XXIII named the conservative Archbishop of Guadalajara, José Garibi Rivera, as Mexico's first Cardinal, questions were asked as to whether this appointment was a rebuff to the official anticlericals of the PRI and the liberal attitude of Archbishop Primate Miguel Dario Miranda of Mexico City. *Hispanic American Report*, XI, No. 11 (November, 1958), 597.

Catholic Church in Mexico has consistently warned against its lure, although it has perhaps been too prone to attribute to Communist influence anticlerical policies of Revolutionary administrations. There have been ample occasions, however, for warranted Catholic anti-Communist action. The Church has also been alive to the external danger. One such example was a Catholic demonstration before the Basilica of Guadalupe in condemnation of Cuba's swing to communism. Said Archbishop Miranda of Mexico City: "Recent events have awakened Mexicans to the great danger of Communism in Mexico." Catholic support of United States policy vis-à-vis Fidel Castro was counter to an apparent majority view in Mexico.[80]

While not pursuing anticlerical programs, Presidents Ávila Camacho, Miguel Alemán, and their successors were equally friendly to Protestant efforts in Mexico. Responding to a benevolent atmosphere, the Evangelical Church experienced phenomenal growth. In 1957 Father Considine reported: "Protestant activity in Mexico is at an all-time high." In 1960 the total number of Protestants in Mexico was 645,145, and the number of their clergy, 911.[81] Of the many sects, the Pentecostals, who worked with the lower classes, were by far the most successful. Despite the claims for Protestant growth in Mexico, it represented only 1.9 per cent of the total population, which was small compared with Brazil and Chile. Despite the fact that Protestantism is commonly considered in Mexico as connected with progress, it has nowhere successfully linked social revolution with the Evangelical faith.

It is a remarkable fact that "Mexico, which has produced so many martyrs, is the leading Catholic country of Latin America."[82] Father Nevins, who rates Mexico among the few Latin-American countries where Catholicism is in a healthy condition, writes: "Nowhere else in the world is there as strong a faith as that which exists among the masses of Mexico. After each wave of persecution, the people of that country restored and rebuilt the Church there. Mexican Catholicism is not the traditional Catholicism found elsewhere in Latin America, but a Catholicism of courage and heroism; it is a Catholicism purified by martyrdom and suffering."[83] Here the clergy is genuinely beloved by the people,

80. *Hispanic American Report*, XIV, No. 6 (June, 1961), 481; XV, No. 1 (January, 1962), 17; XVI, No. 7 (June, 1962), 495.

81. John J. Considine, *New Horizons in Latin America* (New York, 1958), p. 176; W. Stanley Rycroft and Myrtle M. Clemmer, *A Factual Study of Latin America* (New York, 1963), p. 234.

82. Erik Von Kuehnelt-Leddihn, "Catholics in Latin America," *The Commonweal*, June 23, 1961, pp. 322-25.

83. Albert J. Nevins, M.M., "How Catholic is Latin America?" *The Sign*, Vol. 36, No. 2 (September, 1956), 14.

which is quite a contrast to the regard for the clergy in other Latin-American countries.

Although Church-State relationships are no longer a major preoccupation of the people and their government in Mexico, it would be hazardous to inscribe *finis* to the history of the issue. It should not be forgotten that the drastic and intolerable anticlerical legislation, although unenforced, cannot be removed from the statute books because of a substantial anticlerical opposition. The status of the Catholic Church in Mexico is prosperous and expanding—but precarious.

Chapter XVII

Conclusion

When embarking upon their independent careers the nations of Latin America adhered for a time to uniformity in religious policy, i.e., Catholicism continued to be the State religion. Indeed, with the sole exception of Argentina (then called the United Provinces of La Plata), religious toleration to the extent of allowing the public exercise of dissident faiths was not among the guarantees of the first national constitutions. Thus, when the youthful nations of Latin America undertook the direction of their own destinies, they were faithful to the religious policy of the Motherland.

Yet, in a short time opposition to the favored cult appeared, and it began to be shorn of its old-time privileges. In the decades of the 1820's and 1830's the Catholic Church was subjected to attack in many of the republics, particularly in Argentina, Chile, Mexico, and the Federation of Central America. What was the cause of this radical change in ecclesiastical policy?

The basis of this early opposition to the Roman Catholic organization—not the Roman Catholic religion—was largely political. The abolition of tithes, suppression of religious orders, confiscation of ecclesiastical property, and like measures, were as a rule acts of vengeance wreaked upon the clergy by their political opponents. As was explained in the first chapter, the Spanish crown leaned heavily upon the members of the ecclesiastical organization for the governance of the Indies. Prelates and clerics held official positions high and low; they were a component part of the political organization. If it is not charitable to criticize too severely the failure of Latin Americans to govern successfully under representative political institutions, considering their tutelage for centuries under an absolute monarch, it is likewise unfair to expect the clergy to abandon immediately their ancient practice of participating in governmental affairs. It was inconceivable that this habit should be changed forthwith when independence was established.

Church authorities and their lay partisans insisted that the only unifying constructive tradition upon which the republics could establish order and achieve progress was the Catholic tradition of colonial times. Churchmen tended to interpret any attempt to alter the *status quo* as inimical to religion itself. Believing, quite correctly, that their ancient rights and privileges would be endangered with the establishment of representative republics, the ecclesiastics plunged into politics in alliance with the other conservative elements, notably the landholding élite, who also sought the preservation of the *status quo.* The principal questions which divided Church and State were—in addition to the issue of ecclesiastical patronage—control of education, control of the marriage ceremony, the disposition of Church property, control of the register of vital statistics, and toleration of dissenting sects. Unfortunately for the Church, without the sanction and prestige of its old alliance with the Spanish crown, it could no longer overawe obedience to its will.

Opposed to clerical pretensions were those liberals who insisted that the Catholic tradition was one of sterility and oppression. They advocated restricting the Church to its strictly religious sphere because it was regarded as an obstacle to modern progress. This was the meaning of anticlericalism, which was not antireligious, but merely sought to deprive the Church of those means and privileges which enabled it to exercise political power. An extreme anticlerical view was that the record of the Church in regard to political interference made it impossible for a Catholic to be a good citizen.

These early anticlericals were not reformers in the proper sense of the term. Their opposition was not based on spiritual, social, or economic causes. Recruited almost exclusively from the creoles, they had no complaint with Catholic dogmas and tenets; representatives of a privileged social class, they manifested little interest in the welfare of the lower classes; and if they regarded clerical wealth as an evil, it was because this wealth made the Church powerful politically. The pose of the anticlericals as champions of representative government, the rights of the masses, and purity of faith was often insincere and untrue. Usually their sole object was to get control of the government and make it impossible to oust them. It is conceded that there were sincere anticlerical reformers like Valentín Gómez Farías, but such men were exceptional, and moreover they were impractical idealists who by unwise and precipitate action caused much more harm than good.

In such fashion, therefore, the lines were drawn, and the struggle between liberal anticlerical forces and conservative proclerical groups was violent and protracted. Since the clergy who adhered to the colonial tradition and chose to take part in political issues were often so unfortunate as to be on the losing side, they frequently suffered the fate of the defeated opposition. The opposition, let it be known, was usually regarded as an enemy of the State and was meted the punishment of traitors. The fortunes of Church and clergy ebbed and flowed with the rise and fall of political factions.

With the passing of the mid-nineteenth century, the position of the Catholic Church in Latin America became increasingly unstable. In Mexico, Guatemala, Colombia, Chile, Ecuador, and Venezuela, severe anticlerical laws were put into force, and in several of the republics Church and State were separated. The first republic to proclaim separation was Colombia in 1853. This status, however, proved to be temporary. The first republic to disestablish the Church permanently was Mexico in 1859. But Mexico, distrusting the reactionary clergy, was unwilling to release the Church and continued to exercise an oppressive supervision over it. Soon after Mexico, some of the Central American republics disestablished the Church, but intolerantly burdened it with State control. In 1890, in Brazil, the alliance of Church and State, inherited by the Empire from the Kingdom of Portugal, was dissolved.

In the early twentieth century the trend toward separation continued. Cuba and Panama, states which came into existence under the tutelage of the United States, provided in their constitutions for complete separation. In Ecuador, only a quarter of a century after a most extreme clerical reaction when García Moreno created a veritable theocratic state, ecclesiastical policy was carried to the other extreme by the Liberal leader Eloy Alfaro, who severed official ties between the spiritual and temporal orders. In 1917 Uruguay, and in 1925 Chile, formally separated Church and State.

Separation was not necessarily the objective of anticlericalism for in some of the countries in which the Church was reduced to impotency, anticlerical opinion did not insist on disestablishment. With its dominance assured, as was the case in Venezuela, the State was willing to maintain friendly relations with the Roman Church, and so made no attempt to alter its nominal status as the official cult. Moreover, many anticlericals insisted on union as the means whereby the State could best maintain surveillance over the Church. Thus, it does not necessarily follow that, if certain countries concede a constitutionally preferred status to Roman Catholicism, this represents any important concession to clerical pretensions. This status of nominal union contributes little to the material and temporal strength of the Church. In fact, it may be a burden.

The revolutionary step of disestablishing the Church was accomplished peacefully in Brazil, Chile, and Uruguay. In these three important countries the Church was allowed to retain its property unconditionally and to go its own way without governmental interference. Apparently the policy of releasing the Church properties and observing a minimum of surveillance contributed to the peaceful and seemingly successful transition. In Mexico, however, a contrary policy was adopted with most unfortunate consequences. Since the position occupied by the Catholic Church in that republic was not appreciably different than in other Latin-American countries, it does not necessarily follow that the bestowal of complete independence upon the Mexican Church would have been followed by the same happy results. The activities of the clergy during the Maximilian period certainly proved that the time had not arrived to establish an independent Church. Since that time, however, the Mexican clergy evidently learned their lesson, and it would probably be safe to allow the Catholic Church the same rights it enjoys in Brazil and Chile.

Citizens of the United States unacquainted with the facts have been too prone to regard Mexico as the only rebellious member of the Catholic flock in Latin America. That this is not true has been conclusively demonstrated in the preceding chapters. In Venezuela, Colombia, Ecuador, and Chile, the Church was attacked, sometimes with considerable animosity. In several of the lesser countries, too, like Guatemala, El Salvador, and Honduras, the same vicissitudes were suffered. Although the attacks in Mexico were more bitter and the results more disastrous, to say that the Mexican remedies were more severe because the abuses were more glaring would not be absolutely true. In other countries the Church was quite as wealthy, relatively speaking, and as much of a political factor.

A significant feature of the religious conflicts has been the uncompromising attitude of the opposing factions. The difficulty intrinsically is not insuperable, as is evidenced by its satisfactory settlement in several of the countries through the application of a policy of mutual respect and fair play. But in many of the nations of Central and South America the intolerance of clericals and anticlericals alike made a solution well nigh impossible. Neither side was willing to concede any errors in its own program or virtues in that of the opposition. Consequently, as history reveals, there has been a constant ebb and flow of clerical and anticlerical oppression.

Americans are often puzzled to find the Church in admittedly Catholic countries subjected to more restrictive legislation than even in Prostestant lands. The questions arise: Why is it necessary to hedge the Church by such restrictions? and, Why do the Catholics who constitute the majority tolerate such measures? The first question has already been answered. But, to repeat, the habit of the clergy of meddling in politics and assuming an inordinate supervision over the lives of their parishioners make restriction necessary. The clergy of Latin America are quite different from the priesthood in the United States. This fact must be borne in mind if the Latin-American religious situation is to be understood.

As for the second question, it is indeed astonishing that an overwhelmingly Catholic populace should tolerate religious oppression. There were many prophecies in 1926, when the drastic anticlerical legislation was enforced in Mexico, that there would be a popular uprising. It is true that isolated revolts took place but a general uprising failed to materialize. One could reasonably expect that if the Latin Americans are as devoted to the faith as they are supposed to be, the antireligious laws would be impossible of enforcement. The most loyal Catholics are to be numbered among the women and the members of the lowest classes—those least capable of offering opposition to the government's edicts. Most of the men of the higher classes are "nominal" Catholics, that is, they abstain from contact with the sacraments until the time for the ministration of extreme unction. These men would not fight to the death for the faith. It should be noted, furthermore, that the lowest classes, principally Indians, entertain a profound respect for authority; obedience to superior will has been taught them for centuries, and therefore they would not be apt to oppose the will of the officials—particularly when they are backed by the power of the army. Thus it comes about that in Catholic countries the religion of the majority can be persecuted.

It is difficult to classify the religious policies of the various Latin-American countries for they present great diversity. In their attempted settlement of the religious question the different countries have not followed a uniform pattern, and so there is no general or common policy. Nevertheless, we can group these policies into two categories: the union of Church and State, and the separation of Church and State. With respect to the first category, the constitutions of ten republics provide in one way or another a degree of union of Church and State. These republics are: Argentina, Bolivia, Colombia, Costa Rica, Dominican Republic, El Salvador, Haiti, Paraguay, Peru, and Venezuela. In all of these states the Catholic Church is the official and preferred Church, but the extent of State control on the one hand, and Church privileges on the other, vary greatly in the different countries. The existence of concordats or *modus vivendi* are not vital to the union of Church and State. Thus, several of the countries in this category do not at present have concordats with the papacy. Nor is diplomatic representation at the Vatican vital to union, although in fact all of the republics of this category maintain relations with the Holy See.

Constitutional separation of Church and State exists in ten of the republics: Brazil, Chile, Cuba, Ecuador, Guatemala, Honduras, Mexico, Nicaragua, Panama, and Uruguay. In these countries there is supposed to be separation, but in some the Church cannot be said to be free of State control. The nearest approximation to "free Church-free State," such as obtains in the United States, is found in Brazil, Chile, and Uruguay. Of those countries where there has been a dissolution of the connection between Church and State, but where in reality the Church has been put under strict State surveillance, Mexico is the best example, although Mexico in recent years does not enforce the anticlerical laws. Separation has not prevented most of the countries in this category from diplomatic representation at the Vatican.

Undoubtedly there will be further disestablishment of the Catholic Church in Latin America, although there is no anticlerical crusade directed to that end. In fact most of the people regard the whole matter with great impassivity. There is not now, and has not been for a number of years, a "religious question" in Latin-American politics. The status of the Catholic Church, which was a burning issue in the nineteenth century, faded from view ere the dawn of the mid-twentieth century. In fact since about 1950 there has been a pronounced trend, particularly in Central America, Ecuador, and Venezuela, to relax old restrictions on the Catholic Church, and to move closer to the ideal of a free Church in a free State.

* * *

An over-all view of the religious aspects of Latin America today is here presented, in conclusion, for a better understanding of the meaning and significance of the contemporary legal settlement of the Church-State issue. A Catholic lay authority on Latin-American affairs has written: "Latin America is what it is because Catholicism is what it is. Its culture, its expression, its art and its thought bear the unmistakable imprint of the Church. Customs, habits, and daily living are a faithful reflection of Catholic life."[1] This is true. But, it is an anomalous fact that Roman Catholics are only a minority in Latin America—referring to "practicing" Catholics as distinguished from "nominal" Catholics. These terms need to be clarified.

1. Richard Pattee, *Catholicism in Latin America* (Washington, D.C., 1945), p. 9.

The "practicing" Catholics are those who with some degree of regularity perform their religious duties. They attend mass, receive the sacraments, and perform special devotions. The practicing Catholics who observe the fundamental laws and precepts of the Church come to between 15 and 30 per cent of the entire population. Most of these are women, for in all classes religion is regarded as properly the sphere and function of women. It is a "sentimental brand" of Roman Catholicism which is largely practiced by "pious ladies whose religious attitude is one of resignation and complete trust." It is a Catholicism which has little, if any, effect on society and is unrelated to the problems of life.

Those who are Catholics in name only are called "twilight Catholics." Although more than 90 per cent of Latin Americans are baptized Catholics, and so are claimed by the Church, more than two-thirds never make their first communion. Most of these, plus many of those who after the release of parental control no longer continue to be observing Catholics, make up that large body of "nominal" Catholics. Only most infrequently do they attend mass or observe any of the religious duties. Yet, it is an interesting fact that the majority would be offended if their Catholic status were questioned. An emotional attachment to Catholicism is the sufficient basis for the individual's self-qualification as a Catholic. His personal commitment goes only as far as acknowledged belief, but not necessarily the performance of duties.

Most of the nominal Catholics and non-Catholics are men. It appears that there is a widespread repudiation of many aspects of Church activity by Latin-American men, particularly those of the middle and upper classes. Devotion is not regarded as a positive element in the Latin-American ideal of masculinity.[2] Certainly, a very large percentage of Latin-American men refuse to attend mass and reject the dictates of the hierarchy in most of the fields of human conduct.

Unfortunately, Catholic intellectuals are all too few, for most of the intellectuals and university students profess religious indifference which has had some effect on the cultural, social, and political life of the countries. Perhaps nowhere else in the world is this phenomenon of religious indifference so pronounced. Because of the apostasy of the intellectual classes it is very important that the Church retain and recruit those who can fight its battles intellectually.

The sad fact is that Roman Catholicism in Latin America is nothing more than a tradition for a vast majority of the people. It is well that

2. In Latin America the image of the priest is incompatible with the *machismo* ideal. See Andrew Weigert, S.J., "*Machismo* and the Priestly Vocation," in *The Catholic World*, Vol. 199, No. 1,191 (June, 1964), 152-58.

we take a closer look at the strictly religious aspects of Latin-American Catholicism today.

Hispanic-American Catholicism, to the eye of the American, appears gaudy, ornate, and external. The Church of Latin America seeks to save souls by teaching form, ceremony, and ritual which, when learned, should be repeated as frequently as possible. The extreme preoccupation with ritual and ceremony minimizes the extent to which the individual is encouraged to use the life of Christ and the truths of the Gospel as a means of solving personal problems and those of the community. It is a religion which demands little thought and invites no questions.

Roman Catholicism with its pageantry, ceremonies, and fiestas provides the Indian with emotional release. The religious fiestas with their pronounced social aspects such as dancing and drinking enable the Indian to forget the drabness and squalor of his daily life. By and large, Roman Catholicism has done very little to uplift the Indian in three hundred years. Overawed by ritual, and impressed by the images and pictures, he can attach no relationship between all that and his daily existence; there is a divorce between religion and life. There is very little comprehension of the meaning of Christianity.

Latin America lacks the moral and spiritual foundations of Christianity in its culture. In the daily lives of most Latin Americans religion is not a strong force. The typical attitude, in terms of religious practice, is one of relative indifference.

Whatever may be the tradition of Catholicism in Latin America it reflects no real grasp of fundamental religious principles and suppositions. The dominant characteristics of the Catholic laity seem to be a low level of general knowledge of basic tenets of the faith, and laxity in its practice. Even Roman Catholic churchmen, particularly in the United States, concede that the Church in Latin America is in a very critical situation.[3] One of these, writing in 1956, described the status of Roman Catholicism in Latin America as follows:

1. Areas where the Church is strong and has vitality: Mexico, Costa Rica, Colombia, and Argentina.
2. Areas where the Church is standing still: Guatemala, Nicaragua, El Salvador, Chile, Venezuela, Peru, and Uruguay.

3. For example, see William J. Coleman, *Latin American Catholicism: A Self Evaluation* (Maryknoll, N.Y., 1958); John J. Considine, *New Horizons in Latin America* (New York, 1958); John J. Kennedy, "The Force of the Church," in John J. TePeske and Sydney N. Fisher, *Explosive Forces in Latin America* (Columbus, Ohio, 1964); and Albert J. Nevins, "How Catholic is Latin America?" in *The Sign*, Vol. 36, No. 2 (September, 1956), 11-18.

3. Areas where the Church is dying: Bolivia, Brazil, Cuba, Dominican Republic, Ecuador, Haiti, Honduras, and Panama.[4]

According to Father Nevins parish life hardly exists for there is no intensive life of worship. A gulf separates the priests and the people. The Maryknoll Father believes that one of the greatest problems facing the Catholic Church in Latin America is the scarcity of clerical personnel.

Because of the lack of adequate vocations of native clergy, foreign priests have had to supplement the local secular clergy in most of the countries. Most of the foreign priests are Spaniards. Father John Considine estimates that it would take four thousand new priests to revitalize and adequately serve the Catholic Church in Latin America. Obviously great reliance on foreign clergy is unhealthy, for like any other institution, the dependence of the Church on foreign support and personnel arouses nationalistic suspicions and resentments. No native church can exist without native priests. Nevertheless, however undesirable dependence on foreign clergy may be, this can be expected to continue, since the prospects of any increase in native vocations are not bright.

Some Catholic writers refer to Latin America as a "de-Christianized continent." A distinguished Protestant churchman, Dr. John A. Mackay, says that "the basic spiritual problem of Latin America is secularization, the tragedy being that both governments and people had reacted so violently, some cynically, against the very concept of God and Religion."[5] It can certainly be affirmed that now Latin America is really a mission continent. Not Catholicism alone, but Christianity needs to be reclaimed. How are Christians, Catholic and Protestant, answering the challenge?

Since World War II the Catholic Church in many parts of Latin America has been disassociating itself from the forces of conservatism. There is a ferment and restiveness within the Church, unlike the old unyielding dedication to the *status quo*. The Church no longer blindly supports dictators, nor is it unmindful of the desperate need to improve the living conditions of the people.

Probably the most important and significant aspect of the changing attitude of the Church has been the effort to identify itself more closely with the social movement sweeping Latin America. The Archbishop of Manaos stated the problem frankly: "Social reform will come about whether through our efforts or in spite of them. But in the latter case,

4. Nevins, *op. cit.*, pp. 14, 67.
5. John A. Mackay, *The Latin American Churches and the Ecumenical Movement* (New York, 1963), p. 12.

it will be anti-Catholic." Thus, in its own self-interest, plus we trust, honest conviction, the Church generally throughout Latin America has taken a definite stand on behalf of land reform and the social doctrine expressed in papal encyclicals.[6]

The profound influence of Pope John XXIII's encyclicals, *Mater et Magistra* and *Pacem in Terris,* was revealed by the numerous pastorals on the social question issued by the prelates of many of the Latin-American countries. One of the best known and most liberal of church thinkers on social issues is Bishop Manuel Larraín of Talca, Chile. According to the Bishop: "Only one possibility exists today of improving living conditions in Latin America: a rapid and radical transformation of its economic and social institutions to bring them in line with the principles of Christian social teaching." Because he implemented the encyclicals he was accused of being a Red.[7]

The position taken by the hierarchy has provoked a split between the Church and the conservative forces. On various occasions these forces reacted rather violently. For the most part the rich, the majority of whom are practicing Catholics, are more interested in perpetuating the *status quo* and their superior positions than in advancing the Church. It is difficult to say, at least at this stage, whether the Church has reaped any advantages from its new role as social champion. The Church is in the unfortunate position of possessing no political powers to implement the program. In fact, in most of the countries where the Church is expected to be non-political, its advocacy of social and economic reform is regarded as political intervention.

The identification of Roman Catholicism with conservatism seems to be disappearing. According to Alberto Lleras Camargo, distinguished Colombian Liberal statesman and publicist, "One may already assert that the Catholic Church in Latin America is no longer a reactionary and capitalistic force as it would have been described only a few decades ago."[8] Reflective of the new clerical reorientation, leftist political parties made their appearance in Latin America after World War II under the general designation of "Christian Democracy." The first was COPEI in Venezuela, which became under the leadership of Rafael Caldera the second party in the country. In Chile the *Partido Demó-crata Cristiano,* under the leadership of President Eduardo Frei, suc-

6. See "Latin America Looks to Catholic Action for a Program of Social Reform," in Lewis Hanke, ed., *Mexico and the Caribbean* (New York, 1959), pp. 111-15.

7. Nevins, *op. cit.,* p. 13.

8. Alberto Lleras, "La Iglesia Cambiante," in *Visión,* Vol. 28, No. 5 (December 25, 1964), 19; "La Herencia de Juan XXIII," *ibid.,* pp. 20-26.

ceeded, in the election of March 7, 1965, in routing the Communist-leaning *Frente de Acción Popular*.

The two pillars of the Christian Democratic program are: (1) concern for the dignity of man and the improvement of his condition, as urged in papal encyclicals from *Rerum Novarum* to *Mater et Magistra*, and (2) a technical approach to economic problems. They regard as impediments to social and economic progress such structural imbalance as unequal distribution of wealth and lopsided landownership. Christian Democracy is not a Catholic party, nor do clerics exercise control. According to Caldera, it is in no sense a religious movement, nor does it have a confessional character. In its membership are, in addition to Catholics, Protestants, Jews, and agnostics. The name Christian does not represent a religious position, but a conviction that Christian values and the spirit of Christianity are fundamental for success in achieving social justice and the routing of communism.[9]

Another aspect of the Catholic reaction in Latin America is the "re-Catholicization" program. This involves not only Catholic missionary work in Latin America, but revitalization of the Church and the cult. According to Father John J. Considine, Director of the Latin American Bureau of the National Catholic Welfare Conference, "the Catholic Church in Latin America today is in deep trouble."

As we have already noted Latin America, because it has become "de-Christianized," is really a mission continent. But, from the point of view of the Roman Catholic Church, it is the best mission continent in the entire world, for its Catholic traditions ease the work of the missionary. It is conceded that a restoration of Catholicism demands an apostolic attitude of missionary penetration, much more than it requires an attitude of conservation of a badly understood traditionalism. Nearly 40 per cent of all United States Catholic missionaries are in Latin America. In 1961 they numbered 2,751.[10] Probably the most effective are the Maryknoll Fathers, an exclusively missionary organization. Yet these represented only 7 per cent of the total Catholic missionary force in Latin America. In addition to the Americans there are thousands of Spanish, Belgian, French, Canadian, and Italian missionary priests flooding into the Americas. From Spain alone there are more than 18,000.

In 1960 the Holy See appealed for lay persons to serve as volunteer missionaries to Latin America. These "Papal Volunteers for Apostolic Collaboration in Latin America" dedicate themselves to years of hard

9. Based on materials distributed by Center of Christian Democratic Action, 321 E. 48th St., New York City.

10. *U.S. Catholic Missionary Personnel Overseas* (1962), pp. viii-x.

work (like the Peace Corps) "to serve Latin America by serving religion."[11]

In further efforts to rekindle faith left dormant for years there was organized in 1955 the Latin American Bishops' Conference (CELAM), to stimulate and coördinate Catholic life everywhere on the continent. Working closely with the Catholic hierarchy is Catholic Action, the lay apostolate dedicated to the re-Christianization of Latin-American society. It must be confessed, however, that there is little evidence that Catholic Action has had any significant influence on society as a whole.

Although the challenge of Protestantism has been frankly conceded as one of the responsible reasons for the Catholic reactivating movement, the reality of this alleged threat needs to be examined.

With the loss of mission fields in Asia thousands of Protestant missionaries have in recent years turned toward Latin America. Today one in four of all North American Protestant missionaries overseas is in Latin America. In 1960 there was a Protestant missionary body of 13,416. The number of native-born ministers has greatly increased. In fact the indigenization of the Protestant Churches in Latin America is proceeding rapidly as a policy of prudence and practical operation. Today the Protestant community in Latin America has passed the ten million mark, with 90 per cent of this growth within the last 35 years. It can be said that about 5 per cent of the total population of Latin America is Protestant.[12] According to the latest estimates, there are almost two million Pentecostals in Brazil and over 700,000 in Chile. Roughly one third of the Protestants in Latin America are Pentecostals. Perhaps their greater success is due to the fact that they are the only really indigenous Protestant sect in Latin America. Most of their converts are from the lower classes.

Although the numerical increase of Protestants in Latin America has been phenomenal on a purely percentage basis, in most of the countries the Protestant communities are still small minorities, ranging from .03 per cent of the total population of Ecuador, to 11 per cent in Chile. Protestantism makes its appeal mostly to the middle and lower classes. It seems that most converts are made in areas where there is a scarcity or absence of priests.

The impression which Protestantism had made on the minds and culture of Latin Americans is difficult to measure. Dr. John A. Mackay says of Brazil: "Evangelical Christianity has become one of the chief

11. "World of the Papal Volunteers," in *Latin America Calls* (Latin American Bureau, NCWC), Vol. 2, No. 3 (February, 1965), 2.

12. W. Stanley Rycroft and Myrtle M. Clemmer, *A Factual Study of Latin America* (New York, 1963), p. 234.

spiritual forces in the national life." The situation in Brazil, with the possible addition of Chile, is exceptional, for the Evangelical churches have scarcely taken root in the soil of Latin America and in the hearts and minds of its people. The "Protestant peril," voiced by alarmed Catholic clericals is gross exaggeration. The real threat is the wave of secularism, religious apathy, and indifference.

At any rate, since the Catholic Church chooses to regard Evangelical Christianity as a threat this is a good thing for the Church itself. It is one of the responsible causes of the recent efforts by the Church to re-vitalize itself. It is now endeavoring to prove that it can be as helpful as the Protestants—and the Communists—in fulfilling "this worldly" aspiration of the people. Whether an expanding and aggressive Protestantism and a socially-conscious and reinvigorated Roman Catholicism will succeed in their great task of re-Christianizing Latin America remains for history to reveal.

Bibliography

A. PRIMARY SOURCES

I. MANUSCRIPTS

Archivo Bazaine: Correspondencia de Achille François Bazaine, 1862-1867.
26 vols. An invaluable collection of some 60,000 pages on the French
Intervention in Mexico. Contains numerous allusions to the reactionary
policy of the Mexican clergy.

Gómez Farías Papers. Letters and papers, official and private, of the Gómez
Farías family, covering the period 1820 to 1857. The collection yielded
items relating to politico-ecclesiastical relations in Mexico particularly for
the premature reform régime of 1834.

Riva Palacio Papers. The private correspondence of a notable Mexican
publicist and historian. Contains information relating to the religious
question in the Revolution of Ayutla and the Wars of the Reform.

(Note: The above documents are to be found in the Latin American Collection in the Library of the University of Texas. This collection contains
a wealth of documentary materials on the religious question beyond the
needs of the present study.)

II. OFFICIAL DOCUMENTS AND OTHER PRINTED SOURCES

Álvarez Lejarza, Emilio, comp. *Las Constituciones de Nicaragua.* Madrid,
1958. Vol. 9 of *Las Constituciones Hispanoamericanas* (Ediciones Cultura Hispánica).

Anguita, Ricardo, comp. *Leyes promulgadas en Chile desde 1810 hasta el 1°
de Junio de 1912.* Santiago, 1912-13. 4 vols.

Annaes do Parliamento Brasileiro, Assembléa Constituinte, 1823. Rio de
Janeiro, 1876-84. 6 vols.

Arancel Eclesiástico de la Diócesis de La Paz. La Paz, 1927. An interesting
schedule of fees for various religious services.

Archivo Santander. Bogotá, 1924-25. 4 vols. Correspondence of General
Santander. Throws new light on his policies with respect to the Church.

Arosemena, Justo. *Estudios Constitucionales sobre los gobiernos de la Améri-*

ca Latina. Paris, 1888. 2 vols. A collection of the constitutions in force at the time of date of publication.

Balderrama, Luis C. *El Clero y el Gobierno de México.* Mexico, 1927. 2 vols. Collection of documents of a varied nature, to explain the religious crisis of 1926. A government propaganda publication.

Branch, H. N., trans. *The Mexican Constitution of 1917 compared with the Constitution of 1857.* Supplement to *Annals of the American Academy of Political and Social Science,* 1917. Constitutional articles arranged in parallel columns. Enables one to ascertain easily the additions made in 1917 to the religious clauses of 1857.

Cabañas, Joaquín Ramírez, ed. *Las Relaciones entre México y el Vaticano.* Mexico, 1928. Number 27 of the *Archivo Histórico Diplomático Mexicano.*

Camara dos Deputados, Exposição Commemorativa do Centenario da 1ª Constituinte do Brasil. Rio de Janeiro, 1923. The religious question in the first Brazilian constitutional convention.

Carranza, Adolfo P., ed. *El Clero Argentino de 1810 á 1830.* Buenos Aires, 1907. 2 vols. A collection of patriotic orations, allocutions, and panegyrics by La Platan clerics.

Cleven, N. A. N. *Readings in Hispanic American History.* New York, 1927. Contains important bulls and decrees relating to the Church in Colonial Spanish America.

Codificación de los Decretos del C. Venustiano Carranza. Mexico, 1915. In the "Pre-Constitutional" decrees of the First Chief, herein contained, are detected the germs of the anticlerical provisions of the Constitution of 1917.

Colección Completa de Leyes Nacionales Sancionadas por el Honorable Congreso durante los Años 1852 á 1917. Buenos Aires, 1918.

Colección de los Decretos y Ordenes del Soberano Congreso Mexicano. Mexico, 1825.

Colección Eclesiástica Mejicana. Mexico, 1834. 4 vols.

Diario de los Debates del Congreso Constituyente. Mexico, 1916-17. 2 vols. The debates in the Querétaro Convention show the anticlerical temper of the Constituents. It was an extremely prejudiced body.

Diario de Sesiones de la H. Convención N. Constituyente de la República Oriental del Uruguay. Montevideo, 1918. Contains the debates on separation of Church and State.

Dictamen de la Comisión de Patronato. Mexico, 1823. Report of the first committee on the patronage. It upheld national rights.

Dictamen sobre Provisión de Benefices Eclesiásticos. Mexico, 1824. Report of the committee on the patronage to the Mexican Constituent Congress. It was regalistic in nature.

Documentos para a Historia da Independencia. Rio de Janeiro, 1923. Contains information on the participation of the clergy and the Masons in the independence movement.

Documentos relativos á la organización constitucional de la República Argentina. Buenos Aires, 1911. 3 vols. The documents cover the period 1851-83. Vol. 3 contains exclusively documents relating to the general constituent congress of 1853.

Dublán, Manuel, y Lozano, José María, eds. *Legislación Mexicana ó Colección completa de las Disposicionas legislativas expedidas desde la Independencia de la República.* Mexico, 1876-90. 19 vols.

Encinas, Diego de. *Provisiones, Cédulas, Capítulos de Ordenanzas ... tocantes al buen gobierno de las Indias.* Madrid, 1596. 4 vols. Contains *cédulas* and other documents emanating from the Council of the Indies not found in the *Recopilación de Leyes de los Reynos de las Indias.*

Fitzgibbon, Russell H. *The Constitutions of the Americas.* Chicago, 1948. As of January 1, 1948. For a list of earlier published collections of Latin-American constitutions, see p. vii.

Gamboa, José M. *Leyes Constitucionales de México Durante el siglo XIX.* Mexico, 1901. Contains not only all the National Constitutions with their amendments, but the Constitution of Cádiz, the Constitution of Apatzingán, and the *Plan de Iguala.*

García, Genaro, ed. *El Clero de México durante la Dominación Española, según el Archivo Inédito Archiepiscopal Metropolitano.* Mexico, 1906.

———. *El Clero de México y la Guerra de Independencia.* Mexico, 1906. Published by García in an effort to refute the claim that the clergy supported the Revolution.

———. *La Inquisición de México.* Mexico, 1906. Collection of documents on the Inquisition in New Spain. This is Vol. 5 of the *Documentos Inéditos ó Muy Raros.* (36 vols. 1906-13.)

Gibbons, William J., S.J., comp. *Basic Ecclesiastical Statistics for Latin America,* 1960. Maryknoll Publications, World Horizon Reports, No. 25.

———. *Seven Great Encyclicals.* Glen Rock, N.J.: Paulist Press, 1963. Encyclicals of Popes Leo XIII, Pius XI, and John XXIII.

Gibson, William M. *The Constitutions of Colombia.* Durham, N.C., 1948.

Goytia, Víctor F., comp. *Las Constituciones de Panamá.* Madrid, 1954. Vol. 7 of *Las Constituciones Hispanoamericanas.* (Ediciones Cultura Hispánica).

Gros Espiell, Héctor, ed. *Constitución Uruguaya Anotada.* 2nd ed. Montevideo, 1958.

"Hearings before a Select Committee on Haiti and Santo Domingo," United States Senate. Sen. Res. 112, 67 Cong., Washington, 1922. Contains information on the religious and educational situations in the two republics.

Hernáez, Francisco Javier. *Colección de Bulas, Breves, y Otros Documentos relativos á la Iglesia de América y Filipinas.* Brussels, 1879. 2 vols. An invaluable work for the ecclesiastical history of the Americas. Contains all bulls for the colonial and republican periods to the date of publication.

Hernandez y Dávalos, J. E., ed. *Colección de Documentos para la Historia de la Guerra de Independencia de México de 1808 á 1821.* Mexico, 1877-82. 6 vols.

Instrucciones Reservadas que los Virreyes de Nueva España Dejaron á sus Sucesores. Mexico, 1867. The state of the Church and ecclesiastical business always occupied a prominent position in the instructions of the viceroys to their successors.

Investigation of Mexican Affairs. Hearing before a subcommittee of the Committee on Foreign Relations, United States Senate, Sixty-sixth Congress, first session, pursuant to S. Res. 106 directing the Committee on Foreign Relations to investigate the matter of outrages on citizens of the United States in Mexico. Washington, 1919. 3 vols. The famous Fall Report.

Lazcano y Mazón, Andrés María. *Constitución de Cuba.* Havana, 1941. With the debates in the constitutional convention.

Lecuna, Vicente, ed. *Cartas del Libertador.* Caracas, 1929-30. 10 vols. A remarkably well edited work and contains an excellent index (Vol. 10). Bolívar's attitude toward the Church and religion, during his last years, shown in a new light, according to these letters.

———. *Documentos Referentes á la Creación de Bolivia.* Caracas, 1924. 2 vols.

Léfèvre, Eugène. *Historia de la Intervención Francesa en Méjico.* Brussels and London, 1869. 2 vols. Official documents from the private secretariat of Maximilian. Published by order of President Juárez.

Legón, Faustino J., and Medrano, Samuel W., comp. *Las Constituciones de la República Argentina.* Madrid, 1953. Vol. 3 of *Las Constituciones Hispanoamericanas* (Ediciones Cultura Hispánica).

Leyes, Decretos y Reglamentos Vigentes del Registro del Estado Civil. Montevideo, 1921.

Magoon, Charles E. *Republic of Cuba: Report of the Provisional Administration.* Havana, 1908. Used for report on the status of the confiscated Church properties agreement.

Mariñas Otero, Luis, comp. *Las Constituciones de Honduras.* Madrid, 1962. Vol. 15 of *Las Constituciones Hispanoamericanas* published under direction of Manuel Fraga Iriborne (Ediciones Cultura Hispánica).

Mateos, Juan A. *Historia Parlamentaria de los Congresos Mexicanos de 1821 á 1857.* Mexico, 1877-1912. 25 vols.

Melgarejo Randolf, L., y Fernandez Rojas, J., eds. *El Congreso Constituyente de 1916 y 1917. Reseña histórico de los debate á que dieron las reformas de la constitución de 1857.* Mexico, 1917. For the religious question in the Convention.

Memorándum del General Guzmán Blanco. Caracas, 1876. Letters written by Guzmán Blanco while on campaign during the years 1870-73. There are frequent references to clerical opposition.

Memoria de la Conducta Pública y Administrativa de Manuel José Arce. Mexico, 1830. Arce's defense of his administration as president of the Confederation of Central America.

Memorias de la Secretaría de Gobernación. Mexico, 1926-32. 7 vols. Contains reports of federal and state legislation concerning the Church.

Memoria que Presente el Ministro de Relaciones Interiores al Congreso Nacional en 1909. Caracas, 1909. Contains a discussion of a controversy relating to the delimitation of ecclesiastical jurisdiction. Illustrates the *Patronato Nacional.*

Mensaje Leido por S. E. el Presidente de la República. Santiago, June 1, 1923. President Arturo Alessandri proposes separation of Church and State in Chile.

Mensaje Leido por S. E. el Vicepresidente de la República en la Apertura del Congreso Nacional el 21 de Mayo de 1927. Santiago, 1927. Vice-President Carlos Ibañez, on concessions made to Church schools.

Mercati, Angelo, ed. *Raccolta di Concordati su Materie Ecclesiastiche tra la Santa Sede e la Autorità Civili.* Rome, 1919. A collection of all the concordats entered into with the papacy to the time of publication. Invaluable for a history of politico-ecclesiastical relations. Cited in text as *Raccolta di Concordati.*

Ministerio del Interior, Actas Oficiales de las Sesiones celebradas por la Comisión y Subcomisiones encargadas del estudio del Proyecto de Nueva Constitución Política de la República. Santiago, 1925.

Ministerio de Relaciones Exteriores y Culto, Circular Informativa Mensual. Buenos Aires, 1924. Contains discussion of the controversy over the appointment to the archiepiscopal see of Buenos Aires.

Nueva Recopilación. Madrid, 1775. 2 vols. Both an abridgment and continuation of the *Recopilación de Leyes de los Reynos de las Indias.*

Olivo, Juan F. *Constituciones del Perú, 1821-1919.* Lima, 1922.

Páez, José Antonio. *Autobiografía de General José Antonio Páez.* New York, 1867-69. 2 vols.

Pareja Paz-Soldám, José, ed. *Las Constituciones del Perú.* Madrid, 1954. Vol. 6 of *Las Constituciones Hispanoamericanas* (Ediciones Cultura Hispánica).

Peña y Reyes, Antonio de la. *León XII y Los Paises Hispano-Americanos.* Mexico, 1924. Vol. IX of the *Archivo Histórico Diplomático Mexicano.*

Pérez Lugo, J., ed. *La Cuestión Religiosa en México. Recopilación de Leyes Disposiciones Legales y Documentos para el Estudio de este Problema Político.* Mexico, 1927. A carefully selected, but essentially impartial, set of source materials to aid in explaining the religious crisis of 1926. Is best for the period 1857-76. Contains a brief introduction of a rather marked anticlerical tone. Was published as government propaganda.

Pombo, Manuel Antonio, y Guerra, José Joaquín. *Constituciones de Colom-*

bia. Bogotá, 1911. 2 vols. A useful collection of all the national and state constitutions.

Proyecto de Constitución para la República de Bolivia y Discurso del Libertador. Buenos Aires, 1826. The argument of the Liberator in support of his model constitution for the new state of Bolivia, contains some remarkable observations regarding religious toleration and separation of Church and State.

Pruvonena, P., ed. *Memorias y Documentos para la Historia de la Independencia del Perú*. Paris, 1858.

Ramírez Cabañas, Joaquín, ed. *Las Relaciones entre México y el Vaticano*. Mexico, 1928. No. 27, *Archivo Histórico Diplomático Mexicano*. A useful collection of documents illustrative of Mexican relations with the papacy from 1822 to 1861.

Recopilación de Leyes de los Reynos de las Indias. 2nd ed. 2 vols. Madrid, 1756. In the Laws of the Indies can be seen the intimate relations which existed between Church and State in the Spanish colonies. An indispensable source for the history of the *Real Patronato de las Indias*. For a history of this work together with an analysis of its contents, see H. H. Bancroft, *History of Central America*, I, 285-88.

Report of the President's Commission for the Study and Review of Conditions in the Republic of Haiti, March 26, 1930. Washington, 1930. Contains an informative statement on the status of the Catholic Church in Haiti.

Rodríguez, J. I. *American Constitutions*. Washington, 1906. 2 vols. A collection of Latin-American constitutions, in original languages and in translation.

Roure, Agenor de. *A Constituinte Republicana*. Rio de Janeiro, 1920. The religious question and separation of Church and State in the Republican Constitutional Convention of 1890.

Salazár, Francisco Ignacio. *Actas de la Convención Nacional del Ecuador, Año de 1835*. Quito, 1891.

Tercera Semana Inter-Americana de Acción Católica. Lima y Chimbote, Peru, 1953. An objective and realistic self-evaluation of Latin-American Catholicism.

Uribe, Antonio José, ed. *Anales Diplomáticos y Consulares de Colombia*. Bogotá, 1920. Volume VI of Public Treaty Series contains the concordat of 1887, and supplementary conventions.

Vera, Fortino Hipólito, ed. *Colección de Documentos Eclesiásticos de México*. Amecameca, 1887. 3 vols. Laws and regulations of the Mexican hierarchy for both the colonial and republican periods.

Zarco, Francisco. *Historia del Congreso Estraordinario Constituyente de 1856 y 1857*. Mexico, 1857. 2 vols. A very useful work for the attitude of the constituents toward the religious question. An index to the above is Basilio Pérez Gallardo, *Guía para consultar la Historia del Congreso Constituyente de 1857*. Mexico, 1878.

B. SECONDARY REFERENCES

Abad y Queipo, Manuel. *Breve Exposición sobre el Real Patronato.* Madrid, 1820.

Abreu e Lima, José Ignacio de. *Compendio da Historia do Brasil.* Rio de Janeiro, 1843. 2 vols.

Agüero, Raúl. *Guatemala, La Revolución Liberal de 1871 y las Administraciones del Lcdo don Manuel Estrada Cabrera.* San José de Costa Rica, 1914. Exaggerated praise of the liberal cause and its leaders.

Aguirre, Joaquín. *Curso de Disciplina Eclesiástica General.* Madrid, 1871. 4 vols. Used for the origins and early history of the patronage.

Akers, Charles E. *A History of South America, 1854-1904.* London, 1912.

Alamán, Lucas. *Historia de Méjico.* Mexico, 1849-50. 5 vols. Since Alamán was a conservative supporter of the Church, his data on the wealth of the colonial Church and frank confession of corruption in clerical ranks can be accepted as the truth.

Alberdi, Juan B. *Bases y Puntos de Partida para la Organización de la República Argentina.* Buenos Aires, 1914. This was the famous model used by the Convention of Santa Fé in 1853 in framing the present constitution of the Argentine Republic. Alberdi presents an able argument in favor of religious toleration.

Alessandri, Arturo. *Reformas Constitucionales.* Santiago, 1925. President Alessandri defends separation of Church and State in Chile.

Altamira y Crevea, Rafael. *Historia de España y de la Civilización Española.* Barcelona, 1900-14. 4 vols. Useful for the origins and early history of the Patronato Español.

Amunátegui, Miguel Luis. *Los Precursores de la Independencia de Chile.* Santiago, 1870. 3 vols. As one of the contributing causes of the Wars for Independence, the abuses of the ecclesiastical governments of the colonies are discussed. Some of the observations appear to be radical and are not accepted by Galdames.

Araneda Bravo, Fidel. *El Arzobispo Errázuriz y la evolución política y social en Chile.* Santiago, 1956. Especially noteworthy are the chapters on "Churchmen and Politics," and "Separation of Church and State."

Arguedas, Alcides. *Historia General de Bolivia.* La Paz, 1922. The best modern history of Bolivia.

Arosemena, Justo. *Estudios Constitucionales sobre los gobiernos de la América Latina.* Paris, 1888. 2 vols. Commentaries on the existing (1888) Latin-American constitutions with observations on the religious clauses. Is particularly useful for discussions of the constitutional development of each country.

Artaud de Montor, Alexis François. *Histoire du Pape León XII.* Paris, 1873.

Ayarragaray, Lucas. *La Iglesia en América y la Dominación Española.* Buenos Aires, 1920. A scholarly and valuable work. Is one of the first studies of the kind based on materials in the Vatican archives.

Azeredo, Magalhães de. "Dom Pedro II. Traços da sua Physionomia Moral," in *Revista do Instituto Historico e Geographico Brasileiro.* Tomo Especial, 1925.

Azevedo, Thales de. *O catolicismo no Brasil.* Rio de Janeiro, 1955. "Um campo para a pesquisa social."

———. *Social Change in Brazil.* Gainesville, Fla., 1963. An excellent discussion (Chap. III) of the contemporary status of religion in Brazil.

Balderrama, Luis C. *El Clero y el Gobierno de México.* Mexico, 1927. 2 vols. Volume one, "Apuntes Para La Historia de La Crisis en 1926," contains a vigorous pro-government discussion of the religious issue.

Bancroft, Hubert Howe. *History of Central America.* San Francisco, 1882-87. 3 vols. This is the most adequate and accurate history of Central America up to the date of publication. References to the ecclesiastical subjects are rather scattered.

———. *History of Mexico.* San Francisco, 1883-87. 5 vols.

Baralt, Rafael María, y Díaz, Ramón. *Resumen de la Historia de Venezuela.* Curazao, 1887. 3 vols. Comprehends the period 1797 to 1837.

Barboza Lima, Alexandre José. "Um Grande Brasileiro, Frei Vital," in *Rev. do Inst. Hist. e Geog.,* LXXI, Pt. II, pp. 145-52. A eulogy of the Bishop of Olinda, major figure in the religious crisis of 1873.

Barrantes, Francisco Montero. *Elementos de Historia de Costa Rica.* San José de Costa Rica, 1892.

Beals, Carleton. *Porfirio Díaz.* Philadelphia and London, 1932. Not as much attention as one might properly expect is devoted to Díaz's religious policy.

Berthe, A. *García Moreno, President de L'Equateur.* Paris, 1887. The "Catholic President" of Ecuador is glorified by his clerical biographer. The work is extravagantly eulogistic and strongly ultramontane.

Bialek, Robert W. *Catholic Politics, a History Based on Ecuador.* New York, 1963. See particularly Chapter V, "The Twentieth Century" (1905-37).

Biesanz, John and Mavis. *Costa Rican Life.* New York, 1949. Chapter VIII for a graphic description of "Religion."

Braga, Erasmo, and Grubb, Kenneth G. *The Republic of Brazil: A Survey of the Religious Situation.* New York, 1932.

Bravo, Joaquín Rodríguez. *Estudios Constitucionales.* Santiago de Chile, 1888. A commentary on the Constitution of 1833. Contains certain useful observations on the patronage.

Brown, Lyle C. "Mexican Church-State Relations, 1933-1940," in *A Journal of Church and State* (Baylor University), VI, No. 2 (Spring, 1964), 202-22.

Browning, Webster E. *The River Plate Republics.* London, 1928. A leading Evangelical missionary describes religious conditions in Argentina, Paraguay, and Uruguay. Is characterized by considerable sympathetic understanding and tolerance.

Browning, W. E., Ritchie, John, and Grubb, K. G. *The West Coast Republics of South America.* London, 1930. The status of Catholicism and the progress of Protestantism in Peru, Bolivia, and Chile is discussed by Evangelical missionaries. Severe critics of the Church, their conclusions can be accepted with only minor reservations.

Bruno, Cayetano. *El Derecho Público de la Iglesia en la Argentina.* Buenos Aires, 1956. 2 vols. Vol. I, *El Estado Católico*; Vol. II, *Relaciones entre la Iglesia y el Estado.*

Bulnes, Francisco. *El Verdadero Díaz y la revolución.* Mexico, 1920. An attack on Díaz; a companion work of the author's *Juárez.*

———. *Juárez y las Revoluciones de Ayutla y de Reforma.* Mexico, 1905. A scathing attack on Juárez and the Liberals of 1857. A valuable work in that it has helped to tone down the eulogisms of Juárez.

Cabrera, Luis. *The Religious Question in Mexico.* New York, 1915. Cabrera, a member of the Catholic Party, discusses clerical political action under Madero and Huerta. Is prejudiced and must be used with caution.

Cadavid G., J. Ivan. *Los fueros de la iglesia ante el liberalismo y el conservatismo en Colombia.* Medellín, Colombia, 1955. A review of the politico-religious policies of the two major Colombian parties, 1837-1955.

Caldera Rodríguez, Rafael. *Moldes para la fragua.* Buenos Aires, 1962. Collection of articles by Venezuela's Christian Democratic (COPEI) leader.

Callcott, Wilfred Hardy. *Church and State in Mexico, 1822-1857.* Durham, 1926. A useful and trustworthy work. There are serious omissions, however: for example, there is no reference to the patronage problem or to papal relations.

———. *Liberalism in Mexico, 1857-1929.* Stanford University, 1931. This is a continuation of the author's *Church and State in Mexico, 1822-1857.* Although politico-ecclesiastical relations are not emphasized to the extent that they were in the first volume, these matters are always devoted prime consideration.

Calogeras, João Pandiá. *A History of Brazil.* Transl. and ed. by Percy A. Martin. Chapel Hill, N.C., 1939.

Cárcano, Ramón J. *Primeras Luchas entre La Iglesia y El Estado en la Gobernación de Tucumán, Siglo XVI.* Buenos Aires, 1929. Vol. IV of the series, *Biblioteca de Historia Argentina y Americana.* Illustrative of the actual relations between the civil and ecclesiastical powers in a frontier Spanish colony in South America.

Cardozo, Manoel. "The Holy See and the Question of the Bishop-Elect of Rio, 1833-1839," in *The Américas*, X, No. 1 (July, 1953), 3-75.

Casiello, Juan. *Iglesia y Estado en La Argentina.* Buenos Aires, 1948. A comprehensive survey.

Castillo de Aza, Zenón. *Trujillo y otros benefactores de la iglesia.* Ciudad Trujillo, 1961. A propaganda piece.

Cevallos, Pedro Fermín. *Resumen de la Historia del Ecuador desde su origin hasta 1845.* Guayaquil, 1886-89. 6 vols. The first five volumes comprise the period of the title. Volume VI is a political geography of Ecuador in 1887.

Chacaltana, Cesáreo. *Patronato Nacional Argentino.* Buenos Aires, 1885. A defense of the national prerogatives as against the pretensions of the ultraclericals. The immediate occasion for this study was the controversy concerning Señor Clara, vicar of Córdoba.

Chapman, Charles E. *A History of the Cuban Republic.* New York, 1927. A scholarly work in which the facts are fearlessly told. Contains a brief statement concerning the religious issue at the time of the establishment of the republic.

Cline, Howard F. *Mexico: Revolution to Evolution, 1940-1960.* New York, 1963. Consult index.

———. *The United States and Mexico.* Cambridge, Mass., 1953.

Coleman, William J. *The First Apostolic Delegation in Rio de Janeiro and Its Influence in Spanish America: A Study in Papal Policy, 1830-1840.* Washington, D.C., 1950. A history of the interesting but futile efforts of the first resident apostolic delegation to the Spanish American republics.

———. *Latin-American Catholicism: A Self-Evaluation.* Maryknoll, N.Y., 1958. A frank discussion of the meeting of 300 representatives of Catholic Action from 20 Latin-American countries in Chimbote, Peru, in 1953.

Colmenares Díaz, Luis. *La espada y el incensario: la iglesia bajo Pérez Jiménez.* Caracas, 1961. Marxist account of Church and State in Venezuela, 1948-57.

Considine, John J. *New Horizons in Latin America.* New York, 1958. Religio-social portraits of the people of South and Middle America by a moderate Catholic author.

———., ed. *The Church in the New Latin America.* Notre Dame, Ind., 1964. Papers delivered at the 1964 CICOP conference (Catholic Inter-American Coöperation Program).

———., ed. *The Missionary's Role in Socio-Economic Betterment.* New York, 1960. Sponsored by Fordham University Institute of Human Studies and the International Rural Life Movement.

Corti, Count Egon Caesar. *Maximilian and Charlotte of Mexico.* New York, 1928. 2 vols. (Catherine Alison Phillips, translator). This is a foremost work on the Emperor Maximilian. His relations with the Mexican clergy are treated in a most adequate manner.

Crivelli, Camilo. *Los Protestantes y la América Latina.* Rome, 1931. The author, a Jesuit, is obsessed with the idea that the United States is using Protestant missionary enterprise to prepare the way for the absorption of Latin America.

Cuevas, Mariano. *Historia de la Iglesia en México.* Mexico, El Paso, 1921-28. 5 vols. A work representative of considerable industry and not without value. The first four volumes, on colonial New Spain, are more accurate and trustworthy than Volume 5 which was written when Father

Cuevas was an exile in the United States and embittered toward the Mexican government.

Cunningham Graham, R. B. *A Vanished Arcadia.* New York, 1901. A sympathetic treatment of the Jesuit Republic of Paraguay.

Curtis, William E. *Venezuela.* New York, 1896. Used for the Church-State conflict during the régime of Guzmán Blanco. Contains many inaccuracies, but useful nevertheless.

Damboriena, Prudencio. *El Protestantismo en América Latina.* Bogotá, 1962. A FERES study which views Protestantism as a threat.

Dávalos y Lissón, Pedro. *La Primera Centuria; Causas geográficas, políticas y económicas que han detenido el progreso moral y material del Perú en el primer siglo de su vida independiente.* Lima, 1919-26. 4 vols. This work is sincere and accurate. It contains a searching criticism of religious conditions in Peru.

Delgado Román, Ricardo. *Valentín Gómez Farías: ideario reformista.* Guadalajara, 1958.

Dellhora, Guillermo. *La Iglesia Católica ante la Crítica en el Pensamiento y en el Arte.* Mexico, 1929. Excerpts of anticlerical thought culled from the works of the masters in arts, letters, and sciences. Venomously antagonistic toward the Church and particularly the pope. A government publication.

Dewart, Leslie. *Christianity and Revolution.* New York, 1963. A Canadian Roman Catholic layman indicts his own Church for tragic insensitivity to the Cuban situation.

Diccionario Historico, Geographico e Ethnographico do Brasil. Rio de Janeiro, 1922. 2 vols. Commemorative of the first centenary of independence. Published by Instituto Historico e Geographico Brasileiro.

Dornas, João. *O padroado e a igreja brasiliera.* São Paulo, 1938. A documented and objective account of the relations of Church and State under the Empire.

Egaña, Antonio de. *La teoría del regio Vicariato Español en Indias.* Rome, 1958. Canonical interpretation.

Ellis, L. Elthan. "Dwight Morrow and the Church-State Controversy in Mexico," in *Hisp. Am. Hist. Rev.,* Vol. 38, No. 4 (November, 1958), 482-505. Detailed account, based on Morrow, Kellogg, and State Department papers.

Enock, C. R. *Ecuador.* London, 1914.

Enríquez, Andrés. *La Reforma y Juárez.* Mexico, 1906.

Espinosa, Julio Bañados. *Balmaceda, su Gobierno, y la Revolución de 1891.* Paris, 1894. Contains a very good discussion of the anticlerical legislation of the 1880's.

Estrada, José Manuel de. *La Iglesia y el Estado y otros Ensayos Políticos y de Crítica Literaria.* Buenos Aires, 1929. Volume XXVII of the series, *Grandes Escritores Argentinos.* A defense of the State-Church system in Argentina, somewhat ultramontane in view.

Fabié, Antonio María. *Ensayo Histórico de la Legislación Española.* Madrid, 1896. Used for a study of the origins of *Real Patronato de las Indias.*

Fermandoiz, José Luis. *El Conflicto Eclesiástico de Tacna.* Santiago, 1923. A full, and fair discussion of the difficult and delicate problem of ecclesiastical jurisdiction in Tacna and Arica after the War of the Pacific.

Fermoso E., P. Paciano. *Catolicismo de la Juventud Colombiana.* Bogotá, 1961.

Fisher, Lillian Estelle. *Viceregal Administration in the Spanish-American Colonies.* Berkeley, 1926. An excellent and informative section of this book is devoted to the viceroy as vice-patron.

Fitzgibbon, Russell H. "Catholicism, Protestantism and Politics in Latin America," in *Hanover Forum* (Hanover College, Ind.), Vol. II, No. 1 (Winter, 1956), 3-13. The changing political position of the Church.

———. *Uruguay, Portrait of a Democracy.* New Brunswick, N.J., 1954. Ch. XVI, "Uruguay Worships."

Fletcher, James C., and Kidder, D. O. *Brazil and the Brazilians.* Boston, 1866. The authors were Protestant missionaries in Brazil in the 1840's. Their criticism of religious conditions in the Empire is remarkably fair and temperate.

Fluharty, Vernon L. *Dance of the Millions: Military Rule and Social Revolution in Colombia, 1930-1956.* Pittsburgh, 1957.

Foreign Areas Studies Division. *U.S. Army Area Handbook for Bolivia* (Special Operations Research Office, The American University, Washington, D.C., August, 1963). Chap. 10, "Religion."

———. *U.S. Army Area Handbook for Colombia* (Special Operations Research Office, The American University, Washington, D.C., July, 1961). Chap. 11, "Religion."

———. *Special Warfare Area Handbook for Cuba* (Special Operations Research Office. The American University, Washington, D.C., June, 1961). Chap. 11, "Religion."

———. *Special Warfare Area Handbook for Panama* (Special Operations Research Office, The American University, Washington, D.C., March, 1962). Chap. 5, "Religion."

———. *U.S. Army Area Handbook for Venezuela* (Special Operations Research Office, The American University, Washington, D.C., February, 1964). Chap 11, "Religion."

Frasso, Pedro. *De Regio Patronato.* Madrid, 1677. Frasso was one of the foremost lay defenders of *regalismo* during the colonial period.

Frizzi de Longoni, Haydee E. *Rivadávia y la Reforma Eclesiástica.* Buenos Aires, 1947. Analytic study of an anticlerical.

Furlong, Guillermo. *La Santa Sede y la Emancipación Hispanoamericana.* Buenos Aires, 1957. A summary of Father Pedro Leturia's studies.

———. *La Tradición Religiosa en la Escuela Argentina.* Buenos Aires, 1957. An assault on Ley 1420 (1884) which established lay education in Argentina.

Galdames, Luis. *A History of Chile.* Trans. and ed. by Isaac J. Cox. Chapel Hill, N.C., 1941.

——. *Estudio de la Historia de Chile.* Santiago, 1911. The best short history of Chile. In matters relating to the Church is tolerant.

——. *Historia de Chile: La Evolución Constitucional 1810-1925.* Santiago, 1926. Vol. I. Volume I covers the period 1810-33.

Gallardo, Ricardo. *Divorcio, Separación de Cuerpos y Nulidad del Matrimonio en las Naciones Latino-Americanas.* Madrid, 1957.

García Calderón, Francisco. *Latin America, Its Rise and Progress.* London, 1913. An interpretative discussion of Latin-American history by a brilliant Peruvian litterateur.

——. *Le Pérou Contemporain.* Paris, 1907.

——. *Les démocraties latines de l'Amérique.* Paris, 1912. Insofar as the Church and religious problems are discussed, these are treated sympathetically.

García Gutiérrez, Jesús. *Acción anticatólica en México.* Mexico, 1956.

——. *Apuntes para la historia del origen y desenvolvimiento del Regio Patronato Indiano hasta 1857.* Mexico, 1941. Supports canonical view.

——. *La Iglesia Mejicana en el segundo imperio.* Mexico, 1955.

Geographia do Brasil. Sociedade de Geographia do Rio de Janeiro, 1923, Vol. X.

Gil Fortoul, José. *Historia Constitucional de Venezuela.* Berlin, 1907-9. 2 vols. A superior political history of Venezuela to about 1870. For the most part is accurate and trustworthy. Is an invaluable reference for the history of Great Colombia.

Gómez, Hernán F. *Instituciones de la Provincia de Corrientes.* Buenos Aires, 1922. This work proved to be valuable for the study of the relation of the Church to the provincial governments.

Gómez Hoyos, Rafael. *La Iglesia de América en las Leyes de Indias.* Madrid, 1961. Examines the legal provisions dealing with the affairs of the Church in the Indies with special reference to the influence of canon law.

González Blanco, Edmundo. *Carranza y La Revolución de México.* Madrid, 1916. "An examination of the Mexican Revolution from the economic and political point of view." A defense before the Spanish people of the Constitutional cause.

González Blanco, Pedro. *De Porfirio Díaz á Carranza.* Madrid, 1916. Lectures delivered in the Ateneo (Madrid) "explaining" the Mexican Revolution. Contains interesting material on clerical persecution by the Constitutionalists.

Groot, José Manuel. *Historia Eclesiástica y Civil de Nueva Granada.* Bogotá, 1889-93. 4 vols. Originally intended to be an ecclesiastical history, but resolved into a political work (to 1830) as well. Written designedly to "correct" contemporary anticlerical histories.

Grose, Howard B. *Advance in the Antilles.* New York, 1910. A very prejudiced (anti-Catholic) discussion of missionary problems in Cuba and Porto Rico.

Gruening, Ernest. *Mexico and Its Heritage.* New York, 1928. The chapters on the Catholic Church which manifest a pronounced anti-Church bias are the least satisfactory part of an otherwise useful book.

Guerra, Flavio. *A questão religiosa do sugundo imperio brasileiro; fundamentos historicos.* Rio de Janeiro, 1952.

Guerra, José Guillermo. *La Constitución de 1925.* Santiago, 1929. Señor Guerra, a member of the Constituent Convention, discusses the new Constitution and incidentally the act of separation which he supported.

Haring, C. H. *Empire in Brazil.* Cambridge, Mass., 1958. Contains a short, but useful, discussion of the Church in the Empire.

Henao, Jesús María, y Arrubla, Gerardo. *Historia de Colombia.* Bogotá, 1912. 2 vols.

————. *History of Colombia.* Trans. and ed. by J. Fred Rippy. Chapel Hill, N.C., 1938.

Holleran, Mary P. *Church and State in Guatemala.* New York, 1949. A useful survey.

Holme, John G. *The Life of Leonard Wood.* New York, 1920. Contains a discussion of Wood's handling of religious problems in Cuba.

Houtart, Francisco. *El cambio social en América Latina.* Bogotá, 1964. Estudios Socio-Religiosos Latino Americanos, No. 18. A product of FERES (Federación International de Institutos Católicos de Investigaciones Sociales y Socio-religiosas).

Howard, George P. *Religious Liberty in Latin America?* Philadelphia, 1944. The negative answer is supported by evidence.

Humboldt, Alexander von. *Ensayo Político sobre el Reyno de la Nueva España.* Madrid, 1811. 2 vols. Translated from the original French. A valuable reference for the economic status of the Church and the clergy in New Spain on the eve of independence.

Huneeus y Gana, Dr. Jorge. *Obras de Don Jorge Huneeus.* Santiago, 1890. 2 vols. A noted commentator on the Chilean constitution. He makes interesting observations (Vol. I) on the religious article (Article 5).

Ibarra, R. P. Gabriel de. *El Concordato de Colombia.* Bogotá, 1941.

Icazbalceta, Joaquín García. *Biografía de don Fr. Juan de Zumárraga.* Mexico, 1881. For the early political status of the Church in New Spain.

Infante Vial, Gerardo. *Personalidad juridica de la Iglesia en Chile.* Santiago, 1962.

Ingenieros, José. *La Evolución de las Ideas Argentinas.* Buenos Aires, 1918. A scholarly work which contains much valuable information regarding the early relations of the Church and State in Argentina.

Inman, Samuel Guy. *South America Today.* New York, 1921. A discussion of the religious outlook in South America by the Secretary of the Committee on Coöperation in Latin America (An Evangelical Missionary organization).

Ireland, Gordon, and Galindez, Jesús de. *Divorce in the Americas.* Buffalo, N.Y., 1947.

James, Earle K. "Church and State in Mexico," in *Foreign Policy Association Reports*, XI, No. 9 (July 3, 1935), 106-16. Study of the religious issue in Mexico since the adoption of the Constitution of 1917.

James, Herman G. *Brazil After a Century of Independence.* New York, 1925.

————. *The Constitutional System of Brazil.* Washington, 1923. A scholarly study. Contains copies of both the imperial and the republican constitutions.

Kelley, Francis Clement. *Blood-drenched altars: Mexican study and comment.* Milwaukee, 1936. The religious persecution in Mexico.

Kennedy, John J. *Catholicism, Nationalism, and Democracy in Argentina.* Notre Dame, Ind., 1958. Doubts decisive influence of the Church.

Larrea, Juan Ignacio. *La iglesia y el estado en el Ecuador.* Sevilla, 1954. The personality of the Church recognized in the *modus vivendi* with the Holy See.

Lea, H. C. *The Inquisition in the Spanish Dependencies.* New York, 1908. A classic treatment of the subject.

Lee, John. *Religious Liberty in South America.* New York, 1907. Useful for religious legislation in Ecuador under President Eloy Alfaro.

Léger, J. N. *Haiti, Her History and Her Detractors.* New York, 1907. Written by the Haitian minister to the United States in an effort to present "the facts" to the American people. Somewhat colored by prejudice, but as a whole is a very acceptable work.

Legón, Faustino J. *Doctrina y Ejercicio del Patronato Nacional.* Buenos Aires, 1920. According to Father Leturia (*La acción diplomática*, p. 42, n. 25) this is "a book of solid doctrine (ultramontane), exact historical method, and based on a great quantity of materials, printed and unprinted, although the latter are only from the Buenos Aires archives." The book, says the Jesuit historian, is somewhat deficient because of failure to use the Vatican archives.

Leturia, P. Pedro. "Alusiones en la Cámara Argentina al Origen Histórico del Patronato de Indias," in *Razón y Fé*, 1927, Vol. 78, pp. 326-35.

————. "El Origen Histórico del Patronato de Indias," in *Razón y Fé*, 1927, Vol. 78, pp. 20-36.

————. *La Acción Diplomática de Bolívar ante Pío VII, 1820-1823.* Madrid, 1925. An excellent work of research based almost exclusively on materials in the Vatican archives.

————. "La Célebre Encíclica de León XII sobre la independencia de la América española en 21 de septiembre de 1824," in *Razón y Fé*, May, 1925.

————. "Gregorio XVI y la emancipación de la América Española," in *Rivista de Historia de América.* Instituto Panamericano de Geografía é Historia. Mexico D.F., No. 26 (Dic., 1948), 309-77.

——. *Relaciones entre la Santa Sede é Hispano-América.* Caracas, 1959. A collection of studies, all relating to the independence period.

Levene, Ricardo. *Lecciones de Historia Argentina.* Buenos Aires, 1919. 2 vols. Contains only a summary discussion of the Church in Argentina.

——. *A History of Argentina.* Trans. and ed. by William S. Robertson. Chapel Hill, N.C., 1937.

Lewin, Boleslao. *La Inquisición en Hispano-américa.* Buenos Aires, 1962. An exposition of inquisitional absolutism.

Lippmann, Walter. "Church and State in Mexico. The American Mediation," in *Foreign Affairs,* VIII, No. 2 (January, 1930), 182-208. An account of the mediation of Ambassador Morrow in the Church-State conflict in Mexico.

Long, Eula Kennedy. "Catholic Renewal in Brazil," in *The Christian Century,* LXXVIII, No. 38 (September, 1961), 1120-22. A discussion of the "stimulants" calling the Catholic Church to action.

Lorente, Sebastián. *Historia del Perú bajo los Borbones.* Lima, 1871. Contains statements on ecclesiastical conditions in the viceroyalty of Peru on the eve of independence.

Macfarland, Charles Stedman. *Chaos in Mexico, the Conflict of Church and State.* New York, 1935.

MacGaffey, Wyatt, and Barnett, Clifford R. *Cuba: its people, its society, its culture.* New Haven, Conn., 1962.

Mackay, John A. "A Fresh Look at Cuba," in *The Christian Century,* LXXXI, No. 32 (August 5, 1964), 983-89. The Cuban situation not as bad as pictured.

——. *The Latin American Churches and the Ecumenical Movement.* New York, 1963. For the Committee on Coöperation in Latin America, Division of Foreign Missions, National Council of the Churches of Christ in the U.S.A.

——. *The Other Spanish Christ.* New York, 1933. A study of the spiritual history of Spain and South America.

Magalhães, Basilio de. "D. Pedro II e a Egreja," in *Revista do Instituto Historico e Geographico Brasileiro,* Vol. 152 (1928), 385-409.

Marsal S., Pablo. *Perón y la Iglesia.* Buenos Aires, 1955. Useful data on the anti-Catholic campaign of 1954, whether soundly interpreted or not.

Martin, P. A. "Causes of the Collapse of the Brazilian Empire," in *The Hispanic American Historical Review,* IV (1921), 4-48.

Martin, Percy F. *Mexico of the Twentieth Century.* London, 1907.

——. *Maximilian in Mexico.* New York, 1914. Useful for religious policies and relations during the Second Empire.

——. *Peru in the Twentieth Century.* London, 1911.

Marure, Alejandro. *Bosquejo Histórico de las Revoluciones de Centro-América desde 1811 hasta 1834.* Guatemala, 1877-78. 2 vols. A Liberal, and partisan, history written by order of President Mariano Gálvez of Guatemala.

Matienzo, José N. *Cuestiones de Derecho Público Argentino.* Buenos Aires, 1924. One of the "cases" discussed in this work is that of the patronage.

Mecham, J. Lloyd. "Latin America's Fight Against Clerical Domination," in *Current History,* XXIX, No. 4 (January, 1929), 565-70.

———. "The Origins of Real Patronato de Indias," in *The Catholic Historical Review,* VIII, No. 2 (July, 1928), 205-28.

———. "The Papacy and Spanish-American Independence," in *The Hispanic American Historical Review,* IX, No. 2 (May, 1929), 154-75.

———. "The Religious Question in Mexico," in S. D. Myres, Jr., ed., *Mexico and the United States.* Dallas, 1938, pp. 118-37.

Medina, José Toribio. *Historia del Tribunal del Santo Oficio de la Inquisición en México.* Santiago, 1905. A master work on the Inquisition.

Medina Ascensio, Luis. *La Santa sede y la emancipación Mexicana.* Guadalajara, 1946.

Menéndez Mena, Rodolfo. *The Work of the Clergy and the Religious Persecution in Mexico.* New York, 1916. Revelations of anticlerical outrages by the Constitutionalists.

Miranda Ribadeneira, Francisco. *Política cristiana.* Quito, 1955. A view of the relations between religion and politics, especially as they exist in Ecuador.

Moctezuma, Aquilas P. *El conflicto religioso de 1926; sus origines, su desarrollo, su solución.* 2nd ed. Mexico, 1960.

Monsalve, José D. *El Ideal Político del Libertador Simón Bolívar.* Madrid, 1917. 2 vols. The final chapter in this original work (II, Chap. 26) is devoted to Bolívar's religious ideals. Bolívar, according to Monsalve, was a sincere Catholic, and were it not for this he would never have been Liberator.

Montúfar, Lorenzo. *El General Francisco Morazán.* Guatemala, 1896. The life and career of the great Liberal written in a partisan manner by a notable Liberal historian.

———. *Reseña Histórica de Centro-América.* Guatemala, 1878 81. A Liberal history. Designed to supplement the work of Marure. A violently anticlerical work. Extends to about 1850.

Moore, R. C. *Piety and Poverty in Chile.* Nashville, Tenn., 1946. A study of the economic and social effects of Roman Catholicism in Chile.

Moraes, Eugenio Vilhena de. "O Patriotismo e o Clero no Brasil," in *Revista do Instituto Historico e Geographico Brasileiro.* Rio de Janeiro, 1925. Tomo 99. Vol. 153, pp. 113-68.

Moses, Bernard. *Spain's Declining Power in South America.* Berkeley, 1919. Allusions to the ecclesiastical state of South America in the middle of the eighteenth century.

———. *The Spanish Dependencies in South America.* New York, 1914. 2 vols. "The Church in Relation to the Civil Government" (Chap. XII, Vol. II) is one of the best short discussions of the *real patronato.*

Mossé, Benjamin. *Dom Pedro II.* Paris, 1889.

Munro, Dana G. *The Five Republics of Central America.* New York, 1918. After Bancroft this is the most acceptable history of Central America. The discussions of the religious issues, however, are inadequate.

Nevins, Albert J., "How Catholic is Latin America?" *The Sign,* Vol. 36, No. 2 (September, 1956), 11-18. The answer is not encouraging to Catholicism.

Niemeyer, E. V. "Anticlericalism in the Mexican Constitutional Convention, 1916-1917," in *The Americas,* XI, No. 1 (July, 1954), 31-49.

Núñez, Rafael. *La Reforma Política en Colombia.* Bogotá, 1886. The famous Colombian President reveals somewhat incidentally his ideas on religious policy.

O'Leary, Daniel F. *Bolívar y la Emancipación de Sud-América.* Madrid, 1915. 2 vols. *Memorias* of General O'Leary, comrade of the Liberator. Translated from English by his son Simón B. O'Leary.

Oliveira Lima, Manuel. *Formation Historique de la Nationalité Brazilienne.* Paris, 1911.

Otero, Mariano. *Ensayo sobre la Cuestión Social.* Mexico, 1842. An acceptable discussion, with statistical data, of the religious situation in Mexico after the establishment of the Republic.

Parsons, Wilfred. *Mexican Martyrdom.* New York, 1936.

Pattee, Richard. *Catholicism in Latin America.* Washington, D.C., 1945. A frank discussion sponsored by the National Catholic Welfare Conference.

———. *Gabriel García Moreno y el Ecuador de su tiempo.* Quito, 1941.

Pérez, Ángel Gabriel. *El Patronato Español en el Virreyno del Perú durante el Siglo XVI.* Tournai, Belgium, 1937. A contribution to colonial ecclesiastical history.

Phipps, Helen. *Some Aspects of the Agrarian Question in Mexico.* University of Texas *Bulletin,* No. 2515. Austin, 1925. A very useful study of the land problem in Mexico during the colonial and republican periods. Since the extensive ecclesiastical holdings was a major issue, considerable attention is devoted to agrarian legislation as it affected the Church.

Piaggio, Agustín. *La Influencia del Clero en la Independencia Argentina, 1810-1820.* Barcelona, 1912. An exposition of the contribution of the clergy of La Plata to the winning of independence.

Pike, Frederick B. "The Catholic Church in Central America," in *Review of Politics,* Vol. 21, No. 1 (January, 1959), 83-113. A discussion of Church-State relations in Central America. The author believes that the role of the Church is comparatively unimportant.

———., ed. *The Conflict Between Church and State in Latin America.* New York, 1964. A collection of essays covering the colonial, independence, and contemporary periods.

———. "The Modernized Church in Peru: Two Aspects," in *The Review of Politics,* Vol. 26, No. 3 (July, 1964), 307-18. The dangers of clerical preoccupation with economic reform.

Portes Gil, Emilio. *The Conflict Between the Civil Power and the Clergy.* Mexico, 1935. An historical and legal essay by the Mexican Attorney General.

Puig Casauranc, José Manuel. *La Cuestión religiosa en relación con la educación pública en México.* Mexico, 1928.

Rebello, Annibal Velloso. "García Moreno," in *Revista do Instituto Historico e Geographico Brasileiro,* Rio de Janeiro, 1920, CXLI, 75-214.

Renan, Ernest. *Histoire des Origines du Christianisme.* Paris, 1863-99. 7 vols. Renan describes (VI, 93 ff.) early episcopal elections.

Restrepo, José Manuel. *Historia de la Revolución de la República de Colombia.* Besançon, 1858. 4 vols. An excellent history of the Revolution to the breakup of Great Colombia.

Restrepo, Juan Pablo. *La Iglesia y el Estado en Colombia.* London, 1881. The status of the Church in its relation to the State is fully discussed from every angle. This is one of the most comprehensive and scholarly treatments the writer has seen.

Ribadencyra, Antonio Joaquín de. *Manual Compendio de el Regio Patronato Indiano.* Madrid, 1755. Ribadeneyra was the outstanding exponent of regalism during the colonial period. His study was "official."

Rice, Elizabeth Ann. *The Diplomatic Relations Between the United States and Mexico, as Affected by the Struggle for Religious Liberty in Mexico, 1925-1929.* Washington, D.C., 1959.

Río, Ángel del, ed. *Responsible Freedom in the Americas.* New York, 1955. Articles by Jorge Mañach, "Religion and Freedom in the Americas," pp. 349-61, and William Stokes, "Catholicism and Democracy in Latin America," pp. 361-81.

Riva Palacio, Vicente, ed. *México á Través de Los Siglos.* Mexico, Barcelona, 1888-89. 5 vols. The extensive reproduction of sources makes it to a large extent a collection of source materials. This work is conspicuous among Mexican histories for its balanced judgment.

Robertson, William Spence. *History of the Latin-American Nations.* New York, 1925.

———. *Rise of the Spanish-American Republics.* New York, 1918.

Roldán, Alcibiades. *Elementos de Derecho Constitucional de Chile.* Santiago, 1917. Commentaries on the Chilean Constitution. A useful reference for the political status of the established cult. Contains interesting observations on the patronage.

Romaña, José María. "Iglesia y estado en la política peronista," in *Estudios Americanos* (Sevilla, España) 11:55 (April, 1956), 377-89. Strongly anti-Perón, from the Roman Catholic Church point of view, but sets forth basic issues.

Rowe, Leo S. *The Federal System of the Argentine Republic.* Washington, 1921.

Ryan, Edwin. *The Church in the South American Republics.* New York, 1932.

Rycroft, W. Stanley, and Clemmer, Myrtle M. *A Factual Study of Latin America.* New York, 1963. Published by the Commission on Ecumenical Mission and Relations of the United Presbyterian Church in the U.S.A.

Rycroft, W. Stanley. *Religion and Faith in Latin America.* Philadelphia, 1958. The development and promise of the Evangelical movement in Latin America.

Saldías, Adolfo. *Historia de la Confederación Argentina, Rosas y su Época.* Buenos Aires, 1911. 5 vols. Used particularly for a study of the Church under the Rosas dictatorship. The author is remarkably sympathetic toward Rosas, and seeks to defend his religious policy.

Sallusti, José. *Historia de las Misiones Apostólicas de Monseñor Juan Muzi en el Estado de Chile.* Santiago, 1906. A full account of the famous mission of Apostolic Delegate Muzi to Chile in 1823.

Sánchez, George I. *Mexico: A Revolution by Education.* New York, 1936. Ch. VI, The Socialistic School, and Ch. VIII, Church, State, and Education.

Sánchez Espejo, Carlos. *El Patronato en Venezuela.* Caracas, 1953.

Sánchez Viamonte, Carlos. *El pensamiento liberal Argentino en siglo XIX.* Buenos Aires, 1957. Part I is concerned with freedom of education and the pervasive role of the Catholic Church in this field.

Sanguinetti, Manuel Juan. *La representación diplomática del Vaticano en los paises del Plata.* Buenos Aires, 1954.

Sarsfield, Dalmacio Vélez. *Relaciones del Estado con la Iglesia en la Antigua América Española.* Buenos Aires, 1889. A vigorous defence of *patronato nacional* by one of Argentina's leading constitutional lawyers.

Schoenrich, Otto. *Santo Domingo.* New York, 1918.

Schmitt, Karl M. "Catholic Adjustment to the Secular State: The Case of Mexico, 1867-1911," in *Cath. Hist. Rev.,* XLVIII, No. 2 (July, 1962), 182-204.

Scholes, Walter V. "Church and State in the Mexican Constitutional Convention, 1856-1857," in *The Américas,* IV, No. 2 (October, 1947), 151-74.

Service, Elman R. and Helen S. *Tobati: Paraguayan Town.* Chicago, 1954. Ch. XIII: The Church as a social institution.

Shea, J. J. *The Life of Pope Pius IX.* New York, 1877.

Shiels, W. E. *King and Church: The Rise and Fall of the Patronato Real.* Chicago, 1961.

Shuck, L. Edward, Jr. "Church and State in Argentina," in *The Western Political Quarterly,* II, No. 4 (December, 1949), 527-44. A pro-Perón view.

Silva, J. Francisco V. *El Libertador Bolívar y el Deán Funes en la Política Argentina.* Madrid, 1918. This work, devoted to the support of Bolívar's plan of Spanish-American unity by the famous dean, contains some information on ecclesiastical policy in La Plata.

Silveria Camargo, Mons. Paulo Floriencio da. *Historia Eclesiastica do Brasil.* Petropolis, 1955.

Solórzano y Pereyra, Juan de. *Política Indiana.* Madrid, 1776. 2 vols. This was the foremost commentary on the Laws of the Indies. Solórzano, like Ribadeneyra, defended *regalismo.*

Stanger, Francis Merriman. "Church and State in Peru," in *The Hispanic American Historical Review,* VII, No. 4 (November, 1927), 410-37.

Stoddard, Lathrop. *The French Revolution in San Domingo.* New York, 1914.

Stuart, Graham H. *The Governmental System of Peru.* Washington, 1925.

Thornton, Sister Mary Crescentia. *The Church and Freemasonry in Brazil, 1872-1875. A Study in Regalism.* Washington, D.C., 1948.

Tobar Donoso, Julio. *La iglesia ecuatoriana en el siglo XIX.* Quito, 1934.

———. *Las relaciónes entre la iglesia y el estado ecuatoriano; resumen histórico.* Quito, 1938.

Tormo, Leandro, y Aizpuru, Pilar Gonzalbo. *La Iglesia en la crisis de la independencia.* Madrid, 1961. Vol. III of *La Historia de la Iglesia en América Latina.* No. 10.

Toro, Alfonso. *La Iglesia y El Estado en México.* Mexico, 1927. A publication of the *Archivo General de la Nación, Secretaría de Gobernación.* A survey of the conflicts between the Catholic clergy and the Mexican governments from independence to 1926. A very cursory treatment of the events since 1901. This work was one of the numerous "official" studies published in defense of the anticlerical program of the Calles administration.

Tucker, William P. *The Mexican Government Today.* Minneapolis, Minn., 1957. Ch. 3, "Church and State."

Uroz, Antonio. *La Cuestión Religiosa en México.* Mexico, 1926. A defense of the policy of President Calles in the crisis of 1926.

Van Sickle, H. Gordon. "The Background of Protestant Suppression in Colombia," in *The Iliff Review,* XI, No. 3 (Fall, 1954), 3-20.

Vargas Urgarte, Rubén. *Historia de la iglesia en el Perú.* Burgos, 1953-61. 4 vols. A comprehensive treatment of the action of the Church in colonial Peru.

Vedia, Agustín de. *Constitución Argentina.* Buenos Aires, 1907. An able commentary.

Vedia y Mitre, Mariano de. *De Rivadavia á Rosas.* Buenos Aires, 1930. Volume V of the series, *Biblioteca de Historia Argentina y Americana,* presents a brief discussion of the reforms of Rivadavia.

———. *El Gobierno del Uruguay: Estudio Constitucional de la Reforma de 1917.* Buenos Aires, 1919.

Vera-Estañol, Jorge. *Carranza and His Bolshevik Régime.* Los Angeles, Cal., 1920. A severe attack on Carranza's policies, including his antireligious measures.

Vergara, Ignacio. *El protestantismo en Chile.* Santiago, 1962.

Vianna, Oliveira. "A Queda do Imperio," in *Rev. do Inst. Hist. e Geog.* Tomo Especial, 1925, pp. 787-887.

Viveiros de Castro, A. O. "Contribuições para a Biographia de D. Pedro II," in *Rev. do Inst. Hist. e Geog.* Tomo Especial, 1925, pp. 477-534.

Wagley, Charles. *An Introduction to Brazil.* New York, 1963. For a good discussion of "Religion and the State," see pp. 232-67.

Walsh, R. *Notices of Brazil in 1828 and 1829.* Boston, 1831. 2 vols.

Ward, H. G. *Mexico in 1827.* London, 1828. 2 vols. Britain's first minister to Mexico does not neglect brief mention in his well-known book of the religious situation in Mexico.

Warren, Harris Gaylord. *Paraguay: An Informal History.* Norman, Oklahoma, 1949.

Washburn, Charles A. *A History of Paraguay.* Boston, 1871. 2 vols.

Watters, Mary. "The Present Status of the Church in Venezuela," in the *Hispanic American Historical Review,* XIII (February, 1933), 23-45.

———. "Bolívar and the Church," in *Catholic Historical Review,* XXI (1935), 299-313.

———. *A History of the Church in Venezuela, 1810-1930.* Chapel Hill, N.C., 1933. In explanation of the virtual impotence of the Church in spite of the fact that it is still established.

Welles, Sumner. *Naboth's Vineyard, The Dominican Republic, 1844-1924.* New York, 1928. 2 vols. The best history of the Dominican Republic. There are scattered references to the Church and the clergy.

Wheeler, W. R., and Browning, W. E. *Modern Missions on the Spanish Main.* Philadelphia, 1925. A discussion of Protestant missionary enterprise in Colombia and Venezuela. A searching, and sometimes too severe criticism of the deficiencies of Roman Catholicism in the two republics.

Whetten, Nathan L. *Guatemala, the Land and the People.* New Haven, Conn., 1961. "Religion and the Church," pp. 286-311.

Whitaker, Arthur P. *Argentine Upheaval: Perón's Fall and the New Régime.* New York, 1956.

Williams, Mary W. "The Ecclesiastical Policy of Francisco Morazán and Other Central American Liberals," in *The Hispanic American Historical Review,* III, No. 2 (May, 1920), 119-43.

Wood, Eric F. *Leonard Wood.* New York, 1920. There is a brief discussion in this work of Wood's able management of Church problems in Cuba.

Wright, Almon R. "Argentina and the Papacy, 1810-1827," in *Hisp. Am. Hist. Rev.,* Vol. 18 (1938), pp. 15-42.

Zamora, Matías Gómez. *Regio Patronato Español é Indiano.* Madrid, 1897. A very scholarly study of patronato. Is perhaps the leading work written from the ultramontane viewpoint.

Zavala, Lorenzo de. *Ensayo Histórico de las Revoluciones de México desde 1808 hasta 1830.* Mexico, 1945. 2 vols. Zavala's anticlerical bias often leads him to extravagant and ludicrous limits. Is a useful work for factual information but one must be on guard against the conclusions.

Ziegler, Aloysius K. *Church and State in Visigothic Spain.* Washington, D.C., 1930.

Zubieta, Pedro A. *Apuntaciones sobre las Primeras Misiones Diplomáticas de Colombia.* Bogotá, 1924. This work contains in Chapter XXX an excellent discussion of Colombian relations with the papacy until the time of papal recognition.

C. PERIODICALS AND NEWSPAPERS

The Americas, Washington, D.C., 1947, 1953, 1954, 1959.
Anales de la Facultad de Derecho, Buenos Aires, 1915.
Annuario Catholico de Brasil, Rio de Janeiro, 1928.
Boletín Informativo Demócrata Cristiano, New York, 1962-64.
Boletín Oficial, Buenos Aires, 1955.
Brazilian Bulletin, New York, June 1, 1963.
Catholic Historical Review, Washington, D.C., 1928, 1942, 1962.
Catholic World, Glen Rock, N.J., June, 1964.
Chicago Tribune, Chicago, August 24, 1929.
Christian Century, Chicago, August 5, 1964.
Christian Science Monitor, Boston, 1918-65.
Christianity Today, Washington, D.C., July 19, 1963.
The Commonweal, New York, March 25 and April 1, 1931; June 23, 1961.
Current History Magazine, New York, 1920-33.
Diario Oficial, Bogotá, January 19, 1928.
Diario Oficial, Mexico, 1916, 1920-34.
Excelsior, Mexico, 1917-33.
Foreign Policy Association Reports, New York, July 3, 1935.
Gaceta Oficial, Caracas, June 17, 1924.
Gaceta Oficial, Ciudad Trujillo, 1954, 1955.
Hispanic American Historical Review, Durham, N.C., 1921, 1927, 1933, 1958.
Hispanic American Report. A monthly report on developments in Latin America by the Hispanic World Affairs Seminar of Stanford University, 1948-63.
Iliff Review, Denver, Fall, 1954.
Journal of Church and State, Waco, Texas, 1964, 1965.
Missionary Review of the World, New York, March, 1938.
El Nacional, Caracas, March 7, 1964.
La Nación, Santiago, Chile, 1920-30.
The News, Mexico, April 10, 1965.
New York Herald Tribune, February 24, 1926.
New York Times, 1910-65.
Our Sunday Visitor, The National Catholic Action Weekly, Huntington, Ind., January 19, 1964.
La Prensa, Buenos Aires, 1923-28, 1945, 1947.
La Prensa, New York, 1927-29.

Razón y Fé, Madrid, 1927.
Review of Politics, Notre Dame, Ind., 1959, 1964.
Revista de Instrucción Pública, Caracas, February, 1910.
Revista de Instituto Historico e Geographico Brasileiro, Rio de Janeiro, 1925.
The Sign, Union City, N.J., September, 1956.
El Universal, Mexico, 1926-33.
Visión, New York, December 25, 1964.

Index

A

Date Due